D0057526

LANGENSCHEIDT'S
UNIVERSAL DICTIONARY

ENGLISH-GERMAN
GERMAN-ENGLISH

New edition

LANGENSCHEIDT

NEW YORK · BERLIN · MUNICH
VIENNA · ZURICH

Contents

Abbreviations Used in this Dictionary

Die Tilde (~, bei veränderter Schreibung des Anfangsbuchstabens 2) ersetzt entweder das ganze Stichwort oder den vor dem senkrechten Strich (|) stehenden Teil davon oder ein bereits mit einer Tilde gebildetes Stichwort, z. B. birth ... ~day = birthday; approv|al ... ~e = approve; after ...noon: good ~ = good afternoon; lord ... the 2 = the Lord.

The tilde (~, when the initial letter changes: 2) stands for the catchword at the beginning of the entry or the part of it preceding the vertical bar (|) or for a catchword already having a tilde. Examples: birth ... ~day = birthday; approv|al ...~e = approve; after ...noon: good ~ = good afternoon; lord ... the 2 = the Lord.

a. auch, *also.*

abbr. abbreviation, Abkürzung.

acc accusative (case), Akkusativ.

adj adjective, Adjektiv.

adv adverb, Adverb.

aer. aeronautics, Luftfahrt.

agr. agriculture, Landwirtschaft.

Am. American English, amerikanisches Englisch.

anat. anatomy, Anatomie.

appr. approximately, etwa.

arch. architecture, Architektur.

ast. astronomy, Astronomie.

attr attributively, attributiv.

biol. biology, Biologie.

bot. botany, Botanik.

Brit. British English, britisches Englisch.

bsd. besonders, *especially.*

chem. chemistry, Chemie.

cj conjunction, Konjunktion.

colloq. colloquial, umgangssprachlich.

comp comparative, Komparativ.

cond conditional, Konditional.

contp. contemptuously, verächtlich.

dat dative (case), Dativ.

4

dem demonstrative, Demonstrativ...

ea. einander, *one another, each other.*

eccl. ecclesiastical, kirchlich.

econ. economics, Wirtschaft.

e-e, e-e eine, *a (an).*

electr. electricity, Elektrizität.

e-m, e-m einem, *to a (an).*

e-n, e-n einen, *a (an).*

e-r, e-r einer, *of a (an), to a (an).*

e-s, e-s eines, *of a (an).*

et., et. etwas, *something.*

etc. et cetera, *and so on,* und so weiter.

f feminine, weiblich.

fig. figuratively, bildlich.

gen genitive *(case),* Genitiv.

geogr. geography, Geographie.

geol. geology, Geologie.

ger gerund, Gerundium.

gr. grammar, Grammatik.

hist. history, Geschichte.

hunt. hunting, Jagd.

ichth. ichthyology, Ichthyologie.

impers impersonal, unpersönlich.

indef indefinite, Indefinit...

inf infinitive *(mood),* Infinitiv.

int. interjection, Interjektion.

interr interrogative, Interrogativ...

irr irregular, unregelmäßig.

j-m, j-m jemandem, *to someone.*

j-n, j-n jemanden, *someone.*

j-s, j-s jemandes, *someone's.*

jur. jurisprudence, Recht.

konkr. konkret, *concretely.*

ling. linguistics, Sprachwissenschaft.

lit. literary, literarisch.

m masculine, männlich.

mar. maritime terminology, Schiffahrt.

math. mathematics, Mathematik.

m-e, m-e meine, *my.*

med. medicine, Medizin.

metall. metallurgy, Metallurgie.

meteor. meteorology, Meteorologie.

mil. military terminology, Militärwesen.

min. mineralogy, Mineralogie.

mot. motoring, Kraftfahrwesen.

mst meistens, *mostly, usually.*

mus. music, Musik.

n neuter, sächlich.

od. oder, *or.*

opt. optics, Optik.

orn. ornithology, Ornithologie.

o.s., o.s. oneself, sich.

paint. painting, Malerei.

parl. parliamentary term, parlamentarischer Ausdruck.

pass passive voice, Passiv.

ped. pedagogy, Pädagogik.

phls. philosophy, Philosophie.

phot. photography, Fotografie.

phys. physics, Physik.

physiol. physiology, Physiologie.

pl plural, Plural.

poet. poetical, dichterisch.

pol. politics, Politik.

poss possessive, Possessiv...

post. postal service, Post-
wesen.

pp past participle, Partizip
Perfekt.

pred predicative, prädika-
tiv.

pres present, Präsens.

pres p present participle,
Partizip Präsens.

pret preterit(e), Präteritum.

print. printing, Buchdruck.

pron pronoun, Pronomen.

prp preposition, Präposition.

psych. psychology, Psycho-
logie.

rail. railway, Eisenbahn-
wesen.

rel relative, Relativ...

rhet. rhetoric, Rhetorik.

S., S. Sache, thing.

s. siehe, see, refer to.

Scot. Scottish, schottisch.

s-e, s-e seine, his, one's.

sg singular, Singular.

sl. slang, Slang.

*s-m, s-m seinem, to his, to
one's.*

s-n, s-n seinen, his, one's.

s.o., s.o. someone, jemand
(-en).

sp. sports, Sport.

*s-r, s-r seiner, of his, of one's,
to his, to one's.*

*s-s, s-s seines, of his, of
one's.*

s.th., s.th. something, etwas.

sub substantive, noun, Substantiv.

subj subjunctive (mood), Konjunktiv.

sup superlative, Superlativ.

tech. technology, Technik.

tel. telegraphy, Telegrafie.

teleph. telephony, Fern-
sprechwesen.

thea. theatre, Theaterwesen.

u., u. und, and.

univ. university, Hochschul-
wesen.

v/aux auxiliary verb, Hilfsverb.

vb verb, Verb.

vet. veterinary medicine,
Tiermedizin.

v/i verb intransitive, intransi-
tives Verb.

v/refl verb reflexive, reflexi-
ves Verb.

v/t verb transitive, transitives
Verb.

vulg. vulgar, vulgär.

zo. zoology, Zoologie.

Zs., zs. zusammen, together.

*Zssg(n) Zusammensetzung
(-en), compound word(s).*

Key to English Pronunciation

The length of vowels is indicated by [:] following the vowel symbol, the stress by ['] preceding the stressed syllable.

[ɑ:]	as in *father*	[uə]	as in *poor*
[ʌ]	as in *but, come*	[u]	as in *put*
[æ]	as in *man*	[r]	as in *rose*
[ɛə]	as in *bare*	[ʒ]	as in *jazz*
[ai]	as in *I, sky*	[ʃ]	as in *shake*
[au]	as in *house*	[θ]	as in *thin*
[ei]	as in *date*	[ð]	as in *father*
[e]	as in *bed*	[s]	as in *see*
[ə]	as in *ago, butter*	[z]	as in *zeal*
[i:]	as in *sea*	[ŋ]	as in *ring*
[i]	as in *big*	[w]	as in *will*
[iə]	as in *here*	[f]	as in *fast*
[əu]	as in *boat*	[v]	as in *vast*
[ɔ:]	as in *door*	[j]	as in *yes*
[ɔ]	as in *god*	[ɑ̃]	as in French *blanc*
[ɔi]	as in *boy*	[ɔ̃]	as in French *bonbon*
[ə:]	as in *girl*	[ɛ̃]	as in French *vin*
[u:]	as in *shoe*		

Numerals

Cardinal Numbers

0	*nought, zero, cipher* null	50	*fifty* fünfzig
1	*one* eins	60	*sixty* sechzig
2	*two* zwei	70	*seventy* siebzig
3	*three* drei	80	*eighty* achtzig
4	*four* vier	90	*ninety* neunzig
5	*five* fünf	100	*a or one hundred* hundert
6	*six* sechs	101	*a hundred and one* hundert(und)eins
7	*seven* sieben	200	*two hundred* zweihundert
8	*eight* acht.		
*9	*nine* neun	572	*five hundred and seventy-two* fünfhundert(und)zweiundsiebzig
10	*ten* zehn		
11	*eleven* elf		
12	*twelve* zwölf		
13	*thirteen* dreizehn	1000	*a or one thousand* tausend
14	*fourteen* vierzehn		
15	*fifteen* fünfzehn	1972	*nineteen hundred and seventy-two* neunzehnhundertzweiundsiebzig
16	*sixteen* sechzehn		
17	*seventeen* siebzehn		
18	*eighteen* achtzehn		
19	*nineteen* neunzehn		
20	*twenty* zwanzig	500000	*five hundred thousand* fünfhunderttausend
21	*twenty-one* einundzwanzig		
22	*twenty-two* zweiundzwanzig	1 000 000	*a or one million* eine Million
23	*twenty-three* dreiundzwanzig	2 000 000	*two million* zwei Millionen
30	*thirty* dreißig	1 000 000 000	*a or one milliard (Am. billion)* eine Milliarde
40	*forty* vierzig		

Ordinal Numbers

1st	*first* erste	
2nd	*second* zweite	
3rd	*third* dritte	
4th	*fourth* vierte	
5th	*fifth* fünfte	
6th	*sixth* sechste	
7th	*seventh* siebente	
8th	*eighth* achte	
9th	*ninth* neunte	
10th	*tenth* zehnte	
11th	*eleventh* elfte	
12th	*twelfth* zwölfte	
13th	*thirteenth* dreizehnte	
14th	*fourteenth* vierzehnte	
15th	*fifteenth* fünfzehnte	
16th	*sixteenth* sechzehnte	
17th	*seventeenth* siebzehnte	
18th	*eighteenth* achtzehnte	
19th	*nineteenth* neunzehnte	
20th	*twentieth* zwanzigste	
21st	*twenty-first* einundzwanzigste	
22nd	*twenty-second* zweiundzwanzigste	

23rd	*twenty-third* dreiundzwanzigste	
30th	*thirtieth* dreißigste	
40th	*fortieth* vierzigste	
50th	*fiftieth* fünfzigste	
60th	*sixtieth* sechzigste	
70th	*seventieth* siebzigste	
80th	*eightieth* achtzigste	
90th	*ninetieth* neunzigste	
100th	*(one) hundredth* hundertste	
101st	*(one) hundred and first* hundert(und)erste	
200th	*two hundredth* zweihundertste	
572nd	*five hundred and seventy-second* fünfhundert(und)zweiundsiebzigste	
1000th	*(one) thousandth* tausendste	
1970th	*nineteen hundred and seventieth* neunzehnhundert(und)siebzigste	
500 000th	*five hundred thousandth* fünfhunderttausendste	
1 000 000th	*(one) millionth* millionste	
2 000 000th	*two millionth* zweimillionste	

Fractional Numbers and other Numerical Values

$^1/_2$ *one half, a half* halb
half a mile eine halbe
Meile

$1^1/_2$ *one and a half* anderthalb *or* eineinhalb

$2^1/_2$ *two and a half* zweieinhalb

$^1/_3$ *one or a third* ein Drittel

$^2/_3$ *two thirds* zwei Drittel

$^1/_4$ *one fourth, one or a quarter* ein Viertel

$^3/_4$ *three fourths, three quarters* drei Viertel

$1^1/_4$ *one hour and a quarter* ein und eine viertel Stunde

$^1/_5$ *one or a fifth* ein Fünftel

$3^4/_5$ *three and four fifths* drei vier Fünftel

.4 *point four* null Komma vier (0,4)

2.5 *two point five* zwei Komma fünf (2,5)

einfach *single*
zweifach *double, twofold*
dreifach *threefold, treble, triple*
vierfach *fourfold, quadruple*

fünffach *fivefold, quintuple*
einmal *once*
zweimal *twice*
drei-, vier-, fünfmal *three or four or five times*
zweimal soviel(e) *twice as much or many*

erstens, zweitens, drittens *first(ly), secondly, thirdly; in the first or second or third place*

$2 \times 3 = 6$ *twice three are or make six, two multiplied by three are or make six* zwei mal drei ist sechs, zwei multipliziert mit drei ist sechs

$7 + 8 = 15$ *seven plus eight are fifteen* sieben plus acht ist fünfzehn

$10 - 3 = 7$ *ten minus three are seven* zehn minus drei ist sieben

$20 : 5 = 4$ *twenty divided by five make four* zwanzig (dividiert) durch fünf ist vier

German Weights and Measures

I. Linear Measure

1 mm   *Millimeter* millimetre = 0.039 inch

1 cm   *Zentimeter* centimetre = 10 mm = 0.394 inch

1 m   *Meter* metre = 100 cm = 1.094 yards = 3.281 feet

1 km   *Kilometer* kilometre = 1000 m = 0.621 mile

II. Square Measure

1 mm²   *Quadratmillimeter* square millimetre = 0.002 square inch

1 cm²   *Quadratzentimeter* square centimetre = 100 mm² = 0.155 square inch

1 m²   *Quadratmeter* square metre = 10000 cm² = 1.196 square yards = 10.764 square feet

1 a   *Ar* are = 100 m² = 119.599 square yards

1 ha   *Hektar* hectare = 100 a = 2.471 acres

III. Cubic Measure

1 cm³   *Kubikzentimeter* cubic centimetre = 1000 mm³ = 0.061 cubic inch

1 m³   *Kubikmeter* cubic metre = 1 000 000 cm³ = 35.315 cubic feet = 1.308 cubic yards

1 RT   *Registertonne* register ton = 2,832 m³ = 100 cubic feet

IV. Measure of Capacity

1 l   *Liter* litre = 1.760 pints = U.S. 1.057 liquid quarts *or* 0.906 dry quart

1 hl   *Hektoliter* hectolitre = 100 l = 2.75 bushels = U.S. 26.418 gallons

V. Weight

1 g   *Gramm* gram(me) = 15.432 grains

1 Pfd.   *Pfund* pound (German) = 500 g = 1.102 pounds avdp.

1 kg   *Kilogramm* kilogram(me) = 1000 g = 2.205 pounds avdp. = 2.679 pounds troy

1 Ztr.   *Zentner* centner = 100 Pfd. = 0.984 hundredweight = 1.102 U.S. hundredweights

1 dz   *Doppelzentner* = 100 kg = 1.968 hundredweights = 2.204 U.S. hundredweights

1 t   *Tonne* ton = 1000 kg = 0.984 long ton = U.S. 1.102 short tons

A

a [ei, ə] ein(e); **not ~(n)** kein(e).

aback [ə'bæk] zurück; **taken ~** überrascht, bestürzt.

abandon [ə'bændən] aufpreisgeben; verlassen; überlassen; **~ment** Aufgabe f, Preisgabe f.

abashed [ə'bæʃt] verlegen.

abate [ə'beit] verringern, abnehmen, nachlassen; *Mißstand* abstellen.

abb|ess ['æbis] Äbtissin f; **~ey** ['~i] Abtei f; **~ot** ['~ət] Abt m.

abbreviat|e [ə'bri:vieit] (ab)kürzen; **~ion** Abkürzung f.

ABC ['eibi:'si:] Abc n.

abdicate ['æbdikeit] aufgeben; abdanken.

abdomen ['æbdəmen] Unterleib m.

abduct [æb'dʌkt] entführen.

abhor [əb'hɔ:] verabscheuen; **~rence** [~ərəns] Abscheu m; **~rent** verabhaßt, zuwider; abstoßend.

abide [ə'baid] (*irr*) bleiben; (v)ertragen; warten auf.

ability [ə'biliti] Fähigkeit f.

abject ['æbdʒekt] niedrig, gemein; *fig.* äußerst.

abjure [əb'dʒuə] abschwören; entsagen.

able ['eibl] fähig; geschickt; **be ~ to** imstande sein zu, können.

abnormal [æb'nɔ:məl] abnorm.

aboard [ə'bɔ:d] an Bord.

abode [ə'boud] *pret u. pp von* **abide**; Aufenthalt m; Wohnung f.

aboli|sh [ə'bɔliʃ] abschaffen; **~tion** [æbəu'liʃən] Abschaffung f.

A-bomb ['eibɔm] Atombombe f.

abominable [ə'bɔminəbl] abscheulich.

abortion [ə'bɔ:ʃən] Fehlgeburt f; Abtreibung f.

abound [ə'baund]: **~ in, ~ with** voll sein von; wimmeln von.

about [ə'baut] *prp räumlich*: um, um ... herum; in ... umher; *zeitlich, größen-, mengenmäßig*: ungefähr, etwa, gegen (**~ this time, ~ my height**); bei (**I haven't any money ~ me**); im Begriff, dabei; *adv* umher, herum; in der Nähe, da; ungefähr, etwa.

above [ə'bʌv] *prp* über, oberhalb; *fig.* erhaben über; **~ all** vor allem; *adv* oben; darüber; *adj* obig, obenerwähnt.

abreast [ə'brest] nebeneinander. [kürzen.]

abridge [ə'bridʒ] (ver-){

abroad [ə'brɔːd] im od. ins Ausland; überall(hin).

abrupt [ə'brʌpt] jäh; zs.-hanglos; schroff.

abscess ['æbsis] Geschwür n.

absence ['æbsəns] Abwesenheit f; Mangel m; ~ of mind Zerstreutheit f.

absent ['æbsənt] abwesend; **be** ~ fehlen; ~-**minded** zerstreut, geistesabwesend.

absolute ['æbsəluːt] absolut; unumschränkt.

absolve [əb'zɔlv] frei-, lossprechen.

absorb [əb'sɔːb] aufsaugen; *fig.* ganz in Anspruch nehmen.

abst|ain [əb'stein] sich enthalten; ~**ention** [~'stenʃən] Enthaltung f.

abstinen|ce ['æbstinəns] Enthaltsamkeit f; ~**t** enthaltsam.

abstract ['æbstrækt] abstrakt; Auszug m; [~'strækt] abziehen; trennen; ~**ed** zerstreut.

absurd [əb'sɔːd] absurd; lächerlich.

abundan|ce [ə'bʌndəns] Überfluß m; Fülle f; ~**t** reichlich.

abus|e [ə'bjuːs] Mißbrauch m; Beschimpfung f; [~z] mißbrauchen; beschimpfen; ~**ive** ausfallend; Schimpf...

abyss [ə'bis] Abgrund m.

academ|ic(al) [ækə'demik(əl)] akademisch; ~**y** [ə'kædəmi] Akademie f.

accelerat|e [æk'seləreit] beschleunigen; *mot.* Gas geben; ~**or** Gaspedal n.

accent ['æksənt] Akzent m.

accept [ək'sept] annehmen; (freundlich) aufnehmen; hinnehmen; ~**able** annehmbar; ~**ance** Annahme f; (freundliche) Aufnahme f.

access ['ækses] Zugang m; ~**ary** [ək'sesəri] Mitwisser(in), Mitschuldige m, f; ~**ible** [ək'sesəbl] zugänglich; ~**ion** [ək'seʃən] Zuwachs m; Zunahme f; Antritt m; ~ **to the throne** Thronbesteigung f.

accessory [ək'sesəri] Zubehör(teil) n; s. **accessary.**

access road Zufahrtsstraße f; Autobahneinfahrt f.

accident ['æksidənt] Zufall m; Un(glücks)fall m; **by** ~ zufällig; ~**al** [~'dentl] zufällig; nebensächlich.

acclimatize [ə'klaimətaiz] (sich) akklimatisieren od. eingewöhnen.

accommodat|e [ə'kɔmədeit] anpassen; unterbringen; versorgen; j-m aushelfen; ~**ion** Anpassung f; Versorgung f; (*Am. pl:*) Unterkunft f; Unterbringung f.

accompan|iment [ə'kʌm-panimənt] Begleitung *f*; **~y** begleiten.

accomplice [ə'kɔmplis] Komplice *m*.

accomplish [ə'kɔmpliʃ] vollenden; ausführen; **~ed** vollendet, perfekt; **~ment** Vollendung *f*; Ausführung *f*; Leistung *f*; Fähigkeit *f*.

accord [ə'kɔːd] übereinstimmen, gewähren; Übereinstimmung *f*; **with one~** einstimmig; **~ing:** **~ to** gemäß; nach; **~ingly** (dem)entsprechend.

account [ə'kaunt] Rechnung *f*; Berechnung *f*; Konto *n*; Bericht *m*; Rechenschaft *f*; **on no ~** auf keinen Fall; **on ~ of** wegen; **take into ~** berücksichtigen; **call to ~** zur Rechenschaft ziehen; **~ for** Rechenschaft über *et.* ablegen; (sich) erklären; **~ant** Buchhalter *m*; **~ing** Buchführung *f*.

accumulate [ə'kjuːmjuleit] (sich) (an)häufen od. ansammeln.

accura|cy [ˈækjurəsi] Genauigkeit *f*; **~te** [ˈ~it] genau; richtig.

accus|ation [ækjuː(ː)'zei-ʃən] Anklage *f*, Beschuldigung *f*; **~ative (case)** [əˈkjuːzətiv] *gr.* Akkusativ *m*, 4. Fall; **~e** [əˈkjuːz] anklagen, beschuldigen; **~ed: the ~** der *od.* die Angeklagte; **~er** Kläger (-in).

accustom [əˈkʌstəm] gewöhnen; **~ed** gewohnt, üblich; gewöhnt.

ace [eis] As *n* (*a. fig.*).

ache [eik] schmerzen; *anhaltender* Schmerz.

achieve [əˈtʃiːv] ausführen; erreichen; **~ment** Ausführung *f*; Leistung *f*.

acid [ˈæsid] sauer; Säure *f*.

acknowledg|e [əkˈnɔlidʒ] anerkennen; zugeben; *Empfang* bestätigen; **~(e)ment** Anerkennung *f*; Bestätigung *f*; Eingeständnis *n*.

acoustics [əˈkuːstiks] *pl* Akustik *f*.

acquaint [əˈkweint] bekannt machen; **~ s.o. with s.th.** j-m et. mitteilen; **be ~ed with** kennen; **~ance** Bekanntschaft *f*; Bekannte *m*, *f*.

acquire [əˈkwaiə] erwerben.

acquisition [ækwiˈziʃən] Erwerbung *f*; Errungenschaft *f*.

acquit [əˈkwit] freisprechen; **~tal** Freispruch *m*.

acre [ˈeikə] Morgen *m* (4047 *qm*).

acrid [ˈækrid] scharf.

acrobat [ˈækrəbæt] Akrobat *m*.

across [əˈkrɔs] *prp* (quer) durch *od.* über; jenseits, über, auf der anderen Seite von; **come ~, run ~** stoßen auf; *adv* (quer) durch; herüber; quer durch; drüben; über Kreuz.

act [ækt] handeln; wirken; funktionieren; *thea.:* spielen; aufführen; Tat *f*; *thea.* Akt *m*; **~ion** Handlung *f* (*a. thea.*); Tätigkeit *f*; Tat *f*; Wirkung *f*; Klage *f*, Prozeß *m*; Gefecht *n*; Mechanismus *m*.

activ|e [æktiv] aktiv; tätig; wirksam; **~e (voice)** *gr.* Aktiv *n*, Tätigkeitsform *f*; **~ity** Tätigkeit *f*; Betriebsamkeit *f*.

act|or [æktə] Schauspieler *m*; **~ress** Schauspielerin *f*.

actual [æktʃuəl] wirklich. **acute** [ə'kju:t] spitz; scharf (-sinnig); brennend (*Frage*); *med.* akut.

adapt [ə'dæpt] anpassen; bearbeiten.

add [æd] hinzufügen; addieren; hinzukommen.

addict [ædikt] Süchtige *m*, *f*; **~ed** [ə'diktid]: **~ to** dem *Rauschgift etc.* verfallen, ... süchtig.

addition [ə'diʃən] Hinzufügen *n*; Zusatz *m*; Addition *f*; in **~** außerdem; **in ~** to außer; **~al** zusätzlich.

address [ə'dres] *Worte etc.* richten (**to** an), das Wort richten an, *j-n* ansprechen; adressieren; Adresse *f*, Anschrift *f*; Ansprache *f*; **~ee** [ædre'si:] Empfänger *m*.

adequate [ædikwit] angemessen.

adhe|re [əd'hiə] haften

(**to** an), **~sive** [~'hi:siv] Klebstoff *m*; **~sive tape** *od.* **plaster** Heftpflaster *n*.

adjacent [ə'dʒeisənt] benachbart.

adjective [ædʒiktiv] *gr.* Adjektiv *n*, Eigenschaftswort *n*.

adjoin [ə'dʒɔin] angrenzen an.

adjourn [ə'dʒə:n] (sich) vertagen.

adjust [ə'dʒʌst] in Ordnung bringen; anpassen; *tech.* einstellen.

administ|er [əd'ministə] verwalten, führen; spenden; *Arznei* (ein)geben; *Recht* sprechen; **~ration** Verwaltung *f*; Regierung *f*; *bsd. Am.* Amtsperiode *f*; **~rative** [~trətiv] Verwaltungs...; **~rator** [~treitə] (Vermögens)Verwalter *m*.

admirable [ædmərəbl] bewundernswert, großartig.

admiral [ædmərəl] Admiral *m*.

admir|ation [ædmə'reiʃən] Bewunderung *f*; **~e** [əd'maiə] bewundern; verehren; **~er** Verehrer *m*.

admiss|ible [əd'misəbl] zulässig; **~ion** Zulassung *f*; Eintritt(sgeld *n*) *m*; Eingeständnis *n*; **~ion fee** Eintrittsgeld *n*.

admit [əd'mit] (her)einlassen; zulassen; zugeben; **~tance** Zutritt *m*.

admonish [əd'mɔniʃ] ermahnen; warnen.

ado [ə'du:] Getue n.

adolescent [ædəu'lesnt] Jugendliche m, f.

adopt [ə'dɔpt] adoptieren; sich aneignen; **~ion** Adoption f.

ador|able [ə'dɔ:rəbl] liebenswert; entzückend; **~ation** [ædɔ:'reiʃən] Anbetung f; **~e** [ə'dɔ:] anbeten.

adorn [ə'dɔ:n] schmücken.

adult [ˈædʌlt] erwachsen; Erwachsene m, f.

adulter|ate [ə'dʌltəreit] (ver)fälschen; **~y** Ehebruch m.

advance [əd'va:ns] vorrücken; Fortschritte machen; vorbringen; Geld leihen; Preis erhöhen; Vorrücken n; Fortschritt m; Vorschuß m; Erhöhung f; **in ~** im voraus; **~ booking** Brit. Voranmeldung f; **~d** vorgerückt, fortgeschritten; **~ payment** Vorauszahlung f; **~ reservation** bsd. Am. Voranmeldung f.

advantage [əd'va:ntidʒ] Vorteil m; Gewinn m; **take ~ of** ausnutzen; **~ous** [ædvən'teidʒəs] vorteilhaft.

adventur|e [əd'ventʃə] Abenteuer n; **~er** Abenteurer m; **~ous** abenteuerlich.

adverb ['ædvə:b] gr. Adverb n, Umstandswort n.

advers|ary ['ædvəsəri] Gegner m; **~e** ['ə:s] ungünstig.

advertis|e ['ædvətaiz] inserieren; Reklame machen (für); werben (für); **~ement** [əd'və:tismənt] (Zeitungs)Anzeige f, Inserat n; Reklame f; **~ing** Reklame f, Werbung f.

advice [əd'vais] Rat (-schlag) m; **take ~** e-n Rat folgen.

advis|able [əd'vaizəbl] ratsam; **~e** j-n beraten; j-m raten; **~er** Ratgeber(in).

advocate ['ædvəkeit] befürworten. [Antenne f.]

aerial ['ɛəriəl] Luft...;]

aero|nautics [ɛərə'nɔ:tiks] sg Luftfahrt f; **~plane** Flugzeug n.

aesthetic(al) [i:s'θetik (-əl)] ästhetisch.

affair [ə'fɛə] Angelegenheit f, Sache f; Geschäft n; (Liebes)Verhältnis n.

affect [ə'fekt] sich auswirken auf; (be)rühren; med. angreifen, befallen; vortäuschen; affektiert; **~ed** gerührt; affektiert; **~ion** Liebe f, (Zu)Neigung f; **~ionate** [~ʃnit] liebevoll.

affinity [ə'finiti] chem. Affinität f; (geistige) Verwandtschaft.

affirm [ə'fə:m] behaupten; bestätigen; **~ation** [æfə:'meiʃən] Bestätigung f; **~ative** [ə'fə:mətiv] bejahend; sub: **answer in the ~ative** bejahen.

afflict [ə'flikt] betrüben; plagen; **~ion** Elend n; Leiden n.

affluen|ce ['æfluəns] Überfluß *m*; Wohlstand *m*; ~t reich(lich).

afford [ə'fɔ:d] liefern; bieten; **I can ~ it** ich kann es mir leisten; *(gung f.)*

affront [ə'frʌnt] Beleidigen.

afraid [ə'freid]: **be ~ (of)** sich fürchten *od.* Angst haben (vor).

African ['æfrikən] afrikanisch; Afrikaner(in).

after ['ɑ:ftə] *prp räumlich:* hinter (... her), nach; *zeitlich,fig.:* nach; ~ **all** schließlich; doch; ~ **that** danach; *adv* nachher, hinterher, danach; *adj* später, künftig; *cj* nachdem; ~**noon** Nachmittag *m;* **good ~** guten Tag *(nachmittags);* **in the ~** nachmittags; **this ~** heute nachmittag; ~**ward(s)** ['~wəd(z)] nachher; später.

again [ə'gen] wieder (-um); ~ **and** ~, **time and** ~ immer wieder.

against [ə'genst] gegen; an, vor.

age [eidʒ] alt werden *od.* machen; Alter *n;* Zeit(alter *n) f;* **old** ~ Greisenalter *n;* **of** ~ mündig; ... **years of** ~ ... Jahre alt; **at the** ~ **of** ... im Alter von ... Jahren; **for** ~**s** *colloq.* e-e Ewigkeit, ewig; ~**d** ['eidʒid] alt, bejahrt; [eidʒd]: ~ **twenty** 20 Jahre alt.

agen|cy ['eidʒənsi] Tätigkeit *f;* Vermittlung *f;* Vertretung *f,* Agentur *f;* Büro *n;* ~**t** Agent *m,* Vertreter *m;* wirkende Kraft.

aggress|ion [ə'greʃən] Angriff *m;* ~**ive** aggressiv; ~**or** Angreifer *m.*

agile ['ædʒail] flink, behend.

agitat|e ['ædʒiteit] agitieren; bewegen; *fig.* erregen; ~**ion** Agitation *f,* Erregung *f;* ~**or** Agitator *m.*

ago [ə'gəu] vor *(zeitlich);* **long** ~ vor langer Zeit; **a year** ~ vor e-m Jahr.

agon|izing ['æɡənaizɪŋ] qualvoll; ~**y** Qual *f.*

agree [ə'gri:] zustimmen, einwilligen; sich einigen; übereinkommen; übereinstimmen; bekommen *(Essen);* ~**able** [~i-] angenehm; ~**ment** [~i:-] Abkommen *n,* Vereinbarung *f;* Verständigung *f;* Übereinstimmung *f.*

agricultur|al [æɡri'kʌltʃərəl] landwirtschaftlich; ~**e** ['~ʃə] Landwirtschaft *f;* ~**ist** Landwirt *m.*

ague ['eigju:] Wechselfieber *n;* Schüttelfrost *m.*

ahead [ə'hed] vorwärts; vor, voraus; vorn; **straight** ~ geradeaus.

aid [eid] helfen; Hilfe *f.*

ailing ['eiliŋ] kränkelnd.

aim [eim] Ziel *n;* Absicht *f;* zielen; *fig.* beabsichtigen; ~ **at** *Waffe* richten auf; ~**less** ziellos.

air¹ [ɛə] Luft *f;* Luftzug *m;* **by** ~ auf dem Luftwege; **in the open** ~ im Freien; **on the** ~ im Rundfunk.

air² Miene f; Aussehen n; **give o.s.** ~s vornehm tun.

air³ Weise f, Melodie f.

air| base Luftstützpunkt m; **~bed** Luftmatratze f; **~brake** Druckluftbremse f; **~conditioned** mit Klimaanlage; **~craft** Flugzeug (a pl) n; **~craft carrier** Flugzeugträger m; **~crew** Flugzeugbesatzung f; **~cushion** Luftkissen n; ~ **force** Luftwaffe f; **~hostess** Stewardeß f; **~letter** Luftpostbrief m; **~lift** Luftbrücke f; **~line** Fluggesellschaft f, Luftverkehrsgesellschaft f; **~liner** Verkehrsflugzeug n; ~ **mail** Luftpost f; **~plane** Am. Flugzeug n; **~pocket** Luftloch n; **~port** Flughafen m; ~ **raid** Luftangriff m; **~route** Flugstrecke f; **~show** Luftfahrtschau f; **~sick** luftkrank; **~taxi** Lufttaxi n; ~ **terminal** Fluggastabfertigungsgebäude n (in der Innenstadt); **~tight** luftdicht; **~traffic** Flugverkehr m; ~ **traffic control** Flugsicherung f; ~ **traffic controller** Fluglotse m; **~way** s. **airline; ~y** luftig.

aisle [ail] Seitenschiff n; Gang m.

ajar [ə'dʒɑː] halb offen, angelehnt.

akin [ə'kin] verwandt (**to** mit).

alacrity [ə'lækriti] Bereitwilligkeit f, Eifer m.

alarm [ə'lɑːm] alarmieren; beunruhigen; Alarm(zeichen n) m; Angst f; **give the** ~ Alarm schlagen; **~clock** Wecker m.

alcohol ['ælkəhɔl] Alkohol m; **~ic** alkoholisch.

ale [eil] Ale n, helles englisches Bier.

alert [ə'lɔːt] wachsam; sub: **on the** ~ auf der Hut.

alibi ['ælibai] Alibi n.

alien ['eiljən] fremd; Ausländer(in).

alight [ə'lait] ab-, aussteigen; sich niederlassen (Vogel); aer. landen.

alike [ə'laik] gleich, ähnlich; gleich, ebenso.

alimony ['æliməni] Unterhalt m.

alive [ə'laiv] am Leben, lebend; lebhaft, belebt; **be still** ~ noch leben.

all [ɔːl] all; ganz; jede(r, -s); alles; alle pl; ganz, völlig; ~ **of us** wir alle; **two** ~ sp. 2:2; **at** ~ überhaupt; **not at** ~ überhaupt nicht; keine Ursache!; nichts zu danken!; **for** ~ **I care** meinetwegen; **for** ~ **I know** soviel ich weiß; ~ **at once** auf einmal; ~ **the better** desto besser; ~ **but** fast.

alleged [ə'ledʒd] angeblich.
alleviate [ə'li:vieit] lindern.
alley ['æli] Gäßchen *n*;
Allee *f*; (Durch)Gang *m*.
alliance [ə'laiəns] Bündnis *n*.
allot [ə'lɔt] zuteilen; **~ment** Zuteilung *f*; Parzelle *f*; Schrebergarten *m*.
allow [ə'lau] erlauben; bewilligen, gewähren; zugeben; **~ for** berücksichtigen; **be ~ed** dürfen; **~ance** Erlaubnis *f*; Bewilligung *f*; Taschengeld *n*, Zuschuß *m*.
alloy ['ælɔi] Legierung *f*.
all-round vielseitig.
allu|de [ə'lu:d]: **~ to** anspielen auf; **~re** [ə'ljuə] (an-, ver)locken; **~sion** [ə'lu:ʒən] Anspielung *f*.
ally [ə'lai] (sich) vereinigen; sich verbünden; ['ælai] Verbündete *m*, *f*; **the Allies** *pl* die Alliierten *pl*.
almighty [ɔːl'maiti] allmächtig. [del *f*.]
almond ['ɑːmənd] Mandel-
almost ['ɔːlməust] fast, beinahe.
alms [ɑːmz], *pl* **~** Almosen *f*.
aloft [ə'lɔft] (hoch) oben.
alone [ə'ləun] allein; **let** *od.* **leave ~** in Ruhe *od.* bleiben lassen; **let ~** geschweige denn.
along [ə'lɔŋ] *prp* entlang, längs; *adv* weiter, vorwärts; **all ~** die ganze Zeit; **~ with** zs. mit;

come ~ mitkommen;
~side Seite an Seite, neben.
aloud [ə'laud] laut.
alphabet ['ælfəbit] Alphabet *n*, Abc *n*; **~ical** [~'betikəl] alphabetisch.
already [ɔːl'redi] bereits, schon.
also ['ɔːlsəu] auch, ebenfalls.
altar ['ɔːltə] Altar *m*.
alter ['ɔːltə] (sich) verändern; ab-, umändern; **~ation** Änderung *f*.
alternat|e [ɔːl'tɔːneit] abwechseln (lassen); [~'tɔːnit] abwechselnd; **~ing current** Wechselstrom *m*; **~ive** [ɔːl'tɔːnətiv] Alternative *f*, Wahl *f*.
although [ɔːl'ðəu] obgleich, obwohl.
altitude ['æltitjuːd] Höhe *f*.
altogether [ɔːltə'geðə] völlig; alles in allem.
alumin|ium [ælju'minjəm], *Am.* **~um** [ə'luːminəm] Aluminium *n*.
always ['ɔːlweiz] immer.
am [æm, əm] *1. sg pres von* **be**.
amateur ['æmətə(:)] Amateur *m*; (Kunst- *etc.*) Liebhaber *m*.
amaz|e [ə'meiz] erstaunen, verblüffen; **~ement** Erstaunen *n*, Verblüffung *f*; **~ing** erstaunlich, verblüffend.
ambassador [æm'bæsədə] Botschafter *m*. [*m*.]
amber ['æmbə] Bernstein-

ambiguous [æm'bigjuəs]
zwei-, vieldeutig; un-
klar.

ambiti|on [æm'biʃən]Ehr-
geiz m; ~ous ehrgeizig.

ambulance ['æmbjuləns]
Krankenwagen m.

ambush ['æmbuʃ] Hinter-
halt m; auflauern.

amen ['ɑː'men] Amen n.

amend [ə'mend] (ver-)
bessern; Gesetz (ab)än-
dern; sich bessern; ~ment
(Ver)Besserung f; Än-
derung(santrag m) f; ~s
sg (Schaden)Ersatz m;
make ~s Schadenersatz
leisten.

American [ə'merikən]
amerikanisch; Amerikaner
(-in); Amerikanisch n.

amiable ['eimjəbl] liebenswürdig.

amicable ['æmikəbl]
gütlich.

amid(st) [ə'mid(st)]
(mitten) in od. unter.

amiss [ə'mis] verkehrt;
falsch; **take** ~ übelnehmen.

ammunition [æmju'ni-
ʃən] Munition f.

amnesty ['æmnisti] Amnestie f.

among(st) [ə'mʌŋ(st)]
(mitten) unter, zwischen.

amount [ə'maunt] Be-
trag m; Menge f; Be-
deutung f; ~ **to** sich belaufen auf; hinauslaufen
auf, bedeuten.

ample ['æmpl] weit, groß;
reichlich.

amplif|ier ['æmplifaiə]

electr. Verstärker m; ~y
['~ai] verstärken.

amputate ['æmpjuteit]
amputieren.

amulet ['æmjulit] Amulett n.

amus|e [ə'mjuːz] amüsie-
ren, unterhalten; ~ement
Unterhaltung f, Zeitver-
treib m; ~ing lustig, amü-
sant.

an [æn, ən] ein(e).

an(a)emia [ə'niːmjə]
Blutarmut f.

an(a)esthetic [ænis'θetik]
Betäubungsmittel n.

analog|ous [ə'næləgəs]
analog, ähnlich; ~y [~dʒi]
Analogie f.

analy|se, Am. a. ~ze
['ænəlaiz] analysieren, zerlegen; ~sis [ə'næləsis]
Analyse f.

anatom|ize [ə'nætəmaiz]
zergliedern; ~y Anatomie f.

ancest|or ['ænsistə] Vor-
fahr m, Ahn m; ~ry Ab-
stammung f; Ahnen pl.

anchor ['æŋkə] Anker m.

anchovy ['æntʃəvi] Sar-
delle f.

ancient ['einʃənt] (ur)alt,
antik; sub: **the** ~s pl die
Alten (Griechen u. Römer).

and [ænd, ənd] und; ~ **so**
on und so weiter.

anecdote ['ænikdəut]
Anekdote f.

anew [ə'njuː] von neuem.

angel ['eindʒəl] Engel m.

anger ['æŋgə] Zorn m,
Ärger m. [gina f.]

angina [æn'dʒainə] An-

angle ['æŋgl] Winkel *m*; *fig.* Standpunkt *m*; angeln.

Anglican ['æŋglikən] anglikanisch.

Anglo-Saxon ['æŋglou-'sæksən] angelsächsisch; Angelsachse *m*.

angry ['æŋgri] zornig, böse, ärgerlich (**with** *s.o.,* **at** *s.th.* über).

anguish ['æŋgwiʃ] (Seelen)Qual *f.*

angular ['æŋgjulə] winkelig; eckig.

animal ['æniməl] Tier *n*; tierisch.

animat|e ['ænimeit] beleben; anregen, aufmuntern; **~ed cartoon** Zeichentrickfilm *m*; **~ion** Lebhaftigkeit *f*; Zeichentrickfilm *m.*

animosity [æni'mɔsiti] Feindseligkeit *f.*

ankle ['æŋkl] (Fuß)Knöchel *m.*

annex(e) ['æneks] Anhang *m*; Anbau *m*, Nebengebäude *n.*

annihilate [ə'naiəleit] vernichten.

anniversary [æni'vɔːsəri] Jahrestag *m.*

annotation [ænəu'teiʃən] Anmerkung *f.*

announce [ə'nauns] ankündigen; ansagen; **~ment** Ankündigung *f*; Durchsage *f*; Anzeige *f*; **~r** Ansager(in).

annoy [ə'nɔi]: **be ~ed** sich ärgern; **~ance** Ärger (-nis *n*) *m.*

annual ['ænjuəl] jährlich; Jahrbuch *n.*

annuity [ə'nju(ː)iti] Jahresrente *f.*

annul [ə'nʌl] annullieren.

anodyne ['ænoudain] schmerzstillend(es Mittel).

anomalous [ə'nɔmələs] anomal.

anonymous [ə'nɔniməs] anonym.

another [ə'nʌðə] ein anderer; ein zweiter; noch ein; **with one ~** miteinander; **for ~ day** noch e-n Tag.

answer ['ɑːnsə] Antwort *f*; beantworten; antworten (auf *od.* **to** auf; Zweck erfüllen; **~ for** einstehen für; **~ to** entsprechen.

ant [ænt] Ameise *f.*

antagonist [æn'tægənist] Gegner(in).

antelope ['æntiləup] Antilope *f.*

anthem ['ænθəm] Hymne *f.*

anti|... ['ænti] Gegen...; gegen...; **~aircraft** Fliegerabwehr...; **~biotic** ['.bai'ɔtik]Antibiotikum *n.*

anticipate [æn'tisipeit] vorwegnehmen; zuvorkommen; voraussehen, ahnen; erwarten; **~ion** Vorwegnahme *f*; Erwartung *f*; **in ~ion** im voraus.

anti|cyclone ['ænti'saikləun] Hoch(druckgebiet) *n*; **~dote** ['.dəut] Gegengift *n*; **~freeze** *mot.* Frostschutzmittel *n.*

antipathy [æn'tipəθi] Abneigung *f*.

antiquated ['æntikweitid] veraltet.

antique|e [æn'ti:k] antik, alt; **~ity** [~ikwiti] Altertum *n*.

antiseptic [ænti'septik] antiseptisch(es Mittel).

antlers ['æntləz] *pl* Geweih *n*.

anvil ['ænvil] Amboß *m*.

anxiety [æŋ'zaiəti] Angst *f*; Sorge *f*.

anxious ['æŋkʃəs] ängstlich, besorgt (**about** um, wegen); gespannt (**for** auf); bestrebt (**to** zu).

any ['eni] (irgend)ein(e), (irgend)welche *pl*; jede(r, ~s) (beliebige); irgend (-wie), etwas; **not ~** kein; **not ~ longer** nicht länger, nicht mehr; **not ~ more** nicht(s) mehr; **~body** jeder; jemand; **~how** irgendwie; trotzdem, jedenfalls; **~one** *s*. **~body**; **~thing** (irgend) etwas; alles; **~thing but** alles andere als; **~thing else?** (sonst) noch (irgend) etwas?; **not ~thing** nichts; *s*. **~way** ohnehin; **~where** irgendwo(hin); überall; **not ~where** nirgends.

apart [ə'pɑːt] auseinander, getrennt; für sich; beiseite; **~ from** abgesehen von.

apartment [ə'pɑːtmənt] Zimmer *n*; *Am. a.* Wohnung *f*; *pl Brit.* (möblierte) (Miet)Wohnung, Apart-

ment *n*; **~ house** *Am.* Mietshaus *n*.

apathetic [æpə'θetik] apathisch, gleichgültig.

ape [eip] (Menschen-) Affe *m*.

apiece [ə'piːs] (für) das Stück, je.

apolog|ize [ə'plədʒaiz] sich entschuldigen; **~y** Entschuldigung *f*.

apoplexy ['æpəupleksi] Schlag(anfall) *m*.

apostle [ə'pɒsl] Apostel *m*.

apostrophe [ə'pɒstrəfi] Apostroph *m*.

appal(l) [ə'pɔːl] entsetzen.

apparatus [æpə'reitəs] Apparat *m*.

apparent [ə'pærənt] anscheinend, scheinbar; klar.

appeal [ə'piːl] *jur.* Berufung einlegen; **~ to** appellieren an, sich wenden an; wirken auf, zusagen; *jur.* Revision *f*, Berufung *f*; Aufruf *m*, dringende Bitte; Reiz *m*.

appear [ə'piə] erscheinen; sich zeigen; *öffentlich* auftreten; scheinen, aussehen; **~ance** Erscheinen *n*, Auftreten *n*; Aussehen *n*, Äußere *n*; Anschein *m*.

appease [ə'piːz] beschwichtigen; stillen.

appendi|citis [əpendi'saitis] Blinddarmentzündung *f*; **~x** [ə'pendiks] Anhang *m*; (**vermiform**) **~x** Blinddarm *m*.

appeti|te ['æpitait]: **~** (**for**) Appetit *m* (auf); *fig.* Ver-

langen *n* (nach); **~zing**
appetitanregend.
applau|d [ə'plɔ:d] applau-
dieren; loben; **~se** [~z]
Applaus *m*, Beifall *m*.
apple ['æpl] Apfel *m*; **~-pie**
gedeckter Apfelkuchen; **~-
sauce** Apfelmus *n*.
appliance [ə'plaiəns] Vorrichtung *f*, Gerät *n*.
applica|nt ['æplikənt] Be-
werber(in); **~tion** Auf-,
Anlegen *n*; Anwendung *f*;
Gesuch *n*; Bewerbung *f*.
apply [ə'plai] auf-, anlegen; anwenden; ver-
wenden; zutreffen, gelten;
sich wenden (to an);
~ o.s. to sich widmen;
~ for sich bewerben um;
beantragen.
appoint [ə'pɔint] festsetzen; ernennen; **~ment**
Verabredung *f*, Termin
m; Ernennung *f*; Stellung
f, Stelle *f*.
apportion [ə'pɔ:ʃən] ver-
zuteilen.
appreciat|e [ə'pri:ʃieit]
schätzen; würdigen, zu
schätzen wissen; **~ion**
Würdigung *f*; Verständ-
nis *n*; Anerkennung *f*.
apprehen|d [æpri'hend]
festnehmen;begreifen, verstehen; befürchten; **~sion**
Festnahme *f*; Verstand *m*;
Besorgnis *f*; **~sive** ängstlich, besorgt.
apprentice [ə'prentis]
Lehrling *m*; *vb*: **be ~d to**
in der Lehre sein bei; **~ship**
[~iʃip] Lehre *f*.

approach [ə'prəutʃ] sich
nähern; herantreten an;
(Heran)Nahen *n*; Annähe-
rung *f*; Zugang *m*, Zu-,
Auffahrt *f*; **~ road** Zufahrtsstraße *f*.
appropriate [ə'prəupriit]
angemessen; passend.
approv|al [ə'pru:vəl] Bil-
ligung *f*; **~e** billigen.
approximate [ə'prɔksi-
mit] annähernd.
apricot ['eiprikɔt] Aprikose *f*.
April ['eiprəl] April *m*.
apron ['eiprən] Schürze *f*.
apt [æpt] passend; begabt; **~ to** neigend zu.
aquarium [ə'kwɛəriəm]
Aquarium *n*.
aquatic [ə'kwætik] Wasser...;**~ sports** *pl* Wasser-
sport *m*.
aqueduct ['ækwidʌkt]
Aquädukt *n*.
aquiline ['ækwilain] Adler...
Arab ['ærəb] Araber(in);
~ic arabisch; Arabisch *n*.
arbitrary ['ɑ:bitrəri] will-
kürlich; eigenmächtig.
arbo(u)r ['ɑ:bə] Laube *f*.
arc [ɑ:k] Bogen *m*; **~ade**
[ɑ:'keid] Arkade *f*.
arch[1] [ɑ:tʃ] Bogen *m*; Gewölbe *n*; (sich) wölben.
arch[2] Haupt...; Erz...
arch[3] schelmisch.
arch(a)eolog|ist [ɑ:ki-
'ɔlədʒist] Archäologe *m*;
~y Archäologie *f*.
archaic [ɑ:'keiik] veraltet.
arch|angel ['ɑ:k-] Erz-

engel *m*; **~bishop** ['a:tʃ'-] Erzbischof *m*.

archer ['a:tʃə] Bogenschütze *m*; **~y** Bogenschießen *n*.

architect ['a:kitekt] Architekt *m*; **~ure** Architektur *f*.

archives ['a:kaivz] *pl* Archiv *n*.

archway (Tor)Bogen *m*.

arctic ['a:ktik] arktisch.

ard|ent ['a:dənt] begeistert; glühend, feurig; **~o(u)r** *fig.*: Eifer *m*; Glut *f*.

are [a:] *pres pl u. 2. sg von* **be**.

area ['ɛəriə] Fläche *f*; Gebiet *n*.

Argentine ['a:dʒəntain] argentinisch; Argentinier (-in).

argu|e ['a:gju:] erörtern; beweisen; behaupten; streiten; Einwände machen; Argument *n*, (Beweis)Grund *m*; Erörterung *f*; **~mentation** Beweisführung *f*.

arise [ə'raiz] (*irr* **rise**) entstehen, sich ergeben; sich erheben.

arithmetic [ə'riθmətik] Rechnen *n*.

ark [a:k] Arche *f*.

arm[1] [a:m] Arm *m*; Armlehne *f*; Ärmel *m*.

arm[2] (sich) bewaffnen; **~ament** [a:'məmənt] Aufrüstung *f*; **~ament race** Wettrüsten *n*.

armchair Sessel *m*.

armistice ['a:mistis] Waffenstillstand *m* (*a. fig.*).

armo(u)r ['a:mə] Rüstung *f*; Panzer *m* (*a. zo.*); panzern; **~ed car** Panzerwagen *m*.

armpit Achselhöhle *f*.

arms [a:mz] *pl* Waffen *pl*.

army ['a:mi] Heer *n*, Armee *f*.

around [ə'raund] *prp* um, um ... her(um), rund um; *Am. colloq.* etwa; *adv* (rund)herum; überall.

arouse [ə'rauz] aufwecken; *fig.* aufrütteln; erregen.

arrange [ə'reindʒ] (an-) ordnen; vereinbaren, abmachen; festsetzen; **~ment** Anordnung *f*; Übereinkommen *n*; Vorkehrung *f*.

arrears [ə'riəz] *pl* Rückstand *m*; Schulden *pl*.

arrest [ə'rest] Verhaftung *f*; verhaften; hemmen; *fig.* fesseln.

arriv|al [ə'raivəl] Ankunft *f*; Ankömmling *m*; **~e: ~ (at, in)** (an)kommen (in), eintreffen (in); **~e at** *fig.* kommen zu, erreichen.

arrogan|ce ['ærəugəns] Anmaßung *f*; **~t** anmaßend.

arrow ['ærəu] Pfeil *m*.

arsenic ['a:snik] Arsen(ik) *n*; [a:'senik] Arsen...

arson ['a:sn] *jur.* Brandstiftung *f*.

art [a:t] Kunst(erziehung) *f*; *pl* List *f*; *pl* Geisteswissenschaften *pl*.

arter|ial [a:'tiəriəl] Arterien...; **~ial road** Ausfallstraße f; **~y** ['ɑːtəri] Arterie f, Pulsader f; *fig.* (Haupt)Verkehrsader f.

artful schlau, verschlagen.

article ['ɑːtikl] Artikel m (a. *Zeitung*), Gegenstand m, Ware f; *gr.* Artikel m, Geschlechtswort n.

articulate [ɑː'tikjuleit] deutlich (aus)sprechen; [~t] deutlich; gegliedert.

artificial [ɑːti'fiʃl] künstlich, Kunst...

artillery [ɑː'tiləri] Artillerie f.

artisan [ɑːti'zæn] Handwerker m.

artist ['ɑːtist] Künstler (-in) f; **~e** [ɑː'tiːst] Artist(in) f; **~ic** [ɑː'tistik] künstlerisch, Kunst...

artless ungekünstelt; arglos.

as [æz, əz] so, (ebenso wie; als; als, während; da, weil; (so) wie; **~ ... ~** (eben)so ... wie; **~ many ~** nicht weniger als; **~ well** auch; **~ well ...** sowohl ... als auch; **~ for** was ... (an)betrifft.

ascen|d [ə'send] (auf-, herauf-, hinauf)steigen; be-, ersteigen; **~sion** Aufsteigen n; **♀sion (Day)** Himmelfahrt(stag m) f; **~t** Aufstieg m, Besteigung f; Steigung f.

ascertain [æsə'tein] feststellen.

ascetic [ə'setik] asketisch.

ascribe [əs'kraib] zuschreiben.

aseptic [æ'septik] aseptisch(es Mittel).

ash¹ [æʃ] Esche f.

ash², **~es** pl ['æʃiz] Asche f.

ashamed [ə'ʃeimd] beschämt; **be** *od.* **feel ~ of** sich *e-r S. od. j-s* schämen.

ash can *Am.* Mülleimer m.

ashore [ə'ʃɔː]: **go ~ an** Land gehen.

ash|-tray Asch(en)becher m; **♀ Wednesday** Aschermittwoch m.

Asiatic [eiʃi'ætik] asiatisch; Asiat(in) f.

aside [ə'said] beiseite; **~ from** *Am.* abgesehen von.

ask [ɑːsk] fragen (**s.th.** nach et.,); verlangen; bitten; **~ a question** e-e Frage stellen; **~ s.o. to dinner** j-n zum Essen einladen; **~ for** bitten um, fragen nach.

askew [əs'kjuː] schief.

asleep [ə'sliːp] schlafend; **be (fast) ~** (fest) schlafen; **fall ~** einschlafen.

asparagus [əs'pærəgəs] Spargel m.

aspect ['æspekt] Aussehen n; Lage f; Aspekt m.

aspire [əs'paiə]: **~ (after, to)** streben (nach).

ass [æs] Esel m.

assail [ə'seil] angreifen, überfallen; befallen (*Zweifel*); **~ant** Angreifer(in).

assassin [ə'sæsin] Attentäter(in); **~ate** [~eit] ermorden; **~ation** politischer Mord, Attentat n.

assault [ə'sɔːlt] Angriff m; angreifen.

assembl|age [ə'semblidʒ] *tech.* Montage f; **~e** (ˌ~bl) (sich) versammeln; *tech.* montieren; **~y** Versammlung f; *tech.* Montage f; **~y line** Fließband n.

assent [ə'sent] Zustimmung f; **~ to** zustimmen, billigen.

assert [ə'səːt] behaupten; geltend machen.

assess [ə'ses] *Kosten etc.* festsetzen; besteuern.

assets ['æsets] pl Vermögen n; *econ.* Aktiva pl.

assign [ə'sain] an-, zuweisen; bestimmen; **~ment** Anweisung f.

assimilate [ə'simileit] (sich) angleichen; (sich) assimilieren.

assist [ə'sist] beistehen, helfen; unterstützen; **~ance** Hilfe f; **~ant** Assistent(in); Verkäufer(in).

assizes [ə'saiziz] pl *Brit. periodisches* Schwurgericht (*bis 1971*).

associat|e [ə'səuʃieit] vereinigen; verbinden; assoziieren; verkehren; Teilhaber m; Gefährte m; **~ion** Vereinigung f; Verbindung f; Verein m; (Handels)Gesellschaft f; Genossenschaft f; **~ion football** (Verbands)Fußball m.

assort|ed [ə'sɔːtid] gemischt; **~ment** Auswahl f; Mischung f.

assume [ə'sjuːm] annehmen.

assur|ance [ə'ʃuərəns] Versicherung f; Zusicherung f; Zuversicht f, Gewißheit f; Selbstsicherheit f; **~e** (ˌ~uə) (ver)sichern; **~ed** Versicherte m, f.

asthma ['æsmə] Asthma n.

astir [ə'stəː] auf (den Beinen); in Aufregung.

astonish [əs'tɔniʃ] überraschen; be **~ed** erstaunt sein (**at** über); **~ing** erstaunlich; **~ment** (Er-) Staunen n, Verwunderung f.

astray [əs'trei]: **lead ~** irreführen, verleiten.

astride [əs'traid] rittlings.

astringent [əs'trindʒənt] zs.-ziehend(es Mittel).

astronaut ['æstrənɔːt] Astronaut m, Raumfahrer m.

asunder [ə'sʌndə] auseinander; entzwei.

asylum [ə'sailəm] Asyl n.

at [æt, ət] *räumlich:* an, auf, bei, in, zu; *zeitlich:* an, auf, bei, in, im Alter von, mit, um, zu; *Richtung, Ziel:* auf, gegen, nach; *fig.* auf, bei, für, von, mit, nach, über, um, zu.

ate [et] *pret von* **eat**.

athlet|e ['æθliːt] (Leicht-) Athlet m; **~ic** [-'letik] athletisch; **~ics** sg Leichtathletik f.

Atlantic [ət'læntik] atlantisch; **~ (Ocean)** Atlantik m, Atlantischer Ozean.

atlas ['ætləs] Atlas m.

atmosphere ['ætməsfiə] Atmosphäre f.

atom ['ætəm] Atom n; **~ bomb** Atombombe f.

atomic [ə'tɔmik] atomar, Atom...; **~ age** Atomzeitalter n; **~ bomb** Atombombe f; **~ pile** Kernreaktor m; **~ powered** durch Atomkraft betrieben, Atom...

atomize ['ætəumaiz] atomisieren; zr Zerstäuber m.

atone [ə'təun]: **~ for** wiedergutmachen.

atrocious [ə'trəuʃəs] scheußlich; grausam; **~ty** [‿ɔsiti] Greueltat f.

attach [ə'tætʃ] anheften, befestigen; Wert beimessen; **be ~ed to** hängen an; **~ o.s.** to sich anschließen an; **~ment** Anhänglichkeit f.

attack [ə'tæk] angreifen; Angriff m; med. Anfall m.

attempt [ə'tempt] versuchen; Versuch m.

attend [ə'tend] bedienen; pflegen; med. behandeln; teilnehmen an; Vorlesung etc. besuchen; anwesend sein; fig. begleiten; **~ance** Begleitung f, Gefolge n; Bedienung f; med. Behandlung f; Besuch m (e-r Schule etc.); **~ant** Begleiter(in); Wärter(in); tech. Wart m; pl Gefolge n.

attention [ə'tenʃən] Aufmerksamkeit f; **~ive** aufmerksam.

attest [ə'test] bescheinigen.

attic ['ætik] Mansarde f.

attitude ['ætitju:d] (Ein-) Stellung f; Haltung f.

attorney [ə'tə:ni] Bevollmächtigte m; Am. (Rechts-) Anwalt m.

attract [ə'trækt] anziehen; Aufmerksamkeit erregen, auf sich lenken; **~ion** Anziehung(skraft) f; fig. Reiz m; **~ive** reizvoll.

attribute [ə'tribju(:)t] beimessen; zurückführen (**to** auf); ['ætribju:t] Attribut n, Merkmal n; gr. Attribut n, Beifügung f.

auburn ['ɔ:bən] kastanienbraun.

auction ['ɔ:kʃən] Auktion f; msr **~ off** versteigern.

audacious [ɔ:'deiʃəs] kühn; unverschämt; **~ty** [ɔ:'dæsiti] Unverschämtheit f.

audible ['ɔ:dəbl] hörbar.

audience ['ɔ:djəns] Publikum n, Zuhörer pl, Zuschauer pl; Leser(kreis m) pl; Audienz f.

aught [ɔ:t]: **for ~ I care** meinetwegen.

August ['ɔ:gəst] August m.

august [ɔ:'gʌst] erhaben.

aunt [u:nt] Tante f.

au pair girl [əu 'pɛə] Au-pair-Mädchen n.

austere [ɔs'tiə] streng; einfach; **~ity** [‿'teriti] Strenge f; Einfachheit f.

Australian [ɔs'treiljən] australisch; Australier(in).

Austrian ['ɔstriən] österreichisch; Österreicher(in).

authentic [ɔːˈθentik] authentisch, zuverlässig, echt.

author [ˈɔːθə] Urheber (-in); Autor(in), Schriftsteller(in), Verfasser(in); **~itative** [ɔːˈθɔritətiv] maßgebend; gebieterisch; zuverlässig; **~ity** Autorität f; Vollmacht f; Fachmann m; mst pl Behörde f; **~ize** [ˈ~ɔraiz] bevollmächtigen; **~ship** Urheberschaft f.

auto|graph [ˈɔːtəgrɑːf] Autogramm n; **~mat** [ˈ~mæt] Automatenrestaurant n; **~matic** [ˌ~ˈmætik] automatisch; **~mation** Automation f.

autumn [ˈɔːtəm] Herbst m.

auxiliary [ɔːˈziljəri] Hilfs...; **~ (verb)** gr. Hilfsverb n.

avail [əˈveil] nützen, helfen; **~ o.s. of** sich e-r S. bedienen; Nutzen m; **of no ~** nutzlos; **~able** verfügbar, vorhanden, benutzbar; gültig.

avalanche [ˈævəlɑːnʃ] Lawine f.

avaric|e [ˈævəris] Geiz m; Habsucht f; **~ious** [ˌ~ˈriʃəs] geizig; habgierig.

avenge [əˈvendʒ] rächen.

avenue [ˈævinjuː] Allee f; bsd. Am. Prachtstraße f.

average [ˈævəridʒ] Durchschnitt m; durchschnittlich, Durchschnitts...

avers|e [əˈvəːs] abgeneigt **(to, from** dat); **~ion** Widerwille m.

avert [əˈvəːt] abwenden; vermeiden.

aviat|ion [eiviˈeiʃən] Fliegen n; Luftfahrt f; **~or** [ˈ~tə] Flieger m.

avoid [əˈvɔid] (ver)meiden.

avow [əˈvau] bekennen, (ein)gestehen; **~al** Bekenntnis n, (Ein)Geständnis n.

await [əˈweit] erwarten.

awake[1] [əˈweik] wach, munter.

awake[2] (irr) (auf)wecken; auf-, erwachen; **~ to** s.th. sich e-r S. bewußt werden; **~n** fig. erwecken.

award [əˈwɔːd] Urteil n; Preis m; zusprechen; verleihen.

aware [əˈwɛə]: **be ~ of** wissen von, sich e-r S. bewußt sein.

away [əˈwei] weg, fort; immerzu, darauflos.

awe [ɔː] (Ehr)Furcht f, Scheu f; (Ehr)Furcht einflößen; einschüchtern.

awful [ˈɔːful] furchtbar, schrecklich.

awhile [əˈwail] e-e Weile.

awkward [ˈɔːkwəd] ungeschickt, linkisch; unangenehm; unpraktisch.

awning [ˈɔːniŋ] Plane f, Markise f.

awoke [əˈwəuk] pret u. pp von **awake**[2].

awry [əˈrai] schief; **go ~** schiefgehen.

ax(e) [æks] Axt f, Beil n.

axis [ˈæksis], pl **axes** [ˈ~iːz] Achse f.

axle(-tree) ['æksl(-)](Rad-) Achse *f*.

azure ['æʒə] azur-, himmelblau.

B

babble ['bæbl] stammeln, plappern; Geplapper *n*.

babe [beib] Baby *n*, kleines Kind.

baboon [bə'bu:n] Pavian *m*.

baby ['beibi] Säugling *m*, kleines Kind, Baby *n*; Baby..., Kinder...; klein; **~ carriage** *Am.* Kinderwagen *m*; **~hood** erste Kindheit.

bachelor ['bætʃələ] Junggeselle *m*.

back [bæk] Rücken *m*; Rückseite *f*; Rücklehne *f*; Rücksitz *m*; Fußball: Verteidiger *m*; Hinter..., Rück...; rückwärtig; rückständig; zurück; hinten grenzen an; rückwärts fahren; unterstützen; sich rückwärts bewegen, zurückgehen, -fahren; **~bone** Rückgrat *n*; **~door** Hintertür *f*; **~fire** Fehlzündung *f*; **~ground** Hintergrund *m*; **~ number** alte Nummer (*e~r Zeitung*); **~ seat** Rücksitz *m*; **~stairs** Hintertreppe *f*; **~stroke** Rückenschwimmen *n*; **~ tyre** Hinterreifen *m*; **~ ward** ['~wəd] Rück(wärts)...; zurückgeblieben, rückständig; zurückhaltend; **~ward(s)** rückwärts, zurück; **~ wheel** Hinterrad *n*.

bacon ['beikən] Speck *m*; **~ and eggs** Spiegeleier mit Speck.

bacterium [bæk'tiəriəm], *pl* **~ia** [~iə] Bakterie *f*.

bad [bæd] schlecht, böse, schlimm; **not (too)** ~ nicht schlecht!; **that's too** ~ ach wie dumm!, so ein Pech!; **he is ~ly off** es geht ihm sehr schlecht (*finanziell*); **~ly wounded** schwerverwundet; **want ~ly** dringend brauchen.

bade [bæd] *pret von* **bid.**

badge [bædʒ] Abzeichen *n*.

badger ['bædʒə] Dachs *m*.

badminton ['bædmintən] Federballspiel *n*.

baffle ['bæfl] verwirren; vereiteln.

bag [bæg] Beutel *m*, Sack *m*; Tüte *f*; Tasche *f*.

baggage ['bægidʒ] *Am.* (Reise)Gepäck *n*; **~ check** *Am.* Gepäckschein *m*.

baggy ['bægi] bauschig; ausgebeult; **~pipes** *pl* Dudelsack *m*.

bail [beil] Kaution *f*; **~ out** gegen Kaution freibekommen.

bailiff ['beilif] Gerichtsvollzieher *m*, -diener *m*; (Guts)Verwalter *m*.

bait [beit] Köder *m* (*a. fig.*).

bak|e [beik] (über)backen; braten; *Ziegel* brennen; **~er** Bäcker *m*; **at the ~er's** beim Bäcker; **~ery** Bäckerei *f*; **~ing-powder** Backpulver *n*.

balance ['bæləns] Waage *f*; Gleichgewicht *n* (*a. fig.*); Unruh(e) *f* (*Uhr*); ab-, erwägen; (aus)balancieren; *econ.* (sich) ausgleichen; **~ wheel** Unruh(e) *f* (*Uhr*).

balcony ['bælkəni] Balkon *m*.

bald [bɔ:ld] kahl.

bale [beil] *econ.* Ballen *m*.

balk [bɔ:k] Balken *m*; Hindernis *n*; verhindern, -eiteln; scheuen (*bsd. Pferd*).

ball [bɔ:l] Ball *m*; Kugel *f*; (Hand-, Fuß)Ballen *m*; Knäuel *m, n*; Kloß *m*; Ball *m*, Tanzveranstaltung *f*.

ballad ['bæləd] Ballade *f*.

ballast ['bæləst] Ballast *m*.

ball-bearing(s *pl*) *tech.* Kugellager *n*.

ballet ['bælei] Ballett *n*.

ballistic [bə'listik] ballistisch.

balloon [bə'lu:n] Ballon *m*.

ballot ['bælət] Wahlzettel *m*; (geheime) Wahl; **~box** Wahlurne *f*.

ball(-point)-pen Kugelschreiber *m*.

balm [bɑ:m] Balsam *m*; *fig.* Trost *m*.

balmy ['bɑ:mi] mild; heilend.

balustrade [bæləs'treid] Geländer *n*.

bamboo [bæm'bu:] Bambus *m*.

ban [bæn] (amtliches) Verbot; Bann *m*, Acht *f*; verbieten.

banana [bə'nɑ:nə] Banane *f*.

band [bænd] Band *n*; Streifen *m*; Schar *f*; Bande *f*; (Musik)Kapelle *f*.

bandage ['bændidʒ] Binde *f*; Verband *m*; bandagieren, verbinden.

band|master Kapellmeister *m*; **~stand** Musikpavillon *m*.

bang [bæŋ] Knall *m*; heftiger Schlag; Pony *m* (*Frisur*); Tür zuschlagen.

banish ['bæniʃ] verbannen; **~ment** Verbannung *f*.

banisters [bænistəz] *pl* Treppengeländer *n*.

banjo ['bændʒou] Banjo *n*.

bank [bæŋk] Böschung *f*; Ufer *n*; (Sand-, Wolken-) Bank *f*; *econ.* Bank(haus *n*) *f*; *Geld* auf die Bank legen; **~bill** Bankwechsel *m*; *Am.* Banknote *f*; **~er** Bankier *m*; ein Bank...; **~note** Banknote *f*; *pl* Papiergeld *n*; **~rate** Diskontsatz *m*; **~rupt** ['~rʌpt] bankrott.

banner ['bænə] Banner *n*, Fahne *f*; Transparent *n*.

banns [bænz] *pl* Aufgebot *n*.

banquet ['bæŋkwit] Festessen *n*.

bapti|sm ['bæptizəm] Taufe *f*; **~ze** [~'taiz] taufen.

bar [bɑ:] Stange *f*; (Gitter)Stab *m*; Riegel *m*; Tafel *f* (*Schokolade*); Schranke *f*; Schanktisch *m*; Bar *f* (*Hotel*); verriegeln, -sperren; ausschließen, verbieten.

barb [bɑ:b] Widerhaken *m*.

barbar|ian [bɑ:'bɛəriən] Barbar(in); **~ous** ['~bərəs] barbarisch.

barbed wire Stacheldraht *m*.

barber ['bɑ:bə] (Herren-) Friseur *m*; **at** *od.* **to the ~'s** beim *od.* zum Friseur.

bare [bɛə] nackt, bloß; kahl; leer; entblößen; **~-foot(ed)** barfuß; **~-headed** barhäuptig; **~ly** kaum, gerade (noch), bloß.

bargain ['bɑ:gin] Geschäft *n*, Handel *m*; (vorteilhafter) Kauf; (ver)handeln, übereinkommen.

barge [bɑ:dʒ] Lastkahn *m*.

bark¹ [bɑ:k] Borke *f*, Rinde *f*.

bark² bellen; Bellen *n*.

barley ['bɑ:li] Gerste *f*.

barn [bɑ:n] Scheune *f*; *Am.* Stall *m*.

barometer [bə'rɔmitə] Barometer *n*.

barracks ['bærəks] *sg*, *pl* Kaserne *f*.

barrel ['bærəl] Faß *n*; (Gewehr)Lauf *m*; Walze *f*; **~-organ** Drehorgel *f*.

barren ['bærən] unfruchtbar; öde.

barricade [bæri'keid]

Barrikade *f*; verbarrikadieren, sperren.

barrier ['bæriə] Schranke *f* (*a. fig.*), Sperre *f*; *fig.* Hindernis *n*.

barrister ['bæristə] Rechtsanwalt *m*, Barrister *m*.

barrow ['bærəu] Karre(n *m*) *f*.

barter ['bɑ:tə] Tausch *m*; tauschen.

base¹ [beis] gemein; minderwertig.

base² Basis *f*; Fundament *n*; Stützpunkt *m*; *fig.* stützen; **~ball** Baseball(-spiel *n*) *m*; **~less** grundlos; **~ment** Fundament *n*; Keller(geschoß *n*) *m*.

bashful ['bæʃful] schüchtern.

basic ['beisik] grundlegend, Grund...

basin ['beisn] Becken *n*; Schüssel *f*.

bask [bɑ:sk] sich sonnen.

basket ['bɑ:skit] Korb *m*; **~ball** Korbball(spiel *n*) *m*.

bass [beis] Baß *m*.

bastard ['bæstəd] unehelich; unecht; Bastard *m*.

baste¹ [beist] Braten begießen.

baste² (an)heften.

bat¹ [bæt] Fledermaus *f*.

bat² Schlagholz *n*, Schläger *m*.

bath [bɑ:θ] *j-n* baden; Bad *n*; baden; **take** *od.* **have a ~** ein Bad nehmen, baden.

bathe [beið] baden (*a. im Freien*).

bathing ['beɪðɪŋ] Baden *n*; Bade...; **~cap** Badekappe *f*, -mütze *f*; **~costume**, **~suit** Badeanzug *m*; **~trunks** *pl* Badehose *f*.

bath|robe Bademantel *m*; **~room** Badezimmer *n*; **~towel** Badetuch *n*; **~tub** Badewanne *f*.

baton ['bætən] Stab *m*; Taktstock *m*.

battalion [bə'tæljən] Bataillon *n*.

batter ['bætə] Rührteig *m*; heftig schlagen; **~ed** verbeult; **~y** Batterie *f*.

battle ['bætl] Schlacht *f*; **~ship** Schlachtschiff *n*.

baulk [bɔ:k] *s.* **balk.**

Bavarian [bə'vɛəriən] bay(e)risch; Bayer(in).

bawl [bɔ:l] brüllen; johlen, grölen.

bay¹ [beɪ] rotbraun.

bay² Bai *f*, Bucht *f*; Erker *m*; **~window** Erkerfenster *n*.

baza(a)r [bə'zu:] Basar *m*.

be [bi:, bɪ] (*irr*) sein; **there is, there are** es gibt; **he wants to ~ ...** er möchte ... werden; **~ reading** gerade lesen; **I am to** ich soll od. muß; *zur Bildung des Passivs:* werden.

beach [bi:tʃ] Strand *m*; **on the ~** am Strand; **~ hotel** Strandhotel *n*; **~wear** Strandkleidung *f*.

beacon ['bi:kən] Blinklicht *n*, Leuchtfeuer *n*.

bead [bi:d] Perle *f*; Tropfen *m*.

beak [bi:k] Schnabel *m*.

beam [bi:m] Balken *m*; Strahl *m*; Leitstrahl *m*; strahlender Blick; (aus-) strahlen.

bean [bi:n] Bohne *f*.

bear¹ [bɛə] Bär *m*.

bear² (*irr*) tragen; gebären; ertragen; **~ out** bestätigen.

beard [bɪəd] Bart *m*; *bot.* Granne *f*.

bear|er ['bɛərə] Überbringer(in); **~ings** *pl* Richtung *f*.

beast [bi:st] Vieh *n*; Tier *n*; *fig.* Bestie *f*; **~ly** viehisch; scheußlich; **~ of prey** Raubtier *n*.

beat [bi:t] (*irr*) schlagen; verprügeln; besiegen; übertreffen; **~ it!** *sl.* hau ab!; Schlag *m*; Pulsschlag *m*; *mus.*: Takt *m*; Beat *m*; Runde *f* (*e-s Polizisten*); **~en** *pp von* **beat.**

beauti|ful ['bju:təful] schön; **~fy** ['~ɪfaɪ] verschönern.

beauty ['bju:tɪ] Schönheit *f*; **~ parlo(u)r** Schönheitssalon *m*.

beaver ['bi:və] Biber *m*; Biberpelz *m*.

because [bɪ'kɔz] weil; **~ of** wegen.

beckon ['bekən] (zu)winken.

become [bɪ'kʌm] (*irr* **come**) werden (**of** aus); sich schicken für; kleiden

(*Hut etc.*); ~ing schicklich; kleidsam.

bed [bed] Bett *n*; Lager (-statt *f*) *n*; Unterlage *f*; *agr.* Beet *n*; ~clothes *pl* Bettzeug *n*; ~ding Bettzeug *n*; Streu *f*; ~linen Bettwäsche *f*; ~ridden bettlägerig; ~room Schlafzimmer *n*; ~side: at the ~ am (Kranken)Bett; ~side table Nachttisch *m*; ~spread Bett-, Tagesdecke *f*; ~stead Bettgestell *n*; ~time Schlafenszeit *f*.

bee [bi:] Biene *f*.

beech [bi:tʃ] Buche *f*.

beef [bi:f] Rindfleisch *n*; ~steak Beefsteak *n*; ~ tea (klare) Fleischbrühe.

bee|hive Bienenkorb *m*, -stock *m*; ~keeper Imker *m*; ~line kürzester Weg.

been [bi:n, bin] *pp von* be.

beer [biə] Bier *n*.

beet [bi:t] Runkelrübe *f*, Bete *f*.

beetle ['bi:tl] Käfer *m*.

beetroot rote Rübe.

befall [bi'fɔ:l] (*irr* **fall**) zustoßen.

before [bi'fɔ:] *adv* voran; vorher; (schon) früher; *prp* vor; *cj* bevor, ehe; ~hand vorher; (im) voraus.

befriend [bi'frend] sich *j*-s annehmen.

beg [beg] bitten; ~ (~for) betteln *od.* bitten um.

began [bi'gæn] *pret von* begin.

beget [bi'get] (*irr*) (er-) zeugen.

beggar ['begə] Bettler (-in); *colloq.* Kerl *m*.

begin [bi'gin] (*irr*) beginnen, anfangen; **to ~ with** um es vorwegzusagen, erstens; ~ner Anfänger(in); ~ning Anfang *m*.

begot [bi'gɔt] *pret*, ~ten *pp von* beget.

begun [bi'gʌn] *pp von* begin.

behalf [bi'hɑ:f]: **on ~ od. in ~ of** im Namen von; **on s.o.'s ~** um *j*-s willen.

behav|e [bi'heiv] sich benehmen; ~io(u)r [~jə] Benehmen *n*.

behind [bi'haind] *prp* hinter; *adv* hinten, dahinter; zurück.

being ['bi:iŋ] (Da)Sein *n*; Wesen *n*.

belated [bi'leitid] verspätet.

belch [beltʃ] rülpsen; Feuer, Rauch ausspeien.

belfry ['belfri] Glockenturm *m*; Glockenstube *f*.

Belgian ['beldʒən] belgisch; Belgier(in).

belie|f [bi'li:f] Glaube *m* (in an); ~ve [~v] glauben (in an); trauen; **make ~ve** vorgeben; ~ver Gläubige *m*, *f*.

bell [bel] Glocke *f*; Klingel *f*.

belligerent [bi'lidʒərənt] kriegführend; *fig.* streitlustig.

bellow ['beləu] brüllen;
~s [~z] pl Blasebalg m.

belly ['beli] Bauch m.

belong [bi'lɔŋ] gehören; ~
to (an)gehören, gehören zu;
~ings pl Habseligkeiten pl.

beloved [bi'lʌvd] geliebt.

below [bi'ləu] adv unten; prp unter(halb).

belt [belt] Gürtel m, Gurt
m; tech. Treibriemen m;
Gebiet n, Zone f.

bench [bentʃ] Bank f.

bend [bend] Biegung f,
Kurve f; (irr) (sich) biegen; (sich) beugen.

beneath [bi'ni:θ] s. **below**.

bene|diction [beni-
'dikʃn] Segen m; ~**factor**
['~fæktə] Wohltäter m;
~**ficent** [bi'nefisənt] wohltätig; ~**ficial** [~'fiʃəl]
wohltuend; nützlich; ~**fit**
['~fit] Wohltat f; Nutzen
m, Vorteil m; Unter-
stützung f; nützen; Vor-
teil haben; ~**volent** [bi-
'nevələnt] mildtätig, gü-
tig; wohlwollend.

bent [bent] Hang m, Neigung f; pret u. pp von
bend; ~ **on** entschlossen zu.

benzene ['benzi:n] Ben-
zol n.

benzine ['benzi:n] Benzin n.

bequeath [bi'kwi:ð] vermachen; ~**est** [~'kwest]
Vermächtnis n.

ber|eave [bi'ri:v] (irr)
berauben; ~**eft** [~'reft]
pret u. pp von **bereave**.

beret ['berei] Baskenmütze f.

berry ['beri] Beere f.

berth [bə:θ] Koje f; Bett
n (Zug).

beside [bi'said] neben;
~ **o.s.** außer sich (**with**
vor); ~**s** adv außerdem;
prp außer, neben.

besiege [bi'si:dʒ] belagern.

best [best] adj best; größt;
~ **wishes** beste Wünsche,
herzliche Glückwünsche;
adv am besten, am meisten;
~ **of all** am allermeisten;
der, die, das Beste; die
Besten pl; **all the** ~ alles
Gute; **do one's** ~ sein
möglichstes tun; **at** ~
höchstens, bestenfalls.

bestow [bi'stəu] geben,
spenden, schenken, ver-
leihen.

bet [bet] Wette f; (irr)
wetten.

betray [bi'trei] verraten;
~**al** Verrat m; ~**er** Ver-
räter(in).

better ['betə] besser; **he
is** ~ es geht ihm besser;
so much the ~ desto
besser; **the Bessere; get
the** ~ **of** die Oberhand
gewinnen über; überwin-
den; vb: ~ (**o.s.** sich) verbessern.

between [bi'twi:n] adv
dazwischen; prp zwischen;
unter.

beverage ['bevəridʒ] Getränk n.

beware [bi'wɛə] sich in
acht nehmen; ~ **of the**

dog! Vorsicht, bissiger Hund!

bewilder [bi'wildə] verwirren; **~ment** Verwirrung f, Bestürzung f.

bewitch [bi'witʃ] bezaubern; verzaubern.

beyond [bi'jɔnd] adv darüber hinaus; prp jenseits; über (...hinaus); mehr als; außer.

bias ['baiəs] beeinflussen; **~(s)ed** befangen.

bib [bib] Lätzchen n.

Bible ['baibl] Bibel f.

bicycle ['baisikl] Fahrrad n; radfahren.

bid [bid] Gebot n, Angebot n; (irr) befehlen; Karten: reizen; **~ farewell** Lebewohl sagen; **~den** pp von **bid**.

bier [biə] (Toten)Bahre f.

big [big] groß, dick, stark; **~ talk ~** prahlen; **~ business** Großunternehmertum n; **~wig** colloq. hohes Tier (Person).

bike [baik] colloq. (Fahr-)Rad n.

bilateral [bai'lætərəl] bilateral.

bile [bail] Galle f (a. fig.).

~ious ['biljəs] Gallen...

bill¹ [bil] Schnabel m.

bill² Gesetzentwurf m; Rechnung f; Plakat n; Am. Banknote f; econ. Wechsel m; **~board** Am. Anschlagbrett n; Reklamefläche f; **~fold** Am. Brieftasche f.

billiards ['biljədz] sg Billard(spiel) n.

billion ['biljən] Milliarde f; früher Brit. Billion f.

bill of exchange Wechsel m; **~ of fare** Speisekarte f.

billow ['bilau] Woge f; wogen.

bin [bin] Behälter m, Kasten m.

bind [baind] (irr) (an-, ein-, um-, auf-, fest-, ver)binden; verpflichten; **~ing** bindend; Binden n; Einband m; Einfassung f; (Ski)Bindung f.

binoculars [bi'nɔkjuləz] pl Feldstecher m, Fern-, Opernglas n.

biography [bai'ɔgrəfi] Biographie f.

biology [bai'ɔlədʒi] Biologie f, Naturkunde f.

birch [bə:tʃ] Birke f.

bird [bə:d] Vogel m; **~ of passage** Zugvogel m; **~ of prey** Raubvogel m; **~'s-eye view** Vogelperspektive f; allgemeiner Überblick.

birth [bə:θ] Geburt f; Herkunft f; **give ~ to** gebären, zur Welt bringen; **date of ~** Geburtsdatum n; **~-control** Geburtenregelung f; **~day** Geburtstag m; **happy ~day to you** ich gratuliere dir recht herzlich zum Geburtstag; **~day party** Geburtstagsgesellschaft f, -feier f; **~place** Geburtsort m.

biscuit ['biskit] Keks m, n.

bishop ['biʃəp] Bischof *m.*

bison ['baisn] Wisent *m*; Bison *m.*

bit [bit] Gebiß *n* (*am Zaum*); Bißchen *n*, Stückchen *n*; kleine Münze; *pret von* **bite.**

bitch [bitʃ] Hündin *f.*

bite [bait] Biß *m*; Bissen *m*; (*irr*) (an)beißen; *fig.* beißen, schneiden.

bitten ['bitn] *pp von* **bite.**

bitter ['bitə] bitter; *fig.* verbittert; **~s** *pl* Magenbitter *m.*

black [blæk] schwarz; dunkel; finster; schwärzen; *Schuhe* wichsen; Schwarz *n*; Schwärze *f*; Schwarze *m*, *f* (*Neger*); **~berry** Brombeere *f*; **~bird** Amsel *f*; **~board** (Wand)Tafel *f*; **~en** schwärzen; schwarz werden; **~ eye** blaues Auge; **~head** Mitesser *m*; **~mail** Erpressung *f*; erpressen; **~ market** schwarzer Markt; **~ pudding** Blutwurst *f*; **~smith** Schmied *m.* [Blase *f.*]

bladder ['blædə] *anat.*]

blade [bleid] *bot.* Blatt *n* (*a. Säge, Schulter etc.*), Halm *m*; Flügel *m* (*Propeller*); Klinge *f.*

blame [bleim] Schuld *f*; Tadel *m*; tadeln, die Schuld geben; **be to ~ for** schuld sein an; **~less** tadellos.

blank [blæŋk] leer (*a. fig.*); nicht ausgefüllt, un-

beschrieben; *fig.* verdutzt; leerer Raum, Lücke *f*; Niete *f*; *fig.* Leere *f.*

blanket ['blæŋkit] Wolldecke *f.*

blasphemy ['blæsfimi] Gotteslästerung *f.*

blast [blɑːst] Windstoß *m*; Luftdruck *m* (*Explosion*); Ton *m* (*Blasinstrument*); (*in die Luft*) sprengen; zerstören (*a. fig.*); **~ (it)!** verdammt!; **~furnace** Hochofen *m.*

blaze [bleiz] flammen, lodern; leuchten; Flamme (*n pl*) *f*; Feuer *n*; **~r** Blazer *m*, Klub-, Sportjacke *f.*

bleach [bliːtʃ] bleichen.

bleak [bliːk] öde, kahl; rauh; *fig.* freudlos, finster, trüb(e).

blear [bliə] trüb(e); trüben.

bleat [bliːt] Blöken *n*; blöken.

bled [bled] *pret u. pp von* **bleed.**

bleed [bliːd] (*irr*) bluten (*a. fig.*); *fig.* schröpfen.

blemish ['blemiʃ] Fehler *m*; Makel *m*; verunstalten.

blend [blend] (*irr*) (sich) (ver)mischen; Mischung *f*; Verschnitt *m.*

blent [blent] *pret u. pp von* **blend.**

bless [bles] segnen; preisen; **~ my soul!** *colloq.* du meine Güte!; **~ed** ['blesid] gesegnet; selig; **~ing** Segen *m.*

blew [bluː] *pret von* **blow².**

blight [blait] Mehltau *m.*

blind [blaind] blind (*fig.*
to gegenüber); Jalousie *f*,
Rouleau *n*; ~ **alley** Sackgasse *f*; ~**fold** *j–m* die Augen
verbinden; *fig.* blindlings.

blink [bliŋk] blinzeln, zwinkern; blinken; schimmern.

bliss [blis] Seligkeit *f*.

blister ['blistə] Blase *f*.

blithe [blaið] *mst poet.*
lustig, fröhlich, munter.

blizzard ['blizəd] Schneesturm *m*.

bloate|d ['bləutid] aufgedunsen; *fig.* aufgeblasen;
~**r** Bückling *m*.

block [blɔk] (*Stein-, Häuser- etc.*)Block *m*; Klotz
m; Verstopfung *f*, (*Verkehrs*)Stockung *f*; blokkieren; ~ (**up**) (ab-, ver-)
sperren.

blockade [blɔ'keid] Blokkade *f*; blockieren.

block|letters *pl* Druck-,
Blockschrift *f*; ~ **of flats**
Brit. Mietshaus *n*.

blond(e) [blɔnd] blond;
Blondine *f*.

blood [blʌd] Blut *n*; **in
cold** ~ kaltblütig; ~**shed**
Blutvergießen *n*; ~**shot**
blutunterlaufen; ~**vessel**
Blutgefäß *n*; ~**y** blutig.

bloom [blu:m] Blüte *f*;
blühen.

blossom ['blɔsəm] Blüte
f; blühen.

blot [blɔt] Klecks *m*,
Fleck *m*; *fig.* Makel *m*; beklecksen, beflecken; (ab-)
löschen; ~ **out** ausstreichen; ~**ter** Löscher *m*; ~-

ting-paperLöschpapier*n*.

blouse [blauz] Bluse *f*.

blow[1] [bləu] Schlag *m*,
Stoß *m*.

blow[2] (*irr*) blasen; wehen;
schnaufen; durchbrennen
(*Sicherung*); ~ **out** ausblasen; ~ **up** in die Luft
fliegen; (in die Luft)
sprengen; *phot.* vergrößern; ~**one's nose** sich
die Nase putzen; ~**n** *pp
von* **blow**[2].

blue [blu:] blau; *colloq.*
traurig, schwermütig;
Blau *n*; ~**bell** Glockenblume*f*; ~**s** *pl mus.* Blues *m*;
colloq. Trübsinn *m*.

bluff [blʌf] Irreführung *f*;
bluffen.

bluish ['blu:iʃ] bläulich.

blunder ['blʌndə] Fehler
m, Schnitzer *m*; stolpern;
(ver)pfuschen.

blunt [blʌnt] stumpf;
plump, grob.

blur [blə:] Fleck(en) *m*;
fig. undeutlicher Eindruck;
verschmieren; verschwommen machen *od.* werden;
trüben.

blush [blʌʃ] Erröten *n*;
Schamröte *f*; erröten, rot
werden. [*m*.]

boar [bɔ:] Eber *m*, Keiler*f*

board [bɔ:d] Brett *n*;
(Wand)Tafel *f*; Pappe
f; Ausschuß *m*; Amt *n*,
Behörde *f*; Verpflegung
f; **full** ~ Vollpension *f*;
on ~ an Bord; dielen; verschalen; beköstigen; an
Bord gehen, einsteigen in;

in Kost sein; **~er** Kostgänger(in); Internatsschüler(in); Pensionsgast *m*; **~ing-house** (Fremden)Pension *f*, Fremdenheim *n*; **~ing-school** Internat *n*; **~walk** *Am.* Strandpromenade *f*.

boast [bəust] Prahlerei *f*; Stolz *m*; sich rühmen, prahlen.

boat [bəut] Boot *n*; Schiff *n*; **~ing** Bootsfahrt *f*; **~race** Ruderregatta *f*, Bootsrennen *n*.

bob [bɔb], *pl ~s, sl. alte Währung:* Schilling *m*; sich auf und ab bewegen; **~(bed hair)** Bubikopf *m*.

bobby ['bɔbi] *Brit. colloq.* Polizist *m*.

bob-sleigh ['bɔb-] Bob (-sleigh) *m*.

bodice ['bɔdis] Mieder *n*.

bodily ['bɔdili] körperlich.

body ['bɔdi] Körper *m*, Leib *m*; Leichnam *m*; *mot.* Karosserie *f*; Gruppe *f*; Körperschaft *f*; **~guard** Leibwache *f*. [Moor *n.*]

bog [bɔg] Sumpf *m*,

boil [bɔil] Furunkel *m*; kochen, sieden; **~ over** überkochen; **~ed eggs** *pl* gekochte Eier *pl*; **~er** (Dampf)Kessel *m*; Boiler *m*.

boisterous ['bɔistərəs] rauh; lärmend, laut.

bold [bəuld] kühn; keck, dreist.

bolster ['bəulstə] Keilkissen *n*; Polster *n*.

bolt [bəult] Bolzen *m*; Riegel *m*; Blitz(strahl) *m*; verriegeln; durchgehen (*Pferd*); davonlaufen; **~ upright** kerzengerade.

bomb [bɔm] Bombe *f*; mit Bomben belegen; bombardieren.

bombard [bɔm'bɑːd] bombardieren.

bond [bɔnd] Bündnis *n*; *econ.* Obligation *f*; *pl* Fesseln *pl*.

bone [bəun] Knochen *m*; Gräte *f*.

bonfire ['bɔnfaiə] (Freuden)Feuer *n*.

bonnet ['bɔnit] Haube *f*; Mütze *f*, Kappe *f*; (Motor)Haube *f*.

bonn|ie, ~y ['bɔni] hübsch, schön; gesund, rosig.

bonus ['bəunəs] *econ.* Prämie *f*; Gratifikation *f*; Zulage *f*.

bony ['bəuni] knöchern; knochig.

book [buk] Buch *n*; Heft *n*; Block *m*; (Namens-) Liste *f*; buchen, *Platz etc.* (vor)bestellen, reservieren lassen; eintragen; *Fahrkarte etc.* lösen, kaufen; *Gepäck* aufgeben; **~ed up** ausgebucht, -verkauft; voll besetzt (*Hotel*); **~case** Bücherschrank *m*, **~regal** *n*; **~ing-clerk** Schalterbeamt|e *m*, -in *f*; **~ing-office** Fahrkartenausgabe *f*, -schalter *m*; **~keeper** Buchhalter *m*; **~keeping** Buchführung

_f_; **~let** ['~lit] Broschüre
_f_; **~seller** Buchhändler _m_;
~shop Buchhandlung _f_.

boom [bu:m] Aufschwung
_m_, Hochkonjunktur _f_,
Hausse _f_.

boomerang ['bu:məræŋ]
Bumerang _m_.

boor [buə] Lümmel _m_.

boost [bu:st] _tech._ Schub
_m_; hochstieben; _fig._
fördern.

boot [bu:t] Stiefel _m_; _mot._
Kofferraum _m_; **~ee** ['~ti:]
(Damen)Halbstiefel _m_.

booth [bu:ð] (Markt- _etc._)
Bude _f_; Wahlzelle _f_; _Am._
Telephonzelle _f_.

booty ['bu:ti] Beute _f_.

border ['bɔ:də] Rand _m_,
Einfassung _f_, Grenze _f_;
einfassen; begrenzen; grenzen (**upon** an).

bore[1] [bɔ:] bohren; lang-
weilen; langweiliger _od._
lästiger Mensch; lang-
weilige _od._ lästige Sache.

bore[2] _pret von_ **bear**[2].

born [bɔ:n] _pp von_ **bear**[2]:
gebären; **she was ~ on** ...
sie wurde am ... geboren;
~e _pp von_ **bear**[2]: tragen.

borough ['bʌrə] _Brit._:
Stadtgemeinde _f_; Stadt _f_
mit eigener Vertretung
im Parlament.

borrow ['bɔrəu] (aus)bor-
gen, (ent)leihen.

bosom ['buzəm] Busen _m_.

boss [bɔs] _colloq._ Boß _m_,
Chef _m_.

botany ['bɔtəni] Botanik _f_,
Pflanzenkunde _f_.

botch [bɔtʃ] Flickwerk _n_;
verpfuschen.

both [bəuθ] beide(s); **~ ...
and** sowohl ... als (auch).

bother ['bɔðə] Plage _f_,
Mühe _f_; belästigen, plagen; **~ about** sich Ge-
danken machen wegen,
sich sorgen um.

bottle ['bɔtl] in Flaschen
abfüllen; Flasche _f_; **a
~ of ...** e-e Flasche ...

bottom ['bɔtəm] Boden _m_,
Grund _m_; Fuß _m_ (_Berg_);
(unteres) Ende; _colloq._
Hintern _m_.

bough [bau] Ast _m_.

bought [bɔ:t] _pret u. pp
von_ buy. [block _m_.\]

boulder ['bəuldə] Geröll-

bounce [bauns] Sprung _m_;
Aufprallen _n_; (hoch)sprin-
gen.

bound [baund] _pret u. pp
von_ bind; unterwegs (**for**
nach); Sprung _m_; Grenze
_f_; (hoch)springen; (an-,
auf-, ab)prallen; begren-
zen; **~less** grenzenlos.

bouquet [bu'kei] (Blumen)Strauß _m_; Blume _f_
(_Wein_).

bout [baut] _med._ Anfall
_m_; (Wett)Kampf _m_.

bow[1] [bau] _mar._ Bug _m_;
Verbeugung _f_; sich (ver-)
beugen (**to** vor); biegen;
beugen, neigen.

bow[2] [bəu] Bogen _m_;
Schleife _f_.

bowels ['bauəlz] _pl_ Eingeweide _pl_.

break

bower ['bauə] Laube f.

bowl[1] [bəul] Schüssel f; Schale f; Humpen m; (Pfeifen)Kopf m.

bowl[2] Kugel f; Ball, Kugel rollen, werfen.

box [bɔks] Büchse f, ·Schachtel f, Kasten m; thea. Loge f; Box f (für Pferde etc.); boxen; **~ s.o.'s ear(s)** j-n ohrfeigen; **~er** Boxer m; **~ing** Boxen n; **2ing Day** zweiter Weihnachtsfeiertag; **~ing-match** Boxkampf m; **~-office** Theaterkasse f.

boy [bɔi] Junge m, Bursche m.

boycott ['bɔikət] boykottieren.

boy|-friend Freund m; **~hood** Knabenalter m; **~ish** knabenhaft; kindisch; **2 Scout** Pfadfinder m.

bra [brɑː] colloq. Büstenhalter m.

brace [breis] Strebe f; pl Hosenträger m; verstreben; **~ (o.s.) [up]** sich) zs.-nehmen.

bracelet ['breislit] Armband n.

bracket ['brækit] tech. Winkelstütze f; print. Klammer f; einklammern.

brag [bræg] prahlen; **~gart** ['...] Prahler m.

braid [breid] (Haar)Flechte f; Borte f; Tresse f; flechten; mit Borte besetzen.

brain [brein] Gehirn n;

fig. Verstand m; **~ wave** colloq. Geistesblitz m.

brake [breik] Bremse f; bremsen.

bramble ['bræmbl] Brombeerstrauch m.

branch [brɑːntʃ] Zweig m (a. fig.), Ast m; Gebiet n, Fach n; Zweigstelle f, Filiale f; sich verzweigen; abzweigen.

brand [brænd] (Feuer)Brand m; Brandmal n; econ.: Handelsmarke f, Sorte f; einbrennen; fig. brandmarken.

bran(d)-new nagelneu.

brass [brɑːs] Messing n; **~ band** Blaskapelle f.

brassière ['bræsiə] Büstenhalter m.

brave [breiv] tapfer, mutig; trotzen; **~ry** Tapferkeit f.

Brazilian [brə'ziljən] brasilianisch; Brasilianer(in).

breach [briːtʃ] Lücke f; fig. Bruch m, Verletzung f; durchbrechen.

bread [bred] Brot n; **~and-butter letter** Dankbrief m.

breadth [bredθ] Breite f, Weite f.

break [breik] Bruch(stelle f) m; Öffnung f, Lücke f; Pause f; (Tages)Anbruch m; (zer)brechen; (zer-)reißen (Seil); ruinieren; Pferd zureiten; Bank sprengen; Reise etc. unterbrechen; Nachricht schonend mitteilen; los-, an-, aufbre-

chen; umschlagen (*Wetter*);
~ away sich losreißen; **~
down** niederreißen; zs.-
brechen (*a. fig.*), einstürzen; *mot.* e-e Panne haben;
~ in Pferd zureiten; einbrechen; **~ off** abbre-
chen; **~ out** ausbrechen; **~
up** zerbrechen, -stören;
schließen, in die Ferien
gehen; *fig.*: (sich) auflösen; verfallen; **~able**
zerbrechlich; **~down** Zs.-
bruch *m*; Maschinen-
schaden *m*; *mot.* Panne *f*;
~down service
Abschlepp-, Pannendienst *m*.

breakfast ['brekfəst]
Frühstück *n*; **bed and ~**
Zimmer mit Frühstück;
at od. for ~ beim *od.* zum
Frühstück; **(have) ~** früh-
stücken.

breast [brest] Brust *f*; **~
stroke** Brustschwimmen *n*.

breath [breθ] Atem(zug)
m; Hauch *m*; **hold one's
~** den Atem anhalten;
~e [bri:ð] (ein- u. aus-)
atmen; wehen; hauchen;
flüstern; **~ing** ['bri:ðiŋ]
Atmen *n*, Atmung *f*;
~less ['breθlis] atemlos.

bred [bred] *pret u. pp von*
breed.

breeches ['britʃiz] *pl*
Knie-, Reithosen *pl.*

breed [bri:d] Zucht *f*;
Rasse *f*; Herkunft *f*; (*irr*)
züchten; auf-, erziehen;
brüten; sich fortpflanzen;
~er Züchter(in); **~ing**
(Tier)Zucht *f*; Erziehung *f.*

breeze [bri:z] Brise *f.*

brew [bru:] brauen; sich
zs.-brauen; **~ery** Brau-
erei *f.*

bribe [braib] Bestechungs-
geld *n*, -geschenk *n*) *f*; bestechen; **~ry** Bestechung *f.*

brick [brik] Ziegel(stein)
m; **~layer** Maurer *m*;
~work Mauerwerk *n*;
~works *sg* Ziegelei *f.*

bridal ['braidl] Braut...

bride [braid] Braut *f*,
Neuvermählte *f*; **~groom**
Bräutigam *m*, Neuver-
mählte *m*; **~smaid** Braut-
jungfer *f.*

bridge [bridʒ] Brücke *f*;
e-e Brücke schlagen über;
~ over *fig.* überbrücken.

bridle ['braidl] Zaum *m*;
Zügel *m*; (auf)zäumen;
zügeln (*a. fig.*); **~path**,
~road Reitweg *m.*

brief [bri:f] kurz, bündig;
~case Aktenmappe *f.*

brigade [bri'geid] Brigade *f.*

bright [brait] hell, glänzend; strahlend; *fig.* gescheit; **~en** (sich) aufhellen; erhellen; aufhei-
tern; **~ness** Helligkeit *f*;
Glanz *m*; Aufgewecktheit *f.*

brillian|ce, ~cy ['bril-
jəns, '-si] Glanz *m*;
glänzend; *fig.* ausgezeichnet; geistreich; Brillant *m.*

brim [brim] Rand *m*;
Krempe *f*; **~ful(l)** ganz voll.

bring [briŋ] (*irr*) (mit-)
her)bringen; *j-n* veranlassen, dazu bringen; **~ an**

action against s.o. j-n
verklagen; ~ **about** zustande bringen; ~ **forth**
hervorbringen; ~ **in** (her-)
einbringen; ~ **up** auf-,
erziehen.

brink [briŋk] Rand *m.*

brisk [brisk] lebhaft, flink.

bristle ['brisl] Borste *f;*
sich sträuben.

Brit|ish ['britiʃ] britisch,
selten: englisch; *sub:* **the ~
ish** *pl* die Briten *pl;* **~on**
['~tn] Brit|e *m,* -in *f.*

brittle ['britl] spröde.

broach [brəutʃ] *Thema*
anschneiden.

broad [brɔːd] breit; weit;
hell (*Tag*); deutlich (*Wink*);
allgemein; liberal; **~cast**
(*irr* **cast**) *Radio:* senden;
Rundfunksendung *f;* ~
minded großzügig.

brochure ['brəuʃjuə] Broschüre *f;* Prospekt *m.*

broke [brəuk] *pret von*
break; *sl.* pleite, ohne
e-n Pfennig; **~n** *pp von*
break; zerbrochen, kaputt; zerrüttet; **~r** Makler *m.*

bronze [brɔnz] Bronze *f;*
bronzen, Bronze...

brooch [brəutʃ] Brosche *f.*

brood [bruːd] Brut *f;*
Zucht...; brüten (*a. fig.*).

brook [bruk] Bach *m.*

broom [bruːm] Besen *m.*

broth [brɔθ] (Fleisch-)
Brühe *f.*

brothel ['brɔθl] Bordell *n.*

brother ['brʌðə] Bruder
m; **~(s) and sister(s)**

Geschwister *pl;* **~-in-law**
Schwager *m;* **~ly** brüder-
lich.

brought [brɔːt] *pret u.
pp von* **bring.**

brow [brau] (Augen)Braue
f; Stirn *f.*

brown [braun] braun;
Braun *n;* ~ **paper** Pack-
papier *n.*

bruise [bruːz] *med.* Quet-
schung *f;* blauer Fleck;
(zer)quetschen.

brush [brʌʃ] Bürste *f;*
Pinsel *m;* (*Fuchs*)Rute *f;*
Unterholz *n;* (ab-, aus-)
bürsten; putzen; fegen;
streifen; ~ **up** *fig.* auffrischen.

Brussels sprouts ['brʌsl-
'sprauts] *pl* Rosenkohl *m.*

brut|al ['bruːtl] brutal,
roh; **~ality** ['tæliti] Bru-
talität *f;* **~e** [bruːt] Vieh
n; fig. Scheusal *n.*

bubble ['bʌbl] Blase *f;*
sprudeln.

buck [bʌk] Bock *m; Am.
sl.* Dollar *m;* bocken.

bucket ['bʌkit] Eimer *m.*

buckle ['bʌkl] Schnalle *f;*
(um-, zu)schnallen; ~ **on**
anschnallen.

buckskin Wildleder *n.*

bud [bʌd] Knospe *f,* Auge
n; fig. Keim *m;* knospen.

buddy ['bʌdi] *Am. colloq.*
Kamerad *m.*

budget ['bʌdʒit] Haus-
haltsplan *m,* Etat *m.*

buffalo ['bʌfələu] Büffel *m.*

buffer ['bʌfə] *tech.* Puffer *m.*

buffet ['bʌfit] Büfett *n,*

Anrichte f; ['bufei] Büfett n, Theke f.

bug [bʌg] Wanze f; Am. Insekt n, Käfer m.

bugle ['bju:gl] Wald-, Signalhorn n.

build [bild] (irr) (er-)bauen, errichten; **~er** Baumeister m; Bauunternehmer m; **~ing** Bau m, Gebäude n; Bau...

built [bilt] pret u. pp von **build.**

bulb [bʌlb] Zwiebel f, Knolle f; (Glüh)Birne f.

bulge [bʌldʒ] (Aus)Bauchung f; Beule f, Buckel m; sich (aus)bauchen; hervorquellen.

bulk [bʌlk] Umfang m, Masse f; **the ~** der Hauptteil; **~y** umfangreich; sperrig.

bull [bul] Bulle m, Stier m.

bullet ['bulit] Kugel f, Geschoß n.

bulletin ['bulitin] Tagesbericht m; **~ board** Am. Schwarzes Brett.

bullion ['buljən] (Gold-etc./)Barren m.

bully ['buli] tyrannisieren.

bum [bʌm] Am. Vagabund m.

bumble-bee ['bʌmbl-] Hummel f.

bump [bʌmp] Schlag m; Beule f; holperige Stelle; (zs.-)stoßen; holpern; **~er** mot. Stoßstange f; volles Glas (Wein).

bun [bʌn] Rosinenbrötchen n; (Haar)Knoten m.

bunch [bʌntʃ] Bund n;

Bündel n; Strauß m; Büschel n; colloq. Haufen m; **~ of grapes** Weintraube f.

bundle ['bʌndl] Bündel n; vb: **~ up** (zs.-)bündeln, zs.-binden.

bungalow ['bʌngələu] Bungalow m.

bungle ['bʌngl] Pfuscherei f; (ver)pfuschen.

bunion ['bʌnjən] entzündeter Fußballen.

bunk [bʌŋk] (Schlaf)Koje f; **~ bed** Etagenbett n.

bunny ['bʌni] Kaninchen n, Häschen n.

buoy [bɔi] Boje f.

burden ['bə:dn] Last f; Bürde f; mus. Kehrreim m, Refrain m; belasten.

bureau ['bjuərəu] Büro n; Geschäftsstelle f; Schreibtisch m; Am. (Spiegel-)Kommode f.

burglar ['bə:glə] Einbrecher m; **~y** Einbruch(sdiebstahl) m.

burial ['beriəl] Begräbnis n.

burly ['bə:li] stämmig, kräftig.

burn [bə:n] Brandwunde f; (irr) (ver-, an)brennen; **~er** Brenner m; **~ing** brennend (a. fig.); **~t** pret u. pp von **burn.**

burst [bə:st] Bersten n; Bruch m; Ausbruch m; **~ of laughter** Lachsalve f; (irr) sprengen; bersten, platzen; zerspringen, explodieren; **~ into flames** in Flammen aufgehen;

~ **into tears** in Tränen ausbrechen.

bury ['beri] begraben, beerdigen; vergraben, verbergen. [Bus m.]

bus [bʌs] (Omni-, Auto-)

bush [buʃ] Busch m, Strauch m; Gebüsch n; Busch m, Urwald m; **~el** ['~ʃl] Scheffel m (36,371); **~y** buschig.

business [biznis] Geschäft n; Handel m; Angelegenheit f; Aufgabe f; Recht n; **on ~** geschäftlich; **mind one's own ~** sich um s-e eigenen Angelegenheiten kümmern; **talk ~** über geschäftliche Dinge reden; **~ hours** pl Geschäftszeit f; **~ letter** Geschäftsbrief m; **~-like** geschäftsmäßig, sachlich; **~man** Geschäftsmann m; **~ tour, ~ trip** Geschäftsreise f.

bus stop Bushaltestelle f.

bust [bʌst] Büste f.

bustle ['bʌsl] geschäftiges Treiben; hetzen; hasten; sich beeilen.

busy ['bizi] beschäftigt; geschäftig, fleißig; Am. teleph. besetzt; **be ~ doing s.th.** mit et. beschäftigt sein; **~ o.s.** sich beschäftigen.

but [bʌt, bət] cj aber, jedoch; sondern; außer; ohne daß; adv nur, bloß; prp außer; **I cannot ~** ich muß; **all ~** fast; **the last ~ one** der vorletzte; **the next ~ one** der über-

nächste; **~ for** wenn nicht ... gewesen wäre; ohne; **~ that** wenn nicht; **~ then** andererseits.

butcher ['butʃə] Schlächter m, Fleischer m, Metzger m.

butt [bʌt] (Gewehr)Kolben m; Stummel m, Kippe f; Zielscheibe f (a. fig.); **~ in** colloq. sich einmischen.

butter ['bʌtə] Butter f; mit Butter bestreichen; **~cup** Butterblume f; **~fly** Schmetterling m.

buttocks ['bʌtəks] pl Gesäß n.

button ['bʌtn] Knopf m; (a. **~ up** zu)knöpfen; **~hole** Knopfloch n.

buttress ['bʌtris] Strebepfeiler m.

buxom ['bʌksəm] drall.

buy [bai] (irr) (an-, ein-)kaufen; **~er** Käufer(in).

buzz [bʌz] Summen n; Stimmengewirr n; summen, surren. [m.]

buzzard ['bʌzəd] Bussard m.

by [bai] prp bei; an; neben; durch; über; an ... entlang od. vorbei; bis (zu); von; mit; um; nach; **~ o.s.** allein; **~ twos** zu zweien; **~ the dozen** dutzendweise; **~ the end** gegen Ende; **~ land** zu Lande; **go ~ bus (rail, train)** mit dem Bus (Zug, der Bahn) fahren; **day ~ day** Tag für Tag; adv nahe, dabei; vorbei, -über; beiseite; **~ and ~** bald;

nach und nach, allmählich.

by- [bai] Neben..., Seiten...
bye-bye ['bai'bai] *s.* goodbye (*int.*).
by|election Nachwahl *f;*
~**gone** vergangen; ~**name** Beiname *m;* Spitzname *m;* ~**pass** Umgehungsstraße *f;* ~**product**
Nebenprodukt *n;* ~**road**
Seitenstraße *f;* ~**stander**
Zuschauer(in); ~**street**
Neben-, Seitenstraße *f;*
~**word** Inbegriff *m;* Gespött *n.*

C

cab [kæb] Taxi *n,* Droschke *f.* [(-kopf) *m.* \
cabbage ['kæbidʒ] Kohl/
cabin ['kæbin] Hütte *f;*
mar. Kabine *f* (*a. aer.*),
Kajüte *f;* **three-berth** ~
Dreibettkabine *f.*
cabinet ['kæbinit] Kabinett *n;* Schrank *m;* Vitrine
f; ~**maker** (Kunst-)
Tischler *m,* Schreiner *m.*
cable ['keibl] Kabel *n;*
Ankerkette *f; tel.* kabeln;
~**car** Drahtseilbahn *f.*
cab|man Taxifahrer *m;*
~**stand** Taxistand *m.*
cackle ['kækl] gackern,
schnattern.
cact|us ['kæktəs], *pl* ~**uses**
['~siz], ~**i** ['~tai] Kaktus *m.*
café ['kæfei] Café *n;*
Restaurant *n.*
cafeteria [kæfi'tiəriə]
Selbstbedienungsrestaurant
n.
cage [keidʒ] Käfig *m;*
Förderkorb *m.*
cake [keik] Kuchen *m;* Riegel *m,* Stück *n;* **a** ~ **of
soap** ein Stück Seife; *zs.-*
backen; ~**tin** Kuchenform *f.*

calamity [kə'læmiti] Unglück *n,* Katastrophe *f.*
calculat|e ['kælkjuleit]
(be-, aus-, er)rechnen;
~**ion** Kalkulation *f,* Berechnung *f;* Überlegung *f.*
calendar ['kælində] Kalender *m.*
calf [kɑːf], *pl* **calves**
[~vz] Kalb *n;* Wade *f.*
calib|re, *Am.* ~**er** ['kælibə]
Kaliber *n.*
call [kɔːl] Ruf *m; teleph.*
Anruf *m,* Gespräch *n;* Besuch *m;* Aufforderung *f;*
Forderung *f;* ~ **for help**
Hilferuf *m;* (herbei)rufen;
(ein)berufen; *teleph.* anrufen; nennen; **be** ~**ed**
heißen; **s.o. names** j-n
beschimpfen, beleidigen;
~ **back** *teleph.* wieder anrufen; ~ **at** besuchen,
gehen zu; *rail.* halten in;
Hafen anlaufen; ~ **for**
rufen nach, rufen um
(*Hilfe*); *et.* (an)fordern;
abholen; ~ **on s.o.** j-n besuchen; ~ **up** *teleph.* anrufen; *mil.* einberufen;
~**box** Telephonzelle *f;*
~**er** Anrufer(in); Besu-

cher(in); **~ing** Beruf *m*.

callous ['kæləs] schwielig; *fig.* gefühllos, gleichgültig.

calm [ka:m] still, ruhig; (Wind)Stille *f*; Ruhe *f*; besänftigen; beruhigen; **~ down** sich beruhigen.

calorie ['kæləri] Kalorie *f*.

calves [ka:vz] *pl von* **calf**.

cambric ['keimbrik] Batist *m*.

came [keim] *pret von* **come**.

camel ['kæməl] Kamel *n*.

camera ['kæmərə] Kamera *f*, Photoapparat *m*.

camomile ['kæməmail] Kamille *f*.

camouflage ['kæmuflɑ:ʒ] Tarnung *f*; tarnen.

camp [kæmp] (Zelt)Lager *n*; *mil.* Feldlager *n*; lagern; **~(out)** zelten; **~aign** [~'pein] Feldzug *m*; **~bed** Feldbett *n*; **~er** Zelt-, Lagerbewohner *m*; **~ground** *Am.* für **~ing-ground**; **~ing** Camping *n*, Zelten *n*; **go ~ing** zelten (gehen); **~ing-ground** Camping-, Zeltplatz *m*.

campus ['kæmpəs] *Am.* Universitäts-, Schulgelände *n*.

can¹ [kæn] *v aux* kann (*du etc.*: kann(st) *etc.*, darf(st) *etc.*

can² Kanne *f*; *Am.* (Konserven)Dose *f*, (-)Büchse *f*; eindosen.

Canadian [kə'neidjən] kanadisch; Kanadier(in).

canal [kə'næl] Kanal *m*.

canary [kə'nɛəri] Kanarienvogel *m*.

cancel ['kænsəl] (durch-) streichen; entwerten; absagen; rückgängig machen; **be ~(l)ed** ausfallen; **~ out** sich aufheben.

cancer ['kænsə] Krebs *m*.

candid ['kændid] aufrichtig, offen.

candidate ['kændidit] Kandidat *m*. [diert.]

candied ['kændid] kan-]

candle ['kændl] Kerze *f*; **~stick** Kerzenleuchter *m*.

candy ['kændi] *Am.* Süßigkeiten *pl*.

cane [kein] *bot.* Rohr *n*; (Rohr)Stock *m*.

cann|ed [kænd] *Am.* Büchsen...; **~ery** *Am.* Konservenfabrik *f*.

cannibal ['kænibəl] Kannibale *m*.

cannon ['kænən] Kanone *f*.

cannot ['kænɔt] nicht können *od.* dürfen.

canoe [kə'nu:] Kanu *n*; Paddelboot *n*.

canopy ['kænəpi] Baldachin *m*.

cant [kænt] Jargon *m*; Heuchelei *f*.

can't [ka:nt] *s.* **cannot**.

canteen [kæn'ti:n] Kantine *f*; *Am.* Feldflasche *f*; Kochgeschirr *n*.

canvas ['kænvəs] Segeltuch *n*; Zeltleinwand *f*; *paint.* Leinwand *f*.

canvass ['kænvəs] Stimmen, Abonnenten werben.

cap [kæp] Kappe *f*, Mütze

f; Haube *f*; Verschluß (-kappe *f*) *m*.

capab|ility [keipə'biliti] Fähigkeit *f*; **~le** fähig (of zu).

capacity [kə'pæsiti] (Raum)Inhalt *m*, Fassungsvermögen *n*; Kapazität *f*; Aufnahme-, (Leistungs)Fähigkeit *f*.

cape¹ [keip] Kap *n*, Vorgebirge *n*.

cape² Cape *n*, Umhang *m*.

caper ['keipə]: **(cut a)** ~ cut ~s Luftsprünge *od*. Kapriolen machen.

capital ['kæpitl] Hauptstadt *f*; Kapital *n*; Kapital...; Haupt...; *colloq*. vortrefflich; ~ **crime** Kapitalverbrechen *n*; ~**ism** Kapitalismus *m*; ~ **(letter)** großer Buchstabe *m*; ~ **punishment** Todesstrafe *f*.

capricious [kə'priʃəs] launenhaft.

capsize [kæp'saiz] kentern; zum Kentern bringen.

capsule ['kæpsju:l] Kapsel *f*.

captain ['kæptin] Führer *m*; Kapitän *m*; *mil.* Hauptmann *m*.

caption ['kæpʃən] Überschrift *f*, Titel *m*; Bildunterschrift *f*; *Film:* Untertitel *m*.

captiv|ate ['kæptiveit] *fig.* fesseln; **~e** Gefangene *m*, *f*; **~ity** [~'tiviti] Gefangenschaft *f*.

capture ['kæptʃə] Gefangennahme *f*; fangen, ge-

fangennehmen; erbeuten; *mar.* kapern; erlangen, gewinnen; *fig.* fesseln.

car [ka:] Auto *n*; (*bsd. Am.* Eisenbahn-, Straßenbahn-) Wagen *m*; Gondel *f*, Kabine *f*.

caravan ['kærəvæn] Karawane *f*; Wohnwagen *m*.

carbohydrate ['ka:bou'haidreit] Kohlehydrat *n*.

carbon ['ka:bən] *chem.* Kohlenstoff *m*; ~ **dioxide** ['~dai'ɔksaid] Kohlendioxyd *n*; ~ **paper** Kohlepapier *n*.

carbure|tter, ~t(t)or ['ka:bjuretə] *mot.* Vergaser *m*.

car-carrier Autoreisezug *m*.

carca|se, ~ss ['ka:kəs] Kadaver *m*.

card [ka:d] (Post-, Geschäfts-, Visiten-, Spiel-) Karte *f*; **~board** Pappe *f*, **~board box** (Papp)Karton *m*.

cardigan ['ka:digən] Wolljacke *f*.

cardinal ['ka:dinl] Kardinal *m*; Haupt...; ~ **number** Grundzahl *f*.

card index Kartei *f*.

car documents *pl* Wagenpapiere *pl*.

care [kɛə] Sorge *f*; Sorgfalt *f*; Fürsorge *f*, Obhut *f*, Pflege *f*; Aufsicht *f*; sich et. aus *e-r* S. machen; Lust haben; ~ **of** ... *abbr. c/o* bei ...; **take ~ of** acht(geb)en auf, sich kümmern um, sorgen für; **with**

~! Vorsicht!; *vb:* **~ for** sorgen für, sich kümmern um; sich etwas machen aus; **I don't ~!** meinetwegen!

career [kəˈriə] Karriere *f*; Laufbahn *f*; rasen.

care|free sorgenfrei; **~ful** vorsichtig; umsichtig; sorgfältig; **~less** sorglos; nachlässig, unachtsam; leichtsinnig.

caress [kəˈres] Liebkosung *f*; liebkosen.

care|taker (Haus)Verwalter(in); **~worn** abgehärmt, verhärmt.

car ferry Autofähre *f*.

cargo [ˈkɑːgəu] Ladung *f*.

caricature [ˈkærikəˈtjuə] Karikatur *f*.

car-mechanic Automechaniker *m*.

carnation [kɑːˈneiʃən] Nelke *f*.   [neval *m.*\

carnival [ˈkɑːnivəl] Kar-\

carol [ˈkærəl] (Weihnachts)Lied *n*.

carp [kɑːp] Karpfen *m*.

car-park Parkplatz *m*.

carpenter [ˈkɑːpintə] Zimmermann *m*, Tischler *m*.

carpet [ˈkɑːpit] Teppich *m*.

carriage [ˈkæridʒ] (Eisenbahn- *etc.*)Wagen *m*; Transport *m*; Fracht(geld *n*) *f*; (Körper)Haltung *f*; **~free** frachtfrei; **~way** Fahrbahn *f*.

carrier [ˈkæriə] Träger *m*, Bote *m*; Fuhrunternehmer *m*; (Krankheits)Überträger *m*; Gepäckträger *m*

(*Fahrrad*); **~bag** Einkaufstüte *f*, Tragbeutel *m*.

carrion [ˈkæriən] Aas *n*; Aas...

carrot [ˈkærət] Karotte *f*, Mohrrübe *f*, Möhre *f*.

carry [ˈkæri] tragen, bringen, befördern; (bei sich) haben; **~ on** fortsetzen, weiterführen; *Geschäft etc.* betreiben; **~ out** aus-, durchführen.

cart [kɑːt] Fuhrwerk *n*; Karren *m*, Wagen *m*; karren, fahren; **~er** Fuhrmann *m*; **~-horse** Zugpferd *n*.

carton [ˈkɑːtən] Karton *m*, (Papp)Schachtel *f*.

cartoon [kɑːˈtuːn] Karikatur *f*; **(animated) ~** Zeichentrickfilm *m*; **~ist** Karikaturist *m*.

cartridge [ˈkɑːtridʒ] Patrone *f*.

cart-wheel Wagenrad *n*; **turn ~s** radschlagen.

carve [kɑːv] *Fleisch* zerlegen, tranchieren; schnitzen; meißeln; **~r** Schnitzer *m*; **~ing** Schnitzerei *f*.

cascade [kæsˈkeid] Wasserfall *m*.

case¹ [keis] Behälter *m*; Kiste *f*; Etui *n*; Schachtel *f*; kleiner Koffer; Tasche *f*.

case² Fall *m* (*a. med., jur.*); *gr.* Kasus *m*, Fall *m*; Sache *f*, Angelegenheit *f*; **in any ~** auf jeden Fall.

casement [ˈkeismənt] Fensterflügel *m*.

cash [kæʃ] einlösen; Bargeld *n*; Geld *n*, Kasse *f*; **~ down** gegen bar; **~ on delivery** per Nachnahme, zahlbar bei Lieferung; **~ desk** Kasse *f* (*Bank etc.*); **~ier** Kassier *m* Kassierer (-*in*); **~ register** (Registrier)Kasse *f*.

casing ['keisiŋ] Umhüllung *f*; Verkleidung *f*.

cask [ku:sk] Faß *n*; **~et** ['~it] Kästchen *n*; *Am.* Sarg *m*.

cassock ['kæsək] Soutane *f*.

cast [ku:st] Wurf *m*; *tech.* Guß(form *f*) *m*; Abguß *m*, Abdruck *m*; *thea.* (Rollen-)Besetzung *f*; (*irr*) (ab-, aus)werfen; *tech.* gießen; *thea.* Stück besetzen; Rollen verteilen; **be ~ down** niedergeschlagen sein.

caste [ku:st] Kaste *f*.

cast| iron Gußeisen *n*; **~-iron** gußeisern.

castle ['ku:sl] Burg *f*, Schloß *n*.

castor ['ku:stə] (Salz- *etc.*) Streuer *m*.

castor oil Rizinusöl *n*.

cast| steel Gußstahl *m*; **~-steel** aus Gußstahl.

casual ['kæʒuəl] zufällig; gelegentlich; zwanglos; flüchtig; **~ty** Unfall *m*; Verunglückte *m*, *f*; *pl* Opfer *pl*, *mil.* Verluste *pl*.

cat [kæt] Katze *f*.

catalog(ue) ['kætələg] Katalog *m*.

cataract ['kætərækt] Wasserfall *m*.

catarrh [kə'ta:] Katarrh *m*; Schnupfen *m*.

catastrophe [kə'tæstrəfi] Katastrophe *f*.

catch [kætʃ] Fang(en *n*) *m*; Beute *f*; *tech.* Haken *m* (*a. fig.*), Klinke *f*.); (*irr*) fangen; fassen; ertappen; Zug *etc.* erreichen; bekommen; sich *Krankheit* zuziehen, holen; *fig.* erfassen; einschnappen (*Schloß*); sich verfangen, hängenbleiben; **~ (a) cold** sich erkälten; **~ up (with)** einholen, überholen; **~er** Fänger *m*; **~ing** packend; *med.* ansteckend; **~word** Schlagwort *n*; Stichwort *n*.

category ['kætigəri] Kategorie *f*.

cater ['keitə]: **~ for** Lebensmittel liefern für; sorgen für.

caterpillar ['kætəpilə] *zo.* Raupe *f*.

cathedral [kə'θi:drəl] Dom *m*, Kathedrale *f*.

Catholic ['kæθəlik] katholisch; Katholik(in).

cattle ['kætl] (Rind)Vieh *n*, Rinder *pl*.

caught [kɔ:t] *pret u. pp von* **catch**.

ca(u)ldron ['kɔ:ldrən] Kessel *m*.

cauliflower ['kɔliflauə] Blumenkohl *m*.

cause [kɔ:z] Ursache *f*, Grund *m*; Sache *f*; verursachen, -anlassen; bereiten; **~less** grundlos.

caution ['kɔ:ʃən] Vorsicht *f*; (Ver)Warnung *f*; (ver)warnen; **~ous** behutsam, vorsichtig.

cav|e [keiv], **~ern** ['kævən] Höhle *f*; **~ity** ['kæviti] Höhle *f*; Loch *n*.

cease [si:s] aufhören; **~less** unaufhörlich.

ceiling ['si:liŋ] (Zimmer-) Decke *f*; *Preise*: Höchstgrenze *f*.

celebrat|e ['selibreit] feiern; **~ed** berühmt; **~ion** Feier *f*.

celebrity [si'lebriti] Berühmtheit *f*.

celery ['seləri] Sellerie *m*.

celibacy ['selibəsi] Zölibat *n*.

cell [sel] Zelle *f*; *Element n*.

cellar ['selə] Keller *m*.

Celt [kelt] Kelt|e *m*, -in *f*; **~ic** keltisch; *das* Keltische.

cement [si'ment] Zement *m*; Kitt *m*; zementieren; kitten.

cemetery ['semitri] Friedhof *m*.

censor ['sensə] zensieren; **~ship** Zensur *f*.

censure ['senʃə] Tadel *m*; tadeln.

cent [sent] *Am.* Cent *m*; **per ~** Prozent *n*; **~enary** [~'ti:nəri], **~ennial** [~'tenjəl] hundertjährig; Hundertjahrfeier *f*.

centi|grade ['sentigreid]: **10 degrees ~** 10 Grad Celsius; **~metre**, *Am.* **~meter** Zentimeter *n*, *m*.

central ['sentrəl] zentral;

Mittel...; ♀ **Europe** Mitteleuropa *n*; **~ heating** Zentralheizung *f*; **~ize** zentralisieren.

cent|re, *Am.* **~er** ['sentə] Zentrum *n*, Mittelpunkt *m*; (sich) konzentrieren; **~re-forward** Mittelstürmer *m*; **~rehalf** Mittelläufer *m*.

century ['sentʃuri] Jahrhundert *n*.

cereals ['siəriəlz] *pl* Frühstückskost *f* (*aus Getreide*).

cerebral ['seribrəl] Gehirn...

ceremon|ial [seri'məunjəl] Zeremoniell *n*; **~ial**, **~ious** zeremoniell; förmlich; **~y** ['~məni] Zeremonie *f*, Feierlichkeit *f*; Förmlichkeit(en *pl*) *f*.

certain ['sə:tn] sicher, gewiß, bestimmt; gewisse(r, -s); **~ly** sicher(lich), bestimmt, gewiß; **~ty** Gewißheit *f*.

certi|ficate [sə'tifikit] Bescheinigung *f*, Attest *n*; Schein *m*, Urkunde *f*; Zeugnis *n*; **~fy** ['sə:tifai] bescheinigen; **~tude** ['~tju:d] Gewißheit *f*.

chafe [tʃeif] reiben; (sich) wund reiben; **~** sich reiben; toben.

chaff [tʃɑ:f] Spreu *f*; Häcksel *n*.

chaffinch ['tʃæfintʃ] Buchfink *m*.

chagrin ['ʃægrin] Ärger *m*.

chain [tʃein] Kette *f*; (an-) ketten.

chair [tʃeə] Stuhl *m*, Sessel

chalk 50

_m_; Lehrstuhl _m_; Vorsitz _m_;
~-lift Sessellift _m_; **~man**
Vorsitzende _m_.
chalk [tʃɔːk] Kreide _f_.
challenge ['tʃælindʒ] Herausforderung _f_; _mil._ Anruf
_m_; herausfordern; anrufen; anzweifeln.
chamber ['tʃeimbə] Kammer _f_; **~maid** Zimmermädchen _n_.
chamois ['ʃæmwɑː] Gemse _f_; **~-leather** ['ʃæmi-] Sämischleder _n_.
champagne [ʃæm'pein]
Champagner _m_.
champion ['tʃæmpjən]
Vorkämpfer _m_, Verfechter
_m_; _sp._ Meister(in); **~ship**
Meisterschaft _f_.
chance [tʃɑːns] zufällig;
Zufall _m_; Glück _n_; Chance
_f_; (günstige) Gelegenheit;
by ~ zufällig, durch Zufall; **give s.o. a ~** j-m
eine Chance geben; **take
one's ~** es darauf ankommen
lassen.
chancellor ['tʃɑːnsələ]
Kanzler _m_.
chandelier [ʃændi'liə]
Kronleuchter _m_.
change [tʃeindʒ] Veränderung _f_, Wechsel _m_, Abwechs(e)lung _f_; Wechselgeld _n_; Kleingeld _n_; **for
a ~** zur Abwechs(e)lung;
(sich) (ver)ändern; (aus)wechseln, (um)tauschen;
(sich) verwandeln; sich
umziehen; **~ one's mind**
sich anders entschließen;
~ (trains) umsteigen;

~able veränderlich.
channel ['tʃænl] Kanal _m_
(_a. fig._); Rinne _f_; _aer._
Flugsteig _m_; **the (English)** ~ der (Ärmel)Kanal.
chaos ['keiɔs] Chaos _n_.
chap [tʃæp] _colloq._ Bursche _m_, Kerl _m_.
chapel ['tʃæpəl] Kapelle _f_.
chaplain ['tʃæplin] Kaplan _m_.
chapter ['tʃæptə] Kapitel _n_.
character ['kæriktə] Charakter _m_; Schrift(zeichen
_n_) _f_; _thea._, _Roman_: Person _f_; Ruf _m_; Zeugnis _n_;
~istic charakteristisch;
Kennzeichen _n_; **~ize** charakterisieren.
charge [tʃɑːdʒ] laden;
Batterie (auf)laden; beauftragen; befehlen; ermahnen; beschuldigen, anklagen; fordern, verlangen,
berechnen; _electr._ Ladung
_f_; (Spreng)Ladung _f_; Obhut _f_; Schützling _m_; Anklage _f_; Preis _m_; _pl_ Kosten
_pl_; **be in ~ of** verantwortlich sein für, versorgen,
betreuen; **free of ~**
kostenlos.
chariot ['tʃæriət] zweirädriger (Streit-, Triumph-)
Wagen.
charit|able ['tʃæritəbl]
wohltätig; **~y** Nächstenliebe _f_; Wohltätigkeit _f_.
charm [tʃɑːm] Zauber _m_;
Talisman _m_; _fig. a._ Reiz
_m_; bezaubern, entzücken;
~ing bezaubernd, reizend.

chew

chart [tʃɑːt] Seekarte *f*; Tabelle *f*.

charter ['tʃɑːtə] Urkunde *f*; chartern, mieten; **~plane** Chartermaschine *f*.

charwoman ['tʃɑːwumən] Putzfrau *f*.

chase [tʃeis] Jagd *f*; Verfolgung *f*; jagen; verfolgen; *colloq.* eilen.

chasm ['kæzəm] Kluft *f* (*a. fig.*).

chast|e [tʃeist] rein, keusch; **~ity** ['tʃæstiti] Keuschheit *f*.

chat [tʃæt] Geplauder *n*; plaudern; **~ter** plappern, schwatzen, schwätzen; klappern; Geplapper *n*; **~terbox** Plappermaul *n*.

chauffeur ['ʃəufə] Chauffeur *m*.

cheap [tʃiːp] billig (*a. fig.*); **~en** (sich) verbilligen; *fig.* herabsetzen.

cheat [tʃiːt] Betrug *m*; Betrüger(in); betrügen.

check [tʃek] Hemmnis *n*, Einhalt *m*; Kontrolle *f*; Kontroll-, Garderobenmarke *f*; (Gepäck)Schein *m*; *Am.* Rechnung *f* (*Restaurant*); *Am.* Scheck *m*; karierter Stoff; hemmen, hindern, aufhalten; kontrollieren, (nach)prüfen; *Am.* Mantel in der Garderobe abgeben; *Am.* Gepäck aufgeben; **~ in** *Am.* in e-m Hotel absteigen; **~ out** *Am.* abreisen (*Hotel*); **~ed** kariert; **~room** *Am.*: Gar-

derobe *f*; Gepäckaufbewahrung *f*.

cheek [tʃiːk] Backe *f*, Wange *f*; Unverschämtheit *f*; **~y** frech.

cheer [tʃiə] gute Laune; Hoch(ruf *m*) *n*; Beifall (-sruf) *m*; (zu)jubeln; **~ (on)** anfeuern; **~ (up)** ermuntern, aufheitern; **~ up** Mut fassen; **~ful,** heiter; **~io** ['ʃiə'rɪəu] *colloq.* mach's gut!, tschüs!; **~less** freudlos, trüb; **~y** heiter.

cheese [tʃiːz] Käse *m*.

chef [ʃef] Küchenchef *m*.

chemical ['kemikəl] chemisch; **~s** *pl* Chemikalien *pl*.

chemise [ʃə'miːz] (Frauen)Hemd *n*.

chemist ['kemist] Chemiker *m*; Apotheker *m*; Drogist *m*; **~ry** Chemie *f*; **~'s shop** Drogerie *f*; Apotheke *f*.

cheque [tʃek] Scheck *m*.

chequ|ered ['tʃekəd] kariert; *fig.* bunt.

cherish ['tʃeriʃ] hegen.

cherry ['tʃeri] Kirsche *f*.

chess [tʃes] Schach(spiel) *n*; **~board** Schachbrett *n*; **~man** Schachfigur *f*.

chest [tʃest] Kiste *f*, Truhe *f*, Kasten *m*; *anat.* Brustkorb *m*.

chestnut ['tʃesnʌt] Kastanie *f*; kastanienbraun.

chest of drawers Kommode *f*.

chew [tʃuː] kauen; **~ing-gum** Kaugummi *m*.

chicken ['tʃikin] Huhn *n*; Hühnchen *n*, Hähnchen *n*; Küken *n*; **⁓pox** ['⁓pɔks] Windpocken *pl*.

chief [tʃi:f] oberst; Ober..., Haupt...; hauptsächlich; Chef *m*; Anführer *m*; Häuptling *m*; **...in-** Ober...

chilblain ['tʃilblein] Frostbeule *f*.

child [tʃaild], *pl* **⁓ren** Kind *n*, **⁓hood** Kindheit *f*; **⁓ish** kindlich; kindisch; **⁓less** kinderlos; **⁓like** kindlich; **⁓ren** ['tʃildrən] *pl von* **child.**

chill [tʃil] Frost *m*, Kälte (-gefühl *n*) *f*; Erkältung *f*; (ab)kühlen; **be ⁓ed** durch-(ge)froren sein; **⁓y** kalt; *fig.* frostig.

chime [tʃaim] *mst pl* Glockenspiel *n*; Geläut *n*; läuten.

chimney ['tʃimni] Schornstein *m*; **⁓-sweep(er)** Schornsteinfeger *m*.

chin [tʃin] Kinn *n*.

china ['tʃainə] Porzellan *n*.

Chinese ['tʃai'ni:z] chinesisch; Chinese(n *pl*) *m*; Chinesin *f*; Chinesisch *n*.

chink [tʃiŋk] Ritz *m*, Spalt *m*.

chip [tʃip] Splitter *m*, Span *m*, Schnitzel *n*; dünne Scheibe; Spielmarke *f*; *pl* Pommes frites *pl*; schnitzeln; an-, abschlagen.

chirp [tʃə:p] zirpen, zwitschern.

chisel ['tʃizl] Meißel *m*; meißeln.

chivalr|ous ['ʃivəlrəs] ritterlich; **⁓y** Rittertum *n*; Ritterlichkeit *f*.

chive [tʃaiv] Schnittlauch *m*.

chlor|ine ['klɔ:ri:n] Chlor *n*; **⁓oform** ['klɔrəfɔ:m] Chloroform *n*; chloroformieren.

chocolate ['tʃɔkəlit] Schokolade *f* (*a. Getränk*); Praline *f*; *pl* Pralinen *f*, Konfekt *n*; **box of ⁓s** Schachtel *f* Pralinen.

choice [tʃɔis] (Aus)Wahl *f*; auserlesen, vorzüglich.

choir ['kwaiə] Chor *m*.

choke [tʃəuk] (er)würgen; drosseln; ersticken; **⁓down** hinunterwürgen; **⁓up** verstopfen; *sub: mot.* Starterklappe *f*.

choose [tʃu:z] (*irr*) (aus-) wählen; vorziehen.

chop [tʃɔp] Hieb *m*; Kotelett *n*; hauen, (zer-) hacken; **⁓down** niederhauen; *Baum* fällen.

chord [kɔ:d] Saite *f*; *mus.* Akkord *m*; *anat.* Band *n*, Strang *m*.

chorus ['kɔ:rəs] Chor *m*; Kehrreim *m*.

chose [tʃəuz] *pret*, **⁓n** *pp von* **choose.**

Christ [kraist] Christus *m*.

christen ['krisn] taufen; **⁓ing** Taufe *f*.

Christian ['kristjən] Christ (-in) *n*; christlich; **⁓ity** [⁓i'æniti] Christentum *n*; **⁓ name** Vorname *m*.

Christmas ['krisməs] Weihnachten n; Weihnachts...; **Father** ~ Weihnachtsmann m; **Merry** ~ Fröhliche Weihnachten!; ~ **Day** erster Weihnachtsfeiertag m; ~ **Eve** Heiliger Abend. [Chrom n.]

chromium ['krəumjəm] ∫

chronic ['krɔnik] chronisch; ~le Chronik f.

chronological [krɔnə-'lɔdʒikəl] chronologisch.

chubby ['tʃʌbi] pausbackig.

chuck [tʃʌk] colloq. schmeißen.

chuckle ['tʃʌkl] in sich hineinlachen.

chum [tʃʌm] (Stuben-) Kamerad m; guter Freund.

church [tʃəːtʃ] Kirche f; Gottesdienst m; Kirch(en)...; ~**warden** Kirchenvorsteher m; ~**yard** Kirch-, Friedhof m.

churn [tʃəːn] Butterfaß n; Brit. Milchkanne f; buttern; aufwühlen.

chute [ʃuːt] Stromschnelle f; Rutschbahn f, Rutsche f; colloq. Fallschirm m.

cider ['saidə] Apfelwein m.

cigar [si'gɑː] Zigarre f.

cigaret(te) [sigə'ret] Zigarette f.

cinder ['sində] Schlacke f; pl Asche f; Ձella [~'relə] Aschenbrödel n; ~**track** sp. Aschenbahn f.

cine-camera ['sini-] Filmkamera f; ~**ma** [~'əmə] Kino n; Film(kunst f) m.

go to the ~**ma** ins Kino gehen; ~**projector** Filmprojektor m.

cipher ['saifə] Ziffer f; Null f (a. fig.); Chiffre f; chiffrieren.

circle ['səːkl] Kreis(lauf m; thea. Rang m; (um-) kreisen.

circuit ['səːkit] Rundflug m, ~gang m, ~reise f; Stromkreis m; **short** ~ Kurzschluß m.

circular ['səːkjulə] kreisförmig; Kreis...; ~ **(letter)** Rundschreiben n.

circulat|**e** ['səːkjuleit] umlaufen, zirkulieren, kreisen; verbreiten; ~**ing library** Kreisbücherei f; ~**ion** Kreislauf m; econ. Umlauf m; Verbreitung f; Auflage f (Zeitung).

circum|**ference** [sə'kʌmfərəns] (Kreis)Umfang m; ~**navigate** [səːkəm'-] umsegeln; ~**scribe** ['~skraib] umschreiben; fig. begrenzen; ~**stance** Umstand m; pl (a. finanzielle) Verhältnisse pl.

circus ['səːkəs] Zirkus m; (runder) Platz.

cistern ['sistən] Wasserbehälter m.

cite [sait] zitieren; jur. vorladen.

citizen ['sitizn] (Staats-) Bürger(in); Städter(in); ~**ship** Staatsangehörigkeit f.

city ['siti] (Groß)Stadt f; **the** Ձ London: die City,

civics   54

das Geschäftsviertel; ~
centre Innenstadt f,
Stadtmitte f; ~ **guide**
Stadtplan m; ~ **hall** bsd.
Am. Rathaus n.

civics ['siviks] sg Staats-
bürgerkunde f.

civil ['sivl] bürgerlich, Bürger...; zivil; höflich; ~**ian**
[si'viljən] Zivilist m; ~**ity**
Höflichkeit f; ~**ization**
Zivilisation f, Kultur f; ~**ize**
zivilisieren; ~ **marriage**
standesamtliche Trau-
ung; ~ **rights** pl Bürger-
rechte pl; ~ **Service**
Staatsdienst m; ~ **war**
Bürgerkrieg m.

clad [klæd] pret u. pp
von **clothe**; gekleidet.

claim [kleim] Anspruch
m; Anrecht n; beanspru-
chen, fordern; ~**ant** Anwärter m.

clammy ['klæmi] feucht-
kalt, klamm.

clamo(**u**)**r** ['klæmə] Geschrei n; schreien; ~**rous**
lärmend, schreiend.

clamp [klæmp] Klammer f.

clan [klæn] Clan m, Sippe f.

clandestine [klæn'destin]
heimlich.

clank [klæŋk] Gerassel n,
Geklirr n; rasseln od.
klirren (mit).

clap [klæp] Klatschen n;
Knall m; schlagen od.
klatschen (mit).

claret ['klærət] Rotwein m.

clari|fy ['klærifai] (sich)
klären; ~**ty** Klarheit f.

clash [klæ] Geklirr n;

Zs.-stoß m; Widerstreit
m; klirren; zs.-stoßen.

clasp [klɑ:sp] Haken m;
Spange f; Umklamme-
rung f; Umarmung f; ein-
haken, schließen; um-
klammern, umfassen;
~**knife** Klapp-, Taschenmesser n.

class [klɑ:s] Klasse f;
Stand m, Schicht f; Un-
terricht m, Stunde f;
Kurs(us) m; Am. univ.
Jahrgang m; (in Klassen)
einteilen, einordnen; ~
mate Klassenkamerad(in);
~**room** Klassen-, Schul-
zimmer n.

classic ['klæsik] Klas-
siker m; erstklassig; klassisch; ~**al** klassisch.

classi|fication [klæsifi-
'keiʃən] Klassifizierung
f, Einteilung f; ~**fy** ['~fai]
klassifizieren, ~einstufen.

clatter ['klætə] Geklapper
n, Poltern n, Getrappel n;
klappern.

clause [klɔ:z] Klausel f;
gr. Satz(teil) m.

claw [klɔ:] Klaue f, Kralle f.

clay [klei] Ton m.

clean [kli:n] rein, sauber;
völlig; reinigen, sauber-
machen, putzen; ~ **out**
reinigen, säubern; ~ **up**
aufräumen; ~**er** Reiniger
m; (**dry**) ~**ers** pl (chemische) Reinigung; ~**ing**
Reinigung f, Putzen n;
~**liness** ['klenlinis] Rein-
lichkeit f; ~**ly** ['klenli]
reinlich; ~**ness** ['kli:nnis]

Sauberkeit f; ~se [klenz] reinigen, säubern; ~ shaven glattrasiert.

clear [kliə] klar; hell; rein; frei; ganz, voll; rein, netto; reinigen; roden; *Tisch* abräumen; räumen, leeren; freisprechen; ~ away wegräumen; ~ up auf-, abräumen; (sich) aufklären; ~ing Lichtung f, Rodung f.

cleave [kli:v] festhalten (to an); (irr) (sich) spalten.   [sel m.]

clef [klef] (Noten)Schlüs-|

cleft [kleft] Spalte f; pret u. pp von cleave.

clemency ['klemənsi] Milde f.

clench [klentʃ] Lippen zs.-pressen; *Zähne* zs.-beißen; *Faust* ballen.

clergy ['klə:dʒi] Geistlichkeit f; ~man Geistliche m.   [lich.]

clerical ['klerikəl] Geist-|

clerk [klɑ:k] Schreiber (-in); Büroangestellte m, f; (Bank-, Post- etc.)Beamt|e m, -in f; Am. Verkäufer(in).

clever ['klevə] gescheit, klug; gewandt, geschickt.

click [klik] Klicken n, Knacken n; klicken, knakken; (zu-, ein)schnappen.

client ['klaiənt] Klient (-in); Kund|e m, -in f.

cliff [klif] Klippe f.

climate ['klaimit] Klima n.

climax ['klaimæks] Höhepunkt m.

climb [klaim] klettern od. steigen auf; ~ up hinaufsteigen, -klettern; ~er Kletterer m; bot. Kletterpflanze f.

clinch [klintʃ] Umklammerung f.

cling [kliŋ] (irr) sich (an-) klammern (to an).

clinic ['klinik] Klinik f.

clink [kliŋk] klingen (lassen).

clip¹ [klip] (Büro)Klammer f; Spange f.

clip² Schur f; ab-, beschneiden; *Schafe etc.* scheren; ~pings pl (Zeitungs- etc.) Ausschnitte pl.

cloak [klouk] Mantel m, Umhang m; ~room Garderobe f; Gepäckaufbewahrung f; Toilette f.

clock [klɔk] (Wand- etc.) Uhr f; ~wise im Uhrzeigersinn.   [m.]

clod [klɔd] (Erd)Klumpen|

clog [klɔg] Klotz m; Holzschuh m; verstopfen; belasten.

cloister ['klɔistə] Kreuzgang m; Kloster n.

close [klous] geschlossen; nah; eng; dicht; knapp; streng; genau, sorgfältig; schwül, dumpf; geizig; verschwiegen; ~ to od. by dicht od. nahe bei, an; Einfriedung f, Hof m; [~z] (Ab)Schluß m, Ende n; [~z] (ab-, ein-, ver-, zu)schließen; beenden; sich schließen; ~ down *Fabrik etc.* schließen; ~ in hereinbrechen (*Nacht*).

closet ['klɔzit] kleines Zimmer; (*Wand*)Schrank *m*; *s.* **water-closet.**

close-up ['klousʌp] Großaufnahme *f*.

closing-time ['klouziŋ-] Geschäftsschluß *m*.

clot [klɔt] Klumpen *m*, Klümpchen *n*; gerinnen (lassen), Klumpen bilden.

cloth [klɔθ] Stoff *m*, Tuch *n*; **lay the ~** den Tisch decken; **~-bound** in Leinen (gebunden).

clothe [klouð] (*irr*) (an-, be-, ein)kleiden.

clothes [klouðz] *pl* Kleider *pl*, Kleidung *f*; Wäsche *f*; **~-brush** Kleiderbürste *f*; **~-hanger** Kleiderbügel *m*; **~-line** Wäscheleine *f*; **~-peg**, **~-pin** Wäscheklammer *f*.   [dung *f*.]

clothing ['klouðiŋ] KleiーⅠ

cloud [klaud] Wolke *f*; (sich) bewölken; *fig.* (sich) trüben; **~y** wolkig, Wolken...; trüb.

clove¹ [klouv] Gewürznelke *f*.   [**cleave.**]

clove² *pret*, **~n** *pp von*∫

clover ['klouvə] Klee *m*.

clown [klaun] Clown *m*, Hanswurst *m*.

club [klʌb] Keule *f*, Knüppel *m*; Klub *m*, Verein *m*; **~s** *pl*) *Karten*: Kreuz *n*.

clue [klu:] Anhaltspunkt *m*.

clumsy ['klʌmzi] unbeholfen, ungeschickt; plump.

clung [klʌŋ] *pret u. pp von* **cling.**

cluster ['klʌstə] Traube *f*; Büschel *n*; Haufen *m*; sich zs.-drängen; ranken.

clutch [klʌtʃ] Griff *m*; Kupplung *f*; packen, (er-)greifen; **~ pedal** Kupplungspedal *n*.

coach [koutʃ] Kutsche *f*, Karosse *f*; (Eisenbahn-) Wagen *m*; Überland-, Reisebus *m*; Nachhilfelehrer *m*, Einpauker *m*; Trainer *m*; Nachhilfeunterricht geben, einpauken; trainieren.

coagulate [kou'ægjuleit] gerinnen (lassen).

coal [koul] Kohle *f*; **~field** Kohlenrevier *n*.

coalition [kouə'liʃən] Koalition *f*.

coal|-mine Kohlengrube *f*; **~-mining** Kohlenbergbau *m*; **~-pit** Kohlengrube *f*.

coarse [kɔːs] grob; ungeschliffen.

coast [koust] Küste *f*; die Küste entlangfahren; im Freilauf fahren; rodeln; **~guard** Küsten(zoll)wache *f*.

coat [kout] überziehen, anstreichen; umkleiden; Jackett *m*, Jacke *f*, Rock *m*; Mantel *m*; Fell *n*, Pelz *m*; (*Farb- etc.*)Überzug *m*, Anstrich *m*; **~-hanger** Kleiderbügel *m*; **~ing** Überzug *m*, Anstrich *m*; Mantelstoff *m*; **~ of arms** Wappen(schild) *n*.

coax [kouks] beschwatzen.

cob [kɔb] Maiskolben *m*.

cobra ['kəubrə] Brillen-
schlange f, Kobra f.

cobweb ['kɔbweb] Spinn-
(en)gewebe n.

cock [kɔk] Hahn m; Ge-
wehrhahn spannen; **~(up)**
aufrichten; **~a'too** [ə'tu:]
Kakadu m; **~chafer** Mai-
käfer m; **~le** Herzmuschel
f; **~ney** ['~ni] Cockney m,
(echter) Londoner m;
(Flugzeug)Kanzel f; **~-
roach** ['~rəutʃ] (Küchen-)
Schabe f; **~sure** tod-
sicher; überheblich; **~tail**
Cocktail m.   [palme f.]

coco ['kəukəu] Kokos-.]

cocoa ['kəukəu] Kakao m.

coconut ['kəukənʌt] Kokosnuß f.

cocoon [kə'ku:n] Kokon m.

cod [kɔd] Kabeljau m,
Dorsch m.

coddle ['kɔdl] verhätscheln.

code [kəud] Gesetzbuch n;
Kodex m; Code m, Schlüs-
sel m; chiffrieren.

cod-liver oil Lebertran m.

coexist ['kəuig'zist] gleichzeitig bestehen; **~ence**
Koexistenz f.

coffee ['kɔfi] Kaffee m;
~bean Kaffeebohne f;
~mill Kaffeemühle f;
~pot Kaffeekanne f;
~stall Kaffeestube f,
Imbißstube f, -wagen m.

coffin ['kɔfin] Sarg m.

cog-wheel ['kɔg-] Zahn-
rad n.

coherence [kəu'hiərəns],
~cy Zs.-hang m; **~t** zs.-
hängend.

cohesive [kəu'hi:siv] zs.-
hängend.   [sur f.]

coiffure [kwu:'fjuə] Fri-]

coil [kɔil] Rolle f, Spirale f; electr. Spule f;
Windung f; **~(up)** auf-
rollen, (-)wickeln; **~o.s.**
up sich zs.-rollen.

coin [kɔin] Münze f,
Geldstück n; prägen (a.
fig.); münzen; **~age** Prä-
gung f.

coincide [kəuin'said] zs.-
treffen; übereinstimmen;
~nce [kəu'insidəns] Zs.-
treffen n; Übereinstim-
mung f.

coke [kəuk] Koks m; sl.
Koks m (Kokain).

cold [kəuld] kalt; Kälte f;
Erkältung f; **bad ~** starke
Erkältung; **~ness** Kälte
f; **~-storage room** Kühlraum m.

colic ['kɔlik] Kolik f.

collaborate [kə'læbəreit]
zs.-arbeiten; **~ion** Zs.-ar-
beit f; **in ~ion** gemeinsam.

collapse [kə'læps] zs.-,
einfallen; zs.-brechen; Zs.-
bruch m; **~ible** zs.-klapp-
bar, Klapp..., Klapp...

collar ['kɔlə] Kragen m;
Halsband n; Kummet n;
beim Kragen packen; **~-
bone** Schlüsselbein n.

colleague ['kɔli:g] Kolleg|e
m, -in f.

collect [kə'lekt] (ein-)
sammeln; Gedanken etc.
sammeln; einkassieren;
abholen; sich an- od.

versammeln; **~ed** *fig.* gefaßt; **~ion** (An)Sammlung *f*; *econ.* Einziehung *f*; Leerung *f* (*Briefkasten*); **~ive** kollektiv, gesamt; **~or** Sammler *m*; Einnehmer *m*; Einsammler *m*.

college ['kɔlidʒ] College *n*; Hochschule *f*; höhere Lehranstalt.

collide [kə'laid] zs.-stoßen.

colliery ['kɔljəri] (Kohlen-) Zeche *f*.

collision [kə'liʒən] Zs.-stoß *m*.

colloquial [kə'laukwiəl] umgangssprachlich.

colon ['kəulən] Doppelpunkt *m*.

colonel ['kə:nl] Oberst *m*.

colonial [kə'ləunjəl] Kolonial...; **~ism** Kolonialismus *m*.

colon|ist ['kɔlənist] Siedler(in); **~ize** kolonisieren; besiedeln; **~y** Kolonie *f*; Ansiedlung *f*.

colo(u)r ['kʌlə] Farbe *f*; *fig.* Anschein *m*; *pl* Fahne *f*, Flagge *f*; färben; (an-) streichen; *fig.* beschönigen, entstellen; sich (ver-) färben; erröten; **~ bar** Rassenschranke *f*; **~ed** gefärbt; farbig, bunt; farbig, Neger...; **~ed man** Farbige *m*; **~ed people** Farbige *pl*; **~ful** farbenreich, -freudig; bunt; **~ing** Färbung *f*; Farbton *m*; **~less** farblos; **~ line** *Am.* Rassenschranke *f*; **~print** Farbabzug *m*.

colt [kəult] (Hengst)Füllen *n*.

column ['kɔləm] Säule *f*; *print.* Spalte *f*; *mil.* Kolonne *f*. [kämmen.)

comb [kəum] Kamm *m*;}

combat ['kɔmbət] Kampf *m*; (be)kämpfen; **~ant** Kämpfer *m*.

combin|ation [kɔmbi-'neiʃən] Verbindung *f*; **~e** [kəm'bain] (sich) verbinden; **~e-harvester** Mähdrescher *m*.

combust|ible [kəm'bʌstəbl] brennbar; **~ion** [~stʃən] Verbrennung *f*.

come [kʌm] (*irr*) kommen; **~ about** sich zutragen, zustande kommen; **~ across** *od. j—n od. et.* stoßen, *j—m od. et.* begegnen; **~ along** mitkommen; **~ at** erreichen; **~ by** vorbeikommen, zu *et.* kommen; **~ for** abholen kommen; **~ loose** sich ablösen, abgehen; **~ off** ab-, losgehen; abfärben; stattfinden; **~ on!** los!, vorwärts!, komm!; **~ round** vorbeikommen; wieder zu sich kommen; **~ to see** besuchen; **~ up to** entsprechen; **~back** Comeback *m*.

comed|ian [kə'mi:djən] Komiker(in); **~y** ['kɔmidi] Lustspiel *n*.

comet ['kɔmit] Komet *m*.

comfort ['kʌmfət] Bequemlichkeit *f*; Behaglichkeit *f*; Trost *m*; trösten; **~able** behaglich, bequem, komfortabel; **~er** Wollschal *m*; Schnuller *m*.

comic|(al) ['kɔmik(əl)] komisch; **~ strips** *pl* (lustige) Bildergeschichte(n *pl*).

comma ['kɔmə] Komma *n*.

command [kə'mɑ:nd] Herrschaft *f*, Beherrschung *f* (*a.* fig.); Befehl *m*, Aufforderung *f*; *mil.* Kommando *n*, (Ober-)Befehl *m*; befehl(ig)en; verfügen über; beherrschen; **~er** Kommandeur *m*, Befehlshaber *m*; **~er-in-chief** Oberbefehlshaber *m*; **~ment** Gebot *n*.

commemorate [kə'meməreit] gedenken, feiern.

commence [kə'mens] anfangen, beginnen; **~ment** Anfang *m*.

commend [kə'mend] empfehlen; loben; anvertrauen.

comment ['kɔment] Kommentar *m*, An-, Bemerkung *f*; **~ (up)on** kommentieren; **~ary** ['~əntəri] Kommentar *m*; **~ator** ['~enteitə] Kommentator *m*; Rundfunkreporter *m*.

commerc|e ['kɔmə(:)s] Handel *m*; **~ial** [kə'mɔ:ʃəl] *Rundfunk etc.:* Reklame-, Werbesendung *f*; kaufmännisch; Handels...; **~ial travel(l)er** Handlungsreisende *m*.

commiseration [kəmizə-'reiʃən] Mitleid *n*.

commission [kə'miʃən] Auftrag *m*; Vollmacht *f*;

Provision *f*; Kommission *f*; beauftragen; bevollmächtigen; **~ [~ʃnə]** Bevollmächtigte *m*, *f*; Kommissar *m*.

commit [kə'mit] anvertrauen, übergeben; *Tat* begehen, verüben; verpflichten, festlegen; **~ment** Verpflichtung *f*; **~tee** [~'ti] Ausschuß *m*, Komitee *n*.

commodity [kə'mɔditi] Ware *f*, Gebrauchsartikel *m*.

common ['kɔmən] gemeinsam; allgemein; gewöhnlich (*a.* fig.); Gemeindeland *n*; **in ~** gemeinsam; **~er** Bürger *m*; **~ law** Gewohnheitsrecht *n*; **~ market** Gemeinsamer Markt; **~place** Gemeinplatz *m*; alltäglich; **~s** *pl*: **House of ~s** *Brit. parl.* Unterhaus *n*; **~ sense** gesunder Menschenverstand; **~wealth** Staat (-enbund) *m*; Republik *f*; **the (British) ~wealth** das Commonwealth.

commotion [kə'məuʃən] Aufruhr *m*; Aufregung *f*.

commune ['kɔmju:n] Gemeinde *f*; Kommune *f*.

communica|te [kə'mju:nikeit] mitteilen; in Verbindung stehen; **~ion** Mitteilung *f*; Verständigung *f*; Verbindung *f*; **~ive** [~ətiv] gesprächig.

communion [kə'mju:njən] Gemeinschaft *f*; **2 Abendmahl** *n*.

communis|m ['kɔmju-nizəm] Kommunismus *m*; **~t** Kommunist(in); kommunistisch.

community [kə'mju:niti] Gemeinschaft *f*; Gemeinde *f*.

commute [kə'mju:t] aus-, ein-, umtauschen; *Strafe* umwandeln; *rail. etc.* pendeln.

compact ['kɔmpækt] (Kompakt)Puderdose *f*; [kəm'pækt] dicht, fest; knapp, bündig.

companion [kəm'pænjən] Gefährt|e *m*, -in *f*, Begleiter(in); Gesellschafter (-in); **~ship** Gesellschaft *f*.

company ['kʌmpəni] Gesellschaft *f*; Handelsgesellschaft *f*; *thea.* Truppe *f*.

compar|able ['kɔmpərəbl] vergleichbar; **~ative** [kəm'pærətiv] verhältnismäßig; **~ative (degree)** *gr.* Komparativ *m*, 1. Steigerungsstufe; **~e** [kəm'peə] vergleichen; sich vergleichen (lassen); *sub*: **beyond (without, past) ~e** unvergleichlich; **~ison** [.'pærisn] Vergleich *m*; *gr.* Steigerung *f*.

compartment [kəm-'pɑːtmənt] Abteilung *f*; Fach *n*; *rail.* Abteil *n*.

compass ['kʌmpəs] Kompaß *m*; Bereich *m*; **(pair of) ~es** *pl* Zirkel *m*.

compassion [kəm'pæʃən] Mitleid *n*; **~ate** [.it] mitleidig.

compatible [kəm'pætəbl] vereinbar.

compatriot [kəm'pætriət] Landsmann *m*.

compel [kəm'pel] (er-) zwingen.

compensat|e ['kɔmpen-seit] entschädigen; **~ion** Ausgleich *m*; Entschädigung *f*, (Schaden)Ersatz *m*.

compère ['kɔmpeə] Conférencier *m*.

compete [kəm'piːt] sich mitbewerben **(for** um); konkurrieren.

competen|ce ['kɔmpitəns], **~cy** Befähigung *f*; Zuständigkeit *f*; **~t** (leistungs)fähig; ausreichend; zuständig.

competit|ion [kɔmpi-'tiʃən] Wettbewerb *m*, -kampf *m*; *econ.* Konkurrenz *f*; Preisausschreiben *n*; **~or** [kəm'petitə] Konkurrent(in); *sp.* Teilnehmer(in).

compile [kəm'pail] zs.-stellen.

complacent [kəm'pleisnt] selbstzufrieden, -gefällig.

complain [kəm'plein] (sich be)klagen; **~t** Klage *f*, Beschwerde *f*; *med.* Leiden *n*.

complet|e [kəm'pliːt] vollständig, ganz; vollzählig; vervollständigen, ergänzen; beenden; **~ion** Vervollständigung *f*; Abschluß *m*.

complexion [kəm'plek-ʃən] Aussehen *n*; Gesichtsfarbe *f*, Teint *m*.

complicate ['komplikeit] komplizieren, erschweren.

compliment ['komplimənt] Kompliment n; pl Grüße pl; ['⁓mənt] beglückwünschen.

comply [kəm'plai]: ⁓ (with) sich fügen (dat.)

component [kəm'pəunənt] Bestandteil m.

compos|e [kəm'pəuz] zusetzen; komponieren, verfassen; ⁓e o.s. sich beruhigen od. fassen; ⁓ed besonnen sein aus; ⁓ed ruhig, gesetzt; ⁓er Komponist(in); ⁓ition [kompə'ziʃən] Zs.-setzung f; Abfassung f; Komposition f; Aufsatz m; ⁓ure [kəm'pəuʒə] Fassung f.

compote ['kompət] Kompott n.

compound ['kompaund] zs.-gesetzt; Zs.-setzung f; [kəm'paund] zs.-setzen.

comprehen|d [kompri'hend] begreifen; ⁓sible verständlich; ⁓sion [⁓ʃən] Verständnis n; Fassungskraft f; ⁓sive umfassend; ⁓sive school Gesamtschule f.

compress [kəm'pres] zs.-drücken.

comprise [kəm'praiz] bestehen aus.

compromise ['kompramaiz] Kompromiß m; bloßstellen; einen Kompromiß schließen.

compuls|ion [kəm'pʌlʃən] Zwang m; ⁓ory obligatorisch; Pflicht...

compunction [kəm'pʌŋkʃən] Gewissensbisse pl; Reue f.

computer [kəm'pju:tə] Computer m.

comrade ['komrid] Kamerad m, Genosse m; ⁓ship Kameradschaft f.

conceal [kən'si:l] verbergen; verschweigen.

conceit [kən'si:t] Einbildung f; ⁓ed eingebildet.

conceiv|able [kən'si:vəbl] denkbar; ⁓e Kind empfangen; sich denken; planen.

concentrate ['konsəntreit] (sich) konzentrieren.

conception [kən'sepʃən] Begreifen n; Vorstellung f; biol. Empfängnis f.

concern [kən'sə:n] Angelegenheit f; econ. Geschäft n; Interesse n; Sorge f; betreffen, angehen; beteiligen; beunruhigen; ⁓ed besorgt.

concert ['konsət] Konzert n.

concession [kən'seʃən] Zugeständnis n; Konzession f.

concilia|te [kən'silieit] aus-, versöhnen; ⁓ory [⁓ətəri] versöhnlich.

concise [kən'sais] kurz, knapp.

conclu|de [kən'klu:d] (ab-, be)schließen; folgern; ⁓sion [⁓ʒən] Schluß m, Ende n; Abschluß m; Folgerung f; ⁓sive [⁓siv] endgültig.

concord ['kɔnkɔ:d] Eintracht *f*; Übereinstimmung *f*; Harmonie *f*.

concrete ['kɔnkri:t] Beton *m*.

concur [kən'kə:] zs.-treffen, zs.-wirken; übereinstimmen.

concussion (of the brain) [kən'kʌʃən] Gehirnerschütterung *f*.

condemn [kən'dem] verurteilen; verdammen; verwerfen; **~ation** [kɔndem'neiʃən] Verurteilung *f*; Verdammung *f*.

condense [kən'dens] (sich) verdichten, kondensieren; *fig.* kürzen, zs.-drängen; **~r** Kondensator *m*.

condescend [kɔndi'send] sich herablassen, geruhen; **~sion** [-diʃən] Herablassung *f*.

condition [kən'diʃən] Zustand *m*; Bedingung *f*; *pl* Verhältnisse *pl*; bedingen; **~al** bedingend; **~al clause** *gr.* Bedingungssatz *m*; **~al (mood)** *gr.* Konditional *m*, Bedingungsform *f*.

condole [kən'dəul] kondolieren; **~nce** Beileid *n*.

conduct ['kɔndʌkt] Führung *f*; Verhalten *n*, Betragen *n*; [kən'dʌkt] führen; leiten; *mus.* dirigieren; **~ o.s.** sich benehmen; **~ed tour** Führung *f*; Gesellschaftsreise *f*; **~ion** [kən'dʌkʃən] Leitung *f*; **~or** [kən'dʌktə] Führer *m*; Leiter *m*; Schaffner *m*; Dirigent *m*.

cone [kəun] Kegel *m*; *bot.* Zapfen *m*.

confection [kən'fekʃən] Konfekt *n*; **~er** [-ʃnə] Konditor *m*; **~ery** Konditorwaren *pl*; Konditorei *f*.

confedera|cy [kən'fedərəsi] Staatenbund *m*; **~te** [-it] verbündet; Bundesgenosse *m*; [-eit] (sich) verbünden; **~tion** Bund *m*, Bündnis *n*; Staatenbund *m*.

confer [kən'fə:] verleihen; sich beraten; **~ence** ['kɔnfərəns] Konferenz *f*.

confess [kən'fes] gestehen, bekennen; beichten; **~ion** Geständnis *n*; Beichte *f*; **~or** Beichtvater *m*.

confide [kən'faid] (sich) anvertrauen; vertrauen; **~nce** ['kɔnfidəns] Vertrauen *n*; Zuversicht *f*; **~nt** zuversichtlich; **~ntial** [-'denʃəl] vertraulich.

confine [kən'fain] beschränken; einsperren; **be ~d** niederkommen; **~ment** Haft *f*; Niederkunft *f*.

confirm [kən'fə:m] bestätigen; konfirmieren; firmen; **~ation** [kɔnfə'meiʃən] Bestätigung *f*; Konfirmation *f*; Firmung *f*.

confiscate ['kɔnfiskeit] beschlagnahmen.

conflagration [kɔnflə'greiʃən] Großbrand *m*.

conflict ['kɔnflikt] Konflikt *m*; [kən'flikt] im Konflikt stehen.

conform [kən'fɔ:m] (sich) anpassen; **~ity** Übereinstimmung *f*.

confound [kən'faund] verwechseln; ~ **it!** colloq. verdammt!

confront [kən'frʌnt] gegenüberstehen; konfrontieren.

confus|e [kən'fju:z] verwechseln; verwirren; ~ion [~ʒən] Verwirrung f; Durcheinander n; Verwechs(e)lung f.

congeal [kən'dʒi:l] erstarren od. gerinnen (lassen).

congestion [kən'dʒestʃən] (Blut)Andrang m; ~ **of traffic** Verkehrsstockung f.

congratulat|e [kən'grætjuleit] beglückwünschen; j–m gratulieren; ~ion Glückwunsch m.

congregat|e ['kɔŋgrigeit] (sich) (ver)sammeln; ~ion Versammlung f; eccl. Gemeinde f.

congress ['kɔŋgres] (Am. parl. 2) Kongreß m.

conjecture [kən'dʒektʃə] Vermutung f; vermuten.

conjugal ['kɔndʒugəl] ehelich.

conjugat|e ['kɔndʒugeit] gr. konjugieren, beugen; ~ion gr. Konjugation f, Beugung f.

conjunction [kən'dʒʌŋkʃən] Verbindung f; Zs.-treffen n; gr. Konjunktion f, Bindewort n.

conjunctive (mood) [kən-'dʒʌŋktiv] gr. Konjunktiv m, Möglichkeitsform f.

conjure[1] [kən'dʒuə] beschwören.

conjur|e[2] ['kʌndʒə] zaubern; ~**er** Zauberer m; ~**ing trick** Zauberkunststück n; ~**or** s. conjurer.

connect [kə'nekt] verbinden; electr. anschließen an); ~**ed** zs.-hängend; rail. Anschluß haben (**with** an); ~**ion** Verbindung f; Anschluß m; Zs.-hang m.

connexion [kə'nekʃən] s. connection.

conquer ['kɔŋkə] erobern; (be)siegen; ~**or** Eroberer m; Sieger m.

conquest ['kɔŋkwest] Eroberung f.

conscien|ce ['kɔnʃəns] Gewissen n; ~**tious** [~i'enʃəs] gewissenhaft; ~**tious objector** Kriegsdienstverweigerer m.

conscious ['kɔnʃəs] bewußt; **be** ~ **of** sich bewußt sein; ~**ness** Bewußtsein n.

consecrate ['kɔnsikreit] weihen.

consecutive [kən'sekjutiv] auf-ea.-folgend.

consent [kən'sent] Einwilligung f, Zustimmung f; einwilligen, zustimmen.

consequen|ce ['kɔnsikwəns] Folge f, Konsequenz f; Bedeutung f; ~**tly** folglich, daher.

conserv|ative [kən'sɜː-vətiv] konservativ; Konservative m, f; ~**e** erhalten, bewahren; mst ~**es** pl Eingemachte n, Marmelade f.

consider [kən'sidə] betrachten; erwägen, ...

consign 64

überlegen;berücksichtigen; denken, meinen; **~able** beträchtlich; **~ably** bedeutend, (sehr) viel; **~ate** [~rit] rücksichtsvoll; **~ation** Überlegung f; Rücksicht f.

consign [kən'sain] liefern; anvertrauen; **~ment** Versand m; Sendung f.

consist [kən'sist] bestehen (of aus); **~ency** Festigkeit f; Übereinstimmung f; Konsequenz f; **~ent** übereinstimmend; konsequent.

consol|ation [kɔnsə'lei-ʃən] Trost m; **~e** [kən'səul] trösten.

consolidate [kən'sɔlideit] (sich) festigen; vereinigen.

consonant ['kɔnsənənt] ling. Konsonant m, Mitlaut m.

conspicuous [kən'spik-juəs] deutlich sichtbar; auffallend; hervorragend.

conspir|acy [kən'spirəsi] Verschwörung f; **~ator** Verschwörer m; **~e** [~'spaiə] sich verschwören; planen.

constable ['kʌnstəbl] Polizist m.

constant ['kɔnstənt] (be-)ständig; treu.

consternation [kɔnstə(:)-'neiʃən] Bestürzung f.

constipation [kɔnsti'pei-ʃən] med. Verstopfung f.

constituen|cy [kən'stitju-ənsi] Wählerschaft f; Wahlkreis m; **~bezirk** m; **~t** Bestandteil m; Wähler(in).

constitut|e ['kɔnstitju:t] ernennen, einsetzen; bevollmächtigen; einrichten; ausmachen; (in Zu-)setzung f; körperliche Verfassung, Konstitution f; pol. Verfassung f, Grundgesetz n; **~ional** verfassungsmäßig, konstitutionell.

constrain [kən'strein] (er-)zwingen; **~t** Zwang m.

construct [kən'strʌkt] bauen; **~ion** Bau(en n) m; Konstruktion f; **~ive** aufbauend, konstruktiv; **~or** Erbauer m, Konstrukteur m.

consul ['kɔnsəl] Konsul m; **~ar** ['~julə] Konsular...; **~ate** ['~julit] Konsulat n; **~-general** Generalkonsul m.

consult [kən'sʌlt] konsultieren, um Rat fragen; in e-m Buch nachschlagen; sich beraten; **~ation** [kɔnsəl'teiʃən] Konsultation f; Beratung f; Rücksprache f; **~ing hours** pl Sprechstunde f.

consume [kən'sju:m] verzehren; verbrauchen; **~r** Verbraucher m.

consummate [kən'sʌmit] vollenden; ['kɔnsəmeit] vollenden, -ziehen.

consumption [kən'sʌmp-ʃən] Verbrauch m; med. Schwindsucht f.

contact ['kɔntækt] Berührung f; Kontakt m; Verbindung f; [kən'tækt] sich in Verbindung setzen mit; **~ lenses** pl Haft-, Kontaktschalen pl.

contagious [kən'teidʒəs] ansteckend.

contain [kən'tein] enthalten; **~er** Behälter m; Großbehälter m, Container m.

contaminat|e [kən'tæmineit] verunreinigen; verseuchen; **~ion** Verunreinigung f; Verseuchung f.

contemplat|e ['kontempleit] betrachten; beabsichtigen; **~ion** Betrachtung f; Nachdenken n; **~ive** nachdenklich; beschaulich.

contemporary [kən'tempərəri] zeitgenössisch; Zeitgenoss|e m, -in f.

contempt [kən'tempt] Verachtung f; **~ible** verachtenswert; **~uous** [-tjuəs] geringschätzig, verächtlich.

contend [kən'tend] kämpfen.

content [kən'tent] zufrieden; befriedigen; **~ o.s.** sich begnügen; Zufriedenheit f; **to one's heart's** nach Herzenslust; **~ed** zufrieden; **~s** ['kontents] pl Inhalt(sverzeichnis n) m.

contest ['kontest] Wettkampf m, -bewerb m; [kən'test] bestreiten, anfechten.

context ['kontekst] Zusammenhang m.

continent ['kontinent] Kontinent m, Erdteil m; Festland n; **~al** [‿'nentl] kontinental; Kontinental...

continu|al [kən'tinjuəl] fortwährend, unaufhörlich; **~ance** (Fort)Dauer f; **~ation** Fortsetzung f; Fortdauer f; **~e** [‿u(ː)] (sich) fortsetzen; (fort)dauern; fortfahren; **to be ~ed** Fortsetzung folgt; **~ous** ununterbrochen.

contort [kən'tɔːt] verzerren; verdrehen.

contour ['kontuə] Umriß m.

contraceptive [kɔntrə'septiv] empfängnisverhütend(es Mittel).

contract [kən'trækt] (sich) zs.-ziehen; e-n Vertrag schließen, sich vertraglich verpflichten; ['kontrækt] Vertrag m; **~or** [kən'træktə] Unternehmer m.

contradict [kɔntrə'dikt] widersprechen; **~ion** Widerspruch m; **~ory** (sich) widersprechend.

contrary ['kɔntrəri] entgegengesetzt; ungünstig; **~ to** zuwider; gegen; sub: Gegenteil n; **on the ~** im Gegenteil.

contrast ['kɔntrɑːst] Gegensatz m; [kən'trɑːst] gegenüberstellen, vergleichen; sich unterscheiden.

contribut|e [kən'tribju(ː)t] beitragen, -steuern; **~ion** [kɔntri'bjuːʃən] Beitrag m; **~or** [kən'tribjutə] Mitarbeiter(in) (an e-r Zeitung).

contrite ['kɔntrait] zerknirscht.

contriv|ance [kən'traivəns] Vorrichtung f; Erfindung(sgabe) f; Plan m; ～e erfinden; planen; es fertigbringen.

control [kən'trəul] Kontrolle f; Aufsicht f; Herrschaft f, Beherrschung f; Kontrollvorrichtung f; kontrollieren; (nach)prüfen; beherrschen; econ. lenken; ～ler Kontrolleur m, Prüfer m, Aufseher m.

controvers|ial [kɔntrə'və:ʃəl] umstritten; ～y ['.və:si] Streit(frage f) m.

contuse [kən'tju:z] quetschen.

convalesce [kɔnvə'les] genesen; ～nce Genesung f; ～nt Genesende m, f.

conveni|ence [kən'vi:njəns] Bequemlichkeit f; **at your earliest ～ce** sobald wie möglich; **public ～ce** öffentliche Bedürfnisanstalt; ～ent bequem; passend; brauchbar.

convent ['kɔnvənt] (Nonnen)Kloster n; ～ion [kən-'venʃən] Versammlung f; Abkommen n; ～ional konventionell.

conversation [kɔnvə-'seiʃən] Gespräch n, Unterhaltung f; ～e [kən-'və:s] sich unterhalten.

conver|sion [kən'və:ʃən] Um-, Verwandlung f; eccl. Bekehrung f; ～t um-, verwandeln; eccl. bekehren; ～tible umwandelbar; mot. Kabrio(lett) n.

convey [kən'vei] befördern; übermitteln; mitteilen; Sinn ausdrücken; ～ance Beförderung f, Transport m; Übermittlung f; Verkehrsmittel n; ～er od. ～or belt Förderband n.

convict ['kɔnvikt] Sträfling m, Zuchthäusler m; [kən'vikt] überführen (**of** gen); überzeugen (of gen); jur.: Überführung f; Verurteilung f.

convince [kən'vins] überzeugen.

convoy ['kɔnvɔi] Geleit n; Geleitzug m; geleiten.

convuls|ion [kən'vʌlʃən] Krampf m; ～ive krampfhaft, -artig.

cook [kuk] Koch m, Köchin f; kochen; ～ing Kochen n; Küche f (Kochweise).

cool [ku:l] kühl; fig. gelassen; (sich) abkühlen; ～er Kühler m; Kühlraum m; ～ness Kühle f (a. fig.).

co-op ['kəuɔp] colloq. s. **co-operative (society, store).**

co(-)operat|e [kəu'ɔpəreit] zs.-arbeiten; beitragen; ～ion Zs.-arbeit f, Mitwirkung f; ～ive [.ətiv] zs.-arbeitend; genossenschaftlich; ～ive society Konsum(genossenschaft f) m; ～ive store Konsum(laden) m; ～or Mitarbeiter (-in).

co(-)ordinate [kəu'ɔ:dineit] koordinieren; auf-ea. abstimmen.

corroborate

cop [kɔp] *sl.* Polyp *m*, Bulle *m* (*Polizist*).

co-partner ['kou'pɑːtnə] Teilhaber *m*.

cope [koup]: ~ **with** fertigwerden mit.

co-pilot ['kou'pailət] Kopilot *m*. [(-lich).]

copious ['koupjəs] reich∫

copper ['kɔpə] Kupfer *n*; Kupfermünze *f*; kupfern, Kupfer...

copy ['kɔpi] kopieren; abschreiben; nachbilden, -ahmen; Kopie *f*; Abschrift *f*; Durchschlag *m*; Muster *n*; (*Buch*)Exemplar *n*; (*Zeitungs*)Nummer *f*, Ausgabe *f*; druckfertiges Manuskript; **fair** ~ Reinschrift *f*; **rough** ~ erster Entwurf; **~-book** Schreibheft *n*; **~right** Verlagsrecht *n*, Copyright *n*.

coral ['kɔrəl] Koralle *f*.

cord [kɔːd] Schnur *f*, Strick *m*; *anat.* Band *n*, Strang *m*; (zu)schnüren, binden.

cordial ['kɔːdjəl] herzlich; (herz)stärkend; Likör *m*; **~ity** [ˌ~i'æliti] Herzlichkeit *f*.

corduroys ['kɔːdərɔiz] *pl* Kordhose *f*.

core [kɔː] Kerngehäuse *n*; *fig.* Herz *n*, Kern *m*.

cork [kɔːk] Kork(en) *m*; zukorken; **~screw** Korkenzieher *m*.

corn [kɔːn] Korn *n*; Getreide *n*; *Am.* Mais *m*; *med.* Hühnerauge *n*; (ein-)pökeln.

corner ['kɔːnə] Ecke *f*, Winkel *m*; *fig.* Enge *f*; Eck...; *fig.* in die Enge treiben; **~ed** *in Zssgn*: ...eckig.

cornet ['kɔːnit] Eistüte *f*.

corn flakes *pl* geröstete Maisflocken *pl*.

coronation [ˌkɔrə'neiʃən] Krönung *f*.

coroner ['kɔrənə] *jur.* Untersuchungsrichter *m*, **~'s inquest** Gerichtsverhandlung *f* (*zur Feststellung der Todesursache in Fällen gewaltsamen od. plötzlichen Todes*).

corpora|l ['kɔːpərəl] körperlich; Unteroffizier *m*; **~tion** Körperschaft *f*; Stadtbehörde *f*; *Am.* Aktiengesellschaft *f*.

corpse [kɔːps] Leiche *f*.

corpulent ['kɔːpjulənt] beleibt.

corral [kɔː'rɑːl, *Am.* kə'ræl] Korral *m*, Hürde *f*.

correct [kə'rekt] korrekt, richtig; korrigieren; bestrafen; **~ion** Verbesserung *f*; Korrektur *f*; Strafe *f*.

correspond [kɔris'pɔnd] entsprechen (**with**, **to** *dat*); korrespondieren; **~ence** Übereinstimmung *f*; Briefwechsel *m*; **~ent** Korrespondent(in).

corridor ['kɔridɔː] Korridor *m*, Flur *m*, Gang *m*.

corrigible ['kɔridʒəbl] zu verbessern(d).

corroborate [kə'rɔbəreit] bestätigen.

corro|de [kə'rəud] zer-
fressen; wegätzen; **~sion**
[~ʒən] Korrosion *f*.

corrugate ['kɔrugeit] runzeln; welly; **~d iron**
Wellblech *n*.

corrupt [kə'rʌpt] verwor-
fen; bestechlich; verder-
ben; bestechen; **~ion** Fäulnis *f*; Verderben *n*; Ver-
dorbenheit *f*; Korruption
f; Bestechung *f*.

corset ['kɔ:sit] Korsett *n*.

cosmetic [kɔz'metik] kos-
metisch; Kosmetik(artikel
m) *f*; **~ian** [~ə'tiʃən] Kos-
metiker(in).

cosmonaut ['kɔzmənɔ:t]
Kosmonaut *m*, Raumfah-
rer *m*.

cost [kɔst] Preis *m*; Kosten
pl; Schaden *m*; (*irr*) kosten; **~ly** kostbar; kost-
spielig.

costume ['kɔstju:m] Kostüm *n*; Tracht *f*.

cosy ['kəuzi] gemütlich.

cot [kɔt] Feldbett *n*; Kinderbett *n*.

cottage ['kɔtidʒ] Hütte *f*;
kleines Wohnhaus; kleines
Landhaus; Sommerhaus *n*.

cotton ['kɔtn] Baumwolle
f; (Näh-*etc*.)Garn *n*; Baum-
woll...; **~ wool** Watte *f*.

couch [kautʃ] Lager *n*;
Couch *f*, Sofa *n*; in Worte
fassen; (sich) kauern.

cough [kɔf] Husten *m*;
husten. [*von ~nal* cond]

could [kud] *pret u. cond*]

council ['kaunsl] Rat(sver-
sammlung *f*) *m*; **~(l)or**

['~silə] Ratsmitglied *n*,
Stadtrat *m*.

counsel ['kaunsəl] *j-m od.*
zu *et.* raten; Beratung *f*;
Rat(schlag) *m*; Anwalt *m*;
~ for the defence Verteidiger *m*; **~ for the pros-
ecution** Anklagevertreter
m; **~(l)or** ['~slə] Ratgeber
m; *Am. u. Irland* Anwalt *m*.

count¹ [kaunt] Zählen *n*;
(End)Zahl *f*; *jur.* Anklage-
punkt *m*; zählen, rechnen;
~ up zs.-zählen.

count² *nichtbritischer* Graf *m*.

count-down ['kauntdaun]
Countdown *m*, *n*.

countenance ['kaunti-
nəns] Gesichtsausdruck *m*;
Fassung *f*.

counter¹ ['kauntə] Zähler
m; Spielmarke *f*; Laden-
tisch *m*; Theke *f*; Schalter *m*.

counter² entgegen, zuwider (*to dat*); **~act** [~'rækt]
entgegenwirken, bekämp-
fen; **~balance** [~'bæləns]
Gegengewicht *n*; ['~bæ-
ləns] aufwiegen, ausglei-
chen; **~espionage** Spionageabwehr *f*; **~feit** ['~fit]
nachgemacht, gefälscht;
Fälschung *f*; nachmachen,
fälschen; **~foil** ['~foil]
Kontrollabschnitt *m*; **~in-
telligence** ['~rinteli-
dʒəns] Spionageabwehr
(-dienst *m*) *f*; **~pane**
['~pein] Tagesdecke *f*; **~-
part** Gegenstück *n*.

countess ['kauntis] Gräfin *f*.

count|ing-house Kontor *n*, Büro *n*; **~less** zahllos.

country ['kʌntri] Land *n*; Gegend *f*; Heimatland *n*; Land..., ländlich; **in the ~** auf dem Land; **~-house** Landsitz *m*; **~man** Landmann *m* (*Bauer*); Landsmann *m*; **~seat** Landsitz *m*; **~side** Gegend *f*; Landschaft *f*; **~town** Kleinstadt *f*.

county ['kaunti] Grafschaft *f*, Kreis *m*.

coupl|e ['kʌpl] (zs-, ver-) koppeln; kuppeln; (ver-) binden; (sich) paaren; (Ehe)Paar *n*; Koppel *f* (*Jagdhunde*); **a ~ of** zwei, *colloq.* ein paar; **~ing** Kupplung *f*; *Radio*, *electr.*: Kopplung *f*.

coupon ['ku:pɔn] Abschnitt *m*; Bon *m*; (Gut-) Schein *m*.

courage ['kʌridʒ] Mut *m*; **~ous** [kəˈreidʒəs] mutig.

courier ['kuriə] Kurier *m*; Reiseleiter(in).

course [kɔːs] Lauf *m*; Weg *m*, Route *f*; *mar.*, *fig.* Kurs *m*; Rennbahn *f*; Gang *m* (*Speisen*); Kurs(us) *m*; **of ~** selbstverständlich, natürlich; **matter of ~** Selbstverständlichkeit *f*.

court [kɔːt] Hof *m* (*a. e-s Fürsten*); Gericht(shof *m*) *n*; *j-m* den Hof machen; werben um; **~eous** ['kɔːtjəs] höflich; **~esy** ['kɔːtisi] Höflichkeit *f*; Gefälligkeit *f*; **~ier** ['kɔːtjə] Höf-

ling *m*; **~ martial** Militärgericht *n*; **~ of justice** Gericht(shof *m*) *n*; **~-room** Gerichtssaal *m*; **~ship** Werbung *f*; **~yard** Hof *m*.

cousin ['kʌzn] Vetter *m*, Cousin *m*; Base *f*, Cousine *f*.

cover ['kʌvə] Decke *f*; Hülle *f*; Deckel *m*; Umschlag *m*; (Buch)Einband *m*; Mantel *m* (*Bereifung*); Gedeck *n*; Deckung *f*; Schutz *m*; Vorwand *m*; (be-, zu)decken; beziehen; verbergen, verhüllen; schützen; *Weg* zurücklegen; *Gebiet* bereisen, versorgen; *econ.* decken; umfassen; *Fin.* erfassen; *Zeitung:* berichten über; **~age** Berichterstattung *f*; **~ing** Decke *f*; Be-, Überzug *m*; Dach *n*.

covet ['kʌvit] begehren; **~ous** begehrlich.

cow [kau] Kuh *f*.

coward ['kauəd] Feigling *m*; **~ice** ['~is] Feigheit *f*; **~ly** feig(e).

cowboy ['kaubɔi] Cowboy *m*, Rinderhirt *m*.

cower ['kauə] kauern; sich ducken.

cow|herd Kuhhirt *m*; **~hide** Rind(s)leder *n*; **~house** Kuhstall *m*; **~shed** Kuhstall *m*; **~slip** Schlüsselblume *f*; *Am.* Sumpfdotterblume *f*.

coxcomb ['kɔkskəum] Geck *m*.

coxswain ['kɔkswein,

mar. ['kɔksn] Bootsführer *m*; Steuermann *m*.

coy [kɔi] schüchtern; spröde.

crab [kræb] Krabbe *f*.

crack [kræk] Krach *m*, Knall *m*; Riß *m*, Sprung *m*; derber Schlag; (zer-)sprengen; knallen (mit); knacken *od.* krachen (lassen); (auf)knacken; platzen, (zer)springen; brechen (*a. Stimme*); **~ a joke** e-n Witz reißen; **~er** Knallbonbon *m*, *n*, Schwärmer *m*; Keks *m* (*ungesüßt*); **~le** knattern, knistern.

cradle ['kreidl] Wiege *f*; wiegen; betten.

craft [krɑːft] Handwerk *n*; *mar.* Schiff(e *pl*) *n*, Fahrzeug(e *pl*) *n*; List *f*; **~sman** (Kunst)Handwerker *m*; **~y** gerissen, schlau.

crag [kræg] Klippe *f*, spitzer Fels.

cram [kræm] (voll)stopfen.

cramp [kræmp] Krampf *m*; *tech.* Krampe *f*; (ver-)krampfen; einengen, hemmen.

cranberry ['krænbəri] Preiselbeere *f*.

crane [krein] *orn.* Kranich *m*; Kran *m*; (den Hals) recken.

crank [kræŋk] Kurbel *f*; komischer Kauz; **~ up** *Motor* anwerfen.

crape [kreip] Krepp *m*; Trauerflor *m*.

crash [kræʃ] Krach(en *n*) *m*; Zs.-stoß *m*; *aer.* Absturz *m*; krachen(*d* fallen *od.* einstürzen) *od.* einstürzen); *aer.* abstürzen; **~-helmet** Sturzhelm *m*; **~-landing** Bruchlandung *f*.

crate [kreit] Lattenkiste *f*.

crater ['kreitə] Krater *m*; (Bomben)Trichter *m*.

crave [kreiv] dringend bitten *od.* flehen um; sich sehnen (**for** nach).

crawfish ['krɔːfiʃ] Flußkrebs *m*.

crawl [krɔːl] kriechen; schleichen; wimmeln; *Schwimmen:* kraulen.

crayfish ['kreifiʃ] Flußkrebs *m*.

crayon ['kreiən] Zeichenstift *m*.

crazy ['kreizi] verrückt (**about** nach).

creak [kriːk] knarren, quietschen.

cream [kriːm] Rahm *m*, Sahne *f*; Creme *f*; Auslese *f*, *das* Beste; den Rahm abschöpfen von; sahnig rühren; **~ cheese** Weich-, Schmelzkäse *m*; **~y** sahnig.

crease [kriːs] (Bügel-)Falte *f*; falten; (zer-)knittern.

creat|e [kriː(:)'eit] (er-)schaffen; verursachen; **~ion** Schöpfung *f*; **~ive** schöpferisch; **~or** Schöpfer *m*; **~ure** ['kriːtʃə] Geschöpf *n*; Kreatur *f*.

credentials [kri'denʃəlz]

pl Beglaubigungsschreiben *n*; Zeugnisse *pl*.

credible ['kredəbl] glaubwürdig; glaubhaft.

credit ['kredit] Glaube(n) *m*; Ruf *m*; Ansehen *n*; Ehre *f*; Guthaben *n* Kredit *m*; *j—m* glauben; *j—m* (zu)trauen; *Betrag* gutschreiben; **~able** ehrenvoll (*to* für); **~ card** Scheckkarte *f*; **~or** Gläubiger *m*.

credulous ['kredjuləs] leichtgläubig.

creed [kri:d] Glaubensbekenntnis *n*.

creek [kri:k] Bucht *f*; *Am.* kleiner Fluß.

creep [kri:p] (*irr*) kriechen; schleichen; **it made my flesh ~** ich bekam *e—e* Gänsehaut; **~er** Kletterpflanze *f*.

cremate [kri'meit] einäschern.

crept [krept] *pret u. pp von* **creep**.

crescent ['kresnt] Halbmond *m*.

cress [kres] Kresse *f*.

crest [krest] (Hahnen-, Berg)Kamm *m*; (*Wellen-*)Kamm *m*; Federbusch *m*; Wappenverzierung *f*; **family** **~** Familienwappen *n*; **~fallen** niedergeschlagen.

crevasse [kri'væs] (Gletscher)Spalte *f*.

crevice ['krevis] Riß *m*, Spalte *f*.

crew[1] [kru:] Schar *f*;

mar., aer. Besatzung *f*, Mannschaft *f*.

crew[2] *pret von* **crow**.

crib [krib] Raufe *f*; *bsd. Am.* Kinderbett *n*; *Schule:* Klatsche *f*; abschreiben.

cricket ['krikit] *zo.* Grille *f*; *sp.* Kricket *n*.

crime [kraim] Verbrechen *n*.

criminal ['kriminl] verbrecherisch; Straf...; Verbrecher(in).

crimson ['krimzn] karmesin-, feuerrot. [ken.]

cringe [krindʒ] sich dukken.]

cripple ['kripl] Krüppel *m*; verkrüppeln; *fig.* lähmen.

cris|is ['kraisis], *pl* **~es** ['~i:z] Krise *f*; Wende-, Höhepunkt *m*.

crisp [krisp] knusp(e)rig; kraus; forsch; *Luft:* scharf, frisch; **(potato)** **~s** *pl* Kartoffelchips *pl*.

critic ['kritik] Kritiker (-in); **~al** kritisch; bedenklich; **~ism** ['~sizəm] Kritik *f*; **~ize** ['~saiz] kritisieren; tadeln.

croak [krouk] krächzen; quaken.

crochet ['krouʃei] häkeln.

crockery ['krɔkəri] Steingut *n*.

crocodile ['krɔkədail] Krokodil *n*.

crofter ['krɔftə] Kleinbauer *m*.

crook [kruk] Krümmung *f*; *sl.* Gauner *m*; (*pret, pp* [krukt]) (sich)

crop

krümmen; **~ed** [' **~**id]
krumm, schief; unehrlich.

crop [krɔp] Kropf *m*;
Ernte *f*; kurzer Haar-
schnitt; *Haar* kurz schneiden; *Acker* bebauen; **~ up**
auftauchen.

cross [krɔs] Kreuz *n*;
biol. Kreuzung *f*; ärgerlich, böse; (sich) kreuzen
(*a. biol.*); durch-, überqueren; *fig.* durchkreu-
zen; **~ off** *od.* **out** ausstreichen; **~ o.s.** sich be-
kreuzigen; **keep one's
fingers ~ed** den Dau-
men halten; **~Channel
boat** Kanalfähre *f*; **~
examination** Kreuz-
verhör *n*; **~ing** Überfahrt
f; (*Bahn-, Fußgänger-*)
Übergang *m*; Kreuzung *f*;
~road Querstraße *f*; **~
roads** *sg* (Straßen)Kreu-
zung *f*; **~word (puzzle)**
Kreuzworträtsel *n*. [ken.]

crouch [krautʃ] sich ducken.[

crow [krou] Krähe *f*;
Krähen *n*; (*irr*) krähen;
triumphieren; **~bar**
Brecheisen *n*.

crowd [kraud] Ansamm-
lung *f*, Haufen *m*; (Menschen)Menge *f*; **~s** *pl* **of
people** Menschenmas-
sen *pl*; sich drängen;
(über)füllen, vollstopfen;
~ed überfüllt, verstopft,
voll.

crown [kraun] Krone *f*;
Kranz *m*; krönen.

crucial ['kru:ʃəl] ent-
scheidend, kritisch.

cruci|fixion [kru:si'fikʃən]
Kreuzigung *f*; **~fy** ['~fai]
kreuzigen.

crude [kru:d] roh; un-
fertig; grob; Roh...

cruel [kruəl] grausam;
hart; **~ty** Grausamkeit *f*;
~ty to animals Tier-
quälerei *f*.

cruet ['kru(:)it] Essig-,
Ölfläschchen *n*.

cruise [kru:z] Kreuzfahrt
f; kreuzen; **~r** Kreuzer *m*;
Jacht *f*.

crumb [krʌm] Krume *f*;
~le ['~bl] zerkrümeln,
-bröckeln; zerfallen.

crumple ['krʌmpl] zerknittern; **~ up** zerknül-
len.

crunch [krʌntʃ] (zer)kauen;
zermalmen; knirschen.

crusade [kru:'seid] Kreuz-
zug *m*; **~r** Kreuzfahrer *m*.

crush [krʌʃ] Gedränge *n*;
(Frucht)Saft *m*; sich
drängen; (zer-, aus)quet-
schen; zermalmen; zer-
knittern; *fig.* vernichten;
~ barrier Absperrgitter *n*.

crust [krʌst] Kruste *f*,
Rinde *f*; verkrusten; **~
(over)** (sich) überkru-
sten; verharschen.

crutch [krʌtʃ] Krücke *f*.

cry [krai] schreien, (aus-)
rufen; weinen; Schrei *m*,
Ruf *m*; Geschrei *n*; Weinen *n*; **~ of rage** Wut-
geschrei *n*.

crypt [kript] Gruft *f*.

crystal ['kristl] Kristall
m, *n*; *Am.* Uhrglas *n*.

~line ['~slain] kristallen;
~lize kristallisieren.
cub [kʌb] *(Raubtier)* Junge *n.*
cube [kju:b] Würfel *m.;*
Kubikzahl *f;* **~ root** Kubikwurzel *f.*
cubicle ['kju:bikl] kleiner
abgeteilter (Schlaf-)
Raum; Kabine *f.* [*m.*\]
cuckoo ['kuku:] Kuckuck *m.*\
cucumber ['kju:kʌmbə]
Gurke *f.*
cuddle ['kʌdl] hätscheln.
cudgel ['kʌdʒəl] Knüppel
m; prügeln. [*(Wink m.*\]
cue [kju:] Stichwort *n;*\
cuff [kʌf] Manschette *f;*
(Ärmel-, *Am. a.* Hosen-)
Aufschlag *m;* Schlag *m;*
~links *pl* Manschettenknöpfe *pl.*
culminat|e ['kʌlmineit]
gipfeln; **~ion** *fig.* Höhepunkt *m.*
culprit ['kʌlprit] Schuldige *m, f.*
cultivat|e ['kʌltiveit] kultivieren; an-, bebauen;
pflegen; **~ion** Bestellung
f; Anbau *m;* Pflege *f;* **~or**
Landwirt *m;* Kultivator *m*
(Gerät).
cultur|al ['kʌltʃərəl] kulturell; **~** Kultur...; **~e**
['~tʃə] Kultur *f;* Pflege *f;*
Zucht *f;* **~ed** kultiviert.
cumulative ['kju:mjulətiv]
sich (an)häufend.
cunning ['kʌniŋ] schlau,
listig; *Am.* reizend; List *f,*
Schlauheit *f.*
cup [kʌp] Becher *m;* Tasse
f; Kelch *m; sp.* Pokal *m;*

a ~ of tea e–e Tasse Tee;
~board ['kʌbəd] Schrank
m.
cupola ['kju:pələ] Kuppel *f.*
cur [kə:] Köter *m.*
curable ['kjuərəbl] heilbar.
curate ['kjuərit] Hilfsgeistliche *m.*
curb [kə:b] *s.* **kerb(stone).**
curd [kə:d] *oft pl* Quark *m;*
~le gerinnen (lassen).
cure [kjuə] Heilung *f;* Kur
f; Heilmittel *n;* heilen;
pökeln; räuchern.
curfew ['kə:fju:] Ausgangssperre *f.*
curio ['kjuəriəu] Rarität *f;* **~sity** ['~ɔsiti] Neugier *f;* Rarität *f;* **~us**
['~əs] neugierig; merkwürdig.
curl [kə:l] Locke *f;* (sich)
kräuseln *od.* locken *od.*
ringeln; **~ up** sich hochringeln *(Rauch);* sich zs.-
rollen; **~y** lockig.
currant ['kʌrənt] Johannisbeere *f;* Korinthe *f.*
curren|cy ['kʌrənsi] Umlauf *m;* Kurs *m;* Währung
f; **~t** laufend; gegenwärtig, aktuell; geläufig,
allgemein bekannt; gültig
(Geld); Strom *m (a.
electr.);* Strömung *f.*
curricul|um [kə'rikjuləm], *pl* **~a** [~ə] Lehr-,
Studienplan *m;* **~um
vitae** ['~'vaiti:] Lebenslauf *m.*
curse [kə:s] Fluch *m;*
(ver)fluchen; **~d** ['~id]
verflucht.

curt [kə:t] kurz; barsch.

curtail [kə:'teil] (ab-ver)kürzen.

curtain ['kə:tn] Vorhang *m*; Gardine *f*.

curts(e)y ['kə:tsi] Knicks *m*; knicksen (**to** vor).

curve [kə:v] Kurve *f*, Krümmung *f*, Biegung *f*; (sich) krümmen *od.* biegen.

cushion ['kuʃən] Kissen *n*; Polster *n*; polstern.

custody ['kʌstədi] Haft *f*; Obhut *f*.

custom ['kʌstəm] Gewohnheit *f*, Brauch *m*, Sitte *f*; Kundschaft *f*; **~ary** üblich; **~er** Kund|e *m*, -in *f*; **~house** Zollamt *n*; **~made** *Am.* maßgearbeitet.

customs ['kʌstəmz] *pl* Zoll (-abfertigung *f*) *m*; **~ clearance** Zollabfertigung *f*; **~ declaration** Zollerklärung *f*; **~ examination** Zollkontrolle *f*.

cut [kʌt] Schnitt *m*; Hieb *m*; Stich *m*; Schnittwunde *f*; Schnitte *f*, Scheibe *f*; Holzschnitt *m*; Schliff *m*; Kürzung *f*; **cold ~** *pl* Aufschnitt *m*; **power ~** Stromsperre *f*; **short ~** Abkürzung(sweg *m*) *f*; (*irr*) (ab-, an-, be-, durch-, zer)schneiden; schnitzen; *Edelstein* schleifen; *Karten* abheben; *Betrag etc.* kürzen; *j-n beim Begegnen* schneiden; *Zahn* bekommen; **~ down** fällen;

mähen; kürzen; *Preis* herabsetzen; **~ in** unterbrechen; *mot.* schneiden; **~ off** abschneiden, -schlagen, -hauen; unterbrechen, trennen; *Strom* sperren; *a.* ausschneiden; zuschneiden; **be ~ out for** das Zeug zu *et.* haben.

cute [kju:t] schlau; *Am. colloq. a.* reizend.

cuticle ['kju:tikl] Oberhaut *f*; Nagelhaut *f*; **~ scissors** *pl* Hautschere *f*.

cutlery ['kʌtləri] (Tisch-, Eß)Besteck *n*.

cutlet ['kʌtlit] Kotelett *n*.

cut|**off** *Am.* Abkürzung(sweg *m*) *f*; **~ purse** Taschendieb(in); **~ter** Zuschneider(in); Schneidewerkzeug *n*, **~ machine** Kutter *m*; **~ting** schneidend, scharf; Schneiden *n*; *Film:* Schnitt *m*; (Zeitungs)Ausschnitt *m*.

cycl|**e** ['saikl] Zyklus *m*; Kreis *m*; Fahrrad *n*; radfahren, radeln; **~ist** Radfahrer(in).

cyclone ['saikləun] Wirbelsturm *m*.

cylinder ['silində] Zylinder *m*, Walze *f*; *tech.* Trommel *f*.

cynic ['sinik] Zyniker *m*; **~al** zynisch.

cypress ['saipris] Zypresse *f*.

cyst [sist] Zyste *f*.

Czech [tʃek] Tschech|e *m*, -in *f*; tschechisch.

dash

Czechoslovak ['tʃekəu-'sləʊvæk] Tschechoslo-wak|e *m*, -in *f*; tschecho-slowakisch.

D

dab [dæb] betupfen.

dachshund ['dækshund] Dackel *m*.

dad [dæd], **~dy** ['ˑi] Papa *m*, Vati *m*; **~dy-longlegs** Schnake *f*; *Am*. Weberknecht *m*.

daffodil ['dæfədil] Gelbe Narzisse.

daft [dɑːft] *colloq*. doof.

dagger ['dægə] Dolch *m*.

daily ['deili] täglich; Tageszeitung *f*.

dainty ['deinti] lecker; zart, fein; wählerisch.

dairy ['dɛəri] Molkerei *f*; Milchgeschäft *n*; **~man** Milchmann *m*.

daisy ['deizi] Gänseblümchen *n*.

dale [deil] Tal *n*.

dally ['dæli] herumtrödeln; schäkern; spielen.

dam [dæm] (Stau)Damm *m*, Deich *m*; (ab-, ein)dämmen.

damage ['dæmidʒ] Schaden *m*; *pl jur*. Schadenersatz *m*; (be)schädigen; schaden.

dame [deim] Dame *f* (*alte Form*).

damn [dæm] verdammen; **~ation** [~'neiʃən]Verdammung *f*; Verdammnis *f*.

damp [dæmp] feucht; Feuchtigkeit *f*; an-, befeuchten; **~(en)** dämp-

fen, niederdrücken.

danc|e [dɑːns] Tanz *m*; Ball *m*; tanzen; **~er** Tänzer(in); **~ing** Tanzen *n*; Tanz...

dandelion ['dændilaiən] Löwenzahn *m*.

dandruff ['dændrʌf] (Kopf)Schuppen *pl*.

Dane [dein] Dän|e *m*, -in *f*.

danger ['deindʒə] Gefahr *f*; **~ous** ['~dʒrəs] gefährlich.

dangle ['dæŋgl] baumeln (lassen), hin- und herschlenkern.

Danish ['deiniʃ] dänisch.

dar|e [dɛə] es *od*. *et*. wagen; **~ing** verwegen.

dark [dɑːk] dunkel; finster; Dunkel(heit *f*) *n*; **~ brown** dunkelbraun; **~en** (sich) verdunkeln; **~ness** Dunkelheit *f*, Finsternis *f*.

darling ['dɑːliŋ] Liebling *m*.

darn [dɑːn] stopfen.

dart [dɑːt] Satz *m*; Wurfpfeil *m*; *pl* Pfeilwerfen *n*; schleudern; schießen, stürzen.

dash [dæʃ] Schlag *m*; (An)Sturm *m*; Klatschen *n* (*Wellen*); Prise *f* (*Salz etc.*); Schuß *m* (*Rum etc.*); Federstrich *m*; Gedankenstrich *m*; schleudern; (be)spritzen; *Hoff-nung* vernichten; stürzen, stürmen, jagen, rasen; **~board** Armaturenbrett n; **~ing** schneidig.

data ['deitə] *pl* Tatsachen *pl*; Daten *pl*, Angaben *pl*, Informationen *pl*; Meßwerte *pl*; **~ processing** Datenverarbeitung *f*.

date [deit] datieren; **~ from** (her)stammen aus *od.* von; *bot.* Dattel *f*; Datum *n*; Termin *m*; Zeit *f*; *colloq.* Verabredung *f*; **out of ~** veraltet, unmodern; **up to ~** zeitgemäß, modern; auf dem laufenden.

dative (case) ['deitiv] *gr.* Dativ *m*, 3. Fall.

daub [dɔ:b] (be)schmieren.

daughter ['dɔ:tə] Tochter *f*; **~-in-law** Schwiegertochter *f*.

dawdle ['dɔ:dl] ~ **(away** ver)trödeln.

dawn [dɔ:n] Dämmerung *f*; dämmern, tagen.

day [dei] Tag *m*; *oft pl* (Lebens)Zeit *f*; ~ **off** (dienst)freier Tag; **by ~** am Tage; **all ~ long** den ganzen Tag (lang, über); **to this ~** bis heute; **the other ~** neulich; **this week** heute in einer Woche; **in the old ~s** in alten Zeiten; früher; **~break** Tagesanbruch *m*; **~ excursion** Tagesausflug *m*; **~labo(u)rer** Tagelöhner *m*; **~light**

Tageslicht *n*; **~school** Tagesschule *f*.

daze [deiz] betäuben.

dazzle ['dæzl] blenden.

dead [ded] tot; unempfindlich (**to** für); völlig; plötzlich; *sub:* **the ~** die Toten *pl*; **in the ~of winter** im tiefsten Winter; **~en** abstumpfen; dämpfen, (ab)schwächen; ~ **end** Sackgasse *f* (*a. fig.*); **~line** letzter Termin; Stichtag *m*; **~lock** *fig.* toter Punkt; **~ loss** Totalverlust *m*; **~ly** tödlich; Tod...; ~ **tired** todmüde.

deaf [def] taub; **~en** taub machen; **~mute** taubstumm.

deal [di:l] Menge *f*, Teil *m*; Abmachung *f*; *colloq.* Handel *m*; **a good ~, a great ~** sehr *od.* ziemlich viel; (*irr*) (aus-, ver-, zu-)teilen; handeln (**in** mit *e-r Ware*); ~ **with** behandeln; sich befassen mit; **~er** Händler *m*; **~ing** Geschäftsverkehr *m*; *pl* Umgang *m*; **~t** [delt] *pret u. pp* von **deal**.

dean [di:n] Dekan *m*.

dear [diə] teuer; lieb; Teure *m*, *f*, Liebling *m*; ♀ **Sir** Sehr geehrter Herr (*in Briefen*); **oh ~!, ~ me!** du liebe Zeit!, ach herrje!

death [deθ] Tod(esfall) *m*; **~ly** tödlich; [Ben.]

debar [di'bɑ:] ausschließen;

debase [di'beis] verderben; verschlechtern.

debate [di'beit] Debatte *f*; debattieren.

debauchery [di'bɔːtʃəri] Ausschweifung *f*.

debit ['debit] *econ.* Debet *n*, Schuld *f*; belasten.

debris ['deibriː] Trümmer *pl.*

debt [det] Schuld *f*; **~or** Schuldner(in).

decade ['dekeid] Jahrzehnt *n*.

decadence ['dekədəns] Verfall *m*.

decapitate [di'kæpiteit] enthaupten.

decay [di'kei] Verfall *m*; Fäulnis *f*; (ver-)faulen.

decease [di'siːs] *bsd. jur.* Ableben *n*; sterben.

deceit [di'siːt] Täuschung *f*, Betrug *m*; **~ful** (be-) trügerisch; falsch.

deceive [di'siːv] betrügen, täuschen; **~r** Betrüger(in).

decelerate [diː'seləreit] s-e Geschwindigkeit verringern, langsamer fahren, *mot. a.* Gas wegnehmen.

December [di'sembə] Dezember *m*.

decen|cy ['diːsnsi] Anstand *m*; **~t** anständig.

deception [di'sepʃən] Täuschung *f*.

decide [di'said] (sich) entscheiden; sich entschließen; beschließen; **~d** entschieden.

decimal ['desiməl] Dezimal...; ziffern.

decipher [di'saifə] ent-

decisi|on [di'siʒən] Entscheidung *f*; Entschluß *m*; **~ve** [di'saisiv] entscheidend; entschieden.

deck [dek] (Ver)Deck *n*; **~ chair** Liegestuhl *m*.

declar|ation [deklə-'reiʃən] Erklärung *f*; **Declaration of Independence** Unabhängigkeitserklärung *f*; **~e** [di'kleə] erklären; behaupten; deklarieren, verzollen.

declension [di'klenʃən] *gr.* Deklination *f*, Beugung *f*.

decline [di'klain] Abnahme *f*; Verfall *m*; *gr.* deklinieren, beugen; ablehnen; sich neigen; abnehmen; verfallen.

declivity [di'kliviti] (Ab-) Hang *m*.

decode ['diː'kəud] entschlüsseln.

decorat|e ['dekəreit] (ver)zieren, schmücken; tapezieren, anstreichen; dekorieren; **~ion** Verzierung *f*; Schmuck *m*, Dekoration *f*; Orden *m*; **~ive** [-rətiv] dekorativ, Zier...; **~or** Dekorateur *m*; Maler *m*.

decoy ['diːkɔi] Lockvogel *m* (*a. fig.*); Köder *m*; [di'kɔi] ködern, locken.

decrease ['diːkriːs] Abnahme *f*; [diː'kriːs] (sich) vermindern, abnehmen.

decree [di'kriː] Dekret *n*, Erlaß *m*; beschließen.

decrepit [di'krepit] altersschwach.

dedicat|e ['dedikeit] widmen; **~ion** Widmung f.

deduce [di'dju:s] ableiten; folgern.

deduct [di'dʌkt] abziehen; **~ion** Abzug m; (Schluß-) Folgerung f.

deed [di:d] Tat f; Heldentat f; Urkunde f.

deep [di:p] tief; verschlagen, schlau; Tiefe f; **~en** (sich) vertiefen; (sich) verstärken; **~freeze** tiefkühlen; Gefrierfach n; Gefrier-, Tiefkühltruhe f; **~ness** Tiefe f.

deer [diə] Hirsch m; Reh n; Rotwild n.

deface [di'feis] entstellen.

defame [di'feim] verleumden.

defeat [di'fi:t] Niederlage f; besiegen; vereiteln.

defect [di'fekt] Defekt m, Fehler m; Mangel m; **~ive** mangelhaft; fehlerhaft.

defen|ce, Am. **~se** [di'fens] Verteidigung f; Schutz m; **~celess**, Am. **~seless** schutzlos, wehrlos.

defen|d [di'fend] verteidigen; schützen; **~dant** Angeklagte m, f; Beklagte m, f; **~der** Verteidiger(in); **~sive** Defensive f; Verteidigungs-.

defer [di'fə:] auf-, verschieben.

defiant [di'faiənt] herausfordernd, trotzig.

deficien|cy [di'fiʃənsi] Unzulänglichkeit f; Mangel m; Fehlbetrag m; **~t** mangelhaft, unzureichend.

deficit ['defisit] Fehlbetrag m.

defile [di'fail] Engpaß m.

defin|e [di'fain] definieren, erklären; **~ite** ['definit] bestimmt, klar; **~ition** (Begriffs)Bestimmung f; Erklärung f; **~itive** [di'finitiv] endgültig.

deflate [di'fleit] Luft od. Gas ablassen aus.

deflect [di'flekt] ablenken.

deform [di'fɔ:m] entstellen, verunstalten; **~ed** mißgestaltet.

defrost ['di:'frɔst] entfrosten, -eisen, abtauen.

defy [di'fai] trotzen; standhalten; herausfordern.

degenerate [di'dʒenərit] entartet, verderbt.

degrade [di'greid] degradieren; erniedrigen.

degree [di'gri:] Grad m; Rang m; fig. Stufe f; **five ~s centigrade** 5 Grad Celsius (abbr. 5°C); **by ~s** allmählich.

dejected [di'dʒektid] niedergeschlagen.

delay [di'lei] Aufschub m, Verzögerung f; aufschieben, verzögern; aufhalten; sich verspäten.

delegate ['deligeit] abordnen; übertragen; ['~it] Abgeordnete m, f; **~ion** ['~geiʃn] Abordnung f.

deliberate [di'libərit] überlegen; sich beraten; ['~it] vorsätzlich.

delica|cy ['delikəsi] Lekkerbissen *m*; Zartheit *f*; Feinheit *f*; **~te** ['~it] schmackhaft; zart; fein; empfindlich; **~tessen** [~'tesn] Feinkost(geschäft *n*) *f*.

delicious [di'lifəs] köstlich.

delight [di'lait] Freude *f*; entzücken, erfreuen; **~ful** wunderbar.

delinquen|cy [di'liŋkwənsi] Vergehen *n*; Kriminalität *f*; **~t** Verbrecher(in) *m*.

deliver [di'livə] befreien; aus-, abliefern, aushändigen; *Briefe* zustellen; *Botschaft* ausrichten; *Rede* halten; *med.* entbinden; **~ance** Befreiung *f*; **~er** Befreier(in); **~y** *med.* Entbindung *f*; (Ab)Lieferung *f*; *Post:* Zustellung *f*; Vortrag *m*.

deluge ['delju:dʒ] Überschwemmung *f*; **the** 2 die Sintflut.

delus|ion [di'lu:ʒən] Täuschung *f*; Wahn(vorstellung *f*) *m*; **~ive** [~siv] trügerisch.

demand [di'mɑ:nd] Forderung *f*; Nachfrage *f*, Bedarf *m*; verlangen, fordern; fragen nach.

demeano(u)r [di'mi:nə] Benehmen *n*.

demented [di'mentid] wahnsinnig. [halb...]

demi- ['demi-] Halb...,]

demilitarized [di:'militəraizd] entmilitarisiert.

demise [di'maiz] *jur.* Ableben *n*.

demobilize [di:'məubilaiz] demobilisieren.

democra|cy [di'mɔkrəsi] Demokratie *f*; **~t** ['deməkræt] Demokrat(in); **~tic** [~'krætik] demokratisch.

demolish [di'mɔliʃ] nieder-, abreißen.

demon ['di:mən] Dämon *m*.

demonstrat|e ['demənstreit] demonstrieren; darlegen, zeigen; vorführen; **~ion** Demonstration *f*; Darlegung *f*, -stellung *f*; Vorführung *f*; **~ive** [di'mɔnstrətiv] demonstrativ.

den [den] Höhle *f*; Hütte *f*, Loch *n*; *colloq.* Bude *f*.

denial [di'naiəl] Leugnen *n*; Ablehnung *f*, Verweigerung *f*, abschlägige Antwort.

denomination [dinɔmi'neiʃən] Konfession *f*.

denounce [di'nauns] anzeigen; *Vertrag* kündigen.

dens|e [dens] dicht, dick (*Nebel*); **~ity** Dichte *f*.

dent [dent] Beule *f*; ver-, einbeulen.

dent|al ['dentl] Zahn...; **~al surgeon**, **~ist** Zahnarzt *m*; **~ure** (künstliches) Gebiß.

deny [di'nai] (ver)leugnen; verweigern, abschlagen.

depart [di'pɑːt] abreisen, abfahren; **~ment** Abteilung *f*; *Am.* Ministerium *n;* ~**ment store** Warenhaus *n;* ~**ure** Abreise *f,* Abfahrt *f;* *aer.* Abflug *m.*

depend [di'pend]: ~ **(up-) on** abhängen von; angewiesen sein auf; **that** ~**s, it all** ~**s** *colloq.* es kommt (ganz) darauf an; ~**ence** Abhängigkeit *f;* ~**ent:** ~ **(up)on** abhängig von; angewiesen auf.

deplor|able [di'plɔ:rəbl] beklagenswert; ~**e** bedauern.

depopulate [di:'pɔpjuleit] entvölkern.

deport [di'pɔ:t] ausweisen; ~ **o.s.** sich benehmen.

depose [di'pəuz] *j–n* absetzen; (unter Eid) aussagen.

deposit [di'pɔzit] *geol.* Ablagerung *f,* (Erz)Lager *n;* Einzahlung *f;* Anzahlung *f;* (nieder-, ab-, hin)legen; Geld einzahlen; Geld anzahlen; (sich) ablagern; ~**or** Kontoinhaber(in).

depot [di'pəu] Depot *n;* Lager(haus) *n.*

depraved [di'preivd] verdorben, -kommen.

depress [di'pres] herunterdrücken; bedrücken; ~**ed** niedergeschlagen; ~**ion** Vertiefung *f,* Flaute *f,* Wirtschaftskrise *f; meteor.* Tief *n* (-druckgebiet) *n;* Niedergeschlagenheit *f.*

deprive [di'praiv] berauben; entziehen.

depth [depθ] Tiefe *f.*

deputy ['depjuti] (Stell-) Vertreter(in); Abgeordnete *m, f.*

derail [di'reil]: **be** ~**ed** entgleisen.

derange [di'reindʒ] durcheinanderbringen.

deri|de [di'raid] verspotten; ~**sion** [~'riʒən] Spott *m;* ~**sive** [~aisiv] spöttisch.

derive [di'raiv]: ~ **(from)** herleiten (von); Nutzen *etc.* ziehen (aus).

derogatory [di'rɔgətəri] nachteilig (**to** für); abfällig; herabsetzend.

descend [di'send] herhinuntersteigen, -kommen; *aer.* niedergehen; **be** ~**ed** abstammen; ~**ant** Nachkomme *m.*

descent [di'sent] Hinuntersteigen *n,* Abstieg *m;* Gefälle *n; aer.* Niedergehen *n;* Abstammung *f.*

descri|be [dis'kraib] beschreiben; ~**ption** [~'krip-ʃən] Beschreibung *f.*

desegregate [di:-'segrigeit] *Am.* die Rassentrennung aufheben in.

desert¹ ['dezət] Wüste *f;* öde; Wüsten...

desert² [di'zə:t] verlassen; im Stich lassen; desertieren; ~**ed** verlassen; einsam; ~**er** Deserteur *m;* ~**ion** Verlassen *n;* Fahnenflucht *f.*

deserve [di'zə:v] verdienen.

design [di'zain] Plan *m,* Entwurf *m;* Zeichnung *f;*

devastate

Muster *n*; Ausführung *f*;
Absicht *f*; entwerfen; planen.
designate ['dezigneit] bezeichnen; bestimmen.
designer [di'zainə] (Muster)Zeichner(in); Kon-
strukteur *m*.
desir|able [di'zaiərəbl]
wünschenswert; ['~it] an-
genehm; ~e [~aiə] Verlangen
n; verlangen; ~ousbegierig.
desk [desk] Pult *n*; Schul-
bank *f*; Schalter *m*;
Schreibtisch *m*; ~ set
Schreibtischgarnitur *f*.
desolat|e ['desəleit] ver-
wüsten; ['~it] öde; ver-
wüstet; verlassen, einsam;
~ion Verwüstung *f*; Ver-
lassenheit *f*.
despair [dis'pεə] Verzweiflung *f*; verzweifeln
(of an); ~ing verzweifelt.
desperat|e ['despərit] ver-
zweifelt; hoffnungslos;
~ion Verzweiflung *f*.
despise [dis'paiz] verachten. [of trotz.]
despite [dis'pait]: (in) ~ ∫
despond [dis'pond] ver-
zagen; ~ent verzagt.
dessert [di'zə:t] Nachtisch
m, Dessert *n*.
destin|ation [desti'nei-
∫ən] Bestimmung(sort *m*)
f; Reiseziel *n*; ~e ['~in]
bestimmen; ~y Schicksal *n*.
destitute ['destitju:t] mittellos.
destroy [dis'trɔi] zerstören, vernichten; ~er Zer-
störer *m*.

destruct|ion [dis'trʌk∫ən]
Zerstörung *f*; ~ive zer-
störend, vernichtend.
detach [di'tæt∫] losma-
chen, (ab)lösen; ~ed ein-
zeln (stehend); unbeein-
flußt.
detail ['di:teil] Einzelheit *f*.
detain [di'tein] zurück-,
auf-, abhalten.
detect [di'tekt] entdecken;
~ion Entdeckung *f*; ~ive
Detektiv *m*, Kriminal-
beamte *m*; ~ive story
Kriminalroman *m*.
detention [di'ten∫ən] Haft
f; Arrest *m*.
deter [di'tə:] abschrecken.
detergent [di'tə:dʒənt]
Reinigungsmittel *n*.
deteriorate [di'tiəriəreit]
(sich) verschlechtern.
determin|ation [ditə:mi-
'nei∫ən] Entscheidung *f*;
Bestimmung *f*; Entschlos-
senheit *f*; ~e [di'tə:min]
bestimmen; (sich) ent-
scheiden; sich entschlie-
ßen.
deterrent [di'terənt] Ab-
schreckungsmittel *n*.
detest [di'test] verabscheu-
en; ~able abscheulich.
detonate ['detəuneit] explodieren (lassen).
detour ['di:tuə] Umleitung *f*.
devalu|ation [di:vælju-
'ei∫ən] Abwertung *f*; ~e
['~vælju:] abwerten.
devastate ['devəsteit] verwüsten.

develop [di'veləp] (sich) entwickeln; erschließen; **~ment** Entwicklung f; phot. Entwickeln n; Erschließung f.

deviate ['di:vieit] abweichen.

device [di'vais] Plan m; Erfindung f; Trick m; Vor-, Einrichtung f; Gerät n.

devil ['devl] Teufel m; **~ish** teuflisch.

devise [di'vaiz] ausdenken.

devoid [di'vɔid]: **~** of ohne.

devot|e [di'vəut] widmen; **~ed** ergeben; zärtlich; **~ion** Ergebenheit f; Hingabe f; Liebe f; pl Andacht f.

devour [di'vauə] verschlingen.

devout [di'vaut] fromm; innig. [betaut.]

dew [dju:] Tau m; **~y**]

dext|erity [deks'teriti] Gewandtheit f; **~(e)rous** ['(ə)rəs] gewandt.

dial ['daiəl] Zifferblatt n; teleph. Wählscheibe f; Skala f; teleph. wählen.

dialect ['daiəlekt] Mundart f.

dialog(ue) ['daiələg] Dialog m, Gespräch n.

diameter [dai'æmitə] Durchmesser m.

diamond ['daiəmənd] Diamant m; **~s** pl) Karten: Karo n.

diaper ['daiəpə] Am. Windel f.

diaphragm ['daiəfræm] Zwerchfell n; opt. Blende f; teleph. Membran(e) f.

diarrh(o)ea [daiə'riə] med. Durchfall m.

diary ['daiəri] Tagebuch n.

dice [dais] pl von die²; würfeln.

dictat|e [dik'teit] diktieren; fig. vorschreiben; **~ion** Diktat n; Vorschrift f; **~or** Diktator m; **~orship** Diktatur f.

dictionary ['dikʃənri] Wörterbuch n.

did [did] pret von do.

die¹ [dai] sterben, umkommen; absterben; **~ of cold** erfrieren. [fel m.]

die², pl **dice** [dais] Würfel m.]

diet ['daiət] Landtag m; Diät f; Nahrung f, Kost f; **auf Diät setzen**; diät leben.

differ ['difə] sich unterscheiden; auseinandergehen (Meinungen); **~ence** ['difrəns] Unterschied m; Differenz f; Meinungsverschiedenheit f; **~ent** verschieden.

difficult ['difikəlt] schwierig, schwer; **~y** Schwierigkeit f.

diffident ['difidənt]schüchtern.

diffuse [di'fju:z] verbreiten.

dig [dig] (irr) (um)graben.

digest [di'dʒest] verdauen; verdaut werden; ['daidʒest] Überblick m; Auswahl f; **~ible** [di'dʒestibl] verdaulich; **~ion**[di'dʒestʃən] Verdauung f.

diggings ['digiŋz] *pl colloq.*
Bude *f*, Zimmer *n*.

digni|fied ['dignifaid]
würdevoll; **~ty** Würde *f*.

digress [dai'gres] abschweifen.

digs [digz] *pl colloq.* Bude
f, Zimmer *n*.

dike [daik] Deich *m*,
Damm *m*; Graben *m*.

dilapidated [di'læpidei-
tid] verfallen, baufällig.

dilate [dai'leit] (sich) ausdehnen *od.* (aus)weiten.

diligen|ce ['dilidʒəns]
Fleiß *m*; **~t** fleißig.

dilute [dai'lju:t] verdünnen.   (trüben.)

dim [dim] trüb(e); (sich)|

dime [daim] *Am.* Zehn-
centstück *n*.

dimension [di'menʃən]
Dimension *f*, Abmessung
f; *pl a.* Ausmaß *n*.

dimin|ish [di'miniʃ] (sich)
verringern; **~utive** [.~jutiv]
winzig.

dimple ['dimpl] Grübchen
n.

dine [dain] speisen; **~r**
Gast *m*; *rail.* Speisewagen
m.

dining-car ['dainiŋ-]
Speisewagen *m*; **~-room**
Speise-, Eßzimmer *n*;
~-table Eßtisch *m*.

dinner ['dinə] Hauptmahlzeit *f*, (Mittag-, Abend-)
Essen *n*; **for ~** zum Essen;
have ~ zu Mittag *od.*
Abend essen; **~ bed
and breakfast** Halb-
pension *f*; **~-jacket** Smo-

kingjacke *f*; **~-party**
Tischgesellschaft *f*.

dip [dip] (ein-, unter-)
tauchen; schöpfen; *mot.*
abblenden; sich senken;
Eintauchen *n*; *colloq.* kur-
zes Bad; Senkung *f*, Nei-
gung *f*.   (Diphtherie *f*.)

diphtheria [dif'θiəriə]|

diploma [di'pləumə] Diplom *n*, Abgangszeugnis
n; **~cy** Diplomatie *f*; **~t**
['.~əmæt] Diplomat *m*;
~tic [.~ə'mætik] diploma-
tisch; **~tist** [di'pləumətist]
Diplomat *m*.

direct [di'rekt] direkt; gerade; unmittelbar; offen,
deutlich; *adv s.* **directly**;
Weg zeigen; lenken,
leiten; adressieren; an-
ordnen; richten; **~ cur-
rent** Gleichstrom *m*; **~ion**
Richtung *f*; Leitung *f*;
Direktion *f*; **~ions** (*for use*)
Adresse *f*; Anweisung(en
pl) *f*; **~ions** (*for use*)
Gebrauchsanweisung *f*;
~ly gerade; sofort, gleich.

director [di'rektə] *Film:*
Regisseur *m*; *thea.* Intendant *m*; Direktor *m*, Leiter
m; **board of ~s** Direktion *f*, Aufsichtsrat *m*;
~y Adreßbuch *n*.

dirigible ['diridʒəbl] lenk-
bar.

dirt [də:t] Schmutz *m*;
~-cheap spottbillig; **~y**
schmutzig; beschmutzen.

disabled [dis'eibld] dienst-
unfähig; körperbehindert;
kriegsbeschädigt.

disadvantage [disəd-
'vɑ:ntidʒ] Nachteil *m*;
~ous [disædvɑ:n'teidʒəs]
nachteilig.

disagree [disə'gri:] nicht
übereinstimmen; anderer
Meinung sein (**with** als);
nicht bekommen (**with**
s.o. j-m); **~able** [.əbl]
unangenehm; **~ment** Un-
stimmigkeit *f*; Meinungsverschiedenheit *f*.

disappear [disə'piə] ver-
schwinden; **~ance** Ver-
schwinden *n*.

disappoint [disə'pɔint]
enttäuschen; **~ment** Enttäuschung *f*.

disapprov|al [disə'pru:-
vəl] Mißbilligung *f*; **~e**
mißbilligen (**of** s.th. et.).

disarm [dis'ɑ:m] entwaf-
nen; abrüsten; **~ament**
Abrüstung *f*.

disarrange ['disə'reindʒ]
in Unordnung bringen.

disast|er [di'zɑ:stə] Un-
glück *n*, Katastrophe *f*;
~rous katastrophal.

disbelief ['disbi'li:f] Unglaube *m*, Zweifel *m*; **~ve**
['.'li:v] nicht glauben.

disc [disk] Scheibe *f*;
(Schall)Platte *f*.

discern [di'sə:n] unterscheiden; erkennen.

discharge [dis'tʃɑ:dʒ] ent-,
ab-, ausladen; abson-
dern; ausströmen; ab-
feuern; *Pflicht* erfüllen;
Schuld bezahlen; entlassen; freisprechen; (sich)
entladen; abfließen; Aus-

laden *n*; Entladung *f*; Ausströmen *n*, Abfluß *m*; Ab-
sonderung *f* (*Eiter*), Aus-
fluß *m*; Abfeuern *n*; Entlassung *f*; Bezahlung *f*.

discipl|e [di'saipl] Schüler
m; Jünger *m*; **~ine** ['disi-
plin] Disziplin *f*.

disc jockey Ansager *m*
(*e-r Schallplattensendung*).

dis|claim [dis'kleim] (ab-)
leugnen; **~close** aufdek-
ken; enthüllen; **~colo(u)r**
(sich) verfärben; **~com-
fort** Unbehagen *n*; **~com-
pose** beunruhigen; **~con-
cert** [.kən'sə:t] aus der
Fassung bringen; *Pläne*
zunichte machen.

disconnect [diskə'nekt]
trennen; *electr. a.* abschal-
ten; **~ed** zs.-hanglos.

disconsolate [dis'kɔn-
səlit] untröstlich.

discontent ['diskən'tent]
Unzufriedenheit *f*; **~ed** unzufrieden.

discontinue ['diskən-
'tinju(:)] aufhören.

discord ['diskɔ:d], **~ance**
[.'kɔ:dəns] Mißklang *m*.

discotheque ['diskəutek]
Diskothek *f*.

discount ['diskaunt] Diskont *m*; Rabatt *m*.

discourage [dis'kʌridʒ]
entmutigen; abschrecken.

discover [dis'kʌvə] entdecken; **~er** Entdecker
(-in); **~y** Entdeckung *f*.

dis|credit [dis'kredit]
schlechter Ruf; Schande
f; Zweifel *m*; anzweifeln;

in Mißkredit bringen;
~creet [.'kri:t] diskret,
verschwiegen; ~crepancy
[.'krepənsi] Widerspruch
m; ~cretion [.'kreʃən]
Verschwiegenheit *f*; Vorsicht *f*; Ermessen *n*; ~
criminate [.'krimineit]
unterscheiden; ~**criminate against** benachteiligen.

discuss [dis'kʌs] diskutieren, besprechen; ~**ion** Diskussion *f*, Besprechung *f*.

disdain [dis'dein] Verachtung *f*; verachten.

disease [di'zi:z] Krankheit *f*; ~**d** krank.

disembark ['disim'bɑ:k]
ausschiffen; an Land gehen.

disengage ['disin'geidʒ]
los-, freimachen; ~**d** frei.

dis|entangle ['disin'tæŋgl] entwirren; ~**favo(u)r** Mißfallen *n*; Ungnade *f*; ~**figure** entstellen.

disgrace [dis'greis] Ungnade *f*, Schande *f*; entehren; ~**ful** schändlich.

disguise [dis'gaiz] verkleiden; *Stimme* verstellen; verbergen; Verkleidung *f*; Maske *f*; Verstellung *f*.

disgust [dis'gʌst] Ekel *m*, Abscheu *m*; anekeln; empören; ~**ing** ekelhaft.

dish [diʃ] Schüssel *f*, Platte *f*, Schale *f*; Gericht *n*, Speise *f*; *the* ~**es** *pl* Geschirr *n*; ~**cloth** Spüllappen *m*.

dishevel(l)ed [di'ʃevəld]
zerzaust, wirr.

dishonest [dis'ɔnist] unehrlich; ~**y** Unehrlichkeit *f*.

dishono(u)r [dis'ɔnə]
Schande *f*; entehren;
Wechsel nicht honorieren;
~**able** schändlich; unehrlich.

dish|**-washer** Geschirrspülmaschine *f*; ~**-water** Spülwasser *n*.

dis|illusion [disi'lu:ʒən]
Ernüchterung *f*, Enttäuschung *f*; ernüchtern; ~**inclined** abgeneigt.

disinfect [disin'fekt] desinfizieren; ~**ant** Desinfektionsmittel *n*.

dis|inherit ['disin'herit]
enterben; ~**integrate**
(sich) auflösen; ~**interested** uneigennützig.

disk [disk] *s.* **disc**.

dis|like [dis'laik] Abneigung *f*; nicht mögen; ~**locate** *med.* verrenken;
~**loyal** treulos.

dismal [dizməl] düster,
trüb(e), trostlos.

dis|mantle [dis'mæntl] demontieren; ~**may** [.'mei]
Schrecken *m*, Bestürzung
f; ~**member** zerstückeln.

dismiss [dis'mis] entlassen; wegschicken; aufgeben; ~**al** Entlassung *f*.

dismount ['dis'maunt] abmontieren; absteigen.

disobedien[ce] [disə'bi:-
djəns] Ungehorsam *m*;
~**t** ungehorsam.

dis|obey ['disə'bei] nicht

gehorchen; nicht befolgen; **~oblige** ungefällig sein gegen.

disorder [dis'ɔːdə] Unordnung f; Unruhe f; med. Störung f; **~ly** unordentlich; gesetzwidrig; aufrührerisch.

dis|own [dis'əun] nicht anerkennen; verleugnen; **~parage** [.'pæridʒ] herabsetzen; **~passionate** leidenschaftslos.

dispatch [dis'pætʃ] Erledigung f; Absendung f; Eile f; (amtlicher) Bericht; (ab)senden; (schnell) erledigen; töten.

dispens|able [dis'pensəbl] entbehrlich; **~e** austeilen; **~e with** auskommen ohne.

dis|perse [dis'pəːs] (sich) zerstreuen; **~place** verrücken, -schieben; absetzen; ersetzen.

display [dis'plei] Entfaltung f; Zurschaustellen n; (Schaufenster)Auslage f; Ausstellung f; zeigen; ausstellen; entfalten.

displeas|e [dis'pliːz] mißfallen; **~ed** ungehalten; **~ure** [.'eʒə] Mißfallen n.

dispos|al [dis'pəuzəl] Anordnung f; Verfügung(s-recht n) f; Beseitigung f; Veräußerung f; **~e** (an-)ordnen; veranlassen; **~e of** verfügen über; veräußern; beseitigen; erledigen; **~ed** geneigt; **~ition** [.zi'ziʃən] Anordnung f; freie Ver-

fügung; Neigung f; Wesen n, Gemütsart f.

disproportionate [disprə'pɔːʃnit] unverhältnismäßig.

dispute [dis'pjuːt] Debatte f; Streit m; (sich) streiten; anzweifeln.

dis|qualify [dis'kwɔlifai] ausschließen; **~regard** nicht beachten; **~reputable** verrufen; schändlich; **~respectful** respektlos; unhöflich; **~rupt** [.'rʌpt] spalten.

dissatisf|action [dissætis'fækʃən] Unzufriedenheit f; **~ied** unzufrieden.

dissen|sion [di'senʃən] Zwietracht f; **~t** anderer Meinung sein (**from** als).

dis|similar ['di'similə] verschieden (**to** von); **~sipate** ['.sipeit] (sich) zerstreuen; **~sociate** [.'səuʃieit] trennen; **~sociate o.s.** sich distanzieren.

dissol|ute ['disəluːt] ausschweifend, liederlich; **~ution** Auflösung f; **~ve** [di'zɔlv] (sich) auflösen.

dissuade [di'sweid] j-m abraten.

distan|ce ['distəns] Abstand m, Entfernung f; Ferne f; Strecke f; fig. Distanz f; **in the ~ce** in der Ferne; **~t** entfernt; zurückhaltend; Fern...

distaste ['dis'teist] Wider-

wille *m*; Abneigung *f*; **~ful**
[~'teistful] unangenehm.

distend [dis'tend] (sich)
ausdehnen; aufblähen.

distinct [dis'tiŋkt] verschieden; getrennt; deut-
lich, klar; **~ion** Unter-
scheidung *f*; Unterschei-
dung *f*; Auszeichnung *f*; Rang
m; **~ive** besonder.

distinguish [dis'tiŋgwiʃ]
unterscheiden; auszeich-
nen; **~ed** berühmt; ausgezeichnet; vornehm.

distort [dis'tɔ:t] verzerren; verdrehen.

distract [dis'trækt] ablenken, zerstreuen; **~ed**
verwirrt; von Sinnen; **~ion**
Ablenkung *f*; Wahnsinn *m*.

distress [dis'tres] Schmerz
m; Elend *n*; Not *f*; beunruhigen; bekümmern; **~ed** besorgt,
bekümmert; notleidend.

distribut|e [dis'tribju(:)t]
aus-, verteilen; verbreiten;
~ion [~'bju:ʃən] Verteilung *f*; Verbreitung *f*.

district ['distrikt] Bezirk
m; Gegend *f*, Gebiet *n*.

distrust [dis'trʌst] Mißtrauen *n*; mißtrauen; **~ful**
mißtrauisch.

disturb [dis'tə:b] stören;
beunruhigen; **~ance** Störung *f*; Unruhe *f*.

disused [dis'ju:zd] außer
Gebrauch, ausgedient.

ditch [ditʃ] Graben *m*.

dive [daiv] (unter)tauchen;
e-n Kopfsprung (*aer.*
Sturzflug) machen; (ha-
stig) hineingreifen; (Kopf-)

Sprung *m*; *aer.* Sturzflug
m; **~r** Taucher *m*.

diverge [dai'və:dʒ] aus-
ea.-laufen; abweichen.

divers|e [dai'və:s] ver-
schieden; **~ion** Ablen-
kung *f*; Umleitung *f*; Zeitvertreib *m*; **~ity** Verschiedenheit *f*; Mannigfaltigkeit *f*.

divert [dai'və:t] ablenken;
j-n zerstreuen; umleiten.

divide [di'vaid] (sich) teilen; (sich) trennen; ein-
teilen; dividieren (**by**
durch); Wasserscheide *f*.

divine [di'vain] ahnen;
Geistliche *m*; göttlich.

diving ['daiviŋ] Tauchen
n; Kunstspringen *n*; Taucher...

divinity [di'viniti] Gottheit *f*; Göttlichkeit *f*;
Theologie *f*.

divis|ible [di'vizəbl] teil-
bar; **~ion** [~ʒən] (Ein-)
Teilung *f*; Trennung *f*;
mil., math. Division *f*.

divorce [di'vɔ:s] (Ehe-)
Scheidung *f*; *j-n* scheiden;
sich scheiden lassen von.

dizzy ['dizi] schwind(e)lig.

do [du:] (*irr*) tun; machen; *Speisen* zubereiten;
Zimmer (sauber)machen;
handeln; sich verhalten;
genügen; **~ you know
him?** ~ **No, I don't**
kennst du ihn? - Nein;
~ not (don't) nicht; **~ be
quick!** beeile dich doch!;
what can I ~ for you?
was kann ich für Sie tun?;

docile   88

~ **London** colloq. London besichtigen; **have one's hair done** sich die Haare machen od. frisieren lassen; **have done reading** fertig sein mit Lesen; **that will ~** das genügt; ~ **away with** abschaffen, beseitigen; ~ **well** s-e Sache gut machen; ~ **up** instand setzen; zurechtmachen; einpacken; **I could ~ with …** ich könnte … gebrauchen od. vertragen; ~ **without** auskommen ohne.   [fügsam.)

docile ['dəusail] gelehrig;)

dock [dɔk] Dock n; pl Hafenanlagen pl; ~**yard** Werft f.

doctor ['dɔktə] Doktor m; Arzt m; ~**'s help** Arzthelferin f.

doctrine ['dɔktrin] Doktrin f; Lehre f.

document ['dɔkjumənt] Urkunde f; ~**ary** (**film**) Dokumentar-, Kulturfilm m.

dodge [dɔdʒ] rasches Ausweichen; Schlich m, Kniff m; ausweichen; sich drücken (vor).

doe [dəu] Hirschkuh f; (Reh)Geiß f; Häsin f.

dog [dɔg] Hund m; ~**eared** mit Eselsohren (Buch); ~**gie** f; ~**gy**Hündchen n.

dogma ['dɔgmə] Dogma n, Glaubenssatz m.

dog tired hundemüde.

doings ['du(:)iŋz] pl colloq.

Ereignisse pl; Treiben n.

dole [dəul] Spende f; colloq. Arbeitslosenunterstützung f.

doll [dɔl] Puppe f.

dollar ['dɔlə] Dollar m.

doll's | ~**house** Puppenhaus n; ~ **pram** Puppenwagen m.

dolorous ['dɔlərəs] schmerzlich, traurig.

dolphin ['dɔlfin]Delphin m.

dome [dəum] Kuppel f.

domestic [dəu'mestik] häuslich; Inlands…; einheimisch; Innen…; ~ **animal** Haustier n; ~**ate** [.eit] zähmen; ~ **servant** Hausangestellte m, f.

domicile ['dɔmisail]Wohnsitz m.

dominate ['dɔmineit] beherrschen, herrschen über; ~**ation** (Vor)Herrschaft f; ~**eer** [.'niə] (despotisch) herrschen; ~**eering** herrisch; tyrannisch.

donate [dəu'neit] spenden; ~**ion** Spende f.

done [dʌn] pp von **do**; getan; erledigt; fertig; gar.

donkey ['dɔŋki] Esel m.

donor ['dəunə] Spender (-in) (a. med.).

doom [du:m] Verhängnis n; verurteilen; ~**sday** der Jüngste Tag.

door [dɔː] Tür f; ~**handle** Türgriff m, -klinke f; ~**keeper**, Am. a. ~**man** Pförtner m, Portier m; ~**mat** Fußmatte f; ~**way** Türöffnung f.

dope [dəup] *colloq.* Rauschgift *n*; Rauschgift geben; betäuben; dopen.

dormer(-window) ['dɔːmə('-)] Dachfenster *n*.

dormitory ['dɔːmitri] Schlafsaal *m*; *bsd. Am.* Studenten(wohn)heim *n*.

dose [dəus] Dosis *f*.

dot [dɔt] Punkt *m*; punktieren, tüpfeln; verstreuen.

dote [dəut]: ~ **(up)on** vernarrt sein in.

double ['dʌbl] doppelt, Doppel..., zweifach; Doppelte *n*; Doppelgänger(in *f*); ~(s *pl*) *Tennis*: Doppel *n*; (sich) verdoppeln; ~ **up** zs.-falten, zs.-rollen; sich krümmen; ~ **bed** Doppelbett *n*; französisches Bett; ~**breasted** zweireihig (*Jackett*); ~**decker** *colloq.* Doppeldecker *m*; ~**park** in zweiter Reihe parken; ~ **room** Doppel-, Zweibettzimmer *n*.

doubt [daut] zweifeln (an); bezweifeln; Zweifel *m*; no ~ ohne Zweifel; ~**ful** zweifelhaft; ~**less** ohne Zweifel.

douche [du:ʃ] *med.*: Spülung *f*; (aus)spülen.

dough [dəu] Teig *m*; ~**nut** ~-e *e* Art Schmalzgebackenes.

dove [dʌv] Taube *f*.

down[1] [daun] Daune *f*; Flaum *m*; Düne *f*; *pl* Hügelland *n*.

down[2] nieder; her-, hinunter; *aer.* abschießen; ~**cast** niedergeschlagen; ~**fall** *fig.* Sturz *m*; ~**hill** bergab; ~**pour** Regenguß *m*; ~**right** glatt (*Lüge etc.*); ~**stairs** (die Treppe) hinunter; unten; ~**town** *bsd. Am.* Geschäftsviertel *n*; ~ **train** Zug *m* von London; ~**ward(s)** ['~wəd(z)] abwärts, nach unten.

downy ['dauni] flaumig.

dowry ['dauəri] Mitgift *f*.

doze [dəuz] dösen; Schlummer *m*.

dozen ['dʌzn] Dutzend *n*.

drab [dræb] eintönig.

draft [drɑːft] Entwurf *m*; *econ.* Tratte *f*; *Am. mil.* Einberufung *f*; *s. draught*; entwerfen; aufsetzen; *Am. mil.* einziehen; ~**sman** (technischer) Zeichner.

drag [dræg] schleppen, ziehen, zerren.

dragon ['drægən] Drache *m*; ~**fly** Libelle *f*.

drain [drein] Abfluß(rohr *n*, -kanal *m*); Entwässerungsgraben *m*; entwässern; ~ **away**, ~ **off** abfließen; ~**age** Abfluß *m*; Entwässerung *f*; Kanalisation *f*.

drake [dreik] Enterich *m*, Erpel *m*.

drama ['drɑːmə] Drama *n*; ~**tic** [drə'mætik] dramatisch; ~**tist** ['dræmətist] Dramatiker *m*. [**drink**.]

drank [dræŋk] *pret von*

drape [dreɪp] drapieren; in Falten legen.

drastic ['dræstik] drastisch.

draught, *Am.* **draft** [drɑːft] Ziehen *n*, Zug *m*; Fischzug *m*; Luftzug *m*; Zugluft *f*; Schluck *m*; ~ **beer** Faßbier *n*; ~**sman** *s.* **draftsman**; ~**y** zugig.

draw [drɔː] Lotterie: Ziehung *f*; unentschiedenes Spiel; Attraktion *f*; Zugnummer *f*; (*irr*) (heraus-, zu)ziehen; herausholen); *Geld* abheben; anziehen; zeichnen; unentschieden spielen; *Luft* schöpfen; ~ **near** sich nähern, heranrücken; ~ **out** in die Länge ziehen; ~ **up** *Schriftstück* aufsetzen; halten; vorfahren; ~**back** Nachteil *m*; Hindernis *n*; ~**er** Zeichner *m*; Aussteller *m* (*e-s Wechsels*); [drɔː] Schublade *f*; (**a pair of**) ~**ers** [drɔːz] *pl* (e-e) Unterhose; (ein) Schlüpfer.

drawing ['drɔːiŋ] Ziehen *n*; Ziehung *f*; Zeichnung *f*; ~**pin** Reißzwecke *f*; ~**room** Salon *m*.

drawn [drɔːn] *pp von* **draw**; unentschieden; verzerrt.

dread [dred] Furcht *f*, Schrecken *m*; fürchten, sich fürchten vor; ~**ful** schrecklich, furchtbar.

dream [driːm] Traum *m*;

(*irr*) träumen; ~**t** [dremt] *pret u. pp von* **dream**; ~**y** verträumt.

dreary ['driəri] trostlos.

dregs [dregz] *pl* Bodensatz *m*; [nässen.]

drench [drentʃ] durch-

dress [dres] Anzug *m*; Kleid(ung *f*) *n*; zurechtmachen; (sich) ankleiden *od.* anziehen; schmücken; *med.* verbinden; frisieren; ~ **circle** *thea.* erster Rang; ~ **designer** Modezeichner(in), -schöpfer(in).

dressing ['dresiŋ] An-, Zurichten *n*; Ankleiden *n*; Verband *m*; (*Salat*)Soße *f*; Füllung *f*; ~**case** Reisenecessaire *n*; ~**cubicle** Umkleidekabine *f*; ~**gown** Morgenrock *m*; ~**table** Frisierkommode *f*.

dressmaker Schneiderin*f*.

drew [druː] *pret von* **draw**.

drift [drift] Treiben *n*; (*Schnee*)Verwehung *f*; Tendenz *f*; (dahin)treiben; wehen.

drill [dril] Bohrer *m*; (*Acker*)Furche *f*; Sämaschine *f*; Drill *m*; Exerzieren *n*; bohren; drillen; (ein)exerzieren.

drink [driŋk] (*irr*) trinken; (geistiges) Getränk *n*; **have a** ~ et. trinken.

drip [drip] tropfen *od.* tröpfeln (lassen); ~**dry** bügelfrei; ~**ping** Bratenfett *n*.

drive [draiv] (Spazier-

Fahrt *f*; Auffahrt *f*; *tech.* Antrieb *m*; Tatkraft *f*, Schwung *m*; (*irr*) (an-)treiben; fahren; ~ **away** vertreiben, -jagen; ~ **out** vertreiben; **what is he driving at?** worauf will er hinaus?

drive-in *Am.* Autokino *n*; Autorestaurant *n*; Auto...; ~ **cinema** Autokino *n*.

drive|n ['drivn] *pp von* **drive;** ~**r** ['draivə] Fahrer *m*.

driving| lesson ['draiviŋ] Fahrstunde *f*; ~ **licence** Führerschein *m*; ~ **school** Fahrschule *f*.

drizzle ['drizl] Sprühregen *m*; sprühen, nieseln.

drone [drəun] Drohne *f*.

droop [dru:p] sinken lassen; (schlaff) herabhängen; (lassen).

drop [drɔp] Tropfen *m*; (Frucht)Bonbon *m*, *n*; *econ.* Sinken *n*; tropfen (lassen); fallen lassen; *Brief* einwerfen; *Fahrgast* absetzen; senken; (herab-)fallen; sich legen (*Wind*); ~ **s.o. a few lines** j-m ein paar Zeilen schreiben; ~ **in** unerwartet kommen, vorbeikommen.

drove [drəuv] *pret von* **drive.**

drown [draun] ertrinken; ertränken; *fig.* übertönen; **be ~ed** ertrinken.

drowsy ['drauzi] schläfrig; einschläfernd.

drudge [drʌdʒ] sich (ab-)plagen.

drug [drʌg] Droge *f*; Rauschgift *n*; Drogen beimischen; (mit Drogen) betäuben; (mit Drogen od. Rauschgift) nehmen; ~ **addict** Rauschgiftsüchtige *m*, *f*; ~**gist** ['~gist] Drogist *m*; Apotheker *m*; ~ **store** *Am.* Drugstore *m*.

drum [drʌm] Trommel *f*; trommeln; ~**mer** Trommler *m*.

drunk [drʌŋk] *pp von* **drink;** betrunken; ~**ard** ['~əd] Trinker *m*, Säufer *m*; ~**en** betrunken; ~**en-driving** Trunkenheit *f* am Steuer.

dry [drai] trocken; herb (*Wein*); (ab)trocknen; dörren; ~ **up** austrocknen; ~**-clean** chemisch reinigen; ~ **goods** *pl Am.* Textilien *pl*.

dual ['dju:(:)əl] doppelt.

duchess ['dʌtʃis] Herzogin *f*.

duck [dʌk] Ente *f*; *colloq.* Liebling *m*; (unter)tauchen; (sich) ducken.

dude [dju:d] *Am.* Geck *m*; ~ **ranch** *Am.* Ferienranch *f*.

due [dju:] Zustehende *n*, Anspruch *m*; ~**s** pl Gebühren *pl*; fällig; zustehend; gebührend; angemessen, sorgfältig; erwartet; ~ **to** zuzuschreiben, verursacht durch; **be ~ to** sollen,

müssen; in ~ time recht-
zeitig.

duel ['dju(:)əl] Duell *n*,
Zweikampf *m*. **{dig.}**

dug [dʌg] *pret u. pp von*

duke [dju:k] Herzog *m*.

dull [dʌl] dumm;
dumpf; trüb(e); schwach
(*Gehör*); langweilig;
träg(e); dumm; *econ.* flau.

duly ['dju:li] ordnungs-
gemäß; rechtzeitig.

dumb [dʌm] stumm;
sprachlos; *Am. colloq.*
blöd(e); ~**founded** sprachlos.

dummy ['dʌmi] At-
trappe *f*; nachgemacht;
Schein...

dump [dʌmp] auskippen;
Schutt etc. abladen;
Schutthaufen *m*; Schutt-
abladeplatz *m*.

dun [dʌn] *Schuldner*
mahnen, drängen.

dune [dju:n] Düne *f*.

dung [dʌŋ] Dung *m*;
düngen.

dungeon ['dʌndʒən] Ker-
ker *m*.

dupe [dju:p] anführen,
täuschen.

duplicate ['dju:plikit]
genau gleich; doppelt;
Duplikat *n*; ['~eit] kopieren; verdoppeln.

dura|ble ['djuərəbl]
dauerhaft; ~**tion** Dauer *f*.

duress(e) [djuə'res]
Zwang *m*.

during ['djuəriŋ] während.

dusk [dʌsk] Dämmerung *f*.

dust [dʌst] Staub *m*; abstauben; Staub wischen;
(be)streuen; ~**bin** Mülleimer *m*; ~**cart** Müll-
wagen *m*; ~**er** Staub-
lappen *m*; ~**jacket**
Schutzumschlag *m*; ~**man**
Müllabfuhrmann *m*; ~**pan**
Kehrschaufel *f*; ~**y** staubig.

Dutch [dʌtʃ] holländisch;
Holländisch *n*; **the ~** *pl*
die Holländer *pl*; ~**man**
Holländer *m*; ~**woman**
Holländerin *f*.

duty ['dju:ti] Pflicht *f*,
Aufgabe *f*; Zoll *m*; **be
off ~** dienstfrei haben;
be on ~ Dienst haben,
im Dienst sein; ~**free**
zollfrei.

dwarf [dwɔ:f] Zwerg *m*.

dwell [dwel] (*irr*)
wohnen; verweilen [**up-**
on bei); ~**ing** Wohnung *f*.

dwelt [dwelt] *pret u. pp*
von **dwell.**

dwindle ['dwindl] schwinden.

dye [dai] Farbe *f*; färben.

dying ['daiiŋ] *pres p von*
die[1].

dyke [daik] *s.* **dike.**

dynam|ic [dai'næmik]
dynamisch; ~**ics** *sg*
Dynamik *f*; ~**ite** ['~əmait]
Dynamit *n*; ~**o** ['~əmou]
Dynamo(maschine *f*) *m*,
Lichtmaschine *f*.

dysentery ['disntri] *med.*
Ruhr *f*.

E

each [i:tʃ] jede(r, -s); ~ **other** einander.

eager ['i:gə] begierig; eifrig; **~ness** Begierde f; Eifer m.

eagle ['i:gl] Adler m.

ear [iə] Ohr n; Gehör n; Ähre f; Henkel m; **~drum** Trommelfell n.

earl [ə:l] britischer Graf.

early ['ə:li] früh...; erst; bald. [bringen.]

earn [ə:n] verdienen; ein-]

earnest ['ə:nist] ernst (-haft); **in** ~ ernsthaft.

earnings ['ə:niŋz] pl Verdienst m, Einkommen n.

ear|-phone Kopfhörer m; **~shot** Hörweite f.

earth [ə:θ] Erde f; Land n; electr. erden; **~en** irden; **~enware** Steingut n; irden; **~ly** irdisch; **~quake** Erdbeben n; **~worm** Regenwurm m.

ease [i:z] erleichtern; lindern; beruhigen; sich entspannen (Lage); Bequemlichkeit f; Entspannung f; Ungezwungenheit f;Leichtigkeit f; **at** ~ bequem, behaglich.

easel ['i:zl] Staffelei f.

east [i:st] Ost(en m); östlich, nach Osten, Ost...

Easter ['i:stə] Ostern n; Oster...; **~ly** östlich, nach Osten, Ost...; **~n** östlich.

eastward(s) ['i:stwəd(z)] ostwärts.

easy ['i:zi] leicht, einfach; bequem; ruhig; ungezwungen; **take it** ~! immer mit der Ruhe!; ~ **chair** Lehnstuhl m, Sessel m.

eat [i:t] (irr) essen; (zer-) fressen; ~ **up** aufessen; **~en** pp von **eat**.

eaves [i:vz] pl überhängende Dachkante; **~drop** lauschen, horchen.

ebb(-tide) ['eb('~)] Ebbe f.

ebony ['ebəni] Ebenholz n.

eccentric [ik'sentrik] exzentrisch; fig. a. überspannt; Sonderling m.

ecclesiastical [ikli:zi'æstikəl] kirchlich, geistlich.

echo ['ekəu] Echo n, Widerhall m; widerhallen; fig. echoen, nachsprechen.

eclipse [i'klips] (Sonnen-, Mond)Finsternis f.

economic [i:kə'nɔmik] (volks)wirtschaftlich, Wirtschafts...; **~al** wirtschaftlich, sparsam; **~s** sg Volkswirtschaft(slehre) f.

econom|ist [i(:)'kɔnəmist] Volkswirt m; **~ize** sparen; **~y** Wirtschaft f; Sparsamkeit f; pl Einsparung f; ~ **class** aer. Economy-Klasse f, Touristenklasse f.

ecstasy ['ekstəsi] Ekstase f.   [wirbeln.]

eddy ['edi] Wirbel m;]

edg|e [edʒ] schärfen; (um)säumen; Schneide *f*; Rand *m*; Kante *f*; **be on ~e** gereizt *od.* nervös sein; **~ing** Rand *m*; Einfassung *f*; **~y** gereizt, nervös.

edible ['edibl] eßbar.

edifice ['edifis] Gebäude *n*.

edifying ['edifaiiŋ] erbaulich.

edit ['edit] Buch, Zeitung herausgeben; **~ion** [i'diʃən] Ausgabe *f*; Auflage *f*; **~or** ['editə] Herausgeber *m*; Redakteur *m*; **~orial** [edi'tɔːriəl] Leitartikel *m*; Redaktions...

educat|e ['edju(ː)keit] erziehen, unterrichten, ausbilden; **~ion** Erziehung *f*; (Aus)Bildung *f*; Schulwesen *n*; **~ional** erzieherisch, Erziehungs...; **~or** Erzieher(in).

eel [iːl] Aal *m*.

effect [i'fekt] bewirken; ausführen; Wirkung *f*; Eindruck *m*, Effekt *m*; *pl* Habe *f*; **in ~** tatsächlich; *jur.* in Kraft; **take ~** in Kraft treten; **~ive** wirksam; eindrucksvoll; tatsächlich.

effeminate [i'feminit] verweichlicht; weibisch.

effervescent [efə'vesnt] sprudelnd, schäumend.

efficien|cy [i'fiʃənsi] Leistungsfähigkeit *f*; **~t** tüchtig, (leistungs)fähig.

effort ['efət] Anstrengung *f*, Bemühung *f*.

effusive [i'fjuːsiv] überschwenglich.

egg [eg] Ei *n*; **~cup** Eierbecher *m*; **~head** Am. sl. Intellektuelle *f*.

egoism ['egouizəm] Egoismus *m*, Selbstsucht *f*.

egress ['iːgrəs] Ausgang *m*; *fig.* Ausweg *m*.

Egyptian [i'dʒipʃən] ägyptisch; Ägypter(in).

eider-down ['aidə-] Eiderdaunen *pl*; Daunendecke *f*.

eight [eit] acht; Acht *f*; **~een(th)** ['ei'tiːn(θ)] achtzehn(te); **~fold** achtfach; **~h** [eitθ] achte; Achtel *n*; **~hly** achtens; **~ieth** ['~tiiθ] achtzigste; **~y** achtzig; Achtzig *f*.

either ['aiðə, Am. 'iːðə] jede(r, -s) (von zweien), beide; irgendeine(r, -s) (von zweien); **... or ~** entweder ... oder; **not ... ~** auch nicht.

ejaculate [i'dʒækjuleit] Worte etc. ausstoßen.

eject [i(ː)'dʒekt] ausstoßen; vertreiben; ausweisen.

elaborate [i'læbərit] sorgfältig ausgearbeitet; [~eit] sorgfältig ausarbeiten.

elapse [i'læps] vergehen, -streichen (Zeit).

elastic [i'læstik] elastisch, dehnbar; Gummiband *n*.

elated [i'leitid] freudig erregt.

elbow ['elbou] Ell(en)bogen *m*; Biegung *f*; tech. Knie *n*; mit dem Ellbogen stoßen, drängen.

elder[1] ['eldə] Holunder *m*.

elde|r² älter; *der, die* Ältere; **~rly** ältlich; **~st** [´~ist] älteste.

elect [i´lekt] designiert; wählen; **~ion** Wahl *f*; **~or** Wähler *m*; *Am.* Wahlmann *m*.

electric [i´lektrik] elektrisch; **~al engineer** Elektroingenieur *m*, -techniker *m*; **~ chair** elektrischer Stuhl; **~ian** [~´triʃən] Elektriker *m*; **~ity** [~´trisiti] Elektrizität *f*.

electrify [i´lektrifai] elektrisieren; elektrifizieren.

electrocute [i´lektrəkju:t] durch elektrischen Strom töten.   [tron *n*.\

electron [i´lektron] Elek-}

elegan|ce [´eligəns] Eleganz *f*; Anmut *f*; **~t** elegant, geschmackvoll.

element [´elimənt] Element *n*; *pl* Anfangsgründe *pl*; **~al** [~´mentl] elementar; **~ary** [~´mentəri] elementar; Anfangs...; **~ary school** Volks-, Grundschule *f*.   [*m*.\

elephant [´elifənt] Elefant }

elevat|e [´eliveit] (hoch-, er)heben; **~ion** Erhebung *f*; Erhöhung *f*; Höhe *f*; Erhabenheit *f*; **~or** *Am.* Fahrstuhl *m*; *aer.* Höhenruder *n*.

eleven [i´levn] elf; Elf *f*; **~th** [~θ] elfte.   [eignet.\

eligible [´elidʒəbl] ge-}

eliminat|e [i´limineit] entfernen, ausmerzen; ausscheiden; **~ion** Entfernung

f, Ausmerzung *f*; Ausscheidung *f*.

elk [elk] Elch *m*; *Am.* Elk *m*, Wapiti *m*.

ellipse [i´lips] Ellipse *f*.

elm [elm] Ulme *f*.

elongate [i´lɔŋgeit] (sich) verlängern.

elope [i´ləup] davonlaufen, durchbrennen (*Frau*).

eloquen|ce [´eləkwəns] Beredsamkeit *f*; **~t** beredt.

else [els] sonst; weiter; andere; **what ~?** was sonst noch?; **~where** anderswo(hin).

elu|de [i´lu:d] ausweichen, sich entziehen; **~sive** ausweichend; schwer faßbar.

emaciated [i´meiʃieitid] abgemagert, abgezehrt.

emancipate [i´mænsipeit] emanzipieren, befreien.

embalm [im´bɑ:m] einbalsamieren.

embankment [im´bæŋkmənt] Damm *m*; Bahndamm *m*; befestigte Uferstraße.

embargo [em´bɑ:gəu] (Hafen-, Handels)Sperre *f*.

embark [im´bɑ:k] (sich) einschiffen (**for** nach); verladen (**for** nach); **~(up)on** *et.* anfangen.

embarrass [im´bærəs] behindern; verwirren, in Verlegenheit bringen; **~ing** unangenehm, peinlich; **~ment** (Geld)Verlegenheit *f*.

embassy [´embəsi] Botschaft *f*; Gesandtschaft *f*.

embedded [im'bedid] (ein)gebettet, eingeschlossen.

embellish [im'beliʃ] verschönern; (aus)schmücken.

embers ['embəz] pl glühende Asche, Glut f.

embezzle [im'bezl] Geld unterschlagen.

embitter [im'bitə] verbittern.

emblem ['embləm] Sinnbild n, Symbol n.

embody [im'bɔdi] verkörpern.

embolism ['embəlizəm] Embolie f.

embrace [im'breis] (sich) umarmen; Umarmung f.

embroider [im'brɔidə] sticken; fig. ausschmücken; ~y Stickerei f.

emerald ['emərəld] Smaragd(grün n) m.

emerge [i'mɜːdʒ] auftauchen; fig. hervorgehen.

emergency [i'mɜːdʒənsi] Not(lage) f, ~fall m; Not...; ~ brake Notbremse f; ~ call Notruf m; ~ chute aer. Notrutsche f; ~ exit Notausgang m; ~ landing aer. Notlandung f; make an ~ landing aer. notlanden.

emigra|nt ['emigrənt] Auswanderer m; ~te ['~eit] auswandern; ~tion Auswanderung f.

eminent ['eminənt] berühmt; außergewöhnlich; ~ly (ganz) besonders.

emit [i'mit] aussenden, -strömen, -stoßen.

emotion [i'məuʃən] (Gemüts)Bewegung f, Gefühl n, Rührung f; ~al gefühlsmäßig; gefühlvoll; gefühlsbetont.

emperor ['empərə] Kaiser m.

empha|sis ['emfəsis] Nachdruck m; ~size ['~saiz] (nachdrücklich) betonen; ~tic [im'fætik] nachdrücklich, betont.

empire ['empaiə](Kaiser-) Reich n.

employ [im'plɔi] beschäftigen, anstellen; an-, verwenden; sub: in the ~ of angestellt bei; ~ee [emplɔi'i:] Angestellte m, f, Arbeitnehmer(in); ~er Arbeitgeber(in); ~ment Beschäftigung f, Arbeit f; ~ment agency Stellenvermittlungsbüro n; ~ment exchange Arbeitsamt n. |rin f.|

empress ['empris] Kaiserin f.

empt|iness ['emptinis] Leere f; ~y leer; (aus-, ent)leeren; sich leeren.

emulate ['emjuleit] wetteifern mit, nacheifern.

enable [i'neibl] es j-m ermöglichen; ermächtigen.

enact [i'nækt] erlassen; verfügen; thea. spielen.

enamel [i'næməl] Email (-le f) n; Glasur f; Lack m; Zahnschmelz m.

encase [in'keis] umhüllen; verschalen.

engrave

enchant [in'tʃɑːnt] be-, verzaubern.

encircle [in'sɔːkl] umgeben; einkreisen.

enclos|e [in'kləuz] einzäunen; einschließen; beifügen; **~ure** [ˌʒə] Einzäunung f; Anlage f (Brief).

encounter [in'kauntə] Begegnung f; begegnen; auf Schwierigkeiten etc. stoßen.

encourage [in'kʌridʒ] ermutigen; unterstützen; **~ment** Ermutigung f; Unterstützung f.

encumber [in'kʌmbə] belasten; behindern.

end [end] enden; beend(ig)en; Ende n; Ziel n, Zweck m; **no ~ of** sehr viel(e); **in the ~** schließlich; **stand on ~** zu Berge stehen (Haare).

endanger [in'deindʒə] gefährden.

endear [in'diə] lieb od. teuer machen (**to s.o.** j-m).

endeavo(u)r [in'devə] Bemühung f; sich bemühen.

end|ing ['endiŋ] Ende n, Schluß m; gr. Endung f; **~less** endlos, unendlich.

endorse [in'dɔːs] Dokument auf der Rückseite beschreiben; et. vermerken; billigen, unterstützen.

endow [in'dau] ausstatten; stiften.

endur|ance [in'djuərəns] Ausdauer f; Ertragen n; **~e** (aus-, fort)dauern; durchhalten; ertragen.

enemy ['enimi] Feind m; feindlich.

energ|etic [enə'dʒetik] energisch; **~y** Energie f.

enervate ['enəːveit] entnerven, -kräften.

enfold [in'fəuld] umfassen.

enforce [in'fɔːs] er-, aufzwingen; durchführen.

enfranchise [in'fræntʃaiz] das Wahlrecht verleihen.

engage [in'geidʒ] anstellen; mil. angreifen; sich verpflichten, versprechen, garantieren; sich beschäftigen (**in** mit); **be ~d** verlobt sein (**to** mit); beschäftigt sein (**in** mit); besetzt sein; **~ment** Verpflichtung f; Verlobung f; Verabredung f.

engine ['endʒin] Maschine f; Motor m; Lokomotive f; **~-driver** Lokomotivführer m.

engineer [endʒi'niə] Ingenieur m, Techniker m; Maschinist m; Am. Lokomotivführer m; mil. Pionier m; **~ing** Maschinenbau m; Ingenieurwesen n; technisch.

engine trouble Motorschaden m.

English ['iŋgliʃ] englisch; Englisch n; **the ~** pl die Engländer m pl; **~man** Engländer m; **~woman** Engländerin f.

engrav|e [in'greiv] gravieren, eingraben; fig. einprägen; **~ing** (Kupfer-)

Stahl)Stich *m*; Holzschnitt
m.

engross [in'grəus] ganz in
Anspruch nehmen.

enigma [i'nigmə] Rätsel *n*.

enjoin [in'dʒɔin] vorschrei-
ben, befehlen.

enjoy [in'dʒɔi] sich erfreuen an; genießen; **did
you ~ it?** hat es Ihnen
gefallen?; **~ o.s.** sich
amüsieren *od.* gut unterhalten; **~ment** Genuß *m*,
Freude *f*.

enlarge [in'lɑːdʒ] (sich)
vergrößern; **~ment** Ver-
größerung *f*.

enlighten [in'laitn] *fig.*
aufklären; belehren.

enlist [in'list] gewinnen
(*zur Mitarbeit*); *mil.* an-
werben; sich (freiwillig)
melden.

enliven [in'laivn] beleben.

enmity ['enmiti] Feindschaft *f*. [geheuer.)

enormous [i'nɔːməs] un-)

enough [i'nʌf] genug.

enquir|e [in'kwaiə], **~y** *s.*
inquire, inquiry.

enrage [in'reidʒ] wütend
machen; **~d** wütend.

enrapture [in'ræptʃə] entzücken. [reichern.)

enrich [in'ritʃ] be-)

enrol(l) [in'rəul] *j-s Namen* eintragen; aufnehmen.

ensue [in'sjuː] folgen, sich
ergeben. [garantieren.)

ensure [in'ʃuə] sichern;)

entangle [in'tæŋgl] ver-
wickeln, -wirren.

enter ['entə] (ein)treten

in; betreten; einfahren in;
eindringen in; eintragen;
anmelden; sich einschrei-
ben; **~ (up)on** *Amt etc.*
antreten.

enterpris|e ['entəpraiz]
Unternehmen *n*; Unter-
nehmungslust *f*; **~ing** un-
ternehmungslustig.

entertain [entə'tein] unterhalten; bewirten; *Zwei-
fel etc.* hegen; **~er** Unter-
haltungskünstler *m*;
~ment Bewirtung *f*; Veranstaltung *f*; Unterhal-
tung *f*.

enthusias|m [in'θjuːzi-
æzəm] Begeisterung *f*;
~t [~st] Enthusiast(in),
Schwärmer(in), **~tic**
[~stik] begeistert.

entice [in'tais] (ver)locken;
verleiten.

entire [in'taiə] ganz; vollständig; **~ly** völlig.

entitle [in'taitl] betiteln;
berechtigen.

entrails ['entreilz] *pl* Eingeweide *pl*.

entrance ['entrəns] Ein-,
Zutritt *m*; Einfahrt *f*; Ein-
gang *m*; Einlaß *m*; **~ fee**
Eintrittsgeld *n*.

entreat [in'triːt] (*et.* er-)
bitten; **~y** dringende Bitte.

entrust [in'trʌst] anvertrauen; betrauen.

entry ['entri] Eintritt *m*;
Einreise *f*; Eintragung *f*;
sp. Meldung *f*; **~ permit**
Einreisegenehmigung *f*.

enumerate [i'njuːməreit]
aufzählen.

envelop [in'veləp] einhüllen; einwickeln; **~e** ['enveləp] Briefumschlag *m*.

envi|able ['enviəbl] beneidenswert; **~ous** neidisch.

environ|ment [in'vaiərənment] Umgebung *f*; **~mental pollution** Umweltverschmutzung *f*; **~s** ['enviranz] *pl* Umgebung *f* (*e-r Stadt*).

envoy ['envɔi] Gesandte *m*.

envy ['envi] Neid *m*; beneiden.

epidemic (disease) [epi'demik] Seuche *f*.

epidermis [epi'də:mis] Oberhaut *f*. [lepsie *f*.]

epilepsy ['epilepsi] Epi-]

epilog(ue) ['epilog] Epilog *m*, Nachwort *n*.

episode ['episəud] Episode *f*.

epitaph ['epitɑ:f] Grabschrift *f*.

epoch ['i:pɔk] Epoche *f*.

equal ['i:kwəl] Gleichgestellte *m*, *f*; gleiche; gleich; **be ~ to** e-r S. gewachsen sein; **~ity** [i(:)-'kwɔliti] Gleichheit *f*, -berechtigung *f*; **~ize** gleichmachen, -stellen; ausgleichen.

equanimity [ekwə'nimiti] Gleichmut *m*.

equat|ion [i'kweiʒən] Ausgleich *m*; *math.* Gleichung *f*; **~or** Äquator *m*.

equilibrium [i:kwi'libriəm] Gleichgewicht *n*.

equip [i'kwip] ausrüsten;

~ment Ausrüstung *f*; Einrichtung *f*, Anlage *f*.

equivalent [i'kwivələnt] gleichwertig; entsprechend (**to** *dat*); Äquivalent *n*, Gegenwert *m*.

era ['iərə] Ära *f*, Zeitrechnung *f*, -alter *n*.

erase [i'reiz] ausradieren, -streichen, (-)löschen.

ere [ɛə] ehe, bevor; vor.

erect [i'rekt] aufrecht; aufrichten, -stellen; errichten; **~ion** Auf-, Errichtung *f*; Gebäude *n*.

erosion [i'rəuʒən] Zerfressen *n*; *geol.* Erosion *f*.

erotic [i'rɔtik] erotisch.

err [ə:] (sich) irren.

errand ['erənd] Botengang *m*, Auftrag *m*; **run ~s** Besorgungen machen.

erro|neous [i'rəunjəs] irrig, falsch; **~r** ['erə] Irrtum *m*, Fehler *m*.

erupt [i'rʌpt] ausbrechen (*Vulkan*); **~ion** Ausbruch *m* (*e-s Vulkans*; *a. fig.*); Hautausschlag *m*.

escalat|ion [eskə'leiʒən] Eskalation *f*; **~or** ['..tə] Rolltreppe *f*.

escape [is'keip] entgehen; entkommen; *j-m* entfallen; Entkommen *n*, Flucht *f*.

escort ['eskɔ:t] Eskorte *f*; Begleiter(in); [is'kɔ:t] eskortieren; begleiten.

especial [is'peʃəl] besonder; **~ly** besonders.

espionage [espiə'nɑ:ʒ] Spionage *f*.

espy [is'pai] erspähen.

essay ['esei] Aufsatz m, Essay m, n.

essen|ce ['esns] Wesen n (e-r Sache); Essenz f; **~tial** [i'senʃəl] wesentlich.

establish [is'tæbliʃ] errichten, aufbauen, gründen; **~ o.s.** sich niederlassen od. einrichten; **~ment** Er-, Einrichtung f, Gründung f; pol. die etablierte Macht, die herrschende Schicht; Firma f.

estate [is'teit] (Grund-) Besitz m; **~ agent** Immobilienhändler m; **~ car** Kombiwagen m.

esteem [is'ti:m] Achtung f; achten, schätzen.

estimat|e ['estimeit] beurteilen, schätzen, veranschlagen; ['~it] Beurteilung f; Kostenanschlag m; **~ion** Urteil n, Meinung f; Achtung f.

estrange [is'treindʒ] entfremden.

estuary ['estjuəri] Flußmündung f (ins Meer).

etern|al [i(:)'tə:nl] ewig; **~ity** Ewigkeit f.

ether ['i:θə] Äther m.

ethics ['eθiks] sg Sittenlehre f, Ethik f; pl Moral f.

etymology [eti'mɔlədʒi] Etymologie f.

European [juərə'pi(:)ən] europäisch; Europäer(in).

evacuate [i'vækjueit] entleeren; evakuieren; räumen.

evade [i'veid] ausweichen.

evaporate [i'væpəreit] verdunsten od. verdampfen (lassen).

evasi|on [i'veiʒən] Ausweichen n; Ausflucht f; **~ve** [~siv] ausweichend.

eve [i:v] Vorabend m, -tag m.

even¹ ['i:vən] eben; glatt; gleichmäßig; ausgeglichen; gerade (Zahl).

even² selbst, sogar; **not ~** nicht einmal; **~ if, ~ though** selbst wenn.

evening ['i:vniŋ] Abend m; **this ~** heute abend; **~ dress** Abendanzug m; Abendkleid n; **~ paper** Abendzeitung f.

evensong ['i:vənsɔŋ] Abendandacht f.

event [i'vent] Ereignis n; sp.: Veranstaltung f; (Programm)Nummer f; **at all ~s** auf alle Fälle; **in the ~ of** im Falle; **~ful** ereignisreich.

eventual [i'ventʃuəl] schließlich; **~ly** schließlich.

ever ['evə] je(mals); immer; **~ after, ~ since** von der Zeit an, seitdem; **for ~** für immer; **~lasting** ewig; dauerhaft; **~more** immerfort.

every ['evri] jede(r, -s); all; **~ other day** jeden zweiten Tag; **~ few od. ten minutes** alle paar od. zehn Minuten; **~body** jeder(mann), alle; **~day** (all)täglich; Alltags...; **~one** jeder(mann), alle; **~thing** alles; **~where** überall.

eviden|ce ['evidəns] Beweis(material n) m; Zeugenaussage f; **give ~ce** aussagen; **~t** augenscheinlich, klar.

evil ['iːvl] übel, schlecht, schlimm, böse; Übel n; das Böse.

evince [i'vins] zeigen.

evoke [i'vəuk] (herauf)beschwören; hervorrufen.

evolution [iːvə'luːʃən] Entwicklung f.

evolve [i'vɔlv] (sich) entwickeln.

ewe [juː] Mutterschaf n.

ex- [eks-] ehemalig, früher.

exact [ig'zækt] genau; Zahlung eintreiben; (er-)fordern; **~itude** [~itjuːd] s. **exactness**; **~ly** genau; **~ness** Genauigkeit f.

exaggerat|e [ig'zædʒəreit] übertreiben; **~ion** Übertreibung f.

exalt [ig'zɔːlt] erhöhen, erheben; verherrlichen.

exam [ig'zæm] colloq. abbr. für **~ination** Examen n, Prüfung f; Untersuchung f; Vernehmung f; **~ine** [~in] untersuchen; prüfen; vernehmen, -hören.

example [ig'zɑːmpl] Beispiel n; Vorbild n; **for ~** zum Beispiel.

exasperate [ig'zɑːspəreit] ärgern, reizen.

excavate ['ekskəveit] ausgraben, -heben.

exceed [ik'siːd] überschreiten; übertreffen; **~ingly** außerordentlich.

excel [ik'sel] übertreffen; **~lence** ['eksələns] hervorragende Leistung; Vorzug m; **2lency** Exzellenz f; **~lent** ausgezeichnet.

except [ik'sept] ausnehmen; ausgenommen; abgesehen von; **~ for** Ausnahme f; **~ion** Ausnahme f; **~ional(ly)** außergewöhnlich.

excess [ik'ses] Übermaß n; Exzeß m; **~ fare** Zuschlag m; **~ive** übermäßig, -trieben; **~ luggage** Übergewicht n (Gepäck); **~ postage** Nachgebühr f.

exchange [iks'tʃeindʒ] (aus-, ein-, um)tauschen (**for** gegen); wechseln; (Aus-, Um)Tausch m; (Geld)Wechsel m; Börse f.

exchequer [iks'tʃekə]: **the 2 Brit.** das Finanzministerium.

excit|able [ik'saitəbl] reizbar; **~e** erregen; aufreizen; (auf)reizen; **~ed** aufgeregt; **~ement** Auf-, Erregung f; Reizung f; **~ing** erregend; aufregend, spannend.

exclaim [iks'kleim] ausrufen.

exclamation [eksklə'meiʃən] Ausruf m; **~ mark** Ausrufezeichen n.

exclu|de [iks'kluːd] ausschließen; **~sion** [~ʒən] Ausschluß m; **~sive** [~siv] ausschließlich; exklusiv.

excursion [iks'kəːʃən] Ausflug m.

excuse [iks'kjuːz] entschuldigen; **~ me** entschuldige(n Sie)!; [~s] Entschuldigung f.

execut|e ['eksikju:t] ausführen; mus., thea. vortragen, spielen; hinrichten; **~ion** Ausführung f; mus. Vortrag m; Hinrichtung f; **~ive** [ig'zekjutiv] vollziehend; Exekutive f; econ. leitender Angestellter, Geschäftsführer m.

exemplary [ig'zempləri] vorbildlich; abschreckend.

exempt [ig'zempt] befreit; befreien.

exercise ['eksəsaiz] Übung (-sarbeit) f; körperliche Bewegung; Ausübung f, Gebrauch m; **take** ~ sich Bewegung machen; vb: gebrauchen; (aus)üben; bewegen; sich Bewegung machen; **~-book** (Schul-, Übungs)Heft n.

exert [ig'zə:t] Einfluß etc. ausüben; **~ o.s.** sich anstrengen od. bemühen; **~ion** Anwendung f; Anstrengung f.

exhale [eks'heil] ausatmen, -dünsten; ausströmen.

exhaust [ig'zɔ:st] entleeren, auspumpen; erschöpfen; Abgas n; Auspuff m; **~ fumes** pl Auspuffgase pl; **~ion** Erschöpfung f; **~-pipe** Auspuffrohr n.

exhibit [ig'zibit] ausstellen; zeigen, aufweisen; Ausstellungsstück n; Beweisstück n; **~ion** [eksi-'biʃən] Ausstellung f; Zur-

schaustellung f; Brit. Stipendium m; **~ion grounds** pl Ausstellungsgelände n.

exile ['eksail] Exil n, Verbannung f; Verbannte m, f; verbannen.

exist [ig'zist] existieren, bestehen; leben; **~ence** Existenz f, Bestehen n, Leben n; **in ~ence, ~ent** vorhanden.

exit ['eksit] Ausgang m; Ausfahrt f; thea. Abgang m; thea. (geht) ab; **~ (road)** Autobahnausfahrt f; **~ visa** Ausreisevisum n.

expan|d [iks'pænd] (sich) ausbreiten od. ausdehnen od. erweitern; **~se** [~s] Ausdehnung f, Weite f; **~sion** Ausbreitung f; Ausdehnung f; Erweiterung f; **~sive** ausdehnungsfähig; ausgedehnt, weit.

expect [iks'pekt] erwarten; colloq. annehmen; **~ation** [ekspek'teiʃən] Erwartung f.

expedi|ent [iks'pi:djənt] zweckmäßig; Hilfsmittel n, (Not)Behelf m; **~tion** [ekspi'diʃən] Eile f; Expedition f, Forschungsreise f.

expel [iks'pel] vertreiben; ausstoßen, -schließen.

expen|d [iks'pend] Geld ausgeben; verwenden; verbrauchen; **~se** [~s] (Geld-)Ausgabe f; pl Unkosten pl, Spesen pl; **at the ~se of** auf Kosten von; **~sive** kostspielig, teuer.

experience [iks'piəriəns]

Erfahrung f; Erlebnis n; erfahren, erleben; **~d** erfahren.

experiment [iks'periment] Experiment n, Versuch m; [~ment] experimentieren.

expert ['ekspə:t] Experte m, Sachverständige m, Fachmann m; ['~, pred a. ~'pə:t] erfahren, geschickt; fachmännisch.

expir|ation [ekspaiə'reiʃən] Ausatmen n; Ablauf m; **~e** [iks'paiə] ausatmen; ablaufen; verfallen.

expl|ain [iks'plein] erklären, erläutern (**to s.o.** j-m); **~anation** [eksplə'neiʃən] Erklärung f.

explicit [iks'plisit] deutlich.

explode [iks'pləud] explodieren (lassen).

exploit [iks'plɔit] ausverwerten; ausbeuten.

explor|ation [eksplɔ:-'reiʃən] Erforschung f; **~e** [iks'plɔ:] erforschen; **~er** Forscher m.

explosi|on [iks'pləuʒən] Explosion f; fig. Ausbruch m; **~ve** [~siv] explosiv; Sprengstoff m.

export [iks'pɔ:t] exportieren, ausführen; ['~] Export m, Ausfuhr f; **~ation** Ausfuhr f; **~er** Exporteur m.

expos|e [iks'pəuz] aussetzen; ausstellen; phot. belichten; aufdecken; entlarven, bloßstellen; **~ition**

[ekspəu'ziʃən] Ausstellung f; **~ure** [iks'pəuʒə] Ausgesetztsein n; phot. Belichtung f; Enthüllung f, -larvung f; **~ure meter** Belichtungsmesser m.

express [iks'pres] ausdrücklich, deutlich; Expreß..., Eil...; Eilbote m; Schnellzug m; äußern, ausdrücken; auspressen; **~ion** Ausdruck m; **~ive** ausdrückend (**of** acc); ausdrucksvoll; **~ly** ausdrücklich, eigens; **~ train** Schnellzug m; **~way** Am. Schnellstraße f.

expulsion [iks'pʌlʃən] Vertreibung f; Ausschluß m; Ausweisung f.

exquisite [iks'kwizit] vorzüglich, ausgezeichnet.

extant [eks'tænt] (noch) vorhanden.

exten|d [iks'tend] ausdehnen; ausstrecken; vergrößern; verlängern; sich erstrecken; **~sion** Ausdehnung f; Verlängerung f; Anbau m; teleph. Nebenanschluß m; fig. Vergrößerung f, Erweiterung f; **~sive** ausgedehnt, umfassend; **~t** Ausdehnung f, Weite f, Größe f, Länge f; fig. Umfang m, Grad m; **to some ~t** einigermaßen.

exterior [eks'tiəriə] äußere, Außen...; Äußere n.

exterminate [iks'tə:mineit] ausrotten, vertilgen.

external [eks'tə:nl] äußere, äußerlich; Außen...

extinct [iks'tiŋkt] erlöschen; ausgestorben.

extinguish [iks'tiŋgwiʃ] (aus)löschen; vernichten.

extirpate ['ekstə:peit] ausrotten; *med.* entfernen.

extra ['ekstrə] zusätzlich, Extra..., Sonder..., Neben...; extra, besonders; Zusätzliche *n; pl* Nebenkosten *pl,* Zuschlag *m;* ~ **charge** Mehrpreis *m.*

extract ['ekstrækt] Auszug *m;* [iks'trækt] (heraus-)ziehen; entlocken; e-n Auszug machen; *tech.* gewinnen; ~**ion** (Heraus-)Ziehen *n;* Herkunft *f.*

extradite ['ekstrədait] *Verbrecher* ausliefern.

extraordinary [iks-'trɔ:dnri] außerordentlich; ungewöhnlich.

extravagan|ce [iks'trævigəns] Verschwendung *f;*

Überspanntheit *f;* ~**t** übertrieben; verschwenderisch.

extrem|e [iks'tri:m] äußerst, größt, höchst; Äußerste *n,* Extrem *n;* ~**ity** [~emiti] Äußerste *n;* (höchste) Not; *pl* Gliedmaßen *pl; mst pl* äußerste Maßnahmen *pl.*

exuberant [ig'zju:bərənt] üppig; überschwenglich.

exult [ig'zʌlt] frohlocken, jubeln.

eye [ai] Auge *n;* Öhr *n;* Öse *f; fig.* Blick *m;* ansehen, mustern; ~**ball** Augapfel *m;* ~**brow** Augenbraue *f;* ~**d** *in Zssgn:* ...äugig; (a pair of) ~**glasses** *pl* (e-e) Brille; ~**lash** (Augen)Wimper *f;* ~**lid** Augenlid *n;* ~**sight** Augen(licht *n) pl,* Sehkraft *f;* ~**witness** Augenzeug|e *m, -in f.*

F

fable ['feibl] Fabel *f.*

fabric ['fæbrik] Gewebe *n,* Stoff *m;* Gebäude *n; fig.* Struktur *f;* ~**ate** ['~eit] erfinden; fälschen.

fabulous ['fæbjuləs] sagenhaft, unglaublich.

façade [fə'sɑːd] Fassade *f.*

face [feis] Gesicht *n;* Oberfläche *f;* Vorderseite *f;* Zifferblatt *n;* Stirn *f;* **make** *od.* **pull a** ~ *od.* ~**s** Fratzen schneiden; *vb:* ansehen; gegenüberstehen; (hinaus)gehen

auf (*Fenster*); die Stirn bieten; einfassen; ~**cloth** Waschlappen *m.*

facil|itate [fə'siliteit] *et.* erleichtern; ~**ity** Leichtigkeit *f;* Gewandtheit *f; pl* Einrichtung(en *pl) f,* Anlage(n *pl) f;* Erleichterung(en *pl) f.*

fact [fækt] Tatsache *f;* Wirklichkeit *f,* Wahrheit *f;* **in** ~ in der Tat, tatsächlich.

factor ['fæktə] Faktor *m,* Umstand *m;* ~**y** Fabrik *f.*

faculty ['fækəlti] Fähigkeit f; Gabe f; univ. Fakultät f.

fade [feid] (ver)welken od. verblassen (lassen); schwinden.

fail [feil] fehlen; nachlassen; versagen; mißlingen, fehlschlagen; versäumen, unterlassen; Kanditat: durchfallen (lassen); im Stich lassen; **he cannot ~ to** er muß (einfach); **~ure** ['~jə] Fehlschlag m, Mißerfolg m; Ausbleiben n, Versagen n; Unterlassung f; Versager m.

faint [feint] schwach, matt; in Ohnmacht fallen.

fair¹ [feə] (Jahr)Markt m; Messe f, Ausstellung f.

fair² gerecht, ehrlich, anständig, fair; recht gut; reichlich; schön (Wetter); günstig (Wind); blond; hellhäutig; sauber, in Reinschrift; schön, hübsch (Frau); **play ~** ehrlich od. fair spielen; fig. ehrlich sein; **~ly** ziemlich; **~ness** Gerechtigkeit f, Fairneß f.

fairy ['fɛəri] Fee f; Elf(e f) m; **~tale** Märchen n.

faith [feiθ] Glaube m; Vertrauen n; Treue f; **~ful** treu; genau; **Yours ~fully** hochachtungsvoll; **~less** treulos.

fake [feik] Schwindel m; Fälschung f; Schwindler m; fälschen.

falcon ['fɔːlkən] Falke m.

fall [fɔːl] Fall(en n) m; Sturz m; Verfall m; Am. Herbst m; pl Wasserfall m; (irr) (ab-, ein-, zer-, ver)fallen; sinken; nachlassen (Wind); **~ back on** zurückgreifen auf; **~ ill**, **~ sick** krank werden; **~ in love with** sich verlieben in; **~ out** sich entzweien; **~ short of** den Erwartungen etc. nicht entsprechen; **~en** pp von **fall**.

false [fɔːls] falsch; **~hood** Lüge f. [fälschen.]

falsify ['fɔːlsifai] (ver-)/

falter ['fɔːltə] schwanken; zaudern; straucheln; stocken (Stimme); stammeln.

fame [feim] Ruhm m, Ruf m; **~d** berühmt (**for** wegen).

familiar [fə'miljə] vertraut; gewohnt; ungezwungen; Vertraute m, f; **~ity** [~i'æriti] Vertrautheit f; (plumpe) Vertraulichkeit; **~ize** vertraut machen.

family ['fæmili] Familie f; Familien...; **~ name** Familien-, Nachname m; **~ tree** Stammbaum m.

famine ['fæmin] Hungersnot f; Mangel m; **~sh** verhungern.

famous ['feiməs] berühmt.

fan¹ [fæn] Fächer m; Ventilator m.

fan² colloq. begeisterter Anhänger, Fan m.

fanatic [fə'nætik] Fanatiker(in); **~(al)** fanatisch.

fanciful ['fænsiful] phantasievoll; phantastisch.

fancy ['fænsi] Phantasie *f*; Einbildung(skraft) *f*; Idee *f*, Laune *f*; Vorliebe *f*; Phantasie...; sich vorstellen; sich einbilden; gern mögen; ~ **cake** Torte *f*; ~ **be** *v/refl.* sich vorgehen (*Uhr*).

fang [fæŋ] Fangzahn *m*; Giftzahn *m*.

fantastic [fæn'tæstik] phantastisch.

far [fɑ:] fern, entfernt; weit; (sehr) viel; **as ~ as** bis; soweit; **by ~** bei weitem, weitaus; ~ **from** weit entfernt von; **~away** weitentfernt.

fare [fɛə] Fahrgeld *n*; Fahrgast *m*; Kost *f*; (er-)gehen; ~ **well** lebe(n Sie) wohl!; Abschied *m*, Lebewohl *n*.

far-fetched weithergeholt.

farm [fɑ:m] Bauernhof *m*, Farm *f*, Gehöft *n*; *Land* bewirtschaften; **~er** Bauer *m*, Landwirt *m*; **~hand** Landarbeiter(in); **~house** Bauern-, Gutshaus *n*; **~ing** Landwirtschaft *f*; **~worker** Landarbeiter(in).

far-sighted weitsichtig; *fig.* weitblickend.

farthe|r ['fɑ:ðə] *comp von* **far**; **~st** ['~ist] *sup von* **far**.

fascinat|e ['fæsineit] bezaubern; **~ion** Zauber *m*, Reiz *m*.

fashion ['fæʃən] Mode *f*; Art *f*, Stil *m*; herstellen, machen; **~able** ['~ʃnəbl] modern, modisch, elegant.

fast[1] [fɑ:st] schnell; fest; treu; echt, beständig (*Farbe*); **be ~** vorgehen (*Uhr*).

fast[2] Fasten *n*; fasten.

fasten ['fɑ:sn] befestigen, festbinden, -schnallen, anbinden; *Augen etc.* richten (**on** auf); sich schließen lassen; **~er** Verschluß *m*.

fastidious [fæs'tidiəs] anspruchsvoll, wählerisch.

fast train Eilzug *m*.

fat [fæt] fett; dick; Fett *n*.

fat|al ['feitl] tödlich; verhängnisvoll (**to** für); **~e** [feit] Schicksal *n*; Verhängnis *n*.

father ['fɑ:ðə] Vater *m*; **~hood** Vaterschaft *f*; **~in-law** Schwiegervater *m*; **~less** vaterlos; **~ly** väterlich.

fathom ['fæðəm] Klafter *m*, *n*; *mar.* Faden *m*; loten; *fig.* ergründen; **~less** unergründlich.

fatigue [fə'ti:g] Ermüdung *f*; Strapaze *f*; ermüden.

fatten ['fætn] fett machen *od.* werden; mästen.

faucet ['fɔ:sit] *Am. tech.* Hahn *m*.

fault [fɔ:lt] Fehler *m*, Defekt *m*; Schuld *f*; **find ~ with** et. auszusetzen haben an; **~less** fehlerfrei, tadellos; **~y** fehler-, mangelhaft.

favo(u)r ['feivə] begünsti-

fen

gen; Gunst(bezeigung) f;
Gefallen m; **in ~ of** zugunsten von; **do s.o. a ~**
j-m e-n Gefallen tun;
~able günstig; **~ite** ['-rit]
Günstling m, Liebling m,
sp. Favorit(in); bevorzugt,
Lieblings...

fawn [fɔːn] (Reh)Kitz n;
Rehbraun n.

fear [fiə] Furcht f, Angst f;
(be)fürchten, sich fürch-
ten vor; **~ful** furchtsam;
furchtbar; besorgt; **~less**
furchtlos.

feast [fiːst] Fest(tag m) n,
Feiertag m; Festmahl n,
Schmaus m; (festlich)
bewirten; schmausen;
sich weiden.

feat [fiːt] Helden-, Großtat
f; Kunststück n.

feather ['feðə] Feder f;
pl Gefieder n; mit Federn
schmücken; **~bed** (Feder-)
Unterbett n; **~ed** be-,
gefiedert; **~y** federartig.

feature ['fiːtʃə] (Ge-
sichts-, Charakter)Zug m;
(charakteristisches) Merkmal; Haupt-, Spielfilm
m; Zeitung, Rundfunk:
Feature n; pl Gesicht n.

February ['februəri]
Februar m.

fed [fed] pret u. pp von
feed.

federal ['fedərəl] Bun-
des...; **~tion** Staatenbund
m; Verband m.

fee [fiː] Gebühr f; Honorar f.

feeble ['fiːbl] schwach.

feed [fiːd] Futter n, Nah-

rung f; Fütterung f; tech.
Zuführung f, Speisung f;
(irr) (ver)füttern; (er-)
nähren, speisen, zu essen
geben; tech. speisen, zu-
führen; weiden; **be fed
up with** sl. et. satt haben;
~er road Zubringer-
straße f; **~ing-bottle**
Saugflasche f.

feel [fiːl] (irr) (sich) fühlen;
befühlen; empfinden;
sich anfühlen; **~ for**
tasten nach; **~ well** od.
bad sich wohl od. elend
fühlen; Gefühl n; Emp-
findung f; **~er** Fühler m;
~ing mitfühlend; Gefühl n.

feet [fiːt] pl von **foot.**

fell [fel] pret von **fall;**
niederschlagen; fällen.

felloe ['feləu] (Rad)Felge f.

fellow ['feləu] Gefährt|e
m, -in f, Kamerad(in);
colloq. Kerl m, Bursche m;
Gegenstück n; Mit...;
~ being Mitmensch m;
~citizen Mitbürger m;
~countryman Lands-
mann m; **~ship** Gemein-
schaft f; Kameradschaft f.

felon ['felən] Schwer-
verbrecher m; **~y** Kapitalverbrechen n.

felt¹ [felt] pret u. pp von
feel.

felt² Filz m.

female ['fiːmeil] weiblich;
zo. Weibchen n.

feminine ['feminin] weiblich.

fen [fen] Fenn n, Marsch f;
Moor n.

fence

fenc|e [fens] Zaun *m*; fechten; **~e (in)** ein-, umzäunen; **~ing** Fechten *n*.

fend [fend]: **~ for** sorgen für; **~ off** abwehren; *~er Am.* Kotflügel *m*.

ferment [fɜː'ment] Ferment *n*; [fəː'ment] gären (lassen); **~ation** Gärung *f*.

fern [fɜːn] Farn(kraut *n*) *m*.

ferocity [fə'rɒsiti] Grausamkeit *f*; Wildheit *f*.

ferry ['feri] Fähre *f*; übersetzen; **~-boat** Fähre *f*.

fertil|e ['fɜːtail] fruchtbar; **~ity** [~'tiliti] Fruchtbarkeit *f*; **~ize** ['~ilaiz] befruchten; düngen; **~izer** (Kunst)Dünger *m*.

fervent ['fɜːvənt] glühend (heiß); leidenschaftlich.

fester ['festə] eitern.

festiv|al ['festəvəl] Fest *n*, Feier *f*; Festspiele *pl*; **~e** festlich, heiter; **~ities** [~'tiviti] *pl* Fest *n*.

fetch [fetʃ] holen; *Preis* erzielen.

fetter ['fetə] Fessel *f*.

feud [fjuːd] Fehde *f*.

fever ['fiːvə] Fieber *n*; **~ish** fieb(e)rig; *fig.* fieberhaft.

few [fjuː] wenige; **a ~** einige, ein paar; **quite a ~** e-e ganze Menge.

fiancé [fi'ã:nsei] Verlobte *m*; **~e** [~] Verlobte *f*.

fib [fib] schwindeln.

fib|re, *Am. ~er* ['faibə] Faser *f*; **~rous** faserig.

fickle ['fikl] wankelmütig.

fict|ion ['fikʃən] Erfindung

f; Roman(literatur *f*) *m*; **~itious** [~'tiʃəs] erfunden.

fiddle ['fidl] Fiedel *f*, Geige *f*; fiedeln; herumspielen; *~r* Fiedler *m*, Geiger *m*.

fidelity [fi'deliti] Treue *f*.

fidget ['fidʒit] (herum)zappeln; **~y** unruhig, zappelig.

field [fiːld] Feld *n*; (Sport-)Platz *m*; Gebiet *n*, Bereich *m*; **~ events** *pl sp.* Sprung- u. Wurfwettkämpfe *pl*; **~-glasses** *pl* Fernglas *n*; Feldstecher *m*.

fiend [fiːnd] böser Feind, Teufel *m*; in *Zssgn colloq.* Süchtige *m*, *f*; Fanatiker (-in).

fierce [fiəs] wild; heftig.

fiery ['faiəri] glühend; *fig.* feurig, hitzig.

fife [faif] Querpfeife *f*.

fif|teen(th) ['fif'tiːn(θ)] fünfzehn(te); **~th** [fifθ] fünfte; Fünftel *n*; **~thly** ['~θli] fünftens; **~tieth** ['~tiiθ] fünfzigste; **~ty** fünfzig; Fünfzig *f*.

fig [fig] Feige *f*.

fight [fait] Kampf *m*; Schlägerei *f*; Kampflust *f*; (*irr*) bekämpfen; erkämpfen; kämpfen, sich schlagen; *~er* Kämpfer *m*, Streiter *m*; Jagdflugzeug *n*.

figurative ['figjurətiv] bildlich.

figure ['figə] Figur *f*; Gestalt *f*; Ziffer *f*; abbilden; mit Mustern schmücken; sich *et.* vorstellen; e~e Rolle spielen; **~ out** ausrechnen; verstehen; **~skating** Eiskunstlauf m.

file[1] [fail] Ordner m; Akte f; Akten pl, Ablage f; Reihe f; Briefe etc. einordnen, abheften, -legen; hinter-ea. marschieren.

file[2] Feile f; feilen.

fill [fil] (sich) füllen; an-, aus-, erfüllen; **~ in** Formular ausfüllen; Namen einsetzen; **~ up** an-, vollfüllen, mot. volltanken.

fillet ['filit] Filet n.

filling ['filiŋ] Füllung f; **~ station** Am. Tankstelle f.

filly ['fili] (Stuten)Füllen n.

film [film] Häutchen n; Film m; (ver)filmen.

filter ['filtə] Filter m; filtern.

filth [filθ] Schmutz m; **~y** schmutzig; fig. unflätig.

fin [fin] Flosse f.

final ['fainl] letzt; endgültig; End..., Schluß...; oft pl Schlußprüfung f; oft pl sp. Finale n, Endspiel n; **~ly** endlich, schließlich.

finance [fai'næns] Finanzwesen n; pl Finanzen pl; finanzieren; **~ial** [~ʃəl] finanziell; **~ier** [~siə] Finanzmann m; Financier m.

finch [fintʃ] Fink m.

find [faind] Fund m; (irr) finden, (an)treffen, entdecken; jur. für schuldig erklären; beschaffen; **(out)** herausfinden; **~ings** pl Befund m; Urteil n.

fine[1] [fain] Geldstrafe f; zu e~r Geldstrafe verurteilen.

fine[2] schön; fein; rein; spitz, dünn; vornehm; colloq. gut, bestens; **I am ~** es geht mir gut; **~ry** Putz m, Staat m.

finger ['fiŋgə] Finger m; betasten; **~nail** Fingernagel m; **~print** Fingerabdruck m.

finish ['finiʃ] (be)enden, abschließen, vollenden; polieren, glätten; Ende n; Vollendung f, letzter Schliff; **~ing line** Ziellinie f.

Finn [fin] Finne m, -in f; **~ish** finnisch; Finnisch n.

fir [fə:] Tanne f.

fire ['faiə] an-, entzünden; Ziegel etc. brennen; heizen; colloq. rausschmeißen, entlassen; (ab)feuern, schießen; Feuer n; **catch ~**, **take ~** Feuer fangen; **on ~** in Brand, in Flammen; **~alarm** Feuermelder m; **~arm** Schußwaffe f; **~brigade**, Am. **~ department** Feuerwehr f; **~engine** Löschfahrzeug n; **~escape** Feuerleiter f; Nottreppe f; **~extinguisher** Feuerlöscher m; **~man** Feuerwehrmann m; Heizer m; **~place** Kamin m; **~proof** feuerfest; **~side** Kamin m; **~wood** Brennholz n; **~works** pl Feuerwerk n.

firm

firm [fəːm] fest; standhaft; Firma *f*; **~ness** Festigkeit *f*.

first [fəːst] erst; best; zuerst; erstens; **~ of all** zu allererst; *der, die, das* Erste; **'at ~** zuerst, anfangs; **~ aid** Erste Hilfe; **~-aid box** Verband(s)-kasten *m*; **~-aid kit** Verband(s)zeug *n*; **~-born** erstgeboren; **~ class** erster Klasse; **~-class** erstklassig; **~ floor** erster Stock, *Am.* Erdgeschoß *n*; **~ly** erstens; **~ name** Vorname *m*; **~-rate** erstklassig.

firth [fəːθ] Förde *f*, (weite) Mündung.

fish [fiʃ], *pl* **~(es)** ['~iz] Fisch *m*; fischen, angeln; **~bone** Gräte *f*.

fisher|**man** ['fiʃəmən] Fischer *m*; **~y** Fischerei *f*.

fishing ['fiʃiŋ] Fischen *n*; **~-line** Angelschnur *f*; **~rod** Angelrute *f*; **~tackle** Angelgerät *n*.

fishmonger ['fiʃmʌŋgə] Fischhändler *m*.

fiss|**ion** ['fiʃən] Spaltung *f*; **~ure** ['fiʃə] Spalt(e *f*) *m*, Riß *m*.

fist [fist] Faust *f*.

fit [fit] Anfall *m*; geeignet, passend; schicklich; tauglich; in (guter) Form, fit; passen, sitzen (*Kleid*); passen für *od.* dat; an-passen, geeignet machen; **~ (on)** anprobieren; **~ out** ausrüsten; **~ up** einrichten, ausstatten; **~ness** Gesund-heit *f*; Fähigkeit *f*; Schick-

lichkeit *f*; **~ter** Monteur *m*, Installateur *m*; **~ting** passend; schicklich; In-stallation *f*; Anprobe *f*; *pl* Einrichtung *f*.

five [faiv] fünf; Fünf *f*.

fix [fiks] befestigen; *Augen etc.* richten; fesseln; be-stimmen; fixieren; *Am. colloq.* richten; **~ (up)on** sich entschließen für; **~ up** arrangieren; *j-n* unter-bringen; *colloq.* heikle Lage, Klemme *f*; **~ed** fest; bestimmt; starr; **~tures** *pl* festes Inventar.

fizz [fiz] zischen, sprudeln.

flabbergast ['flæbəgɑːst] *colloq.*: **be ~ed** platt sein.

flabby ['flæbi] schlaff.

flag [flæg] Flagge *f*, Fahne *f*; Fliese *f*; Schwertlilie *f*; beflaggen; schlaff herab-hängen; *fig.* nachlassen; **~stone** Fliese *f*, Platte *f*.

flake [fleik] Flocke *f*; *vb*: **~ off** abblättern.

flame [fleim] Flamme *f*, Feuer *n*; flammen, lodern.

flank [flæŋk] Flanke *f*, flankieren.

flannel ['flænl] Flanell *m*; Waschlappen *m*; *pl* Flanell-hose *f*.

flap [flæp] (*Hut*-)Krempe *f*; Klappe *f*; Klaps *m*, Schlag *m*; schlagen; flattern.

flare [flɛə] flackern; sich bauschen; **~ up** auf-flammen; *fig.* aufbrausen.

flash [flæʃ] Blitz *m*; Auf-blitzen *n*; kurze Meldung;

aufleuchten *od.* -blitzen (lassen); *od.* -blitzen *Blick* werfen; funken; **~bulb** Blitzbirne *f*; **~cube** Blitzwürfel *m*; **~light** Blinklicht *n*; *phot.* Blitzlicht *n*; Taschenlampe *f*; **~ of lightning** Blitzstrahl *m*.

flask [flɑːsk] Taschenflasche *f*; Thermosflasche *f*.

flat [flæt] flach, eben; platt; schal; *econ.* flau; klar; glatt; völlig; Fläche *f*, Ebene *f*; Flachland *n*; *mot.* Plattfuß *m*; *Brit.* (Miet)Wohnung *f*; **~ten** (ein)ebnen; abflachen; flach werden.

flatter ['flætə] schmeicheln; **~y** Schmeichelei *f*.

flavo(u)r ['fleivə] (Bei-)Geschmack *m*; Aroma *n*; würzen.

flaw [flɔː] Sprung *m*, Riß *m*; Fehler *m*; **~less** fehlermakellos.

flax [flæks] Flachs *m*.

flea [fliː] Floh *m*.

fled [fled] *pret u. pp von* **flee.**

fledged [fledʒd] flügge

flee [fliː] *(irr)* fliehen.

fleece [fliːs] Vlies *n*, Schaffell *n*; *fig.* prellen.

fleet [fliːt] schnell; Flotte *f*; ♀ **Street** die (Londoner) Presse.

flesh [fleʃ] Fleisch *n*; **~y** fleischig; dick.

flew [fluː] *pret von* **fly²**.

flexible ['fleksəbl] flexibel, biegsam; *fig.* anpassungsfähig.

flick [flik] leicht u. schnell schlagen; schnellen.

flicker ['flikə] flackern, flimmern; flattern.

flier ['flaiə] s. **flyer.**

flight [flait] Flucht *f*; Flug *m*; Schwarm *m* (*Vögel etc.*); *aer.* Flug(verbindung *f*) *m*; **~ of stairs** Treppe *f*.

flimsy ['flimzi] dünn; *fig.* fadenscheinig.

flinch [flintʃ] zurückweichen.

fling [fliŋ] Wurf *m*; Versuch *m*; *(irr)* eilen, stürzen; werfen, schleudern; **~ open** *Tür* aufreißen.

flint [flint] Kiesel *m*; Feuerstein *m*.

flip [flip] schnipsen.

flippant ['flipənt] frech.

flipper ['flipə] (Schwimm-)Flosse *f*.

flirt [fləːt] flirten, kokettieren; **~ation** Flirt *m*.

flit [flit] flitzen, huschen; (umher)flattern.

float [fləut] Schwimmer *m*; Floß *n*; flottmachen; schwimmen *od.* treiben (lassen); schweben.

flock [flɔk] (*Schaf*)Herde *f* (*a. fig.*); Schar *f*; sich scharen; zs.-strömen.

floe [fləu] Eisscholle *f*.

flog [flɔg] peitschen; prügeln.

flood [flʌd] Flut *f*; Überschwemmung *f*; *fig.* Flut *f*, Strom *m*; überfluten, -schwemmen; **~lights** *pl* Flutlicht *n*; **~-tide** Flut *f*.

floor [flɔ:] Fußboden *m*;
Stock(werk *n*) *m*, Etage *f*;
take the ~ das Wort ergreifen; *vb*: e-n (Fuß-)
Boden legen; zu Boden
schlagen; verwirren; **~
cloth** Putzlappen *m*; **~
lamp** Stehlampe *f*; **~
show** Nachtklubvorstel-
lung *f*.

flop [flɔp]: **~ down** (sich)
hinplumpsen lassen.

florist ['flɔrist] Blumen-
händler(in).

flounder ['flaundə] Flunder *f*.

flour ['flauə] (feines) Mehl.

flourish ['flʌriʃ] Schnörkel
m; Schwingen *n*; Tusch
m; blühen, gedeihen;
schwingen.

flow [fləu] Fließen *n*; Strom
m, Fluß *m*; fließen.

flower ['flauə] Blume *f*;
Blüte *f* (*a. fig.*); blühen.

flown [fləun] *pp von* **fly²**.

fluctuate ['flʌktjueit]
schwanken.

flu [flu:] *colloq. abbr. von*
influenza.

fluent ['flu(:)ənt] fließend,
geläufig.

fluff [flʌf] Flaum *m*; **~y**
flaumig, flockig.

fluid ['flu(:)id] flüssig;
Flüssigkeit *f*. {**fling**.\

flung [flʌŋ] *pret u. pp von*\

flunk [flʌŋk] *Am. colloq.*
durchfallen (lassen).

flurry ['flʌri] Bö *f*; Schauer
m; Aufregung *f*, Unruhe
f; nervös machen, beun-
ruhigen.

flush [flʌʃ] Spülung *f*;
Erröten *n*; Erregung *f*;
überfluten; (aus)spülen;
(er)röten.

fluster ['flʌstə] Aufregung
f; nervös machen, ver-
wirren; sich aufregen.

flute [flu:t] Flöte *f*.

flutter ['flʌtə] Geflatter *n*;
Erregung *f*; flattern (mit).

flux [flʌks] Fließen *n*,
Fluß *m*.

fly¹ [flai] Fliege *f*.

fly² (*irr*) fliegen (lassen);
stürmen, stürzen; flattern,
wehen; verfliegen (*Zeit*);
Drachen steigen lassen;
fliehen aus; **~ north** nach
Norden fliegen; **~
(across)** überfliegen; **~
into a rage** *od.* **passion**
in Wut geraten; **~er**
Flieger *m*.

flying ['flaiiŋ] fliegend;
Flug...; **~ machine** Flug-
apparat *m*, -zeug *n*; **~
squad** Überfallkomman-
do *n*; **~ time** Flugzeit *f*.

fly|-over (Straßen)Über-
führung *f*; **~weight**
Boxen: Fliegengewicht *n*.

foal [fəul] Fohlen *n*.

foam [fəum] Schaum *m*;
schäumen; **~y** schaumig.

focus ['fəukəs] Brennpunkt
m; *opt.* scharf einstellen;
fig. konzentrieren.

foe [fəu] *poet.* Feind *m*.

fog [fɔg] (dichter) Nebel
m; **~gy** neb(e)lig; *fig.* nebel-
haft.

foible ['fɔibl] *fig.* Schwäche *f*.

foil¹ [fɔil] Folie *f; fig.* Kontrast *m,* Hintergrund *m.*

foil² vereiteln.

fold¹ [fəuld] (Schaf)Hürde *f,* Pferch *m; eccl.* Herde *f;* einpferchen.

fold² Falte *f;* falten; *Arme* kreuzen; **~er** Aktendeckel *m,* Schnellhefter *m;* Faltprospekt *m.*

folding ['fəuldiŋ] zs.-legbar, Klapp...; **~ boat** Faltboot *m;* **~ chair** Klappstuhl *m.*

foliage ['fəuliidʒ] Laub (-werk) *n,* Blätter *pl.*

folk [fəuk] *pl* Leute *pl;* **~lore** ['⌒lɔ:] Folklore *f;* **~s** *pl colloq.* Leute *pl* (*Angehörige*)*;* **~song** Volkslied *n.*

follow ['fɔləu] folgen(*dat*)*;* befolgen; *Beruf* ausüben; **~er** Anhänger(in); **~ing** Anhängerschaft *f.*

folly ['fɔli] Torheit *f.*

fond [fɔnd] zärtlich; vernarrt; **be ~ of** gern haben, lieben; **~le** liebkosen, streicheln; **~ness** Zärtlichkeit *f;* Vorliebe *f.*

food [fu:d] Speise *f,* Essen *n,* Nahrung *f;* Nahrungs-, Lebensmittel *pl;* Futter *n.*

fool [fu:l] (herum)spielen; zum Narren halten; betrügen; verleiten; Narr *m,* Närrin *f,* Dummkopf *m;* Hanswurst *m;* **make a ~ of o.s.** sich lächerlich machen; **~hardy** tollkühn; **~ish** töricht, dumm; **~ishness** Torheit

f; **~proof** narrensicher.

foot [fut], *pl* **feet** [fi:t] Fuß *m;* Fußende *n;* **on ~** zu Fuß; *fig.* im Gange; **~ the bill** die Rechnung bezahlen; **~ball** Fußball *m;* **~baller** Fußballspieler *m;* **~board** Trittbrett *n;* **~ brake** Fußbremse *f;* **~hills** *pl* Vorgebirge *n;* **~hold** fester Stand; **~ing** Stand *m,* Halt *m; fig.* Stellung *f;* (*Kampf etc.*) *f;* **~lights** *pl* Rampenlicht *n;* **~path** (Fuß-) Pfad *m,* Gehweg *m;* **~print** Fußspur *f;* **~step** Fußstapfe *f;* Schritt *m.*

for [fɔ:, fə] für; als; *Zweck, Ziel, Richtung:* zu, nach; *warten, hoffen etc. auf; sich sehnen etc. nach; Grund:* aus, vor, wegen; **~ three days** drei Tage lang; seit drei Tagen; **walk ~ a mile** eine Meile (weit) gehen.

forbade [fə'bæd] *pret von* **forbid.**

forbear [fɔ:'bɛə] (*irr*) unterlassen, sich enthalten.

forbid [fə'bid] (*irr*) verbieten; **~den** *pp* verboten; **~ding** abstoßend.

forbore [fɔ:'bɔ:] *pret,* **~ne** *pp von* **forbear.**

force [fɔ:s] Kraft *f,* Gewalt *f;* Zwang *m;* Nachdruck *m;* **armed ~s** *pl* Streitkräfte *pl;* **come of.** Kraft treten *od.* setzen; *vb:* (er-) zwingen; **~ (open)** auf-

forceps

brechen; **~d landing**
Notlandung f.

forceps ['fɔ:seps], pl ~
med. Zange f.

forcible ['fɔ:səbl] gewaltsam; überzeugend.

ford [fɔ:d] Furt f; durchwaten.

fore [fɔ:] vorder, Vorder...;
~boding [~'bəudiŋ]
Ahnung f; **~cast** Voraus-,
Vorhersage f; (irr **cast**)
vorhersehen, voraussagen;
~fathers pl Vorfahren
pl; **~finger** Zeigefinger
m; **~foot** Vorderfuß m;
~ground Vordergrund m;
~head ['fɔrid] Stirn f.

foreign ['fɔrin] fremd;
ausländisch; **~** currency
Devisen pl; **~er** Ausländer
(-in), Fremde m, f; **~**
exchange Devisen pl;
2 Office Brit. Außenministerium n; **~** **policy**
Außenpolitik f; **~** **trade**
Außenhandel m.

fore|leg Vorderbein n;
~man Vorarbeiter m,
Werkmeister m; jur.
Sprecher m (der Geschworenen); **~most** vorderst; erst; zuerst; **~noon**
Vormittag m; **~see** (irr
see) vorhersehen; **~sight**
Voraussicht f, Vorsorge f.

forest ['fɔrist] Wald m (a.
fig.), Forst m; **~er** Förster
m; **~ry** Forstwirtschaft f.

fore|taste Vorgeschmack
m; **~tell** (irr **tell**) vorhersagen.   [mer.]

forever [fə'revə] (für) im-

foreword Vorwort n.

forfeit ['fɔ:fit] einbüßen,
verscherzen; Strafe f.

forge [fɔ:dʒ] Schmiede f;
schmieden; fälschen;
~ry Fälschung f.

forget [fə'get] (irr) vergessen; **~ful** vergeßlich; **~me-not** Vergißmeinnicht n.

forgiv|e [fə'giv] (irr **give**)
vergeben, -zeihen; **~eness**
Verzeihung f; **~ing** versöhnlich.

forgot [fə'gɔt] pret, **~ten**
pp von **forget**.

fork [fɔ:k] Gabel f; sich
gabeln, abzweigen.

forlorn [fə'lɔ:n] verloren,
-lassen; unglücklich.

form [fɔ:m] Form f; Gestalt f; Formular n;
(Schul)Bank f (Schul)-
Klasse f; Kondition f;
(sich) formen od. bilden
od. gestalten.

formal ['fɔ:məl] förmlich;
formell; äußerlich; **~ity**
[~'mæliti] Förmlichkeit f,
Formalität f.

format|ion [fɔ:'meiʃən]
Bildung f; **~ive** [~'mətiv]
formend, gestaltend.

former ['fɔ:mə] früher,
ehemalig; **the ~** der
erstere; **~ly** früher.

formidable ['fɔ:midəbl]
schrecklich; ungeheuer.

formulate ['fɔ:mjuleit]
formulieren.

for|sake [fə'seik] (irr) verlassen; aufgeben; **~saken**
pp, **~sook** [fə'suk] pret
von **forsake**.

fort [fɔ:t] Fort n.

forth [fɔ:θ] heraus; weiter, fort(an); **~com-ing** bevorstehend; **~with** sogleich. [ste.]

fortieth ['fɔ:tiiθ] vierzig-ʃ

fortify ['fɔ:tifai] befestigen; fig. stärken.

fortnight ['fɔ:tnait] vierzehn Tage; **today** heute in vierzehn Tagen.

fortress ['fɔ:tris] Festung f.

fortunate ['fɔ:tʃnət] glücklich; **~ly** glücklicherweise.

fortune ['fɔ:tʃən] Glück n; Schicksal n; Vermögen n.

forty ['fɔ:ti] vierzig; Vierzig f.

forward ['fɔ:wəd] adj vorwärts; vorder; zeitig; vorlaut; fortschrittlich; adv (selten **~s**) nach vorn, vorwärts; (her)vor; **~** (Ge)Stürmer m; (be)fördern; (ver)senden; Brief etc. nachsenden.

foster|-child ['fɔstətʃaild] Pflegekind n; **~-parents** pl Pflegeeltern pl.

fought [fɔ:t] pret u. pp von **fight**.

foul [faul] schmutzig (a. fig.); faul, verdorben; schlecht (a. Wetter); übelriechend; sp. unfair, regelwidrig; Foul n; be-, verschmutzen.

found [faund] pret u. pp von **find**; gründen; stiften; tech. gießen; **~ation** Gründung f; Stiftung f; oft pl Fundament n; fig.

Grundlage f; **~er** Gründer(in); Stifter(in); **~ling** Findelkind n.

fountain ['fauntin] Springbrunnen m; Quelle f (bsd. fig.); **~-pen** Füllfederhalter m.

four [fɔ:] vier; Vier f; **~score** achtzig; **~stroke engine** Viertaktmotor m; **~teen** [~'ti:n(θ)] vierzehn(te); **~th** [fɔ:θ] vierte; Viertel n; **~thly** viertens.

fowl [faul] Haushuhn n; Geflügel n; Vogel m; **~ing-piece** Vogel-, Schrotflinte f.

fox [fɔks] Fuchs m.

fract|ion ['frækʃən] Bruch (-teil) m; **~ure** (bsd. Knochen)Bruch m; brechen. [brechlich.]

fragile ['frædʒail] zer-ʃ

fragment ['frægmənt] Bruchstück n.

fragran|ce ['freigrəns] Wohlgeruch m, Duft m; **~t** wohlriechend, duftend.

frail [freil] ge-, zerbrechlich; schwach; **~ty** fig. Schwäche f.

frame [freim] Rahmen m; Gerüst n; (Brillen)Gestell n; Körper(bau) m; **~ of mind** Gemütsverfassung f; bilden, formen, bauen; (ein)rahmen; **~house** Holzhaus n; **~work** tech. Gerüst n.

franchise ['fræntʃaiz] Wahlrecht n; Bürgerrecht n.

frank [fræŋk] offen, aufrichtig.

frankfurter ['fræŋkfətə] Frankfurter Würstchen.

frankness ['fræŋknis] Offenheit f.

frantic ['fræntik] wild, rasend; wahnsinnig.

fratern|al [frə'tə:nl] brüderlich; **.ity** Brüderlichkeit f; Bruderschaft f.

fraud [frɔ:d] Betrug m; Schwindel m; Schwindler m.

fray [frei] (sich) durchscheuern.

freak [fri:k] (verrückter) Einfall, Laune f; verrückter Kerl, Sonderling m.

freckle ['frekl] Sommersprosse f.

free [fri:] befreien; freilassen; frei; freigebig; **~ and easy** zwanglos; **set ~** freilassen; **.dom** Freiheit f; Offenheit f; Zwanglosigkeit f; (plumpe) Vertraulichkeit; **.mason** Freimaurer m; **~ port** Freihafen m; **~ ticket** Freikarte f; **~ time** Freizeit f; **.way** Am. Schnellstraße f; **.wheel** Freilauf m.

freez|e [fri:z] (irr) (ge-) frieren; erstarren; zum Gefrieren bringen; Fleisch etc. einfrieren, tiefkühlen; **.ing point** Gefrierpunkt m.

freight [freit] Fracht(geld n, -gut n) f; Am. Güter...; beladen; **.er** Frachter m.

French [frentʃ] französisch;

Französisch n; **the ~** pl die Franzosen pl; **.man** Franzose m; **~ window** Balkon-, Glastür f; **.woman** Französin f.

frequen|cy ['fri:kwənsi] Häufigkeit f; phys. Frequenz f; **.t** häufig; [fri'kwent] (oft) be- od. aufsuchen.

fresh [freʃ] frisch; neu; unerfahren; **.man** Student m im ersten Jahr; **.ness** Frische f; Neuheit f; **.water** Süßwasser...

fret [fret] (sich) ärgern.

friar ['fraiə] (Bettel)Mönch m.

friction ['frikʃən] Reibung f; fig. Spannung f.

Friday ['fraidi] Freitag m.

fridge [fridʒ] colloq. Kühlschrank m.

fried [fraid] gebraten, gebacken, Brat..., Back...

friend [frend] Freund(in); Bekannte m, f; **make ~s** Freundschaft schließen; **.ly** freund(schaft)lich; **.ship** Freundschaft f.

frig|e [fridʒ] s. **fridge**.

fright [frait] Schreck(en) m; zum erschrecken; **.ened: be ~ of** colloq. sich fürchten vor; **.ful** schrecklich. {stig.}

frigid ['fridʒid] kalt, frostig.

frill [fril] Krause f, Rüsche f.

fringe [frindʒ] Franse f; Rand m; Pony m (Frisur).

frisk [frisk] hüpfen; **.y** lebhaft, munter.

fro [frəu]: **to and ~** hin und her, auf und ab.

frock [frɔk] Kutte f; Kleid n.

frog [frɔg] Frosch m.

frolic ['frɔlik] scherzen, spaßen; **~some** ['~səm] vergnügt, ausgelassen.

from [frɔm, frəm] von; aus, von ... aus od. her, aus ... heraus, von ... herab; aus, vor, infolge von; **~ ... to** von ... bis.

front [frʌnt] gegenüberstehen, -liegen, mit der Front nach ... zu liegen; Vorderseite f; Front f (a. mil.); Strandpromenade f; Vorder...; **in ~** vorn; **in ~ of** räumlich: vor; **~door** Haus-, Vordertür f; **~ garden** Vorgarten m; **~ier** ['~iə] Grenze f; Grenz...; **~ page** Titelseite f; **~ seat** Vordersitz m; **~ tyre** Vorderreifen m; **~ wheel** Vorderrad n; **~-wheel drive** Vorderradantrieb m.

frost [frɔst] Frost m; Reif m; mit Reif od. Eis überziehen; mit Puderzucker bestreuen; glasieren; mattieren; **~bite** Erfrierung f; **~ed glass** Milchglas n; **~y** eisig, frostig.

froth [frɔθ] Schaum m; schäumen; **~y** schaumig.

frown [fraun] die Stirn runzeln; finster blicken.

froze [frəuz] pret, **~n** pp von **freeze**; **~n meat** Gefrierfleisch n.

frugal ['fru:gəl] sparsam, bescheiden.

fruit [fru:t] Frucht f; Früchte pl; Obst n; **~erer** Obsthändler m; **~ful** fruchtbar; **~less** unfruchtbar; fig. vergeblich.

frustrate [frʌs'treit] vereiteln; enttäuschen.

fry [frai] braten, backen; **~ing-pan** Bratpfanne f.

fuchsia ['fju:ʃə] Fuchsie f.

fuel [fjuəl] Brenn-, Treib-, Kraftstoff m.

fugitive ['fju:dʒitiv] flüchtig; Flüchtling m.

fulfil(l) [ful'fil] erfüllen; ausführen; **~ment** Erfüllung f.

full [ful] voll; vollständig; ganz; ausführlich; völlig, ganz; gerade; genau; **~ of** voller ...; voll von; erfüllt von; **~ up** voll, besetzt; **in ~** voll(ständig); **~ board** Vollpension f; **~ stop** Punkt m.

full(l)ness ['fulnis] Fülle f.

full-time employment, **~ job** Ganztagsbeschäftigung f.

fumble ['fʌmbl] umhertasten, (herum)fummeln.

fume [fju:m] Dunst m, Dampf m; rauchen, dampfen; fig. wütend sein.

fun [fʌn] Scherz m, Spaß m; **for ~,** in **~** zum Spaß; **it is ~** es macht Spaß; **make ~ of** sich lustig machen über.

function ['fʌŋkʃən] Funktion f; Aufgabe f; Ver-

anstaltung *f*; funktionieren; **~ary** Funktionär *m*.
fund [fʌnd] Kapital *n*,
Geldsumme *f*, Fonds *m*;
pl a. (Geld)Mittel *f/n*; *fig.*
Vorrat *m*.
fundamental [fʌndə-
'mentl] grundlegend.
funeral ['fjuːnərəl] Be-
erdigung *f*; Trauer..., Begräbnis...
fun fair Rummelplatz *m*.
funicular (railway)
[fju(:)'nikjulə] (Draht-)
Seilbahn *f*.
funnel ['fʌnl] Trichter *m*;
Licht-, Luftschacht *m*;
mar., *rail.* Schornstein *m*.
funny ['fʌni] spaßig, komisch, lustig.
fur [fəː] Pelz *m*, Fell *n*;
Belag *m* (*auf der Zunge*).
furious ['fjuəriəs] wütend;
wild.
furl [fəːl] zs.-rollen; sich
zs.-rollen lassen.
furnace ['fəːnis] Schmelz-,
Hochofen *m*; (Heiz)Kessel
m.

furnish ['fəːniʃ] versorgen;
liefern; möblieren; aus-
statten.
furniture ['fəːnitʃə] Möbel
pl, Einrichtung *f*.
furrow ['fʌrəu] Furche *f*;
pflügen; furchen.
further ['fəːðə] weiter; ferner, überdies; fördern;
~more ferner, überdies.
furtive ['fəːtiv] verstohlen.
fury ['fjuəri] Zorn *m*, Wut
f; Furie *f*.
fuse [fjuːz] (ver)schmelzen;
electr. durchbrennen; *electr.*
Sicherung *f*; Zünder *m*.
fuselage ['fjuːzilɑːʒ] (Flugzeug)Rumpf *m*.
fusion ['fjuːʒən] Ver-
schmelzung *f*; Fusion *f*.
fuss [fʌs] Aufregung *f*, Getue *n*; viel Aufhebens
machen; (sich) aufre-
gen.
futile ['fjuːtail] nutzlos.
future ['fjuːtʃə] (zu)künf-
tig; Zukunft *f*; **~ (tense)**
gr. Futur *n*, Zukunft *f*.

G

gab [gæb] *colloq.* Geschwätz *n*; **have the gift
of the ~** ein gutes Mund-
werk haben.
gable ['geibl] Giebel *m*.
gad-fly ['gædflai] *zo.* Bremse *f*.
gag [gæg] Knebel *m*; Gag
m; kneb(e)ln.
gage [geidʒ] *s.* **gauge.**
gai|ety ['geiəti] Fröhlich-

keit *f*; **~ly** *adv von* **gay.**
gain [gein] Gewinn *m*;
Zunahme *f*; gewinnen; bekommen; zunehmen (*Ge-
wicht*); vorgehen (*Uhr*).
gait [geit] Gang(art *f*) *m*;
~er Gamasche *f*.
gale [geil] Sturm *m*.
gall [gɔːl] Galle *f*.
gallant ['gælənt] stattlich;
tapfer; galant, höflich.

gallery ['gæləri] Galerie f; Empore f.

galley ['gæli] Galeere f; Kombüse f; **~proof** (Korrektur) Fahne f.

gallon ['gælən] Gallone f (4,54 Liter, Am. 3,78 Liter).

gallop ['gæləp] Galopp m; galoppieren (lassen).

gallows ['gæləuz] sg Galgen m.

galore [gə'lɔ:] im Überfluß.

gamble ['gæmbl] spielen; **~r** Spieler(in).

gambol ['gæmbəl] Luftsprung m; (herum)hüpfen.

game [geim] Spiel n (a. Wettkampf, -spiel); Wild n; **~keeper** Wildhüter m.

gander ['gændə] Gänserich m.

gang [gæŋ] Gruppe f, Trupp m; Bande f; **~ up** sich zs.-rotten od. zs.-tun.

gangster ['gæŋstə] Gangster m.

gangway ['gæŋwei] (Durch)Gang m; Gangway f, Laufplanke f.

gaol [dʒeil] Gefängnis n; einsperren; **~er** (Gefängnis)Wärter m.

gap [gæp] Lücke f; Spalt (e f) m; fig. Kluft f.

gape [geip] gähnen; gaffen; klaffen.

garage ['gæra:dʒ] Garage f; Auto-, Reparaturwerkstatt f; Auto einstellen.

garbage [ga:bidʒ] Abfall m.

garden ['ga:dn] Garten

m; **~er** Gärtner(in); **~ing** Gartenarbeit f.

gargle ['ga:gl] Mund ausspülen; gurgeln.

garland ['ga:lənd] Girlande f, Kranz m. [m.\]

garlic ['ga:lik] Knoblauch

garment ['ga:mənt] Kleidungsstück n, Gewand n.

garnish ['ga:niʃ] garnieren.

garret ['gærət] Dachstube f, Mansarde f.

garrison ['gærisn] Garnison f, Besatzung f.

garter ['ga:tə] Strumpfband n; Am. Sockenhalter m.

gas [gæs] Gas n; Am. mot. Benzin n; **~eous** ['~jəs] gasförmig; **~ fire** Gasheizung f.

gash [gæʃ] klaffende Wunde.

gasket ['gæskit] tech. Dichtung f.

gas| -meter Gasuhr f; **~oline** ['gæsəli:n] Am. mot. Benzin n.

gasp [ga:sp] Keuchen n; keuchen, schnaufen.

gas| station Am. Tankstelle f; **~stove** Gasherd m; **~works** sg Gaswerk n.

gate [geit] Tor n; Pforte f; Schranke f, Sperre f; aer. Flugsteig m; **~way** Tor(weg m) n, Einfahrt f.

gather ['gæðə] sich versammeln; sich zs.-ballen (Wolken); eitern (Abszeß); (ein-, ver)sammeln; ernten, pflücken; raffen; fig.

schließen (**from** aus); ~
speed schneller werden;
~ing Versammlung f.

gaudy ['gɔːdi] grell; protzig.

gauge [geidʒ] (Normal-)
Maß n; rail. Spurweite f;
Meßgerät n; eichen; (aus-)
messen.

gaunt [gɔːnt] hager; finster.   [m.]

gauze [gɔːz] Gaze f; Mull |

gave [geiv] pret von **give**.

gay [gei] lustig, fröhlich,
heiter; bunt, lebhaft.

gaze [geiz] (fester, starrer)
Blick; ~ **at** anstarren.

gear [giə] tech. Getriebe
n; mot. Gang m; Gerät
n; ~-change Gangschal-
tung f; ~-defect Getriebe-
schaden m; ~ing Getriebe
n; Übersetzung f; ~-lever
Schalthebel m.

geese [giːs] pl von **goose**.

gem [dʒem] Edelstein m.

gender ['dʒendə] gr. Genus n.

general ['dʒenərəl] allgemein; Haupt...; General
m; Feldherr m; ~ize ver-
allgemeinern; ~ly im all-
gemeinen; gewöhnlich.

generat|e ['dʒenəreit] er-
zeugen; ~ion Erzeugung
f; Generation f; Men-
schenalter n; ~or Gene-
rator m; mot. Licht-
maschine f.

gener|osity [dʒenə'rɒsiti]
Großmut f; Großzügig-
keit f; ~ous großzügig;
edel; reichlich.

genial ['dʒiːnjəl] freundlich.

genitive (**case**) ['dʒeni-
tiv] gr. Genitiv m, 2. Fall.

genius ['dʒiːnjəs] Genie n;
fig. Geist m.

gentle ['dʒentl] sanft, mild,
zart; vornehm; ~man
Herr m, Gentleman m;
~manlike, ~manly vor-
nehm, fein, gebildet; ~
ness Güte f, Milde f,
Sanftheit f; ~woman
Dame f.

gentry ['dʒentri] niederer
Adel; gebildete und be-
sitzende Stände pl.

genuine ['dʒenjuin] echt.

geography [dʒi'ɒgrəfi]
Geographie f, Erdkunde f.

geolog|ist [dʒi'ɒlɒdʒist]
Geologe m; ~y Geologie f.

geometry [dʒi'ɒmitri]
Geometrie f.

germ [dʒəːm] Keim m;
Bakterie f.

German ['dʒəːmən]
deutsch; Deutsche m, f;
Deutsch n.

germinate ['dʒəːmineit]
keimen.

gerund ['dʒerənd] gr. Gerundium n.

gesticulate [dʒes'tikju-
leit] gestikulieren.

gesture ['dʒestʃə] Geste f,
Gebärde f.

get [get] (irr) erhalten, bekommen, colloq. kriegen;
(sich) besorgen; holen;
bringen; erwerben; verdienen; ergreifen, fassen, fangen; veranlassen; colloq.

verstehen; gelangen; (an-)kommen, geraten; *mit adj:* werden; ~ **about** herumkommen; ~ **auf den Beinen** sein; sich verbreiten (*Gerücht*); ~ **along** auskommen; vorwärtskommen; ~ **away** loskommen; entkommen; ~ **in** einsteigen; ~ **off** aussteigen; ~ **on** einsteigen in; ~ **on with s.o.** mit j-m auskommen; ~ **out** aussteigen; ~ **out of** heraus- *od.* hinauskommen aus; ~ **to** kommen nach; ~ **together** zs.-kommen; ~ **up** aufstehen; ~ **by heart** auswendig lernen; ~ **one's hair cut** sich die Haare schneiden lassen; ~ **ready** sich fertigmachen; ~ **to know** kennenlernen; **have got to** haben od. müssen; **have got to** müssen.

geyser ['gaizə] Geiser *m*, Geysir *m*; ['gi:zə] Boiler *m*.

ghastly ['gɑ:stli] gräßlich, schrecklich; (toten)bleich.

gherkin ['gə:kin] Gewürzgurke *f*.

ghost [gəust] Geist *m*, Gespenst *n*; ~**ly** geisterhaft.

giant ['dʒaiənt] riesig, gigantisch, Riesen...; Riese *m*.

gibbet ['dʒibit] Galgen *m*.

gibe [dʒaib] (ver)spotten.

giblets ['dʒiblits] *pl* Gänse-, Hühnerklein *n*.

giddy ['gidi] schwind(e)lig; schwindelnd; *fig.* leichtsinnig.

gift [gift] Geschenk *n*;

Begabung *f*, Talent *n*; ~**ed** begabt.

gigantic [dʒai'gæntik] riesig, gigantisch.

giggle ['gigl] kichern; Gekicher *n*.

gild [gild] (*irr*) vergolden; verschöne(r)n.

gill [gil] Kieme *f*; *bot.* Lamelle *f*.

gilt [gilt] *pret u. pp von* **gild**; Vergoldung *f*.

gin [dʒin] Gin *m*, Wacholderschnaps *m*.

ginger ['dʒindʒə] Ingwer *m*; *colloq.* Schneid *m*, Feuer *n*; rötlich-gelb; ~**bread** Pfefferkuchen *m*; ~**ly** sachte, behutsam; zimperlich.

gipsy ['dʒipsi] Zigeuner (-in).

giraffe [dʒi'rɑ:f] Giraffe *f*.

gird [gə:d] (*irr*) (um)gürten; umgeben.

girder ['gə:də] Träger *m*, Tragbalken *m*.

girdle ['gə:dl] Gürtel *m*; Hüfthalter *m*, -gürtel *m*.

girl [gə:l] Mädchen *n*; ♀ **Guide** Pfadfinderin *f*; ~**hood** Mädchenjahre *pl*; ~**ish** mädchenhaft; ♀ **Scout** *Am.* Pfadfinderin *f*; ~**'s name** Mädchenname *m*.

girt [gə:t] *pret u. pp von* **gird**.

girth [gə:θ] (Sattel)Gurt *m*; Umfang *m*.

give [giv] (*irr*) (ab-, weiter)geben; schenken; hergeben; widmen; geben, reichen; liefern; verursachen, bereiten; zugestehen, erlauben; nachgeben; **~ away** verschenken; verteilen; verraten; **~ in** nach-, aufgeben; *Gesuch etc.* einreichen; **~ up** aufgeben; *j-n* ausliefern; **~ (up)on** sich stellen; **~ o.s. up** (**to**) gehen nach, hinausgehen auf (*Fenster etc.*); **~ way** zurückweichen, Platz machen; **~** *n pp* gegeben; ergeben, verfallen (**to** *dat.*).

glacier ['glæsjə] Gletscher *m.*

glad [glæd] froh, erfreut; **be ~** sich freuen; **~ly** gern(e); **~ness** Freude *f.*

glam|orous ['glæmərəs] bezaubernd; **~o(u)r** Zauber *m*, Reiz *m.*

glance [gla:ns] flüchtiger Blick; Aufblitzen *n*; **~ at** (schnell, flüchtig) blicken auf.

gland [glænd] Drüse *f.*

glare [glɛə] blendendes Licht; wilder *od.* funkelnder Blick; grell leuchten *od.* scheinen; **~ at** (wild) anstarren.

glass [gla:s] (Trink-, Fern-, Opern)Glas *n*; Spiegel *m*; Barometer *n*; **a ~ of** ... ein Glas ...; (**a pair of**) **~es** *pl* (e--e) Brille; gläsern, Glas...; **~y** gläsern; glasig.

glaz|e [gleiz] Glasur *f*; verglasen; glasieren; glasig werden (*Auge*); **~ier** ['glæziə] Glaser *m.*

gleam [gli:m] schwacher

Schein, Schimmer *m*; leuchten, schimmern.

glee [gli:] Fröhlichkeit *f*, Freude *f*; mehrstimmiges Lied.

glen [glen] enges Tal, Bergschlucht *f.*

glib [glib] glatt, gewandt, zungenfertig.

glide [glaid] Gleiten *n*; *aer.* Gleitflug *m*; gleiten; segeln; **~r** Segelflugzeug *n.*

glimmer ['glimə] Schimmer *m*; schimmern.

glimpse [glimps] flüchtiger Blick; flüchtig (er-) blicken.

glint [glint] schimmern, glitzern.

glisten ['glisn] schimmern, glänzen, glitzern.

glitter ['glitə] glitzern, glänzen, funkeln.

gloat [gləut]: **~ (up)on, ~ over** sich weiden an.

globe [gləub] (Erd)Kugel *f*; Globus *m.*

gloom [glu:m] Düsterkeit *f*, Dunkel *n*; düstere Stimmung, Schwermut *f*; **~y** dunkel, düster; niedergeschlagen.

glor|ify ['glɔ:rifai] verherrlichen; **~ious** herrlich; ruhmvoll; **~y** Ruhm *m*, Ehre *f*; Herrlichkeit *f.*

gloss [glɔs] Glanz *m.*

glossary ['glɔsəri] (Spezial)Wörterbuch *n.*

glossy ['glɔsi] glänzend.

glove [glʌv] Handschuh *m.*

glow [gləu] Glühen *n*;

Glut *f*; glühen; **~worm** Glühwürmchen *n*.

glue [glu:] Leim *m*; Klebstoff *m*; leimen; kleben.

glutton ['glʌtn] Vielfraß *m*; **~ous** gefräßig; **~y** Gefräßigkeit *f*.

gnarled [nɑːld] knorrig, knotig, gichtig (*Finger*).

gnash [næʃ] knirschen mit (*Zähnen*).

gnat [næt] (Stech)Mücke*f*.

gnaw [nɔː] zernagen, nagen an; nagen (**at** an).

go [gəu] (*irr*) gehen, fahren; verkehren (*Fahrzeuge*); (fort)gehen, abfahren; vergehen (*Zeit*); kaputtgehen; ausgehen; ablaufen, ausfallen; gehen, arbeiten, funktionieren; reichen; passen; werden; gelten; läuten, ertönen (*Glocke*); **~ to bed** ins Bett gehen; **~ to school** zur Schule gehen; **~ to see** besuchen; **~ to loslassen**; **~ at** losgehen auf; **~ by** sich richten nach; **~ for** holen; angreifen; **~ for a walk** spazierengehen; **~ in** hineingehen, eintreten; **~ in for an examination** e-e Prüfung machen; **~ off** fortgehen; **~ on** weitergehen, -fahren; *fig*.: fortfahren (**doing** zu tun); vor sich gehen, vorgehen; **~ through** durchgehen; durchmachen; **~ up** steigen; hinaufsteigen, -gehen; **~ without** auskommen ohne; *sub: colloq*. Schwung *m*; **have a ~ at** es versuchen mit.

goad [gəud] anstacheln.

goal [gəul] Ziel *n*; *Fußball*: Tor *n*; **~keeper** Torwart *m*.

goat [gəut] Ziege *f*.

go-between Vermittler (-in).

goblet ['gɔblit] Kelchglas *n*.

goblin ['gɔblin] Kobold *m*.

god [gɔd] (*eccl*. 2) Gott *m*; *fig*. (Ab)Gott *m*; **~child** Patenkind *n*; **~dess** Göttin *f*; **~father** Pate *m*; **~less** gottlos; **~mother** Patin *f*.

goggles ['gɔglz] *pl* Schutzbrille *f*.

going ['gəuiŋ]: **be ~ to** im Begriff sein zu, gleich *tun* wollen od. werden.

gold [gəuld] Gold *n*; golden, Gold...; **~digger** Goldgräber *m*; **~en** golden (*a*. *fig*.), goldgelb; **~plated** vergoldet; **~smith** Goldschmied *m*.

golf [gɔlf] Golf(spiel) *n*; Golf spielen; **~course**, **~links** *pl* Golfplatz *m*.

gondola ['gɔndələ] Gondel *f*.

gone [gɔn] *pp von* go; fort, weg, *colloq*. futsch.

good [gud] Gut; artig, lieb (*Kind*); gütig; **~ at** gut in, geschickt in; **make s.th. ~** et. wiedergutmachen; Gute *n*, Wohl *n*; Vorteil *m*, Nutzen *m*; *pl* Waren *pl*, Güter *pl*; **that's no ~** das nützt

nichts; **for** ~ für immer;
~by(e) ['bai] Lebe-
wohl n; int. ['~'bai] (auf)
Wiedersehen!; **~for-
nothing** Taugenichts m;
♀ **Friday** Karfreitag m;
~natured gutmütig;
~ness Güte f; **thank
~ness!** Gott sei Dank!;
~will Wohlwollen n, guter
Wille.

goose [guːs], pl **geese**
[giːs] Gans f (a. fig.).

goose|berry ['guzbəri]
Stachelbeere f; **~flesh**
['guːs~] fig. Gänsehaut f.

gopher ['gəufə] Taschen-
ratte f.

gorge [gɔːdʒ] enge (Fels-)
Schlucht; Mageninhalt m;
gierig verschlingen; (sich)
vollstopfen.

gorgeous ['gɔːdʒəs]
prächtig; colloq. großartig.

gospel ['gɔspəl] Evange-
lium n.

gossip ['gɔsip] Klatsch m;
Geplauder n; Klatsch-
base f; klatschen.

got [gɔt] pret u. pp von **get**.

Gothic ['gɔθik] gotisch.

gotten ['gɔtn] Am. pp von
get.

gourd [guəd] Kürbis m.

gout [gaut] Gicht f.

govern ['gʌvən] regieren;
(be)herrschen; verwal-
ten, lenken, leiten; **~ess**
Erzieherin f; **~ment** Regierung f; pol. Kabinett n;
~or Gouverneur m; colloq.
Alte m (Vater, Chef).

gown [gaun] (Damen-)

Kleid n; Robe f, Talar m.

grab [græb] (hastig) (er-)
greifen; an sich reißen,
packen.

grace [greis] Gnade f;
Gunst f; jur., econ. Frist f;
Grazie f, Anmut f; An-
stand m; Tischgebet n;
Your ♀ Euer Gnaden;
~ful anmutig.

gracious ['greiʃəs] gnädig;
gütig; **good ~!** du meine
Güte!

grade [greid] Grad m,
Stufe f; Rang m; Qualität
f; Am. Schule: Klasse f;
Note f; einstufen; planie-
ren; **~ crossing** Am.
schienengleicher Bahn-
übergang; **~ school** Am.
Grundschule f.

gradient ['greidjənt]
Steigung f, Gefälle n.

gradual| ['grædʒuəl] all-
mählich, stufenweise;
~te ['~djueit] ein-, (sich)
abstufen; in Grade ein-
teilen; promovieren; e-n
akademischen Grad ver-
leihen od. erlangen;
['~djueit] Graduierte m,
f, Promovierte m, f; Am.
Absolvent(in f) m; **~tion** [~dju-
'eiʃən] Abstufung f; Grad-
einteilung f; Promotion f;
Am. Abschlußfeier f.

graft [grɑːft] Pfropfreis n;
pfropfen; med. verpflan-
zen.

grain [grein] (Samen-)
Korn n; Getreide n; fig.
Spur f.

gram [græm] s. **gramme**.

gramma|r ['græmə] Grammatik f; **~r-school** appr. Gymnasium n; **~tical** [grə'mætikəl] grammati(kali)sch.

gramme [græm] Gramm n.

gramophone ['græmə-fəun] Grammophon n, Plattenspieler m.

grand [grænd] großartig; erhaben; groß, bedeutend; Groß..., Haupt...; **~child** ['~ntʃ-] Enkel(in); **~daughter** ['~ndɔː-] Enkelin f; **~eur** ['~ndʒə] Größe f, Hoheit f; Erhabenheit f; Herrlichkeit f; **~father** ['~df-] Großvater m; **~father('s) clock** Standuhr f; **~ma** ['~nmɑː] colloq. Oma f; **~mother** ['~nm-] Großmutter f; **~pa** ['~npɑː] colloq. Opa m; **~parents** ['~np-] pl Großeltern pl; **~son** ['~ns-] Enkel m; **~stand** Tribüne f.

granny ['græni] colloq. Oma f.

grant [grɑːnt] Unterstützung f, Zuschuß m; Stipendium n; bewilligen; Bitte etc. erfüllen; zugeben; **take for ~ed** als selbstverständlich annehmen.

granulated sugar ['grænjuleitid] Kristallzucker m.

grape [greip] Weinbeere f, -traube f; **~fruit** Grapefruit f, Pampelmuse f; **~-sugar** Traubenzucker m.

graphic ['græfik] graphisch; anschaulich.

grasp [grɑːsp] Griff m; fig. Verständnis n; (er)greifen, packen; fig. verstehen; greifen (**at** nach).

grass [grɑːs] Gras n; Rasen m; Weide f; **~hopper** Heuschrecke f; **~ widow** Strohwitwe f.

grate [greit] (Feuer)Rost m; (zer)reiben; knirschen (mit).

grateful ['greitful] dankbar.

grater ['greitə] Reibeisen n.

grati|fication [grætifi-'keiʃən] Befriedigung f; Freude f; **~fy** ['~fai] befriedigen; erfreuen.

grating ['greitiŋ] rauh; unangenehm; Gitter n.

gratitude ['grætitjuːd] Dankbarkeit f.

gratuit|ous [grə-'tjuː(:)itəs] unentgeltlich; freiwillig; **~y** Gratifikation f; Trinkgeld n.

grave [greiv] ernst; Grab n; **~digger** Totengräber m.

gravel ['grævəl] Kies m.

graveyard Friedhof m.

gravit|ation [grævi-'teiʃən] Schwerkraft f; **~y** ['~ti] Ernst m; Schwere f; Schwerkraft f.

gravy ['greivi] Bratensoße f.

gray [grei] bsd. Am. für **grey**.

graz|e [greiz] (ab)weiden; (ab)grasen; streifen;

schrammen; *Haut* abschürfen; **~ing-land** Weideland *n*.

greas|e [gri:s] Fett *n*; Schmiere *f*; [~z] (be-, ab)schmieren; **~y** ['~zi] fettig, schmierig, ölig.

great [greit] groß; Groß...; *colloq.* großartig; **~coat** Überzieher *m*; **~grandchild** Urenkel(in); **~grandfather** Urgroßvater *m*; **~grandmother** Urgroßmutter *f*; **~ly** sehr; **~ness** Größe *f*; Bedeutung *f*.

greed [gri:d] Gier *f*; **~y** (be)gierig; habgierig.

Greek [gri:k] griechisch; Grieche *m*, -in *f*; Griechisch *n*; **it's ~ to me** das sind böhmische Dörfer für mich.

green [gri:n] grün (*a. fig.*); unreif; *fig.* unerfahren, neu; Grün *n*; Grünfläche *f*; *pl* grünes Gemüse; **~grocer** Gemüsehändler(in); **~horn** Grünschnabel *m*, Neuling *m*; **~house** Gewächshaus *n*; **~ish** grünlich.

greet [gri:t] (be)grüßen; **~ing** Gruß *m*, Begrüßung *f*.

grenade [gri'neid] Hand-, Gewehrgranate *f*.

grew [gru:] *pret von* **grow**.

grey [grei] grau; Grau *n*; **~hound** Windhund *m*.

grid [grid] Gitter *n*; *electr.* Überlandleitungsnetz *n*; **~(iron)** (Brat)Rost *m*.

grief [gri:f] Kummer *m*.

griev|ance ['gri:vəns] Grund *m* zur Klage, Mißstand *m*; **~e** bekümmern, kränken; bekümmert sein; **~ous** schmerzlich; schwer.

grill [gril] grillen; (Brat-) Rost *m*, Grill *m*; gegrilltes Fleisch; **~(-room)** Grill (-room) *m*.

grim [grim] grimmig.

grimace [gri'meis] Fratze *f*, Grimasse *f*; Grimassen schneiden.

grim|e [graim] Schmutz *m*; **~y** schmutzig.

grin [grin] Grinsen *n*; grinsen.

grind [graind] (*irr*) zerreiben; (zer)mahlen; schleifen; *Kaffeemühle etc.* drehen; mit den Zähnen knirschen; **~stone** Schleifstein *m*.

grip [grip] packen (*a. fig.*), fassen; Griff *m* (*a. fig.*).

gripes [graips] *pl* Kolik *f*.

gristle ['grisl] Knorpel *m*.

grit [grit] Kies *m*, Sand *m*; *fig.* Mut *m*.

groan [groun] stöhnen.

grocer ['grousə] Lebensmittel-, Kolonialwarenhändler *m*; **~ies** ['~riz] *pl* Lebensmittel *pl*; **~y** Lebensmittelgeschäft *n*.

groin [groin] *anat.* Leiste *f*.

groom [grum] Reit-, Pferdeknecht *m*; Bräutigam *m*; pflegen.

groove [gru:v] Rinne *f*; Rille *f*.

grope [grəup] tasten.

gross [grəus] dick, fett; grob; derb; Brutto...; Gros *n* (*12 Dutzend*).

ground[1] [graund] *pret u. pp von* **grind**.

ground[2] [graund] Boden *m*, Erde *f*; Gebiet *n*; (*Spiel- etc.*) Platz *m*; Meeresboden *m*; *fig.* Grund *m*; *pl* Grundstück *n*, Park *m*, Gartenanlage *f*; *pl* (*Kaffee*)Satz *m*; (be)gründen; *electr.* erden.

ground| control *aer.* Bodenkontrollstation *f*; ⁓ **crew** *aer.* Bodenpersonal *n*; ⁓**floor** Erdgeschoß *n*; ⁓**glass** Mattglas *n*; ⁓**hog** Amerikanisches Murmeltier; ⁓**less** grundlos; ⁓**nut** Erdnuß *f*; ⁓**staff** *aer.* Bodenpersonal *n*.

group [gru:p] Gruppe *f*; (sich) gruppieren.

grove [grəuv] Hain *m*, Gehölz *n*.

grow [grəu] (*irr*) wachsen; werden; anbauen; (sich) wachsen lassen.

growl [graul] knurren, brummen; grollen (*Donner*).

grow|n [grəun] *pp von* **grow**; ⁓**n-up** erwachsen; Erwachsene *m*, *f*; ⁓**th** [⁓θ] Wachstum *n*; (An-)Wachsen *n*; Entwicklung *f*; Wuchs *m*; Produkt *n*; Erzeugnis *n*; *med.* Wucherung *f*.

grub [grʌb] Larve *f*, Made *f*; ⁓**by** schmierig.

grudge [grʌdʒ] Groll *m*; mißgönnen; ungern geben.

gruel [gruəl] Haferschleim *m*.

gruff [grʌf] grob, schroff, barsch.

grumble ['grʌmbl] murren, brummen; grollen (*Donner*); ⁓**r** Nörgler *m*.

grunt [grʌnt] grunzen.

guarant|ee [gærən'ti:] Bürgschaft *f*, Garantie *f*; Kaution *f*, Sicherheit *f*; Bürge *m*; (sich ver-) bürgen für; garantieren; ⁓**or** [⁓'tɔ:] Bürge *m*; ⁓**y** ['⁓ti] Bürgschaft *f*, Garantie *f*; Kaution *f*, Sicherheit *f*.

guard [gɑ:d] bewachen, (be)schützen; ⁓ **against** sich hüten vor; Wache *f*; Aufseher *m*, Wächter *m*, Wärter *m*; *rail.* Schaffner *m*; Schutzvorrichtung *f*; **on one's** ⁓ auf der Hut; **off one's** ⁓ unachtsam; ⁓**ian** ['⁓jən] *jur.* Vormund *m*; Schutz...; ⁓**ianship** *jur.* Vormundschaft *f*; ⁓**s** *pl in England*: Garde *f*.

guess [ges] Vermutung *f*; vermuten; (er)raten; *Am.* denken.

guest [gest] Gast *m*; ⁓**house** (Hotel)Pension *f*, Fremdenheim *n*; ⁓**room** Gäste-, Fremdenzimmer *n*.

guidance ['gaidəns] Führung *f*; (An)Leitung *f*.

guide [gaid] Führer *m*; Fremdenführer *m*; führen; lenken, leiten, steuern; **~-book** (Reise)Führer *m*.

guild [gild] Gilde *f*, Zunft *f*, Innung *f*; Vereinigung *f*; **2-hall** Rathaus *n* (*in London*).

guileless ['gaillis] arglos.

guilt [gilt] Schuld *f*; **~less** schuldlos; **~y** schuldig.

guinea-pig ['gini-] Meerschweinchen *n*.

guitar [gi'tɑ:] Gitarre *f*.

gulf [gʌlf] Meerbusen *m*, Golf *m*; Abgrund *m*, Kluft *f*.

gull [gʌl] Möwe *f*.

gullet ['gʌlit] Speiseröhre *f*; Gurgel *f*.

gulp [gʌlp] (großer) Schluck; **~ down** hinunterschlingen, -stürzen.

gum [gʌm] Gummi *n*; Klebstoff *m*; *pl* Zahnfleisch *n*; gummieren; kleben.

gun [gʌn] Gewehr *n*,

Flinte *f*; Geschütz *n*, Kanone *f*; *Am. colloq.* Revolver *m*; **~powder** Schießpulver *n*.

gurgle ['gə:gl] gluckern, gurgeln, glucksen.

gush [gʌʃ] Strom *m*, Guß *m*; *fig.* Erguß *m*; sich ergießen, schießen.

gust [gʌst] Windstoß *m*, Bö *f*.

guts [gʌts] *pl* Eingeweide *pl*; *fig.* Schneid *m*.

gutter ['gʌtə] Dachrinne *f*; Gosse *f* (*a. fig.*), Rinnstein *m*.

guy [gai] *Am. sl.* Kerl *m*.

gym [dʒim] *sl. abbr. für* **gymnasium**, **gymnastics**; **~nasium** [~'neizjəm] Turnhalle *f*; **~nastics** [~'næstiks] *pl* Turnen *n*; Gymnastik *f*.

gyn(a)ecologist [gaini-'kɔlədʒist] Frauenarzt *m*.

gypsy ['dʒipsi] *bsd. Am. für* **gipsy**.

H

haberdasher ['hæbədæʃə] Kurzwarenhändler *m*; *Am.* Herrenausstatter *m*; **~y** Kurzwaren(geschäft *n*) *pl*; *Am.* Herrenbekleidungsartikel *pl*; *Am.* Herrenmodengeschäft *n*.

habit ['hæbit] (An)Gewohnheit *f*; **~ation** Wohnen *n*; Wohnung *f*; **~ual** [hə'bitjuəl] gewohnt, üblich; gewohnheitsmäßig.

hack [hæk] (zer)hacken.

hackney-carriage ['hækni-] (Pferde)Droschke *f*.

hack-saw ['hæk-] Metallsäge *f*.

had [hæd] *pret u. pp von* **have**.

haddock ['hædək] Schellfisch *m*.

h(a)emorrhage ['heməridʒ] Blutung *f*.

hag [hæg] Hexe *f*.

haggard ['hægəd] verhärmt.

hail [heil] Hagel m; hageln; begrüßen; anrufen.

hair [hɛə] Haar n; **~brush** Haarbürste f; **~cut** Haarschnitt m; **~do** Frisur f; **~dresser** (bsd. Damen)Friseur m; **at the ~dresser's** beim Friseur; **~dryer** Trockenhaube f; Föhn m; **~less** kahl; **~pin** Haarnadel f; **~y** haarig, behaart.

half [hɑ:f] halb; **~an hour** e-e halbe Stunde; **~a pound** ein halbes Pfund; **~way up** auf halber Höhe; **~past ten** halb elf (Uhr); **~,** pl **halves** [~vz] Hälfte f; **~back** Fußball: Läufer m; **~breed,** **~caste** Mischling m, Halbblut n; **~penny** ['heipni] halber Penny; **~time** sp. Halbzeit f; **~way** auf halbem Weg od. in der Mitte (liegend).

halibut ['hælibət] Heilbutt m.

hall [hɔ:l] Halle f; Saal m; (Haus)Flur m, Diele f.

hallo [hə'ləu] int. hallo!

halo ['heiləu] ast. Hof m; Heiligenschein m.

halt [hɔ:lt] Halt(estelle f) m; Stillstand m; (an-)halten.

halter ['hɔ:ltə] Halfter m, n; Strick m (zum Hängen).

halve [hɑ:v] halbieren; **~s** [~z] pl von **half.**

ham [hæm] Schinken m.

hamburger ['hæmbə:gə]

Am. deutsches Beefsteak; mit deutschem Beefsteak belegtes Brötchen.

hamlet ['hæmlit] Weiler m.

hammer ['hæmə] Hammer m; (ein)hämmern.

hammock ['hæmək] Hängematte f.

hamper ['hæmpə] Geschenk-, Eßkorb m; (be-)hindern.

hamster ['hæmstə] Hamster m.

hand [hænd] Hand f (a. fig.); Handschrift f; (Uhr-)Zeiger m; Mann m, Arbeiter m; Karten: Blatt n; **at ~** nahe, bei der Hand; **at first ~** aus erster Hand; **on ~** vorrätig; **on the one ~** einerseits; **on the other ~** andererseits; **on the right ~** rechter Hand, rechts; **change ~s** den Besitzer wechseln; **lend a ~** (mit) anfassen; vb: **~** geben, (-)reichen; **~** zurückgeben; **~ down** überliefern; **~ in** einhändigen, -reichen; **~ over** aushändigen, -liefern; **~bag** Handtasche f; **~-bill** Hand-, Reklamezettel m; **~brake** Handbremse f; **~cuffs** pl Handschellen pl; **~ful** Handvoll f; colloq. Plage f.

handi|cap ['hændikæp] Handikap n; Nachteil m; (be)hindern, benachteiligen; **~craft** Handwerk n.

handkerchief ['hæŋkətʃiː(ː)f] Taschentuch n; Halstuch n.

handle ['hændl] Griff m; Stiel m; Henkel m; (Tür-) Klinke f; anfassen; handhaben; umgehen mit; behandeln; **~bar** Lenkstange f.

hand|luggage Handgepäck n; **~made** handgearbeitet; **~rail** Geländer n; **~shake** Händedruck m; **~some** ['hænsəm] hübsch; beträchtlich, ansehnlich; **~work** Handarbeit f; **~writing** (Hand)Schrift f; **~y** geschickt; handlich; zur Hand.

hang [hæŋ] (irr) (auf-, be-, ein)hängen; Tapete ankleben; (pret u. pp ~ed) (auf-, er)hängen; **~ about** (Am. around) herumlungern; **~ out** (her-aushängen; **~ up** aufhängen.

hangar ['hæŋə] Flugzeughalle f.

hang|ings ['hæŋiŋz] pl Wandbehang m; **~man** Henker m; **~over** Katzenjammer m, Kater m.

hanky ['hæŋki] colloq. Taschentuch n.

haphazard ['hæp'hæzəd] Zufall m; **at ~** aufs Geratewohl.

happen ['hæpən] sich ereignen, geschehen, vorkommen; **he ~ed to be at home** er war zufällig zu Hause; **~ (up)on** zu-

fällig treffen auf od. finden; **~ing** Ereignis n.

happ|ily ['hæpili] glücklich(erweise); **~iness** Glück n; **~y** glücklich; froh; erfreut; **~y-go-lucky** unbekümmert.

harass ['hærəs] belästigen, quälen; aufreiben.

harbo(u)r ['hɑːbə] Hafen m; Zuflucht(sort m) beherbergen; Groll hegen.

hard [hɑːd] hart; schwer, schwierig; kräftig, mühsam; fleißig; streng, stark, heftig; Am. stark (Spirituosen); fest; **~ by** ganz nahe; **~ up** schlecht bei Kasse; **~ of hearing** schwerhörig; **try ~** sich alle Mühe geben; **work ~** schwer od. fleißig arbeiten; **~en** härten; hart machen; hart werden, erhärten; (sich) abhärten; fig. (sich) verhärten; **~-headed** praktisch, nüchtern; **~-hearted** hart(herzig), herzlos; **~ly** kaum; **~ness** Härte f; Strenge f; **~ship** Härte f, Not f; Mühsal f, Beschwerde f; **~ware** Eisenwaren pl; **~y** kühn; widerstandsfähig, abgehärtet.

hare [hɛə] Hase m; **~bell** Glockenblume f.

hark [hɑːk] horchen.

harm [hɑːm] Schaden m, Unrecht n; schaden, schädigen, verletzen; **~ful** schädlich; **~less** harmlos, unschädlich.

harmon|ious [hɑ:'məun-jəs] harmonisch; **~ize** ['~ənaiz] in Einklang bringen; harmonieren; **~y** Harmonie f.

harness ['hɑ:nis] (Pferde-)Geschirr n; anschirren.

harp [hɑ:p] Harfe f; Harfe spielen; **~ on** fig. herumreiten auf.

harpoon [hɑ:'pu:n] Harpune f; harpunieren.

harrow ['hærəu] Egge f; eggen.

harsh [hɑ:ʃ] rauh; hart; streng, grausam.

hart [hɑ:t] Hirsch m.

harvest ['hɑ:vist] Ernte (-zeit) f; Ertrag m; ernten; **~er** Mähbinder m.

has [hæz] 3. sg pres von **have**.

hash [hæʃ] Haschee n; Fleisch zerschneiden, -hakken.

haste [heist] Eile f; Hast f; **make ~** (sich be)eilen; **~en** ['~sn] (sich be)eilen; j-n antreiben; et. beschleunigen; **~y** (vor)eilig; hastig; hitzig.

hat [hæt] Hut m.

hatch [hætʃ] Luke f; Durchreiche f; Brut f; (Junge) ausbrüten; ausschlüpfen.

hatchet ['hætʃit] Beil n.

hat|e [heit] Haß m; hassen; **~eful** verhaßt; widerlich; **~red** ['~rid] Haß m.

haught|iness ['hɔ:tinis] Hochmut m, Stolz m; **~y** hochmütig, stolz.

haul [hɔ:l] Ziehen n; Fischzug m; (Transport)Strecke f; ziehen, schleppen; transportieren.

haunch [hɔ:ntʃ] zo. Keule f.

haunt [hɔ:nt] (bsd. Lieblings)Platz m; Schlupfwinkel m; heimsuchen; spuken in; **this place is ~ed** hier spukt es.

have [hæv, həv] (irr) haben; bekommen; (haben) mögen, essen, trinken, nehmen; ausführen, machen; lassen; vor inf: müssen; **I had my hair cut** ich ließ mir das Haar schneiden; **I had better go** es wäre besser, wenn ich ginge; **I had rather** ich möchte lieber; **~ on** anhaben, tragen; **~ come** gekommen sein; **~ got** colloq. haben.

haven ['heivn] (mst fig. sicherer) Hafen.

havoc ['hævək] Verwüstung f; **make ~ of, play ~ with** od. **among** verwüsten, übel zurichten.

hawk [hɔ:k] Habicht m; Falke m.

hawthorn ['hɔ:θɔ:n] Weiß-, Rotdorn m.

hay [hei] Heu n; **~cock** Heuschober m, -haufen m; **~ fever** Heuschnupfen m; **~loft** Heuboden m; **~rick, ~stack** Heuschober m.

hazard ['hæzəd] Zufall m; Gefahr f, Wagnis n, Risiko n; wagen; **~ous** Gewagt, riskant.

haze [heiz] Dunst *m*.

hazel ['heizl] Haselnuß (-strauch *m*) *f*; nußbraun; **~-nut** Haselnuß *f*.

hazy ['heizi] dunstig, diesig; *fig.* verschwommen.

H-bomb ['eitʃbɔm] H-Bombe *f*, Wasserstoffbombe *f*.

he [hi:] er; *in Zssgn:* männlich, ...männchen *n*.

head [hed] an der Spitze stehen von; (an)führen; *Fußball:* köpfen; losgehen, zusteuern (auf for); Kopf...., Ober...; Kopf *m*, Haupt *n* (*a. fig.*); Leiter *m*, Chef *m*; Direktor *m* (*Schule*); Spitze *f*; oberes Ende; Kopfende *n* (*Bett*); Kopfseite *f* (*Münze*); Vorgebirge *n*, Kap *n*; Bug *m*; Hauptpunkt *m*, Abschnitt *m*; ~ *pl* Stück *pl* (*Vieh*); ~ **over heels** Hals über Kopf; *fig.* völlig; **at the ~ of** an der Spitze (*gen*); **off one's ~** verrückt, übergeschnappt; **come to a ~** aufbrechen (*Geschwür*); *fig.* sich zuspitzen; **I cannot make ~ or tail of it** ich kann daraus nicht schlau werden; **~ache** Kopfschmerz(en *pl*) *m*, -weh *n*; **~gear** Kopfbedeckung *f*; **~ing** Überschrift *f*, Titel *m*; Thema *n*, Punkt *m*; **~land** Vorgebirge *n*, Kap *n*; **~light** Scheinwerfer *m*; **~line** Überschrift *f*, Schlagzeile *f*; **~long** kopfüber; **~master** Direktor

m (*Schule*); **~mistress** Direktorin *f* (*Schule*); **~phone** Kopfhörer *m*; **~quarters** *pl mil.* Hauptquartier *n*; Hauptsitz *m*, Zentrale *f*; **~strong** eigensinnig, halsstarrig; **~word** Stichwort *n* (*Wörterbuch*).

heal [hi:l] heilen; ~ **up**, ~ **over** (zu)heilen.

health [helθ] Gesundheit *f*; ~ **resort** Kurort *m*; **~y** gesund.

heap [hi:p] Haufe(n) *m*; *colloq.* Haufen *m*, Menge *f*; (an-, auf)häufen (*a.* ~ **up**); *fig.* überhäufen, -schütten.

hear [hiə] (*irr*) (an-, ver-, zu-, *Lektion* ab)hören; **~d** [hə:d] *pret u. pp von* **hear**; **~er** (Zu)Hörer(in); **~ing** Gehör *n*; Anhören *n*; Hörweite *f*; **~say** Hörensagen *n*; Gerücht *n*.

hearse [hə:s] Leichenwagen *m*.

heart [hɑ:t] Herz *n* (*a. fig.*); Innere *n*; Kern *m*; Mut *m*; Liebling *m*; **~s** (*pl Karten:* Herz *n*; **by** ~ auswendig; **~breaking** herzzerbrechend; **~burn** Sodbrennen *n*. (*fig.*).

hearth [hɑ:θ] Herd *m* (*a. fig.*).

heart|less ['hɑ:tlis] herzlos; **~ transplant** Herzverpflanzung *f*; **~y** herzlich; aufrichtig; gesund; herzhaft.

heat [hi:t] Hitze *f*; *fig.* Eifer *m*; *zo.* Läufigkeit *f*, Brunst *f*; *sp.:* Durchgang *m*; Lauf *m*, Einzelrennen *n*; heizen; (sich) erhitzen (*a. fig.*); **~er** Heizgerät (*n*) *f*.); **~er** Heizgerät *n*; Erhitzer *m*; Ofen *m*.

heath [hi:θ] Heide(kraut *n*) *f*.

heathen ['hi:ðən] Heid|e *m*, -*in f*; heidnisch.

heather ['heðə] Heidekraut *n*; *f*; Heiz...|.

heating ['hi:tiŋ] Heizung *f*.

heave [hi:v] (*irr*) (hoch-) heben; *Anker* lichten; *Seufzer* ausstoßen; sich heben und senken, wogen.

heaven ['hevn] Himmel *m*; *mst pl* Himmel *m*, Firmament *n*; **good ~s!** du lieber Himmel!; **~ly** himmlisch.

heaviness ['hevinis] Schwere *f* (*a. fig.*); Druck *m*.

heavy ['hevi] schwer; heftig (*Regen*); trüb(e) (*Himmel*); unwegsam (*Straße*); drückend, lästig; schwerfällig; bedrückt, traurig; Schwer...; **~ current** Starkstrom *m*; **~-handed** ungeschickt; **~ traffic** starker *od.* dichter Verkehr; **~-weight** Schwergewicht(ler *m*) *n*.

hectic ['hektik] hektisch.

hedge [hedʒ] Hecke *f*; **~hog** Igel *m*; *Am.* Stachelschwein *n*.

heed [hi:d] beachten, achten auf; Beachtung *f*, Aufmerksamkeit *f*; **take ~ of**, **give** *od.* **pay ~ to** achten auf, beachten; **~less**: **~ of** ungeachtet.

heel [hi:l] Ferse *f*; Absatz *m*; **take to one's ~s** Reißaus nehmen.

he-goat Ziegenbock *m*.

heifer ['hefə] Färse *f* (*junge Kuh*).

height [hait] Höhe *f*; Höhepunkt *m*; **~en** erhöhen; vergrößern.

heinous ['heinəs] abscheulich. [Erbin *f*.]

heir [ɛə] Erbe *m*; **~ess**)

held [held] *pret u. pp von* **hold**.

helicopter ['helikɔptə] Hubschrauber *m*.

hell [hel] Hölle *f*.

hello [he'ləu] *int.* hallo!

helm [helm] Ruder *n*, Steuer *n*.

helmet ['helmit] Helm *m*.

help [help] Hilfe *f*; (Dienst)Mädchen *n*, Hilfe *f*; helfen; geben, reichen (*bei Tisch*); **~ o. s.** to sich bedienen mit, sich nehmen; **I can't ~ it** ich kann es nicht ändern, ich kann nichts dafür; **I cannot ~ laughing** ich muß (einfach) lachen; **~er** Helfer(in); Gehilf|e *m*, -*in f*; **~ful** hilfreich, -bereit; nützlich; **~ing** Portion *f*; **~less** hilflos; **~lessness** Hilflosigkeit *f*.

helter-skelter ['heltə-'skeltə] holterdipolter.

hem [hem] Saum *m*; säumen; sich räuspern, stokken (*beim Reden*); **~ in** einschließen.

hemisphere ['hemisfiə]

Halbkugel f, Hemisphäre f.

hemline Saum m.

hemlock ['hemlɔk] Schierling m.

hemp [hemp] Hanf m.

hemstitch Hohlsaum m.

hen [hen] Henne f, Huhn n; (*Vogel*)Weibchen n.

hence [hens] von jetzt an, binnen; daher, deshalb; **~forth**, **~forward** von nun an, künftig.

hen|-coop ['henku:p]Hühnerstall m; **~house** Hühnerhaus n; **~pecked** unter dem Pantoffel stehend; **~pecked husband** Pantoffelheld m.

her [hə:] sie; ihr; ihr(e); sich.

herald ['herəld] Herold m; Vorbote m; ankündigen; einführen; **~ry** Wappenkunde f, Heraldik f.

herb [hə:b] Kraut n.

herd [hə:d] Herde f (a. fig.); **~sman** Hirt m.

here [hiə] hier; hierher; **~'s to ...!** auf das Wohl von ...!; **~ you are** hier (bitte)!; (*da hast du es!*); **~after** künftig; **~by** hierdurch;

hereditary [hi'reditəri] erblich, Erb... [von.\
here|in hierin; **~of** hier-]

heresy ['herəsi] Ketzerei f.

here|upon hierauf, darauf (-hin); **~with** hiermit.

heritage ['heritidʒ] Erbe n, Erbschaft f.

hermit ['hə:mit] Einsiedler m.

hero ['hiərəu] Held m; **~ic** [hi'rəuik] heroisch; **~ine** ['herəuin] Heldin f; **~ism** ['herəuizəm] Heldentum n, Heroismus m.

heron ['herən] Reiher m.

herring ['heriŋ] Hering m.

hers [hə:z] ihr, der, die, das ihr(ig)e.

herself [hə:'self] sich (selbst); sie *od.* ihr selbst; **by ~** allein.

hesitat|e ['heziteit] zögern, Bedenken tragen; **~ion** Zögern n, Bedenken n.

hew [hju:] (*irr*) hauen, hacken; **~n** *pp von* **hew.**

hey [hei] *int.* he! heda!

heyday ['heidei] Höhepunkt m, Blüte f.

hi [hai] *int.* he!, heda!; *Am.* hallo!

hicc|ough, **~up** ['hikəp] Schlucken m; den Schlucken haben.

hid [hid] *pret u. pp*, **~den** *pp von* **hide.**

hide [hid] (*Tier*)Haut f; (*irr*) (sich) verbergen *od.* -stecken; **~-and-seek** Versteckspiel n.

hideous ['hidiəs] abscheulich.

hiding[1] ['haidiŋ] Tracht f Prügel.

hiding[2] Versteck n; **be in ~** sich versteckt halten; **~ place** Versteck n.

hi-fi ['hai'fai] *colloq. s.* **high-fidelity.**

high [hai] *meteor.* Hoch(druckgebiet) n;

hoch; stark, heftig; schrill; teuer; äußerst; angegangen (*Fleisch*); bedeutend, Haupt..., Hoch..., Ober...; erhaben, vornehm, edel; arrogant, hochmütig; **be ~** *sl.* angeheitert sein; im Drogenrausch sein; **~ up** hoch oben; **in ~ spirits** guter Laune, in gehobener Stimmung; **~ time** höchste Zeit; **~brow** Intellektuelle *m, f*; (betont) intellektuell; **~ diving** Turmspringen *n*; **~fidelity** mit höchster Wiedergabetreue, Hi-Fi; **~ jump** Hochsprung *m*; **~lands** *pl* Hochland *n*; **~lights** *pl* Höhepunkt(e *pl*) *m*; **~ly** hoch, sehr; **think ~ly of** viel halten von; **~ness** *fig.:* Höhe *f*; **2ness** Hoheit *f* (*Titel*); **~-pitched** schrill (*Ton*); steil (*Dach*); **~-power(ed)** Hochleistungs..., Groß...; **~-pressure area** Hochdruckgebiet *n*; **~road** Hauptstraße *f*; **~ school** *Am. appr.* höhere Schule (*bis Mittlere Reife*), Mittelschule *f*; **~ street** *Brit.* Hauptstraße *f*; **~ tea** kaltes Abendessen mit Tee; **~ tide** Flut *f*; **~way** Landstraße *f*; **2way Code** Straßenverkehrsordnung *f*.

hijack ['haidʒæk] (be-) rauben; entführen.

hike [haik] *colloq.* wandern; Wanderung *f*; **~r** Wanderer *m*.

hilarious [hi'lɛəriəs] vergnügt, ausgelassen.

hill [hil] Hügel *m*, Anhöhe *f*; **~billy** ['~bili] Hinterwäldler *m*; **~side** (Ab-) Hang *m*; **~y** hügelig.

hilt [hilt] Heft *n*, Griff *m*.

him [him] ihn; ihm; ihm; den(-), dem(jenigen); sich; **~self** sich (selbst); (er, ihn, ihm) selbst; **by ~self** allein.

hind¹ [haind] Hirschkuh *f*.

hind² Hinter...; **~er** ['hində] (ver)hindern, abhalten; **~ leg** Hinterbein *n*; **~rance** ['hindrəns] Hindernis *n*.

hinge [hindʒ] (Tür)Angel *f*, Scharnier *n*.

hinny ['hini] Maulesel *m*.

hint [hint] Wink *m*, Hinweis *m*, Tip *m*; Anspielung *f*; andeuten; anspielen.

hinterland ['hintəlænd] Hinterland *n*.

hip [hip] Hüfte *f*.

hippopotamus [hipə'pɔtəməs] Fluß-, Nilpferd *n*.

hire ['haiə] mieten; *j-n* anstellen; ~ *out* vermieten; *sub:* Miete *f*; (Arbeits-) Lohn *m*; **for ~** zu vermieten; frei (*Taxi*); **on ~** zu vermieten; **~(d) car** Mietauto *n*, -wagen *m*.

his [hiz] sein(e); seine(r, -s), der, die, das sein(ig)e.

hiss [his] zischen; auszischen, -pfeifen; Zischen *n*.

histor|ian [his'tɔ:riən] Historiker *m*; **~ic** [~'tɔrik] historisch (berühmt od. bedeutsam); **~ical** historisch, geschichtlich (belegt), Geschichts...; **~y** ['ɔːri] Geschichte f.

hit [hit] Schlag m, Stoß m; Treffer m; thea., mus. Schlager m; (irr) schlagen, stoßen; treffen (a. fig.); auf et. stoßen; **~ (up)on** (zufällig) auf et. stoßen, et. treffen od. finden; **~and-run driving** Fahrerflucht f.

hitch [hitʃ] Ruck m; fig. Haken m; ziehen; festmachen, -haken; hängenbleiben; **~hike** per Anhalter fahren **~hiker** Anhalter m.

hither ['hiðə] hierher; **~to** bisher.

hive [haiv] Bienenkorb m, -stock m; Bienenvolk n.

hoard [hɔːd] Vorrat m, Schatz m; horten.

hoar-frost ['hɔː'-] (Rauh-) Reif m.

hoarse [hɔːs] heiser, rauh.

hoax [həuks] Schabernack m, Streich m; foppen.

hobble ['hɔbl] humpeln; e-m Pferd die Vorderbeine fesseln.

hobby ['hɔbi] Steckenpferd n, Hobby n; **~horse** Schaukelpferd n; Steckenpferd n. [Kobold m.]

hobgoblin ['hɔbgɔblin]∫

hobo ['həubəu] Am. Wanderarbeiter m, Landstreicher m. [wein.]

hock¹ [hɔk] weißer Rhein-∫

hock² zo. Sprunggelenk n.

hockey ['hɔki] Hockey n.

hoe [həu] Hacke f; hacken.

hog [hɔg] Schwein n.

hoist [hɔist] (Lasten)Aufzug m; hochziehen; hissen.

hold [həuld] (irr) (ab-, an-, auf-, aus-, be)halten; besitzen; Amt innehaben; Stellung halten; fassen, enthalten; Ansicht vertreten, haben; meinen; beibehalten; halten für; fig. fesseln; (stand)halten; (an-, fort)dauern; **~ one's ground, ~ one's own** sich behaupten; **~ tight** sich festhalten; **~ on** sich festhalten; aushalten, -harren; fortdauern; teleph. am Apparat bleiben; **~ s.th. on** et. (an s-m Platz fest)halten; **~ to** festhalten an; **~ up** hochheben, halten, stützen; aufrechterhalten; überfallen; sub: Halt m; Griff m; Gewalt f, Einfluß m; Lade-, Frachtraum m; **catch (get, lay, seize, take) ~ of** (er)fassen, ergreifen; **keep ~ of** festhalten; **~er** oft in Zssgn: Halter m; Pächter m; Inhaber(in) (bsd. econ.); **~ing** Pachtgut n; mst pl Besitz m (an Effekten etc.); **~up** Raubüberfall m; Aufhalten n, (Verkehrs)Stockung f.

hole [həul] Loch n; Höhle f, Bau m; durchlöchern.

holiday ['hɔlədi] Feiertag

m; freier Tag, Ferientag *m; mst pl* Ferien *pl,* Urlaub *m;* on ~ in den Ferien, auf Urlaub; **~makers** *pl* Urlauber *pl;* **~ village** Feriendorf *n.*

hollow ['hɔləu] Höhle *f,* (Aus)Höhlung *f;* Loch *n;* Mulde *f,* Tal *n;* hohl (*a. fig.*); ~ **(out)** aushöhlen.

holly ['hɔli] Stechpalme *f.*

holy ['həuli] heilig; 2 **Thursday** Gründonnerstag *m;* 2 **Week** Karwoche *f.*

home [həum] Heim *n;* Wohnung *f;* Heimat *f;* **at** ~ zu Hause; **make o.s. at** ~ es sich bequem machen; **take s.o.** ~ j-n nach Hause bringen; einheimisch, inländisch, Inland(s)...; nach Hause; **~ Counties** *pl die* Grafschaften um London; **~less** heimatlos; obdachlos, **~ly** anheimelnd, häuslich; *fig.* hausbacken; schlicht; **~made** selbstgemacht; 2 **Office** Brit. Innenministerium *n;* 2 **Secretary** Brit. Innenminister *m;* **~sick: be** ~ Heimweh haben; **~sickness** Heimweh *n;* **~ team** *sp.* Gastgeber *pl;* **~ trade** Binnenhandel *m;* **~ward** ['~wəd] heimwärts; Heim...; **~wards** heimwärts; **~work** Hausaufgabe(n *pl*) *f,* Schularbeiten *pl.*

homicide ['hɔmisaid] Totschlag *m;* Mord *m.*

honest ['ɔnist] ehrlich; aufrichtig; **~y** Ehrlichkeit *f;* Aufrichtigkeit *f.*

honey ['hʌni] Honig *m;* *fig.* Liebling *m;* **~comb** (Honig)Wabe *f;* **~moon** Flitterwochen *pl;* die Flitterwochen verbringen.

honk [hɔŋk] *mot.* hupen.

honorary ['ɔnərəri] Ehren...; ehrenamtlich.

hono(u)r ['ɔnə] Ehre *f;* (Hoch)Achtung *f;* Ansehen *n;* *fig.* Zierde *f; pl* Auszeichnung *f,* Ehrung *f;* (be)ehren; Scheck *etc.* einlösen; **~able** ehrenwert; ehrlich; ehrenvoll.

hood [hud] Kapuze *f; mot.* Verdeck *n; Am.* (Motor-) Haube *f; tech.* Kappe *f.*

hoodlum ['hu:dləm] *Am. colloq.* Rowdy *m,* Strolch *m.*

hoodwink ['hudwiŋk] täuschen.

hoof [hu:f], *pl* ~s, **hooves** [~vz] Huf *m.*

hook [huk] (Angel)Haken *m;* Sichel *f;* an-, ein-, fest-, zuhaken; angeln (*a. fig.*); sich (zu)haken lassen; sich festhaken.

hoop [hu:p] (Faß- *etc.*) Reif(en) *m.*

hooping-cough ['hu:piŋ-] Keuchhusten *m.*

hoot [hu:t] heulen, johlen; *mot.* hupen; auspfeifen.

Hoover ['hu:və] (*Fabrikmarke*): Staubsauger *m;* staubsaugen.

hooves [hu:vz] *pl von* **hoof.**

hop [hɔp] *bot.* Hopfen *m*; Sprung *m*; hüpfen, hopsen.

hope [həup] Hoffnung *f*; hoffen (**for** auf); *~ful* hoffnungsvoll; *~less* hoffnungslos, verzweifelt.

horizon [hə'raizn] Horizont *m*; *~tal* [hɔri'zɔntl] horizontal, waag(e)recht.

horn [hɔːn] Horn *n*; *mot.* Hupe *f*; *pl* Geweih *n*.

hornet ['hɔːnit] Hornisse *f*.

horny ['hɔːni] aus Horn; schwielig.

horr|ible ['hɔrəbl] schrecklich, entsetzlich; *~id* ['~id] schrecklich; *~ify* ['~ifai] entsetzen; *~or* Entsetzen *n*; Abscheu *m* (**of** vor).

horse [hɔːs] Pferd *n*; Bock *m*, Gestell *n*; *~back*: **on ~** zu Pferde; *~hair* Roßhaar *n*; *~man* Reiter *m*; *~power* Pferdestärke *f*; *~race* Pferderennen *n*; *~racing* Pferderennsport *m*, -rennen *n*; *~radish* Meerrettich *m*; *~shoe* Hufeisen *n*.

horticulture ['hɔːtikʌltʃə] Gartenbau *m*.

hos|e [həuz] Schlauch *m*; *~e pl* Strümpfe *pl*; *~iery* ['~iəri] Strumpfwaren *pl*.

hospitable ['hɔspitəbl] gast(freund)lich.

hospital ['hɔspitl] Krankenhaus *n*, Klinik *f*; *~ity* [~'tæliti] Gastfreundschaft *f*.

host [həust] Gastgeber *m*; Hausherr *m*; (Gast)Wirt *m*; *fig.* (Un)Menge *f*; Heer *n*; *eccl.* Hostie *f*.

hostage ['hɔstidʒ] Geisel *f*.

hostel ['hɔstəl] Herberge *f*; Studenten(wohn)heim *n*.

hostess ['həustis] Gastgeberin *f*; (Gast)Wirtin *f*.

hostil|e ['hɔstail] feindlich; feindselig; *~ity* [~'tiliti] Feindseligkeit *f*.

hot [hɔt] heiß; scharf; warm; hitzig; heftig.

hot dog *colloq.* heißes Würstchen in e-r Semmel.

hotel [hou'tel] Hotel *n*.

hot|head Hitzkopf *m*; *~house* Treibhaus *n*; *~water-bottle* Wärmflasche *f*.

hound [haund] Jagdhund *m*; jagen, hetzen; drängen.

hour ['auə] Stunde *f*; (Tages)Zeit *f*, Uhr *f*; *~ly* stündlich.

house [haus] Haus *n*; **the 2** *colloq.* das Parlament; [~z] unterbringen; *~hold* Haushalt *m*; Haushalts...; *~keeper* Haushälterin *f*; *~keeping* Haushaltung *f*, -wirtschaft *f*; *~warming* Einzugsfeier *f*; *~wife* Hausfrau *f*; *~work* Hausarbeit(en *pl*) *f*, Arbeit *f* im Haushalt.

housing estate ['hauziŋ] (Wohn)Siedlung *f*.

hove [houv] *pret u. pp von* **heave.**

hover ['hɔvə] schweben.

how [hau] wie; *~ do you do? (Begrüßungsformel bei der Vorstellung)*; *~ are*

you? – fine, thank you wie geht es Ihnen? – danke, gut!; **~ about ...?** wie steht's mit ...?; **~ much (many)?** wieviel(e)?; **~ much is it?** was kostet es?; **~ever** wie auch (immer); jedoch.

howl [haul] heulen; wehklagen; pfeifen (*Wind, Radio*); Heulen *n*, Geheul *n*; **~er** *colloq.* grober Fehler.

hub [hʌb] (Rad)Nabe *f*.

hubbub ['hʌbʌb] Stimmengewirr *n*; Tumult *m*, Lärm *m*.

hubby ['hʌbi] *colloq.* (Ehe-) Mann *m*.

huckleberry ['hʌklberi] amerikanische Heidelbeere.

huddle ['hʌdl]: **~ together** (sich) zs.-drängen; **~d up** zs.-gekauert.

hue [hju:] Farbe *f*.

hug [hʌg] Umarmung *f*; umarmen.

huge [hju:dʒ] sehr groß, riesig, ungeheuer.

hull [hʌl] *bot.* Schale *f*, Hülse *f*; (Schiffs)Rumpf *m*; enthülsen, schälen.

hullabaloo [hʌləbə'lu:] Lärm *m*.

hullo ['hʌ'ləu] *int.* hallo!

hum [hʌm] summen, brummen.

human ['hju:mən] menschlich, Menschen...; **~e** [~'mein] human; **~itarian** [~mæni'tɛəriən] Menschenfreund *m*;

humanitär; **~ity** [~'mæniti] Menschheit *f*; Humanität *f*.

humble ['hʌmbl] demütig, bescheiden; niedrig, gering; erniedrigen, demütigen; **~ness** Demut *f*.

humbug ['hʌmbag] Schwindel *m*; Schwindler *m*; beschwindeln.

humdrum ['hʌmdrʌm] eintönig, alltäglich.

humidity [hju(:)'miditi] Feuchtigkeit *f*.

humiliate [hju(:)'milieit] erniedrigen, demütigen; **~ion** Erniedrigung *f*, Demütigung *f*.

humility [hju(:)'militi] Demut *f*.

humming-bird Kolibri *m*.

humorous ['hju:mərəs] humoristisch, humorvoll, komisch.

humo(u)r ['hju:mə] Laune *f*, Stimmung *f*; Humor *m*; *j-m* s-n Willen tun *od.* lassen.

hump [hʌmp] Höcker *m*, Buckel *m*; **~back** Bucklige *m, f*.

hunch [hʌntʃ], **~back** s. hump(back).

hundred ['hʌndrəd] hundert; Hundert *n*; **~th** ['~θ] hundertste; **~weight** *appr.* Zentner *m* (50,8 *kg*).

hung [hʌŋ] *pret u. pp von* hang.

Hungarian [hʌŋ'gɛəriən] ungarisch; Ungar(in); Ungarisch *n*.

hunger ['hʌŋə] Hunger *m*; **hungern (for, after** nach).

hungry ['hʌŋgri] hungrig; **be ~** Hunger haben.

hunt [hʌnt] Jagd *f*; jagen; **~er** Jäger *m*; Jagdpferd *n*; **~ing** Jagen *n*; Jagd...; **~ing-ground** Jagdrevier *n*; **~sman** Jäger *m*.

hurdle ['hɜːdl] Hürde *f* (*a. fig.*); **~r** Hürdenläufer (-in); **~-race** Hürdenlauf *m*.

hurl [hɜːl] schleudern.

hurrah [hu'rɑː], **~y** [ˈ~reɪ] *int.* hurra!

hurricane ['hʌrikən] Hurrikan *m*, Wirbelsturm *m*, Orkan *m*.

hurried ['hʌrid] eilig, hastig, übereilt.

hurry ['hʌri] Eile *f*, Hast *f*; **be in a ~** es eilig haben; *vb*: (an)treiben, drängen (*beide a.* **~ up**); (sich be)eilen; **~ up!** beeile dich!

hurt [hɜːt] Verletzung *f*; Schaden *m*; (*irr*) verletzen (*a. fig.*); schmerzen, weh tun; drücken (*Schuh*) (*j-m*) schaden.

husband ['hʌzbənd] (Ehe)Mann *m*; haushalten mit; **~ry** Landwirtschaft *f*.

hush [hʌʃ] Stille *f*; still sein; zum Schweigen bringen; beruhigen; **~ up** vertuschen; [ʃː] *int.* still!, pst!

husk [hʌsk] (trockene) Hülse, Schote *f*, Schale *f*; enthülsen, schälen; **~y**

heiser; *colloq.* robust, stämmig.

hustle ['hʌsl] stoßen, (sich) drängen; antreiben; Gedränge *n*, Getriebe *n*.

hut [hʌt] Hütte *f*.

hutch [hʌtʃ] (*bsd.* Kaninchen)Stall *m*; Hütte *f*.

hybrid ['haibrid] *biol.* Mischling *m*, Kreuzung *f*.

hydrant ['haidrənt] Hydrant *m*.

hydraulic [hai'drɔːlik] hydraulisch.

hydro- ['haidrəu-] Wasser...; Wasserstoff...

hydro|carbon Kohlenwasserstoff *m*; **~chloric acid** [ˈ~klɔrik] Salzsäure *f*; **~gen** ['ˌidʒən] Wasserstoff *m*; **~gen bomb** Wasserstoffbombe *f*; **~plane** Gleitboot *n*.

hyena [hai'iːnə] Hyäne *f*.

hygiene ['haidʒiːn] Hygiene *f*.

hymn [him] Hymne *f*, Kirchenlied *n*.

hyphen ['haifən] Bindestrich *m*.

hypnotize ['hipnətaiz] hypnotisieren.

hypo|crisy [hi'pɔkrəsi] Heuchelei *f*; **~crite** ['hipəkrit] Heuchler(in); **~critical** [hipəu'kritikəl] heuchlerisch.

hypothesis [hai'pɔθisis] Hypothese *f*.

hysteri|a [his'tiəriə] Hysterie *f*; **~cal** [ˈ~terikəl] hysterisch; **~cs** *pl* hysterischer Anfall.

I

I [ai] ich.

ice [ais] Eis n; gefrieren (lassen); vereisen (a. ~ up); mit od. in Eis kühlen; überzuckern, glasieren; **~age** Eiszeit f; **~berg** ['ɔːbɔːg] Eisberg m; **~cream** (Speise)Eis n.

ic|icle ['aisikl] Eiszapfen m; **~ing** Zuckerguß m; tech. Vereisung f; **~y** eisig (a. fig.); vereist.

idea [ai'diə] Idee f; Vorstellung f, Begriff m, Ahnung f; Gedanke m; Idee f, Einfall m; **~l** ideal; Ideal n.

identical [ai'dentikəl] identisch, gleich(bedeutend).

identi|fication [aidentifi-'keiʃən] Identifizierung f; **~fication papers** pl Ausweis(papiere pl) m; **~fy** [~'dentifai] identifizieren; ausweisen.

identity [ai'dentiti] Identität f; **~ card** (Personal-) Ausweis m, Kennkarte f.

ideological [aidiə'lɔdʒi-kəl] ideologisch.

idiom ['idiəm] Idiom n, Mundart f; Redewendung f.

idiot ['idiət] Idiot(in), Dummkopf m; Schwachsinnige m, f; **~ic** [~'ɔtik] blödsinnig.

idle ['aidl] müßig, untätig; träg(e), faul; nutzlos; faulenzen; tech. leerlaufen;

~away vertrödeln; **~ness** Muße f; Faulheit f.

idol ['aidl] Idol n, Abgott m; Götzenbild n; **~ize** ['ɔːulaiz] vergöttern.

idyl(l) ['idil] Idyll(e f) n.

if [if] wenn, falls; ob; Wenn n.

igloo ['iglu:] Iglu m.

ignit|e [ig'nait] an-, (sich) entzünden; zünden; **~ion** [ig'niʃən] mot. Zündung f; **~ion key** Zündschlüssel m.

ignoble [ig'nəubl] schändlich, gemein.

ignor|ance ['ignərəns] Unwissenheit f; Unkenntnis f; **~ant** ungebildet; nicht wissend od. kennend; **~e** [ig'nɔː] ignorieren; nicht beachten.

ill [il] übel, böse; schlimm, schlecht; krank; **fall ~**, **be taken ~** krank werden; Unglück n; Übel n, Böse n; **~advised** schlechtberaten; unklug; **~bred** ungezogen, -höflich.

il|legal [i'li:gəl] illegal, ungesetzlich; **~legible** unleserlich; **~legitimate** unrechtmäßig; unehelich.

ill-humo(u)red übellaunt.

il|licit [i'lisit] unerlaubt; **~literate** [i'litərit] ungebildet; Analphabet(in).

ill-judged unvernünftig; **~mannered** ungehobelt, mit schlechten Um-

gangsformens; **~natured**
boshaft, bösartig; **~ness**
Krankheit f; **~tempered**
schlechtgelaunt; **~timed**
ungelegen, unpassend; **~
treat** mißhandeln.

illumina|te [i'lju:mineit]
be-, erleuchten; *fig.* erläutern; **~ion** (*pl* Fest-)
Beleuchtung f.

illusion [i'lu:ʒən] Illusion
f, Täuschung f; **~ive,
~ory** illusorisch, trügerisch.

illustrat|e ['iləstreit] illu-
strieren; erläutern; be-
bildern; **~ion** Erläuterung
f; Illustration f; Abbil-
dung f; **~ive** erläuternd.

illustrious [i'lʌstriəs] berühmt.

ill well Feindschaft f.

image ['imidʒ] Bild(nis)
n; Statue f; Ebenbild n;
Vorstellung f; **~ry** Bilder
pl, Bildwerk(e *pl*) n; Bild-
ersprache f.

imagin|able [i'mædʒi-
nəbl] denkbar; **~ary** eingebildet; **~ation** Phantasie
f, Einbildung(skraft) f; **~e**
[~ʤin] sich *j-n od. et.* vorstellen; sich *et.* einbilden.

imbecile ['imbisi:l] geistes-
schwach; dumm; Schwach-
sinnige m, f; Narr m.

imitat|e ['imiteit] nach-
ahmen, imitieren; **~ion**
Nachahmung f; Nachbil-
dung f; unecht, künstlich,
Kunst...

im|material [imə-
'tiəriəl] unwesentlich;

~mature unreif; **~mea-
surable** unermeßlich.

immediate [i'mi:djət]
unmittelbar; unverzüglich,
sofort; **~ly** sofort; unmittelbar.

im|mense [i'mens] unge-
heuer; **~merse**
[~'mə:s]
(ein)tauchen; vertiefen.

immigra|nt ['imigrənt]
Einwander|er m, -in f; **~te**
['~eit] einwandern; **~tion**
Einwanderung f.

imminent ['iminənt] bevorstehend, drohend.

im|mobile [i'məubail] un-
beweglich; **~moderate**
übermäßig, maßlos; **~
modest** unbescheiden; **~
moral** unmoralisch.

immortal [i'mɔ:tl] un-
sterblich
m, f; **~ity** [~'tæliti] Un-
sterblichkeit f.

im|movable [i'mu:vəbl]
unbeweglich; unerschüt-
terlich; **~mune** [i'mju:n]
immun.

imp [imp] Teufelchen n;
Schlingel m.

impact ['impækt] Stoß m,
Zs.-prall m; *fig.* (Ein-)
Wirkung f.

impair [im'pɛə] schwächen; beeinträchtigen.

impart [im'pɑ:t] geben;
mitteilen; **~ial** [~ʃəl] unparteiisch; **~iality** [~ʃi'æ-
liti] Unparteilichkeit f.

im|passable unpassier-
bar; **~passive** teilnahmslos; **~t** ungeduldig.

impatien|ce Ungeduld f;

impediment [im'pedimənt] Behinderung f.

im|pend [im'pend] bevorstehen, drohen; **~penetrable** [~'penitrəbl] undurchdringlich; fig. unzugänglich.

imperative [im'perətiv] unumgänglich, unbedingt erforderlich; befehlend, gebieterisch; **~ (mood)** gr. Imperativ m, Befehlsform f.

imperceptible unmerklich.

imperfect [im'pə:fikt] unvollkommen; unvollendet; **~ (tense)** gr. Imperfekt n, unvollendete Vergangenheit.

imperial [im'piəriəl] kaiserlich; großartig; **~ism** Imperialismus m.

im|peril [im'peril] gefährden; **~perious** [im'piəriəs] herrisch; dringend; **~permeable** undurchlässig.

imperson|al unpersönlich; **~ate** [im'pə:səneit] verkörpern; thea. darstellen.

impertinen|ce [im'pə:tinəns] Unverschämtheit f; **~t** unverschämt.

im|perturbable [impə(:)-'tə:bəbl] unerschütterlich; **~pervious** [~'pə:vjəs] undurchlässig; fig. unzugänglich (to für); **~petuous** [~'petjuəs] ungestüm, heftig; **~placable** [~'plækəbl] unversöhnlich.

implement ['implimənt] Werkzeug n, Gerät n.

implicat|e ['implikeit] verwickeln; **~ion** Verwick(e)lung f; Folge f; tieferer Sinn.

im|plicit [im'plisit] (mit od. stillschweigend) inbegriffen; blind (Glaube etc.); **~plore** [~'plɔ:] j-n dringend bitten an anflehen; **~ply** [~'plai] in sich schließen; bedeuten; andeuten; **~polite** unhöflich.

import ['impɔ:t] Einfuhr f, Import m; pl Einfuhrwaren pl; Bedeutung f; Wichtigkeit f; [~'pɔ:t] einführen, importieren; bedeuten; **~ance** [~'pɔ:təns] Wichtigkeit f, Bedeutung f; **~ant** wichtig, bedeutend; wichtigtuerisch; **~ation** Import m, Einfuhr(ware) f.

importune [im'pɔ:tju:n] dauernd bitten, belästigen.

impos|e [im'pəuz] auferlegen, aufbürden (on, upon dat); **~e upon** j-n täuschen; **~ing** eindrucksvoll, imponierend.

impossib|ility Unmöglichkeit f; **~le** unmöglich.

impostor [im'pɔstə] Hochstapler(in).

impoten|ce ['impətəns] Unvermögen n, Unfähigkeit f; Machtlosigkeit f; med. Impotenz f; **~t** unfähig; machtlos; schwach; med. impotent.

impracticable undurchführbar; unwegsam.

impregnate ['impregneit] schwängern; imprägnieren.

impress ['impres] Ab-, Eindruck m; [~'pres] (auf-) drücken; einprägen (on dat); j-n beeindrucken; **~ion** Eindruck m; Abdruck m; **be under the ~ion** den Eindruck haben; **~ive** eindrucksvoll.

imprint [im'print] (auf-) drücken; aufdrucken; fig. einprägen (on dat); ['~] Abdruck m.

imprison [im'prizn] einsperren; **~ment** Haft f; Gefängnis(strafe f) n.

improbable unwahrscheinlich; **~proper** unpassend; falsch; unanständig.

improve [im'pru:v] verbessern; sich (ver)bessern; **~ment** (Ver)Besserung f; Fortschritt m.

improvise ['improvaiz] improvisieren; **~prudent** [~'pru:dənt] unklug, unüberlegt.

impuden|ce ['impjudəns] Unverschämtheit f, Frechheit f; **~t** unverschämt.

impulse ['impʌls] Antrieb m; fig. a. Impuls m, Drang m; **~ive** (an)treibend; fig. impulsiv.

impunity [im'pju:niti]: **with ~** straflos, ungestraft;

~pure [~'pjuə] unrein (a. fig.); schmutzig; **~pute** [~'pju:t] zuschreiben.

in [in] prp in, auf, an; **~ the street** auf der Straße; **~ 1972** im Jahre 1972; **~ English** auf Englisch; **~ my opinion** meiner Meinung nach; **~ Shakespeare** bei Shakespeare; adv hinein; herein; (dr)innen; zu Hause; da, angekommen; modern.

in|ability Unfähigkeit f; **~accessible** [inæk'sesəbl] unzugänglich; **~accurate** ungenau; falsch.

inactiv|e untätig, **~ity** Untätigkeit f.

in|adequate unangemessen; unzulänglich; **~advertent** [inəd'və:tənt] unachtsam; unabsichtlich; **~alterable** unveränderlich; **~animate** [~'ænimit] leblos; fig. unbelebt; geistlos, langweilig; **~appropriate** unangebracht, unpassend; **~apt** ungeschickt; unpassend; **~articulate** undeutlich; sprachlos.

inasmuch [inəz'mʌtʃ]: **~ as** da, weil.

in|attentive unaufmerksam; **~audible** unhörbar.

inaugura|l [i'nɔ:gjurəl] Antrittsrede f; Antritts...; **~te** [~eit] (feierlich) einführen; einweihen, eröffnen; einleiten, beginnen.

inborn ['in'bɔ:n] angeboren.

incalculable [in'kæl-kjuləbl] unzählbar; unberechenbar.

incapa|ble unfähig; **~citate** [inkə'pæsiteit] unfähig *od.* untauglich machen; **~city** Unfähigkeit *f*, Untauglichkeit *f*.

incautious unvorsichtig.

incendiary [in'sendjəri] Feuer...; Brand...; Brandstifter *m*.

incense¹ ['insens] Weihrauch *m*.

incense² [in'sens] erzürnen, erbosen.

incessant [in'sesnt] unaufhörlich, ständig.

incest ['insest] Blutschande *f*.

inch [intʃ] Zoll *m* (= 2,54 cm).

incident ['insidənt] Vorfall *m*, Ereignis *n*; *bsd.* Zwischenfall *m*; **~al** [~'dentl] beiläufig, nebensächlich; Begleit..., Neben...; **~ally** beiläufig; zufällig.

incinerate [in'sinəreit] (zu Asche) verbrennen.

incis|e [in'saiz] einschneiden; **~ion** [~'iʒən] (Ein-)Schnitt *m*; **~ive** scharf, schneidend; *fig.* **~or** Schneidezahn *m*.

incite [in'sait] anspornen, anregen; aufhetzen.

inclement [in'klemənt] rauh (*Klima, Wetter*).

inclin|ation [inkli'neiʃən] Neigung *f* (*a. fig.*); **~e** [in'klain] (sich) neigen;

abfallen; geneigt sein (**to** *dat*); veranlassen, bewegen; Neigung *f*, Abhang *m*.

inclos|e [in'klouz], **~ure** [~ʒə] *s.* enclose, enclosure.

inclu|de [in'kluːd] einschließen; **~sive** einschließlich (**of** *gen*); **~sive terms** *pl* Pauschalpreis *m*.

incoherent unzs.-hängend.

income ['inkʌm] Einkommen *n*; **~tax** ['~ɔmtæks] Einkommensteuer *f*.

incoming ['inkʌmiŋ] hereinkommend; ankommend.

in|comparable unvergleichlich; **~compatible** unvereinbar; **~competent** unfähig; unbefugt; **~complete** unvollständig; **~comprehensible** unbegreiflich; **~conceivable** unbegreiflich; **~consequent** inkonsequent.

inconsidera|ble unbedeutend; **~te** unüberlegt; rücksichtslos.

in|consistent unvereinbar; widerspruchsvoll; **~consolable** untröstlich; **~constant** unbeständig; wankelmütig.

inconvenien|ce Unbequemlichkeit *f*; Unannehmlichkeit *f*; Ungelegenheit *f*; belästigen; **~t** unbequem; ungelegen, lästig.

incorporate [in'kɔːpəreit] (sich) vereinigen; einver-

leiben; ~ [~rit], ~d [~reitid]
(amtlich) eingetragen.

in|correct unrichtig; ~
corrigible unverbesser-
lich.

increas|e [in'kri:s] zu-
nehmen, größer werden,
(an)wachsen; vermehren,
-größern, erhöhen; ['in-
kri:s] Zunahme f, Ver-
größerung f, Erhöhung
f, Zuwachs m, Steigen n;
~ingly immer mehr.

incred|ible unglaublich;
~ulous ungläubig, skep-
tisch. [neit] belasten.]

incriminate [in'krimi-/

incubator [in'kjubeitə]
Brutapparat m.

incur [in'kə:] sich et. zuziehen; *Verpflichtung* eingehen; *Verlust* erleiden.

in|curable unheilbar;
~debted verschuldet; *fig.*
zu Dank verpflichtet.

indecen|cy Unanständig-
keit f; ~t unanständig; un-
sittlich.

indecis|ion Unentschlos-
senheit f; ~ive nicht ent-
scheidend; unentschlos-
sen.

indeed [in'di:d] in der
Tat, tatsächlich, wirklich;
allerdings; *int.* ach wirklich!, nicht möglich!

in|defatigable [indi-
'fætigəbl] unermüdlich;
~definite unbestimmt;
unbegrenzt; [~'delibl]
[~'delibl] unauslöschlich;
untilgbar; ~delicate un-
fein; taktlos.

indemni|fy [in'demnifai]
entschädigen; sichern;
~ty Entschädigung f;
Sicherstellung f.

indent [in'dent] (ein)ker-
ben, (aus)zacken; ['~] Kerbe f; ~ure [in'dentʃə]
Vertrag m; Lehrvertrag m.

independen|ce Unab-
hängigkeit f; Selbständig-
keit f; ~t unabhängig;
selbständig.

in|describable [indis-
'kraibəbl] unbeschreib-
lich; ~determinate [~-
di'tə:minit] unbestimmt.

index ['indeks] Zeiger m;
(Inhalts-, Namen-, Sach-)
Verzeichnis n, Register n;
fig. (An)Zeichen n; ~
(finger) Zeigefinger m.

Indian [in'djən] indisch;
indianisch; Inder(in);
(Red) ~ Indianer(in); ~
corn Mais m; ~ file:
in ~ im Gänsemarsch; ~
summer Altweibersom-
mer m.

India-rubber [indjə'rʌbə]
Radiergummi m.

indicat|e ['indikeit] (an-)
zeigen; hinweisen auf;
andeuten; ~ion Anzeichen
n; Andeutung f; ~ive
(mood) [in'dikətiv] *gr.*
Indikativ m, Wirklich-
keitsform f; ~or ['~eitə]
Zeiger m; Anzeigevor-
richtung f; *mot.* Blinker
m.

indict [in'dait] anklagen;
~ment Anklage f.

indifferen|ce Gleichgültigkeit f; ⊷t gleichgültig; mittelmäßig.

indigent ['indidʒənt] arm.

indigest|ible unverdaulich; ⊷ion Verdauungsstörung f, Magenverstimmung f.

indign|ant [in'dignənt] entrüstet, empört; ⊷ation Entrüstung f, Empörung f.

indirect indirekt; nicht direkt od. gerade.

indiscre|et unklug; indiskret; ⊷tion Unüberlegtheit f; Indiskretion f.

in|discriminate [indis-'kriminit] wahllos; ⊷dispensable unentbehrlich.

indispos|ed [indis'pəuzd] unpäßlich; abgeneigt; ⊷ition Unpäßlichkeit f; Abneigung f.

in|disputable ['indis-'pju:təbl] unbestreitbar; unbestritten; ⊷distinct undeutlich, unklar.

individual [indi'vidjuəl] persönlich, individuell; einzeln; Individuum n; ⊷ist Individualist m.

indivisible unteilbar.

indolen|ce ['indələns] Trägheit f; ⊷t träge, lässig.

indomitable [in'dɔmitəbl] unbezähmbar, unbeugsam.

indoor ['indɔ:] im Hause; Haus..., Zimmer..., sp. Hallen...; ⊷s ['in'dɔ:z] im od. zu Hause; ins Haus.

indorse [in'dɔ:s] s. **endorse.**

induce [in'dju:s] veranlassen; verursachen.

induct [in'dʌkt] einführen, -setzen.

indulge [in'dʌldʒ] nachsichtig sein gegen; j-m nachgeben; frönen; ⊷ in s.th. sich et. erlauben od. gönnen; ⊷nce Nachsicht f; Befriedigung f; Schwelgen n; ⊷nt nachsichtig.

industrial [in'dʌstriəl] industriell, gewerblich, Industrie..., Gewerbe...; ⊷ area Industriegebiet n; ⊷ city Industriestadt f; ⊷ist Industrielle m; ⊷ize industrialisieren.

industr|ious [in'dʌstriəs] fleißig; ⊷y ['indəstri] Industrie f; Gewerbe n; Fleiß m.

in|effective, ⊷efficient wirkungslos; unfähig; ⊷equality Ungleichheit f.

inert [i'nə:t] träge; ⊷ia [⊷ʃiə] Trägheit f.

in|estimable [in'estiməbl] unschätzbar; ⊷evitable [⊷'evitəbl] unvermeidlich; ⊷excusable unverzeihlich; ⊷exhaustible unerschöpflich; ⊷expensive nicht teuer, preiswert; ⊷experienced unerfahren; ⊷explicable [⊷'eksplikəbl] unerklärlich.

inexpress|ible [iniks-'presəbl] unaussprechlich; ⊷ive ausdruckslos.

infallible [in'fæləbl] unfehlbar.

infam|ous ['infəməs] schändlich; **~y** Niedertracht f; Schande f.

infan|cy ['infənsi] frühe Kindheit; **~t** Säugling m; kleines Kind, Kleinkind n.

infantile ['infəntail] kindlich, Kinder...; kindisch.

infantry ['infəntri] Infanterie f.

infatuated [in'fætjueitid]: **~ with** vernarrt in.

infect [in'fekt] infizieren, anstecken (a. fig.); versuchen; **~ion** Infektion f, Ansteckung f; **~ious** ansteckend.

infer [in'fə:] schließen; **~ence** ['infərəns] Schlußfolgerung f, (Rück)Schluß m.

inferior [in'fiəriə] Untergebene m, f; unter; minderwertig; **~ to** niedriger od. geringer als; untergeordnet; unterlegen; **~ity** [~'ɔriti] Unterlegenheit f; Minderwertigkeit f.

infernal [in'fə:n] höllisch.

infest [in'fest] heimsuchen; plagen, verseuchen.

infidelity Unglaube m; Untreue f.

infiltrate ['infiltreit] einsickern (in); durchsetzen; eindringen.

infinite ['infinit] unendlich.

infinitive (mood) [in-'finitiv] gr. Infinitiv m, Nennform f.

infinity [in'finiti] Unendlichkeit f.

infirm [in'fə:m] schwach, gebrechlich; **~ary** Krankenhaus n; **~ity** Gebrechlichkeit f, (Alters)Schwäche f.

inflame [in'fleim] (sich) entzünden; fig. entflammen, erregen.

inflamma|ble [in'flæməbl] feuergefährlich; **~tion** [~ə'meiʃən] Entzündung f; **~tory** [in'flæmətəri] med. Entzündungs...; fig. aufrührerisch, Hetz...

inflat|e [in'fleit] aufblasen, -pumpen, -blähen; **~ion** econ. Inflation f; fig. Aufgeblasenheit f.

inflect [in'flekt] biegen; gr. flektieren, beugen.

inflex|ible [in'fleksəbl] starr; fig. unbeugsam; **~ion** [~kʃən] Biegung f; gr. Flexion f, Beugung f.

inflict [in'flikt] Leid zufügen; Wunde beibringen; Schlag versetzen; Strafe verhängen; **~ion** Zufügung f; Plage f.

influen|ce ['influəns] Einfluß m; beeinflussen; **~tial** [~'enʃəl] einflußreich.

influenza [influ'enzə] Grippe f.

inform [in'fɔ:m]: **~ (of)** benachrichtigen (von), informieren (über); j-m mitteilen; **~ against s.o.** j-n anzeigen; **~al** zwanglos.

information [infə'meiʃən] Auskunft f; Nachricht f, Information f;

~ bureau Auskunftsbüro *n*; **~ desk** Informationsschalter *m*; **~ office** Auskunftsbüro *n*.

inform|ative [in'fɔ:mətiv] informatorisch; lehrreich; **~er** Denunziant *m*; Spitzel *m*.

infuriate [in'fjuərieit] wütend machen.

infuse [in'fju:z] aufgießen; *fig.* einflößen.

ingeni|ous [in'dʒi:njəs] geistreich, klug; erfinderisch; kunstvoll, raffiniert; **~uity** [ˌ~i'nju(:)iti] Klugheit *f*, Geschicklichkeit *f*.

ingot ['iŋɡət] (*Gold- etc.*) Barren *m*.

ingrati|ate [in'greiʃieit]: **~ o.s.** sich einschmeicheln (**with** bei); **~tude** [ˌ~'grætitju:d] Undank(barkeit *f*) *m*.

ingredient [in'gri:djənt] Bestandteil *m*; *pl* Zutaten *pl*.

inhabit [in'hæbit] bewohnen; **~able** bewohnbar; **~ant** Bewohner(in); Einwohner(in).

inhale [in'heil] einatmen.

inherent [in'hiərənt] innewohnend, angeboren, eigen.

inherit [in'herit] erben; **~ance** Erbe *n*; Erbschaft *f*.

inhibit [in'hibit] hemmen; **~ion** Hemmung *f*.

in|hospitable ungastlich, unwirtlich; **~human** unmenschlich.

initia|l [i'niʃəl] anfänglich, Anfangs..., Ausgangs...,

Anfangsbuchstabe *m*; **~te** [ˌ~ʃieit] beginnen; einführen, -weihen; **~tion** Einleitung *f*; Einführung *f*; **~tive** [ˌ~ʃiətiv] Initiative *f*.

inject [in'dʒekt] einspritzen; **~ion** Injektion *f*, Spritze *f*.

injudicious unklug.

injur|e ['indʒə] beschädigen; schaden; verletzen, -wunden; *fig.* kränken; **~ed:** the *~* pl die Verletzten *pl*; **~ed person** Verletzte *m*, *f*; **~ious** [in-'dʒuəriəs] schädlich; **be ~ious** schaden (**to** *dat*); **~y** ['ʌəri] Verletzung *f*, Wunde *f*; Schaden *m*; *fig.* Beleidigung *f*.

injustice Ungerechtigkeit *f*, Unrecht *n*.

ink [iŋk] Tinte *f*.

inkling ['iŋkliŋ] Andeutung *f*; leise Ahnung.

ink-pot Tintenfaß *n*.

inland ['inlənd]inländisch; Binnen...; Landesinnere *n*; Binnenland *n*; **~** [in'lænd] *adv* im Innern des Landes; landeinwärts.

inlay ['in'lei] (*irr* lay) einlegen.

inlet ['inlet]schmale Bucht; Einlaß *m*; **~** [m, -in *pl*].

inmate ['inmeit] Insass|e *f*.

inmost ['inməust] innerst; *fig. a.* geheimst.

inn [in] Gasthaus *n*, -hof *m*.

innate [i'neit] angeboren.

inner ['inə] inner, Innen...; **~most** s. **inmost**; **~ tube** (*Fahrrad- etc.*)Schlauch *m*.

innkeeper Gastwirt(in).

innocen|ce ['inəsns] Unschuld *f*; **~t** unschuldig; Unschuldige *m*, *f*.

innovation [inəu'veiʃən] Neuerung *f*.

innumerable [i'nju:mərəbl] unzählig, zahllos.

inoculat|e [i'nɔkjuleit] (ein)impfen; **~ion** Impfung *f*.

inoffensive harmlos.

in-patient [inpeiʃənt] Krankenhauspatient(in).

inquest ['inkwest] *jur.* gerichtliche Untersuchung.

inquir|e [in'kwaiə] fragen *od.* sich erkundigen (nach); **~e into** untersuchen; **~y** Erkundigung *f*, Nachfrage *f*; Untersuchung *f*.

inquisitive [in'kwizitiv] neugierig; wißbegierig.

insan|e [in'sein] geisteskrank; **~ity** [in'sæniti] Geisteskrankheit *f*.

insatia|ble [in'seiʃəbl], **~te** [~ʃiit] unersättlich.

inscri|be [in'skraib] (ein-, auf)schreiben; beschriften; **~ption** [~ipʃən] Inschrift *f*.

insect ['insekt] Insekt *n*.

insecure unsicher.

insensi|ble unempfindlich; bewußtlos; unmerklich; gleichgültig; **~tive** unempfindlich.

inseparable untrennbar; unzertrennlich.

insert [in'sə:t] einsetzen, -fügen; (hin)einstecken; *Münze* einwerfen; **~ion**

Einsetzung *f*, Einfügung *f*; Einwurf *m* (*Münze*).

inshore ['in'ʃɔ:] an *od.* nahe der Küste; Küsten...

inside ['in'said] Innenseite *f*; Innere *n*; **turn ~ out** umkrempeln; inner, Innen...; im Innern, drinnen; nach innen, hinein; innerhalb; **~ left** *sp.* Halblinke *m*; **~ right** *sp.* Halbrechte *m*.

insight ['insait] Einblick *m*; Einsicht *f*.

in|significant unbedeutend; **~sincere** unaufrichtig; **~sinuate** [~'sinjueit] zu verstehen geben; andeuten; **~sipid** [~'sipid] geschmacklos, fad.

insist [in'sist]: **~ (up)on** bestehen auf; dringen auf.

in|solent ['insələnt] unverschämt; **~soluble** [~'sɔljubl] unlöslich; *fig.* unlösbar; **~solvent** zahlungsunfähig.

insomnia [in'sɔmniə] Schlaflosigkeit *f*.

insomuch [insəu'mʌtʃ] dermaßen, so (sehr).

inspect [in'spekt] untersuchen, prüfen; inspizieren; **~ion** Prüfung *f*, Untersuchung *f*; Inspektion *f*; **~or** Inspektor *m*.

inspir|ation [inspə'reiʃən] Inspiration *f*, Eingebung *f*; **~e** [in'spaiə] erfüllen; inspirieren.

insta|l(l) [in'stɔ:l] *tech.* installieren; *in ein Amt* einsetzen; **~llation** [~ə'leiʃən] *tech.* Anlage *f*; Installation *f*; (Amts)Einsetzung *f*; **~l(l)ment** [*~*'stɔ:lmənt] Rate *f*, Teilzahlung *f*; Fortsetzung *f* (*Roman*).

instance ['instəns] Ersuchen *n*; Beispiel *n*, Fall *m*; **for ~** zum Beispiel.

instant ['instənt] dringend; sofortig, augenblicklich; Augenblick *m*; **~aneous** [*~*'teinjəs] augenblicklich; **~ly** sofort.

instead [in'sted] statt dessen; **~ of** anstatt, an Stelle von.

instep ['instep] Spann *m*.

instigat|e ['instigeit] anstiften; **~or** Anstifter *m*.

instil(l) [in'stil] einflößen.

instinct ['instiŋkt] Instinkt *m*; **~ive** [in'stiŋktiv] instinktiv.

institut|e ['institju:t] Institut *n* (*a. Gebäude*); (gelehrte *etc.*) Gesellschaft; **~ion** Institut *n*; Institution *f*, Einrichtung *f*.

instruct [in'strʌkt] unterrichten; ausbilden; anweisen; informieren; **~ion** Unterricht *m*, Ausbildung *f*; *pl.* Vorschrift(en *pl*) *f*, Anweisung(en *pl*) *f*; **~ive** lehrreich; **~or** Lehrer *m*; Ausbilder *m*.

instrument ['instrumənt] Instrument *n*; Werkzeug *n*.

in|subordinate [insə'bɔ:dnit] aufsässig; **~sufferable** unerträglich; **~sufficient** unzulänglich, ungenügend.

insulate ['insjuleit] isolieren.

insult ['insʌlt] Beleidigung *f*; [in'sʌlt] beleidigen.

insupportable [insə'pɔ:təbl] unerträglich.

insur|ance [in'ʃuərəns] Versicherung *f*; Versicherungs...; **~ance policy** Versicherungspolice *f*, -schein *m*; **~e** versichern.

insurmountable [insə(:)-'mauntəbl] unüberwindlich.

insurrection [insə'rekʃən] Aufstand *m*.

intact [in'tækt] unberührt; unversehrt, intakt.

integrate ['intigreit] zs.-schließen, vereinigen; eingliedern; integrieren.

integrity [in'tegriti] Integrität *f*, Rechtschaffenheit *f*; Ganzheit *f*, Vollständigkeit *f*.

intellect ['intilekt] Verstand *m*; **~ual** [*~*'lektjuəl] intellektuell, geistig; Intellektuelle *m*, *f*.

intelli|gence [in'telidʒəns] Intelligenz *f*; Verstand *m*; Nachricht *f*; **~ent** intelligent, klug; **~ible** verständlich.

intemperate unmäßig.

intend [in'tend] beabsichtigen; bestimmen.

intens|e [in'tens] intensiv, stark, heftig; angestrengt; **~ify** [*~*ifai] (sich) verstärken *od.* steigern; **~ity** Intensität *f*; **~ive** intensiv.

intent [in'tent] Absicht *f*;

gespannt; ~ **(up)on** bedacht auf, beschäftigt mit; ~**ion** Absicht *f*; ~**ional** absichtlich.

inter [in'tə:] beerdigen.

inter|cede [intə(:)'si:d] vermitteln; ~**cept** [~'sept] abfangen; abhören; ~**cession** [~ə'seʃən] Fürsprache *f*.

interchange [intə(:)-'tʃeindʒ] austauschen; abwechseln; [~'tʃeindʒ] Austausch *m*.

intercourse ['intə(:)kɔ:s] Umgang *m*; Verkehr *m*.

interdict [intə(:)'dikt] untersagen, verbieten.

interest ['intrist] Interesse *n*; Bedeutung *f*; *econ.* Anteil *m*, Beteiligung *f*; Zins (-en *pl*) *m*; **take an** ~ in sich interessieren für; *vb*: interessieren (**in** für); ~**ed** interessiert (**in** an); ~**ing** interessant.

interfere [intə'fiə] sich einmischen; eingreifen; ~ **with** stören; ~**nce** Einmischung *f*, Eingreifen *n*; Störung *f*.

interior [in'tiəriə] inner, Innen...; Innere *n*; **Department of the** ♀ *Am.* Innenministerium *n*; ~ **decorator** Innenarchitekt *m*.

inter|jection [intə(:)'dʒekʃən] Interjektion *f*, Ausruf *m*; ~**lude** ['~lu:d] Zwischenspiel *n*.

intermedia|ry [intə(:)-'mi:djəri] Zwischen...; vermittelnd; Vermittler *m*; ~**te** [~jət] dazwischenliegend, Zwischen..., Mittel...; ~**te landing** *aer.* Zwischenlandung *f*.

inter|mingle (sich) vermischen; ~**mission** Unterbrechung *f*, Pause *f*; ~**mittent fever** [intə(:)-'mitənt] Wechselfieber *n*.

intern [in'tə:n] *Am.* Assistenzarzt *m*; ~**al** [~'tə:nl] inner(lich).

inter|national international; ~**pose** *Veto* einlegen; unterbrechen; dazwischentreten; vermitteln.

interpret [in'tə:prit] interpretieren, auslegen; (ver-)dolmetschen; ~**ation** Interpretation *f*; Auslegung *f*; ~**er** Dolmetscher(in).

interrogat|e [in'terəugeit] (be)fragen; vernehmen, -hören; ~**ion** Vernehmung *f*, -hör *n*; Befragung *f*; **note (mark, point) of** ~**ion** Fragezeichen *n*; ~**ive** [intə-'rɔgətiv] fragend; *ling.* interrogativ, Frage...

interrupt [intə'rʌpt] unterbrechen; ~**ion** Unterbrechung *f*.

intersect [intə(:)'sekt] sich schneiden *od.* kreuzen; ~**ion** Schnittpunkt *m*; (Straßen)Kreuzung *f*.

interval ['intəvəl] Zwischenraum *m*; Abstand *m*; Pause *f*.

interven|e [intə(:)'vi:n] dazwischenkommen; sich

einmischen; vermitteln; **~tion** [˳'venʃən] Eingreifen *n*, Einmischung *f*.

interview ['intəvju:] Unterredung *f*, Interview *n*; interviewen; **~er** Interviewer *m*.

intestines [in'testinz] *pl* Eingeweide *pl*.

intima|cy ['intiməsi] Intimität *f*, Vertrautheit *f*; **~te** ['˳eit] zu verstehen geben; ['˳it] intim; vertraut; gründlich; Vertraute *m*, *f*; **~tion** Andeutung *f*.

intimidate [in'timideit] einschüchtern.

into ['intu, 'intə] in, in ... hinein.

intoler|able unerträglich; **~ant** unduldsam, intolerant.

in|toxicate [in'tɔksikeit] berauschen; **~transitive** *gr.* intransitiv; **~trepid** [˳'trepid] unerschrocken, furchtlos.

intricate ['intrikit] verwickelt, kompliziert.

intrigue [in'tri:g] Intrige *f*; intrigieren; neugierig machen.

introduc|e [intrə'dju:s] einführen; vorstellen (**to** *dat*); **~tion** [˳'dʌkʃən] Einführung *f*; Einleitung *f*; Vorstellung *f*; **letter of ~tion** Empfehlungsschreiben *n*; **~tory** [˳'dʌktəri] einleitend.

intru|de [in'tru:d] (sich) aufdrängen; stören; **~der** Eindringling *m*; Stören-

fried *m*; **~sion** [˳ʒən] Eindringen *n*; Zudringlichkeit *f*.

intuition [intju(:)'iʃən] Intuition *f*, Eingebung *f*.

invade [in'veid] eindringen in, einfallen in; **~r** Angreifer *m*, Eindringling *m*.

invalid[1] ['invəli:d] krank; Kranke *m*, *f*, Invalide *m*.

invalid[2] [in'vælid] (rechts-)ungültig; **~ate** [˳eit] (für) ungültig erklären; entkräften.

invaluable unschätzbar.

invariab|le unveränderlich; **~ly** beständig.

invasion [in'veiʒən] *mil.*: **~ (of)** Einfall *m* (in), Invasion *f* (in), Angriff *m* (auf).

invent [in'vent] erfinden; **~ion** Erfindung *f*; **~ive** erfinderisch; **~or** Erfinder(in).

invers|e ['in'və:s] umgekehrt; **~ion** Umkehrung *f*.

invert [in'və:t] umkehren, umdrehen, umstellen; **~ed commas** *pl* Anführungszeichen *pl*.

invest [in'vest] investieren, anlegen.

investigat|e [in'vestigeit] untersuchen; **~ion** Untersuchung *f*; **~or** Untersuchungsbeamte *m*.

investment [in'vestmənt] Kapitalanlage *f*.

in|vincible [in'vinsəbl] unbesiegbar; unüberwindlich; **~violable** [˳'vaiə-ləbl] unverletzlich, unantastbar; **~visible** unsichtbar.

invit|ation [invi'teiʃən] Einladung f; Aufforderung f; **~e** [in'vait] einladen; auffordern.

invoice ['invɔis] econ. (Waren)Rechnung f.

in|voke [in'vouk] anrufen; beschwören; **~voluntary** unfreiwillig; unwillkürlich; **~volve** [~'vɔlv] verwickeln, -stricken, hineinziehen; mit sich bringen; **~vulnerable** unverwundbar.

inward ['inwəd] inner (-lich); **~(s)** ['~(z)] einwärts, nach innen.

iodine ['aiədi:n] Jod n.

I O U ['aiəu'ju:] (= **I owe you**) Schuldschein m.

irascible [i'ræsibl] jähzornig.

iridescent [iri'desnt] schillernd.

iris ['aiəris] anat. Iris f; bot. Schwertlilie f.

Irish ['aiəriʃ] irisch; Irisch n; **the ~** pl die Iren pl; **~man** Ire m; **~woman** Irin f.

iron ['aiən] Eisen n; Bügeleisen n; eisern, Eisen...; bügeln; plätten.

ironic(al) [ai'rɔnik(əl)] ironisch, spöttisch.

iron|ing ['aiəniŋ] Bügeln n; Plätten n; Bügel..., Plätt...; **~ lung** med. eiserne Lunge; **~monger** Metallwarenhändler m; **~mo(u)ld** Rostfleck m; **~works** sg, pl Eisenhütte f.

irony ['aiərəni] Ironie f.

ir|radiate [i'reidieit] bestrahlen (a. med.); Gesicht aufheitern; et. erhellen; **~rational** unvernünftig; **~reconcilable** unversöhnlich; unvereinbar; **~recoverable** unersetzlich; **~redeemable** econ. nicht einlösbar; fig. unersetzlich; **~regular** unregelmäßig; ungleichmäßig; **~relevant** nicht zur Sache gehörig; **~removable** unabsetzbar; **~reparable** [i'repərəbl] nicht wiedergutzumachen(d); **~replaceable** unersetzlich; **~repressible** kaum zu unterdrücken(d); unbezähmbar; **~reproachable** untadelig; **~resistible** unwiderstehlich; **~resolute** unentschlossen; **~respective:** **~** of ohne Rücksicht auf, unabhängig von; **~responsible** unverantwortlich; verantwortungslos; **~retrievable** unwiederbringlich, unersetzlich; **~reverent** [i'revərənt] respektlos; **~revocable** [i'revəkəbl] unwiderruflich, verbindlich. [sern.]

irrigate ['irigeit] bewäs-∫

irrit|able [i'ritəbl] reizbar; **~ate** ['~eit] reizen; (ver)ärgern; **~ation** Reizung f; Gereiztheit f.

is [iz] 3. sg pres von **be**.

island ['ailənd] Insel f.

isle [ail] Insel f.

isn't ['iznt] = **is not**; ~ **it?** nicht wahr?

isolat|e ['aisəleit] isolieren; ~**ed** abgeschieden; ~**ion** Isolierung f.

issue ['iʃu:] Ausgabe f (Buch etc.); Nummer f (Zeitung); Nachkommen (-schaft f) pl; Ausgang m; (Streit)Frage f; **point at** ~ strittige Frage; vb: Befehle erteilen; ausgeben; Bücher etc. herausgeben; herausströmen, -kommen.

it [it] es; er, sie, es, ihn (für Sachen u. Tiere).

Italian [i'tæljən] italienisch; Italiener(in); Italienisch n.

itch [itʃ] Jucken n; jucken.

item ['aitəm] Punkt m, Posten m; Zeitungsnotiz f.

itinerary [ai'tinərəri] Reiseroute f; Reiseplan m; Reisebericht m.

its [its] von Sachen u. Tieren: sein(e), ihr(e); dessen, deren.

itself [it'self] sich; sich selbst; selbst; **by** ~ allein; von selbst.

ivory ['aivəri] Elfenbein n.

ivy ['aivi] Efeu m.

J

jab [dʒæb] stechen, stoßen.

jack [dʒæk] Wagenheber m; Karten: Bube m; ~**(up)** Auto aufbocken.

jackal ['dʒækɔ:l] Schakal m.

jack|ass ['dʒækæs] Esel m; ['ˌ.ka:s] fig. Esel m, Dummkopf m; ~**daw** ['ˌˌdɔ:] Dohle f.

jacket ['dʒækit] Jacke f, Jackett n; tech. Mantel m; Schutzumschlag m.

jack-in-the-box ['dʒæk-] Schachtelmännchen n; ~**knife** Klappmesser n; ♀ **of all trades** Alleskönner m; ~**pot** Haupttreffer m.

jag [dʒæg] Zacken m; ~**ged** ['ˌgid] zackig.

jaguar ['dʒægjuə] Jaguar m.

jail [dʒeil], ~**er** s. gaol (-er).

jam¹ [dʒæm] Marmelade f.

jam² [dʒæm] quetschen, pressen; versperren; blockieren; Radio: stören; eingeklemmt sein, festsitzen; (sich ver)klemmen; Gedränge n; Stauung f; Stockung f; tech. Blockieren n; colloq. mißliche Lage, Klemme f.

janitor ['dʒænitə] Portier m; Am. Hausmeister m.

January ['dʒænjuəri] Januar m.

Japanese [dʒæpə'ni:z] japanisch; Japaner(in); Japanisch n; **the** ~ pl die Japaner pl.

jar [dʒa:] Krug m, Topf m, (Einmach)Glas n.

jaundice ['dʒɔ:ndis] Gelbsucht f.

javelin ['dʒævlin] Speer m.

jaw [dʒɔ:] Kinnbacken *m*, Kiefer *m*; *pl*: Rachen *m*; Maul *n*; **~bone** Kiefer (-knochen) *m*, Kinnlade *f*.

jay [dʒei] Eichelhäher *m*.

jealous ['dʒeləs] eifersüchtig; **~y** Eifersucht *f*.

jeer [dʒiə] Spott *m*, Stichelei *f*; spotten, höhnen.

jellied ['dʒelid] eingedickt (*Obst*); in Gelee.

jelly ['dʒeli] Gallert(e *f*) *n*; Gelee *n*; gelieren; zum Gelieren bringen; **~fish** Qualle *f*.

jeopardize ['dʒepədaiz] gefährden, aufs Spiel setzen.

jerk [dʒə:k] Ruck *m*; *med.* Zuckung *f*; (plötzlich) stoßen *od.* ziehen, (sich) ruckartig bewegen; werfen, schleudern; **~y** ruckartig; holperig.

jersey ['dʒə:zi] Wollpullover *m*.

jest [dʒest] Scherz *m*; scherzen; **~er** Spaßmacher *m*; Hofnarr *m*.

jet [dʒet] (*Wasser- etc.*) Strahl *m*; Düse *f*; **~ engine**, **~ liner**, **~ plane** hervorschießen; ausstoßen; **~ engine** Strahl-, Düsentriebwerk *n*; **~liner**, **~ plane** Düsenflugzeug *n*; **~propelled** mit Düsenantrieb.

jetty ['dʒeti] Mole *f*; Anlegestelle *f*.

Jew [dʒu:] Jude *m*.

jewel ['dʒu:əl] Juwel *m*, *n*, Edelstein *m*; **~(l)er** Juwe-

lier *m*; **~(le)ry** Juwelen *pl*; Schmuck *m*.

Jew|ess ['dʒu(:)is] Jüdin *f*; **~ish** jüdisch.

jiffy ['dʒifi] *colloq.* Augenblick *m*.

jiggle ['dʒigl] (leicht) rütteln *od.* schaukeln.

jingle ['dʒiŋgl] Klimpern *n*; klimpern (mit).

job [dʒɔb] *ein Stück* Arbeit *f*; *colloq.* Stellung *f*, Arbeit(splatz *m*) *f*, Beschäftigung *f*, Beruf *m*; Aufgabe *f*; Sache *f*; **by the ~** im Akkord; **out of ~** arbeitslos; **~work** Akkordarbeit *f*.

jockey ['dʒɔki] Jockei *m*.

jocular ['dʒɔkjulə] lustig; scherzhaft. [fröhlich.\

jocund ['dʒɔkənd] lustig,\

jog [dʒɔg] (an)stoßen, rütteln; **~ along**, **~ on** dahintrotten, -zuckeln.

join [dʒɔin] Verbindungsstelle *f*; verbinden, vereinigen, zs.-fügen (**to** mit); sich anschließen (an); eintreten in, beitreten; sich vereinigen (mit); **~ in** teilnehmen an, mitmachen bei; einstimmen in.

joiner ['dʒɔinə] Tischler *m*.

joint [dʒɔint] Verbindungsstelle *f*; Gelenk *n*; Braten *m*; *Am. sl.* Spelunke *f*; *sl.* Marihuanazigarette *f*; gemeinsam, Mit...; **~stock company** Aktiengesellschaft *f*.

joke [dʒɔuk] scherzen; Scherz *m*, Spaß *m*; Witz

m; **practical** ~ Streich *m*;
play a ~ on s.o. j-m e-n
Streich spielen; **he cannot take a ~** er versteht
keinen Spaß; **~r** Spaß-
vogel *m*; *Karten:* Joker *m*.

jolly ['dʒɔli] lustig, fidel;
colloq.: nett; sehr.

jolt [dʒəult] stoßen; rütteln; holpern; Ruck *m*,
Stoß *m*, Rütteln *n*.

jostle ['dʒɔsl] (an)rempeln.

jot [dʒɔt]: ~ **down** schnell
notieren.

journal ['dʒə:nl] Tagebuch *n*; Journal *n*; Zeitung *f*; Zeitschrift *f*;
~ism ['~əlizəm] Journa-
lismus *m*.

journey ['dʒə:ni] reisen;
Reise *f*; Fahrt *f*; ~ **there**
Hinfahrt *f*; **~man** Geselle
m. [vergnügt.]

jovial ['dʒəuvjəl] heiter,|

joy [dʒɔi] Freude *f*; **~ful,
~ous** freudig, erfreut; froh.

jubil|ant ['dʒu:bilənt]
frohlockend; **~ee** ['~li:]
(fünfzigjähriges) Jubiläum.

judge [dʒʌdʒ] Richter *m*;
Preis-, Schiedsrichter *m*;
Kenner *m*; urteilen; ein
Urteil fällen über; ent-
scheiden; beurteilen; hal-
ten für; **~(e)ment** Urteil
n; Verständnis *n*, Einsicht
f; Meinung *f*; göttliches
(Straf)Gericht; ♀**(e)ment
Day, Day of** ♀**(e)ment**
Jüngstes Gericht.

judici|al [dʒu(:)'diʃəl] ge-
richtlich, Justiz...; **~** Ge-
richts...; kritisch; un-

parteiisch; **~ous** ver-
nünftig, klug. [*f*.]

jug [dʒʌg] Krug *m*, Kanne|

juggle ['dʒʌgl] Taschen-
spielerei *f*; Schwindel *m*;
jonglieren; verfälschen;
betrügen; **~r** Jongleur *m*.

juic|e [dʒu:s] Saft *m*; **~y**
saftig.

juke-box ['dʒu:k-] Musik-
automat *m*.

July [dʒu(:)'lai] Juli *m*.

jumble ['dʒʌmbl] Durcheinander *n*; **~sale** Wohl-
tätigkeitsbasar *m*.

jump [dʒʌmp] Sprung *m*;
(über)springen; hüpfen;
~ at sich stürzen auf; **~er**
Springer *m*; **~ing jack**
Hampelmann *m*; **~y** nervös.

junct|ion ['dʒʌŋkʃən] Ver-
bindung *f*; *rail.* Knoten-
punkt *m*; **~ure** Verbindungsstelle *f*; (kritischer)
Augenblick *od.* Zeitpunkt.

June [dʒu:n] Juni *m*.

jungle ['dʒʌŋgl] Dschungel *m*.

junior ['dʒu:njə] junior;
jünger; untergeordnet;
Am. Kinder..., Jugend...;
Jüngere *m*, *f*; Junior *m*.

juris|diction [dʒuəris-
'dikʃən] Rechtsprechung
f; Gerichtsbarkeit *f*; **~-
prudence** ['~pru:dəns]
Rechtswissenschaft *f*.

juror ['dʒuərə] Geschworene *m*, *f*.

jury ['dʒuəri] *die* Geschworenen *pl*; Jury *f*,
Preisrichter *pl*.

just [dʒʌst] gerecht; be-
rechtigt; genau, richtig;
gerade, (so)eben; gerade
(noch); nur; ~ **like that**
einfach so; ~ **now** gerade
jetzt.

justice ['dʒʌstis] Gerechtigkeit f; Recht n;
Richter m.

justifI|cation [dʒʌstifi-
'keiʃən] Rechtfertigung f;
~**y** ['~fai] rechtfertigen.

justly ['dʒʌstli] mit Recht.

jut [dʒʌt]: ~ **out** vor-
springen, herausragen.

juvenile ['dʒuːvinail]jung,
jugendlich; ~ Jugend...;
Jugendliche m, f.

K

kangaroo [kæŋgə'ruː]
Känguruh n.

keel [kiːl] Kiel m.

keen [kiːn] scharf (a. fig.);
begeistert, eifrig; heftig;
stark, groß; ~ **on** colloq.
erpicht od. versessen auf.

keep [kiːp] (Lebens)Un-
terhalt m; (irr) (auf-, ab-,
[bei]be-, ein-, er-, fest-,
unter)halten; (auf)be-
wahren; Versprechen hal-
ten; Buch, Ware etc.
führen; Bett hüten; blei-
ben; sich halten; colloq.
wohnen; weiter... (Hand-
lung beibehalten); ~ **doing**
immer wieder tun; ~
going weitergehen; ~
(on) talking weiter-
sprechen; ~ **s.o. com-
pany** j-m Gesellschaft
leisten; ~ **s.o. waiting**
j-n warten lassen; ~ **time**
richtig gehen (Uhr); ~
away (sich) fernhalten;
wegbleiben; ~ **from** ab-,
zurückhalten; et. vorent-
halten; sich fernhalten
von; sich enthalten; ~ **in**
Schüler nachsitzen lassen;

~ **off** (sich) fernhalten,
~ **on** Kleider anbehalten,
Hut aufbehalten; Licht
brennen lassen; ~ **to**
bleiben in; sich halten
an; ~ **up** aufrechter-
halten; Mut nicht sinken
lassen; sich halten; ~ **up**
with Schritt halten mit.

keep|er ['kiːpə] Wächter
m, Aufseher m, Wärter m;
~**ing** Verwahrung f, Obhut f, Pflege f; **be in**
(out of) ~ing with ...
(nicht)übereinstimmen
mit
...; ~**sake** Andenken n
(Geschenk).

keg [keg] kleines Faß.

kennel ['kenl] Hunde-
hütte f; Hundezwinger m.

kept [kept] pret u. pp von
keep. [Bordstein m.]

kerb(stone) ['kəːb(-)]]

kerchief ['kəːtʃif] (Kopf-)
Tuch n.

kernel ['kəːnl] Kern m.

kettle ['ketl] Kessel m;
~**drum** (Kessel)Pauke f.

key [kiː] Schlüssel m (a.
fig.); (Klavier- etc.)Taste
f; (Druck)Taste f; mus-

Tonart f; fig. Ton m;
Schlüssel...; **~board** Kla-
viatur f; Tastatur f; **~hole**
Schlüsselloch n; **~note**
mus. Grundton m (a. fig.).

kick [kik] (Fuß)Tritt m;
Stoß m; colloq. (Nerven-)
Kitzel m; (mit dem Fuß)
stoßen od. treten; e-n
Fußtritt geben; Fußball:
schießen; ausschlagen
(Pferd); **~ off** Fußball:
anstoßen; **~ out** colloq.
hinauswerfen.

kid [kid] Zicklein n;
Ziegenleder n; sl. Kind n;
sl. foppen; **~glove** Glacé-
handschuh m (a. fig.).

kidnap ['kidnæp] ent-
führen; **~(p)er** Kindes-
entführer m, Kidnapper m.

kidney ['kidni] Niere f;
~ bean Weiße Bohne.

kill [kil] töten; schlachten;
vernichten; **~ time** die
Zeit totschlagen; Tötung
f; Jagdbeute f, Strecke f;
~er Mörder m.

kiln [kiln] Brenn-, Darr-
ofen m.

kilo|gram(me) ['kiləu-
græm] Kilo(gramm) n;
~metre, Am. **~meter**
Kilometer m.

kilt [kilt] Kilt m, Schotten-
rock m.

kin [kin] Familie f; pl
(Bluts)Verwandtschaft f.

kind [kaind] gütig, freundlich, nett; Art f; Gattung
f; **what ~ of ...?** was für
ein ...?

kindergarten ['kində-

ɡɑ:tn] Kindergarten m.
kind-hearted gütig.

kindle ['kindl] anzünden,
(sich) entzünden; fig. entflammen.

kind|ly ['kaindli] freund-
lich; **~ness** Güte f, Freund-
lichkeit f; Gefälligkeit f.

kindred ['kindrid] verwandt; Verwandtschaft f;
Verwandte pl.

king [kiŋ] König m; **~dom**
(König)Reich n; **~size**
überlang, -groß.

kins|man ['kinzmən] Ver-
wandte m, **~woman** Ver-
wandte f.

kipper ['kipə] Räucher-
hering m. [küssen.]

kiss [kis] Kuß m; (sich)]

kit[1] [kit] Kätzchen n.

kit[2] Ausrüstung f; Werkzeug n; Werkzeugtasche f.

kitchen ['kitʃin] Küche f;
~ette [.'net] Kochnische
f, Kleinküche f.   [m.]

kite[kait] (Papier)Drachen]

kitten ['kitn] Kätzchen n.

knack [næk] Kniff m,
Dreh m.

knapsack ['næpsæk] Tor-
nister m; Rucksack m.

knave [neiv] Schurke m;
Karten: Bube m; **~ry**
['.əri] Schurkerei f.

knead [ni:d] kneten; massieren.

knee [ni:] Knie n; **~cap**
Kniescheibe f; **~joint**
Kniegelenk n.

kneel [ni:l] (irr) knien;
(sich) hin- od. niederknien
(**to** vor).

knelt [nelt] *pret u. pp von* **kneel.** [**know.**\
knew [nju:] *pret von*]\
knicker|bockers ['nikə-bɔkəz] *pl* Kniehosen *pl*; **~s** *pl colloq.* für **knickerbockers**; (Damen)Schlüpfer *m*.\
knick-knack ['niknæk] Tand *m*; Nippsache *f*.\
knife [naif], *pl* **knives** [\~vz] Messer *n*; schneiden; erstechen.\
knight [nait] Ritter *m*; *Schach:* Springer *m*; zum Ritter schlagen.\
knit [nit] (*irr*) stricken; zs.-fügen, verbinden; **~ the brows** die Stirn runzeln; **~ting** Stricken *n*; Strickzeug *n*; Strick...\
knives [naivz] *pl von* **knife.**\
knob [nɔb] Knopf *m*, Knauf *m*, runder Griff.\
knock [nɔk] Schlag *m*, Stoß *m*; Klopfen *n*, Pochen *n*; **there is a ~** es klopft; *vb:* schlagen; stoßen; (an-)klopfen; pochen; **~ down** niederschlagen; überfahren; **~ out** *Boxen:* k.o.

schlagen; **~ over** umwerfen, umstoßen; **~er** Türklopfer *m*; **~out** *Boxen:* Knockout *m*, K.o. *m*.\
knoll [nəul] kleiner (Erd-)Hügel.\
knot [nɔt] Knoten *m* (*a. mar., bot.*); Schleife *f*; Gruppe *f* (*Menschen*); *fig.* Band *n*; Schwierigkeit *f*; (ver)knoten, -knüpfen; **~ty** knotig; knorrig; *fig.* schwierig, verwickelt.\
know [nəu] (*irr*) wissen; (es) können *od.* verstehen; kennen; (wieder)erkennen, unterscheiden; **~ all about it** genau Bescheid wissen; **~ German** Deutsch können; **~ one's business, ~ a thing or two, ~ what's what** sich auskennen, Erfahrung haben; **~ing** klug; schlau; verständnisvoll, wissend; **~ingly** absichtlich; **~ledge** ['nɔlidʒ] Kenntnis(se *pl*) *f*; Wissen *n*; **to my ~ledge** meines Wissens; **~n** *pp von* **know**; bekannt.\
knuckle ['nʌkl] Knöchel *m*.

L

label ['leibl] Zettel *m*, Etikett *n*, Schildchen *n*; etikettieren, beschriften.\
laboratory [lə'bɔrətəri] Labor(atorium) *n*; **~ assistant** Laborant(in).\
laborious [lə'bɔ:riəs] mühsam; arbeitsam;

schwerfällig (*Stil*).\
labor union [leibə] *Am. pol.* Gewerkschaft *f*.\
labo(u)r ['leibə] (schwer) arbeiten; sich be- *od.* abmühen; (schwere) Arbeit; Mühe *f*; Arbeiter(schaft *f*) *pl*; *med.* Wehen *pl*; Ar-

beiter...; Arbeits...; **Ministry of ♀ Arbeitsministerium** *n*; **～er** (*bsd.* ungelernter) Arbeiter; **♀ Exchange** Arbeitsamt *n*; **Labour Party** *Brit. pol.* Labour Party *f*.

lace [leis] Spitze(n *pl*) *f*; Litze *f*, Schnur *f*; Schnürsenkel *m*; (zu)schnüren; mit Spitze *etc.* besetzen.

lack [læk] Fehlen *n*, Mangel *m*; nicht haben, Mangel haben an; **be ～ing in** fehlen *od.* mangeln an.

laconic [lə'kɔnik] lakonisch.

lacquer ['lækə] Lack *m*; lackieren.　　　　　　　[*m*.\

lad [læd] Bursche *m*, Junge\

ladder ['lædə] Leiter *f*; Laufmasche *f*; **～proof** maschenfest (*Strumpf*).

laden ['leidn] beladen; **～ing** Ladung *f*, Fracht *f*.

ladle ['leidl] Schöpflöffel *m*, Kelle *f*.

lady ['leidi] Dame *f*; Lady *f*; **～ help** Hausangestellte *f*; **～like** damenhaft.

lag [læg] **～ behind** zurückbleiben.

lager ['lɑːgə] Lagerbier *n*.

lagoon [lə'guːn] Lagune *f*.

laid [leid] *pret u. pp von* **lay³**.

lain [lein] *pp von* **lie²**.

lair [lɛə] Lager *n* (*des Wildes*).

lake [leik] See *m*.

lamb [læm] Lamm *n*.

lame [leim] lahm; lähmen.

lament [lə'ment] (Weh-)

Klage *f*; jammern; (be-)klagen; **～able** ['læməntəbl] beklagenswert; erbärmlich; **～ation** [læmen'teifən] (Weh)Klage *f*.

lamp [læmp] Lampe *f*; **～post** Laternenpfahl *m*; **～shade** Lampenschirm *m*.

lance [lɑːns] Lanze *f*; *med.* aufschneiden, -stechen.

land [lænd] landen; Land *n*; Grundbesitz *m*, Grund *m* und Boden *m*; **by ～** auf dem Landweg; **～holder** Grundpächter *m*; Grundbesitzer *m*.

landing ['lændiŋ] *mar.* Anlegen *n*; *aer.* Landung *f*; Treppenabsatz *m*; **～field** *aer.* Landeplatz *m*; **～gear** *aer.* Fahrgestell *n*; **～stage** Landungssteg *m*, Anlegeplatz *m*.

land|lady ['lænleidi] Vermieterin *f*, Wirtin *f*; **～lord** ['læn-] Vermieter *m*; Wirt *m*; Haus-, Grundbesitzer *m*; **～lubber** ['lænd-] *mar.* Landratte *f*; **～mark** ['lænd-] Wahrzeichen *n*; **～owner** ['lænd-] Land-, Grundbesitzer *m*; **～scape** ['lænskeip] Landschaft *f*; **～slide** ['lænd-] Erdrutsch *m* (*a. pol.*); **～slip** ['lænd-] Erdrutsch *m*.

lane [lein] (Feld)Weg *m*, Gasse *f*; *mot.* Fahrbahn *f*, Spur *f*.

language ['læŋgwidʒ] Sprache *f*.

langu|id ['læŋgwid] matt;
träg(e); **~ish** ermatten;
schmachten; dahinsiechen;
~or ['læŋgə] Mattigkeit *f*;
Trägheit *f*; Stille *f*.

lank [læŋk] lang und dünn;
glatt (*Haar*); **~y** schlaksig.

lantern ['læntən] Laterne *f*.

lap [læp] Schoß *m*; (sich)
überlappen; plätschern;
(auf)lecken; schlürfen.

lapel [lə'pel] Rockauf-
schlag *m*, Revers *n*, *m*.

lapse [læps] Verlauf *m*
(*der Zeit*); Versehen *n*.

larceny ['lɑːsəni] Diebstahl *m*.

larch [lɑːtʃ] Lärche *f*.

lard [lɑːd] (Schweine-)
Schmalz *n*; **~er** Speise-
kammer *f*.

large [lɑːdʒ] groß; reichlich; weitgehend; groß-
zügig, -mütig; **at ~** auf
freiem Fuß; ausführlich;
~ly weitgehend; reichlich.

lark [lɑːk] Lerche *f*; *fig.*
Spaß *m*, Streich *m*.

larva ['lɑːvə] *zo.* Larve *f*.

larynx ['læriŋks] Kehl-
kopf *m*.

lascivious [lə'siviəs] lüstern; schlüpfrig.

lash [læʃ] Peitschen-
schnur *f*; (Peitschen)Hieb
m; Wimper *f*; peitschen
(*mit*); schlagen; (fest)bin-
den.

lass [læs] Mädchen *n*.

lasso [læ'suː] Lasso *n*, *m*.

last¹ [lɑːst] *adj* letzt;
vorig; äußerst; neuest;
~ night gestern abend;

~ but one vorletzt; *adv*
zuletzt; as letzte(r,-s);
(but) not least nicht
zuletzt; *sub*: der, die, das
Letzte; **at ~** endlich.

last² dauern; (stand)halten;
(aus)reichen; **~ing** dauerhaft.

last|ly zuletzt; **~ name**
Familien-, Nachname *m*.

latch [lætʃ] Klinke *f*;
Schnappschloß *n*; ein-,
zuklinken.

late [leit] spät; ehemalig;
neuest; verstorben; **be ~**
(zu) spät kommen, sich
verspäten; **at (the) ~st**
spätestens; **as ~ as** erst,
noch; **of ~** kürzlich; **~r on**
später; **~ly** kürzlich.

lath [lɑːθ] Latte *f*.

lathe [leið] Drehbank *f*.

lather ['lɑːðə] (Seifen-)
Schaum *m*; einseifen;
schäumen.

Latin ['lætin] lateinisch;
Latein *n*. [Breite *f*.]

latitude ['lætitjuːd] *geogr.*

latter ['lætə] letzt; letzter.

lattice ['lætis] Gitter *n*.

laudable ['lɔːdəbl] lobenswert.

laugh [lɑːf] Lachen *n*,
Gelächter *n*; lachen; **~ at**
lachen über; **~ in** aus-
lachen; **make s.o. ~** j-n
zum Lachen bringen; **~ter**
Lachen *n*, Gelächter *n*.

launch [lɔːntʃ] *Schiff* vom
Stapel lassen; *Rakete* starten, abschießen; **~ing-
pad** (Raketen)Abschuß-
rampe *f*.

laund|erette [lɔːndəˈret]
Selbstbedienungswaschsalon *m*; **~ry** [ˈ~drі]
Wäscherei *f*; Wäsche *f*.

laurel [ˈlɔrəl] Lorbeer *m*.

lavatory [ˈlævətərі]
Waschraum *m*; Toilette *f*.

lavender [ˈlævіndə] Lavendel *m*.

lavish [ˈlævіʃ] freigebig, verschwenderisch.

law [lɔː] Gesetz *n*; Recht(swissenschaft *f*) *n*; **~ court** Gericht(shof *m*) *n*; **~ful** gesetzlich; rechtmäßig; **~less** gesetzlos; rechtswidrig.

lawn [lɔːn] Rasen *m*.

law|suit [ˈlɔːsjuːt] Prozeß *m*; **~yer** [ˈ~jə] Jurist *m*; (Rechts)Anwalt *m*.

lax [læks] locker; schlaff; **~ative** [ˈ~ətіv] abführend; Abführmittel *n*.

lay¹ [leі] *pret von* **lie²**.

lay² weltlich; Laien...

lay³ Lage *f*; legen (*a. fig.*); *Tisch* decken; (Eier) legen; **~ out** ausbreiten; auslegen; *Geld* ausgeben; *typ.* gestalten; *Garten etc.* anlegen; **~ up** *Vorräte* hinlegen; **be laid up** das Bett hüten müssen.

lay-by [ˈleіbaі] *Brit. mot.* Parkstreifen *m*.

layer [ˈleіə] Lage *f*, Schicht *f*.

layman [ˈleіmən] Laie *m*.

lazy [ˈleіzі] faul, träg(e).

lead¹ [liːd] Führung *f*; *thea.* Hauptrolle *f*; *electr.* Leitung *f*; (Hunde)Leine

f; (*irr*) (an)führen; leiten; *Karte* ausspielen; vorangehen.

lead² [led] Blei *n*; Lot *n*; **~en** bleiern (*a. fig.*), aus Blei, Blei...

lead|er [ˈliːdə] (An)Führer(in); Leiter(in); Leitartikel *m*; **~ing** leitend, maßgebend; **~** führend; erst.

leaf [liːf], *pl* **leaves** [~vz] Blatt *n*; (Tisch)Klappe *f*, Ausziehplatte *f*; **~let** [ˈ~lіt] Blättchen *n*; Flugblatt *n*; Prospekt *m*.

league [liːg] Liga *f*; Bund *m*; *mst poet.* Meile *f*.

leak [liːk] Leck *n*; leck sein; tropfen; **~ out** *fig.* durchsickern; **~age** Lekken *n*; **~y** leck, undicht.

lean¹ [liːn] (*irr*) (sich) lehnen, (sich) neigen.

lean² mager; mageres Fleisch.

leant [lent] *pret u. pp von* **lean¹**.

leap [liːp] Sprung *m*; (*irr*) (über)springen; **~t** [lept] *pret u. pp von* **leap**; **~-year** Schaltjahr *n*.

learn [lɜːn] lernen; erfahren; hören; **~ed** [ˈ~nіd] gelehrt; **~er** Anfänger(in); Fahrschüler(-in); **~ing** Gelehrsamkeit *f*; **~t** [lɜːnt] *pret u. pp von* **learn**.

lease [liːs] Pacht *f*, Miete *f*; Pacht-, Mietvertrag *m*; (ver)pachten, (-)mieten.

leash [liːʃ] (Hunde)Leine *f*.

least [liːst] kleinst, geringst, mindest; **at ~** mindestens, wenigstens.

leather ['leðə] Leder *n*; ledern; Leder...

leave [li:v] Erlaubnis *f*; Abschied *m*; Urlaub *m*; **take (one's) ~** sich verabschieden; *(irr)* (hinter-, über-, übrig-, ver-, zurück)lassen; liegenlassen, vergessen; vermachen; (fort-, weg)gehen; abreisen (von); abfahren.

leaven ['levn] Sauerteig *m*; Hefe *f*.

leaves [li:vz] *pl von* **leaf**; Laub *n*.

lecture ['lektʃə] Vortrag *m*; Vorlesung *f*; Strafpredigt *f*; **e-n** Vortrag *od.* Vorträge halten; e-e Vorlesung *od.* Vorlesungen halten; abkanzeln; **~r** Vortragende *m*, *f*; *univ.* Dozent(in).

led [led] *pret u. pp von* **lead**[1].

ledge [ledʒ] Leiste *f*, Sims *m, n*; Riff *n*.

leech [li:tʃ] Blutegel *m*.

leek [li:k] Lauch *m*, Porree *m*.

leer [liə] (lüsterner *od.* finsterer) Seitenblick; schielen (*at* nach).

left[1] [left] *pret u. pp von* **leave**.

left[2] link(s); **turn ~** links abbiegen; *sub:* Linke *f*; **on the ~** links, auf der linken Seite; **to the ~** nach links; **keep to the ~** sich links halten; *mot.* links fahren;

~-hand link; **on the ~ hand side** links; **~ handed** linkshändig.

left-luggage office Gepäckaufbewahrung *f*.

leg [leg] Bein *n*; Keule *f*; **pull s.o.'s ~** *fig.* j-n auf den Arm nehmen.

legacy ['legəsi] Vermächtnis *n*.

legal [li:gəl] gesetzlich; gesetzmäßig; Rechts...

legation [li'geiʃən] Gesandtschaft *f*.

legend ['ledʒənd] Legende *f*, Sage *f*; Beschriftung *f*, Bildunterschrift *f*; **~ary** sagenhaft.

legible ['ledʒəbl] leserlich.

legion ['li:dʒən] Legion *f*; Unzahl *f*.

legislat|**ion** [ledʒis'leiʃən] Gesetzgebung *f*; **~ive** ['~lətiv] gesetzgebend; **~or** ['~leitə] Gesetzgeber *m*.

legitimate [li'dʒitimit] legitim, rechtmäßig.

leisure ['leʒə] Muße *f*; **~ly** gemächlich.

lemon ['lemən] Zitrone *f*; **~ade** [~'neid] Zitronenlimonade *f*; **~ squash** Zitronenwasser *n*.

lend [lend] *(irr)* (ver-, aus)leihen.

length [leŋθ] Länge *f*; (Zeit)Dauer *f*; **at ~** endlich; **~en** verlängern; länger werden; **~wise** ['~waiz] der Länge nach.

lenient ['li:njənt] mild(e), nachsichtig.

lens [lenz] *opt.* Linse *f*.

lent [lent] *pret u. pp von* **lend;** 2 Fastenzeit *f.*

leopard ['lepəd] Leopard *m.*

leprosy ['leprəsi] Lepra *f.*

less [les] kleiner, geringer; weniger; minus; **~en** (sich) vermindern; abnehmen; herabsetzen; **~er** kleiner, geringer.

lesson ['lesn] Lektion *f;* Aufgabe *f;* (Unterrichts-) Stunde *f; pl* Unterricht *m; fig.* Lehre *f.*

lest [lest] damit nicht, daß nicht; daß.

let [let] (*irr*) lassen; vermieten; sollen; **~ alone** in Ruhe lassen; geschweige denn; **~ down** *j-n* im Stich lassen; **~ go** loslassen; **~ s.o.** *know* j-n wissen lassen.

lethal ['li:θəl] tödlich.

letter ['letə] Buchstabe *m;* Brief *m; pl* Literatur *f;* **~box** Briefkasten *m;* **~ carrier** *Am.* Briefträger *m.*

lettuce ['letis] (Kopf-) Salat *m.*

leuk(a)emia [lju(:)'ki:miə] Leukämie *f.*

level ['levl] Ebene *f,* ebene Fläche *f;* (gleiche) Höhe, Niveau *n,* Stand *m;* eben; waag(e)recht; gleich (-mäßig); ebnen; gleichmachen; ebnen; **~ crossing** *Brit.* schienengleicher Bahnübergang.

lever ['li:və] Hebel *m.*

levity ['leviti] Leichtfertigkeit *f.*

levy ['levi] (Steuer)Erhebung *f; Steuern* erheben.

lewd [lu:d] lüstern; unzüchtig.

liability [laiə'biliti] Verpflichtung *f,* Verbindlichkeit *f;* Haftpflicht *f.*

liable ['laiəbl] verantwortlich, haftbar; verpflichtet; **be ~ to** neigen zu; *e-r Sache* ausgesetzt sein *od.* unterliegen.

liar ['laiə] Lügner(in).

libel ['laibəl] *jur.* Verleumdung *f.*

liberal ['libərəl] liberal (*a. pol.*); freigebig; reichlich.

liberate ['libəreit] befreien; freilassen; **~ion** Befreiung *f;* **~or** Befreier *m.*

liberty ['libəti] Freiheit *f;* **be at ~** frei sein.

librarian [lai'brɛəriən] Bibliothekar(in); **~y** ['~brəri] Bibliothek *f;* Bücherei *f.*

lice [lais] *pl von* **louse.**

licen|ce, *Am.* **~se** ['laisəns] Lizenz *f,* Konzession *f;* lizenzieren, berechtigen; **~see** [~'si:] Lizenzinhaber *m.*

lichen ['laikən] Flechte *f.*

lick [lik] Lecken *n;* Salzlecke *f;* (be)lecken; *colloq.* verdreschen; **~ing** *colloq.* Dresche *f.*

lid [lid] Deckel *m;* (Augen)Lid *n.*

lie¹ [lai] Lüge *f;* lügen.

lie² Lage *f;* (*irr*) liegen; **~ down** sich hin- *od.* nieder-

legen; **~in: have a ~** sich
gründlich ausschlafen.
lieutenant [lefˈtenənt, *mar.*
leˈtenənt, *Am.* luːˈtenənt]
Leutnant *m.*

life [laif], *pl* **lives** [~vz]
Leben *n*; Biographie *f*;
for ~ auf Lebenszeit,
lebenslänglich; **~ assur-
ance** Lebensversicherung
f; **~belt** Rettungsgürtel
m; **~boat** Rettungsboot
n; **~guard** Rettungs-
schwimmer *m*; **~ insur-
ance** Lebensversicherung
f; **~jacket** Schwimm-
weste *f*; **~less** leblos;
matt; **~like** lebensecht;
~ sentence lebensläng-
liche Freiheitsstrafe;
~time Leben(szeit *f*) *n.*

lift [lift] Heben *n*; *phys.,
aer.* Auftrieb *m*; Fahrstuhl
m, Lift *m*, Aufzug *m*;
give s.o. a ~ j-n (im
Auto) mitnehmen; **get a
~** (im Auto) mitgenommen
werden; *vb:* (auf-, er-,
hoch)heben; sich heben;
~off *aer.* Start *m*, Abheben *n.*

ligature [ˈligətʃuə] *med.:*
Abbinden *n*; Verband *m.*

light¹ [lait] Licht *n* (a.
fig.); Gesichtspunkt *m*,
Aspekt *m*; **can you give
me a ~, please?** haben
Sie Feuer?; **put a ~ to**
anzünden; *adj:* licht, hell;
vb (*irr*): leuchten; **~ (up)**
anzünden; be-, erleuch-
ten; **~ up** aufleuchten (*Augen etc.*).

light² leicht; **~en** leichter
machen *od.* werden; er-
hellen; sich aufhellen;
blitzen; **~er** Feuerzeug *n*;
mar. Leichter *m*; **~house**
Leuchtturm *m*; **~ing** Beleuchtung *f*; **~minded**
leichtfertig; **~ness** Leich-
tigkeit *f.*

lightning [ˈlaitniŋ] Blitz
m; **~conductor**, **~rod**
Blitzableiter *m.*

light-weight Leichtge-
wicht *n.*

like [laik] gleich; (so) wie;
ähnlich; **feel ~** Lust haben
zu; **~ that** so; **what is
he ~?** wie sieht er aus?;
wie ist er?; **der, die, das
~** gleiche; *vb:* gern haben,
(gern) mögen; wollen;
how do you ~ it? wie
gefällt es dir?; **if you ~**
wenn du willst.

like|lihood [ˈlaiklihud]
Wahrscheinlichkeit *f*; **~ly**
wahrscheinlich; geeignet;
~ness Ähnlichkeit *f*; (Ab-)
Bild *n*; Gestalt *f*; **~wise**
[ˈ~waiz] gleich-, ebenfalls.

liking [ˈlaikiŋ] Zuneigung
f; Gefallen *n*, Geschmack
m.

lilac [ˈlailək] lila; Flieder
m.

lily [ˈlili] Lilie *f*; **~ of the
valley** Maiglöckchen *n.*

limb [lim] (*Körper*)Glied
n; Ast *m*; *pl* Gliedmaßen
pl.

lime [laim] Kalk *m*;
Limonelle *f*; Linde *f*;
~light *thea.* Scheinwerfer-
licht *n.*

limit ['limit] Grenze *f*; **off ~s** *Am.* Zutritt verboten; **that's the ~!** *colloq.* das ist (doch) die Höhe!; *vb*: begrenzen; beschränken (**to** auf); **~ed liability company** Gesellschaft *f* mit beschränkter Haftung.

limp [limp] hinken; schlaff; weich.

line [lain] Linie *f*; Strich *m*; Reihe *f*; (Menschen-) Schlange *f*; Falte *f*, Runzel *f*; Geschlecht *n*, Linie *f*; Zeile *f*; Vers *m*; Fach *n*, Branche *f* (Eisenbahn-*etc.*)Linie *f*, Strecke *f*; (Verkehrs)Gesellschaft *f*; *teleph.* Leitung *f*; Leine *f*; (Angel)Schnur *f*; *pl* Umriß *m*; **hold the ~** *teleph.* am Apparat bleiben; **stand in ~** anstehen; *vb*: linieren; *Gesicht* zeichnen; einfassen, säumen; *Kleid* füttern; **~ up** (sich) aufstellen.

lineaments ['liniəmənts] *pl* Gesichtszüge *pl*.

linear ['liniə] geradlinig.

linen ['linin] Leinen *n*, Leinwand *f* (*Bett- etc.*) Wäsche *f*; leinen; **~ closet** Wäscheschrank *m*.

liner ['lainə] Passagier-dampfer *m*; Verkehrsflug-zeug *n*.

linger ['liŋgə] zögern; trödeln; verweilen.

lingerie ['læ:nʒəri:] Da-menunterwäsche *f*.

lining ['lainiŋ] (*Kleider-etc.*)Futter *n*.

link [liŋk] (Ketten)Glied

n; *fig.* (Binde)Glied *n*; (sich) verbinden.

links [liŋks] *pl* Dünen *pl*; *sg* Golfplatz *m*.

lion ['laiən] Löwe *m*; **~ess** Löwin *f*.

lip [lip] Lippe *f*; **~stick** Lippenstift *m*.

liquid ['likwid] flüssig; Flüssigkeit *f*.

liquor ['likə] alkoholisches Getränk; Flüssigkeit *f*, Saft *m*. [kritze *f*.]

liquorice ['likəris] La-┘

lisp [lisp] Lispeln *n*; lispeln.

list [list] Liste *f*, Ver-zeichnis *n*; (in e-e Liste) eintragen; verzeichnen.

listen ['lisn] hören, hor-chen, lauschen; **~ in,** **to** *Radio* hören; **~ to** zu-, anhören; hören auf; **~er** Zuhörer(in); (Rundfunk-) Hörer(in).

listless ['listlis] lustlos.

lit [lit] *pret u. pp von* **light**[1].

literal ['litərəl] wörtlich.

litera|ry ['litərəri] litera-risch, Literatur...; **~ture** ['.itrəʃə] Literatur *f*.

lithe [laið] geschmeidig.

lit|re, *Am.* **~er** ['li:tə] Liter *m*, *n*.

litter ['litə] Tragbahre *f*; Abfall *m*; *zo.* Wurf *m*; **~basket, ~bin** Abfall-korb *m*.

little ['litl] klein; wenig; **a ~** bit etwas; **~ one** Kleine *n* (*Kind*); **a ~** ein wenig, ein bißchen, etwas; **~ by ~** nach und nach.

live¹ [liv] leben; wohnen; ~ **on** leben von.

live² [laiv] lebend; lebendig; lebhaft; *Rundfunk, Fernsehen*: Direkt..., Original..., Live...

live|lihood ['laivlihud] Lebensunterhalt *m*; ~ **long: the ~ day** den lieben langen Tag; ~**ly** lebhaft, lebendig.

liver ['livə] Leber *f*.

livery ['livəri] Livree *f*.

live|s [laivz] *pl von* **life**; ~**stock** Vieh(bestand *m*) *n*.

livid ['livid] bläulich, fahl.

living ['liviŋ] lebend(ig); Leben *n*; Lebensweise *f*; Lebensunterhalt *m*; *eccl.* Pfründe *f*; ~**room** Wohnzimmer *n*.

lizard ['lizəd] Eidechse *f*.

load [ləud] Last *f*; Ladung *f*; Belastung *f*; (be-, ver-)laden; *fig.* überhäufen, -laden; ~ **up** aufladen; ~**ing** (Be)Laden *n*; Ladung *f*; Lade...

loaf¹ [ləuf], *pl* **loaves** [~vz] (Brot)Laib *m*.

loaf² herumlungern; ~**er** Herumtreiber(in).

loam [ləum] Lehm *m*.

loan [ləun] Anleihe *f*; Darlehen *n*; (Ver)Leihen *n*; Leihgabe *f*; **on** ~ leihweise; *vb: bsd. Am.* verleihen.

loath [ləuθ] abgeneigt; ~**e** [ləuð] sich ekeln vor; verabscheuen; ~**ing** ['ləuðiŋ] Ekel *m*; Abscheu *m*;

~**some** ['~ðsəm] ekelhaft, -erregend.

loaves [ləuvz] *pl von* **loaf**¹.

lobby ['lɔbi] Vorhalle *f*; *parl.* Wandelgang *m*; *thea.* Foyer *n*.

lobe [ləub] *anat.* Lappen *m*; Ohrläppchen *n*. [*m.*]

lobster ['lɔbstə] Hummer.'

local ['ləukəl] örtlich, lokal, Orts...; *colloq.* Wirtshaus *n* (*am Ort*); ~**ity** [~'kæliti] Örtlichkeit *f*; Lage *f*; ~**ize** lokalisieren; ~ **train** Vorort(s)zug *m*.

locat|e ['ləu'keit] unterbringen; ausfindig machen; **be ~ed** gelegen sein; ~**ion** Lage *f*.

loch [lɔk] *Scot.:* See *m*; Bucht *f*.

lock [lɔk] (*Tür-, Gewehretc.*)Schloß *n*; Schleuse(nkammer) *f*; Locke *f*; (ab-, ver-, zu)schließen, (ver-)sperren; umschließen; *tech.* sperren; bsd. schließen (lassen); ~ **in** einschließen, -sperren; ~ **up** ver-, wegschließen; ~**er** schmaler Schrank; schließfach *n*; ~**et** ['~it] Medaillon *n*; ~**smith** Schlosser *m*.

locomotive ['ləukəməutiv] Fortbewegungs...; Lokomotive *f*.

locust ['ləukəst] Heuschrecke *f*.

lodg|e [lɔdʒ] Häuschen *n*; Sommerhaus *n*; Pförtnerhaus *n*; Jagdhütte *f*; aufnehmen, (für die Nacht) unterbringen; (in Unter-

miete) wohnen; ~er (Unter)Mieter(in); **~ing** Unterkunft f; pl möbliertes Zimmer; **night's ~ing** Nachtquartier n; Übernachtung f.

loft [lɔft] (Dach)Boden m; Heuboden m; Empore f; **~y** hoch; erhaben; stolz.

log [lɔg] Klotz m, Block m; (gefällter) Baumstamm; **~book** Log-, Fahrtenbuch n; **~ cabin** Blockhaus n.

loggia [ˈlɔdʒə] Loggia f.

logic [ˈlɔdʒik] Logik f; **~al** logisch. [denstück n.]

loin [lɔin] Lende f; Lendenstück n.

loiter [ˈlɔitə] schlendern, bummeln, trödeln.

loll [lɔl] (sich) rekeln.

lone|liness [ˈlounlinis] Einsamkeit f; **~ly, ~some** einsam; abgelegen.

long[1] [lɔŋ] lang(e); langfristig; **be ~** lange brauchen; **so ~!** bis dann!, auf Wiedersehen!; **no ~er, not any ~er** nicht mehr, nicht (mehr) länger; sub: Länge f; lange Zeit; **before ~** bald; **for ~** lange (Zeit); **take ~** lange brauchen od. dauern.

long[2] sich sehnen (**for** nach).

long-distance Fern...; Langstrecken...; **~ call** Ferngespräch n.

longing [ˈlɔŋiŋ] sehnsüchtig; Sehnsucht f, Verlangen n.

longitude [ˈlɔndʒitjuːd] geogr. Länge f.

long|jump Weitsprung m; **~shoreman** [ˈ~ʃɔːmən] Hafenarbeiter m; **~sighted** weitsichtig; **~term** langfristig; **~winded** langatmig.

look [luk] Blick m; pl Aussehen n; **have a ~ at s.th.** sich et. ansehen; vb: sehen, blicken, schauen (**at** auf); aussehen; nachsehen; **~ after** nachblicken; aufpassen auf, sich kümmern um; **~ at** ansehen; **~ for** suchen; erwarten; **~ forward to** sich freuen auf; **~ into** untersuchen, prüfen; **~ on** zuschauen; betrachten, ansehen; **~ on (to)** liegen nach, (hinaus)gehen auf (Fenster etc.); **~ out** aufpassen; sich vorsehen; **~ over** et. durchsehen; j-n mustern; **~ round** sich umsehen (a. fig.); **~ up** et. nachschlagen.

look|er-on [ˈlukərˈɔn] Zuschauer(in); **~ing-glass** Spiegel m.

loom [luːm] Webstuhl m; undeutlich zu sehen sein.

loop [luːp] Schlinge f, Schleife f; Schlaufe f; Öse f; **~** et. Schleife machen; in Schleifen legen, schlingen.

loose [luːs] los(e); locker; ungenau; liederlich; lösen; lockern; **~n** [ˈ~sn] (sich) lösen, (sich) lockern.

loot [luːt] plündern; Beute f.

lop [lɔp] schlaff herunterhängen; *Baum* beschneiden; ~ **(off)** abhauen.

lope [ləup]: **at a ~** im Galopp, mit großen Sprüngen.

lord [lɔːd] Herr *m*, Gebieter *m*; Lord *m*; **House of ~s** *Brit. parl.* Oberhaus *n*; **the ~** der Herr (*Gott*); **~ Mayor** *Brit.* Oberbürgermeister *m*; **~'s Prayer** Vaterunser *n*; **~'s Supper** Abendmahl *n*.

lorry ['lɔri] Last(kraft)wagen *m*; *rail.* Lore *f*.

lose [luːz] (*irr*) verlieren; verpassen; nachgehen (*Uhr*); **~ o.s.** sich verirren.

loss [lɔs] Verlust *m*; Schaden *m*; **at a ~** *econ.* mit Verlust; in Verlegenheit, außerstande.

lost [lɔst] *pret u. pp von* **lose**; verloren; *fig.* versunken, -tieft; **~-property office** Fundbüro *n*.

lot [lɔt] Los *n* (*a. fig.*); Anteil *m*; Parzelle *f*; (Waren)Posten *m*; *colloq.* Menge *f*; **cast ~s, draw ~s** losen; **the ~** alles; **a ~ of, ~s of** viel, e-e Menge; **a ~** (sehr) viel.

loth [ləuθ] *s.* **loath.**

lotion ['ləuʃən] (*Haar-, Haut-, Rasier- etc.*)Wasser *n*.

lottery ['lɔtəri] Lotterie *f*.

lotto ['lɔtəu] Lotto *n*.

loud [laud] laut; *fig.* grell, auffallend; **~speaker** Lautsprecher *m*.

lounge [laundʒ] sich re-

keln *od.* lümmeln; Bummel *m*; Wohnzimmer *n*; Hotelhalle *f*.

lous|e [laus], *pl* **lice** [lais] Laus *f*; **~y** ['~zi] verlaust; *colloq.* miserabel.

lout [laut] Tölpel *m*, Lümmel *m*.

love [lʌv] Liebe *f*; Liebling *m*, Schatz *m*; *sp.* null; **give my ~ to her** grüße sie herzlich von mir; **send one's ~ to** j-n grüßen lassen; **~ from** herzliche Grüße von (*Brief*); **in ~ with** verliebt in; **fall in ~ with** sich verlieben in; *vb:* lieben; mögen; **~ to do** gern tun; **we~d having you with us** wir haben uns sehr über deinen Besuch gefreut; **~ly** lieblich, wunderschön, entzückend, reizend; **~r** Liebhaber(in) (*a. fig.*), Geliebte *m, f*; *pl* Liebespaar *n*.   [liebevoll.

loving ['lʌviŋ] liebend,]

low[1] [ləu] niedrig; tief; gering; leise (*Stimme, Ton*); *fig.* niedergeschlagen; *meteor.* Tief(druckgebiet) *n*.

low[2] [ləu] brüllen, muhen (*Rind*).

lower ['ləuə] niedriger, tiefer; unter, Unter...; fallen, sinken; niedriger machen; senken; *Preis* herabsetzen; herunterlassen; *fig.* erniedrigen; **~ House** *Brit. parl.*Unterhaus *n*.

low|lands *pl* Tiefland *n*; **~ly** demütig; einfach; be-

scheiden; **~necked** (tief)
ausgeschnitten   (*Kleid*);
~pressure area Tief
(-druckgebiet) *n*; **~ tide**
Ebbe *f.*   [Treue *f.*\
loyal ['lɔiəl] treu; **~ty**\
lozenge ['lɔzindʒ] Raute
f; Pastille *f.*
lubber ['lʌbə] Tölpel *m.*
lubric|ant   ['lu:brikənt]
Schmiermittel *n*; **~ate**
['~eit] (ab)schmieren, ölen;
~ation (Ab)Schmieren *n*,
Ölen *n.*   [lich.\
lucid ['lu:sid] klar; deut-∫
luck [lʌk] Zufall *m*; Schicksal *n*; **bad (hard, ill) ~**
Unglück *n*, Pech *n*; **good
~** Glück *n*; **~ily** glücklicherweise; **~y** glücklich;
Glücks...; **be ~y** Glück
haben; **~y fellow** Glückspilz *m.*
ludicrous ['lu:dikrəs] lächerlich.
lug [lʌg] zerren, schleppen.
luggage ['lʌgidʒ] (Reise-)
Gepäck *n*; **~-carrier** Gepäckträger *m* (*Fahrrad*);
~ (delivery) office Gepäckausgabe *f*; **~-rack**
Gepäcknetz *n*; **~ (registration) office** Gepäckannahme *f*; Gepäckausgabe *f*; **~ ticket** Gepäckschein *m*; **~-van** Gepäckwagen *m.*
lukewarm ['lu:kwɔ:m] lau
(-warm); *fig.* lau.
lull [lʌl] einlullen; (sich)
beruhigen; sich legen;
(Ruhe)Pause *f*; **~aby**
['~əbai] Wiegenlied *n.*

lumbago   [lʌm'beigəu]
Hexenschuß *m.*
lumber ['lʌmbə] Bau-,
Nutzholz *n*; Gerümpel *n*;
~jack, ~man Holzfäller
m, -arbeiter *m*; **~-room**
Rumpelkammer *f.*
luminous   ['lu:minəs]
leuchtend; Leucht...; klar,
einleuchtend.
lump [lʌmp] Klumpen *m*;
fig. Kloß *m*; **~ of** Stück *n*
(*Zucker etc.*); **in the ~**
in Bausch und Bogen;
~ sugar Würfelzucker *m*;
~ sum Pauschalsumme *f.*
lunar ['lu:nə] Mond...;
~ module Mondfähre *f.*
lunatic ['lu:nətik] irr-,
wahnsinnig; Geisteskranke
m, f.
lunch [lʌntʃ] zu Mittag
essen; Lunch *m*, (leichtes)
Mittagessen; **packed ~**
Lunchpaket *n*; **~-hour**
Mittagspause *f.*
lung [lʌŋ] Lunge(nflügel
m) *f*; **the ~s** *pl* die Lunge.
lunge [lʌndʒ] losstürzen,
-fahren (**at** auf.)
lurch [lə:tʃ] *mar.* schlingern; taumeln, torkeln.
lure [ljuə] Köder *m*; *fig.*
Lockung *f*; ködern, (an-)
locken.
lurk [lə:k] lauern; *fig.* verborgen liegen, schlummern.
luscious ['lʌʃəs] köstlich;
üppig; sinnlich.
lust [lʌst] Begierde *f*;
Gier *f*, Sucht *f.*
lust|re, *Am.* **~er** ['lʌstə]

Glanz *m*; Kronleuchter
m.

lusty ['lʌsti] kräftig, robust.

lute [luːt] Laute *f*.

luxate ['lʌkseit] *med*. ver-
renken.

luxurious [lʌg'zjuəriəs]
luxuriös, üppig, Luxus...;

~y ['lʌkʃəri] Luxus *m*;
Luxusartikel *m*.

lying ['laiiŋ] *pres p von*
lie¹ *u*. **lie²**; lügnerisch.

lymph [limf] Lymphe *f*.

lynch [lintʃ] lynchen.

lynx [liŋks] Luchs *m*.

lyric ['lirik] lyrisch(es Gedicht); *pl* (Lied)Text *m*.

M

ma'am [mæm, məm]
colloq. s. **madam.**

mac [mæk] *colloq. s*.
mackintosh.

machine [mə'ʃiːn] Ma-
schine *f*; **~-made** ma-
schinell hergestellt; **~ery**
Maschinen *pl*; **~ist** Maschinist *m*.

mack [mæk] *colloq*., **~in-
tosh** ['~intɔʃ] Regenmantel *m*.

mad [mæd] wahnsinnig,
verrückt, toll; *bsd. Am*.
wütend; **drive s.o. ~** j-n
verrückt machen; **go ~**
verrückt werden.

madam ['mædəm] gnä-
dige Frau, gnädiges Fräu-
lein.

made [meid] *pret u. pp
von* **make.**

mad|man Verrückte *m*;
~ness Wahnsinn *m*.

magazine [mægə'ziːn]
Magazin *n*; Munitions-
lager *n*; Zeitschrift *f*.

maggot ['mægət] Made *f*.

magic ['mædʒik] Zaube-
rei *f*; *fig*. Zauber *m*; **~(al)**
magisch, Zauber...; **~ian**

[mə'dʒiʃən] Zauberer *m*;
Zauberkünstler *m*.

magistrate ['mædʒis-
treit] (Polizei-, Friedens-)
Richter *m*.

magnanimous [mæg-
'næniməs] großmütig.

magnet ['mægnit] Magnet
m; **~ic** [~'netik] magnetisch.

magnificence [mæg'ni-
fisns] Großartigkeit *f*,
Pracht *f*; **~ficent** großartig, prächtig, herrlich;
~fy ['~fai] vergrößern.

magpie ['mægpai] El-
ster *f*.

maid [meid] (Dienst)Mäd-
chen *n*, Magd *f*; Mädchen
n; **old ~** alte Jungfer; **~en**
unverheiratet; Jungfern...,
Erstlings...; **~enly** mädchenhaft; **~en name** Mädchenname *m* (*e-r Frau*).

mail [meil] Post(dienst *m*) *f*;
Post(sendung) *f*; *Am*. (mit
der Post) schicken, auf-
geben; **~bag** Postsack *m*;
~box *Am*. Briefkasten
m; **~man** *Am*. Briefträger
m; **~order** business

(firm, house) Versandgeschäft n, -haus n.

maim [meim] verstümmeln.

main [mein] Haupt..., größt, wichtigst, hauptsächlich; *mst pl* Haupt- (gas-, -wasser-, -strom-) leitung f; Stromnetz n; **~land** Festland n; **~ly** hauptsächlich; **~ road** Haupt(verkehrs)straße f; **~ street** Am. Hauptstraße f.

maintain [mein'tein] (aufrecht)erhalten; instand halten; unterstützen; unterhalten; behaupten; verteidigen.

maintenance ['meintənəns] Instandhaltung f; tech. Wartung f; Unterhalt m.

maize [meiz] Mais m.

majes|tic [mə'dʒestik] majestätisch; **~y** ['mædʒisti] Majestät f.

major ['meidʒə] größer; wichtig; volljährig; mus. Dur...; der ältere; Major m; Volljährige m, f; Am. Hauptfach n; mus. Dur n; **~ette** [ˌ~'ret] Tambourmajorin f; **~ity** [mə'dʒɔriti] Mehrheit f; Mehrzahl f; Volljährigkeit f; **~ road** Haupt-, Vorfahrt(s)straße f.

make [meik] Ausführung f; Fabrikat n; tech. Typ m, Bauart f; (irr) machen; anfertigen, herstellen, erzeugen; verarbeiten (**into** zu); bilden; (er)geben;

machen zu, ernennen zu; *j-n* veranlassen od. bringen od. zwingen zu; *Geld* verdienen od. colloq. Strecke zurücklegen; colloq. et. erreichen od. schaffen; **~ for** zugehen auf; sich begeben nach; **~ out** Rechnung etc. ausstellen; erkennen, ausmachen; ausfindig machen, feststellen; entziffern; klug werden aus; **~ over** Eigentum etc. übertragen; **~ up** bilden; zs.-setzen; zs.-stellen; (sich) zurechtmachen od. schminken; sich ausdenken, erfinden; **~ up for** ausgleichen, aufholen; wiedergutmachen; **~ up one's mind** sich entschließen; **~ it up** sich versöhnen; **~-believe** So-tun-als-ob n; Verstellung f; **~r** Hersteller m; **2r** Schöpfer m (Gott); **~shift** Notbehelf m; behelfsmäßig; **~up** Schminke f, Make-up n.

malady ['mælədi] Krankheit f.

male [meil] männlich; Mann m; zo. Männchen n.

male|diction [mæli'dikʃən] Fluch m; **~factor** ['ˌfæktə] Übeltäter m; **~volent** [mə'levələnt] übelwollend.

malic|e ['mælis] Bosheit f, Gehässigkeit f; Groll m; **~ious** [mə'liʃəs] boshaft; böswillig.

malignant [mə'lignənt] bösartig (a. med.).

malnutrition ['mælnju(:)-
'triʃən] Unterernährung f.

malt [mɔ:lt] Malz n.

maltreat [mæl'tri:t] mißhandeln. [ma f.]

mam(m)a [mə'mɑ:] Ma-

mammal ['mæməl] Säugetier n.

man [mæn, in Zssgn: mən],
pl **men** [men] Mann m;
Mensch(en pl) m; Menschheit f; Diener m; männlich; bemannen.

manage ['mænidʒ] handhaben; verwalten; leiten;
fertig werden mit; et. fertigbringen; Betrieb etc.
leiten od. führen; auskommen; colloq. (es) schaffen; ~able handlich; lenksam; ~ment Verwaltung
f, Leitung f; Geschäftsleitung f, Direktion f; ~r
Verwalter m, Leiter m;
Manager m; Geschäftsführer m, Direktor m; ~ress
['~ə'res] Geschäftsführerin f.

mane [mein] Mähne f.

maneuver [mə'nu:və] Am.
für manoeuvre.

manger ['meindʒə] Krippe f.

mangle ['mæŋgl] Wäschemangel f; mangeln; übel zurichten; fig. verstümmeln.

manhood ['mænhud]
Mannesalter n; Männlichkeit f; die Männer pl.

mania ['meinjə] Wahn
(-sinn) m; Sucht f, Manie
f; ~c ['~iæk] Wahnsinnige
m, f.

manifest ['mænifest] offenbar; offenbaren; kundtun.

manifold ['mænifould]
mannigfaltig; vervielfältigen.

manipulate [mə'nipjuleit] (geschickt) handhaben od. behandeln; manipulieren.

man|kind [mæn'kaind] die
Menschheit; ['~kaind] die
Männer pl; ~ly männlich.

manner ['mænə] Art f,
Weise f, Art und Weise;
pl Benehmen n, Manieren
pl, Sitten pl.

manoeuvre [mə'nu:və]
Manöver n; manövrieren.

man-of-war ['mænəv-
'wɔ:] Kriegsschiff n.

manor ['mænə] Rittergut
n; lord of the ~ Gutsherr
m; ~house Herrenhaus n.

man|power [mæn] Menschenpotential n; Arbeitskräfte
pl; ~servant Diener m.

mansion ['mænʃən] (herrschaftliches) Wohnhaus.

manslaughter jur. Totschlag m, fahrlässige Tötung.

mantelpiece ['mæntlpi:s]
Kaminsims m.

manual ['mænjuəl] Hand-
...; Handbuch n.

manufacture [mænju-
'fæktʃə] Herstellung f; herstellen, erzeugen; ~r Hersteller m, Erzeuger m,
Fabrikant m.

manure [mə'njuə] Dünger m, Mist m; düngen.

mascot

manuscript ['mænju-skript] Manuskript *n*; Handschrift *f*.

many ['meni] viel(e); manch; **a good ~, a great ~** sehr *od.* ziemlich viel(e).

map [mæp] (Land- *etc.*) Karte *f*;(Stadt- *etc.*)Plan *m*.

maple ['meipl] Ahorn *m*.

marble ['maːbl] Marmor *m*; Murmel *f*; marmorn.

March [maːtʃ] März *m*.

march [maːtʃ] Marsch *m*; marschieren.

mare [mɛə] Stute *f*.

margarine [maːdʒə-'riːn], **~e** [maːdʒ] *colloq.* Margarine *f*.

margin ['maːdʒin] Rand *m*; Grenze *f*; Spielraum *m*; (Gewinn)Spanne *f*.

marine [mə'riːn] Marine *f*; Marineinfanterist *m*; See-...; Marine...; Schiffs-...; **~r** ['mærinə] Seemann *m*.

maritime ['mæritaim] See...; Küsten...

mark [maːk] Markierung *f*, Bezeichnung *f*, Marke *f*; Zeichen *n* (*a. fig.*); (Körper)Mal *n*; Spur *f*; Merkmal *n*; Zensur *f*, Note *f*; Ziel *n*; markieren, kenn-zeichnen; benoten, zen-sieren; sich *et.* merken; achtgeben; **~ out** abgren-zen, bezeichnen; **~ed** deut-lich; auffallend.

market ['maːkit] Markt *m* (*Handel, Absatzgebiet*); Markt(platz) *m*; *Am.* (Le-bensmittel)Geschäft *n*; auf den Markt bringen; ver-kaufen; einkaufen; **~-gar-den** Handelsgärtnerei *f*; **~ing** *econ.* Marketing *n*, Absatzpolitik *f*; **~-place** Marktplatz *m*.

marksman ['maːksmən] (guter) Schütze.

marmalade ['maːmə-leid] (*bsd.* Orangen)Mar-melade *f*.

marmot ['maːmət] Mur-meltier *n*.

marriage ['mæridʒ] Hei-rat *f*, Hochzeit *f*; Ehe (-stand) *f*; **~able** heirats-fähig; **~ articles** *pl* Ehevertrag *m*; **~ certif-icate, ~ lines** *pl* Trau-schein *m*; **~ portion** Mit-gift *f*.

married ['mærid] verhei-ratet; **~ couple** Ehepaar *n*.

marrow ['mærəu] Mark *n*.

marry ['mæri] (ver)heira-ten; trauen; (sich ver)hei-raten.

marsh [maːʃ] Sumpf *m*.

marshal ['maːʃəl] Mar-schall *m*; *Am.* Bezirkspoli-zeichef *m*; ordnen; auf-stellen; (hinein)geleiten.

marshy ['maːʃi] sumpfig.

marten ['maːtin] Marder*m*.

martial ['maːʃəl] Kriegs...,Militär...

martyr ['maːtə] Märtyrer (-in).

marvel ['maːvəl] Wunder *n*; sich wundern; **~(l)ous** wunderbar; fabelhaft.

mascot ['mæskət] Mas-kottchen *n*.

masculine ['mæskjulin] männlich.

mash [mæʃ] zerdrücken, -quetschen; **~ed potatoes** pl Kartoffelbrei m.

mask [mɑːsk] Maske f; maskieren.

mason ['meisn] Steinmetz m; Maurer m; **~ry** Mauerwerk n.

masque [mɑːsk] Maskenspiel n.

mass [mæs] eccl. Messe f; Masse f; Menge f; Massen...; (sich) (an)sammeln.

massacre ['mæsəkə] Blutbad n; niedermetzeln.

massage ['mæsɑːʒ] Massage f; massieren.

massif ['mæsiːf] (Gebirgs-) Massiv m [schwer.]

massive ['mæsiv] massiv; [

mast [mɑːst] Mast m.

master ['mɑːstə] Meister m; Herr m; Gebieter m; Lehrer m; junger Herr (als Anrede); Rektor m (e-s College); Meister...; Haupt...; meistern; beherrschen; **~ly** meisterhaft; **2 of Arts** Magister m Artium; **~ of ceremonies** Am. Conférencier m; **~piece** Meisterstück n, -werk n; **~ship** Meisterschaft f; Herrschaft f; Lehramt n; **~y** Herrschaft f; Oberhand f; Beherrschung f.

mat [mæt] Matte f; Untersetzer m; mattiert, matt.

match¹ [mætʃ] Streichholz n.

match² Partie f; (Wett-) Spiel n, Wettkampf m; **be a ~ for** j–m gewachsen sein; **find** od. **meet one's ~** s–n Meister finden; vb: passen zu; zs.-passen; **to ~** dazu passend; **~less** unvergleichlich; **~maker** Ehestifter(in).

mate [meit] Kamerad m; Gehilfe m; Gatte m, -in f; zo. Männchen n, Weibchen n; mar. Maat m; zo. (sich) paaren.

material [mə'tiəriəl] materiell; körperlich; wesentlich; Material m; Stoff m.

matern|al [mə'təːnl] mütterlich; mütterlicherseits; **~ity** Mutterschaft f; **~ity hospital** Entbindungsanstalt f.

mathematic|ian [mæθimə'tiʃən] Mathematiker m; **~s** [~'mætiks] sg, pl Mathematik f.

maths [mæθs] colloq. abbr. für **mathematics**.

matriculate [mə'trikjuleit] immatrikulieren; sich immatrikulieren (lassen).

matrimony ['mætriməni] Ehe(stand m) f.

matron ['meitrən] ältere (verheiratete) Frau, Matrone f; Wirtschafterin f; Oberin f.

matter ['mætə] von Bedeutung sein; **it doesn't ~** es macht nichts (aus); Materie f, Material n, Stoff m; med. Eiter m; Sache f, Angelegenheit f;

Anlaß m; **a ~ of course**
e-e Selbstverständlichkeit;
a ~ of fact e-e Tatsache;
for that ~ was das betrifft; **no ~** ganz gleich;
what's the ~? was ist
los?; **what's the ~ with
you?** was fehlt dir?; **~-of-
fact** sachlich. [tratze f.\
mattress ['mætris] Ma-
matur|e ['mə'tjuə] reif;
reiflich (erwogen); econ.
fällig; zur Reife bringen;
reifen; econ. fällig werden;
~ity Reife f; econ. Fällig-
keit f.
Maundy   Thursday
['mɔ:ndi] Gründonnerstag
m.
mauve [məuv] hellviolett.
maw [mɔ:] (Tier)Magen m.
maxim ['mæksim] Grundsatz m; **~um** ['..əm]
Maximum n; Höchst...
May [mei] Mai m.
may [mei]v/aux ich, du etc.:
kann(st) etc., mag(st) etc.,
darf(st) etc.; **~be** vielleicht.
may|-beetle, ~-bug Mai-
käfer m; **♀ Day** der 1. Mai.
mayor [mɛə] Bürgermei-
ster m.
maypole Maibaum m.
maze [meiz] Irrgarten m,
Labyrinth n; **in a ~** verwirrt.
me [mi:, mi] mir; mich;
colloq. ich; **it's ~** ich bin's.
meadow ['medəu] Wiese f.
meag|re, Am. **~er** ['mi:-
gə] mager, dürr; dürftig.
meal [mi:l] Mahl(zeit f) n;
Mehl n.

mean¹ [mi:n] gemein; niedrig, gering; armselig;
geizig, knauserig.
mean² Mitte f; Mittel n;
pl (Geld)Mittel pl; **~s** sg
Mittel n; **by all ~s** gewiß;
auf alle Fälle; **by no ~s**
keineswegs; **by ~s of** mit-
tels, durch.
mean³ (irr) meinen; beabsichtigen; bestimmen;
bedeuten; **~ well** od. **ill** es
gut od. schlecht meinen;
~ing bedeutsam; Sinn m,
Bedeutung f; **~ingless**
bedeutungs-, sinnlos.
meant [ment] pret u. pp
von **mean³**.
mean|time, ~while in-
zwischen. [sern n.\
measles ['mi:zlz] sg Ma-\
measure ['meʒə] Maß n
(a. fig.); mus. Takt m;
Maßnahme f; **beyond ~**
über alle Maßen, außer-
ordentlich; **made to ~**
nach Maß gemacht; v/b:
(ab-, aus-, ver)messen;
Maß nehmen; **by no ~**
unermeßlich; **~ment** Mes-
sung f; Maß n; pl Ab-
messungen pl; **~ of capacity** Hohlmaß n.
meat [mi:t] Fleisch n.
mechanic [mi'kænik] Me-
chaniker m; **~al** mecha-
nisch; Maschinen...; **~s** sg
Mechanik f.
mechan|ism ['mekən-
izəm] Mechanismus m; **~-
ize** mechanisieren.
medal ['medl] Medaille f;
Orden m.

meddle ['medl] sich einmischen (**with, in** in in).

mediaeval [medi'i:vəl] s. **medieval**.

mediat|e ['mi:dieit] vermitteln; **~ion** Vermittlung f; **~or** Vermittler m.

medical ['medikəl] medizinisch, ärztlich; **~ certificate** ärztliches Attest.

medicated ['medikeitid] medizinisch.

medicin|al [me'disinl] medizinisch, Heil...; **~e** ['medsin] Medizin f; Arznei f.

medieval [medi'i:vəl] mittelalterlich.

mediocre [mi:di'əukə] mittelmäßig.

meditat|e ['mediteit] nachdenken, grübeln; im Sinn haben; **~ion** Nachdenken n; Meditation f; Betrachtung f; **~ive** ['~tətiv] nachdenklich.

Mediterranean [meditə'reinjən] Mittelmeer n; Mittelmeer...

medium ['mi:djəm] Mitte f; Mittel n; Medium n; mittler, Mittel...

medley ['medli] Gemisch n; mus. Potpourri n.

meek [mi:k] sanftmütig, demütig.

meet [mi:t] (irr) treffen (auf); stoßen auf; begegnen; j-n kennenlernen; bsd. Am. j-n vorstellen; j-n abholen; Verpflichtungen nachkommen; Wunsch etc. befriedigen; sich tref-

fen; sich versammeln; **~ with** stoßen auf; erleiden, erfahren; **~ing** Begegnung f; Treffen n; Versammlung f; Sitzung f; Tagung f.

melancholy ['melənkəli] Schwermut f; schwermütig.

mellow ['meləu] reif; weich; fig. abgeklärt.

melod|ious [mi'ləudjəs] melodisch; **~y** ['melədi] Melodie f; Lied n.

melon ['melən] Melone f.

melt [melt] (zer)schmelzen; fig.: erweichen; zerfließen; weich werden.

member ['membə] (Mit-) Glied n; Angehörige m, f; **~ship** Mitgliedschaft f; Mitgliederzahl f; Mitglieds...

membrane ['membrein] Membran(e) f; Häutchen n.

memo|ir ['memwa:] Denkschrift f; pl Memoiren pl; **~rable** ['~mərəbl] denkwürdig; **~rial** [mi'mɔ:riəl] Denk-, Ehrenmal n; **~rize** ['meməraiz] auswendig lernen; **~ry** ['~əri] Gedächtnis n, Erinnerung f; Andenken n; **in ~ry of** zum Andenken an.

men [men] pl von **man**; Leute pl.

menace ['menəs] (be-) drohen; Drohung f.

mend [mend] ausbessern, flicken, reparieren; (ver-) bessern.   [(Arbeit).]

menial ['mi:njəl] niedrig

mental ['mentl] geistig, Geistes...; **~ arithmetic** Kopfrechnen *n*; **~ home**, **~ hospital** (Nerven)Heilanstalt *f*; **~ity** ['~tæliti] Mentalität *f*.

mention ['menʃən] Erwähnung *f*; erwähnen; **don't ~ it** bitte!

menu ['menju:] Menü *n*; Speisekarte *f*.

meow [mi(:)'au] miauen.

mercantile ['mɔ:kəntail] kaufmännisch; Handels...

mercenary ['mɔ:sinəri] käuflich; gewinnsüchtig; Söldner *m*.

merchan|dise ['mɔ:tʃəndaiz] Waren *pl*; **~t** ['~ənt] Kaufmann *m*; *Am. a.* Krämer *m*; Handels...

merci|ful ['mɔ:siful] barmherzig; **~less** unbarmherzig.

mercury ['mɔ:kjuri] Quecksilber *n*.

mercy ['mɔ:si] Barmherzigkeit *f*, Gnade *f*.

mere [miɔ] bloß, rein; **~ly** bloß, rein, nur.

merge [mɔ:dʒ] verschmelzen (**in** mit).

meridian [mə'ridiən] Meridian *m*.

merit ['merit] Verdienst *n*; Wert *m*; *fig.* verdienen; **~orious** ['~tɔ:riəs] verdienstvoll.   [xe *f.*]

mermaid ['mɔ:meid] Ni-ƒ

merriment ['merimənt] Lustigkeit *f*, Belustigung *f*.

merry ['meri] lustig, fröhlich; **make ~** lustig sein;

~ andrew ['~'ændru:] Hanswurst *m*; **~-go-round** Karussell *n*; **~-making** Lustbarkeit *f*, Fest *n*.

mesh [meʃ] Masche *f*; *pl fig.* Netz *n*, Schlingen *pl*.

mess [mes] Unordnung *f*, *colloq.* Schweinerei *f*; Patsche *f*, Klemme *f*; **what a ~!** so eine schöne Geschichte!; *vb*: **~ (up)** beschmutzen; in Unordnung bringen; verpfuschen

message ['mesidʒ] Botschaft *f*; Mitteilung *f*, Nachricht *f*; **give s.o. a ~**, **give a ~ to s.o.** j-m et. ausrichten *od.* bestellen.

messenger ['mesindʒə] Bote *m*.

met [met] *pret u. pp von* **meet**.

metal ['metl] Metall *n*; **~lic** [mi'tælik] metallisch; Metall...

meteor ['mi:tjə] Meteor *m*; **~ology** ['~rɔlədʒi] Meteorologie *f*.

meter ['mi:tə] Messer *m*, Zähler *m*; *Am. für* **metre**.

method ['meθəd] Methode *f*; **~ical** [mi'θɔdikəl] methodisch.

meticulous [mi'tikjuləs] peinlich genau.

met|re, *Am.* **~er** ['mi:tə] Meter *m, n*; Versmaß *n*.

metric system ['metrik] Dezimalsystem *n*.

metropolitan [metrə'pɔlitən] hauptstädtisch.

mew [mju:] miauen.

miaow 180

miaow [mi(:)'au] miauen.
mice [mais] *pl von* **mouse**.
micro|phone ['maikrə-
fəun] Mikrophon *n*; **~-
scope** Mikroskop *n*.
mid [mid] mittler, Mittel...; in **~ winter** mitten
im Winter; **~day** Mittag
m.
middle ['midl] Mitte *f*;
mittler, Mittel...; **~-aged**
mittleren Alters; ♀ **Ages**
pl Mittelalter *n*; **~ class**
(**-es** *pl*) Mittelstand *m*;
~ name zweiter Vor-
name; **~-sized** mittel-
groß; **~ weight** *Boxen:*
Mittelgewicht *n*.
middling ['midliŋ] mittelmäßig; leidlich.
midge [midʒ] Mücke *f*;
~t ['~it] Zwerg *m*, Knirps
m.
mid|land ['midlənd] bin-
nenländisch; *the* ♀**lands** *pl*
Mittelengland *n*; **~night**
Mitternacht *f*; **~st: in the
~ of** inmitten (*gen*);
~summer Sommerson-
nenwende *f*; Hochsommer
m; **~way** auf halbem
Wege; **~wife** Hebamme *f*.
might [mait] *pret von*
may; Macht *f*, Gewalt *f*;
~y mächtig, gewaltig, groß.
migrat|e [mai'greit] (aus-)
wandern, (fort)ziehen;
~ory ['~ətəri] Zug..., Wander...
mild [maild] mild, sanft,
leicht.
mildew ['mildju:] Mehltau *m*.

mildness ['maildnis] Milde *f*.
mile [mail] Meile *f*
(*1,609 km*).
mil(e)age ['mailidʒ] zu-
rückgelegte Meilenzahl *od.*
Fahrtstrecke; Meilen-, Ki-
lometergeld *n*.
milestone Meilenstein *m*.
military ['militəri] mili-
tärisch, Militär...
milk [milk] melken; Milch
f; **it's no use crying
over spilt ~** geschehen
ist geschehen; **~ing-ma-
chine** Melkmaschine *f*;
~man Milchmann *m*;
~shake Milchmixge-
tränk *n*; **~sop** ['~sɔp]
Weichling *m*; **~y** milchig;
Milch...
mill [mil] Mühle *f*; Fabrik
f; Spinnerei *f*; mahlen;
tech. fräsen; **~er** Müller *m*.
millet ['milit] Hirse *f*.
milliner ['milinə] Putz-
macherin *f*, Modistin *f*.
million ['miljən] Million
f; **~aire** [~'nɛə] Millio-
när *m*; **~th** ['~θ] mil-
lionste; Millionstel *n*.
milt [milt] *ichth.* Milch *f*.
mimic ['mimik] nachahmen, -äffen.
minc|e [mins] zerhacken;
~e(d meat) Hackfleisch
n; **~emeat** *e-e* Pasteten-
füllung; **~e pie** *mit mince-
meat gefüllte Pastete*; **~er**,
~ing-machine Fleisch-
wolf *m*.
mind [maind] Sinn *m*;
Geist *m*, Verstand *m*; Mei-

nung *f*; Absicht *f*, Neigung *f*, Lust *f*; Gedächtnis *n*; **to my ~** meiner Ansicht nach; **out of one's ~** von Sinnen, verrückt; **bear od. keep s.th. in ~** an et. denken; **change one's ~** sich anders besinnen; **give s.o. a piece of one's ~** j-m gründlich die Meinung sagen; **have s.th. on one's ~** et. auf dem Herzen haben; *vb*: merken, beachten, achtgeben auf; achten auf; sich kümmern um; **I don't ~ (it)** ich habe nichts dagegen, meinetwegen; **do you ~ if I smoke?, do you ~ my smoking?** stört es Sie, wenn ich rauche?; **would you ~ opening the window?** würden Sie bitte das Fenster öffnen?; **~ the step!** Achtung Stufe!; **~ your own business!** kümmern Sie sich um Ihre Angelegenheiten!; **~!** gib acht!; **never ~!** macht nichts!; **~ed** geneigt, gewillt; in *Zssgn*: gesinnt; **~ful: be ~ of** achten auf, denken an.

mine¹ [main] meine(-r, -s), der, die, das meine.

mine² Bergwerk *n*, Grube *f*; *mil.* Mine *f*; *fig.* Fundgrube *f*; graben; Erz, Kohle abbauen, gewinnen; *mil.* verminen; **~r** Bergmann *m*.

mineral ['minərəl] Mineral *n*; mineralisch.

mingle ['miŋgl] (ver)mi-

schen; sich mischen *od.* mengen (**with** unter).

miniature ['minjətʃə] Miniatur(gemälde *n*) *f*; Miniatur..., Klein...; **~ camera** Kleinbildkamera *f*.

minimum ['miniməm] Minimum *n*; Mindest...

mining ['mainiŋ] Bergbau *m*.

miniskirt ['miniskə:t] Minirock *m*.

minister ['ministə] Geistliche *m*; Minister *m*; Gesandte *m*; helfen, unterstützen.

ministry ['ministri] geistliches Amt; Ministerium *n*.

mink [miŋk] Nerz *m*.

minor ['mainə] kleiner, geringer; unbedeutend; *mus.* Moll *n*; Minderjährige *m*, *f*; *Am.* Nebenfach *n*; **~ity** [~'nɔriti] Minderjährigkeit *f*; Minderheit *f*.

minster ['minstə] Münster *n*.

minstrel ['minstrəl] *mus. hist.* Spielmann *m*; Sänger, der als Neger geschminkt auftritt.

mint [mint] *bot.* Minze *f*; Münze *f*; münzen, prägen.

minus ['mainəs] minus, weniger; *colloq.* ohne.

minute¹ [mai'nju:t] sehr klein, winzig; sehr genau.

minute² ['minit] Minute *f*; Augenblick *m*; *pl* Protokoll *n*; **in a ~** gleich, sofort; **just a ~** e-n Augenblick;

miracle

182

to the ~ auf die Minute (genau).

mirac|le ['mirəkl] Wunder *n*; **~ulous** [mi'rækjuləs] wunderbar; **~ulously** wie durch ein Wunder.

mirage ['mirɑːʒ] Luftspiegelung *f*, Fata Morgana *f*.

mire [maiə] Schlamm *m*, Sumpf *m*, Kot *m*.

mirror ['mirə] Spiegel *m*; (wider)spiegeln.

mirth [mɜːθ] Fröhlichkeit *f*, Heiterkeit *f*.

miry ['maiəri] schlammig.

mis- [mis-] miß..., falsch, schlecht.

misadventure Mißgeschick *n*; Unfall *m*.

misanthrope ['mizənθrəup], **~ist** [mi'zænθrəpist] Menschenfeind *m*.

mis|apply falsch anwenden; **~apprehend** mißverstehen; **~behave** sich schlecht benehmen; **~calculate** falsch berechnen; sich verrechnen.

miscarr|iage Mißlingen *n*; Fehlgeburt *f*; **~y** mißlingen; e-e Fehlgeburt haben.

miscellaneous [misi'leinjəs] ge-, vermischt; verschiedenartig.

mischie|f ['mistʃif] Unheil *n*, Schaden *m*; Unfug *m*; Übermut *m*; **~vous** ['~vəs] schädlich; boshaft, mutwillig; schelmisch.

mis|deed Missetat *f*, Verbrechen *n*; **~demeano(u)r** Vergehen *n*.

miser ['maizə] Geizhals *m*.

miser|able ['mizərəbl] elend, erbärmlich; unglücklich; **~y** Elend *n*, Not *f*.

mis|fortune Unglück(sfall *m*) *n*; Mißgeschick *n*; **~giving** Befürchtung *f*; **~guided** fehl-, irregeleitet; **~hap** ['~hæp] Unglück *n*, Unfall *m*; **~inform** falsch unterrichten; **~lay** (*irr* **lay**) et. verlegen; **~lead** (*irr* **lead**) irreführen, täuschen; verleiten; **~manage** schlecht verwalten *od.* führen; **~place** *et.* verlegen; an e-e falsche Stelle legen *od.* setzen; *fig.* falsch anbringen; **~print** [~'print] verdrucken; ['~print] Druckfehler *m*; **~pronounce** falsch aussprechen; **~represent** falsch darstellen, verdrehen.

Miss [mis] *mit folgendem Namen:* Fräulein *n*.

miss [mis] Fehlschlag *m*, -schuß *m*, -stoß *m*, -wurf *m*; Versäumen *n*, Entrinnen *n*; verpassen, -säumen, -fehlen; übersehen; (ver)missen; entgehen; nicht treffen; mißlingen; **~ out** auslassen.

missile ['misail] (Wurf-) Geschoß *n*; **(ballistic)** Rakete *f*.

missing ['misiŋ] fehlend,

abwesend; vermißt; **be ~** fehlen.

mission ['miʃən] Auftrag *m*; *eccl.*, *pol.* Mission *f*; *mil.* Einsatz *m*; Berufung *f*; **~ary** ['~nəri] Missionar(in).

mis-spell (*irr* spell) falsch buchstabieren *od.* schreiben.

mist [mist] (feiner) Nebel, feuchter Dunst.

mistake [mis'teik] (*irr* **take**) verwechseln (**for** mit); verstehen; sich irren (in); Mißverständnis *n*; Irrtum *m*, Versehen *n*; Fehler *m*; **by ~** aus Versehen; **~n** falsch; **be ~n** sich irren.

Mister ['mistə] *s.* **Mr.**

mistletoe ['misltəu] Mistel *f*.

mistress ['mistris] Herrin *f*; Lehrerin *f*; Geliebte *f*.

mistrust mißtrauen; Mißtrauen *n*.

misty ['misti] (leicht) neb(e)lig, dunstig; *fig.* unklar.

misunderstand (*irr* **stand**) mißverstehen; **~ing** Mißverständnis *n*.

misuse [mis'ju:z] mißbrauchen; mißhandeln; ['~'ju:s] Mißbrauch *m*.

mite [mait] Milbe *f*.

mitigate ['mitigeit] mildern, lindern.

mitten ['mitn] Fausthandschuh *m*, Fäustling *m*; Halbhandschuh *m* (*ohne Finger*).

mix [miks] (sich) (ver-) mischen; mixen; verkehren (**with** mit); **~ up** durch-ea.-bringen; verwechseln; **be ~ed up with** in *et.* verwickelt sein; **~ture** Mischung *f*.

moan [məun] Stöhnen *n*; stöhnen.

moat [məut] Burg-, Stadtgraben *m*.

mob [mɔb] Pöbel *m*.

mobile ['məubail] beweglich.

mock [mɔk] falsch, Schein...; (ver)spotten; trotzen; **~ery** Spott *m*, Hohn *m*.

mode [məud] (Art und) Weise *f*; Mode *f*.

model ['mɔdl] Modell *n*; Muster *n*; Mannequin *n*; *fig.* Vorbild *n*; Muster...; Modell...; modellieren; (ab)formen.

moderate ['mɔdərit] (mittel)mäßig; ['~eit](sich) mäßigen; *et.* leiten; **~ion** Mäßigung *f*, Maß(halten) *n*.

modern ['mɔdən] modern, neu; **~ize** (sich) modernisieren.

modest ['mɔdist] bescheiden; **~y** Bescheidenheit *f*.

modi|**fication** ['mɔdifi'keiʃən] Ab-, Veränderung *f*; Einschränkung *f*; **~fy** ['~fai] (ab)ändern; mäßigen.

modul|**ate** ['mɔdjuleit] modulieren; **~e** [':u:l] *Raumfahrt:* Kapsel *f*.

moist [mɔist] feucht, naß;

~en ['ˌ~n] an-, befeuchten; **~ure** ['ˌ~stʃə] Feuchtigkeit *f*.

molar (tooth) ['məulə] Backenzahn *m*.

mole [məul] *zo.* Maulwurf *m*; Muttermal *n*; Mole *f*, Hafendamm *m*.

molecule ['mɔlikju:l] Molekül *n*.

molest [məu'lest] belästigen.

mollify ['mɔlifai] besänftigen, beruhigen.

moment ['məumənt] Augenblick *m*, Moment *m*; Bedeutung *f*; **~ary** augenblicklich; vorübergehend.

monarch ['mɔnək] Monarch(in); **~y** Monarchie *f*.

monastery ['mɔnəstəri] (Mönchs)Kloster *n*.

Monday ['mʌndi] Montag *m*.

monetary ['mʌnitəri] Währungs-, ...; Geld...

money ['mʌni] Geld *n*; **~ order** Postanweisung *f*.

monger ['mʌŋgə] *in Zsgn*: ...händler *m*, ...krämer *m*.

monk [mʌŋk] Mönch *m*.

monkey ['mʌŋki] Affe *m*; **~ business** fauler Zauber; **~-wrench** Engländer *m* (*Schraubenschlüssel*).

mono|logue, *Am. a.* **~log** ['mɔnələg] Monolog *m*.

mono|polize [mə'nɔpəlaiz] monopolisieren; *fig.* an sich reißen; **~poly** Monopol *n* (**of** *auf*); **~tonous** [~tnəs] monoton, eintönig; **~tony** [~tni] Monotonie *f*.

monst|er ['mɔnstə] Ungeheuer *n*, Monstrum *n*; Riesen...; Monster...; **~rous** ungeheuer(lich); gräßlich.

month [mʌnθ] Monat *m*; **~ly** monatlich, Monats...; Monatsschrift *f*.

monument ['mɔnjumənt] Monument *n*, Denkmal *n*.

moo [mu:] muhen.

mood [mu:d] Stimmung *f*, Laune *f*; **~y** launisch; übellaunig; niedergeschlagen.

moon [mu:n] Mond *m*; **~light** Mondlicht *n*, **~shine** *m*; **~lit** mondhell.

Moor [muə] Maure *m*, Mohr *m*.

moor¹ [muə] Moor *n*, Heideland *n*.

moor² *mar.* vertäuen; **~ings** *pl mar.*: Vertäuung *f*; Ankerplatz *m*.

moose [mu:s] Elch *m*.

mop [mɔp] Mop *m*; (Haar)Wust *m*; auf-, abwischen.

moral ['mɔrəl] Moral *f*, *pl* Moral *f*, Sitten *pl*; moralisch; Moral..., Sitten...; **~e** [mɔ'rɑ:l] Moral *f* (*e-r Truppe etc.*); **~ity** [mɔ'ræliti] Moralität *f*; Moral *f*; **~ize** ['mɔrəlaiz] moralisieren.

morass [mə'ræs] Morast *m*, Sumpf *m*. [haft.]

morbid ['mɔ:bid] krank-}

more [mɔ:] mehr; noch; **no ~** nicht mehr; **once ~** noch einmal; **(all) the ~ so** (nur) um so mehr; **so**

much the ~ as um so mehr als.

morel [mɔ'rel] Morchel f.

moreover [mɔ:'rəuvə] außerdem, ferner.

morgue [mɔ:g] Leichenschauhaus n.

morning ['mɔ:niŋ] Morgen m; Vormittag m; **this** ~ heute morgen od. früh; **~ tomorrow** ~ morgenfrüh.

morose [mə'rəus] mürrisch.

morph|ia ['mɔ:fjə], **~ine** ['~fi:n] Morphium n.

morsel ['mɔ:səl] Bissen m; Stückchen n, das bißchen.

mortal ['mɔ:tl] sterblich; tödlich; **~ity** [~'tæliti] Sterblichkeit f.

mortar ['mɔ:tə] Mörser m; Mörtel m.

mortgage ['mɔ:gidʒ] Hypothek f; verpfänden.

mortician [mɔ:'tiʃən] Am. Leichenbestatter m.

morti|fication [mɔ:tifi'keiʃən] Kränkung f; **~fy** ['~fai] kränken, demütigen.

mortuary ['mɔ:tjuəri] Leichenhalle f.

mosaic [məu'zeiik] Mosaik n.

mosque [mɔsk] Moschee f.

mosquito [məs'ki:təu] Moskito m; (Stech)Mücke f.

moss [mɔs] Moos n; **~y** moosig, bemoost.

most [məust] meist; die meisten; am meisten; höchst, äußerst; das Äußerste; das meiste; **at**

(the) ~ höchstens; **~ly** hauptsächlich; meistens.

moth [mɔθ] Motte f; **~-eaten** mottenzerfressen.

mother ['mʌðə] Mutter f; **~ country** Vater-, Heimatland n; Mutterland n; **~hood** Mutterschaft f; **~-in-law** Schwiegermutter f; **~ly** mütterlich; **~-of-pearl** Perlmutter f, n; **~'s help** Hausangestellte f; **~ tongue** Muttersprache f.

motif [məu'ti:f] (Leit)Motiv n.

motion ['məuʃən] Bewegung f; Gang m (a. tech.); parl. Antrag m; ~less bewegungslos; ~ **picture** Film m.

motiv|ate ['məutiveit] motivieren, begründen; **~e** Motiv n.

motor ['məutə] Motor m, Motor...; im Auto fahren; **~bicycle**, **~bike** Motorrad n; **~boat** Motorboot n; **~bus** Autobus m; **~car** Auto(mobil) n, (Kraft)Wagen m; **~coach** Reisebus m; **~cycle** Motorrad n; **~cyclist** Motorradfahrer m; **~ing** Autofahren n; **~ist** Autofahrer(in); **~ize** motorisieren; **~lorry** Last(kraft)wagen m; **~scooter** Motorroller m; **~way** Autobahn f.

motto ['mɔtəu] Motto n.

mo(u)ld [məuld] Schimmel m; (Guß)Form f; formen; gießen; **~er (away)**

zerfallen; **~y** schimm(e)lig,
mod(e)rig. [mausern.\
mo(u)lt [məult] (sich)\
mound [maund] Erdhügel
m, -wall *m*.
mount [maunt] Berg *m*;
(Reit)Pferd *n*; be-, erstei-
gen; hinaufgehen; mon-
tieren; (auf-, hinauf)stei-
gen; aufs Pferd steigen.
mountain ['mauntin] Berg
m; *pl* Gebirge *n*; Berg...,
Gebirgs...; **~eer** [ˌ~'niə]
Bergbewohner(in); Berg-
steiger(in); **~ous** bergig,
gebirgig.
mourn [mɔːn] trauern (**for**,
over um); betrauern, trauern um; **~er** Leidtragende
m, *f*; **~ful** traurig; **~ing**
Trauer *f*.
mouse [maus], *pl* **mice**
[mais] Maus *f*.
moustache [məs'tɑːʃ]
Schnurrbart *m*.
mouth [mauθ], *pl* **~s**
[mauðz] Mund *m*; Maul
n; Mündung *f*; **~ful** Mund-
voll *m*; **~-organ** Mund-
harmonika *f*; **~piece**
Mundstück *n*; *fig.* Sprach-
rohr *n*; **~-wash** Mundwasser *n*.
move [muːv] bewegen;
(weg)rücken; *fig.* rühren;
et. beantragen; sich (fort-)
bewegen; sich rühren;
(um)ziehen (**to** nach); **~ in**
einziehen; **~ on** weitergehen; **~ out** ausziehen;
Schach: Zug *m*; Bewegung
f; *fig.* Schritt *m*; **~ment**
Bewegung *f*.

movies ['muːviz] *pl colloq.*
Kino *n*.

moving ['muːviŋ] beweglich; treibend; *fig.* rührend.

mow [məu] (*irr*) mähen;
~er Mäher(in); Mähma-
schine *f*; **~n** *pp von* **mow**.
Mr, Mr. ['mistə] *abbr. von*
Mister: Herr *m* (*vor Familiennamen od. Titeln*).

Mrs, Mrs. ['misiz] *mit
folgendem Familiennamen*:
Frau *f*.

much [mʌtʃ] viel; sehr;
fast; *vor comp*: viel; *vor
sup*: bei weitem; **too ~**
zuviel; **very ~** sehr; **I
thought as ~** das dachte
ich mir; **make ~ of** viel
Wesens machen von.

mucus ['mjuːkəs] *biol.*
Schleim *m*.

mud [mʌd] Schlamm *m*;
Schmutz *m*.

muddle ['mʌdl] verwirren; **~ (up)**, **~ (together)** durcheinanderbringen;
Durcheinander *n*.

mud|dy ['mʌdi] schlam-
mig; trüb(e); **~guard**
Kotflügel *m*.

muff [mʌf] Muff *m*.

muffle ['mʌfl]: **~ (up)** einwickeln; *Stimme etc.* dämpfen; **~r** Halstuch *n*, Schal
m; *Am. mot.* Auspuff-
topf *m*.

mug [mʌg] Krug *m*;
Becher *m*.

mulberry ['mʌlbəri] Maul-
beerbaum *m*; Maulbeere *f*.

mule [mjuːl] Maultier *n*.

mull [mʌl] Mull *m*.

mulled| claret [mʌld], **~ wine** Glühwein *m*.

mullion ['mʌliən] Fensterpfosten *m*.

multi|ple ['mʌltipl] vielfach; mehrere, viele; **~plication** [-pli'keiʃən] Vermehrung *f*; Multiplikation *f*; **~plication table** Einmaleins *n*; **~ply** ['~plai] (sich) vermehren; multiplizieren; **~tude** ['~tju:d] (Menschen)Menge *f*.

mumble ['mʌmbl] murmeln; mummeln (*mühsam essen*).

mummy[1] ['mʌmi] Mumie *f*.

mummy[2] Mami *f*, Mutti *f*.

mumps [mʌmps] *sg* Ziegenpeter *m*, Mumps *m*, *f*.

munch [mʌntʃ] mit vollen Backen kauen, mampfen

municipal [mju(:)'nisipəl] städtisch, Gemeinde..., Stadt...; **~ity** ['~pæliti] Stadtverwaltung *f*.

mural ['mjuərəl] Mauer..., Wand...

murder ['mə:də] Mord *m*; (er)morden; **~er** Mörder *m*; **~ess** Mörderin *f*; **~ous** mörderisch; Mord...

murmur ['mə:mə] Murmeln *n*; Gemurmel *n*; Murren *n*; murmeln; murren.

musc|le ['mʌsl] Muskel *m*; **~le-bound: be ~** Muskelkater haben; **~ular** ['~kjulə] Muskel...; muskulös.

muse [mju:z] (nach)sinnen, (-)grübeln.

museum [mju:(:)'ziəm] Museum *n*.

mush [mʌʃ] (*Am.* Mais-) Brei *m*.

mushroom ['mʌʃrum] Pilz *m*, *bsd.* Champignon *m*.

music ['mju:zik] Musik *f*; Noten *pl*; **~al** Musical *n*; Musik...; musikalisch; wohlklingend; **~al box** *Brit.*, **~ box** *Am.* Spieldose *f*; **~hall** Varieté(theater) *n*; **~ian** [~'ziʃən] Musiker *m*; **~stand** Notenständer *m*; **~stool** Klavierstuhl *m*.

musk [mʌsk] Moschus *m*, Bisam *m*.

musket ['mʌskit] Muskete *f*.

musk-rat Bisamratte *f*.

Muslim ['muslim] mohammedanisch; Moslem *m*.

muslin ['mʌzlin] Musselin *m*.

musquash ['mʌskwɔʃ] Bisamratte *f*; Bisampelz *m*.

mussel ['mʌsl] (Mies-) Muschel *f*.

must[1] [mʌst] Muß *n*; *v/aux* ich, du *etc.*: muß(t) *etc.*, darf(st) *etc.*; *pret* mußte(st) *etc.*, durfte(st) *etc.*; **I ~ not** ich darf nicht.

must[2] Schimmel *m*, Moder *m*; Most *m*.

mustache ['mʌstæʃ] *Am.* Schnurrbart *m*.

mustard ['mʌstəd] Senf *m*.

muster ['mʌstə] versammeln; **~ (up)** aufbieten.

musty ['mʌsti] mod(e)rig, muffig.

mute [mju:t] stumm;

mutilate ['mju:tileit] verstümmeln.

mutin|eer [mju:ti'niə] Meuterer *m*; **~ous** ['~nəs] meuternd, rebellisch; **~y** ['~ni] Meuterei *f*; meutern.

mutter ['mʌtə] Gemurmel *n*; murmeln; murren.

mutton ['mʌtn] Hammel-, Schaffleisch *n*; **~ chop** Hammelkotelett *n*.

mutual ['mju:tʃuəl] gegen-, wechselseitig; gemeinsam.

muzzle ['mʌzl] Maul *n*, Schnauze *f*; Maulkorb *m*;

(*Gewehr*)Mündung *f*; e-n Maulkorb anlegen; *fig.* den Mund stopfen.

my [mai] mein(e).

myrrh [mə:] Myrrhe *f*.

myrtle ['mə:tl] Myrte *f*.

myself [mai'self] (ich) selbst; mir, mich; mir *od.* mich selbst; **by ~** allein.

myster|ious [mis'tiəriəs] geheimnisvoll; **~y** ['~təri] Geheimnis *n*; Rätsel *n*.

mystify ['mistifai] verwirren, -blüffen.

myth [miθ] Mythos *m*, Mythe *f*, Sage *f*.

N

nag [næg] nörgeln; **~ (at)** herumnörgeln an.

nail [neil] Nagel *m*; (an-, fest)nageln.

naked ['neikid] nackt; bloß; kahl.

name [neim] (be)nennen; erwähnen; ernennen; Name *m*; **what is your ~?** wie heißen Sie?; **my ~ is** ... ich heiße ...; **call s.o. ~s** j-n beschimpfen; **~less** namenlos; unbekannt; **~ly** nämlich.

nanny ['næni] Kindermädchen *n*; **~-goat** Ziege *f*.

nap [næp] Schläfchen *n*; **have od. take a ~** ein Nickerchen machen.

nape (**of the neck**) [neip] Genick *n*, Nacken *m*.

nap|kin ['næpkin] Serviette *f*; *Brit.* Windel *f*; **~py** *Brit. colloq.* Windel *f*.

narcosis [nɑ:'kəusis] Narkose *f*.

narcotic [nɑ:'kɔtik] Betäubungsmittel *n*; Rauschgift *n*.

narrat|e [næ'reit] erzählen; **~ion** Erzählung *f*; **~ive** ['~ətiv] Erzählung *f*; **~or** ['~'reitə] Erzähler *m*.

narrow ['nærəu] eng, schmal; beschränkt; *fig.* knapp; (sich) verengen; **~-minded** engherzig, -stirnig.

nasty ['nɑ:sti] schmutzig; widerlich; unangenehm; böse; häßlich.

nation ['neiʃən] Nation *f*, Volk *n*.

national ['næʃənl] national, National...; Landes...; Volks...; Staats...; Staatsangehörige *m*, *f*; **~ity** ['~'næliti] Nationalität *f*,

Staatsangehörigkeit f; **ity plate** mot. Nationalitätskennzeichen n; **ize** ['ʃnɔlaiz] einbürgern; verstaatlichen.

native ['neitiv] Eingeborene m, f; angeboren; eingeboren; einheimisch; gebürtig; heimatlich, Heimat...; **language** Muttersprache f.

nativity [nɔ'tiviti] Geburt f (bsd. eccl.).

natural ['nætʃrɔl] natürlich; angeboren, unehelich; **ize** einbürgern; **science** Naturwissenschaft f.

nature ['neitʃɔ] Natur f.

naught [nɔ:t] Null f; **y** frech, ungezogen, unartig.

nausea ['nɔ:sjɔ] Übelkeit f; Ekel m; **ting** ['ɪeitiŋ] ekelerregend.

nautical ['nɔ:tikɔl] nautisch; **mile** Seemeile f.

naval ['neivɔl] See..., Marine...; **base** Flottenstützpunkt m.

nave[1] [neiv] (Kirchen-) Schiff n.

nave[2] [Rad]Nabe f.

navel ['neivɔl] Nabel m; fig. Mittelpunkt m.

naviga|ble ['nævigɔbl] schiffbar; fahrbar; lenkbar; **te** [ʃɪeit] (be)fahren; navigieren, steuern; **tion** Schiffahrt f; Navigation f; **tor** Steuermann m; Seefahrer m.

navy['neivi]Kriegsmarine f.

nay [nei] nein; ja sogar.

near [niɔ] nahe; in der Nähe (von); nahe verwandt; eng befreundet; knapp; geizig; nahe an od. bei; sich nähern; **by** bsd. Am. in der Nähe, nahe; **ly** nahe; fast, beinahe; annähernd; **ness** Nähe f; **sighted** kurzsichtig.

neat [ni:t] ordentlich; sauber; **ness** Sauberkeit f.

necess|ary ['nesisɔri] notwendig; **itate** [ni'sesiteit] erfordern, verlangen; **ity** [ni'sesiti] Notwendigkeit f; Bedürfnis n; Not f.

neck [nek] Hals m; Nacken m, Genick n; sl. (sich) (ab-)knutschen; **erchief** ['ɪkɔtʃif] Halstuch n; **lace** ['ɪlis] Halskette f; **tie** Krawatte f.

née [nei] geborene.

need [ni:d] nötig haben, brauchen; müssen; Not f; Notwendigkeit f; Bedürfnis n; Mangel m; **in** ~ in Not; **be** od. **stand in** ~ **of** dringend brauchen.

needle ['ni:dl] (Näh-, Strick)Nadel f; Zeiger m.

needy ['ni:di] bedürftig.

negat|e [ni'geit] verneinen; **ion** Verneinung f; **ive** ['negɔtiv] negativ; verneinen(d); Verneinung f; phot. Negativ n; **answer in the ive** verneinen.

neglect [ni'glekt] vernachlässigen.

negligent ['neglidʒɔnt] nachlässig.

negotiat|e [ni'gɔuʃieit]

verhandeln (über); **~ion**
Ver-, Unterhandlung _f_.
Negr|ess ['ni:gris] Negerin
_f_; **~o** [‚'~ou], _pl_ **~oes** Neger
_m_. [wiehern.]
neigh [nei] Wiehern _n_;
neighbo(u)r ['neibə]
Nachbar(in); Nächste _m_;
~hood Nachbarschaft _f_,
Umgebung, Nähe _f_;
~ing benachbart.
neither ['naiðə, _Am._ 'ni:ðə]
kein(e, -er, -es) (von beiden); auch nicht; **~ ...
nor ...** weder ... noch ...
neon ['ni:ɔn] Neon _n_; **~
sign** Neonreklame _f_.
nephew ['nevju(:)]Neffe _m_.
nerve [nə:v] Nerv _m_;
(_Blatt_)Rippe _f_; Mut _m_;
get on s.o.'s ~s j-m auf
die Nerven gehen.
nervous ['nə:vəs] nervös;
Nerven...; **~ness** Nervo-
sität _f_.
nest [nest] Nest _n_; **~le**
['nesl]: **~ (down)** sich behaglich niederlassen; **~
up to** sich anschmiegen an.
net[1] [net] Netz _n_.
net[2] netto; Rein...
nettle ['netl] _bot._ Nessel _f_;
ärgern.
network ['netwə:k] (_Stra-
ßen-_etc.)Netz _n_; _Radio:_
Sendernetz _n_, -gruppe _f_.
neurosis [njuə'rousis] Neu-
rose _f_.
neuter ['nju:tə] _gr._: sächlich; Neutrum _n_.
neutral ['nju:trəl] neutral;
unparteiisch; Neutrale _m_,
_f_; _mot._ Leerlauf(stellung _f_)

_m_; **~ gear** _mot._ Leerlauf
(-gang) _m_; **~ity** [‚'træliti]
Neutralität _f_; **~ize** neu-
tralisieren. [tron _n_.]
neutron ['nju:trɔn] Neu-
never ['nevə] nie(mals);
gar nicht; **~more** nie
wieder; **~theless** nichts-
destoweniger, dennoch.
new [nju:] neu; frisch;
unerfahren; **~-born** neu-
geboren; **~comer** Neu-
ankömmling _m_; Neuling _m_.
news [nju:z] _sg_ Neuig-
keit(en _pl_) _f_, Nachricht(en
_pl_) _f_; **~agent** Zeitungs-
händler _m_; **~cast** _Radio:_
Nachrichtensendung _f_; **~
paper** Zeitung _f_; Zei-
tungs...; **~reel** _Film:_ Wo-
chenschau _f_; **~stand** Zei-
tungskiosk _m_.

new| year Neujahr _n_, _das
neue Jahr_; ♀ **Year's Day**
Neujahrstag _m_; ♀ **Year's
Eve** Silvester _m_.
next [nekst] _adj_ nächst;
(the) ~ day am nächsten
Tag; **~ door** nebenan;
~ to neben; **~ but one**
übernächst; _adv_ als näch-
ste(r, -s); _das_ nächste Mal;
prp gleich neben _od._ bei
_od._ an; _sub:_ der, die, _das_
nächste.
nibble ['nibl]: **~ (at)** nagen
an, knabbern an.
nice [nais] nett; hübsch;
schön; fein; angenehm;
heikel; (peinlich) genau;
~ly gut, ausgezeichnet;
~ty ['~iti] Feinheit _f_; Genauigkeit _f_.

niche [nitʃ] Nische f.

nick [nik] Kerbe f.; (ein-)kerben.

nickel ['nikl] min. Nickel n; Am. Nickel m (Fünfcentstück); vernickeln.

nick-nack ['niknæk] s. **knick-knack.**

nickname ['nikneim] Spitzname m; j—m den Spitznamen ... geben.

niece [niːs] Nichte f.

niggard ['nigəd] Geizhals m.

night [nait] Nacht f; Abend m; at ~, by ~, in the ~ bei Nacht, nachts; **~cap** Nachtmütze f; Schlaftrunk m; **~club** Nachtklub m, -lokal n; **~dress, ~gown** (Damen-)Nachthemd n; **~ingale** ['~iŋgeil] Nachtigall f; **~ly** nächtlich; jede Nacht od. jeden Abend (stattfindend); **~mare** ['~mɛə] Alptraum m; **~school** Abendschule f; **~shirt** (Herren)Nachthemd n; **~y** colloq. (Damen-, Kinder)Nachthemd n.

nil [nil] bsd. sp. null.

nimble ['nimbl] flink, behend(e).

nine [nain] neun; Neun f; **~pins** sg Kegel(spiel n) pl; **~teen** ['~'tiːn(θ)] neunzehn(te); **~tieth** ['~tiiθ] neunzigste; **~ty** neunzig; Neunzig f.

ninth [nainθ] neunte; Neuntel n; **~ly** neuntens.

nip [nip] scharfer Frost; Schlückchen n; kneifen, zwicken, klemmen; schneiden (Kälte); sl. flitzen; nippen (an).

nipple ['nipl] Brustwarze f.

nit|re, Am. **~er** ['naitə] Salpeter m; **~rogen** ['~trədʒən] Stickstoff m.

no [nəu] nein; nein; Nein n; kein(e); ~ **one** keiner.

nobility [nəu'biliti] Adel m.

noble ['nəubl] adlig; edel; vornehm; Adlige m, f; **~man** Adlige m, Edelmann m.

nobody ['nəubədi] niemand, keiner.

nod [nɔd] nicken (mit); (im Sitzen) schlafen; sich neigen; Nicken n, Wink m.

noise [nɔiz] Lärm m; Geräusch n; Geschrei n; **~less** geräuschlos.

noisy ['nɔizi] geräuschvoll; laut; lärmend.

nomin|al ['nɔminl] nominell, nur dem Namen nach; **~ate** ['~eit] ernennen; nominieren, vorschlagen; **~ation** Ernennung f; Nominierung f.

nominative (case) ['nɔminətiv] gr. Nominativ m, 1. Fall.

non- [nɔn-] in Zssgn: nicht..., Nicht..., un...

non|-alcoholic alkoholfrei; **~commissioned officer** Unteroffizier m; **~committal** unverbindlich; **~conductor** electr. Nichtleiter m; **~conformist** Dissident(in), Freikirchler

(-in); **~descript** ['~di-skript] schwer zu beschreiben(d); nichtssagend.

none [nʌn] kein(e, -er, -es); keineswegs.

non|-existence Nicht(da)-sein n; das Fehlen; **~-fiction** Sachbücher pl.

nonsense ['nɔnsəns] Unsinn m.

non|-skid rutschfest, -sicher; **~-smoker** Nichtraucher(in) m; rail. Nichtraucher(abteil n) m; **~-stop** Nonstop m, rail. durchgehend, aer. ohne Zwischenlandung; **~-union** nicht organisiert (Arbeiter); **~-violence** (Politik f der) Gewaltlosigkeit f.

noodle ['nu:dl] Nudel f.

nook [nuk] Ecke f, Winkel m.

noon [nu:n] Mittag m; Mittags...; **at (high) ~** um 12 Uhr mittags.

noose [nu:s] Schlinge f.

nor [nɔ:] noch; auch nicht.

norm [nɔ:m] Norm f, Regel f; **~al** normal; **~alize** normalisieren; normen.

Norman ['nɔ:mən] normannisch; Normann|e m, -in f.

north [nɔ:θ] Nord(en m); nördlich, Nord...; **~east** Nordost; **~east(ern)** nordöstlich; **~erly** ['~-ɔ-], **~ern** ['~ɔ-] nördlich, Nord...; **~erner** ['~ɔ-] bsd. Am. Nordstaatler(in); ♀ **Pole** Nordpol m; ♀ **Sea**

Nordsee f; **~ward(s)** ['~-wəd(z)] nördlich, nordwärts; **~west** Nordwest; **~west(ern)** nordwestlich.

Norwegian [nɔ:'wi:dʒən] norwegisch; Norweger (-in); Norwegisch n.

nose [nəuz] Nase f; Spitze f; Schnauze f; riechen; schnüffeln; **~gay** ['~gei] (Blumen)Strauß m.

nostril ['nɔstril] Nasenloch n, Nüster f.

nosy ['nəuzi] sl. neugierig.

not [nɔt] nicht; **~ a** kein(e).

notable ['nəutəbl] bemerkenswert.

notary ['nəutəri] oft **~ public** Notar m.

notation [nəu'teiʃən] Bezeichnung(ssystem n) f.

notch [nɔtʃ] Kerbe f; Am. Engpaß m; (ein)kerben.

note [nəut] bemerken, be-(ob)achten; **~ down** notieren; Zeichen n; Notiz f; Note f (a. mus.); Briefchen n, Zettel m; print. Anmerkung f; Banknote f; mus. Ton m; **take ~** sich Notizen machen; **~-book** Notizbuch n; **~d** bekannt; **~paper** Briefpapier n; **~worthy** bemerkenswert.

nothing ['nʌθiŋ] nichts; **~ but** nichts als, nur; **~ for** umsonst; **good for ~** zu nichts zu gebrauchen; **say ~ of** geschweige denn; **there is ~ like** es geht nichts über.

notice ['nəutis] bemerken, be(ob)achten; Notiz

f; Nachricht *f*, Bekanntmachung *f*, Anschlag *m*; Anzeige *f*, Ankündigung *f*; Kündigung *f*; Aufmerksamkeit *f*; **at short ~** kurzfristig; **without ~** fristlos; **give ~ that** bekanntgeben, daß; **give (a week's) ~** (acht Tage vorher) kündigen; **take ~ of** Notiz nehmen von; **~able** wahrnehmbar; beachtlich.

noti|fication [nəutifi'keiʃən] Anzeige *f*, Meldung *f*; Bekanntmachung *f*; **~fy** ['~fai] *et.* anzeigen, melden; benachrichtigen.

notion ['nəuʃən] Begriff *m*, Vorstellung *f*; *pl Am.* Kurzwaren *pl*.

notorious [nəu'tɔːriəs] notorisch; berüchtigt.

notwithstanding [nɔtwiθ'stændiŋ] ungeachtet, trotz.   [*f.*\]

nought [nɔːt] nichts; Null\]

noun [naun] *gr.* Substantiv *n*, Hauptwort *n*.

nourish ['nʌriʃ] (er)nähren; *fig.* hegen; **~ing** nahrhaft; **~ment** Ernährung *f*; Nahrung(smittel *n*) *f.*\

novel ['nɔvəl] neu; Roman *m*; **~ist** Romanschriftsteller(in); **~ty** Neuheit *f.*

November [nəu'vembə] November *m*.

novice ['nɔvis] Neuling *m*; *eccl.* Novize *m*.

now [nau] nun; jetzt; eben; **just ~** soeben; **~ and again, (every) ~ and then** dann u. wann.

nowadays ['nauədeiz] heutzutage.   [gends.\]

nowhere ['nəuweə] nir-\]

noxious ['nɔkʃəs] schädlich.   [Mundstück *n.*\]

nozzle ['nɔzl] Düse *f*;\]

nuclear ['njuːkliə] Kern...; **~ fission** Kernspaltung *f*; **~ power plant od. station** Atomkraftwerk *n*; **~ reactor** Kernreaktor *m*.

nucleus ['njuːkliəs] Kern *m*.

nude [njuːd] nackt; *paint.* Akt *m.*

nudge [nʌdʒ] *j-n* heimlich anstoßen; Rippenstoß *m.*

nugget ['nʌgit] (*bsd.* Gold-)Klumpen *m.*

nuisance ['njuːsns] Ärgernis *n*, Unfug *m*, Plage *f.*

null [nʌl]: **~ and void** null u. nichtig, ungültig.

numb [nʌm] starr, taub.

number ['nʌmbə] Nummer *f*; (An)Zahl *f*; Heft *n*, Ausgabe *f*, Nummer *f*; (*Autobus- etc.*)Linie *f*; zählen; numerieren; **~less** zahllos; **~ plate** *mot.* Nummernschild *n.*

numer|al ['njuːmərəl] Ziffer *f*; *ling.* Numerale *n*, Zahlwort *n*; **~ous** zahlreich.

nun [nʌn] Nonne *f*; **~nery** (Nonnen)Kloster *n.*

nuptials ['nʌpʃəlz] *pl* Hochzeit *f.*

nurse [nəːs] Kindermädchen *n*, Säuglingsschwester *f*; Amme *f*; Krankenpflegerin *f*; Krankenschwester f; stillen, nähren; großziehen; pflegen.

nursery ['nɜːsəri] Kinderzimmer n; Baum-, Pflanzschule f; **~ rhyme** Kinderlied n, -reim m; **~ school** Kindergarten m; **~ school teacher** Kindergärtnerin f; **~ slope** Ski: Idiotenhügel m.

nursing ['nɜːsiŋ] Stillen n; Krankenpflege f; **~ home** Privatklinik f.

nut [nʌt] Nuß f; (Schrau-ben)Mutter f; **be ~s** sl. verrückt sein; **~crackers** pl Nußknacker m; **~meg** ['~meg] Muskatnuß f.

nutri|ment ['njuːtrimənt] Nahrung f; **~tion** Ernährung f; **~tious** nahrhaft.

nut|shell Nußschale f; **in a ~shell** in aller Kürze; **~ty** nußartig; sl. verrückt.

nylon ['nailən] Nylon n; pl Nylonstrümpfe pl.

nymph [nimf] Nymphe f.

O

o [əu] int. o(h)!, ach!; bsd. teleph. Null f.

oak(-tree) ['əuk(-)]Eiche f.

oar [ɔː] Ruder n, Riemen m; rudern; **~sman** Ruderer m.

oas|is [əu'eisis], pl **~es** [~iːz] Oase f (a. fig.).

oast [əust] Darre f; **~house** Darrhaus n.

oat [əut] mst pl Hafer m; **sow one's wild ~s** sich die Hörner abstoßen.

oath [əuθ], pl **~s** [əuðz] Eid m, Schwur m; Fluch m; **on ~** unter Eid.

oatmeal Hafermehl n, -flocken pl.

obedien|ce [ə'biːdjəns] Gehorsam m; **~t** gehorsam.

obey [ə'bei] gehorchen; Befehl etc. befolgen.

obituary [ə'bitjuəri] Todesanzeige f; Nachruf m.

object ['ɔbdʒikt] Gegen-

stand m; Ziel n, Zweck m; Absicht f; Objekt n; gr. Objekt n, Satzergänzung f; [əb'dʒekt:] **~ (to)** einwenden (gegen); protestieren (gegen); et. dagegen haben; **~ion** Einwand m, -spruch m; **~ive** objektiv, sachlich; Ziel n; opt. Objektiv n.

obligation [ɔbli'geiʃən] Verpflichtung f; Verbindlichkeit f; econ. Schuldverschreibung f; **be under an ~ to s.o.** j-m (zu Dank) verpflichtet sein.

oblig|e [ə'blaidʒ] (zu Dank) verpflichten; nötigen, zwingen; **much ~ed** sehr verbunden, danke bestens; **~ing** gefällig, zuvorkommend. [schräg.)

oblique [ə'bliːk] schief,)

obliterate [ə'blitəreit] auslöschen; ausstreichen.

oblivi|on [ə'bliviən] Vergessenheit *f*; **~ous: be ~ of** s.th. et. vergessen (haben).

oblong ['ɔblɔŋ] länglich; rechteckig. [ständig.]

obscene [əb'si:n] unan-]

obscure [əb'skjuə] dunkel; *fig.* dunkel, unklar; unbekannt; verdunkeln.

obsequies ['ɔbsikwiz] *pl* Trauerfeierlichkeiten *pl*.

observ|ance [əb'zə:vəns] Befolgung *f*, Einhaltung *f*; Brauch *m*; **~ant** aufmerksam; **~ant of** befolgend; **~ation** Beobachtung *f*; Bemerkung *f*; Beobachtungs..., Aussichts...; **~atory** [~tri] Observatorium *n*; Stern-, Wetterwarte *f* **~e** be(ob)achten; sehen; (ein)halten; befolgen; bemerken, (sich) äußern; **~er** Beobachter (-in).

obsess [əb'ses]: **~ed by, ~ed with** besessen von; **~ion** Besessenheit *f*.

obsolete ['ɔbsəli:t] veraltet. [dernis *n*.]

obstacle ['ɔbstəkl] Hin-]

obstina|cy ['ɔbstinəsi] Eigensinn *m*; Hartnäckigkeit *f*; **~te** [~it] eigensinnig; hartnäckig.

obstruct [əb'strʌkt] versperren, -stopfen, blokkieren; behindern.

obtain [əb'tein] erlangen, erhalten, erreichen, bekommen; **~able** erhältlich.

obtrusive [əb'tru:siv] aufdringlich.

obvious ['ɔbviəs] offensichtlich, augenfällig, klar.

occasion [ə'keiʒən] veranlassen, -ursachen; Gelegenheit *f*; Grund *m*, Ursache *f*; Anlaß *m*; **on the ~ of** anläßlich; **~al** gelegentlich, Gelegenheits...

Occident ['ɔksidənt] *the ~* Okzident *m*, Abendland *n*.

occup|ant ['ɔkjupənt] Bewohner(in); Insass|e *m*, -in *f*; **~ation** Besitznahme *f*; *mil.* Besatzung *f*, Besetzung *f*; Beruf *m*; Beschäftigung *f*; **~y** ['~pai] einnehmen, in Besitz nehmen; bewohnen; *mil.* besetzen; besitzen; in Anspruch nehmen; beschäftigen.

occur [ə'kə:] vorkommen; sich ereignen; **it ~red to me** es fiel mir ein; **~rence** [ə'kʌrəns] Vorkommen *n*; Vorfall *m*, Ereignis *n*.

ocean ['ouʃən] Ozean *m*, Meer *n*.

o'clock [ə'klɔk]: **(at) five ~ (um)** fünf Uhr.

October [ɔk'toubə] Oktober *m*.

ocul|ar ['ɔkjulə] Augen...; **~ist** Augenarzt *m*.

odd [ɔd] ungerade (*Zahl*); einzeln; etwas darüber; überzählig; gelegentlich; sonderbar; **~s** *pl* (Gewinn-) Chancen *pl*; Vorteil *m*; Unterschied *m*; **the ~s are that** es ist sehr wahrscheinlich, daß; **at ~s with** im Streit mit, un-

einig mit; **~s and ends** Krimskrams *m*; Reste *pl.*
odo(u)r [ˈəudə] Geruch *m.*
of [ɔv, əv] von; *Ort:* bei; um (**cheat s.o. ~ s.th.**) *Herkunft:* von, aus; *Material:* aus, von; von, an (**die ~**); aus (**~ charity**); vor (**afraid ~**); auf (**proud ~**); über (**glad ~**); nach (**smell ~**); von, über (**speak ~ s.th.**); an (**think ~ s.th.**); **the city ~ London** die Stadt London; **the works ~ Dickens** D's Werke; **your letter ~ ...** Ihr Schreiben vom ...; **five minutes ~ twelve** *Am.* fünf Minuten vor zwölf.

off [ɔf] *adv* fort, weg; ab, herunter(-), los(-,-); entfernt; *Zeit:* bis, hin; aus(-), ab(geschaltet) (*Licht etc.*), zu (*Hahn etc.*); ab(-), los (-gegangen) (*Knopf etc.*), frei (*von Arbeit*); ganz, zu Ende; *econ.* flau; verdorben (*Fleisch etc.*); *fig.* aus, vorbei; **be ~** fort *od.* weg sein; (weg)gehen; *prp* fort von, weg von; von (... ab, weg, herunter); abseits von, entfernt von; frei von (*Arbeit*); *adj* (weiter) entfernt; Seiten..., Neben...; (arbeits-, dienst)frei; *econ.* flau, still, tot; *int.* fort!, weg!

offen|ce, *Am.* **~se** [əˈfens] Vergehen *n*, Verstoß *m*; Beleidigung *f*, Anstoß *m*; Angriff *m*; **~d** beleidi-

gen, verletzen; verstoßen (**against** gegen); **~der** Übeltäter(in); Straffällige *m*, *f*; **~sive** beleidigend; anstößig; ekelhaft; Angriffs...; Offensive *f.*

offer [ˈɔfə] Angebot *n*; Anerbieten *n*; anbieten; (sich) bieten; darbringen; *Widerstand* leisten; **~ing** Opfer(n) *n*; Angebot *n.*

office [ˈɔfis] Büro *n*; Geschäftsstelle *f*; ⚹ Amt *n*; Ministerium *n*; **~r** Beamt|e *m*, -in *f*; Polizist *m*, Polizeibeamte *m*; *mil.* Offizier *m.*

official [əˈfiʃəl] offiziell, amtlich, Amts..., Dienst...; Beamt|e *m*, -in *f.*

officious [əˈfiʃəs] aufdringlich.

off|-licence Schankerlaubnis *f* außer der Straße; **~side** *sp.* abseits; **~spring** Nachkomme(nschaft *f*) *m.*

often [ˈɔfn] oft, häufig.

oh [əu] *int.* oh!, ach!

oil [ɔil] Öl *n*; Erdöl *n*; ölen, schmieren; **~cloth** Wachstuch *n*; **~y** ölig, fettig, schmierig. [be *f.*]

ointment [ˈɔintmənt] Sal-]

O.K., OK, okay [ˈəuˈkei] *colloq.* richtig, gut, in Ordnung.

old [əuld] alt; **ten-year-zehnjährig**; **~ age** (das) Alter; **~-age** Alters...; **~-fashioned** altmodisch; **~ town** Altstadt *f.*

olive [ˈɔliv] Olive *f*; Olivgrün *n.*

Olympic Games [əu'lim-pik] *pl* Olympische Spiele *pl.* [lett(e *f*) *n.*|

omelet(te) ['ɔmlit] Omelett *n.*|

ominous ['ɔminəs] unheilvoll.

omis|sion [ə'miʃən] Unterlassung *f;* Auslassung *f;* **⁓t** unterlassen; auslassen.

omni|potent [ɔm'nipətənt] allmächtig; **⁓scient** [⁓ʃiənt] allwissend.

on [ɔn] *prp* auf an; in; **⁓ the street** *Am.* auf der Straße; *Richtung, Ziel:* auf ... (hin), an; *fig.* auf ... (hin) (**⁓ demand**); *gehörig* zu, *beschäftigt* bei; *Zustand:* in, auf, zu (**⁓ duty, ⁓ fire**); *Thema:* über; *Zeitpunkt:* an (**⁓ Sunday, ⁓ the 1st of April**); bei (**⁓ his arrival**); *adv* an(geschaltet) (*Licht etc.*), eingeschaltet, laufend, auf (*Hahn etc.*); auf(*legen,* **⁓schrauben** *etc.*); *Kleidung:* an(*haben,* **-**ziehen), auf(*behalten*); weiter(*gehen,* **-sprechen** *etc.*); **and so ⁓** und so weiter; **⁓ and ⁓** immer weiter; **⁓ to ...** auf ... (hinaus); **be ⁓** im Gange sein, los sein; *thea.* gespielt werden; laufen (*Film*).

once [wʌns] einmal; je (*-mals*); einst; sobald; **⁓ again, ⁓ more** noch einmal; **⁓ in a while** dann u. wann; **⁓ (upon a time) there was** es war einmal; **at ⁓** sofort;

zugleich; **all at ⁓** plötzlich; **for ⁓** diesmal, ausnahmsweise.

one [wʌn] ein; einzig; man; eins; Eins *f;* **Smith** ein gewisser Smith; **⁓ day** eines Tages; **⁓ of these days** demnächst; **⁓ by ⁓** einer nach dem andern; **⁓ another** einander; **the little ⁓s** die Kleinen; **⁓self** sich(selbst) (sich) selbst; einseitig; **⁓-sided** einseitig; **⁓-way street** Einbahnstraße *f.*

onion ['ʌnjən] Zwiebel *f.*

onlooker ['ɔnlukə] Zuschauer(in).

only ['əunli] einzig; nur, bloß; erst.

onto ['ɔntu, '⁓ə] auf.

onward ['ɔnwəd] vorwärts gerichtet; **⁓(s)** vorwärts, weiter.

ooze [u:z] Schlamm *m;* sickern; ausströmen, **-schwitzen**. [durchsichtig.|

opaque [əu'peik] un-|

open ['əupən] offen; geöffnet; auf; frei (*Feld etc.*); öffentlich; aufgeschlossen (**to** für); freimütig; freigebig; **in the ⁓ air** im Freien; *vb:* (er)öffnen; sich öffnen, ausgehen; führen, gehen (*Tür*) (**on** auf); **into** nach; beginnen; **⁓-air** im Freien, Freilicht...; Freiluft...; **⁓er** (*Büchsen-etc.*)Öffner *m;* **⁓handed** freigebig; **⁓ing** (Er)Öffnung *f;* freie Stelle; Möglichkeit *f;* Eröffnungs...;

~-minded aufgeschlossen.
opera ['ɔpərə] Oper f;
~-glasses pl Opernglas n.
operat|e ['ɔpəreit] arbeiten, funktionieren, laufen; med., mil. operieren; Maschine bewirken; **~ion** Operation f; **~ive** ['~ətiv] wirksam; med. operativ; **~or** tech. Bedienungsperson f; Telefonist(in).
opinion [ə'pinjən] Meinung f; Ansicht f; Gutachten n; **in my ~** meines Erachtens.
opponent [ə'pəunənt] Gegner m, Gegenspieler m.
opportunity [ɔpə'tju:niti] (günstige) Gelegenheit.
oppos|e [ə'pəuz] gegenüberstellen; entgegensetzen; sich widersetzen, bekämpfen; **be ~ed to** gegen j-n od. et. sein; **~ite** ['ɔpəzit] gegenüberliegend; entgegengesetzt; gegenüber; Gegenteil n, Gegensatz m; **~ition** [ɔpə'ziʃən] Widerstand m; Gegensatz m; Opposition f.
oppress [ə'pres] unterdrücken; bedrücken; **~ion** Unterdrückung f; Bedrücktheit f; **~ive** (be-, nieder)drückend.
optic|al ['ɔptikəl] optisch; **~ian** [ɔp'tiʃən] Optiker f.
optimism ['ɔptimizəm] Optimismus m.
or [ɔ:] oder; **~ else** sonst.
oral ['ɔ:rəl] mündlich; Mund...

orange ['ɔrindʒ] Orange f, Apfelsine f; Orange n (Farbe); orange(farben); **~ade** ['~'eid] Orangenlimonade f.
orator ['ɔrətə] Redner m.
orbit ['ɔ:bit] (die Erde) umkreisen; Kreis-, Umlaufbahn f.
orchard ['ɔ:tʃəd] Obstgarten m.
orchestra ['ɔ:kistrə] Orchester n.
ordeal [ɔ:'di:l] schwere Prüfung, Qual f.
order ['ɔ:də] Ordnung f; Anordnung f, Reihenfolge f; Klasse f, Rang m; Orden m (a. eccl.); Befehl m; econ.: Bestellung f; (Zahlungs)Auftrag m; **in ~ to** um zu; **in ~ that** damit; **out of ~** nicht in Ordnung, außer Betrieb; befehlen; med. ver)ordnen; bestellen; j-n schicken; **~ly** ordentlich; fig. ruhig; mil. Sanitätssoldat m.
ordinal number ['ɔ:dinl] Ordinal-, Ordnungszahl f.
ordinary ['ɔ:dnri] gewöhnlich; üblich; alltäglich.
ore [ɔ:] Erz n.
organ ['ɔ:gən] Orgel f; Organ n; **~ic** [ɔ:'gænik] organisch.
organiz|ation [ɔ:gənai'zeiʃən] Organisation f; **~e** ['~aiz] organisieren; **~er** Organisator(in).
Orient ['ɔ:riənt] the **~** Orient m, Morgenland n.

orient(ate) ['ɔ:rient(eit)] orientieren.

origin ['ɔridʒin] Ursprung *m*; Anfang *m*; Herkunft *f*; **~al** [ə'ridʒənl] ursprünglich; originell; Original...; Original *n*; **~ality** [əridʒi'næliti] Originalität *f*; **~ate** [ə'ridʒineit] hervorbringen, schaffen; entstehen.

ornament ['ɔ:nəmənt] Verzierung *f*; *fig.* Zierde *f*; ['~ment] verzieren, schmücken; **~al** schmückend, Zier...

orphan ['ɔ:fən] Waise *f*; **~age** Waisenhaus *n*.

oscillate ['ɔsileit] schwingen; *fig.* schwanken.

ostrich ['ɔstritʃ] *orn.* Strauß *m*.

other ['ʌðə] ander; **the ~ day** neulich; **every ~ day** jeden zweiten Tag; **~wise** ['~waiz] anders; sonst.

ought [ɔ:t] *v/aux* ich, du *etc.*: sollte(st) *etc.*; **you ~ to have done it** Sie hätten es tun sollen.

ounce [auns] Unze *f* (28,35 g).

our ['auə] unser; **~s** unsere(r, -s), der, die, das uns(e)re; **~selves** ['selvz] uns (selbst); *wir* selbst.

oust [aust] vertreiben, entfernen, hinauswerfen.

out [aut] *adv* aus; hinaus, heraus; aus(...); außen, draußen; nicht zu Hause; *sp.* aus; aus der Mode; vorbei; erloschen; aus(gegangen), verbraucht; zu

Ende; *prp*: **~ of** aus ... (heraus); hinaus; außer (-halb); (hergestellt) aus; aus *Furcht etc.*; **be ~ of** s.th. et. nicht mehr haben; *int.* hinaus!, 'raus!

out|balance überwiegen, -treffen; **~bid** (*irr* bid) überbieten; **~board** Außenbord...; **~break**, **~burst** Ausbruch *m*; **~cast** Ausgestoßene *m, f*; **~come** Ergebnis *n*; **~cry** Aufschrei *m*; **~door(s)** draußen, im Freien.

outer ['autə] Außen..., äußer; **~most** äußerst.

out|fit Ausrüstung *f*, Ausstattung *f*; **~going** weg-, abgehend; **~grow** (*irr* grow) herauswachsen aus; **~ing** Ausflug *m*; **~last** überdauern, -leben; **~law** Geächtete *m, f*; **~let** Abzug *m*, Abfluß *m*; *econ.* Absatzmarkt *m*; *fig.* Ventil *n*; **~line** Umriß *m*; Entwurf *m*; Abriß *m*; umreißen, skizzieren; **~live** überleben; **~look** Ausblick *m*, -sicht *f*; Auffassung *f*; **~number** an Zahl übertreffen; **~patient** ambulanter Patient; **~put** Produktion *f*, Ertrag *m*.

outrage ['autreidʒ] Ausschreitung *f*; Gewalt(tat) *f*; gröblich verletzen; Gewalt antun; **~ous** abscheulich; empörend.

out|right [*adj* 'autrait, *adv* '~rait] völlig; *fig.* glatt;

~run (*irr* run) schneller laufen als; übertreffen; ~side Außenseite *f*; Äußere *n*; äußer, Außen...; außerhalb, draußen; hinaus; ~side left *sp.* Linksaußen *m*; ~sider Außenseiter(in), -stehende *m, f*; ~side right *sp.* Rechtsaußen *m*; ~size Übergröße *f*; ~skirts *pl* Stadtrand *m*; ~spoken offen, unverblümt; ~spread ausgestreckt; ausgebreitet; ~standing hervorragend (*a. fig.*); ausstehend (*Schuld*); ~stretched *s.* outspread; ~ward ['ɔwəd] äußer (-lich); nach (dr)außen gerichtet, Aus...; ~ward(s) (nach) auswärts, nach außen; ~weigh überwiegen; ~wit überlisten.

oval ['ɔuvəl] oval; Oval *n*.

oven ['ʌvn] Backofen *m*.

over ['ɔuvə] *prp* über; über ... hin(weg); im (~ **the radio**); all ~ **the town** durch die ganze *od.* in der ganzen Stadt, überall in der Stadt; *adv* hinüber; darüber; herüber; drüben; über (*kochen etc.*); um (*fallen, -werfen etc.*); herum(*drehen etc.*); von Anfang bis Ende, durch(*lesen etc.*), ganz, über und über; (*gründlich*) über(*legen etc.*); nochmals, wieder; übermäßig, über...; darüber, mehr; übrig; zu Ende, vorüber, vorbei; aus;

(all) ~ **again** nochmal, (ganz) von vorn; ~ **and** ~ **again** immer wieder.

over|all ['ɔuvərɔ:l] Gesamt...; Kittel *m*; *pl* Arbeitsanzug *m*; ~**board** über Bord; ~**burden** überladen, -lasten; ~**cast** bewölkt, bedeckt; ~**charge** überfordern; Betrag zuviel verlangen; überbelasten, -laden; ~**coat** Mantel *m*; ~**come** (*irr* come) überwinden; ~**wältigen**; ~**crowd** überfüllen; ~**do** (*irr* do) übertreiben; zu stark kochen *od.* braten; ~**draw** (*irr* draw) Konto überziehen; überfällig; ~**due** überfällig; ~**estimate** überschätzen, -bewerten; ~**flow** [~'flɔu] überfluten; überlaufen, -fließen; ['~flɔu] Überschwemmung *f*; Überschuß *m*; ~**grown** überwuchert; übergroß; ~**hang** (*irr* hang) hängen über; überhängen; ~**haul** überholen; ~**head** ['~hed] *adv* oben, droben; ['~hed] *adj* Hoch..., Ober...; ~**hear** (*irr* hear) belauschen, hören; ~**heat** überhitzen, -heizen; ~**joyed** überglücklich; ~**lap** sich überschneiden; überlappen; ~**load** überladen, -lasten; ~**look** Fehler übersehen; überblicken; ~**night** Nacht..., Übernachtungs...; *adv* über Nacht; **stay** ~**night** übernachten; ~**pass** (Straßen)Überführung *f*; **~rate** überschätzen; **~rule** überstimmen; ablehnen; **~run** (*irr* **run**) überschwemmen; überlaufen; überwuchern; **~sea(s)** Übersee...; **~seas** in *od.* nach Übersee; **~see** (*irr* **see**) beaufsichtigen; **~seer** Aufseher *m*; **~shadow** überschatten; **~sight** Versehen *n*; **~sleep** (*irr* **sleep**) verschlafen; **~strain** überanstrengen; **~take** (*irr* **take**) einholen; überholen; **be ~ taken by** überrascht werden von; **~throw** ['~'θrəu] (*irr* **throw**) (um)stürzen; ['~θrəu] Sturz *m*; **~time** Überstunden *pl*; **~top** überragen.

overture ['əuvətjuə] Ouvertüre *f*; Vorschlag *m*, Antrag *m*, Angebot *n*.

over|turn umstürzen; **~weight** Übergewicht *n*; **~whelm** [əuvə'welm] *fig.* überschütten; überwälti-

gen; **~work** ['~'wə:k] Überarbeitung *f*; ['~'wə:k] Mehrarbeit *f*, Überstunden *pl*; ['~'wə:k] (*a. irr* **work**) sich überarbeiten.

owe [əu] schulden; verdanken.

owing ['əuiŋ]: **be ~** zu zahlen sein; **~ to** infolge, wegen.

owl [aul] Eule *f*.

own [əun] eigen; selbst; einzig, innig geliebt; besitzen; zugeben; anerkennen.

owner ['əunə] Eigentümer(in); **~ship** Eigentum(srecht) *n*.

ox [ɔks], *pl* **~en** ['~ən] Ochse *m*; Rind *n*.

oxid|ation [ɔksi'deiʃən] Oxydation *f*; **~e** ['~aid] Oxyd *n*; **~ize** ['~daiz] oxydieren.

oxygen ['ɔksidʒən] Sauerstoff *m*.

oyster ['ɔistə] Auster *f*.

ozone ['əuzəun] Ozon *n*.

P

pace [peis] Schritt *m*; Gang *m*; Tempo *n*; (ab-, durch)schreiten.

Pacific (Ocean) [pə'sifik] Pazifik *m*, Pazifischer *od.* Stiller Ozean.

pacify ['pæsifai] besänftigen; befrieden.

pack [pæk] Pack(en) *m*, Päckchen *n*, Paket *n*, Ballen *m*; Spiel *n* (*Karten*); *Am.* Packung *f* (*Zigaret-*

ten); **a ~ of lies** lauter Lügen; **~ (up)** (zs.-, ver-, ein)packen; **~age** Paket *n*, Pack *m*, Ballen *m*; **~er** Packer(in); **~et** ['~it] Päckchen *n*; Packung *f* (*Zigaretten*); **~ing** Packen *n*; Verpackung *f*; **~thread** Bindfaden *m*. [Pakt *m*.]

pact [pækt] Vertrag *m*, [

pad [pæd] Polster *n*, Schreib-, Zeichenblock *m*;

Abschußrampe *f*; (aus-)polstern; **~ding** Polsterung *f*.

paddle ['pædl] Paddel *n*; paddeln; planschen.

paddock ['pædək] (Pferde)Koppel *f*.

padlock ['pædlɔk] Vorhängeschloß *n*.

pagan ['peigən] heidnisch; Heide *m*, -in *f*.

page [peidʒ] (Buch)Seite *f*; (Hotel)Page *m*.

pageant ['pædʒənt] historisches Festspiel; Festzug *m*. **[pay.**

paid [peid] *pret u. pp von* **|**
pail [peil] Eimer *m*.

pain [pein] *j—n* schmerzen, *j—m* weh tun; Schmerz(en *pl*) *m*; Mühe *f*; **be in ~** Schmerzen haben; **take ~s** sich Mühe geben; **~ful** schmerzhaft; schmerzlich; peinlich; **~less** schmerzlos.

paint [peint] Farbe *f*; Schminke *f*; Anstrich *m*; (an-, be)malen; (an)streichen; sich schminken; **~box** Mal-, Tuschkasten *m*; **~brush** (Maler)Pinsel *m*; **~er** Maler(in); **~ing** Malen *n*, Malerei *f*; Gemälde *n*, Bild *n*.

pair [pɛə] Paar *n*; **a ~ of** ein Paar ...; ein(e) ...; *zo.* (sich) paaren.

pajamas [pə'dʒɑːməz] *pl Am.* Schlafanzug *m*.

pal [pæl] *colloq.* Kumpel *m*, Kamerad *m*, Freund *m*.

palace ['pælis] Palast *m*, Schloß *n*, Palais *n*.

palate ['pælit] Gaumen *m*.

pale[1] [peil] Pfahl.

pale[2] blaß, bleich, fahl; erbleichen; **~ness** Blässe *f*.

pallor ['pælə] Blässe *f*.

palm [pɑːm] Handfläche *f*; Palme *f*.

palpitation [pælpi'teiʃən] Herzklopfen *n*.

pamper ['pæmpə] verzärteln.

pamphlet ['pæmflit] Flugschrift *f*; Broschüre *f*.

pan [pæn] Pfanne *f*, Tiegel *m*; **~cake** Pfann-, Eierkuchen *m*.

pane [pein] (Fenster-)Scheibe *f*.

panel ['pænl] (*Tür*)Füllung *f*, (*Wand*)Täfelung *f*; Gremium *n*; Diskussionsteilnehmer *pl*; täfeln.

pang [pæŋ] plötzlicher Schmerz; *fig.* Angst *f*.

panic ['pænik] panisch; Panik *f*.

pansy ['pænzi] Stiefmütterchen *n*.

pant [pænt] *nach Luft* schnappen, keuchen, schnaufen.

panther ['pænθə] Panther *m*.

panties ['pæntiz] *pl colloq.* (Damen)Schlüpfer *m*; Kinderhöschen *n od. pl.*

pantry ['pæntri] Speise-, Vorratskammer *f*.

pants [pænts] *pl* Hose *f*; Unterhose *f*.

pap [pæp] Brei *m*.

papa [pə'pɑː] Papa *m*.

paper ['peipə] Papier *n*;

Zeitung *f*; ˈPrüfungsaufgabe *f*, -arbeit *f*; *pl* (Ausweis)Papiere *pl*; tapezieren; **~back** Taschenbuch *n*, Paperback *n*; **~bag** Tüte *f*; **~hanger** Tapezierer *m*; **~hangings** *pl* Tapete *f*; **~money** Papiergeld *n*; **~weight** Briefbeschwerer *m*.

parable [ˈpærəbl] Gleichnis *n*.

parachut|e [ˈpærəʃuːt] Fallschirm *m*; **~ist** Fallschirmspringer(in).

parade [pəˈreid] Parade *f*; Zurschaustellung *f*, Vorführung *f*; (Strand)Promenade *f*; antreten (lassen); vorbeimarschieren; **zur Schau stellen.**

paradise [ˈpærədais] Paradies *n*.

paragraph [ˈpærəgrɑːf] *print.* Absatz *m*; kurze Zeitungsnotiz.

parallel [ˈpærəlel] parallel; Parallele *f*.

paraly|se, *Am.* **~ze** [ˈpærəlaiz] lähmen; **~sis** [pəˈrælisis] Lähmung *f*.

paramount [ˈpærəmaunt] übergeordnet, höchst; überragend.

parasite [ˈpærəsait] Schmarotzer *m*.

parcel [ˈpɑːsl] Paket *n*, Päckchen *n*; **~ out** auf-, austeilen.

parch [pɑːtʃ] rösten, (aus)dörren; **~ment** Pergament *n*.

pardon [ˈpɑːdn] verzei-

hen; begnadigen; Verzeihung *f*; Begnadigung *f*; **I beg your ~** entschuldigen Sie bitte!, Verzeihung!; wie bitte?; **~able** verzeihlich.

pare [pɛə] schälen; (be)schneiden.

parent [ˈpɛərənt] Elternteil *m*; Vater *m*; Mutter *f*; *pl* Eltern *pl*; **~al** [pəˈrentl] elterlich.

parenthe|sis [pəˈrenθisis], *pl* **~ses** [ˌ~siːz] (runde) Klammer.

parings [ˈpɛəriŋz] *pl* Schalen *pl*; Schnipsel *pl*.

parish [ˈpæriʃ] Kirchspiel *n*, Gemeinde *f*; Pfarr..., Gemeinde...; **~ioner** [pəˈriʃənə] Gemeindemitglied *n*.

park [pɑːk] Park *m*, Anlagen *pl*; Naturschutzgebiet *n*; parken.

parking [ˈpɑːkiŋ] Parken *n*; **no ~** Parken verboten; **~ garage** Parkhaus *n*; **~ lot** *Am.* Parkplatz *m*; **~ meter** Parkuhr *f*.

parliament [ˈpɑːləmənt] Parlament *n*; **Houses of 2** *Brit.* Parlament(sgebäude) *n*; **Member of 2** *Brit. parl.* Abgeordnete *m*, *f*; **~ary** [ˌ~ˈmentəri] parlamentarisch, Parlaments...

parlo(u)r [ˈpɑːlə] Wohnzimmer *n*; Salon *m*; Empfangs-, Sprechzimmer *n*.

parquet [ˈpɑːkei] Parkett *n* (*Am. a. thea.*)

parrot [ˈpærət] Papagei *m*.

parsley ['pɑ:sli]Petersilie*f*.
parson ['pɑ:sn] Pfarrer *m*,
Pastor*m*; **~age**Pfarrhaus *n*.
part [pɑ:t] trennen; *Haar*
scheiteln; sich trennen
(**with** von); (An-, Be-
stand)Teil *m*; Partei *f*;
thea., *fig*. Rolle *f*; *mus*.
Stimme *f*; *pl* Gegend *f*;
take ~ in teilnehmen an;
for my ~ ich für mein(en)
Teil; **on the ~ of** von
seiten, seitens.
partake [pɑ:'teik] (*irr*
take) teilnehmen, -haben.
partial ['pɑ:ʃəl] teilweise,
Teil...; parteiisch; **~ity**
[~ʃi'æliti] Parteilichkeit *f*;
Vorliebe *f*.
particip|ant [pɑ:'tisipənt]
Teilnehmer(in *f*) *m*; **~ate**[~-
peit] teilhaben, -nehmen;
~ation Teilnahme *f*.
participle ['pɑ:tisipl] *gr*.
Partizip *n*, Mittelwort *n*.
particle ['pɑ:tikl] Teil-
chen *n*.
particular [pə'tikjulə] besonder; einzeln; genau,
eigen; wählerisch; **in ~**
besonders; Einzelheit *f*;
pl Nähere *n*; **(personal) ~s**
pl Personalien *pl*; **~ity**
[~'læriti] Besonderheit *f*;
Ausführlichkeit *f*; Eigen-
heit *f*; **~ly** besonders.
parting ['pɑ:tiŋ] (Haar-)
Scheitel *m*; Trennung *f*;
Abschieds...
partition [pɑ:'tiʃən] Teilung *f*; Trennwand *f*;
Fach *n*; **~ off** abteilen.
partly zum Teil.

partner ['pɑ:tnə] Partner
(-in *f*); **~ship** Teilhaber-,
Partnerschaft *f*.
partridge ['pɑ:tridʒ]Reb-
huhn *n*.
part-time Teilzeit..., Halb-
tags...
party ['pɑ:ti] Partei *f*;
Party *f*, Gesellschaft *f*;
(Reise)Gruppe *f*.
pass [pɑ:s] (Gebirgs)Paß
m; Ausweis *m*, Passierschein *m*; *Fußball*: Paß *m*;
Bestehen *n* (*e-s Examens*);
et. passieren, vorbeigehen
an, -fahren an, -fließen an,
-kommen an, -ziehen an;
überholen (*a. mot.*); überschreiten; durchqueren;
reichen, geben; *Ball* abspielen; *Prüfung* bestehen;
Prüfling durchkommen
lassen; *Gesetz* verabschieden; *Urteil* fällen; *fig*.
übersteigen; vorbeigehen,
-fahren, -kommen, -ziehen
(**by** an); übergehen (**to**
auf; [**in**]**to** in); (den Ball)
zu-, abspielen; (die Prü-
fung) bestehen; *Karten*:
passen; sich zutragen, geschehen; **~ (away)** *Zeit*
verbringen; vergehen (*Zeit*,
Schmerz); sterben; **~ for**
gelten als; **~ out** *colloq*.
ohnmächtig werden; **~
round** herumreichen; **~
through** hindurchgehen,
-fahren, -kommen; **~able**
passierbar; leidlich.
passage ['pæsidʒ] Durchgang *m*; Durchfahrt *f*;
Korridor *m*, Gang *m*; *mus*.

Passage f; (Text)Stelle f;
Reise f, (Über)Fahrt f,
Flug m.

passenger ['pæsɪndʒə]
Passagier m, Fahr-, Flug-
gast m, Reisende m, f,
Insasse m; Passagier...

passer-by ['pɑːsə'baɪ] Pas-
sant(in).

passion ['pæʃən] Leidenschaft f; (Gefühls)Aus-
bruch m; Zorn m; 2 eccl.
Passion f; **~ate** ['~ɪt] leidenschaftlich.

passive ['pæsɪv] passiv (a.
gr.); teilnahmslos; un-
tätig; **~ (voice)** gr. Passiv
n, Leideform f.

pass|port ['pɑːspɔːt] (Rei-
se)Paß m; **~word** Parole f.

past [pɑːst] Vergangenheit f (a. gr.); vergangen,
vorüber; vorbei, vorüber;
nach (zeitlich); an ... vorbei; über ... hinaus; **half
~ two** halb drei; **~ hope**
hoffnungslos.

paste [peɪst] Teig m;
Paste f; Kleister m; (be-)
kleben; **~board** Pappe f.

pastime ['pɑːstaɪm] Zeitvertreib m.

pastry ['peɪstrɪ] (Fein-)
Gebäck n; Blätterteig m.

past tense gr. Vergangenheit f.

pasture ['pɑːstʃə] Weide
(-land n) f; weiden.

pat [pæt] Klaps m; tätscheln, klopfen.

patch [pætʃ] Fleck m;
Flicken m; **~ (up)** (zs.-)
flicken; **~work** Flickwerk n.

patent ['peɪtənt, Am. 'pæ-
tənt] patentiert; Patent n;
patentieren (lassen); **~
leather** Lackleder n.

patern|al [pə'tɜːnl] väter-
lich(erseits); **~ity** Vaterschaft f.

path [pɑːθ], pl **~s** [pɑːðz]
Pfad m; Weg m.

pathetic [pə'θetɪk] pathe-
tisch, rührend.

patien|ce ['peɪʃəns] Ge-
duld f; **~t** geduldig; Pa-
tient(in).

patriot ['peɪtrɪət] Patriot
(-in); **~ic** [pætrɪ'ɒtɪk] pa-
triotisch; **~ism** ['pætrɪə-
tɪzəm] Patriotismus m.

patrol [pə'trəʊl] Pa-
trouille f; (Polizei-)
Streife f; (ab)patrouillie-
ren; **~man** Polizist m auf
Streife; Pannenhelfer m.

patron ['peɪtrən] Förderer
m; Kunde m; **~age**
['pætrənɪdʒ] Schirmherr-
schaft f; Kundschaft f;
~ize ['pætrənaɪz] Kunde
sein bei; fördern.

patter ['pætə] trappeln
(Füße); prasseln (Regen).

pattern ['pætən] Muster n
(a. fig.); Modell n.

paunch [pɔːntʃ] (Dick-)
Bauch m.

pause [pɔːz] Pause f; e-e
Pause machen.

pave [peɪv] pflastern; fig.
Weg bahnen; **~ment** Bürgersteig m; Pflaster n;
~ment café Straßencafé n.

paw [pɔː] Pfote f, Tatze f;
scharren; colloq. betasten.

pawn [pɔ:n] Pfand n; verpfänden; **~broker** Pfandleiher m; **~shop** Leihhaus n.

pay [pei] (Be)Zahlung f; Lohn m; Sold m; (irr) (be)zahlen; (be)lohnen; sich lohnen (für); Besuch abstatten; Aufmerksamkeit schenken; **~down, ~cash** bar bezahlen; **~for** (für) et. bezahlen; **~able** zahlbar; fällig; **~day** Zahltag m; **~ee** [‿'i:] Zahlungsempfänger(in); **~ment** (Be-, Ein-, Aus)Zahlung f; Lohn m.

pea [pi:] Erbse f.

peace [pi:s] Friede(n) m, Ruhe f; **~ful** friedlich.

peach [pi:tʃ] Pfirsich m.

peacock [‿'pi:kɔk] Pfau m.

peak [pi:k] Spitze f; Gipfel m; Mützenschirm m; Spitzen..., Haupt..., Höchst...; **~hours** od. **~time** Hauptverkehrs-, Stoßzeit f.

peal [pi:l] (Glocken)Läuten n; Dröhnen n; läuten; dröhnen, krachen.

peanut [‿'pi:nʌt] Erdnuß f.

pear [pɛə] bot. Birne f.

pearl [pɔ:l] Perle f.

peasant [‿'peznt] Bauer m; bäuerlich, Bauern...

peat [pi:t] Torf m.

pebble [‿'pebl] Kiesel(stein) m.

peck [pek] Viertelscheffel m (9,1 Liter); picken, hacken (**at** nach).

peculiar [pi'kju:ljə] eigen (-tümlich); besonder; seltsam; **~ity** [‿‿li'æriti] Eigen-

heit f, Eigentümlichkeit f.

pedal [‿'pedl] Pedal n; (rad)fahren.

pedestal [‿'pedistl] Sockel m.

pedestrian [pi'destriən] Fußgänger(in); **~crossing** Fußgängerübergang m; **~precinct, ~zone** Fußgängerzone f.

pedigree [‿'pedigri:] Stammbaum m. [m.

pedlar [‿'pedlə] Hausierer [

peel [pi:l] Schale f, Rinde f; (sich) (ab)schälen.

peep [pi:p] neugieriger od. verstohlener Blick; Piepen n; neugierig od. verstohlen blicken; piepen.

peer [piə] spähen, schauen.

peevish [‿'pi:viʃ] gereizt.

peg [peg] Pflock m; Zapfen m; Kleiderhaken m; (Wäsche)Klammer f. [m.

pelican [‿'pelikən] Pelikan [

pelt [pelt] bewerfen; (nieder)prasseln.

pelvis [‿'pelvis] anat. Becken n.

pen [pen] (Schreib)Feder f; Federhalter m; Pferch m; (Schaf)Hürde f; **~in, ~up** einpferchen.

penal [‿'pi:nl] Straf...; **~servitude** Zuchthaus (-strafe f) n; **~ty** [‿'penlti] Strafe f; sp. Strafpunkt m; **~ty area** Strafraum m; **~ty kick** Strafstoß m.

penance [‿'penəns] Buße f.

pence [pens] pl von penny.

pencil [‿'pensl] (Blei-, Farb)Stift m; **~sharpener** Bleistiftspitzer m.

pend|ant ['pendənt] (*Schmuck*)Anhänger *m*; **~ing** *jur.* schwebend; während; bis *a*.

penetrat|e ['penitreit] durch-, vordringen, eindringen (in); **~ion** Durch-, Eindringen *n*;Scharfsinn *m*.

pen-friend Brieffreund(in).

penguin ['peŋgwin] Pinguin *m*.

penholder Federhalter *m*.

peninsula [pi'ninsjulə] Halbinsel *f*.

penitent ['penitənt] reuig; **~iary** [⁓'tenʃəri] Besserungsanstalt *f*; *Am.* Zuchthaus *n*.

penknife Taschenmesser *n*.

penniless ['penilis] ohne e-n Pfennig (Geld), mittellos.

penny ['peni], *pl mst* **pence** [pens]Penny *m*; **~worth**: **a ~ of** für e-n Penny.

pension ['penʃən] Pension *f*, Rente *f*; **~ off** pensionieren. [denklich.]

pensive ['pensiv] nach-

penthouse ['penthaus] Wetterdach *n*; Dachwohnung *f*, Penthouse *n*.

people ['pi:pl] Volk *n*, Nation *f*; **~ pl** Leute *pl*; Angehörige *pl*; man; bevölkern.

pepper ['pepə] Pfeffer *m*; pfeffern; **~mint** Pfefferminze *f*; Pfefferminzbonbon *m*, *n*.

per [pə:] per; pro, für.

perambulator ['præmbjuleitə] Kinderwagen *m*.

perceive [pə'si:v] (be-)

merken, wahrnehmen; erkennen.

per|cent [pə'sent] Prozent *n*; **~centage** Prozentsatz *m*; Prozente *pl*.

percept|ible [pə'septəbl] wahrnehmbar; **~ion** Wahrnehmung(svermögen *n*) *f*.

perch [pə:tʃ] *auf et. Hohem* sitzen.

percussion [pə'kaʃən] Schlag *m*, Erschütterung *f*.

peremptory[pə'remptəri] entschieden, bestimmt.

perfect ['pə:fikt] vollkommen, vollendet, perfekt; **~** (**tense**) *gr.* Perfekt *n*; [pə'fekt] vervollkommnen; **~ion** Vollendung *f*; Vollkommenheit *f*.

perforate ['pə:foreit] durchbohren, -löchern.

perform [pə'fɔ:m] ausführen, tun; *thea., mus.* aufführen, spielen, vortragen; **~ance** *thea., mus.* Aufführung *f*, Vorstellung *f*, Vortrag *m*, Leistung *f*; **~er** Künstler(in).

perfume ['pə:fju:m] Duft *m*; Parfüm *n*; [pə'fju:m] parfümieren.

perhaps [pə'hæps, præps] vielleicht.

peril ['peril] Gefahr *f*; **~ous** gefährlich.

period ['piəriəd] Periode *f* (*a. med.*); Zeitraum *m*; *ling.* Punkt *m*; (Unterrichts)Stunde *f*; **~ic** [⁓'ɔdik] periodisch; **~ical** periodisch; Zeitschrift *f*.

perish ['periʃ]umkommen;

~able leicht verderblich.

perjury ['pɜːdʒəri] Meineid *m*.

perm [pɜːm] *colloq*. Dauerwelle *f*; ~anent (fortdauernd, ständig, dauerhaft, Dauer...; ~anent wave Dauerwelle *f*.

permeable ['pɜːmjəbl] durchlässig.

permission [pə'miʃən] Erlaubnis *f*; ~t [~t] erlauben; [~t] Erlaubnis *f*, Genehmigung *f*; Passierschein *m*.

perpendicular [pɜːpən'dikjulə] senkrecht.

perpetual [pə'petʃuəl] fortwährend, ewig.

persecute ['pɜːsikjuːt] verfolgen; ~ion Verfolgung *f*; ~or Verfolger *m*.

persevere [pɜːsi'viə] beharren, aushalten.

persist [pə'sist] beharren (**in** auf); fortdauern, anhalten; ~ence, ~ency Beharrlichkeit *f*; ~ent beharrlich.

person ['pɜːsn] Person *f*; ~age (hohe) Persönlichkeit; ~al persönlich; Personen...; Personal...; ~ality [~sə'næliti] Persönlichkeit *f*; ~ify [~'sɔnifai] verkörpern; ~nel [~sə'nel] Personal *n*, Belegschaft *f*; ~nel manager, ~nel officer Personalchef *m*.

perspiration [pɜːspə'reiʃən] Schwitzen *n*; Schweiß *m*; ~e [pəs'paiə] schwitzen.

persuade [pə'sweid] überreden; überzeugen; ~sion [~ʒən] Überredung (-skunst) *f*; Überzeugung *f*; ~sive [~siv] überredend; überzeugend.

pert [pɜːt] frech, vorlaut.

perusal [pə'ruːzəl] sorgfältige Durchsicht; ~e (sorgfältig) durchlesen.

pervade [pɜː'veid] durchdringen, -ziehen.

perverse [pə'vɜːs] verkehrt; verderbt; eigensinnig; pervers.

pessimism ['pesimizəm] Pessimismus *m*.

pest [pest] Plage *f*; ~er belästigen, plagen.

pet [pet] Liebling(stier *n*) *m*; Lieblings...

petal ['petl] Blütenblatt *n*.

petition [pi'tiʃən] Bittschrift *f*, Eingabe *f*; bitten, ersuchen; ein Gesuch einreichen.

pet name Kosename *m*.

petrify ['petrifai] versteinern.

petrol ['petrəl] Benzin *n*, Kraft-, Treibstoff *m*; ~ station Tankstelle *f*.

pet shop Zoohandlung *f*.

petticoat ['petikəut] Unterrock *m*.

petty ['peti] klein, geringfügig, unbedeutend.

pew [pjuː] Kirchenbank *f*.

pharmacy ['fɑːməsi] Apotheke *f*.

phase [feiz] Phase *f*.

pheasant ['feznt] Fasan *m*.

philanthropist [fi'lænθrəpist] Menschenfreund(in).

philolog|ist [fi'lɔlədʒist] Philolog|e m, -in f; **~y** Philologie f.

philosoph|er [fi'lɔsəfə] Philosoph m; **~ize** philosophieren; **~y** Philosophie f.

phone [fəun] colloq. für **telephone.**

phonetic [fəu'netik] phonetisch, Laut-.

phon(e)y ['fəuni] sl. falsch, gefälscht, unecht.

photo ['fəutəu] colloq. für **~graph** ['~təgraːf] Foto (-grafie f) n, Bild n, Aufnahme f; fotografieren.

photograph|er [fə'tɔgrəfə] Fotograf(in) f; **~y** Fotografie f.

phrase [freiz] Redewendung f, idiomatischer Ausdruck.

physic|al ['fizikəl] physisch, körperlich; physikalisch; **~ian** [fi'ziʃən] Arzt m; **~ist** ['~sist] Physiker m; **~s** sg Physik f.

physique [fi'ziːk] Körper (-bau) m.

piano [pi'ænəu] Klavier n.

pick [pik] (Aus)Wahl f; hacken; (auf)picken; auflesen, -nehmen; pflücken; Knochen abnagen; bohren in, stochern in; aussuchen; **~ out** (sich) et. auswählen; herausfinden; **~ up** aufhacken; aufheben, -lesen, -nehmen, -picken; colloq. et. aufschnappen; (im Auto) mitnehmen; abholen.

picket ['pikit] Pfahl m;

Streikposten m; Streikposten stehen; Streikposten aufstellen vor.

pickle ['pikl] Lake f; pl Eingepökelte n, Pickles pl; einlegen, (-)pökeln.

pick'pocket Taschendieb m; **~up** Tonabnehmer m.

picnic ['piknik] Picknick n.

pictorial [pik'tɔːriəl] illustriert; Illustrierte f.

picture ['piktʃə] Bild n; Gemälde n; bildschöne Sache od. Person; pl colloq. Kino n; Bilder...; darstellen; beschreiben; sich et. vorstellen; **~ postcard** Ansichtskarte f; **~sque** [~'resk] malerisch.

pie [pai] Pastete f.

piece [piːs] Stück n; Teil m, n (~e-s Services); **by the ~** im Akkord; **a ~ of advice** ein Rat; **a ~ of news** e-e Neuigkeit; **in ~s** entzwei; **take to ~s** auseinandernehmen; **~ work** Akkordarbeit f.

pier [piə] Pfeiler m; Pier m, Landungsbrücke f.

pierce [piəs] durchbohren, -stoßen, -stechen; durchdringen.

piety ['paiəti] Frömmigkeit f.   [kel n.]

pig [pig] Schwein n; Ferkel n.

pigeon ['pidʒin] Taube f; **~hole** (Ablage)Fach n.

pig|-headed dickköpfig; **~skin** Schweinsleder n; **~sty** Schweinestall m; **~tail** (Haar)Zopf m.

pike [paik] Hecht m.

pile [pail] Haufen m; Stapel m, Stoß m; oft ~ up, ~ on (an-, auf)häufen, (auf)stapeln, aufschichten.

pilfer ['pilfə] stehlen.

pilgrim ['pilgrim] Pilger(in) m; ~age Pilger-, Wallfahrt f.

pill [pil] Pille f, Tablette f.

pillar ['pilə] Pfeiler m, Ständer m; Säule f; ~-box Briefkasten m. [m.]

pillion ['piljən] Soziussitz

pillory ['piləri] Pranger m.

pillow ['piləu] (Kopf-)Kissen n; ~case, ~slip (Kissen)Bezug m.

pilot ['pailət] Pilot m; Lotse m; lotsen, steuern.

pimple ['pimpl] Pickel m.

pin [pin] (Steck)Nadel f; Pflock m; Kegel m; (an-)heften, (an)stecken, befestigen.

pincers ['pinsəz] pl (a. **a pair of ~**) (e-e) (Kneif-)Zange.

pinch [pintʃ] Kneifen n; Prise f (Salz etc.); kneifen, zwicken; drücken; colloq. klauen.

pine [pain] Kiefer f, Föhre f; sich abhärmen; sich sehnen, schmachten; ~apple Ananas f.

pinion ['pinjən] Flügelspitze f; Schwungfeder f.

pink [piŋk] Nelke f; Rosa n; rosa(farben).

pinnacle ['pinəkl] Zinne f; Spitzturm m; (Berg)Spitze f; fig. Gipfel m.

pint [paint] 0,57 od. Am. 0,47 Liter.

pioneer [paiə'niə] Pionier m. [dächtig.]

pious ['paiəs] fromm; an-]

pip [pip] (Obst)Kern m; kurzer, hoher Ton.

pipe [paip] Rohr n, Röhre f; Pfeife f (a. mus.); Flöte f; Luftröhre f; Wasser etc. leiten; pfeifen; piep(s)en; ~line Rohr-, Ölleitung f, Pipeline f; ~r Pfeifer m.

pirate ['paiərit] Seeräuber m; unerlaubt nachdrukken.

pistol ['pistl] Pistole f.

piston ['pistən] tech. Kolben m.

pit [pit] Grube f; thea. Parterre n; Am. (Obst)Stein m, Kern m.

pitch [pitʃ] min. Pech n; Wurf m; mar. Stampfen n; Neigung f (e-s Daches); mus. Tonhöhe f; Grad m, Stufe f (a. fig.); Zelt, Lager aufschlagen; werfen, schleudern; mus. stimmen; mar. stampfen (Schiff).

pitcher ['pitʃə] Krug m.

piteous ['pitiəs] mitleiderregend.

pitfall ['pitfɔ:l] Fallgrube f; fig. Falle f.

pith [piθ] Mark n.

pit|iable ['pitiəbl] erbärmlich; ~iful mitleidig; erbärmlich (a. contp.); ~iless unbarmherzig; ~y bemitleiden; Mitleid n; it is a ~y es ist schade; **what a ~y** es ist schade.

pivot ['pivət] tech.: (Dreh-) Punkt m (a. fig.); Zapfen m.

placard ['plækɑ:d] Plakat *n*; anschlagen.

place [pleis] Platz *m*; Ort *m*; Stelle *f*; Stätte *f*; (An-)Stellung *f*; Wohnsitz *m*, Wohnung *f*; in ~ of an Stelle von *od*. *gen*; out of ~ fehl am Platz; **take** ~ stattfinden; *vb*: stellen, legen, setzen; *Auftrag* erteilen; **be** ~**d** *sp*. sich placieren. [ruhig.|

placid ['plæsid] sanft *f*; **plague** [pleig] Pest *f*; Plage *f*; plagen, quälen.

plaice [pleis] *ichth*. Scholle *f*. [Plaid.|

plaid [plæd] *schottisches*]

plain [plein] einfach; unscheinbar; offen, ehrlich; einfarbig; klar, deutlich; *Am*. eben, flach; Ebene *f*; ~**clothes man** Polizist *m od*. Kriminalbeamte *m* in Zivil.

plaint|**iff** ['pleintif] Kläger (-in); ~**ive** klagend.

plait [plæt, *Am*. pleit] Flechte *f*, Zopf *m*; flechten.

plan [plæn] Plan *m*; planen.

plane [plein] flach, eben; (ein)ebnen; (ab)hobeln; Ebene *f*, (ebene) Fläche; *aer*. Tragfläche *f*; Flugzeug *n*, Maschine *f*; Hobel *m*; *fig*. Stufe *f*, Niveau *n*.

planet ['plænit] Planet *m*.

plank [plæŋk] Planke *f*, Bohle *f*, Diele *f*.

plant [plɑ:nt] Pflanze *f*; (Fabrik)Anlage *f*, Fabrik *f*; (an-, ein-, be)pflanzen; an-

legen; ~**ation** [plæn'teiʃən] Pflanzung *f*, Plantage *f*; ~**er** ['plɑ:ntə] Pflanzer *m*, Plantagenbesitzer *m*. [tafel *f*.|

plaque [plɑ:k] Gedenk-|

plaster ['plɑ:stə] *med*. Pflaster *n*; (Ver)Putz *m*; bepflastern; verputzen; ~ **cast** Gipsabdruck *m*; *med*. Gipsverband *m*; ~ **of Paris** Gips *m*.

plastic ['plæstik] plastisch; Plastik...; ~**s** *sg* Plastik *n*, Kunststoff *m*.

plate [pleit] Platte *f*; Teller *m*; (Bild)Tafel *f*; Schild *n*; plattieren; panzern.

platform ['plætfɔ:m] Plattform *f*; Bahnsteig *m*; Podium *n*; *pol*. Parteiprogramm *n*. [Platin *n*.|

platinum ['plætinəm]|

platter ['plætə] (Servier-) Platte *f*.

plausible ['plɔ:zəbl] glaubhaft.

play [plei] Spiel *n*; Schauspiel *n*, (Theater)Stück *n*; Spielraum *m* (*a. fig*.); spielen (gegen); ~ **off** *fig*. *j-n* ausspielen; ~**back** Playback *n*, Abspielen *n*; ~**bill** Theaterzettel *m*; ~**er** (Schau)Spieler(in); ~**fellow** Spielgefährt|e *m*, -in *f*; ~**ful** verspielt; ~**ground** Spielplatz *m*; Schulhof *m*; ~**mate** *s*. playfellow; ~**thing** Spielzeug *n*; ~**time** Freizeit *f*; Zeit *f* zum Spielen; ~**wright** ['~rait] Dramatiker *m*.

plea [pli:] Vorwand m; Gesuch n; jur.: Verteidigung f; Einspruch m.

plead [pli:d] e-e Sache vertreten; plädieren; sich einsetzen; ~ **guilty** sich schuldig bekennen.

pleasant ['pleznt] angenehm, erfreulich; freundlich.

pleas|e [pli:z] (j-m) gefallen od. angenehm sein; zufriedenstellen; ~**e!** bitte!; ~**ed** erfreut, zufrieden; ~**ing** angenehm, gefällig.

pleasure ['pleʒə] Vergnügen n, Freude f.

pleat [pli:t] (Plissee)Falte f; plissieren.

pledge [pledʒ] Pfand n; Versprechen n; verpfänden.

plent|iful ['plentiful] reichlich; ~**y** Fülle f, Überfluß m; ~**y of** reichlich, e-e Menge.

pliable ['plaiəbl] biegsam; fig. nachgiebig.

pliers ['plaiəz] pl (a. **a pair of** ~) (e-e) (Draht-, Kneif-) Zange.

plight [plait] schlechter Zustand, mißliche Lage.

plimsolls ['plimsəlz] pl Turnschuhe pl.

plod [plɔd] sich abmühen; ~ **(along, on)** sich dahinschleppen.

plot [plɔt] Stück n (Land); Plan m; Komplott n, Anschlag m; Handlung f (e-s Romans, Dramas etc.); planen.

plough, Am. **plow** [plau] Pflug m; (um)pflügen; ~-**share** Pflugschar f.

pluck [plʌk] Ruck m; Mut m, Schneid m; pflücken, rupfen; (aus)reißen; ~ **up courage** Mut fassen; ~**y** mutig.

plug [plʌg] Pflock m, Dübel m, Stöpsel m, Zapfen m; electr. Stecker m; ~ **in** electr. einstöpseln, -stecken; ~ **up** zu-, verstopfen.

plum [plʌm] Pflaume f; Rosine f (im Backwerk).

plumage ['plu:midʒ] Gefieder n.

plumb [plʌm] Lot n, Senkblei n; loten; ~**er** Klempner m, Installateur m. [chen m.]

plum cake Rosinenku-}

plume ['plu:m] Feder (-busch m) f.

plummet ['plʌmit] Lot m.

plump [plʌmp] drall, mollig; (hin)plumpsen (lassen). [pudding m.]

plum pudding Plum-}

plunder ['plʌndə] Plünderung f; plündern.

plunge [plʌndʒ] (ein-, unter)tauchen; (sich) stürzen.

plunk [plʌŋk] Saite zupfen.

pluperfect (tense) ['plu:pə'fekt] gr. Plusquamperfekt n, Vorvergangenheit f.

plural ['pluərəl] gr. Plural m, Mehrzahl f.

plus [plʌs] plus, und; positiv; Plus n.

plush [plʌʃ] Plüsch m.

ply [plai] (Garn)Strähne *f*; (Stoff-, Holz- *etc.*)Lage *f*; **~wood** Sperrholz *n*.

pneumatic [nju(:)'mætik] pneumatisch, (Preß)Luft...

pneumonia [nju(:)'məunja] Lungenentzündung *f*.

poach [pəutʃ] wildern; **~ed egg** verlorenes Ei; **~er** Wilddieb *m*, Wilderer *m*.

pocket ['pɔkit] (Hosen- *etc.*)Tasche *f*; einstecken (*a. fig.*); Taschen...; **~book** Notizbuch *n*; Brieftasche *f*; Taschenbuch *n*; **~-knife** Taschenmesser *n*; **~money** Taschengeld *n*.

pod [pɔd] Hülse *f*, Schote *f*.

poem ['pəuim] Gedicht *n*.

poet ['pəuit] Dichter *m*; **~ess** Dichterin *f*; **~ic(al)** [ˌ'etik(əl)] dichterisch; **~ry** ['ˌitri] Dichtkunst *f*; Dichtung *f*.

poignant ['pɔinənt]scharf; *fig.*: bitter; ergreifend.

point [pɔint] Spitze *f*; Punkt *m* (*a. ling.*); *math.* (Dezimal)Punkt *m*, Komma *n*; Kompaßstrich *m*; Punkt *m*, Stelle *f*, Ort *m*; springender Punkt; Pointe *f*; Zweck *m*, Ziel *n*; *pl rail.* Weichen *pl*; **beside the ~** nicht zur Sache gehörig; **on the ~ of** *ger* im Begriff zu *inf*; **to the ~** zur Sache (gehörig), sachlich; **win on ~s** nach Punkten siegen; *vb*: (zu-)spitzen; **~ out** zeigen, hinweisen auf; **~ at** *Waffe* richten auf; zeigen auf;

~ to nach *e-r Richtung* weisen *od.* liegen; zeigen auf; hinweisen auf; **~ed** spitz; *fig.*: scharf; deutlich; **~er** Zeiger *m*; Zeigestock *m*; Vorstehhund *m*; **~ of view** Stand-, Gesichtspunkt *m*, Ansicht *f*.

poise [pɔiz] Gleichgewicht *n*; Haltung *f*; *Kopf etc.* halten; schweben.

poison ['pɔizn] Gift *n*; vergiften; *fig.* vergällen; **~ous** giftig.

poke [pəuk] stoßen; schüren; stecken; stoßen, stechen, stochern; **~r** Schürhaken *m*.

polar ['pəulə] polar, Polar...; **~ bear** Eisbär *m*.

Pole [pəul] Pole *m*, -in *f*.

pole [pəul] Pol *m*; Stange *f*; Mast *m*; Deichsel *f*; (Sprung)Stab *m*.

police [pə'li:s] Polizei *f*; **~man** Polizist *m*; **~officer** Polizeibeamte *m*, Polizist *m*; **~station** Polizeiwache *f*, -revier *n*; **~woman** Polizistin *f*.

policy ['pɔlisi] Politik *f*; Police *f*.

polio ['pəuliəu] spinale Kinderlähmung *f*.

Polish ['pəuliʃ] polnisch; Polnisch *n*.

polish ['pɔliʃ] Politur *f*; Schuhcreme *f*; *fig.* Schliff *m*; polieren; *Schuhe* putzen.

polite [pə'lait] höflich; **~ness** Höflichkeit *f*.

politic|al [pə'litikəl] politisch; **~ian** [pɔli'tiʃən]

Politiker *m*; ~s ['politiks] *sg*, *pl* Politik *f*.

poll [pəul] Umfrage *f*; *pol.* Wahl *f*; **go to the ~s** zur Wahl(urne) gehen. [*m*.)

pollen['pɔlin]Blütenstaub)

pollut|e [pə'luːt] beschmutzen, verunreinigen; **~ion**Verschmutzung *f*.

pomp [pɔmp] Pomp *m*; **~ous** pompös; aufgeblasen; schwülstig.

pond [pɔnd] Teich *m*, Weiher *m*.

ponder ['pɔndə] nachdenken (über); **~ous** schwer (-fällig).

pony ['pəuni] Pony *n*.

poodle ['puːdl] Pudel *m*.

pool [puːl] Teich *m*; Pfütze *f*, Lache *f*; (Schwimm)Becken *n*; (Spiel)Einsatz *m*; (Fußball)Toto *n*.

poor [puə] arm(selig); dürftig; *fig.* schlecht; *sub:* **the ~** *pl* die Armen *pl*; **~ly** kränklich; arm(selig), dürftig.

pop [pɔp] knallen (lassen); *Am.* Mais rösten; schnell *wohin* tun *od.* stecken; **~ in** vorbeikommen (*Besuch*); **~ out** hervorschießen; *sub:* Knall *m*; *colloq.* Schlager *m*; Schlager...

pope [pəup] Papst *m*.

poplar ['pɔplə] Pappel *f*.

poppy ['pɔpi] Mohn *m*.

popul|ar ['pɔpjulə] Volks...; volkstümlich; populär, beliebt; **~arity** [~'læriti] Popularität *f*;

~ate ['~eit] bevölkern; **~ation** Bevölkerung *f*; **~ous** dicht besiedelt.

porch [pɔːtʃ] Vorhalle *f*, Portal *n*; *Am.* Veranda *f*.

porcupine ['pɔːkjupain] Stachelschwein *n*.

pore [pɔː] Pore *f*; **~ over** *et.* eifrig studieren.

pork [pɔːk] Schweinefleisch *n*.

porous ['pɔːrəs] porös.

porpoise ['pɔːpəs] Tümmler *m*; [brei *m.*)

porridge ['pɔridʒ]Hafer-)

port [pɔːt] Hafen(stadt *f*) *m*; *mar.* Backbord *n*; Portwein *m*.

portable ['pɔːtəbl] transportabel; tragbar.

porter ['pɔːtə] Pförtner *m*, Portier *m*; (Gepäck)Träger *m*; Porter(bier *n*) *m*.

portion ['pɔːʃən] (An)Teil *m*; Portion *f* (*Essen*); Erbteil *n*; **~** out austeilen.

portly ['pɔːtli] stattlich.

portrait ['pɔːtrit] Porträt *n*, Bild(nis) *n*.

pose [pəuz] Pose *f*; Modell stehen; posieren.

posh [pɔʃ] *colloq.* schick.

position [pə'ziʃən] Position *f*; Lage *f*; (*fig.* Ein-) Stellung *f*; Stand(punkt) *m*.

positive ['pɔzitiv] bestimmt; sicher; *phot.* Positiv *n*.

possess [pə'zes] besitzen; beherrschen; **~ed** besessen; **~ion** Besitz *m*; **~ive** *gr.* possessiv, besitzanzeigend; **~or** Besitzer(in).

power

possib|ility [pɔsə'biliti] Möglichkeit f; **~le** [''pɔsəbl] möglich; **~ly** möglich(er-weise), vielleicht.

post [pəust] Pfosten m; Posten m; (An)Stellung f, Amt n; Post f; Plakat etc. anschlagen; postieren; Brief etc. einstecken, ab-schicken, aufgeben; **~age** Porto n; **~age stamp** Briefmarke f; **~al card** Postkarte f; **~al order** Postanweisung f; **~box** Briefkasten m; **~card** Post-karte f; **~code** Postleitzahl f.

poster ['pəustə] Plakat n.

poste restante ['pəust 'restɑ̃:nt] postlagernd.

posterity [pɔs'teriti] Nach-welt f; Nachkommen pl.

post-free portofrei.

posthumous ['pɔstjuməs] post(h)um.

post|man Briefträger m, Postbote m; **~mark** Post-stempel m; (ab)stempeln; **~master** Postmeister m; **~ office** Post(amt n) f; **~-office box** Postfach n; **~-paid** frankiert.

postpone [pəust'pəun] ver-, aufschieben.

postscript ['pəusskript] Postskriptum n.

posture ['pɔstʃə] (Körper-) Haltung f, Stellung f.

post-war ['pəust'wɔ:] Nachkriegs...

posy ['pəuzi] Blumenstrauß m, Sträußchen n.

pot [pɔt] Topf m; Kanne f; einmachen; eintopfen.

potato [pə'teitəu], pl **~es** Kartoffel f; **~es** pl (boiled) in their jackets Pell-kartoffeln pl.

potent ['pəutənt] stark.

potion ['pəuʃən] (Arznei-, Gift-, Zauber)Trank m.

potter[1] ['pɔtə]: **~ about** herumwerkeln, -hantieren.

potter[2] Töpfer m; **~y** Töpferei f; Töpferware(n pl) f, Steingut n.

pouch [pautʃ] Beutel m; Tasche f.

poulterer ['pəultərə] Ge-flügelhändler m.

poultice ['pəultis] Brei-umschlag m, -packung f.

poultry ['pəultri] Geflügel n. **~en (on** auf.)

pounce [pauns] sich stür-f

pound [paund] Pfund n; **~ (sterling)** Pfund n (Sterling) (abbr. £); häm-mern, trommeln; (zer-) stampfen.

pour [pɔ:] strömen, rin-nen; gießen, schütten; **~ (out)** Getränk eingießen.

pout [paut] Lippen auf-werfen; fig. schmollen.

poverty ['pɔvəti] Armut f.

powder ['paudə] Pulver n; Puder m; pulverisieren; (sich) pudern; **~-room** Damentoilette f.

power ['pauə] Kraft f; Macht f; Gewalt f; jur. Vollmacht f; math. Potenz f; **~ful** mächtig, stark, kräftig; wirksam; **~less** macht-, kraftlos; **~-plant**, **~-station** Kraftwerk n.

practi|cable ['præktikəbl] durchführbar; begeh-, befahrbar; **~cal** praktisch; **~ce** [_tis] Praxis f; Gewohnheit f; Übung f; Ge Am., ~se ausüben, tätig sein als; (sich) üben; **~tioner** [_'tiʃnə]: **general ~** praktischer Arzt.

prairie ['prɛəri] Prärie f.

praise [preiz] Lob n; loben; **~worthy** lobenswert.

pram [præm] colloq. Kinderwagen m.

prance [prɑːns] sich aufbäumen, tänzeln (Pferd).

prank [præŋk] Streich m.

prattle ['prætl] plappern.

prawn [prɔːn] Garnele f.

pray [prei] beten; bitte(n); **~er** [prɛə] Gebet n; Andacht f; **~er-book** Gebetbuch n.

preach [priːtʃ] predigen; **~er** Prediger(in).

precarious [pri'kɛəriəs] unsicher, bedenklich.

precaution [pri'kɔːʃən] Vorsicht(smaßregel) f.

precede [pri(ː)'siːd] voraus-, vorangehen; **~nce** Vorrang m; **~nt** ['president] Präzedenzfall m.

precept ['priːsept] Vorschrift f, Regel f.

precinct ['priːsiŋkt] Bezirk m; Bereich m, Grenze f; pl Umgebung f.

precious ['preʃəs] kostbar; edel; colloq. äußerst.

precipice ['presipis] Abgrund m.

precipit|ate [pri'sipiteit]

(hinab)stürzen; (plötzlich) herbeiführen; [_it] überstürzt; **~ation** meteor. Niederschlag(smenge f) m; Hast f; **~ous** steil, jäh.

précis ['preisiː], pl **~** [_'siːz] (kurze) Zs.-fassung.

precis|e [pri'sais] genau; **~ion** [_'siʒən] Genauigkeit f.

precocious [pri'kouʃəs] frühreif, altklug.

preconceived ['priːkən-'siːvd] vorgefaßt.

predatory ['predətəri] räuberisch, Raub...

predecessor ['priːdisesə] Vorgänger(in).

predetermine ['priːdi-'təːmin] vorherbestimmen.

predicament [pri'dikəmənt] (mißliche) Lage.

predicate ['predikit] gr. Prädikat n, Satzaussage f.

predict [pri'dikt] vorhersagen; **~ion** Vorhersage f.

predisposition ['priːdispə'ziʃən] Neigung f, Anfälligkeit f.

predomina|nt [pri'dominant] vorherrschend; **~te** [_eit] vorherrschen.

preface ['prefis] Vorwort n.

prefect ['priːfekt] Vertrauens-, Aufsichtsschüler m.

prefer [pri'fəː] vorziehen, bevorzugen, lieber haben od. tun; **~able** ['prefərəbl]: **~ (to)** vorzuziehen(d) (dat); **~ably** vorzugsweise, lieber; **~ence** ['prefərəns] Vorliebe f; Vorzug m;

~ment [pri'fə:mənt] Beförderung f.

prefix [pri'fiks] ling. Präfix n, Vorsilbe f.

pregnan|cy [pregnənsi] Schwangerschaft f; **~t** schwanger.

prejudice ['predʒudis] Vorurteil n; **~** mit **~** im Vorurteil erfüllen; beeinträchtigen, benachteiligen; **~d** (vor)eingenommen.

preliminary [pri'liminəri] vorläufig; einleitend.

prelude ['prelju:d] Vorspiel n.

premature [premə'tjuə] vorzeitig, Früh...; vorschnell.

premeditate [pri(:)'mediteit] vorher überlegen.

premier ['premjə] Premierminister m.

premises ['premisiz] pl Anwesen n; Lokal n.

premium ['pri:mjəm] Prämie f; (Versicherungs-) Prämie f.

preoccupied [pri(:)'ɔkjupaid] beschäftigt; vertieft.

prepar|ation [prepə'reiʃən] Vorbereitung f; Zubereitung f; **make ~ations** Vorbereitungen treffen; **~e** [pri'pεə] (sich) vorbereiten; bereiten.

prepay ['pri:'pei] (irr **pay**) vorausbezahlen; frankieren.

preposition [prepə'ziʃən] gr. Präposition f, Verhältniswort n.

prepossess [pri:pə'zes] günstig stimmen, einneh-

men; **~ing** einnehmend, anziehend.

preposterous [pri'pɔstərəs] absurd; lächerlich.

prescri|be [pris'kraib] vorschreiben; med. verschreiben; **~ption** [~'kripʃən] med. Rezept n.

presence ['prezns] Gegenwart f; Anwesenheit f; **~ of mind** Geistesgegenwart f.

present¹ ['preznt] gegenwärtig; jetzig; anwesend, vorhanden; Gegenwart f; Geschenk n; gr. s. **present tense; at ~** jetzt.

present² [pri'zent] (j-n be)schenken; (über)reichen; (vor)zeigen; präsentieren.

presentation [prezen'teiʃən] Vorstellung f; Überreichung f; Schenkung f; Darbietung f; Vorzeigen n.

presentiment [pri'zentimənt] (mst böse Vor-) Ahnung.

presently ['prezntli] bald; Am. zur Zeit, jetzt.

present| perfect gr. Perfekt n, 2. Vergangenheit; **~ tense** gr. Präsens n, Gegenwart f.

preserv|ation [prezə(:)-'veiʃən] Bewahrung f; Erhaltung f; **~e** [pri'zə:v] bewahren, behüten; erhalten; konservieren; einkochen, -machen; pl Eingemachte n.

preside [pri'zaid] den Vorsitz haben od. führen.

president ['prezidənt] Präsident(in).

press [pres] (*Hände*)Druck *m*; (*Wein- etc.*)Presse *f*; (*Drucker*)Presse *f*; Druckerei *f*; Druck *m* (*an*) *fig.* Druck *m*; **the ~** die Presse (*Zeitungswesen*); (aus)pressen; drücken (auf); plätten, bügeln; (be)drängen; sich drängen; **~for** dringen auf, fordern; **~ing** dringend; **~ure** ['~ʃə] Druck *m*.

prestige [pres'ti:ʒ] Prestige *n*.

presum|able [pri'zju:məbl] vermutlich; **~e** annehmen, vermuten; sich *et.* herausnehmen, sich anmaßen; **~ing** anmaßend.

presumpt|ion [pri'zʌmpʃən] Vermutung *f*; Anmaßung *f*; **~uous** [~tjuəs] anmaßend.

presuppose [pri:sə'pəuz] voraussetzen.

preten|ce, *Am.* **~se** [pri'tens] Vorwand *m*; Anspruch *m*; **~d** vorgeben, vortäuschen, so tun als ob; Anspruch erheben (**to** auf); **~der** (Thron)Prätendent *m*; **~sion** Anspruch *m* (**to** auf); *pl* Ambitionen *pl*.

preterit(e) (tense) ['pretərit] *gr.* Präteritum *n*, 1. Vergangenheit.

pretext ['pri:tekst] Vorwand *m*.

pretty ['priti] hübsch, niedlich; schön; ziemlich.

prev|ail [pri'veil] (vor-)herrschen; **~alent** ['prevələnt] vorherrschend.

prevent [pri'vent] verhindern; *j-n* hindern; **~ion** Verhütung *f*; **~ive** vorbeugend.

previous ['pri:vjəs] vorhergehend, Vor...; **~ to** bevor, vor; **~ly** vorher.

pre-war ['pri:'wɔ:] Vorkriegs...

prey [prei] Raub *m*, Beute *f*; **bird of ~** Raubvogel *m*.

price [prais] Preis *m*; *Waren* auszeichnen; **~less** unschätzbar, unbezahlbar.

prick [prik] Stich *m*; (durch)stechen; **~ up one's ears** die Ohren spitzen; **~le** Stachel *m*, Dorn *m*; **~ly** stach(e)lig.

pride [praid] Stolz *m*, Hochmut *m*.

priest [pri:st] Priester *m*.

primar|ily ['praimərili] in erster Linie; **~y** ursprünglich; hauptsächlich; grundlegend, Grund...; **~y school** Grundschule *f*.

prime [praim] erst, wichtigst, Haupt...; erstklassig; *fig.* Blüte(zeit) *f*; **~ minister** Premierminister *m*, Ministerpräsident *m*; **~r** Elementarbuch *n*.

primitive ['primitiv] erst, Ur...; primitiv.

primrose ['primrəuz] Primel *f*, Schlüsselblume *f*.

prince [prins] Fürst *m*; Prinz *m*; **~ss** [~'ses, *attr*

'~ses] Fürstin f; Prinzessin f.

principal ['prinsəpəl] erst, hauptsächlich, Haupt...; (Schul)Direktor m, Rektor m; (Grund)Kapital n.

principality [prinsi'pæliti] Fürstentum n.

principle ['prinsəpl] Prinzip n, Grundsatz m; **on ~ aus Prinzip.**

print [print] (Ab)Druck m; bedruckter Kattun; Druck m, Stich m; phot. Abzug m; **out of ~** vergriffen; (ab-, auf-, be)drucken; in Druckbuchstaben schreiben; ~ **(off)** phot. abziehen; **~ed matter** Drucksache f; **~er** (Buch- etc.) Drucker m; **~ing-ink** Druckerschwärze f; **~ing office** (Buch)Druckerei f.

prior ['praiə] früher, älter (**to** als); ~ **to** vor; **~ity** [~'ɔriti] Priorität f, Vorrang m.

prison ['prizn] Gefängnis n; **~er** Gefangene m, f, Häftling m; **take s.o. ~er** j-n gefangennehmen.

privacy ['privəsi] Zurückgezogenheit f; Privatleben n.

private ['praivit] privat, Privat...; persönlich; vertraulich; geheim; (gemeiner) Soldat; ~ **hotel** Hotelpension f.

privation [prai'veiʃən] Not f, Entbehrung f.

privilege ['priviliʤ] Privileg n; **~d** privilegiert.

prize [praiz] (Sieges)Preis m, Prämie f; (Lotterie-) Gewinn m; preisgekrönt; Preis...; (hoch)schätzen; **~ winner** Preisträger(in).

pro- [prau-] für, pro...

probability [prɔbə'biliti] Wahrscheinlichkeit f; **~le** ['~əbl] wahrscheinlich.

probation [prə'beiʃən] Probe(zeit) f; jur. Bewährungsfrist f.

probe [prəub] Sonde f; sondieren; untersuchen.

problem ['prɔbləm] Problem n; math. Aufgabe f.

procedure [prə'si:dʒə] Verfahren n.

proceed [prə'si:d] fortfahren; sich begeben (**to** nach); ~ **from** ausgehen von; **~ings** pl jur. Verfahren n; **~s** ['prausi:dz] pl Erlös m.

process ['prauses] Fortgang m; Vorgang m; Prozeß m; Verfahren n; bearbeiten; **~ion** [prə'seʃən] Prozession f.

procla|im [prə'kleim] proklamieren, ausrufen; **~mation** [prɔklə'meiʃən] Proklamation f, Bekanntmachung f.

procure [prə'kjuə] be-, verschaffen.

prodig|ious [prə'didʒəs] ungeheuer; **~y** ['prɔdidʒi] Wunder n (a. Person); mst **infant ~y** Wunderkind n.

produce [prə'dju:s] produzieren; erzeugen, herstellen; hervorbringen;

(vor)zeigen; *fig.* hervor-rufen; ['prɔdjuːs] (Natur-)Produkte *pl*; **~r** [prə'djuː-sə] Hersteller *m*; *Film*, *thea.*: Produzent *m*.

product ['prɔdʌkt] Produkt *n*, Erzeugnis *n*; **~ion** [prə'dʌkʃən] Produktion *f*, Erzeugung *f*, Herstellung *f*; Erzeugnis *n*; Vorlegen *n*; *thea.* Inszenierung *f*; **~ive** [prə'dʌktiv] produktiv, fruchtbar.

profess [prə'fes] (sich) bekennen (zu); erklären; **~ed** erklärt; **~ion** Beruf *m*; Beteuerung *f*; **~ional** Berufs..., beruflich; Berufssportler(in), -spieler(in), Profi *m*; *or* Professor(in) *f*.

proficien|cy [prə'fiʃənsi] Können *n*, Tüchtigkeit *f*; **~t** tüchtig, erfahren.

profile ['prəufail] Profil *n*.

profit ['prɔfit] Nutzen *m*, Gewinn *m*, Profit *m*; *j-m* nützen; **~ by** Nutzen ziehen aus; **~able** gewinnbringend; [gründlich].

profound [prə'faund] tief; **profusion** [prə'fjuːʒən] (Über)Fülle *f*, Überfluß *m*.

prognos|is [prɔg'nəusis], *pl* **~es** [~siːz] Prognose *f*.

program(me) ['prəugræm] Programm *n*; *Radio*: *a.* Sendung *f*.

progress ['prəugres] Fortschritt(e *pl*) *m*; [~'gres] fortschreiten; **~ive** progressiv; fortschreitend; fortschrittlich.

prohibit [prə'hibit] ver-

bieten; **~ion** [prəui'biʃən] Verbot *n*; Prohibition *f*.

project ['prɔdʒekt] Projekt *n*, Vorhaben *n*; [prə-'dʒekt] planen, entwerfen; projizieren; vorstehen; *arch.* Vorsprung *m*; Projektion *f*; **~or** Projektor *m*.

pro|logue, *Am. a.* **~log** ['prəulɔg] Prolog *m*.

prolong [prəu'lɔŋ] verlängern, (aus)dehnen.

promenade [prɔmi'nɑːd, *attr* '~] (Strand)Promenade *f*.

prominent ['prɔminənt] vorstehend; prominent.

promis|e ['prɔmis] Versprechen *n*; versprechen; **~ing** vielversprechend.

promontory ['prɔməntri] Vorgebirge *n*.

promo|te [prə'məut] (be-)fördern; *Am. ped.* versetzen; **~ter** Förderer *m*; **~tion** (Be)Förderung *f*.

prompt [prɔmpt] schnell; bereit; pünktlich; *j-n* veranlassen; *thea.* soufflieren; **~er** Souffleur *m*, -se *f*.

prong [prɔŋ] Zinke *f*.

pronoun ['prəunaun] *gr.* Pronomen *n*, Fürwort *n*.

pron|ounce [prə'nauns] aussprechen; **~unciation** [~nansi'eiʃən] Aussprache *f*.

proof [pruːf] Beweis *m*; Probe *f*, Korrekturfahne *f*; *print.*, *phot.* Probeabzug *m*; fest, (*wasser*)dicht, (*kugel*)sicher.

prop [prɔp]: ~ **(up)** (ab-) stützen.

propaga|te ['prɔpəgeit] (sich) fortpflanzen; verbreiten; ~**tion** Fortpflanzung *f*; Verbreitung *f*.

propel [prə'pel] (an-, vorwärts)treiben; ~**ler** Propeller *m*.

proper ['prɔpə] eigen (-tümlich); passend; richtig; anständig, korrekt; *colloq.* ordentlich, gehörig; ~**ty** Eigentum *n*, (Grund-) Besitz *m*; Eigenschaft *f*.

prophe|cy ['prɔfisi] Prophezeiung *f*; ~**sy** ['~ai] prophezeien; ~**t** Prophet *m*.

proportion [prə'pɔ:ʃən] Verhältnis *n*; *pl* (Aus-) Maße *pl*; ~**al** angemessen.

propos|al [prə'pəuzəl] Vorschlag *m*, Angebot *n*; (Heirats)Antrag *m*; ~**e** vorschlagen; e-n Heiratsantrag machen (**to** *dat*); ~**ition** [prɔpə'ziʃən] Vorschlag *m*; Behauptung *f*.

propriet|ary [prə'praiətəri] gesetzlich geschützt (*Ware*); ~**or** Eigentümer *m*.

propulsion [prə'pʌlʃən] Antrieb *m*.

prose [prəuz] Prosa *f*.

prosecut|e ['prɔsikju:t] verfolgen; ~**ion** Verfolgung *f*; ~**or** (An)Kläger *m*.

prospect ['prɔspekt] Aussicht *f* (*a. fig.*); [prə'spekt] *min.* schürfen *od.* bohren (**for** nach); ~**ive** [prə-'spektiv] (zu)künftig; ~**us**

[prə'spektəs] (Werbe)Prospekt *m*.

prosper ['prɔspə] Erfolg haben, blühen; (*~*periti) Wohlstand *m*; ~**ous** ['~pərəs] erfolgreich; wohlhabend.

prostitute ['prɔstitju:t] Prostituierte *f*, Dirne *f*.

prostrate ['prɔstreit] hingestreckt; *fig.:* erschöpft, daniederliegend; gebrochen.

protect [prə'tekt] (be-) schützen (**from** vor); ~**ion** Schutz *m*; ~**ive** (be)schützend, Schutz...; ~**or** Beschützer *m*.

protest ['prəutest] Protest *m*; [prə'test] protestieren; beteuern; **∑ant** ['prɔtistənt] protestantisch; Protestant(in); ~**ation** [prəutes'teiʃən] Beteuerung *f*.

protract [prə'trækt] in die Länge ziehen, hinziehen.

protrude [prə'tru:d] (her-) vorstehen; herausstrecken.

proud [praud] stolz (**of** auf).

prove [pru:v] be-, nachweisen; sich herausstellen *od.* erweisen (**to** zu).

proverb ['prɔvə:b] Sprichwort *n*; ~**ial** [prə'və:bjəl] sprichwörtlich.

provide [prə'vaid] versehen, -sorgen; verschaffen, besorgen; ~ **for** sorgen; ~**d** (**that**) vorausgesetzt, daß.

providence ['prɔvidəns] Vorsorge *f*; Vorsehung *f*.

provinc|e ['prɒvins] Provinz f; fig. Gebiet n; **~ial** [prə'vinʃəl]Provinz...;provinziell; kleinstädtisch.

provision [prə'viʒən] Vorkehrung f; jur. Bestimmung f; jur. Bedingung f; pl (Lebensmittel)Vorrat m, Lebensmittel pl, Proviant m; **~al** provisorisch.

provo|cation [prɒvə'keiʃən] Herausforderung f; **~cative** [prə'vɒkətiv] herausfordernd; **~ke** [prə-'vəuk] j-n reizen; bewegen, herausfordern; et. hervorrufen.

prowl [praul] herumschleichen; durchstreifen.

proxy ['prɒksi] Stellvertreter m; Vollmacht f.

prud|e [pru:d] Prüde f; **~ence** Klugheit f; Vorsicht f; **~ent** klug; vorsichtig; **~ish** prüde, zimperlich.

prune [pru:n] Backpflaume f; *Bäume etc.* beschneiden.

psalm [sa:m] Psalm m.

pseudonym ['psju:dənim] Pseudonym n, Deckname m.

psychiatr|ist [sai'kaiətrist] Psychiater m; **~y** Psychiatrie f.

psycholog|ical [saikə-'lɒdʒikəl] psychologisch; **~ist** [~'kɒlədʒist] Psychologe m, -in f; **~y** [~'kɒlədʒi] Psychologie f.

pub [pʌb] colloq. Kneipe f.

puberty ['pju:bəti] Pubertät f.

public ['pʌblik] öffentlich;

staatlich, Staats...; Volks-..., allgemein bekannt; das Publikum; Öffentlichkeit f; **in ~** öffentlich; **~ation** Bekanntmachung f; Veröffentlichung f; **~ house** Wirtshaus n; **~ity** [~'lisiti] Öffentlichkeit f; Reklame f, Werbung f; **~ school** Public School f.

publish ['pʌbliʃ] veröffentlichen; *Buch etc.* herausgeben, verlegen; **~er** Herausgeber m, Verleger m; **~ing house** Verlag m.

pudding ['pudiŋ] Pudding m, Süßspeise f.

puddle ['pʌdl] Pfütze f.

puff [pʌf] Zug m (*beim Rauchen*); (Dampf-, Rauch-) Wölkchen f; Puderquaste f; schnaufen, keuchen; (auf)blasen; pusten; paffen; **~ paste** Blätterteig m; **~y** kurzatmig; (an)geschwollen.

pull [pul] Zug m; Ruck m; ziehen; zerren; reißen; zupfen; rudern; **~ down** ab-, niederreißen; **~ in** einfahren (*Zug*); **~ out** hinaus-, abfahren (*Zug*); ausscheren (*Auto*); **~ o.s. together** sich zs.-nehmen; **~ up** Auto anhalten; (an)halten.

pulley ['puli] tech.: Rolle f; Flaschenzug m.

pullover ['puləuvə] Pullover m.

pulp [pʌlp] Brei m; Fruchtfleisch n.

pulpit ['pulpit] Kanzel f.

pulpy ['pʌlpi] breiig; fleischig.

puls|ate [pʌl'seit] pulsieren, pochen; **~e** Puls m.

pulverize ['pʌlvəraiz] pulverisieren, zermahlen.

pump [pʌmp] Pumpe f; Pumps m; pumpen; **j-n** aushorchen; **~ attendant** Tankwart m.

pumpkin ['pʌmpkin] Kürbis m.

pun [pʌn] Wortspiel n.

punch [pʌntʃ] (Faust-) Schlag m; Lochzange f; Locher m; Punsch m; schlagen (*mit der Faust*), boxen; (ein)hämmern auf; (aus)stanzen; lochen.

Punch [pʌntʃ] Kasperle n, m, Hanswurst m; **~ and Judy show** ['dʒuːdi] Kasperletheater n.

punctual ['pʌŋktjuəl] pünktlich.

punctuat|e ['pʌŋktjueit] interpunktieren; **~ion** Interpunktion f, Zeichensetzung f; **~ion mark** Satzzeichen n.

puncture ['pʌŋktʃə] (Ein-) Stich m; Reifenpanne f.

pungent ['pʌndʒənt] scharf, stechend, beißend.

punish ['pʌnɪʃ] (be)strafen; **~ment** Strafe f; Bestrafung f.

pupil ['pjuːpl] Pupille f; Schüler(in); Mündel m, n.

puppet ['pʌpit] Marionette f, Puppe f; **~-play**, **~-show** Puppenspiel n.

puppy ['pʌpi] Welpe m, junger Hund.

purchase ['pəːtʃəs] (An-, Ein)Kauf m; Anschaffung f; (er)kaufen; **~r** Käufer(in).

pure [pjuə] rein; **~bred** Am. reinrassig.

purgat|ive ['pəːgətiv] abführend; Abführmittel n; **~ory** Fegefeuer n.

purge [pəːdʒ] Abführmittel n; pol. Säuberung f; mst fig. reinigen; pol. säubern; med. abführen.

puri|fy ['pjuərifai] reinigen (a. fig.); **~ty** Reinheit f.

purloin [pəː'lɔin] stehlen.

purple ['pəːpl] purpurrot; Purpur m.

purport ['pəːpət] beabsichtigen, vorhaben; Absicht f; Zweck m; Entschlußkraft f; **on ~** absichtlich; **to no ~** vergeblich; **~ful** zielbewußt; **~less** zwecklos; ziellos; **~ly** absichtlich.

purr [pəː] schnurren (*Katze*); summen (*Motor etc.*).

purse [pəːs] Geldbeutel m; Am. Handtasche f; **~ (up)** Lippen spitzen.

pursu|e [pə'sjuː] verfolgen (a. fig.); streben nach; fortsetzen; **~er** Verfolger(in); **~it** [~uːt] Verfolgung f; Streben n (**of** nach); **~pl** Studien pl, Arbeiten pl.

purvey [pəː'vei] liefern; **~or** Lieferant m.

pus [pʌs] Eiter m.

push [puʃ] (An-, Vor)Stoß
m; Anstrengung f; Schwung
m; Tatkraft f; stoßen,
schieben, drücken, drän-
gen; (an)treiben; **along**,
~ **on** weitergehen, -fahren;
~ **on** weitermachen.

puss [pus] Katze f; Kätz-
chen n; ~y(-cat) Katze f,
Kätzchen n, Mieze f.

put [put] (*irr*) legen, setzen,
stellen, stecken, tun; bringen (*ins Bett etc.*); werfen;
Frage stellen; ausdrücken,
sagen; ~ **back** zurück-
stellen (*a. Uhr*); *fig.* aufhalten; ~ **by** Geld zurücklegen; ~ **down** hin-, niederlegen, -stellen, -setzen;
aussteigen lassen; ein-
tragen; aufschreiben; zu-
schreiben; ~ **forth** Kraft
aufbieten; Knospen etc.
treiben; ~ **forward** Uhr
vorstellen; Meinung etc.
vorbringen; ~ **in** herein-,
hineinlegen, -setzen, -stellen,
stellen, -stecken; Wort einlegen; ~ **off** auf-, verschieben; vertrösten; j-n
abbringen; ~ **on** Kleider
anziehen; Hut etc. auf-
setzen; Uhr vorstellen;
an-, einschalten; vortäu-

schen; ~ **on weight** zunehmen; ~ **out** hinaus-
legen, -setzen, -stellen;
herausstrecken; Feuer,
Licht ausmachen, (-)lö-
schen; aus der Fassung
bringen; ~ **through** *teleph.*
j-n verbinden (**to** mit); ~
together zs.-setzen; ~ **up**
hochheben, -schieben, -zie-
hen; Haar hochstecken;
Schirm aufspannen; auf-
stellen, errichten; Gast
unterbringen; Widerstand
leisten; Ware anbieten;
Preis erhöhen; ~ **up at**
absteigen *od.* einkehren
in; ~ **up with** sich abfinden mit.

putr|efy ['pju:trifai] (ver-)
faulen; ~id ['ˌid] faul,
verdorben.

putty ['pʌti] Kitt m; ~ (up)
(ver)kitten.

puzzle ['pʌzl] Rätsel n;
Geduld(s)spiel n; kniffliges
Problem; Verwirrung f;
verwirren; j-m Kopfzer-
brechen machen; sich den
Kopf zerbrechen.

pyjamas [pə'dʒɑ:məz] pl
Schlafanzug m.

pyramid ['pirəmid] Pyra-
mide f.

Q

quack [kwæk] quaken;
Quaken n; ~ (**doctor**)
Quacksalber m.

quadrangle ['kwɔdræŋgl]
Viereck n; Innenhof m.

quadrup|ed ['kwɔdruped]

Vierfüßer m; ~le vierfach;
(sich) vervierfachen; ~lets
['ˌlits] pl Vierlinge pl.

quail [kweil] Wachtel f.

quaint [kweint] wunder-
lich, drollig; anheimelnd.

quake [kweik] beben, zittern; Erdbeben n.

quali|fication [kwɔlifi'keiʃən] Qualifikation f, Befähigung f; Einschränkung f; **~fied** ['~faid] qualifiziert, befähigt; eingeschränkt, bedingt; **~fy** ['~fai] (sich) qualifizieren; befähigen; einschränken; mildern; **~ty** Qualität f; Eigenschaft f.

qualm [kwɑ:m] Übelkeit f; pl Bedenken pl.

quandary ['kwɔndəri] verzwickte Lage, Verlegenheit f.

quantity ['kwɔntiti] Quantität f, Menge f.

quarantine ['kwɔrənti:n] Quarantäne f; unter Quarantäne stellen.

quarrel ['kwɔrəl] Streit m; (sich) streiten; **~some** zänkisch.

quarry ['kwɔri] Steinbruch m; (Jagd)Beute f.

quarter ['kwɔ:tə] vierteln, vierteilig; in vier einquartieren; Viertel n; Viertelpfund n; Viertelzentner m; Am. Vierteldollar m; Quartal n; (Stadt)Viertel n; Gegend f, Richtung f; pl Quartier n (a. mil.); pl fig. Kreise pl; **a ~ (of an hour)** e-e Viertelstunde; **a ~ to** od. **past** Uhrzeit: (ein) Viertel vor od. nach; Vierteljahrsschrift f.

quartet(te) [kwɔ:'tet] mus. Quartett n.

quarto ['kwɔ:təu] Quartformat n.

quaver ['kweivə] zittern.

quay [ki:] Kai m.

queen [kwi:n] Königin f; **~ bee** Bienenkönigin f.

queer [kwiə] sonderbar, seltsam; wunderlich.

quench [kwentʃ] Flammen, Durst löschen; Hoffnung zunichte machen.

querulous ['kwerulə s] quengelig, verdrossen.

query ['kwiəri] Frage(zeichen n) f; (be)fragen; (be-, an)zweifeln.

quest [kwest] Suche f.

question ['kwestʃən] (be-)fragen; jur. vernehmen, -hören; et. bezweifeln; Frage f; Problem n; **in ~** fraglich; **that is out of the ~** das kommt nicht in Frage; **~able** fraglich; fragwürdig; **~mark** Fragezeichen n; **~naire** [~stiə'nɛə] Fragebogen m.

queue [kju:] Schlange f, Reihe f; **~ up** anstehen, Schlange stehen, sich anstellen.

quick [kwik] schnell; rasch; flink; aufgeweckt; lebhaft; aufbrausend; scharf (Auge, Gehör); **be ~** beeil dich!; **~en** (sich) beschleunigen; anregen; **~ly** schnell; **~ness** Schnelligkeit f; (geistige) Gewandtheit f; Schärfe f (Gehör etc.); Lebhaftigkeit f; **~sand** Treibsand m; **~silver** Quecksilber n;

witted schlagfertig, aufgeweckt.

quid [kwid] *sg, pl* sl. Pfund *n* (Sterling).

quiet ['kwaiət] ruhig, still; leise; Ruhe *f*; beruhigen; **~ down** sich beruhigen; **~ness, ~ude** ['~itju:d] Ruhe *f*, Stille *f*.

quill [kwil] Federkiel *m*; Stachel *m* (*des Stachelschweins*); **~(-feather)** Schwung-, Schwanzfeder *f*.

quilt [kwilt] Steppdecke *f*.

quince [kwins] Quitte *f*.

quinine [kwi'ni:n, *Am.* 'kwainain] Chinin *n*.

quintal ['kwintl] Doppelzentner *m*.

quintuple ['kwintjupl] fünffach; (sich) verfünffachen; **~ts** ['~lits] *pl* Fünflinge *pl*.

quit [kwit] frei; verlassen;

aufgeben; *Am.* aufhören mit; aufhören; ausziehen; **give notice to ~** kündigen.

quite [kwait] ganz, völlig; ziemlich, recht; wirklich; ganz; **~ (so)!** ganz recht.

quiver ['kwivə] zittern, beben; Zittern *n*; Köcher *m*.

quiz [kwiz] Prüfung *f*, Test *m*; Quiz *n*; ausfragen; *j-n* prüfen.

quota ['kwoutə] Quote *f*; Kontingent *n*.

quotation [kwou'teiʃən] Zitat *n*; (Börsen-, Kurs-) Notierung *f*; **~ marks** *pl* Anführungszeichen *pl*.

quote [kwout] zitieren, anführen; Preis berechnen; *Börse*: notieren.

quotient ['kwouʃənt] Quotient *m*.

R

rabbi ['ræbai] Rabbi *m*; Rabbiner *m*.

rabbit ['ræbit] Kaninchen *n*. [Pöbel *m*.\]

rabble ['ræbl] Mob *m*, \

rabid ['ræbid] wütend; tollwütig (*Tier*); **~es** ['rei-bi:z] Tollwut *f*.

raccoon [rə'ku:n] *s.* **racoon.**

race [reis] Geschlecht *n*; Rasse *f*; Volk *n*, Nation *f*; (Wett)Rennen *n*, Lauf *m*; Renn...; *fig.* Wettlauf *m*; **the ~s** *pl* das Pferderennen; rennen, rasen; um die

Wette laufen *od.* fahren (mit); **~r** Rennpferd *n*, -boot *n*, -wagen *m*.

racial ['reiʃəl] Rassen...

racing ['reisiŋ] (Pferde-) Rennsport *m*; Renn...

rack [ræk] Gestell *n*; (*Kleider- etc.*)Ständer *m*; (Gepäck)Netz *n*; (Futter-) Raufe *f*; *fig.* quälen; **one's brains** sich den Kopf zermartern.

racket ['rækit] (Tennis-) Schläger *m*; Lärm *m*; Trubel *m*; *colloq.* Schwindel *m*.

racoon [rəˈkuːn] Waschbär *m*.

racy [ˈreisi] kraftvoll, lebendig; rassig; würzig.

radar [ˈreidə] Radar(gerät) *n*.

radia|nce [ˈreidjəns] Strahlen *n*; ~**nt** strahlend; ~**te** [~ˌieit] (aus)strahlen; ~**tion** (Aus)Strahlung *f*; ~**tor** Heizkörper *m*; *mar.* Kühler *m*.

radical [ˈrædikəl] *bot., math.* Wurzel...; radikal; *pol.* Radikale *m, f*.

radio [ˈreidiou] funken, senden; Funk(spruch) *m*; Radio *n*, Rundfunk *m*; Radiogerät *n*; Funk...; **by** ~ über Funk; ~**active** radioaktiv; ~**set** Radiogerät *n*; ~**therapy** Strahlentherapie *f*.

radish [ˈrædiʃ] Rettich *m*; Radieschen *n*.

radius [ˈreidjəs] Radius *m*.

raffle [ˈræfl] Tombola *f*, Verlosung *f*; verlosen.

raft [rɑːft] Floß *n*; ~**er** (Dach)Sparren *m*.

rag [ræg] Lumpen *m*.

rage [reidʒ] toben, rasen; Wut(anfall *m*) *f*, Zorn *m*; Sucht *f* (**for** nach).

ragged [ˈrægid] zerlumpt; struppig, zottig; ausgefranst; zackig.

raid [reid] (feindlicher) Überfall; (Luft)Angriff *m*; Razzia *f*; einbrechen in, plündern; überfallen.

rail¹ [reil] schimpfen.

rail² (Quer)Stange *f*; Geländer *n*; *mar.* Reling *f*; **rail.** Schiene *f*; (Eisen-) Bahn *f*; *pl* Gleis *n*; **by** ~ mit der Bahn; ~ **in** *od.* **off** mit e-m Geländer umgeben *od.* abtrennen; ~**ing(s** *pl*) Geländer *n*; *mar.* Reling *f*; ~**road** *Am.*, ~**way** Eisenbahn *f*; ~**way guide** Kursbuch *n*; ~**wayman** Eisenbahner *m*.

rain [rein] Regen *m*; regnen; ~**bow** Regenbogen *m*; ~**coat** Regenmantel *m*; ~**drop** Regentropfen *m*; ~**proof** wasserdicht; *f* regnerisch, Regen...; **save for a ~y day** für Notzeiten vorsorgen.

raise [reiz] (*oft* ~ **up** auf-, hoch)heben; erheben; aufrichten; *Kinder* aufziehen; *Familie* gründen; züchten; errichten; erhöhen; *Geld* sammeln, beschaffen.

raisin [ˈreizn] Rosine *f*.

rak|e [reik] Rechen *m*, Harke *f*; Wüstling *m*, Lebemann *m*; (zs.-)rechen, (-)harken; ~**ish** schnittig; ausschweifend; *fig.* verwegen.

rally [ˈræli] Massenversammlung *f*; *mot.* Rallye *f*; (sich) sammeln *od.* scharen; sich erholen.

ram [ræm] *zo.* Widder *m*; *tech.* Ramme *f*; (fest)rammen.

ramble [ˈræmbl] Streifzug *m*; umherstreifen.

ramify [ˈræmifai] (sich) verzweigen.

ramp [ræmp] Rampe f; **~art** [´~ɑːt] Wall m.

ran [ræn] pret von **run**.

ranch [rɑːntʃ, Am. ræntʃ] Ranch f, Viehfarm f; Farm f; **~er** Rancher m, Viehzüchter m; Farmer m.

rancid [´rænsid] ranzig.

ranco(u)r [´ræŋkə] Groll m, Haß m.

random [´rændəm]: **at ~** aufs Geratewohl.

rang [ræŋ] pret von **ring**.

range [reindʒ] Reihe f; (Berg)Kette f; Herd m; Schießstand m; Entfernung f; Reichweite f; Bereich m; econ. ausgedehntes Weidegebiet; (ausgedehnte) Fläche; aufstellen; einreihen, (-)ordnen; durchstreifen; sich erstrecken, reichen; (umher)schweifen (Blick); **~r** Aufseher m e-s Forsts etc.; Am.: Förster m; Angehöriger e-r berittenen Schutztruppe.

rank [ræŋk] Reihe f; Rang m (a. mil.), Stand m; mil. Glied n; (ein)ordnen, einreihen; rechnen, zählen; e-n Rang einnehmen; gehören, zählen (**among**, **with** zu); üppig; stinkend; scharf.

ransack [´rænsæk] durchwühlen, -stöbern; plündern.

ransom [´rænsəm] Lösegeld n; Auslösung f; loskaufen, auslösen.

rap [ræp] Klopfen n;

klopfen od. pochen (an, auf). [(hab)gierig.

rapacious [rə´peiʃəs]

rape [reip] Vergewaltigung f; vergewaltigen.

rapid [´ræpid] schnell, rasch, rapid(e); steil; **~ity** [rə´piditi] Schnelligkeit f; **~s** pl Stromschnelle f.

rapt [ræpt] versunken; entzückt; **~ure** Entzücken n.

rar|e [reə] selten; colloq. ausgezeichnet; dünn (Luft); halbgar; **~ity** Seltenheit f.

rascal [´rɑːskəl] Schuft m; **~ly** schuftig.

rash[1] [ræʃ] hastig, überstürzt; unbesonnen.

rash[2] (Haut)Ausschlag m.

rasher [´ræʃə] Speckscheibe f.

rasp [rɑːsp] Raspel f; raspeln; kratzen.

raspberry [´rɑːzbəri] Himbeere f.

rat [ræt] Ratte f; **smell a ~** Lunte od. den Braten riechen; **~s!** sl. Quatsch!

rate [reit] besteuern; (ein)schätzen; rechnen, zählen (**among** zu); gelten (**as** als); (Verhältnis)Ziffer f; Rate f; Verhältnis n; (Aus)Maß n; Preis m, Betrag m; Gebühr f; (Kommunal)Steuer f; Geschwindigkeit f; Klasse f, Rang m; **at any ~** auf jeden Fall; **~ of exchange** (Umrechnungs)Kurs m; **~ of interest** Zinssatz m.

rather [´rɑːðə] eher, lieber; vielmehr, besser gesagt; ziemlich, fast.

ratify ['rætifai] bestätigen; ratifizieren.

ration ['ræʃən] Ration *f*, Zuteilung *f*; rationieren.

rational ['ræʃənl] vernünftig, rational; **~ize** ['~ʃnəlaiz] rationalisieren.

rattle ['rætl] Gerassel *n*; Geklapper *n*; Klapper *f*; rasseln (mit); klappern; rütteln (an); röcheln; **~ off** herunterrasseln; **~snake** Klapperschlange *f*.

ravage ['rævidʒ] Verwüstung *f*; verwüsten; plündern.

rave [reiv] rasen, toben; schwärmen (**about**, **of** von).

raven ['reivn] Rabe *m*.

ravenous ['rævənəs] gefräßig; heißhungrig; gierig.

ravine [rə'vi:n] Schlucht *f*, Klamm *f*, Hohlweg *m*.

ravings ['reiviŋz] *pl* irres Gerede; Delirien *pl*.

ravish ['ræviʃ] entzücken, hinreißen.

raw [rɔ:] roh; Roh...; wund; rauh (*Wetter*); unerfahren.

ray [rei] Strahl *m* (a. *fig.*).

rayon ['reiɔn] Kunstseide *f*.

razor ['reizə] Rasiermesser *n*, -apparat *m*; **~blade** Rasierklinge *f*.

re- ['ri:-] wieder, noch einmal, neu; zurück, wieder.

reach [ri:tʃ] (er)reichen;

(her)langen; sich erstrecken; **~ out** reichen, ausstrecken; Reichweite *f*; Bereich *m*; Fassungskraft *f*; **out of ~** unerreichbar; **within easy ~** leicht zu erreichen.

react [ri(:)'ækt] reagieren; einwirken; **~ion** Reaktion *f*; Rückwirkung *f*; **~ionary** [~ʃnəri] reaktionär; Reaktionär(in); **~or** (Kern-) Reaktor *m*.

read [ri:d] (*irr*) lesen; deuten; (an)zeigen (*Thermometer*); lauten; **~ to s.o.** j-m vorlesen; *pret u. pp von* **read**; **~er** (Vor)Leser(in); Lektor(in); Lesebuch *n*.

readi|ly ['redili] bereitwillig; **~ness** Bereitschaft *f*; Bereitwilligkeit *f*.

reading ['ri:diŋ] Lesen *n*; (Vor)Lesung *f*; Lektüre *f*; Lesart *f*; Auslegung *f*; Lese...

readjust ['ri:ə'dʒʌst] wieder in Ordnung bringen; wieder anpassen.

ready ['redi] bereit; fertig; im Begriff (**to do** zu tun); schnell, rasch; schlagfertig, gewandt; bar (*Geld*); **get ~** (sich) fertigmachen; **~-made** Konfektions...; **~ money** Bargeld *n*.

real [riəl] real, wirklich, tatsächlich; echt; **~ estate** Grundbesitz *m*, Immobilien *pl*; **~ism** Realismus *m*; **~istic** realistisch; **~ity** [ri(:)'æliti] Realität *f*, Wirklichkeit f; **~ization** Realisierung f (a. econ.); Verwirklichung f; Erkenntnis f; **~ize** erkennen, begreifen, einsehen; realisieren (a. econ.); verwirklichen; **~ly** wirklich, tatsächlich; **not ~ly?** nicht möglich!

realm [relm] (König-) Reich n.

realt|or ['rɪəltə] Am. Grundstücksmakler m, Immobilienhändler m; **~y** jur. Grundbesitz m.

reap [ri:p] Getreide schneiden, mähen; fig. ernten; **~er** Schnitter(in); (Getreide)Mähmaschine f.

reappear ['ri:ə'pɪə] wieder erscheinen.

rear [rɪə] auf-, großziehen; (er)heben; sich aufbäumen; Rück-, Hinterseite f; Hintergrund m; mot. Heck n; Hinter..., Rück...; **~guard** mil. Nachhut f; **~lamp, ~light** mot. Rück-, Schlußlicht n.

rearm ['ri:'ɑ:m] (wieder-) aufrüsten; **~ament** (Wieder)Aufrüstung f.

rearmost hinterst.

rear-view mirror mot. Rückspiegel m.

reason ['ri:zn] Vernunft f; Verstand m; Grund m; Ursache f; **for this ~** aus diesem Grund; vb: logisch denken; schließen; argumentieren; **~ out** (logisch) durchdenken; **~ with** gut zureden; **~able** vernünftig; billig; angemessen.

reassure [ri:ə'ʃuə] j-n beruhigen.

rebate ['ri:beit] Rabatt m.

rebel ['rebl] Rebell m, Aufständische m; aufständisch; [ri'bel] rebellieren, sich auflehnen; **~lion** [~'beljən] Rebellion f; **~lious** [~'beljəs] aufständisch; aufsässig.

re-book ['ri:'buk] umbuchen; **[rückprallen.]**

rebound [ri'baund] zu-**]**

rebuff [ri'bʌf] Abfuhr f.

rebuild ['ri:'bild] (irr build) wieder aufbauen.

rebuke [ri'bju:k] Tadel m; tadeln.

recall [ri'kɔ:l] abberufen; sich erinnern an; j-n erinnern (**to** an); widerrufen; Abberufung f; Widerruf m; **beyond ~, past ~** unwiderruflich.

recapture ['ri:'kæptʃə] wieder ergreifen; fig. wiederaufleben lassen.

recede [ri(:)'si:d] zurücktreten.

receipt [ri'si:t] Empfang m; Quittung f; pl Einnahmen pl.

receive [ri'si:v] empfangen, erhalten, bekommen; auf-, annehmen; **~r** Empfänger m; teleph. Hörer m.

recent ['ri:snt] neu, jüngst, frisch; **~ly** kürzlich, vor kurzem, neulich.

reception [ri'sepʃən] Empfang m (a. Funk); Annahme f; Aufnahme f; **~ desk** Empfangsschalter

m, Rezeption *f* (*Hotel*);
~ist Empfangsdame *f*, **-chef**
m; Sprechstundenhilfe *f*.

recess [ri:'ses] Nische *f*;
Am. (Schul)Pause *f*; **~es**
pl fig. Innere *n*; **~ion** Konjunkturrückgang *m*.

recipe ['resipi] Rezept *n*.

recipient [ri'sipiənt] Empfänger(in).

reciprocal [ri'siprəkəl]
wechsel-, gegenseitig.

recit|al [ri'saitl] Bericht
m, Erzählung *f*; *mus.*
(Solo)Vortrag *m*, Konzert
n; **~e** vortragen; aufsagen;
erzählen.

reckless ['reklis] unbekümmert; rücksichtslos.

reckon ['rekən] (be-, er-)
rechnen; halten für; **~ up**
zs.-zählen; **~ing** ['~kniŋ]
(Ab-, Be)Rechnung *f*.

reclaim [ri'kleim] zurückfordern; bekehren; urbar
machen.

recline [ri'klain] (sich)
(zurück)lehnen; liegen.

recogni|tion [rekəg'niʃən]
Anerkennung *f*; Wiedererkennen *n*; **~ze** anerkennen; (wieder)erkennen.

recoil [ri'kɔil] zurückschrecken.

recollect [rekə'lekt] sich
erinnern an; **~ion** Erinnerung *f*.

recommend [rekə'mend]
empfehlen; **~ation** Empfehlung *f*.

recompense ['rekəmpens]
entschädigen; ersetzen.

reconcil|e ['rekənsail] aus-,

versöhnen; in Einklang
bringen; **~iation** [~sili'eiʃən] Ver-, Aussöhnung *f*.

reconsider ['ri:kən'sidə]
nochmals überlegen.

reconstruct ['ri:kən'strʌkt] wieder aufbauen;
rekonstruieren; *fig.* wieder-
aufbauen; **~ion** Wiederaufbau *m*.

record ['rekɔ:d] Aufzeichnung *f*; Protokoll *n*; Urkunde *f*; Register *n*, Verzeichnis *n*; (schriftlicher)
Bericht; Ruf *m*, Leumund
m; Leistung(en *pl*) *f*;
(Schall)Platte *f*; *sp.* Rekord
m; [ri'kɔ:d] auf-, verzeichnen; *auf Schallplatte
etc.* aufnehmen; **~er** [~'k-]
Aufnahmegerät *n*; **~ing**
[~'k-] *Radio etc.* Aufzeichnung *f*, Aufnahme *f*;
~player Plattenspieler *m*.

recourse [ri'kɔ:s]: **have ~
to** s-e Zuflucht nehmen zu.

recover [ri'kʌvə] wiedererlangen, -bekommen;
bergen; wieder gesund
werden; sich erholen; *fig.*
sich fassen; **~y** Wiedererlangung *f*; Bergung *f*;
Genesung *f*, Erholung *f*.

recreation [rekri'eiʃən]
Erholung *f*.

recruit [ri'kru:t] Rekrut *m*.

rectangle ['rektæŋgl]
Rechteck *n*.

rectify ['rektifai] berichtigen; *electr.* gleichrichten.

rector ['rektə] Pfarrer *m*;
Rektor *m*; **~y** Pfarrhaus *n*.

recur [ri'kə:] wiederkeh-

ren; *fig.* zurückkommen
(**to** auf); **~rent** [ri'kΛrənt]
wiederkehrend.

red [red] rot; Rot *n*; ⚥
breast Rotkehlchen *n*; ⚥
Cross das Rote Kreuz; ⚥
deer Rothirsch *m*; **~den**
(sich) röten; erröten; **~**
dish rötlich.

redeem [ri'di:m] freikau-
fen; einlösen; erlösen; ⚥er
Erlöser *m*, Heiland *m*.

redemption [ri'dempʃən]
Einlösung *f*; Erlösung *f*.

red|-handed: catch ~
auf frischer Tat ertappen;
⚥ **Indian** Indianer(in);
~-letter day Festtag *m*;
fig. denkwürdiger Tag.

redouble [ri'dΛbl] (sich)
verdoppeln.

reduc|e [ri'dju:s] redu-
zieren; herabsetzen; ver-
ringern; ermäßigen; **~tion**
[,'dΛkʃən] Herabsetzung
f; Verringerung *f*; Er-
mäßigung *f*.

reed [ri:d] Schilfrohr *n*.

re-education ['ri:edju(:)-
'keiʃən] Umschulung *f*.

reef [ri:f] (Felsen)Riff *n*.

reek [ri:k] stinken, (unangenehm) riechen (**of** nach).

reel [ri:l] (*Garn-, Film-
etc.*) Rolle *f*, (-)Spule *f*; **~**
(**up** auf)wickeln, (-)spulen;
wirbeln; schwanken, tau-
meln.

re|-elect ['ri:i'lekt] wieder-
wählen; **~-enter** wieder
eintreten in; **~-establish**
wiederherstellen.

refer [ri'fə:]: **~ (to)** verwei-

sen (auf, an); übergeben;
zurückführen (auf); sich
beziehen (auf); konsultieren.

referee [refə'ri:] Schiedsrichter *m*; *Boxen*: Ring-
richter *m*.

reference ['refrəns] Refe-
renz *f*, Zeugnis *n*; Verweis *m*; Nachschlagen *n*;
~ book Nachschlagewerk
n; **~ library** Handbiblio-
thek *f*.

refill ['ri:fil] Ersatzfüllung
f, Nachfüllpackung *f*;
['~'fil] auf-, nachfüllen.

refine [ri'fain] raffinieren,
veredeln; (sich) läutern;
(sich) verfeinern (*a. fig.*);
fig. bilden; **~ment** Ver-
feinerung *f*; Feinheit *f*;
Bildung *f*; **~ry** Raffinerie *f*.

reflect [ri'flekt] reflektieren, zurückwerfen, (wider-)
spiegeln; nachdenken (**on,
upon** über); **~ion** Re-
flexion *f*; Reflex *m*; Spie-
gelbild *n*; Überlegung *f*.

reflex ['ri:fleks] Reflex...;
Reflex *m*.

reflexive [ri'fleksiv] *gr.* reflexiv, rückbezüglich.

reform [ri'fɔ:m] Reform *f*;
reformieren, verbessern;
(sich) bessern; **~ation**
[refə'meiʃən] Besserung *f*;
⚥ation *eccl.* Reformation
f; ⚥**er** *eccl.* Reformator *m*;
pol. Reformer *m*.

refract [ri'frækt] *Strahlen*
brechen; **~ory** widerspen-
stig; *med.* hartnäckig.

refrain [ri'frein] unterlassen (**from** acc); Refrain m.

refresh [ri'freʃ]: ~ (**o.s.** sich) erfrischen; auffrischen; ~ment Erfrischung f.

refrigerator [ri'fridʒə-reitə] Kühlschrank m; Kühl... [tanken.]

refuel [ri:'fjuəl] (auf-)]

refuge ['refju:dʒ] Zuflucht (-stätte) f; ~e [͜u(:)'dʒi:] Flüchtling m.

refund [ri:'fʌnd] zurückzahlen.

refus|al [ri'fju:zəl] Ablehnung f; (Ver)Weigerung f; ~e verweigern; abweisen; ablehnen; sich weigern; ['refju:s] Abfall m, Müll m.

refute [ri'fju:t] widerlegen.

regain [ri'gein] wiedergewinnen, -erlangen.

regard [ri'gɑ:d] Achtung f; Rücksicht f; **with** ~ **to** hinsichtlich; **kind** ~s herzliche Grüße; vb: ansehen; (be)achten; betreffen; **as** halten für; **as** ~s was ...betrifft; ~ing hinsichtlich; ~less: ~ **of** ohne Rücksicht auf. [(-in).]

regent ['ri:dʒənt] Regent f]

regiment ['redʒimənt] Regiment n.

region ['ri:dʒən] Gegend f, Gebiet n, Bereich m.

regist|er ['redʒistə] Register n (a. mus.), Verzeichnis n; (sich) eintragen (lassen), einschreiben (lassen); Gepäck aufgeben; sich (an)melden (**with** bei

der Polizei etc.); ~ered letter Einschreibebrief m; ~ration Eintragung f; Anmeldung f.

regret [ri'gret] Bedauern n; bedauern; beklagen; ~table bedauerlich.

regular ['regjulə] regelmäßig; regulär (a. mil.), normal; richtig; ~ity [~'læriti] Regelmäßigkeit f.

regulat|e ['regjuleit] regeln; regulieren; ~ion Regulierung f, pl Vorschrift f; vorgeschrieben.

rehears|al [ri'hə:səl] Probe f; ~e thea. proben; wiederholen.

reign [rein] Regierung f; Herrschaft f (a. fig.); herrschen, regieren.

rein [rein] oft pl Zügel m.

reindeer ['reindiə] sg, pl Ren(ntier) n.

reinforce [ri:in'fɔ:s] verstärken.

reject [ri'dʒekt] wegwerfen; ablehnen; ~ion Ablehnung f.

rejoic|e [ri'dʒɔis] erfreuen; sich freuen (**at** über); ~ing Freude f; pl (Freuden)Fest n.

rejoin ['ri:'dʒɔin] wieder zurückkehren zu; [ri-'dʒɔin] erwidern.

relapse [ri'læps] Rückfall m; wieder fallen (**into** in); rückfällig werden.

relate [ri'leit] erzählen; sich beziehen (**to** auf); ~d verwandt (**to** mit).

relation [ri'leiʃən] Bericht

m, Erzählung *f*; Verhältnis *n*; Verwandte *m*, *f*; *pl* Beziehungen *pl*; **in ~ to** in bezug auf; **~ship** Beziehung *f*; Verwandtschaft *f*.

relative ['relətiv] relativ; verhältnismäßig; bezüglich; Verwandte *m*, *f*; **~ (pronoun)** *gr.* Relativpronomen *n*, bezügliches Fürwort.

relax [ri'læks] lockern; (sich) entspannen.

relay [ri'lei] Relais *n*; *Radio*: Übertragung *f*; *Radio*: übertragen; **~ race** ['ri:lei] Staffellauf *m*.

release [ri'li:s] Freilassung *f*; Befreiung *f*; Freigabe *f*; *tech.*, *phot.* Auslöser *m*; freilassen; befreien; freigeben; *tech.*, *phot.* auslösen.

relent [ri'lent] sich erweichen lassen; **~less** unbarmherzig.

relevant ['relivənt] sachdienlich; zutreffend.

reliab|ility [rilaiə'biliti] Zuverlässigkeit *f*; **~le** zuverlässig.

reliance [ri'laiəns] Vertrauen *n*; Verlaß *m*.

relic ['relik] (Über)Rest *m*; Reliquie *f*.

relie|f [ri'li:f] Relief *n*; Erleichterung *f*; Abwechslung *f*; Unterstützung *f*, Hilfe *f*; Ablösung *f*; *mil.* Entsatz *m*; **~ve** [~v] erleichtern, lindern; unterstützen; ablösen; befreien; *mil.* entsetzen.

religi|on [ri'lidʒən] Religion *f*; **~ous** religiös, Religions...; gewissenhaft.

relinquish [ri'liŋkwiʃ] aufgeben; loslassen.

relish ['reliʃ] (Wohl)Geschmack *m*; *fig.* Reiz *m*; gern essen; Geschmack finden an.

reluctan|ce [ri'lʌktəns] Widerstreben *n*; **~t** widerstrebend, widerwillig.

rely [ri'lai]: **~ (up)on** sich verlassen auf.

remain [ri'mein] (übrig-)bleiben; *pl*: (Über)Reste *pl*; *die* sterblichen Überreste *pl*; **~der** Rest *m*.

remand [ri'mɑ:nd] (in die Untersuchungshaft) zurückschicken; **detention on ~** Untersuchungshaft *f*.

remark [ri'mɑ:k] Bemerkung *f*; bemerken; (sich) äußern; **~able** bemerkenswert.

remedy ['remidi] (Heil-, *jur.* Rechts)Mittel *n*; Abhilfe *f*; heilen; abhelfen.

rememb|er [ri'membə] sich erinnern an; denken an; **~er me to her** grüße sie von mir; **~rance** Erinnerung *f*; Andenken *n*.

remind [ri'maind] erinnern (**of** an); **~er** Mahnung *f*. (sich) erinnern.

reminiscent [remi'nisnt] sich erinnernd.

remiss [ri'mis] nachlässig.

remit [ri'mit] *Schuld etc.* erlassen; überweisen; **~tance** (Geld)Überweisung *f*.

remnant['remnənt](Über-)
Rest *m*.

remodel ['riː'mɔdl] um-
bilden, -formen.

remonstrate ['remən-
streit] protestieren; einwenden.

remorse [ri'mɔːs] Gewissensbisse *pl*, Reue *f*; **~less**
unbarmherzig.

remote [ri'məut] fern, ent-
legen.

remov|al [ri'muːvəl] Ent-
fernen *n*, Beseitigung *f*;
Umzug *m*; **~al van** Möbelwagen *m*; **~e** entfernen,
wegräumen; beseitigen;
(aus-, um-, ver)ziehen;
Schule: Versetzung *f*; **~er**
(*Flecken- etc.*)Entferner *m*;
(Möbel)Spediteur *m*.

Renaissance [rə'neisəns]
die Renaissance. [reißen.]

rend [rend] (*irr*) (zer-)

render ['rendə] berühmt,
möglich etc. machen; wiedergeben; *Dienst etc.* leisten; *Dank* abstatten; übersetzen; *mus.* vortragen;
thea. gestalten, interpretieren; *Rechnung* vorlegen.

renew [ri'njuː] erneuern;
~al Erneuerung *f*.

renounce [ri'nauns] entsagen; verzichten auf; verleugnen.

renovate ['renəuveit] renovieren; erneuern.

renown [ri'naun] Ruhm *m*,
Ansehen *n*; **~ed** berühmt.

rent¹ [rent] *pret u. pp von*
rend; Riß *m*; Spalte *f*.

rent² Miete *f*; Pacht *f*;

(ver)mieten; (ver)pachten.

repair [ri'pɛə] reparieren,
ausbessern; Reparatur *f*;
in good ~ in gutem Zustand; **~ shop** Reparaturwerkstatt *f*.

reparation [repə'reiʃən]
Wiedergutmachung *f*.

repartee [repɑː'tiː] schlag-
fertige Antwort.

repay [riː'pei] (*irr pay*)
zurückzahlen; *er.* vergelten.

repeat [ri'piːt] (sich) wie-
derholen.

repel [ri'pel] *Feind etc.* zurückschlagen; *fig.:* abweisen; *j~n* abstoßen.

repent [ri'pent] bereuen;
~ance Reue *f*; **~ant** reuig.

repetition [repi'tiʃən] Wie-
derholung *f*.

replace [ri'pleis] wieder
hinstellen od. -legen; ersetzen; *j~n* ablösen; **~ment**
Ersatz *m*.

replenish [ri'pleniʃ] (wieder) auffüllen, ergänzen.

reply [ri'plai]: **~ (to)** antworten (auf), erwidern
(auf); Antwort *f*.

report [ri'pɔːt] Bericht *m*;
Nachricht *f*; Gerücht *n*;
Knall *m*; (Schul)Zeugnis
n; berichten (über); (sich)
melden; anzeigen; berich-
ten; **~er** Reporter(in), Be-
richterstatter(in).

repose [ri'pəuz] Ruhe *f*;
(sich) ausruhen; ruhen.

represent [repri'zent] darstellen (*a. fig., thea.*); vertreten; *thea.* aufführen;
~ation Darstellung *f* (*a.*

thea.); Vertretung *f; thea.*
Aufführung *f;* **~ative** darstellend; (stell)vertretend;
repräsentativ; typisch; Vertreter(in); *Am. parl.* Abgeordnete *m;* **House of**
~atives *Am. parl.* Repräsentantenhaus *n.*

repress [ri'pres] unterdrücken; [Aufschub *m*].

reprieve [ri'pri:v] Frist *f.*

reprimand ['reprimɑːnd]
Verweis *m; j-m* e-n Verweis erteilen.

reproach [ri'prəutʃ] Vorwurf *m;* vorwerfen (**s.o.**
with s.th. j—m et.); Vorwürfe machen; **~ful** vorwurfsvoll.

reproduc|e [ri:prə'dju:s]
(sich) fortpflanzen; wiedergeben, reproduzieren; **~**
tion [~'dʌkʃən] Fortpflanzung *f;* Reproduktion *f.*

reproof [ri'pru:f] Vorwurf
m, Tadel *m.*

reprove [ri'pru:v] tadeln.

reptile ['reptail] Reptil *n.*

republic [ri'pʌblik] Republik *f;* **~an** republikanisch; Republikaner(in).

repugnan|ce [ri'pʌgnəns]
Widerwille *m;* **~t** widerlich.

repuls|e [ri'pʌls] Abfuhr
f, Zurückweisung *f;* zurück-, abweisen; **~ive** abstoßend, widerwärtig.

reput|able ['repjutəbl] angesehen; anständig; **~a-**
tion (guter) Ruf; **~e**
[ri'pju:t] Ruf *m.*

request [ri'kwest] Gesuch

n, Bitte *f;* Nachfrage *f;* **by**
~, on ~ auf Wunsch; *vb:*
bitten (um); ersuchen um;
~ stop Bedarfshaltestelle *f.*

require [ri'kwaiə] verlangen; (er)fordern; brauchen; **~d** erforderlich;
~ment (An)Forderung *f;*
Erfordernis *n; pl* Bedarf *m.*

requisite ['rekwizit] erforderlich; (Bedarfs-, Gebrauchs)Artikel *m.*

requite [ri'kwait] vergelten; belohnen.

rescue ['reskju:] Rettung
f; Befreiung *f;* Rettungs...;
retten; befreien.

research [ri'sə:tʃ] Forschung *f,* Untersuchung *f;*
~er Forscher *m.*

resembl|ance [ri'zembləns] Ähnlichkeit *f* (**to**
mit); **~e** gleichen, ähnlich
sein.

resent [ri'zent] übelnehmen; **~ful** übelnehmerisch;
ärgerlich; **~ment** Groll *m.*

reservation [rezə'veiʃən]
Reservierung *f,* Vorbestellung *f; Am.* (Indianer-)
Reservation *f;* Vorbehalt *m.*

reserve [ri'zə:v] Reserve *f;*
Vorrat *m;* Ersatz *m; sp.*
Ersatzmann *m;* Reservat
n; Zurückhaltung *f;* (sich)
aufsparen od. -bewahren;
(sich) zurückhalten mit;
reservieren (lassen), vorbestellen, vormerken; vorbehalten; **~d** *fig.* zurückhaltend, reserviert.

reservoir ['rezəvwɑː] Staubecken *n.*

reside [ri'zaid] wohnen, ansässig sein; ~nce ['rezidəns] Wohnsitz m; ~nce **permit** Aufenthaltsgenehmigung f; ~nt wohnhaft; Einwohner(in).

residue ['rezidju:] Rest m.

resign [ri'zain] zurücktreten; aufgeben; verzichten auf; Amt niederlegen; überlassen; ~o.s. to sich ergeben in, sich abfinden mit; ~ation [rezig'neiʃən] Verzicht m; Rücktritt (-sgesuch n) m; Resignation f; ~ed resigniert.

resin ['rezin] Harz n.

resist [ri'zist] widerstehen; Widerstand leisten; beständig sein gegen; ~ance Widerstand m; tech. Festigkeit f, Beständigkeit f; ~ant widerstehend; widerstandsfähig, beständig (to gegen).

resolut|e ['rezəlu:t] entschlossen; ~ion Entschluß m; Entschlossenheit f; Resolution f.

resolve [ri'zɔlv] auflösen; Zweifel zerstreuen; beschließen; ~(up)on sich entschließen zu; ~d entschlossen.

resonan|ce ['reznəns] Resonanz f; ~t nach-, widerhallend.

resort [ri'zɔ:t] (Aufenthalts-, Erholungs)Ort m; Zuflucht f; ~ **to** oft besuchen; seine Zuflucht nehmen zu.

resound [ri'zaund] widerhallen (lassen).

resource [ri'sɔ:s] Hilfsmittel n; Zuflucht f; Findigkeit f; Zeitvertreib m; Entspannung f; pl natürliche Reichtümer pl, Mittel pl; ~ful findig.

respect [ris'pekt] Beziehung f, Hinsicht f; Achtung f, Respekt m; Rücksicht f; one's ~s pl s-e Grüße od. Empfehlungen pl; achten; schätzen; respektieren; ~able ansehnlich; ehrbar; anständig; ~ful respektvoll, ehrerbietig: yours ~ly hochachtungsvoll; ~ing hinsichtlich; ~ive jeweilig, entsprechend; ~ively beziehungsweise.

respiration [respə'reiʃən] Atmen n, Atmung f; Atemzug m.

respite ['respait] Frist f, Aufschub m; Pause f.

resplendent [ris'plendənt] glänzend, strahlend.

respon|d [ris'pɔnd] antworten, erwidern; ~d to reagieren auf; empfänglich sein für; ~dent jur.: Beklagte m; f beklagt; ~dent to empfänglich für; ~se [~ns] Antwort f, Erwiderung f; fig. Reaktion f.

responsib|ility [rispɔnsə-'biliti] Verantwortung f; ~le verantwortlich; verantwortungsvoll.

rest [rest] Rest m; Ruhe (-pause) f; Rast f; tech.

Stütze f; (aus)ruhen lassen; ruhen; (sich) ausruhen, rasten; (sich) stützen o.d. lehnen; ~ (up)on fig. beruhen auf.

restaurant ['restərɔ:ŋ, '~rɔnt] Restaurant n, Gaststätte f.

rest|ful ruhig; erholsam; ~house Rasthaus n, -stätte f; ~less ruhelos, rastlos; unruhig; ~lessness Ruhe-, Rastlosigkeit f; Unruhe f.

restor|ation [restə'reiʃən] Wiederherstellung f; Wiedereinsetzung f; Restaurierung f; ~e [ris'tɔ:] wiederherstellen; wiedereinsetzen (to in); zurückerstatten, -bringen, -legen; restaurieren.

restrain [ris'trein] zurückhalten; unterdrücken; ~t Zurückhaltung f; Beschränkung f, Zwang m.

restrict [ris'trikt] be-, einschränken; ~ion Be-, Einschränkung f.

result [ri'zʌlt] Ergebnis n, Resultat n; Folge f; sich ergeben (from aus); ~ in zur Folge haben.

resum|e [ri'zju:m] wiederaufnehmen; Sitz wieder einnehmen; ~ption [~'zʌmpʃən] Wiederaufnahme f.

resurrection [rezə'rekʃən] Wiederaufleben n; the ≗ eccl. die Auferstehung.

retail ['ri:teil] Einzelhandel m; Einzelhandels...; [~'teil] im kleinen ver-

kaufen; ~er [~'t~] Einzelhändler(in).

retain [ri'tein] behalten; zurückhalten.

retaliat|e [ri'tælieit] sich rächen; ~ion Vergeltung f.

retell ['ri:'tel] nacherzählen.

retention [ri'tenʃən] Zurückhalten n [ge n.]

retinue ['retinju:] Gefol-[

retire [ri'taiə] (sich) zurückziehen; pensionieren; sich zur Ruhe setzen; in den Ruhestand treten; ~d pensioniert, im Ruhestand (lebend); zurückgezogen; ~ment Ausscheiden n; Ruhestand m; Zurückgezogenheit f.

retort [ri'tɔ:t] erwidern.

retrace [ri'treis] zurückverfolgen; rekonstruieren.

retract [ri'trækt] (sich) zurückziehen; widerrufen.

retreat [ri'tri:t] sich zurückziehen; Rückzug m; beat a ~ fig. es aufgeben.

retribution [retri'bju:ʃən] Vergeltung f.

retrieve [ri'tri:v] wiederbekommen; hunt. apportieren.

retrospect ['retrəuspekt] Rückblick m; ~ive (zu-)rückblickend; rückwirkend.

return [ri'tə:n] zurückgehen, -kehren, -kommen; erwidern; antworten; vergelten; zurückerstatten, -geben, -senden; zurückstellen, -bringen, -tun;

Rück-, Wiederkehr *f*; Rückgabe *f*; *pl* Umsatz *m*; Gegenleistung *f*; Erwiderung *f*; amtlicher Bericht; Rück...; by ~ umgehend; in ~ dafür; on my ~ bei m-r Rückkehr; many happy ~s of the day herzlichen Glückwunsch zum Geburtstag; ~ flight Rückflug *m*; ~ (ticket) Rückfahrkarte *f*.

reunification ['ri:ju:nifi-'keiʃən] Wiedervereinigung *f*.

reunion ['ri:'ju:njən] Wiedervereinigung *f*; Treffen *n*.

revaluation [ri:vælju'ei-ʃən] *econ.* Aufwertung *f*.

reveal [ri'vi:l] enthüllen, zeigen; offenbaren.

revel ['revl] feiern, ausgelassen sein; schwelgen; zechen.

revelation [revi'leiʃən] Enthüllung *f*; Offenbarung *f*.

revenge [ri'vendʒ] Rache *f*; Revanche *f*; rächen; ~ful rachsüchtig.

revenue ['revinju:] Einkommen *f*; *pl* Einkünfte *pl*; ~ office Finanzamt *n*.

revere [ri'viə] (ver)ehren; ~nce ['revərəns] Verehrung *f*; Ehrfurcht *f*; (ver)ehren; ~nd ehrwürdig; Geistliche *m*.

reverse [ri'və:s] Gegenteil *n*; Rückseite *f*; *fig.* Rückschlag *m*; umgekehrt; umkehren; *Meinung etc.* ändern; *Urteil* aufheben; ~

gear *mot.* Rückwärtsgang *m*; ~ side Rückseite *f*; linke (Stoff)Seite.

review [ri'vju:] *mil.* Parade *f*; *Zeitschrift:* Rundschau *f*; Rezension *f*; Rückblick *m*; (über-, nach)prüfen; *mil.* mustern; rezensieren; *fig.* zurückblicken auf; ~er Rezensent(in).

revis|e [ri'vaiz] revidieren; überarbeiten; ~ion [~iʒən] Revision *f*; Überarbeitung *f*.

reviv|al [ri'vaivəl] Wiederbelebung *f*; ~e wiederbeleben.

revoke [ri'vəuk] widerrufen; aufheben.

revolt [ri'vəult] Revolte *f*, Aufstand *m*; revoltieren, sich auflehnen; *fig.* abstoßen.

revolution [revə'lu:ʃən] Umdrehung *f*; *fig.* Revolution *f*, Umwälzung *f*; ~ary revolutionär; Revolutionär(in); ~ist Revolutionär(in); ~ize revolutionieren.

revolv|e [ri'vɔlv] sich drehen; ~ing sich drehend; Dreh...

reward [ri'wɔ:d] Belohnung *f*; belohnen.

rheumatism ['ru:mətizəm] Rheumatismus *m*.

rhubarb ['ru:bɑ:b] Rhabarber *m*.

rhyme [raim] Reim *m*; Vers *m*; (sich) reimen.

rhythm ['riðəm] Rhythmus *m*; ~ic(al) rhythmisch.

rib [rib] Rippe f.

ribbon ['ribən] Band n.

rice [rais] Reis m.

rich [ritʃ] reich (**in** an); kostbar; fruchtbar; voll (*Ton*); schwer, kräftig (*Speise etc.*); *sub:* **the** ~ die Reichen pl; ~**es** ['~iz] pl Reichtümer m; Reichtümer pl; ~**ness** Reichtum m, Fülle f.

rick [rik] (Heu)Schober m.

ricket|**s** ['rikits] sg, pl Rachitis f; ~**y** rachitisch; wack(e)lig, klapp(e)rig.

rid [rid] (*irr*) befreien (**of** von); **get** ~ **of** loswerden.

ridden ['ridn] pp von **ride**.

riddle ['ridl] Rätsel n; grobes Sieb; sieben; durchlöchern, -sieben.

ride [raid] Ritt m; Fahrt f; (*irr*) reiten; fahren; ~**r** Reiter/in.

ridge [ridʒ] (Gebirgs)Kamm m, Grat m; (Dach-)First m.

ridicul|**e** ['ridikjuːl] Verspottung f, Spott m; verspotten; ~**ous** [~'dikjuləs] lächerlich. [Reit...\]

riding ['raidiŋ] Reiten n;\]

rifle ['raifl] Gewehr n, Büchse f.

rift [rift] Riß m, Sprung m; Spalte f.

right [rait] adj recht; recht, richtig; *colloq.* richtig, in Ordnung; **all** ~ in Ordnung, gut!; **that's all** ~ das macht nichts!, schon gut!, bitte!; **I am perfectly all** ~ mir geht

es ausgezeichnet; **that's** ~ richtig!, ganz recht!, stimmt!; **be** ~ recht haben; **put** ~, **set** ~ in Ordnung bringen; adv recht; recht, richtig; gerade(wegs), sofort; direkt; völlig, ganz; genau; ~ **ahead**, ~ **on** geradeaus; ~ **away** sofort; **turn** ~ (sich) nach rechts wenden, rechts abbiegen; vb (aus-, auf-) richten; *j-m* zu s-m Recht verhelfen; Recht n; rechte Hand, Rechte f; **on the** ~ rechts; **to the** ~ (nach) rechts; ~**eous** ['~ʃəs] rechtschaffen; gerecht(fertigt); ~**ful** rechtmäßig; gerecht; ~**-hand** recht; ~**-handed** rechtshändig; ~ **of way** Vorfahrt(srecht n) f.

rigid ['ridʒid] starr, steif; *fig.* streng.

rig|**orous** ['rigərəs] rigoros, streng, hart; ~**o(u)r** Strenge f, Härte f.

rim [rim] Rand m; Felge f.

rind [raind] Rinde f, Schale f; (Speck)Schwarte f.

ring [riŋ] Ring m; Kreis m; Manege f; Arena f; Geläut(e) n; Glockenläuten n; Klang m; Klingeln n; **give s.o. a** ~ *j-n* anrufen; (*irr*) läuten; klingeln; klingen; ~ **the bell** klingeln; ~ **off** (den Hörer) auflegen od. einhängen; ~ **s.o. up** *j-n* od. bei *j-m* anrufen; ~**leader** Rädelsführer m; ~**-master** Zirkusdirektor m.

rink [riŋk] Eisbahn *f*; Rollschuhbahn *f*.

rinse [rins]: **~ (out)** (aus-, ab)spülen.

riot [raiət] Aufruhr *m*; Krawall *m*, Tumult *m*; randalieren, toben; schwelgen; **~ous** aufrührerisch; lärmend.

rip [rip] Riß *m*; auftrennen; (zer)reißen.

ripe [raip] reif; **~n** reifen (lassen); **~ness** Reife *f*.

ripple ['ripl] kleine Welle; Kräuselung *f*; (sich) kräuseln; rieseln.

rise [raiz] (An-, Auf)Steigen *n*; Anhöhe *f*; (Preis-, Gehalts)Erhöhung *f*; Ursprung *m*; *fig.* Aufstieg *m*; (*irr*) sich erheben; aufstehen; auf-, an)steigen; aufgehen (Sonne, Samen); entspringen (Fluß); **~n** ['rizn] *pp von* rise; **~r: early ~** Frühaufsteher(in).

rising ['raiziŋ] *ast.* Aufgang *m*; Aufstand *m*.

risk [risk] riskieren, wagen; Gefahr *f*, Risiko *n*; **run the ~ of** Gefahr laufen zu; **~y** riskant, gewagt.

rite [rait] Ritus *m*.

rival ['raivəl] Rival|e *m*, -in *f*, Konkurrent(in); rivalisierend; wetteifern mit; **~ry** Rivalität *f*.

river ['rivə] Fluß *m*, Strom *m*; **~boat** Flußdampfer *m*; **~side** Flußufer *n*.

rivet ['rivit] *tech.* Niet *m*; (ver)nieten; *fig.* heften.

rivulet ['rivjulit] Flüßchen *n*.

road [rəud] (Auto-, Land-) Straße *f*, Weg *m*; **~ map** Straßenkarte *f*; **~ sign** Verkehrsschild *n*, -zeichen *n*.

roam [rəum] umherstreifen, (-)wandern; durchstreifen.

roar [rɔː] brüllen; brausen, toben; Gebrüll *n*; Brausen *n*, Toben *n*; **~s (pl of laughter)** schallendes Gelächter.

roast [rəust] rösten, braten, schmoren; Braten *m*; geröstet; gebraten, Röst..., Brat...; **~ beef** Rinderbraten *m*; **~ meat** Bratem *m*.

rob [rɔb] (be)rauben; **~ber** Räuber *m*; **~bery** Raub (-überfall) *m*.

robe [rəub] (Amts)Robe *f*, Talar *m*.

robin (redbreast) ['rɔbin] Rotkehlchen *n*.

robot ['rəubɔt] Roboter *m*.

robust [rəu'bʌst] robust, kräftig.

rock [rɔk] Fels(en) *m*; Klippe *f*; Gestein *n*; schaukeln; wiegen.

rocker ['rɔkə] Kufe *f*; *Am.* Schaukelstuhl *m*; Rocker *m*, Halbstarke *m*.

rocket ['rɔkit] Rakete *f*; Raketen...; **~-powered** mit Raketenantrieb; **~ry** Raketentechnik *f*.

rocking-chair Schaukelstuhl *m*.

rocky ['rɔki] felsig, Felsen...

rod [rɔd] Rute f; Stab m; Stange f.

rode [roud] pret von ride.

rodent ['roudənt] Nagetier n.

roe[1] [rou] Reh n.

roe[2] ichth.: **(hard)** ~ Rogen m; **soft** ~ Milch f.

rogu|e [roug] Schurke m; Schelm m; **~ish** schurkisch; schelmisch.

role, rôle [roul] thea. Rolle f (a. fig.).

roll [roul] Rolle f; Walze f; Brötchen n, Semmel f; (Namens)Liste f; (Donner)Rollen n; (Trommel-)Wirbel m; rollen; fahren; schlingern; (g)rollen, dröhnen; (sich) wälzen; walzen; drehen; ~ **up** zs.-, aufrollen; **~er** Rolle f, Walze f; **~er coaster** Am. Achterbahn f; **~er-skate** Rollschuh m; ~ **film** Rollfilm m; **~ing mill** Walzwerk n.

Roman ['roumən] römisch; Römer(in).

roman|ce [rou'mæns] Abenteuer-, Liebesroman m; Romanze f; Romantik f; **~tic** romantisch.

romp [rɔmp] Range f, Wildfang m; Tollen n; umhertollen, sich balgen; **~er(s** pl) Spielanzug m.

roof [ru:f] Dach n; ~ **over** überdachen.

rook [ruk] Saatkrähe f.

room [rum] Raum m; Zimmer n; Platz m; pl Wohnung f; pl Fremdenzimmer pl; **~mate** Zimmergenoss|e m, -in f; **~y** geräumig.

roost [ru:st] Schlafplatz m (von Vögeln); Hühnerstange f; Hühnerstall m; **~er** (Haus)Hahn m.

root [ru:t] Wurzel f; (ein)wurzeln; einpflanzen; (auf)wühlen; ~ **up** ausgraben, -reißen; ~ **out** ausrotten.

rope [roup] Tau n, Seil n, Strick m; Lasso m, n; festbinden; anseilen; ~ **off** (durch ein Seil) absperren.

ros|e [rouz] Rose f; Brause f (e-r Gießkanne); pret von **rise; ~y** rosig.

rot [rɔt] Fäulnis f; faulen lassen; (ver)faulen.

rota|ry ['routəri] sich drehend; Rotations...; **~te** [~'teit] (sich) drehen; rotieren (lassen); **~tion** Umdrehung f.

rotor [routə] aer. Drehflügel m, Rotor m.

rotten ['rɔtn] verfault, faul; morsch; sl. saumäßig.

rotund [rou'tʌnd] rundlich; voll (Stimme).

rough [rʌf] rauh; roh; grob; ungefähr; **~ness** Rauheit f; Roheit f; Grobheit f.

round [raund] Rund n, Kreis m; (Leiter)Sprosse f; Runde f; Rundgang m; Kanon m; adj rund; voll; adv überall; e-e Zeit lang od. hindurch; ~ **(about)** rund-, rings(her)um; prp

rund (um); um *od.* in ...
(herum); *vb* rund machen
od. werden; ~ **off** abrunden; ~ **up** zs.-treiben; ~
about weitschweifig;
Karussell *n*; (Platz *m* mit)
Kreisverkehr *m*; ~ **trip** *Am.*
Hin- u. Rückfahrt *f.*

rouse [rauz] aufwachen;
wecken; ermuntern; ~ **o.s.**
sich aufraffen.

route [ru:t] (Reise-,Fahrt-)
Route *f*,(-)Weg*m*; Strecke*f.*

routine [ru:'ti:n] Routine
f; üblich; Routine...

rove [rəuv] umherstreifen.

row[1] [rau] *colloq.* Krach *m.*

row[2] [rəu] (Häuser-, Sitz-
etc.)Reihe *f*; Ruderpartie
f; rudern; ~-**boat** Ruderboot *n*; ~**er** Ruderer *m*;
~**ing-boat** Ruderboot *n.*

royal [rɔiəl] königlich;
~**ty** Königswürde *f*; Mitglied *n* e-s Königshauses;
(Autoren)Tantieme *f.*

rub [rʌb] reiben; (ab)wischen; ~ **down** abreiben;
~ **in** einreiben; ~ **off** abreiben; ~ **out** ausradieren.

rubber [rʌbə] Gummi *n*,
m; Radiergummi *m*; *pl*
Am. Gummischuhe *pl*;
Gummi...; ~ **plant** Gummibaum *m.*

rubbish [rʌbiʃ] Abfall *m*;
Müll *m*; Schund *m*; ~!
Unsinn!

rubble [rʌbl] Schutt *m.*

ruby [ru:bi] Rubin(rot *n*)*m.*

rucksack [rʌksæk] Rucksack *m.*

rudder [rʌdə] *mar.* (Steu-

er)Ruder *n*; *aer.* Seitenruder *n.*

ruddy [rʌdi] rot(backig).

rude [ru:d] unhöflich;
heftig; grob; roh; ungebildet.

ruff [rʌf] Halskrause *f.*

ruffian [rʌfjən] Rohling
m; Schurke *m.*

ruffle [rʌfl] Krause *f*,
Rüsche *f*; kräuseln; Federn
etc. sträuben; (ver)ärgern.

rug [rʌg] (Reise-, Woll-)
Decke *f*; Vorleger *m.*

Rugby (football) [rʌgbi]
Rugby *n*. ~ [eben.]

rugged [rʌgid] rauh; un-]

rugger [rʌgə] *colloq.* s.
Rugby (football).

ruin [ruin] Ruin *m*, Zs.-
bruch *m*; *pl* Ruine(n *pl*)
f, Trümmer *pl*; vernichten; ruinieren.

rule [ru:l] Regel *f*; Vorschrift *f*; Herrschaft *f*;
Maßstab *m*; **as a** ~ in der
Regel; (be)herrschen;herrschen über; leiten; verfügen; liniieren; ~ **out**
ausschließen; ~**r** Herrscher(in); Lineal *n.*

rum [rʌm] Rum *m.*

rumble [rʌmbl] rumpeln;
grollen (*Donner*).

ruminant [ru:minənt]
Wiederkäuer *m.*

rummage [rʌmidʒ]
Durchsuchung *f*; Ramsch
m; durchsuchen; (durch-)
wühlen; [rückt *n*.]

rumo(u)r [ru:mə] Ge-]

rump [rʌmp] Steiß *m*,
Hinterteil *m*; *fig.* Rumpf *m.*

rumple ['rʌmpl] zerknittern, -knüllen; zerzausen.

run [rʌn] Lauf(en n) m; Rennen n; Spazierfahrt f; Am. Laufmasche f; Serie f; econ. Ansturm m; thea., Film: Laufzeit f; (irr) (aus-, durch-, ver-, zer)laufen; rennen; eilen; fließen; fahren, verkehren (Bus etc.); lauten (Text); gehen (Melodie); tech. arbeiten, laufen, gehen; sp. (um die Wette) laufen (mit); laufen lassen; Geschäft betreiben, leiten; ~ **across** zufällig treffen, stoßen auf; ~ **after** hinterherlaufen; ~ **away** davonlaufen; ~ **down** ablaufen (Uhr); umrennen; überfahren; herunterwirtschaften; j-n schlecht machen; ~ **in** Auto einfahren; ~ **into** hineinlaufen in, prallen gegen; j-n zufällig treffen; geraten in (Schulden etc.); ~ **off** weglaufen; ~ **out** zu Ende gehen, knapp werden, ausgehen; ~ **out of s.th.** j-m geht et. aus od. wird et. knapp; ~ **over** überfliegen, überfliegen, durchlesen; überfahren; ~ **short (of)** s. **run out (of);** ~ **through** durchbohren; (rasch) überfliegen; ~ **up** sich belaufen auf.

rung[1] [rʌŋ] pp von **ring.**
rung[2] (Leiter)Sprosse f.

runner ['rʌnə] Läufer m; (Schlitten- etc.)Kufe f; bot. Ausläufer m; ~**up** sp. Zweite m, f.

running [rʌn] laschend; fließend; **for two days** ~ zwei Tage hintereinander; ~**board** Trittbrett n.

runway ['rʌnwei] aer. Start-, Lande-, Rollbahn f.

rupture ['rʌptʃə] Bruch m, Riß m (beide a. med.).

rural ['ruərəl] ländlich, Land...

rush [rʌʃ] Hetzen n, Stürmen n; Eile f; Andrang m; stürmische Nachfrage; stürzen; jagen, hetzen; stürmen; drängen; ~ **at** sich stürzen auf; ~ **hours** pl Hauptverkehrs-, Stoßzeit f.

Russian ['rʌʃən] russisch; Russ|e m, -in f; Russisch n.

rust [rʌst] Rost m; rosten; verrosten lassen.

rustic ['rʌstik] ländlich, Bauern..., rustikal.

rustle ['rʌsl] rascheln (mit); rauschen; Rascheln n.

rusty ['rʌsti] rostig, verrostet; fig. eingerostet.

rut [rʌt] (Wagen)Spur f; Brunst f, Brunst f.

ruthless ['ruːθlis] unbarmherzig; rücksichts-, skrupellos.

rutt|ed ['rʌtid], ~**y** ausgefahren (Weg).

rye [rai] Roggen m.

S

sable ['seibl]Zobel(pelz) m.

sabotage ['sæbəta:ʒ]
Sabotage f; sabotieren.

sabre ['seibə] Säbel m.

sack [sæk] Plünderung f;
Sack m; give (get) the ~
colloq. entlassen (werden);
vb: plündern; colloq. entlassen, rausschmeißen.

sacrament ['sækrəmənt]
Sakrament n.

sacred ['seikrid] heilig.

sacrifice ['sækrifais] Opfer
n; opfern.

sad [sæd]traurig; schlimm;
~den traurig machen od.
werden; ~ness Traurig-
keit f.

saddle ['sædl] Sattel m;
satteln.

sadness ['sædnis] Traurig-
keit f.

safe [seif] sicher (from
vor); unversehrt, heil; Safe
m, n, Geldschrank m; ~
guard Schutz m; sichern,
schützen.

safety ['seifti] Sicherheit f;
Sicherheits...; ~belt Si-
cherheitsgurt m; ~lock
Sicherheitsschloß n; ~pin
Sicherheitsnadel f; ~ ra-
zor Rasierapparat m.

sag [sæg] durchsacken;
tech. durchhängen.

sagacity [sə'gæsiti]Scharf-
sinn m. [say.\

said [sed] pret u. pp von |

sail [seil] Segel n; segeln,
fahren; auslaufen (Schiff);
~boat Am., ~ing-boat

Segelboot n; ~ing-ship,
~ing-vessel Segelschiff n;
~or Seemann m, Matrose m.

saint [seint] Heilige m, f;
[vor Namen: snt] Sankt ...

sake [seik]: for the ~ of
um ... willen, wegen; for
my ~ meinetwegen.

salad ['sæləd] Salat m.

salary ['sæləri] Gehalt n.

sale [seil] (Aus-, Schluß-)
Verkauf m; econ. Ab-, Um-
satz m; for ~, on ~ zum
Verkauf, zu verkaufen; ~s
department Verkaufsab-
teilung f; ~sman Verkäu-
fer m; ~s manager Ver-
kaufsleiter m; ~swoman
Verkäuferin f.

saliva [sə'laivə] Speichel m.

sallow ['sælou] gelblich.

sally ['sæli]: ~ forth, ~
out sich aufmachen.

salmon ['sæmən] Lachs m,
Salm m.

saloon [sə'lu:n] Salon m;
Am. Kneipe f.

salt [sɔ:lt] Salz n; fig. Würze f; Salz..., salzig; (ein-)
gesalzen, Salz..., Pökel...;
(ein)salzen; pökeln; ~cel-
lar Salzfäßchen n; ~y salzig.

salutation [sælju(:)'tei-
ʃən] Gruß m, Begrüßung f;
~e [sə'lu:t] Gruß m; Salut
m; grüßen; salutieren.

salvation [sæl'veiʃən] Erlösung f; (Seelen)Heil n; 2
Army Heilsarmee f.

salve   246

salve [sɑːv] Salbe f.

same [seim] selb, gleich; **the ~** der-, die-, dasselbe; **all the ~** trotzdem; **it is all the ~ to me** es ist mir ganz gleich.

sample ['sɑːmpl] Probe f, Muster n; probieren.

sanatorium [sænəˈtɔːriəm] (Lungen)Sanatorium n.

sanct|ify ['sæŋktifai] heiligen; weihen; **~ion** Sanktion f; Billigung f; billigen; **~uary** [ˈ~tjuəri] Heiligtum n; Asyl n.

sand [sænd] Sand m.

sandal ['sændl] Sandale f.

sandwich ['sænwidʒ] Sandwich n; **~man** Plakatträger m.

sandy ['sændi] sandig, Sand...; sandfarben; **~ beach** Sandstrand m.

sane [sein] geistig gesund, normal; vernünftig.

sang [sæŋ] pret von sing.

sanitarium [sæniˈtɛəriəm] Am. für sanatorium.

sanit|ary ['sænitəri] hygienisch, Gesundheits...; **~ary napkin**, **~ary towel** Damenbinde f; **~ation** sanitäre Einrichtungen pl; **~y** gesunder Verstand.

sank [sæŋk] pret von sink.

Santa Claus [sæntəˈklɔːz] Nikolaus m, Weihnachtsmann m.

sap [sæp] bot. Saft m; fig. Lebenskraft f; **~py** saftig; fig. kraftvoll.

sarcasm ['sɑːkæzəm] Sarkasmus m, beißender Spott.

sardine [sɑːˈdiːn] Sardine f.

sash [sæʃ] Schärpe f; **~ window** Schiebefenster n.

sat [sæt] pret u. pp von sit.

Satan ['seitən] Satan m.

satchel ['sætʃəl] Schulmappe f [m.]

satellite ['sætəlait] Satellit f

satin ['sætin] Satin m.

satir|e ['sætaiə] Satire f; **~ize** [ˈ~əraiz] verspotten.

satis|faction [sætisˈfækʃən] Befriedigung f; Genugtuung f; Zufriedenheit f; **~factory** befriedigend, zufriedenstellend; **~fy** ['ˈ~fai] befriedigen, zufriedenstellen; überzeugen.

Saturday ['sætədi] Sonnabend m, Samstag m.

sauce [sɔːs] Soße f, Tunke f; Am. Kompott n; **~pan** Kochtopf m; **~r** Untertasse f.

saucy ['sɔːsi] frech.

saunter ['sɔːntə] schlendern, bummeln.

sausage ['sɔsidʒ] Wurst f; Würstchen n.

savage ['sævidʒ] wild; grausam; Wilde m, f.

save [seiv] retten; bewahren; erlösen; (er)sparen; außer; **~** bis auf; **~r** Retter(in); Sparer(in).

saving ['seiviŋ] rettend; sparsam; ...ersparend; pl Ersparnisse pl; **~s-bank** Sparkasse f.

savio(u)r ['seivjə] Retter m; 2 eccl. Heiland m, Erlöser m.

savo(u)r ['seivə] (Wohl-

Geschmack *m*; *fig.* Beige-schmack *m*; **~y** schmack-haft; pikant.

saw¹ [sɔ:] *pret von* **see.**

saw² (*irr*) sägen; Säge *f*; **~dust** Sägespäne *pl*; **~mill** Sägewerk *n*; **~n** *pp von* **saw**².

Saxon ['sæksn] sächsisch; Sachse *m*, Sächsin *f*.

say [sei] (*irr*) (auf)sagen; berichten; *Gebet* sprechen; meinen; **as if to ~** als ob er sagen wollte; **that is to ~** das heißt; **he is said to be ...** er soll ... sein; **no sooner said than done** gesagt, getan; **I ~** ! sag(en Sie) mal!; ich muß schon sagen!; ergo Sprichwort *n*, Redensart *f*; **it goes without ~ing** es versteht sich von selbst.

scab [skæb] Schorf *m*.

scaffold ['skæfəld] (Bau-)Gerüst *n*; Schafott *n*; **~ing** (Bau)Gerüst *n*.

scald [skɔ:ld] verbrühen; *Milch* abkochen.

scale [skeil] Schuppe *f*; Tonleiter *f*; Skala *f*; Maßstab *m*; Waagschale *f*; **(a pair of) ~s** *pl* (~) Waage; (sich) abschuppen *od.* ab-lösen.

scalp [skælp] Kopfhaut *f*; Skalp *m*; skalpieren.

scan [skæn] absuchen, -ta-sten; *fig.* überfliegen.

scandal ['skændl] Skandal *m*; Klatsch *m*; **~ous** ['~dələs] skandalös, an-stößig.

Scandinavian [skændi-'neivjən] skandinavisch; Skandinavier(in).

scant [skænt] knapp; **~y** knapp, spärlich, dürftig.

scapegoat ['skeipgəut] Sündenbock *m*.

scar [skɑ:] Narbe *f*; schrammen; **~ over** ver-narben.

scarce [skɛəs] knapp; selten; **~ely** kaum; **~ity** Mangel *m*, Knappheit *f* (**of** an).

scare [skɛə] erschrecken; **~ away** verjagen, **~scheu-**chen; **be ~d of** Angst haben vor; **~crow** Vogel-scheuche *f*.

scarf [skɑ:f], *pl* **~s** [~fs], **scarves** [~vz] Schal *m*, Hals-, Kopf-, Schulter-tuch *n*.

scarlet ['skɑ:lit] scharlach-rot; **~ fever** Scharlach *m*.

scarred [skɑ:d] narbig.

scarves [skɑ:vz] *pl von* **scarf.**

scathing ['skeiðiŋ] *fig.* ver-nichtend.

scatter ['skætə] (sich) zer-streuen; aus-, verstreuen.

scavenge ['skævindʒ] *Straßen etc.* reinigen.

scene [si:n] Szene *f*; Schau-platz *m*; **~ry** Szenerie *f*.

scent [sent] (Wohl)Geruch *m*, Duft *m*; Parfüm *n*; Fährte *f*; wittern; parfü-mieren.

sceptic ['skeptik] Skepti-ker(in); **~al** skeptisch.

schedule ['ʃedju:l, *Am.* 'skedʒu:l] festsetzen; pla-

scheme 248

nen; Verzeichnis *n; Am.*
Fahr-, Flugplan *m;* **on ~**
(fahr)planmäßig.
scheme [ski:m] Schema *n;*
Plan *m;* planen.
scholar [ˈskɔlə] Gelehrte
m; Stipendiat(in); **~ship**
Stipendium *n.*
school [sku:l] *ichth.*
Schwarm *m;* Schule *f (a.
fig.);* **at ~** auf *od.* in der
Schule; *vb:* schulen; **~boy**
Schüler *m;* **~fellow** Mit-
schüler(in); **~girl** Schüle-
rin *f;* **~ing** (Schul)Ausbil-
dung *f;* **~master** Lehrer
m; **~mate** Mitschüler(in);
~mistress Lehrerin *f;* **~of**
motoring Fahrschule *f.*
schooner [ˈsku:nə] Scho-
ner *m; Am.* Planwagen *m.*
scien|ce [ˈsaiəns] Wissen-
schaft *f;* Naturwissen-
schaft(en *pl);* **~tific** [~-
ˈtifik] (natur)wissenschaft-
lich; **~tist** (Natur)Wissen-
schaftler(in).
scissors [ˈsizəz] *pl (a. **a**
pair of ~)* (e-e) Schere.
scoff [skɔf] spotten (**at**
über).
scold [skəuld] (aus)schel-
ten, ausZANken; schimpfen.
scone [skɔn] weiches Tee-
gebäck.
scoop [sku:p] Schöpfkelle
f; schöpfen, schaufeln.
scooter [ˈsku:tə] (Kinder-)
Roller *m;* (Motor)Roller *m.*
scope [skəup] Bereich *m;*
Spielraum *m.*
scorch [skɔtʃ] versengen,
-brennen.

score [skɔ:] Kerbe *f;* Zeche
f, Rechnung *f; sp.* Spiel-
stand *m,* Punktzahl *f,*
(Spiel)Ergebnis *n;* **20**
Stück; **four ~** achtzig;
(ein)kerben; *sp. Punkte* erzielen, *Tore* schießen.
scorn [skɔ:n] Verachtung *f;*
Spott *m;* verachten; **~ful**
verächtlich.
Scot [skɔt] Schott|e *m,* -in *f.*
Scotch [skɔtʃ] schottisch;
sub: **the ~** die Schotten
pl; **~man, ~woman** *s.*
Scotsman, Scotswom-
an. [straft.]
scot-free [ˈskɔtˈfri:] unge- }
Scots [skɔts] Schottische
n; **~man** Schotte *m;* **~-**
woman Schottin *f.*
scoundrel [ˈskaundrəl]
Schurke *m,* Schuft *m.*
scour [ˈskauə] scheuern;
reinigen.
scout [skaut] Späher *m,*
Kundschafter *m;* Pannen-
helfer *m (e-s Automobil-*
klubs); (aus)kundschaften;
erkunden; **~master** Pfad-
finderführer *m.*
scowl [skaul] finster blik-
ken; finsterer Blick.
scramble [ˈskræmbl] klettern; sich balgen (**for** um);
~d eggs *pl* Rührei *n.*
scrap [skræp] Stückchen *n,*
Fetzen *m;* Abfall *m;*
Schrott *m.*
scrape [skreip] Kratzen *n,*
Scharren *n; fig.* Klemme *f;*
kratzen; scharren; **~ off**
abkratzen; **~ out** auskrat-
zen.

scrap-iron Schrott m.

scratch [skrætʃ] Kratzer m, Schramme f; (zer)kratzen.

scrawl [skrɔ:l] Gekritzel n; kritzeln.

scream [skri:m] Schrei m; Gekreisch n; schreien, kreischen.

screech [skri:tʃ] s. **scream**.

screen [skri:n] (Schutz-) Schirm m; (Film)Leinwand f; Bildschirm m; (Fliegen)Gitter n; (ab-, be)schirmen, (be)schützen; verfilmen; j-n überprüfen.

screw [skru:] Schraube f; schrauben; **~driver** Schraubenzieher m.

scribble ['skribl] Gekritzel n; kritzeln.

script [skript] Manuskript n; Drehbuch n; Schrift f; **the Holy ⸿ures** pl die Bibel...; **the Holy Script**.

scroll [skrəul] Schriftrolle f.

scrub [skrʌb] Gestrüpp n; schrubben, scheuern.

scrup|le ['skru:pl] Skrupel m, Bedenken n; Bedenken haben; **~ulous** ['~pjuləs] gewissenhaft.

scrutin|ize ['skru:tinaiz] (genau) prüfen; **~y** (genaue) Prüfung.

scuffle ['skʌfl] raufen.

sculpt|or ['skʌlptə] Bildhauer m; **~ure** Bildhauerei f; Skulptur f, Plastik f; (heraus)meißeln, formen.

scum [skʌm] (Ab)Schaum m; fig. Abschaum m.

scurf [skə:f] (Kopf)Schuppen pl.

scurvy ['skə:vi] Skorbut m.

scuttle ['skʌtl] Kohleneimer m.

scythe [saið] Sense f.

sea [si:] die See, das Meer; **at ~** auf See; **go to ~** zur See gehen; **~faring** ['~fɛəriŋ] seefahrend; **~food** Meeresfrüchte pl; **~gull** (See)Möwe f.

seal [si:l] Seehund m, Robbe f; Siegel n; tech. Dichtung f; (ver-, fig. be)siegeln; **~ up** (fest) verschließen od. abdichten.

sea level Meeresspiegel m.

seam [si:m] Saum m, Naht f.

seaman ['si:mən] Seemann m, Matrose m.

seamstress ['semstris] Näherin f.

sea|plane Wasserflugzeug n; **~port** Hafenstadt f; **~power** Seemacht f.

search [sə:tʃ] durch-, untersuchen; erforschen; suchen, forschen (**for** nach); Suche f, Forschen n; Durchsuchung f; **in ~ of** auf der Suche nach.

sea|shore See-, Meeresküste f; **~sick** seekrank; **~side** Küste f; **~side resort** Seebad n.

season ['si:zn] Jahreszeit f; Saison f; **dead ~, off ~** Vor-, Nachsaison f; reifen (lassen); würzen; abhärten (**to** gegen); ablagern; **~able** rechtzeitig; **~al** Saison...; **~ing** Würze f;

ticket *rail.* Zeitkarte *f*; *thea.* Abonnement *n.*

seat [si:t] Sitz *m*; Sessel *m*, Stuhl *m*, Bank *f*; (Sitz-) Platz *m*; Landsitz *m*; **take a ~** sich setzen; nehmen Sie Platz!; *vb*: (hin)setzen; fassen, Sitzplätze haben für; **be ~ed** sitzen; nehmen Sie Platz!; **~belt** Sicherheitsgurt *m.*

sea|ward(s) ['si:wəd(z)] seewärts; **~weed** (See-) Tang *m*; **~worthy** seetüchtig.

secession [si'seʃən] Lossagung *f*, Abfall *m.*

seclu|de [si'klu:d] abschließen, absondern; **~ded** abgelegen; **~sion** [~ʒən] Abgeschiedenheit *f.*

second ['sekənd] zweite; der, die, das Zweite; Sekunde *f*; **~ary** sekundär; untergeordnet; **~ary school** höhere Schule; **~ floor** *Am.* erster Stock; **~ hand** aus zweiter Hand; gebraucht; antiquarisch; **~ly** zweitens; **~-rate** zweitklassig.

secre|cy ['si:krisi] Heimlichkeit *f*; Verschwiegenheit *f*; **~t** ['~it] geheim, heimlich; Geheim...; verschwiegen; Geheimnis *n.*

secretary ['sekrətri] Sekretär(in); **♀ of State** *Brit.* Minister *m*; *Am.* Außenminister *m.*

secre|te [si'kri:t] *med.* absondern; **~ion** *med.* Absonderung *f.*

section ['sekʃən] Teil *m*; (Ab)Schnitt *m*; Abteilung *f*; Gruppe *f.*

secular ['sekjulə] weltlich.

secur|e [si'kjuə] sicher; sichern; schützen; sich beschaffen; befestigen; **~ity** Sicherheit *f*; Kaution *f*; *pl* Wertpapiere *pl.*

sedan [si'dæn] Limousine *f.*

sedative ['sedətiv] beruhigend; Beruhigungsmittel *n.*

sediment ['sedimənt] (Boden)Satz *m.*

seduce [si'dju:s] verführen; **~tion** [~'dʌkʃən] Verführung *f*; **~tive** verführerisch.

see [si:] (*irr*) sehen; (sich) ansehen, besichtigen; besuchen; zu *j-m* gehen, *j-n* aufsuchen *od.* konsultieren; sich überlegen; **live to ~** erleben; **~ s.o. home** *j-n* nach Hause bringen *od.* begleiten; **I ~!** ich verstehe!; **~ off** *Besuch* fortbegleiten; **~ out** *Besuch* hinausbegleiten; **~ through** durchschauen; *j-m* über *et.* hinweghelfen; *et.* durchhalten; **~ to** sich kümmern um, dafür sorgen (,daß).

seed [si:d] Samen *m*; Saat *f* (-gut *n*); *fig.* Keim *m.*

seek [si:k] (*irr*) suchen; trachten nach.

seem [si:m] (er)scheinen; **~ing** anscheinend; scheinbar; **~ly** schicklich.

seen [si:n] *pp von* **see.**

seep [si:p] (durch)sickern, tropfen.

seesaw ['si:sɔ:] Wippe *f*, Wippschaukel *f*; wippen.

segment ['segmənt] Abschnitt *m*; Segment *n*.

segregat|**e** ['segrigeit] absondern, trennen; **~ion** Absonderung *f*; (Rassen-) Trennung *f*.

seiz|**e** [si:z] (er)greifen, fassen; nehmen; *fig.* erfassen; **~ure** ['~ʒə] Ergreifung *f*; *jur.* Beschlagnahme *f*.

seldom ['seldəm] selten.

select [si'lekt] auswählen, -suchen; erlesen; **~ion** Auswahl *f*, -lese *f*.

self [self], *pl* **selves** [~vz] Selbst *n*, Ich *n*; *myself, etc. ich selbst etc.*; **~command** Selbstbeherrschung *f*; **~confidence** Selbstvertrauen *n*; **~conscious** befangen, gehemmt; **~control** Selbstbeherrschung *f*; **~defence** Selbstverteidigung *f*, Notwehr *f*; **~employed** selbständig (*Handwerker etc.*); **~government** Selbstverwaltung *f*, Autonomie *f*; **~interest** Eigennutz *m*; **~ish** selbstsüchtig; **~made** selbstgemacht; **~possession** Selbstbeherrschung *f*; **~reliant** selbstbewußt; **~respect** Selbstachtung *f*; **~righteous** selbstgerecht; **~service** Selbstbedienung *f*, Selbstbedienungs...

sell [sel] (*irr*) verkaufen; gehen (*Ware*); **be sold out** ausverkauft sein; **~er** Ver-

käufer(in), Händler(in); *gut- etc.* gehende Ware.

selves [selvz] *pl von* **self**.

semblance ['semblans] Anschein *m*; Ähnlichkeit *f*.

semi|**colon** ['semi'kəulən] Semikolon *n*, Strichpunkt *m*; **~final** *sp.* Halbfinale *n*.

senat|**e** ['senit] Senat *m*; **~or** ['~ətə] Senator *m*.

send [send] (*irr*) senden, schicken; **~ for** kommen lassen, holen (lassen); **~ in** einsenden, **~schicken, ~reichen**; **~er** Absender(in).

senior ['si:njə] älter; rangdienstälter; Ältere *m*; Rang-, Dienstältere *m*.

sensation [sen'seiʃən] Empfindung *f*, Gefühl *n*; Sensation *f*; **~al** sensationell, Sensations...

sense [sens] Sinn *m*; Gefühl *n*; Verstand *m*; Vernunft *f*; **in a** in gewissem Sinne; **in (out of) one's ~s** bei (von) Sinnen; **talk ~** vernünftig reden; *vb*: spüren, fühlen; **~less** bewußtlos; gefühllos; sinnlos.

sensib|**ility** [sensi'biliti] Sensibilität *f*, Empfindungsvermögen *n*; Empfindlichkeit *f*; **~le** spür-, fühlbar; vernünftig; **be ~le of** sich *e-r S.* bewußt sein.

sensitive ['sensitiv] empfindlich (**to** gegen); sensibel, feinfühlig.

sensu|**al** ['sensjuəl] sinnlich; **~ous** sinnlich.

sent [sent] *pret u. pp von* **send**.

sentence ['sentəns] *jur.*Urteil *n*; *gr.* Satz *m*; verurteilen.

sentiment ['sentimənt] (seelische) Empfindung, Gefühl *n*; *pl* Meinung *f*; **⁓al** [⁓'mentl] sentimental, gefühlvoll; **⁓ality** [⁓men-'tæliti] Sentimentalität *f*.

sentry ['sentri] *mil.* Posten *m*.

separa|ble ['sepərəbl] trennbar; **⁓te** ['⁓eit] (sich) trennen; absondern; [⁓prit] getrennt, (ab)gesondert; **⁓tion** Trennung *f*.

September [sep'tembə] September *m*.

septic ['septik] septisch.

sepul|chre, *Am.* **⁓cher** ['sepəlkə] Grab(stätte *f*, -mal *n*) *n*.

sequel ['si:kwəl] Folge *f*; (Roman- *etc.*)Fortsetzung *f*.

sequence ['si:kwəns] (Aufeinander-, Reihen)Folge *f*.

serene [si'ri:n] heiter; klar; ruhig; gelassen.

sergeant ['sɑːdʒənt] *mil.* Feldwebel *m*; (Polizei-) Wachtmeister *m*.

seri|al ['siəriəl] fortlaufend, serienmäßig; Serien-..., Fortsetzungs-...; Fortsetzungsroman *m*; Folge *f*, Serie *f*; **⁓es** ['⁓ri:z], *pl* **⁓** Reihe *f*, Serie *f*, Folge *f*.

serious ['siəriəs] ernst.

sermon ['sɔːmən] (Straf-) Predigt *f*.

serpent ['sɔːpənt] Schlange *f*.

serum ['siərəm] Serum *n*.

servant ['sɔːvənt] Diener (-in); Dienstbote *m*, Dienstmädchen *n*, Hausangestellte *m*, *f*.

serve [sɔːv] dienen; (*j-n*) bedienen; *Speisen* servieren, auftragen; *Tennis:* aufschlagen; *Zweck* erfüllen; nützen; genügen; **⁓ (out)** aus-, verteilen.

service ['sɔːvis] Dienst (-leistung *f*) *m*; Gefälligkeit *f*; Bedienung *f*; Betrieb *m*; *tech.* Wartung *f*, Kundendienst *m*; (Zug-*etc.*)Verkehr *m*; Gottesdienst *m*; Service *f*; *Tennis:* Aufschlag *m*; Nutzen *m*; warten, pflegen; **⁓able** brauchbar, nützlich; **⁓ station** (Reparatur)Werkstatt *f*; Tankstelle *f*.

session ['seʃən] Sitzung(speriode) *f*.

set [set] Satz *m*, Garnitur *f*; Service *n*; Sammlung *f*, Reihe *f*, Serie *f* (*Radio-etc.*)Gerät *n*; Clique *f*; *poet.* (Sonnen)Untergang *m*; fest(gelegt, -gesetzt); bereit; entschlossen; (*irr*) setzen, stellen, legen; *Wecker, Aufgabe* stellen; *Knochenbruch* einrichten; *Tisch* decken; *Haar* legen; *Edelstein* fassen; *Zeitpunkt* festsetzen; *Beispiel* geben; untergehen (*Sonne*); erstarren; **⁓ eyes on** erblicken; **⁓ free** freilassen; **⁓ at ease** beruhigen; **⁓ about doing s.th.** sich daranmachen, et. zu tun; **⁓ off** auf-

brechen; starten; hervor-
heben; **~ out** aufbrechen;
~ to sich daranmachen; **~
up** aufstellen; errichten;
~back Rückschlag *m*; **~
dinner, ~ lunch** Menü *n*,
Gedeck *n*.

settee [se'ti:] *kleines Sofa.*

setting ['setiŋ] Fassung *f
(e-s Edelsteins);* Hintergrund *m*, Umgebung *f*;
*(Sonnen)*Untergang *m.*

settle ['setl] Sitzbank *f*;
(sich) ansiedeln; besiedeln;
Rechnung begleichen; klären, entscheiden; regeln;
Streit beilegen; vereinbaren; vermachen **(on**
dat); beruhigen; sich (ab-)
setzen; **~ (o.s., down)** sich
niederlassen; **~ment** (An-,
Be)Siedlung *f*; Bezahlung
f; Klärung *f*; Schlichtung *f*;
Abmachung *f*; **~r** Siedler *m.*

seven ['sevn] sieben; Sieben
f; **~teen(th)** ['~'ti:n(θ)]
siebzehn(te); **~th** ['~θ]
sieb(en)te; Sieb(en)tel *n*;
~thly sieb(en)tens; **~tieth**
['~tiiθ] siebzigste; **~ty** siebzig; Siebzig *f.*

sever ['sevə] (zer)reißen;
(sich) trennen; *fig.* lösen.

several ['sevrəl] mehrere;
verschiedene; einige.

severe [si'viə] streng;
hart; scharf; rauh *(Wetter)*;
heftig *(Schmerz, Sturm)*;
schwer *(Krankheit)*; **~ity**
[~'eriti] Strenge *f*, Härte *f.*

sew [səu] *(irr)* nähen.

sew|age ['sju(:)idʒ] Ab-
wasser *n*; **~er** Abwasser-

kanal *m*; **~erage** Kanalisation *f.*

sew|ing ['səuiŋ] Nähen *n*;
Näherei *f*; Näh...; **~n** *pp
von* **sew.**

sex [seks] Geschlecht *n*;
(der) Sex.

sexton ['sekstən] Küster *m*
(u. Totengräber *m*).

sexual ['seksjuəl] ge-
schlechtlich, Geschlechts-
..., sexuell, Sexual...

shabby ['ʃæbi] schäbig;
gemein.

shack [ʃæk] Hütte *f*, Bude *f.*

shade [ʃeid] Schatten *m*;
*(Lampen- etc.)*Schirm *m*;
Am. Rouleau *n*; Schattierung *f*; abschirmen, schützen.

shadow ['ʃædəu] Schatten
m; beschatten.

shady ['ʃeidi] schattig; *fig.*
fragwürdig.

shaft [ʃɑ:ft] Schaft *m*;
Stiel *m*; Deichsel *f*;
Schacht *m.*

shaggy ['ʃægi] zottig,
struppig.

shak|e [ʃeik] Schütteln *n*;
Beben *n*; *(irr)* (sch)wan-
ken; beben; zittern; schütteln, rütteln; erschüttern;
~e hands sich die Hand
geben; **~en** *pp von* **shake**;
erschüttert; **~y** wack(e)lig;
zitt(e)rig.

shall [ʃæl] *v/aux* ich, du *etc.;*
soll(st) *etc.; ich werde, wir*
werden.

shallow ['ʃæləu] seicht;
flach; *fig.* oberflächlich;
Untiefe *f.*

sham [ʃæm] vortäuschen; sich verstellen; ~ **ill(ness)** sich krank stellen.

shame [ʃeim] beschämen; j-m Schande machen; Scham f; Schande f; **for** ~!, ~ **on you!** pfui!, schäme dich!; ~**ful** schändlich; ~**less** schamlos.

shampoo [ʃæm'pu:] Haare waschen; Shampoo n; Haarwäsche f; **a** ~ **and set** waschen und legen.

shank [ʃæŋk] Unterschenkel m.

shape [ʃeip] gestalten, formen, bilden; Gestalt f; Form f; **in good** ~ in guter Verfassung; ~**d** geformt; ...förmig; ~**less** formlos; ~**ly** wohlgeformt.

share [ʃɛə] teilen; teilhaben (**in** an); Pflugschar f; (An)Teil m; Aktie f; **go** ~**s** teilen; ~**holder** Aktionär(in).

shark [ʃɑ:k] Hai(fisch) m.

sharp [ʃɑ:p] scharf; spitz; schneidend; stechend; schlau; pünktlich, genau; ~**en** (ver)schärfen; schleifen; spitzen; ~**ener** ['ʃɑ:pnə] (Bleistift)Spitzer m; ~**ness** Schärfe f; ~**-witted** scharfsinnig.

shatter ['ʃætə] zerschmettern; zerstören, -rütten.

shave [ʃeiv] (irr) (sich) rasieren; haarscharf vorbeikommen an; Rasur f; **have (get) a** ~ sich rasieren (lassen); ~**n** pp **von shave.**

shaving ['ʃeiviŋ] Rasieren

n; Rasier...; pl (Hobel-) Späne pl.

shawl [ʃɔ:l] Schal m, Umhängetuch n.

she [ʃi:] sie; **in** Zssgn: zo. ...weibchen n.

sheaf [ʃi:f], pl **sheaves** [~vz] Garbe f; Bündel n.

shear [ʃiə] (irr) scheren.

sheath [ʃi:θ] Scheide f; Futteral n, Hülle f.

sheaves [ʃi:vz] pl **von sheaf.**

shed [ʃed] (irr) Blätter etc. abwerfen; Kleider etc. ablegen; vergießen; verbreiten; Schuppen m; Stall m.

sheep [ʃi:p], pl/~ Schaf(e pl) n; ~**dog** Schäferhund m; ~**ish** einfältig.

sheer [ʃiə] rein; bloß; glatt; steil; senkrecht.

sheet [ʃi:t] Bett-, Leintuch n, Laken n; (Glas- etc.) Platte f; Blatt n, Bogen m (Papier); ~ **iron** Eisenblech n; ~ **lightning** Wetterleuchten n.

shelf [ʃelf], pl **shelves** [~vz] Brett n, Regal n, Fach n.

shell [ʃel] Schale f, Hülse f, Muschel f; Granate f; schälen; enthülsen; beschießen; ~**fish** Schalentier n.

shelter ['ʃeltə] Schutzhütte f; Zufluchtsort m; Obdach n; Schutz m; (be)schützen.

shelves [ʃelvz] pl **von shelf.**

shepherd ['ʃepəd] Schäfer m, Hirt m.

shield [ʃi:ld] (Schutz-)

Schild *m*; (be)schützen (**from** vor).

shift [ʃift] (um-, aus)wechseln; verändern; (sich) verlagern *od.* -schieben; Wechsel *m*; Verschiebung *f*; -änderung *f*; (Arbeits-) Schicht *f*; Ausweg *m*, Notbehelf *m*; Kniff *m*, List *f*; **make ~** sich behelfen; **~y** unzuverlässig; verschlagen.

shilling ['ʃiliŋ] *alte Währung:* Shilling *m*.

shin(-bone) ['ʃin(-)] Schienbein *n*.

shine [ʃain] Schein *m*; Glanz *m*; (*irr*) scheinen, leuchten, glänzen, strahlen; *colloq.* (*pp* **~d**) polieren, putzen.

shingle ['ʃiŋgl] Schindel *f*.

shiny ['ʃaini] blank, glänzend, strahlend.

ship [ʃip] Schiff *n*; verschiffen; **~ment** Verschiffung *f*; Schiffsladung *f*; **~owner** Reeder *m*; **~ping** Verschiffung *f*; Versand *m*; **~ping company** Reederei *f*; **~wreck** Schiffbruch *m*; **~wrecked** schiffbrüchig; **~yard** Werft *f*.

shire ['ʃaiə, *in Zssgn:* ...ʃiə] Grafschaft *f*.　　[(vor.)｜

shirk [ʃə:k] sich drücken |

shirt [ʃə:t] (Herren)Hemd *n*; **~sleeve** Hemdsärmel *m*.

shiver ['ʃivə] Splitter *m*; Schauer *m*, Zittern *n*; zittern; frösteln.

shock [ʃɔk] Erschütterung *f*, Schlag *m*, Stoß *m*; (Nerven)Schock *m*; schockie-

ren, empören; *j-n* erschüttern; **~absorber** Stoßdämpfer *m*; **~ing** schockierend, empörend, anstößig.

shoe [ʃuː] Schuh *m*; **~horn** Schuhanzieher *m*; **~lace** Schnürsenkel *m*; **~maker** Schuhmacher *m*, Schuster *m*; **~string** Schnürsenkel *m*.　　　　　[**shine**.｜

shone [ʃɔn] *pret u. pp von* |

shook [ʃuk] *pret von* **shake**.

shoot [ʃuːt] *bot.* Schößling *m*; (*irr*) (ab)schießen; erschießen; *Film* aufnehmen, drehen; *Knospen etc.* treiben; (dahin-, vorbei)schießen; *bot.* sprießen; filmen; **~er** Schütze *m*.

shooting ['ʃuːtiŋ] Schießen *n*; Schießerei *f*; Jagd (-recht *n*) *f*; *Film:* Dreharbeiten *pl*; **~gallery** Schießstand *m*; **~star** Sternschnuppe *f*.

shop [ʃɔp] Laden *m*, Geschäft *n*; Werkstatt *f*; **talk** ~ fachsimpeln; *vb:* **go ~ping** einkaufen gehen; **~assistant** Verkäufer(in); **~girl** Verkäuferin *f*; **~keeper** Ladeninhaber(in); **~lifter** Ladendieb(in); **~man** Verkäufer *m*; **~ping** Einkauf *m*, Einkaufen *n*; **do one's ~ping** (*s-e*) Einkäufe machen; **~ping centre** Einkaufszentrum *n*; **~steward** *appr.* Betriebsrat *m*; **~walker** Aufsichtsherr *m*, -dame *f*; **~window** Schaufenster *n*.

shore [ʃɔ:] Küste f, Ufer n; Strand m; **on ~** an Land.

shorn [ʃɔ:n] pp von **shear.**

short [ʃɔ:t] adj kurz; klein; knapp; kurz angebunden; mürbe (Gebäck); **make it ~** sich kurz fassen; **~ of** knapp an; adv abgesehen von; **sub: in ~** kurz(um); **~age** Knappheit f; **~coming** Unzulänglichkeit f; **~ cut** Abkürzung(sweg m) f; **~en** (ab-, ver)kürzen; kürzer werden; **~hand** Kurzschrift f, Stenographie f; **~hand typist** Stenotypistin f; **~ly** kurz; bald; **~ness** Kürze f; **~s** pl Shorts pl, kurze Hose; kurze Unterhose; **~story** Kurzgeschichte f; **~sighted** kurzsichtig; **~term** kurzfristig; **~winded** kurzatmig.

shot [ʃɔt] pret u. pp von **shoot;** Schuß m; Schrot (-kugeln pl) m, n; guter etc. Schütze m; (Film-) Aufnahme f; **~gun** Schrotflinte f.

should [ʃud] pret u. cond von **shall.**

shoulder [ˈʃəuldə] Schulter f, Achsel f; schultern.

shout [ʃaut] lauter Schrei od. Ruf; Geschrei n; (laut) rufen, schreien.

shove [ʃʌv] colloq. schieben, stoßen.

shovel [ˈʃʌvl] Schaufel f; schaufeln.

show [ʃəu] (irr) (vor)zeigen; ausstellen; führen;

sich zeigen; **~ (a)round** herumführen; **~ off** angeben, prahlen; **~ up** auftauchen, erscheinen; Zurschaustellung f; Vorführung f, -stellung f, Schau f; Ausstellung f; **~ business** Unterhaltungsindustrie f, Schaugeschäft n.

shower [ˈʃauə] (Regen- etc.)Schauer m; Dusche f; fig. j-n mit et. überschütten od. -häufen; **~bath** Dusche f.

show|n [ʃəun] pp von **show; ~y** prächtig; protzig.

shrank [ʃræŋk] pret von **shrink.**

shred [ʃred] Fetzen m; (irr) zerfetzen.

shrew [ʃru:] zänkisches Weib; **~d** [~d] schlau; klug.

shriek [ʃri:k] Schrei m; Gekreisch(e) n; kreischen; schreien.

shrill [ʃril] schrill, gellend.

shrimp [ʃrimp] Garnele f.

shrine [ʃrain] Schrein m.

shrink [ʃriŋk] (irr) (ein-, zs.-)schrumpfen (lassen); einlaufen; zurückschrecken (**from** vor).

shrivel [ˈʃrivl] (ein-, zs.-) schrumpfen (lassen).

Shrove|tide [ˈʃrəuvtaid] Fastnachtszeit f; **~ Tuesday** Fastnachtsdienstag m.

shrub [ʃrʌb] Strauch m, Busch m; **~bery** Gebüsch n.

shrug [ʃrʌg] die Achseln zucken; Achselzucken n;

silence

shrunk [ʃrʌŋk] *pp von* **shrink; ~en** (ein)geschrumpft; eingefallen.

shudder ['ʃʌdə] schaudern; Schauder *m*.

shuffle ['ʃʌfl] *Karten*: mischen; schlurfen.

shun [ʃʌn] (ver)meiden.

shut [ʃʌt] (*irr*) (ver)schließen, zumachen; sich schließen; **~ down** *Betrieb* schließen; **~ up** ein-, verschließen; einsperren; **~ up!** *colloq.* halt den Mund!; **~ter** Fensterladen *m*; *phot.* Verschluß *m*.

shy [ʃai] scheu; schüchtern; **~ness** Scheu *f*; Schüchternheit *f*.

sick [sik] krank; übel; überdrüssig; **be ~** sich übergeben; **be ~ of** genug haben von; **I feel ~** mir ist schlecht *od.* übel; **~-benefit** Krankengeld *n*; **~en** erkranken, krank werden; anekeln.

sickle ['sikl] Sichel *f*.

sick|-leave Krankenurlaub *m*; **~ly** kränklich; **~ness** Krankheit *f*; Übelkeit *f*; **~room** Krankenzimmer *n*.

side [said] Seite *f*; Seiten...; Neben...; **~ by** Seite an Seite; **take ~s with, ~ with** Partei ergreifen für; **~board** Anrichte *f*, Büfett *n*, Sideboard *n*; **~car** *mot.* Beiwagen *m*; **~d** *in Zssgn*: ...seitig; **~dish** Beilage *f*; **~road** Nebenstraße *f*; **~walk** *Am.* Bürgersteig *m*; **~walk café** *Am.* Straßen-

café *n*; **~ward(s)** ['~wəd(z)], **~ways** seitlich; seitwärts.

siege [si:dʒ] Belagerung *f*.

sieve [siv] Sieb *n*; sieben.

sift [sift] sieben; *fig.* sichten, prüfen. [zen.\

sigh [sai] Seufzer *m*; seuf-\

sight [sait] sehen, erblicken; Sehvermögen *n*, -kraft *f*; Anblick *m*; Sicht *f*; *pl* Sehenswürdigkeiten *pl*; **catch ~ of** erblicken; **know by ~** vom Sehen kennen; **(with)in ~** in Sicht(weite); **...sichtig;** **~seeing** Besichtigung *f* (*von* Sehenswürdigkeiten); Besichtigungs...; **~seeing tour** (Stadt)Rundfahrt *f*; **~seer** Tourist(in).

sign [sain] Zeichen *n*; Wink *m*; Schild *n*; Zeichen geben; unterzeichnen, unterschreiben.

signal ['signl] Signal *n*; signalisieren, Zeichen geben.

signature ['signitʃə] Unterschrift *f*; **~ tune** *Radio*: Kennmelodie *f*.

signboard (Firmen-, Aushänge)Schild *n*.

signet ['signit] Siegel *n*.

significa|nce [sig'nifikəns] Bedeutung *f*; **~nt** bedeutsam; bedeutend (**of** für); **~tion** Bedeutung *f*.

signify ['signifai] andeuten; ankündigen; bedeuten.

signpost Wegweiser *m*.

silence ['sailəns] (Still-)

Schweigen n; Stille f, Ruhe f; ~! Ruhe!; zum Schweigen bringen; ~r Schalldämpfer m; mot. Auspufftopf m.

silent ['sailənt] still; schweigend; schweigsam; stumm.

silk [silk] Seide f; Seiden...; ~en seiden; ~y seidig.

sill [sil] Fensterbrett n.

silly ['sili] dumm; albern; töricht.

silver ['silvə] Silber n; silbern, Silber...; versilbern; ~y silb(e)rig.

similar ['similə] ähnlich, gleich; ~ity [~'læriti]Ähnlichkeit f.

simmer ['simə] leicht kochen, sieden, brodeln.

simple ['simpl] einfach; simpel; schlicht; einfältig.

simpli|city [sim'plisiti] Einfachheit f; Einfalt f; ~fication Vereinfachung f; ~fy [~'fai] vereinfachen.

simply ['simpli] einfach; bloß, nur.

simulate ['simjuleit] vortäuschen; simulieren.

simultaneous [siməl'teinjəs] gleichzeitig.

sin [sin] Sünde f; sündigen. [da (ja), weil.]

since [sins]seit;seit(dem).]

sincer|e [sin'siə] aufrichtig; Yours ~ely Ihr ergebener; ~ity [~'seriti] Aufrichtigkeit f.

sinew ['sinju:] Sehne f; ~y sehnig; fig. kräftig.

sing [siŋ] (irr) (be)singen.

singe [sindʒ] (ver-, an)sengen.

singer ['siŋə] Sänger(in).

single ['siŋgl] einzig; einzeln, Einzel...; einzeln; allein; ledig; vb: ~ out aussuchen, -wählen; sub: einfache Fahrkarte; mst pl Tennis: Einzel m; ~-handed eigenhändig, allein; ~ room Einzel-, Einbettzimmer n; ~ ticket einfache Fahrkarte.

singular ['siŋgjulə] einzigartig; eigentümlich, seltsam; gr. Singular m, Einzahl f; ~ity [~'læriti] Einzigartigkeit f; Eigentümlichkeit f.

sinister ['sinistə] unheilvoll, böse; finster.

sink [siŋk] (irr) (ein-, herab-, ver)sinken; untergehen; sich senken; (ver-) senken; Ausguß m, Spülbecken n; ~ing (Ein-, Ver)Sinken m; Versenken n.

sinner ['sinə] Sünder(in).

sip [sip] Schlückchen n; schlürfen, nippen an od. von.

sir [sə:] (mein) Herr (Anrede); 2 Sir (Titel).

sirloin ['sə:lɔin] Lendenstück n.

sister ['sistə] Schwester f; ~-in-law Schwägerin f.

sit [sit] (irr) sitzen; e-e Sitzung (ab)halten, tagen; setzen; sitzen auf; ~ down sich (hin)setzen; ~ up aufrecht sitzen; sich aufrichten; aufbleiben.

site [sait] Lage *f*; Stelle *f*; Bauplatz *m*.

sitting ['sitiŋ] Sitzung *f*; **~-room** Wohnzimmer *n*.

situat|ed ['sitjueitid] gelegen; **be ~ed** liegen; **~ion** Lage *f*; Stellung *f*; Situation *f*.

six [siks] sechs; Sechs *f*; **~pence** *alte Währung:* Sixpence *m*; **~teen** ['~'ti:n(θ)] sechzehn(te); **~th** [~sθ] sechste; Sechstel *n*; **~thly** sechstens; **~tieth** ['~tiiθ] sechzigste; **~ty** sechzig; Sechzig *f*.

size [saiz] Größe *f*; Format *n*; **~d in** *Zssgn:* ...groß, von *od.* in ... Größe.

sizzle ['sizl] *colloq.* zischen, brutzeln.

skate [skeit] Schlittschuh *m*; Schlitt- *od.* Rollschuh laufen; **~r** Schlittschuh-, Rollschuhläufer(in).

skeleton ['skelitn] Skelett *n*.

skeptic ['skeptik] *bsd. Am. für* **sceptic.**

sketch [sketʃ] Skizze *f*; Entwurf *m*; skizzieren; entwerfen; **~-block**, **~-book** Skizzenbuch *n*.

ski [ski:], *pl* **~(s)** Schi *m*, Ski *m*; Schi *od.* Ski laufen.

skid [skid] Bremsklotz *m*; *aer.* Kufe *f*; *mot.* Rutschen *n*, Schleudern *n*; rutschen, schleudern.

ski|er ['ski:ə] Schi-, Skiläufer(in); **~ing** Schi-, Skilaufen *n* (*m*).

skilful ['skilful] geschickt.

skill [skil] Geschick(lich-

keit *f*) *n*, Fertigkeit *f*; **~ed** geschickt; gelernt, Fach...; **~ed worker** Facharbeiter *m*; **~ful** *Am. für* skilful.

skim [skim] abschöpfen; entrahmen; **~ (through)** *fig.* überfliegen; **~(med) milk** Magermilch *f*.

skin [skin] Haut *f*; Fell *n*; Schale *f*; (ent)häuten; abbalgen; schälen; **~-deep** oberflächlich; **~-diving** Sporttauchen *n*; **~ny** mager.

skip [skip] Hüpfen *n*, Sprung *m*; hüpfen, springen.

skipper ['skipə] *mar.* Schiffer *m*, Kapitän *m*; *aer., sp.* Kapitän *m*.

skirt [skə:t] (Damen)Rock *m*; *pl* Rand *m*, Saum *m*; sich entlangziehen (an).

skittles ['skitlz] *sg* Kegeln *n*; **play (at) ~** kegeln.

skull [skʌl] (Toten)Schädel *m*.

sky [skai] *oft pl* Himmel *m*; **~jacker** ['~dʒækə] Luftpirat *m*; **~light** Oberlicht *n*; Dachfenster *n*; **~line** Horizont *m*; (Stadt- *etc.*)Silhouette *f*; **~scraper** Wolkenkratzer *m*, Hochhaus *n*; **~ward(s)** ['~wəd(z)] himmelwärts.

slab [slæb] Platte *f*, Fliese *f*.

slack [slæk] schlaff; lose; (nach)lässig; *econ.* flau; **~en** nachlassen (in); (sich) lockern; (sich) verlangsamen; **~s** *pl* (lange Damen-) Hose *f*.

slain [slein] *pp von* slay.

slake [sleik] *Durst, Kalk* löschen; *fig.* stillen.

slam [slæm] *Tür etc.* zuschlagen, zuknallen; *et. auf den Tisch etc.* knallen.

slander ['slɑ:ndə] Verleumdung *f;* verleumden.

slang [slæŋ] Slang *m;* lässige Umgangssprache.

slant [slɑ:nt] schräge Fläche; Abhang *m;* sich neigen; schräg liegen *od.* legen.

slap [slæp] Klaps *m,* Schlag *m;* schlagen; **~stick comedy** *thea.* derbe Posse.

slash [slæʃ] Hieb *m;* klaffende Wunde; Schlitz *m;* (auf)schlitzen; (los)schlagen.

slate [sleit] Schiefer *m;* Schiefertafel *f;* **~-pencil** Griffel *m.*

slattern ['slætə(:)n] Schlampe *f.*

slaughter ['slɔ:tə] Schlachten *n;* Gemetzel *n;* schlachten; niedermetzeln.

slave [sleiv] Sklav|e *m,* -in *f;* schuften; **~ry** ['~əri] Sklaverei *f.*

slay [slei] *(irr)* poet. erschlagen, ermorden.

sled(ge) [sled(ʒ)] Schlitten *m;* Schlitten fahren.

sledge(-hammer) Schmiedehammer *m.*

sleek [sli:k] glatt, glänzend; *fig.* geschmeidig.

sleep [sli:p] *(irr)* schlafen; **~ on, ~ over** *et.* beschlafen; Schlaf *m;* **have a**
good, etc. **~** gut etc. schlafen; **go to ~** einschlafen; **~er** Schläfer(in); (Eisenbahn)Schwelle *f;* Schlafwagen(platz) *m;* **~-bag** Schlafsack *m;* **2ing Beauty** Dornröschen *n;* **~ing-car** Schlafwagen *m;* **~ing partner** stiller Teilhaber; **~ing-pill** Schlaftablette *f;* **~less** schlaflos; **~-walker** Schlafwandler(in); **~y** schläfrig; verschlafen.

sleet [sli:t] Schneeregen *m.*

sleeve [sli:v] Ärmel *m;* Plattenhülle *f; tech.* Muffe *f.*

sleigh [slei] *(bsd. Pferde-)* Schlitten *m;* (im) Schlitten fahren.

slender ['slendə] schlank; schmächtig; dürftig.

slept [slept] *pret u. pp von* sleep.

slew [slu:] *pret von* slay.

slice [slais] Schnitte *f,* Scheibe *f,* Stück *n;* **a ~ of bread** e-e Scheibe Brot; in Scheiben schneiden, aufschneiden.

slick [slik] *colloq.* glatt; geschickt, raffiniert; **~er** *Am.* (langer) Regenmantel.

slid [slid] *pret u. pp von* slide.

slide [slaid] *(irr)* gleiten (lassen); rutschen; schlittern; schieben; Gleiten *n;* Rutschbahn *f,* Rutsche *f;* Erd-, Felsrutsch *m; tech.* Schieber *m; phot.* Diapositiv *n;* **~-rule** Rechenschieber *m.*

slight [slait] schmächtig; schwach; gering(fügig); Geringschätzung *f*; geringschätzig behandeln.

slim [slim] schlank, dünn; schlank(er) werden; e-e Schlankheitskur machen.

slim|e [slaim] Schleim *m*; **~y** schleimig.

sling [sliŋ] Schleuder *f*; Tragriemen *m*;(*med.* Arm-) Schlinge *f*; (*irr*) schleudern; auf-, umhängen.

slip [slip] (aus)gleiten, (aus-, ent)rutschen; (hinein-, ent)schlüpfen; gleiten lassen; **have ~ped s.o.'s memory** *od.* **mind** j-m entfallen sein; **~ on** *od.* **off** *Kleid etc.* über- *od.* abstreifen; **~ (up)** (e-n) Fehler machen; (Aus)Gleiten *n*, (-)Rutschen *n*; (Flüchtigkeits)Fehler *m*; Unterkleid *n*; (Kissen)Bezug *m*; Streifen *m*, Zettel *m*, Abschnitt *m*; **~per** Pantoffel *m*, Hausschuh *m*; **~pery** schlüpfrig, glatt.

slit [slit] Schlitz *m*; Spalte *f*; (*irr*) (auf-, zer)schlitzen; reißen.

slobber [´sləbə] sabbern.

slogan [´slougən] Schlagwort *n*, (Werbe)Slogan *m*.

sloop [slu:p] Schaluppe *f*.

slop [sləp] Pfütze *f*; *pl* Spül-, Schmutzwasser *n*; **~ (over)** verschütten; überlaufen.

slop|e [sloup] (Ab)Hang *m*; Neigung *f*, Gefälle *n*; abfallen, schräg verlaufen,

sich neigen; **~ing** schräg, abschüssig, abfallend.

sloppy [´sləpi] naß, schmutzig; *colloq.*: schlampig; sentimental.

slot [slət] Schlitz *m*.

sloth [slouθ] *zo.* Faultier *n*.

slot-machine (Waren-, Spiel)Automat *m*.

slough [slau] Sumpf(loch *n*) *m*.

sloven [´slʌvn] unordentlicher Mensch, Schlampe *f*; **~ly** liederlich, schlampig.

slow [slou] langsam; schwerfällig; träg(e); **be ~** nachgehen (*Uhr*); **~ down** verlangsamen; *et.* verzögern; langsamer werden; **~-motion** Zeitlupe *f*; **~-worm** Blindschleiche *f*.

sluggish [´slʌgiʃ] träg(e).

sluice [slu:s] Schleuse *f*.

slums [slʌmz] *pl* Elendsviertel *n*, Slums *pl*.

slumber [´slʌmbə] *oft pl* Schlummer *m*; schlummern.

slung [slʌŋ] *pret u. pp von* **sling**.

slush [slʌʃ] Schlamm *m*; (Schnee)Matsch *m*.

slut [slʌt] Schlampe *f*; Nutte *f*.

sly [slai] schlau, verschlagen; verschmitzt.

smack [smæk] (Bei)Geschmack *m*; Klatsch *m*, Klaps *m*; Schmatzen *n*; schmecken (of nach); j-m e-n Klaps geben; **~ one's lips** schmatzen.

small [smɔ:l] klein; unbedeutend; niedrig; wenig;

bescheiden; **~ change** Kleingeld *n*; *the* **~ hours** *pl die* frühen Morgenstunden *pl*; **~ish** ziemlich klein; **~ of the back** *anat.* Kreuz *n*; **~pox** ['~pɔks] Pocken (*pl*.); **~s** *pl colloq.* Unterwäsche *f*; **~ talk** oberflächliche Konversation.

smart [smɑːt] klug, gescheit; schlagfertig; gerissen; geschickt; elegant, schick; forsch, flink; hart, scharf.

smash [smæʃ] krachen, zerschlagen, -trümmern; (zer)schmettern; (zer)vernichten; **~ing** *sl.* toll.

smattering ['smætəriŋ] oberflächliche Kenntnis.

smear [smiə] (be)schmieren; *fig.* beschmutzen; Fleck *m*.

smell [smel] Geruch *m*; (*irr*) riechen; duften.

smelt[1] [smelt] *pret u. pp von* **smell**.

smelt[2] Erz schmelzen.

smile [smail] Lächeln *n*; lächeln.

smith [smiθ] Schmied *m*; **~y** ['~ði] Schmiede *f*.

smitten ['smitn] betroffen; *fig.* hingerissen (**with** von).

smock [smɔk] Kittel *m*.

smog [smɔg] Smog *m*, Dunstglocke *f*.

smoke [smuk] Rauch *m*; **have a ~** eine rauchen (*Zigarette etc.*); *vb*: rauchen; räuchern; **~-dried**

geräuchert; **~r** Raucher(in); *rail.* Raucherabteil *n*.

smoking ['smukiŋ] Rauchen *n*; Rauch...; **~-car, ~-carriage, ~-compartment** Raucherabteil *n*.

smoky ['smuki] rauchig; verräuchert.

smooth [smuːð] glatt; ruhig (*a. tech.*); sanft, weich; (sich) glätten; fig. ebnen; **~ down** glattstreichen.

smother ['smʌðə] erstikken.   [schwelen.

smo(u)lder ['smuuldə] |

smudge [smʌdʒ] (be-) schmieren; Fleck *m*.

smuggle ['smʌgl] schmuggeln; **~r** Schmuggler(in).

smut [smʌt] Ruß(fleck) *m*; Zote(n *pl*) *f*; beschmutzen; **~ty** schmutzig.

snack [snæk] Imbiß *m*; **~ bar** Imbißstube *f*.

snail [sneil] Schnecke *f*.

snake [sneik] Schlange *f*.

snap [snæp] schnappen (**at** nach); knallen (mit); zuschnappen (lassen) (*Schloß*); (zer)brechen; zerreißen; *phot.* knipsen; schnappen nach; schnell greifen nach; schnalzen mit; Knacken *n*; Knall *m*; (Zer)Brechen *n*; **cold ~** Kältewelle *f*; **~-fastener** Druckknopf *m*; **~pish** bissig; schnippisch; **~shot** Schnappschuß *m*.

snare [snɛə] Schlinge *f*; Falle *f*.

snarl [snɑːl] wütend

knurren; Knurren *n*, Zäh-
nefletschen *n*.

snatch [snætʃ] schneller
Zugriff; *pl* Bruchstücke *pl*;
schnappen; an sich reißen.

sneak [sni:k] schleichen;
~ers *pl Am.* leichte (Segeltuch)Schuhe *pl*.

sneer [sniə] Hohn(lächeln
n) *m*, Spott *m*; höhnisch
grinsen; spotten. [sen *n*.\

sneeze [sni:z] niesen; Nie-)

sniff [snif] schnüffeln,
schnuppern; die Nase
rümpfen.

snipe [snaip], *pl* **~(s)**
(Sumpf)Schnepfe *f*; **~r**
Scharf-, Heckenschütze *m*.

snivel ['snivl] greinen,
plärren.

snoop [snu:p] Schnüffler
(-in); **~ around** herum-
schnüffeln.

snooze [snu:z] *colloq.*: Nik-
kerchen *n*; dösen.

snore [snɔ:] schnarchen;
Schnarchen *n*.

snort [snɔ:t] schnauben.

snout [snaut] Schnauze *f*;
(*Schweine*)Rüssel *m*.

snow [snəu] Schnee *m*;
schneien; **~-capped**, **~-
clad**, **~-covered** schneebedeckt; **~-drift** Schnee-
wehe *f*; **~drop** Schnee-
glöckchen *n*; **~y** schneeig,
Schnee...; schneebedeckt,
verschneit.

snub [snʌb] verächtlich behandeln; Abfuhr *f*; **~-
nosed** stupsnasig.

snuff [snʌf] Schnupftabak
m; schnupfen.

snug [snʌg] behaglich; **~-
gle** sich schmiegen *od.*
kuscheln.

so [səu] so; deshalb; also;
I hope ~ ich hoffe es; **~
am I** ich auch; **~ far** bisher.

soak [səuk] sickern; einweichen; durchnässen,
-tränken; **~ up** aufsaugen.

soap [səup] Seife *f*; ab-,
einseifen; **~-box** Seifen-
kiste *f*; improvisierte Red-
nerbühne.

soar [sɔ:] sich erheben,
(hoch) aufsteigen.

sob [sɔb] Schluchzen *n*;
schluchzen.

sober ['səubə] nüchtern;
ernüchtern; **~ up** nüchtern
machen *od.* werden.

so-called sogenannt.

soccer ['sɔkə] *colloq.* (Ver-
bands)Fußball *m*.

sociable ['səuʃəbl] gesellig.

social ['səuʃəl] gesellig;
gesellschaftlich; sozial(i-
stisch); Sozial...; **~ insurance** Sozialversiche-
rung *f*; **~ism** Sozialismus
m; **~ist** Sozialist(in); **~-
ist(ic)** sozialistisch; **~ize**
sozialisieren, verstaatlichen.

society [sə'saiəti] Gesellschaft *f*; Verein *m*.

sock [sɔk] Socke *f*; Ein-
legesohle *f*.

socket ['sɔkit] (Augen-,
Zahn)Höhle *f*; *electr.*: Fassung *f*; Steckdose *f*.

sod [sɔd] Grasnarbe *f*;
Rasenstück *n*.

sofa ['səufə] Sofa *n*.

soft [sɔft] weich; mild(e); sanft; leise; *colloq.* einfältig; **~ drink** *colloq.* alkoholfreies Getränk; **~en** ['sɔfn] weich werden *od.* machen; *j-n* rühren.

soil [sɔil] Boden *m*, Erde *f*; (be)schmutzen.

sojourn ['sɔdʒəːn] Aufenthalt *m*; sich aufhalten.

sold [səuld] *pret u. pp von* **sell.**

soldier ['səuldʒə] Soldat *m*.

sole[1] [səul] einzig, allein; **~** *f.* Sohle *f*; besohlen.

sole[2] *ichth.* Seezunge *f*.

solemn ['sɔləm] feierlich; ernst.

solicit [sə'lisit] dringend bitten; **~or** Anwalt *m*; **~ous** besorgt; bestrebt, eifrig bemüht; **~ude** [~tju:d] Besorgnis *f*.

solid ['sɔlid] fest, kompakt; stabil; massiv; *fig.* gründlich, solid(e); **solid|arity** [sɔli'dæriti] Solidarität *f*; **~ity** Festigkeit *f*, Solidität *f*.

soliloquy [sə'liləkwi] Selbstgespräch *n*, Monolog *m*.

solit|ary ['sɔlitəri] einsam; einzeln; **~ude** [~tju:d] Einsamkeit *f*.

solo ['səuljubl] Solo *n*, allein; **~ist** Solist(in).

solu|ble ['sɔljubl] löslich; (auf)lösbar; **~tion** [sə'lu:-ʃən] (Auf)Lösung *f*.

solve [sɔlv] lösen; **~nt** (auf)lösend; zahlungsfähig; Lösungsmittel *n*.

somb|re, *Am.* **~er** ['sɔmbə] düster.

some [sʌm, səm] (irgend-)ein; etwas; *vor pl*: einige, ein paar; manche; etwa; **~ more** noch et.; **~body** ['sʌmbədi] jemand; **~day** eines Tages; **~how** irgendwie; **~one** jemand.

somersault ['sʌməsɔːlt] Salto *m*; Purzelbaum *m*; **turn a ~** e-n Purzelbaum schlagen.

some|thing (irgend) etwas; **~time** irgendwann; ehemalig; **~times** manchmal; **~what** etwas, ziemlich; **~where** irgendwo (-hin).

son [sʌn] Sohn *m*.

song [sɔŋ] Lied *n*; **~-bird** Singvogel *m*; **~-book** Liederbuch *n*; **~ster** ['~stə] Singvogel *m*.

sonic ['sɔnik] Schall...

son-in-law Schwiegersohn *m*.

sonnet ['sɔnit] Sonett *n*.

soon [su:n] bald; früh; **as ~ as** sobald (als, wie); **~er** eher, früher; lieber; **no ~er ... than** kaum ... als; **no ~er said than done** gesagt, getan. (rußen.\

soot [sut] Ruß *m*; ver-\

soothe [su:ð] beruhigen, besänftigen; lindern.

sooty ['suti] rußig.

sophisticated [sə'fistikeitid] kultiviert; intellektuell; anspruchsvoll; blasiert.

soporific [sɔpə'rifik] Schlafmittel *n*.

sorcer|er ['sɔːsərə] Zauberer *m*; **~ess** Zauberin *f*, Hexe *f*; **~y** Zauberei *f*.

sordid ['sɔːdid] schmutzig; schäbig.

sore [sɔː] schlimm, entzündet; weh(e), wund; **~ throat** Halsweh *n*.

sorrow ['sɔrəu] Kummer *m*, Leid *n*; Reue *f*; **~ful** traurig.

sorry ['sɔri] bekümmert; traurig; **(I am) (so)** **~!** es tut mir (sehr) leid!, (ich) bedaure!, Verzeihung!

sort [sɔːt] sortieren, (ein-) ordnen; Sorte *f*, Art *f*.

sought [sɔːt] *pret u. pp von* **seek.**

soul [səul] Seele *f*.

sound [saund] gesund; *econ.* stabil; vernünftig; gründlich; fest, tief (*Schlaf*); *mar.* loten; sondieren; (er)tönen; (er)schallen *od.* (~)klingen (lassen); *fig.* klingen; *med.* abhorchen; (aus)sprechen; Meerenge *f*; Schall *m*, Laut *m*, Ton *m*, Klang *m*; **~less** lautlos; **~proof** schalldicht; **~wave** Schallwelle *f*.

soup [suːp] Suppe *f*.

sour ['sauə] sauer; *fig.* bitter, mürrisch.

source [sɔːs] Quelle *f*; Ursprung *m*.

south [sauθ] Süd (*en m*); südlich, Süd...; **~east** Südost; **~east(ern)** südöstlich.

souther|ly ['sʌðəli], **~n** südlich, Süd...; **~ner** *Am.*

Südstaatler(in); **~nmost** südlichst.

southward(s) ['sauθwəd(z)] südwärts, nach Süden.

southwest Südwest; südwestlich; **~erly** nach *od.* aus Südwesten; **~ern** südwestlich; **~ern** südwestlich.

souvenir ['suːvəniə] (Reise)Andenken *n*, Souvenir *n*.

sovereign ['sɔvrin] Souverän *m*, Monarch(in); **~ty** ['~rənti] Souveränität *f*.

Soviet ['sɔuviət] Sowjet *m*; sowjetisch, Sowjet...

sow[1] [sau] Sau *f*, (Mutter-) Schwein *n*.

sow[2] [səu] (*irr*) (aus)säen; **~n** *pp von* **sow[2].**

spa [spaː] (Heil)Bad *n*.

space [speis] (Welt)Raum *m*; Platz *m*; Zwischenraum *m*, Abstand *m*; Zeitraum *m*; **~craft**, **~ship** Raumschiff *n*; **~suit** Raumanzug *m*.

spacious ['speiʃəs] geräumig; weit, umfassend.

spade [speid] Spaten *m*; **~(s pl)** Karten: Pik *n*.

span [spæn] Spanne *f*; Spannweite *f*; um-, überspannen; *pret von* **spin.**

spangle ['spæŋgl] Flitter *m*; **~d** *fig.* glänzen.

Spani|ard ['spænjəd] Spanier(in); **~sh** spanisch; Spanisch *n*.

spank [spæŋk] verhauen; **~ing** Tracht *f* Prügel.

spanner ['spænə] Schraubenschlüssel *m*.

spare [spɛə] (ver)schonen;

entbehren; (übrig) haben; sparen mit; spärlich; sparsam; übrig; Ersatz..., Reserve...; ~ **(part)** Ersatzteil *n*; ~ **room** Gästezimmer *n*; ~ **time** Freizeit *f*; ~ **wheel** Reserverad *n*.
sparing ['spɛəriŋ] sparsam.

spark [spɑːk] Funke(n) *m*; Funken sprühen; ~**ing-plug** Zündkerze *f*; ~**le** Funke(n) *m*; Funkeln *n*; funkeln, blitzen; schäumen, perlen; ~**plug** Zündkerze *f*.

sparrow ['spærəu] Sperling *m*, Spatz *m*.

sparse [spɑːs] spärlich, dünn.

spasm ['spæzəm] Krampf *m*; ~**odic** [~'mɔdik] krampfhaft, -artig.

spat [spæt] *pret u. pp von* **spit**.

spatter ['spætə] (be)spritzen.   [laichen.]

spawn [spɔːn] Laich *m*; f

speak [spiːk] (*irr*) sprechen, reden (**to** mit, zu); sagen; (aus)sprechen; ~ **out**, ~ **up** laut(er) sprechen; offen reden; ~**er** Sprecher(in), Redner(in).

spear [spiə] Speer *m*; Spieß *m*; aufspießen.

special ['speʃəl] besonder; speziell; Spezial...; Sonder...; Sonderausgabe *f*; Am. (Tages)Spezialität *f*; ~**ist** Spezialist *m*; ~**ity** [~i'æliti] Besonderheit *f*; Spezialität *f*;

~**ize** (sich) spezialisieren; ~**ty** Spezialität *f*.

species ['spiːʃiːz] *pl* ~ Art *f*, Spezies *f*.

speci|fic [spi'sifik] spezifisch; bestimmt; ~**fy** ['spesifai] spezifizieren, einzeln angeben; ~**men** ['spesimin]Exemplar *n*; Muster *n*.

spectacle ['spektəkl] Schauspiel *n*; Anblick *m*; **(a pair of)** ~**s** *pl*(e–e)Brille.

spectacular [spek'tækjulə] eindrucksvoll.

spectator [spek'teitə] Zuschauer *m*.

specula|te ['spekjuleit] Vermutungen anstellen; *econ.* spekulieren; ~**ion** Spekulation *f*.

sped [sped] *pret u. pp von* **speed**.

speech [spiːtʃ] Sprache *f*; Rede *f*; **make a** ~ e–e Rede halten; ~**day** *Schule:* (Jahres)Schlußfeier *f*; ~**less** sprachlos.

speed [spiːd] Geschwindigkeit *f*, Schnelligkeit *f*; Eile *f*; *tech.* Drehzahl *f*; (*irr*) schnell fahren, rasen, (dahin)eilen; ~ **up** (*pret. u. pp* ~**ed**) beschleunigen; ~**limit** Geschwindigkeitsbeschränkung *f*; ~**ometer** [spi'dɔmitə] Tachometer *m*, *n*; ~**y** schnell.

spell [spel] (Arbeits)Schicht *f*; Zeit(abschnitt *m*) *f*, *meteor. a.* Periode *f*; Zauber(spruch *m*) *m*; (*irr*) buchstabieren; richtig schreiben; ~**bound** (wie) gebannt; **~ing** Rechtschreibung f.   **[spell.]**

spelt [spelt] *pret u. pp von*
spend [spend] (*irr*) *Geld
etc.* ausgeben, verbrauchen; verschwenden; verbringen; verwenden.

spent [spent] *pret u. pp
von* **spend**; erschöpft;
verbraucht.

sperm [spə:m] Sperma *n*.

sphere [sfiə] (Erd-, Himmels)Kugel *f; fig.* Sphäre *f*.

spic|e [spais] Gewürz(e *pl*)
n; fig. Würze *f;* würzen;
~y würzig; *fig.* pikant.

spider [ˈspaidə] Spinne *f*.

spike [spaik] *bot.* Ähre *f;*
Stift *m*, Spitze *f*, Dorn *m*,
Stachel *m; pl* Spikes *pl*.

spill [spil] (*irr*) verschütten; überlaufen (lassen).

spilt [spilt] *pret u. pp von*
spill.

spin [spin] (*irr*) spinnen;
(herum)wirbeln; (sich) drehen; Drehung *f*.

spinach [ˈspinidʒ] Spinat *m*.

spinal [ˈspainl] Rückgrat
...; **~ column** Wirbelsäule
f; **~ cord** Rückenmark *n*.

spindle [ˈspindl] Spindel *f*.

spine [spain] *anat.* Rückgrat *n*, Wirbelsäule *f;* Stachel *m*.

spinning-mill Spinnerei *f*.

spinster [ˈspinstə] unverheiratete Frau; alte Jungfer.

spiny [ˈspaini] stach(e)lig.

spiral [ˈspaiərəl] Spirale *f;*
gewunden.

spire [ˈspaiə] (Kirch-)
Turmspitze *f*.

spirit [ˈspirit] Geist *m;*
Gesinnung *f;* Schwung *m*,
Elan *m*, Mut *m; pl* Spirituosen *pl*, alkoholische Getränke *pl;* **in high** *od.*
low ~s *pl* gehobener *od.*
gedrückter Stimmung; **~ed** temperamentvoll, lebhaft; mutig; **~ual** [ˈ.tjuəl]
geistig; geistlich; *mus.*
Spiritual *m, n*.

spit [spit] (Brat)Spieß *m;*
Speichel *m*, Spucke *f;* (*irr*)
(aus)spucken; fauchen.

spite [spait] Bosheit *f;*
Groll *m; in ~ of* trotz; **~ful**
gehässig, boshaft.

spittle [ˈspitl] Speichel *m;*
Spucke *f*.

splash [splæʃ] Spritzer *m;*
Platschen *n;* (be)spritzen;
platschen, planschen; **~down** wassern (*Raumfahrzeug*); **~down** Wasserung *f*.

spleen [spli:n] *anat.* Milz *f;*
schlechte Laune, Ärger *m*.

splend|id [ˈsplendid] glänzend, prächtig, prächtig;
~o(u)r Glanz *m*, Pracht *f*,
Herrlichkeit *f*.

splint [splint] *med.* Schiene
f; schienen; **~er** Splitter *m;*
(zer)splittern.

split [split] Spalt *m*, Riß *m;*
fig. Spaltung *f;* gespalten;
(*irr*) (zer-, auf)spalten;
(zer)teilen; sich (*in et.*)
teilen; sich (auf)spalten;
(zer)platzen; **~ting** heftig,
rasend (*Kopfschmerz*).

splutter [ˈsplʌtə] *Worte*
herausprudeln, -stottern.

spoil [spɔil] *mst pl* (*fig.* Aus)Beute *f*; (*irr*) verderben; verwöhnen; verziehen; **~sport** Spielverderber(in); **~t** *pret u. pp von* **spoil.**

spoke¹ [spəuk] Speiche *f*; (Leiter)Sprosse *f.*

spoke² *pret, ~n pp von* **speak;** **~sman** Wortführer *m.*

spong|e [spʌndʒ] Schwamm *m*; (mit e-m Schwamm) (ab)wischen; *colloq.* schmarotzen; **~e- cake** Biskuitkuchen *m*; **~y** schwammig; locker.

sponsor [spɔnsə] Bürg|e *m*, -in *f*; Pat|e *m*, -in *f*; Förderer *m*; bürgen für.

spontaneous [spɔn'teinjəs] spontan; freiwillig; Selbst...

spook [spu:k] Spuk *m.*

spool [spu:l] Spule *f*; (auf)spulen.

spoon [spu:n] Löffel *m*; **~ up, ~ out** auslöffeln; **~ful** (*ein*) Löffel(voll) *m.*

spore [spɔ:] Spore *f.*

sport [spɔ:t] Vergnügen *n*; Spiel *n*; Spaß *n*; *colloq.* feiner Kerl; *pl* Sport *m*; *colloq.* protzen mit; **~s- man** Sportler *m*; **~s- woman** Sportlerin *f.*

spot [spɔt] Fleck(en) *m*; Tupfen *m*; Tropfen *m*; Pickel *m*; Stelle *f*; Makel *m*; **on the ~** auf der Stelle, sofort; zur Stelle; (be)flecken; ausfindig machen, entdecken, erkennen; **~**

less fleckenlos; **~light** *thea.* Scheinwerfer(licht *n*) *m.*

spout [spaut] Tülle *f*; Schnabel *m*; (Wasser-) Strahl *m*; (heraus)spritzen.

sprain [sprein] Verstauchung *f*; sich *et.* verstauchen.   [spring.]

sprang [spræŋ] *pret von*|

sprat [spræt] Sprotte *f.*

sprawl [sprɔ:l] sich rekeln, ausgestreckt daliegen.

spray [sprei] Gischt *m, f*; Spray *m, n*; zerstäuben; (ver)sprühen; besprühen.

spread [spred] (*irr*) (sich) aus- *od.* verbreiten; (sich) ausdehnen; Butter *etc.* aufstreichen; Brot streichen; Aus-, Verbreitung *f*; (Flügel)Spannweite *f*; (Bett- *etc.*)Decke *f*; (Brot)Aufstrich *m.*

sprig [sprig] kleiner Zweig.

sprightly ['spraitli] lebhaft, munter.

spring [spriŋ] Sprung *m*; Satz *m*; (Sprung)Feder *f*; Quelle *f*; *fig.* Ursprung *m*; Frühling *m*; (*irr*) springen; **~ from** entspringen; **~ board** Sprungbrett *n*; **~time** Frühling *m.*

sprinkle ['spriŋkl] (be-) streuen; (be)sprengen; **~r** Berieselungsanlage *f*; Rasensprenger *m.*

sprint [sprint] sprinten; spurten; Sprint *m*; Endspurt *m*; **~er** Sprinter(in).

sprout [spraut] sprießen; wachsen lassen; Sproß *m.*

spruce [spruːs] schmuck, adrett; ~ **(fir)** Fichte *f*, Rottanne *f*. **[spring.]**

sprung [sprʌŋ] *pp von*

spun [spʌn] *pret u. pp von* **spin.**

spur [spəː] Sporn *m* (*a. zo.*, *bot.*); *fig.* Ansporn *m*; ~ **on** *j-n* anspornen.

sputter ['spʌtə] (hervor-) sprudeln; spritzen; zischen; stottern (*Motor*).

spy [spai] Spion(in); (er-) spähen; (aus)spionieren.

squabble ['skwɔbl] sich zanken.

squad [skwɔd] Gruppe *f*.

squall [skwɔːl] Bö *f*.

squander ['skwɔndə] verschwenden.

square [skwɛə] quadratisch, Quadrat...; viereckig; rechtwink(e)lig; breit, stämmig (*Person*); quitt; ehrlich; Quadrat *n*; Viereck *n*; *öffentlicher* Platz; quadratisch machen; *Zahl* ins Quadrat erheben; *Schultern* straffen; in Einklang bringen *od.* stehen.

squash [skwɔʃ] Gedränge *n*; (*Zitronen-, Orangen-*) Saft *m*; (*zer-, zs.-*)quetschen, (-)drücken.

squat [skwɔt] untersetzt; hocken, kauern.

squeak [skwiːk] quieken; quietschen.

squeal [skwiːl] grell schreien; quieken.

squeamish ['skwiːmiʃ] empfindlich; heikel; penibel.

squeeze [skwiːz] (aus-, zs.-)drücken, (-)pressen; (aus)quetschen; sich zwängen *od.* quetschen; ~**r** (*Frucht*)Presse *f*.

squid [skwid] Tintenfisch *m*.   **[blinzeln.]**

squint [skwint] schielen(|)

squire ['skwaiə] Landedelmann *m*, *a.* Großgrundbesitzer *m*.   **[winden.]**

squirm [skwəːm] sich(|)

squirrel ['skwirəl, *Am.* ˈskwəːrəl] Eichhörnchen *n*.

squirt [skwəːt] spritzen.

stab [stæb] Stich *m*, (Dolch)Stoß *m*; (er)stechen.

stabili|ty [stəˈbiliti] Stabilität *f*; Beständigkeit *f*; ~**ze** ['steibilaiz] stabilisieren.

stable[1] ['steibl] stabil, fest.

stable[2] Stall *m*.

stack [stæk] Schober *m*; Stapel *m*; (auf)stapeln.

stadium ['steidjəm] Stadion *n*.

staff [staːf] Stab *m*, Stock *m*; (Mitarbeiter)Stab *m*; Personal *n*, Belegschaft *f*; Lehrkörper *m*; (mit Personal) besetzen.

stag [stæg] Hirsch *m*.

stage [steidʒ] Bühne *f*; *fig.* Schauplatz *m*; (Fahr-) Strecke *f*; Abschnitt *m*; (Raketen)Stufe *f*; Stadium *n*; inszenieren; ~**coach** Postkutsche *f*; ~**manager** Inspizient *m*.

stagger ['stægə] (sch)wanken, taumeln; erschüttern.

stagnant ['stægnənt] stehend (*Wasser*); stagnierend.

stain [stein] Fleck *m*; *fig.* Makel *m*; beschmutzen, beflecken; **~ed** fleckig; befleckt; bunt, bemalt (*Glas*); **~less** rostfrei; *fig.* fleckenlos.

stair [steə] Stufe *f*; *pl* Treppe *f*; **~case**, **~way** Treppe(nhaus *n*) *f*.

stake [steik] wagen, aufs Spiel setzen; Pfahl *m*; (Spiel)Einsatz *m*; **be at ~** auf dem Spiel stehen.

stale [steil] alt; schal, abgestanden; verbraucht.

stalk [stɔ:k] Stengel *m*, Stiel *m*, Halm *m*.

stall [stɔ:l] (Pferde)Box *f*; (Verkaufs)Stand *m*, (Markt)Bude *f*; *thea.* Sperrsitz *m*; *Motor* abwürgen; aussetzen (*Motor*).

stallion ['stæljən] (Zucht-) Hengst *m*.

stalwart ['stɔ:lwət] stramm, stark; treu.

stammer ['stæmə] stottern, stammeln; Stottern *n*.

stamp [stæmp] Stempel *m*; (Brief)Marke *f*; stampfen; aufstampfen (mit); prägen; stempeln; frankieren; trampeln.

stanch [stɑ:ntʃ] *s.* **staunch**.

stand [stænd] (*irr*) stehen; stellen; aushalten, (v)ertragen; sich *et.* gefallen lassen; *Probe* bestehen; **~ (still)** stehenbleiben, stillstehen; **~ back** zurücktreten; **~ by** dabeistehen; sich bereithalten; zu *j-m* halten *od.* stehen; **~ off** zurücktreten; **~ (up)on** bestehen auf; **~ out** hervortreten; *fig.* sich abheben; **~ up** aufstehen; **~ up for** eintreten für; *sub:* Stehen*n*, Stillstand *m*; (Stand)Platz *m*; (Taxi)Stand(platz) *m*; Ständer *m*; Gestell *n*; Tribüne *f*; (Verkaufs)Stand *m*.

standard ['stændəd] Standarte *f*; Standard *m*, Norm *f*; Maßstab *m*; Niveau *n*; Normal...; **~ize** normen.

standing ['stændiŋ] stehend; (be)ständig; Stehen *n*; Stellung *f*, Rang *m*, Ruf *m*; **of long ~** alt; **~ room** Stehplatz *m*.

stand|-offish ['stænd'ɔfiʃ] reserviert, ablehnend; **~point** Standpunkt *m*; **~still** Stillstand *m*.

stank [stæŋk] *pret von* **stink**.

star [stɑ:] Stern *m*; *thea.* Star *m*; *thea.*, *Film:* die Hauptrolle spielen.

starboard ['stɑ:bəd] Steuerbord *n*.

starch [stɑ:tʃ] (Wäsche-) Stärke *f*; stärken.

stare [steə] starrer Blick; (**~ at** an)starren.

stark [stɑ:k] völlig.

star|ling ['stɑ:liŋ] *orn.* Star *m*; **~lit** sternenklar; **~ry** Stern(en)...;strahlend; **~s and Stripes** Sternenbanner *n*; **~spangled**

sternenbesät; 2-**Spangled Banner** Sternenbanner n.

start [stɑːt] Start m; Anfang m; Aufbruch m, Abreise f, Abfahrt f, aer. Abflug m; fig. Abfahren n, Zs.-fahren n; anfangen (**doing** zu tun); sp. starten; mot. anspringen; aufbrechen; abfahren (Zug), auslaufen (Schiff), aer. abfliegen, starten; auffahren, zs.-fahren; zs.-zucken; stutzen; et. in Gang setzen, tech. a. anlassen; aufmachen, gründen; **~ on a journey** e-e Reise antreten; **~er** sp. Starter m; Läufer(in); mot. Anlasser m.

startle ['stɑːtl] er-, aufschrecken; **~ing** bestürzend; überraschend.

starv|ation [stɑː'veiʃən] (Ver)Hungern n; Hungertod m; **~e** (ver)hungern (lassen).

state [steit] Zustand m; Stand m, Lage f; (pol. 2) Staat m, staatlich, Staats...; darlegen; angeben; feststellen; jur. aussagen; 2 **Department** Am. Außenministerium n; **~ly** stattlich; würdevoll; **~ment** Erklärung f; Behauptung f; Aussage f; Angabe(n pl) f; Darstellung f; econ. Bericht m; **~room** mar. Einzelkabine f; **~side** Am.: amerikanisch, Heimat...; in od. nach den Staaten; **~sman** Staatsmann m.

static ['stætik] statisch.

station ['steiʃən] Platz m; Station f; Bahnhof m; mil. Stützpunkt m; Australien: Schaffarm f; fig. Rang m, Stellung f; aufstellen; mil. stationieren; **~ary** fest (-stehend); gleichbleibend; **~er** Schreibwarenhändler m; **~ery** Schreib-, Papierwaren pl; **~-master** Stationsvorsteher m; **~-waggon** Kombiwagen m.

statistics [stə'tistiks] sg, pl Statistik f.

statue ['stætjuː] Statue f.

statute ['stætjuːt] Statut n, Satzung f; Gesetz n.

staunch [stɔːntʃ] Blut(ung) stillen; treu, zuverlässig; standhaft.

stay [stei] Strebe f, Stütze f; Aufenthalt m; pl Korsett n; bleiben (**with** bei); sich aufhalten, wohnen (**with** bei); **~ away** wegbleiben; **~ up** aufbleiben.

stead [sted]: **in his** ~ an s-r Statt; **~fast** ['~fɑst] fest; unverwandt.

steady ['stedi] fest; gleichmäßig, stetig, (be-)ständig; zuverlässig; ruhig, sicher; fest od. sicher machen od. werden; **~ o.s.** sich stützen.

steal [stiːl] (irr) stehlen; sich stehlen, schleichen.

stealth [stelθ]: **by** ~ heimlich; **~y** verstohlen.

steam [stiːm] Dampf m; Dunst m; Dampf...; dampfen; Speisen dünsten, dämpfen; **~ up** (sich) beschlagen(*Glas*); **~er, ~ship** Dampfer *m*.

steel [sti:l] Stahl *m*; stählern; Stahl...; **~works** *sg*, *pl* Stahlwerk *n*.

steep [sti:p] steil, jäh; steiler Abhang; einweichen, -tauchen; einlegen.

steeple ['sti:pl] (spitzer) Kirchturm.

steer [stiə] steuern, lenken; **~ing-gear** Lenkung *f*; **~ing-wheel** Steuerrad *n*; *mot. a.* Lenkrad *n*.

stem [stem] (Baum-, Wort-) Stamm *m*; Stiel *m*; Stengel *m*.

stench [stentʃ] Gestank *m*.

stenographer [ste'nɔgrəfə] Stenograph(in).

step¹ [step] Schritt *m*; (Treppen)Stufe *f*; schreiten; treten, gehen.

step² in *Zssgn*: Stief..., **~father** Stiefvater *m*; **~mother** Stiefmutter *f*.

stereo ['stiɔriɔu] Stereo *n*.

steril|e ['sterail] unfruchtbar; steril; **~ize** ['~ilaiz] sterilisieren.

sterling ['stə:liŋ] Sterling *m* (*Währung*).

stern [stə:n] streng; *mar.* Heck *n*; **~ness** Strenge *f*.

stew [stju:] schmoren; Schmor-, Eintopfgericht *n*; *colloq.* Aufregung *f*.

steward [stjuəd] Verwalter *m*; Steward *m*; **~ess** Stewardeß *f*.

stick [stik] Stock *m*; (Besen- *etc*.)Stiel *m*; Stange *f*; (dünner) Zweig; (*irr*) ste-

chen mit; (an)stecken; (an)klopfen; *colloq.* ertragen; hängenbleiben; stekkenbleiben; **~ out** ab-, hervorstehen; herausst(r)ecken; **~ to** bei *j—m* *od.* *et.* bleiben; **~ing-plaster** Heftpflaster *n*; **~y** klebrig.

stiff [stif] steif; starr; mühsam; stark (*alkoholisches Getränk*); **~en** (sich) versteifen; erstarren.

stifle ['staifl] ersticken.

stile [stail] Zauntritt *m*.

still [stil] still; (immer) noch; doch; dennoch; stillen, beruhigen; **~ness** Stille *f*, Ruhe *f*.

stilt [stilt] Stelze *f*; **~ed** geschraubt (*Stil*).

stimul|ant ['stimjulənt] Anregungsmittel *n*; Anreiz *m*; **~ate** ['~eit] anregen; **~ating** anregend; **~ation** Anreiz *m*; *med.* Reiz(ung *f*) *m*; **~us** ['~əs] (An)Reiz *m*.

sting [stiŋ] Stachel *m* (*e—s Insekts*); Stich *m*, Biß *m*; (*irr*) stechen; brennen; schmerzen.

stingy ['stindʒi] geizig.

stink [stiŋk] Gestank *m*; (*irr*) stinken.

stipulate ['stipjuleit] ausbedingen, vereinbaren.

stir [stə:] (sich) rühren *od.* bewegen; umrühren; *fig.* erregen; **bügel-**}

stirrup ['stirəp] Steig-}

stitch [stitʃ] Stich *m*; Masche *f*; nähen; heften.

stock [stɔk] Griff *m*; Rohstoff *m*; (Fleisch-, Gemüse)Brühe f; Waren(lager n) pl; Vorrat m; Vieh(bestand m) n; Herkunft f; pl: Effekten pl; Aktien pl; Staatspapiere pl; **in (out of)** ~(nicht) vorrätig; **take** ~ Inventur machen; vorrätig; gängig, Standard... (Größe); ausstatten, versorgen; Waren führen, vorrätig haben; **~breeder** Viehzüchter m; **~broker** Börsenmakler m; **~ex-change** Börse f; **~farm-er** Viehzüchter m; **~holder** Aktionär(in).

stocking ['stɔkiŋ] Strumpf m. [**~y** stämmig.]
stock|-market Börse f;]
stole [stəul] pret, **~n** pp von **steal**.

stomach ['stʌmək] Magen m; Leib m, Bauch m; fig. (v)ertragen.

ston|e [stəun] Stein m; (Obst)Kern m; steinern, Stein...; steinigen; entkernen; **~eware** Steinzeug n; **~y** steinig; fig. steinern.

stood [stud] pret u. pp von **stand**.

stool [stu:l] Schemel m, Hocker m; med. Stuhlgang m. [krumm gehen.]
stoop [stu:p] sich bücken;]
stop [stɔp] aufhören (mit); Zahlungen etc. einstellen; an-, aufhalten, stoppen; hindern; Zahn plombieren; Blut stillen; (an)halten, stehenbleiben, stoppen; aer. zwischenlanden; colloq. bleiben; **~ over** die Fahrt

unterbrechen; **~ (up)** ver-, zustopfen; Halt m; Pause f; Aufenthalt m; Station f, Haltestelle f; tech. Anschlag m; ling. Punkt m; **~page** tech. Hemmung f; (Zahlungs- etc.) Einstellung f; **~per** Stöpsel m; **~ping** med. Plombe f.

storage ['stɔ:ridʒ] Lagerung f; Lager(geld) n.

store [stɔ:] Vorrat m; Lagerhaus n; Am. Laden m, Geschäft n; pl Kauf-, Warenhaus n; versorgen; **~ up** (auf)speichern, lagern; **~house** Lagerhaus n; **~keeper** Am. Ladenbesitzer(in).

stor|ey ['stɔ:ri] Stock(werk n) m; **~eyed**, **~ied** ...stöckig.

stork [stɔ:k] Storch m.

storm [stɔ:m] Sturm m; Gewitter n; stürmen; toben; **~y** stürmisch.

story ['stɔ:ri] Geschichte f; Erzählung f; s. **storey**.

stout [staut] kräftig; dick; starkes Porterbier.

stove [stəuv] Ofen m, Herd m; Treibhaus n.

stow [stəu] verstauen, packen; **~away** blinder Passagier.

straggling ['stræɡliŋ] verstreut (liegend); lose (Haar).

straight [streit] adj gerade; glatt (Haar); ehrlich; **put** ~ in Ordnung bringen; adv gerade(aus); direkt; geradewegs; ehrlich, anständig; ~ **away**, ~ **off** sofort; ~ **ahead**, ~ **on** geradeaus; ~en gerademachen, gerade werden; (gerade)richten; ~**forward** ehrlich; einfach.

strain [strein] (an)spannen; verstauchen, *Muskel etc.* zerren; überanstrengen; durchseihen, filtern; sich anstrengen od. abmühen; Spannung *f*; Belastung *f*; *med.* Zerrung *f*; Überanstrengung *f*, Anspannung *f*; ~**er** Seiher *m*, Sieb *n*.

strait [streit] (*in Eigennamen oft*: ♎s *pl*) Meerenge *f*, Straße *f*; *pl* Not(lage) *f*; ~**en**: **in ~ed circumstances** in beschränkten Verhältnissen.

strand [strænd] Strand *m*; Strang *m*; Strähne *f*; *fig.* stranden (lassen).

strange [streind3] fremd; seltsam, merkwürdig; ~**r** Fremde *m, f*.

strangle [‘stræŋgl] erwürgen, erdrosseln.

strap [stræp] Riemen *m*, Gurt *m*, Band *n*; Träger *m* (*Kleid*); fest~, umschnallen.

strateg|ic [strə‘ti:dʒik] strategisch; ~**y** [‘strætidʒi] Strategie *f*; *pl* Taktik *f*.

straw [strɔ:] Stroh(halm *m*) *n*; Stroh...; ~**berry** Erdbeere *f*.

stray [strei] sich verirren; verirrt; streunend; vereinzelt.

streak [stri:k] streifen;

Strich *m*, Streifen *m*; *fig.* Ader *f*, Spur *f*; ~ **of lightning** Blitzstrahl *m*; ~**y** durchwachsen (*Speck*).

stream [stri:m] Strom *m*, Fluß *m*, Bach *m*; Strömung *f*; strömen; flattern.

street [stri:t] Straße *f*; ~ **car** *Am.* Straßenbahn *f*.

strength [streŋθ] Stärke *f*, Kraft *f*; ~**en** (be)stärken.

strenuous [‘strenjuəs] rührig; tüchtig; anstrengend.

stress [stres] Nachdruck *m*; Betonung *f* (*a. ling.*); Belastung *f*, Streß *m*; betonen.

stretch [stretʃ] (sich) strekken; (sich) dehnen; sich erstrecken; (an)spannen; ~ **out** ausstrecken; (Sich-) Strecken *n*; (Weg)Strecke *f*, Fläche *f*; Zeit(raum *m*) *f*; ~**er** (Trag)Bahre *f*.

strew [stru:] (*irr*) (be-) streuen; ~**n** *pp von* **strew**.

stricken [‘strikən] *pp von* **strike**; heimgesucht; ergriffen.

strict [strikt] streng; genau.

strid|den [‘stridn] *pp von* **stride**; ~**e** [straid] (*irr*) über-, durchschreiten; ausschreiten; großer Schritt.

strife [straif] großer Streit *m*; Kampf *m*.

strike [straik] Schlag *m*, Stoß *m*; (Luft)Angriff *m*; *fig.* Treffer *m*; *econ.* Streik *m*; **be on** ~ streiken; (*irr*) (an-, zu)schlagen; (an-, zu)stoßen; treffen; *Streichholz, Licht* anzünden; stoßen auf; einschlagen (in)

(*Blitz* etc.); *Zelt* abbre-
chen; *die Stunde* etc.
schlagen (*Uhr*); *j-m* einfallen *od.* in den Sinn kommen; *j-m* auffallen; streiken; **~ off, ~ out** (aus-)
streichen; **~r** Streikende
m, f.

striking ['straikiŋ] Schlag-
...; auffallend, eindrucksvoll; verblüffend.

string [striŋ] Schnur *f*,
Bindfaden *m*; Band *n*; Faden *m*, Draht *m*; Reihe *f*,
Kette *f*; *bot.* Faser *f*; (*Bo-*
gen)Sehne *f*; Saite *f*; (*Bo-*
gen)Streichinstrumente *pl*; (*irr*)
(be)spannen; *Perlen* auf-
reihen; *n*; **~y** ['∙ŋi] zäh
(-flüssig); sehnig.

strip [strip] entkleiden (*a.*
fig.), (sich) ausziehen; abziehen, abstreifen; Streifen
m. **[~d** gestreift.)

stripe [straip] Streifen *m*; |

strive [straiv] (*irr*): **~ (for)**
streben (nach), ringen
(um); **~n** ['strivn] *pp von*
strive.

strode [stroud] *pret von*
stride.

stroke [strouk] streichen
über; streicheln; Schlag *m*;
Stoß *m*; *med.* Schlag(anfall) *m*; **~ of luck** Glücks-
fall *m.*

stroll [stroul] schlendern;
Bummel *m*, Spaziergang *m*;
~er Spaziergänger(in); *Am.*
Faltsportwagen *m.*

strong [strɔŋ] stark; kräftig; fest; scharf (*Ge-*
schmack etc.); **~box** Stahl-

kassette *f*; **~room** Tresor
(-raum) *m.* **[strive.**)

strove [strouv] *pret von* |

struck [strʌk] *pret u. pp von*
strike.

structure ['strʌktʃə] Bau
(-werk *n*) *m*; Struktur *f.*

struggle ['strʌgl] sich (ab-)
mühen; kämpfen, ringen;
sich sträuben; Kampf *m*,
Ringen *n.* **(auf.)**

strum [strʌm] klimpern |

strung [strʌŋ] *pret u. pp*
von **string**; **highly ~**
(über)empfindlich, nervös.

strut [strʌt] stolzieren;
Strebe(balken *m*) *f.*

stub [stʌb] (Baum)Stumpf
m; Stummel *m.*

stubble ['stʌbl] Stoppel(n
pl) *f.*

stubborn ['stʌbən] eigensinnig; stur; hartnäckig.

stuck [stʌk] *pret u. pp von*
stick.

stud [stʌd] Beschlagnagel
m; Kragenknopf *m*; Gestüt
n; besetzen, übersäen.

student ['stju:dənt] Stu-
dent(in); Schüler(in).

studio ['stju:diou] Atelier
n; Studio *n*; Aufnahme-,
Senderaum *m*; **~ couch**
Bettcouch *f.*

studious ['stju:djəs] fleißig;
sorgfältig; peinlich.

study ['stʌdi] Studium *n*;
Studier-, Arbeitszimmer *n*;
Studie *f*; (ein)studieren.

stuff [stʌf] Stoff *m*, Material
n; Zeug *n*; (aus)stopfen;
vollstopfen; **~ing** Füllung
f; **~y** muffig; *colloq.* spießig.

stumble ['stʌmbl] stolpern, straucheln; Stolpern n.

stump [stʌmp] Stumpf m, Stummel m; (daher)stampfen.

stun [stʌn] betäuben.

stung [stʌŋ] pret u. pp von sting. [stink.\

stunk [stʌŋk] pret u. pp von\

stunning ['stʌnɪŋ] colloq. toll, hinreißend.

stup|efy ['stju:pifai] betäuben; ~id dumm; ~idity Dummheit f; ~or Erstarrung f, Betäubung f.

sturdy ['stə:di] robust, kräftig.

stutter ['stʌtə] stottern; Stottern n.

sty¹ [stai] Schweinestall m.

sty², ~e med. Gerstenkorn n.

style [stail] Stil m; Mode f; ~ish stilvoll; elegant.

suave [swɑ:v] verbindlich.

subdivision ['sʌbdivɪʒən] Unterteilung f; Unterabteilung f.

subdue [səb'dju:] unterwerfen; dämpfen.

subject ['sʌbdʒikt] Thema n, Gegenstand m; (Lehr-, Schul-, Studien)Fach n; Untertan(in); Staatsbürger (-in), -angehörige m, f; gr. Subjekt n, Satzgegenstand m; ~ to vorbehaltlich; [səb-'dʒekt]: ~ to unterwerfen od. aussetzen (dat); ~ion Unterwerfung f.

subjunctive (mood) [səb-'dʒʌŋktiv] gr. Konjunktiv m, Möglichkeitsform f.

sublime [sə'blaim] erhaben.

submachine-gun ['sʌbmə'ʃi:ŋgən] Maschinenpistole f.

submarine [sʌbmə'ri:n] Unterseeboot n, U-Boot n.

submerge [sab'mə:dʒ] (ein-, unter)tauchen.

submiss|ion [səb'miʃən] Unterwerfung f; ~ive unterwürfig.

submit [səb'mit] : ~ (to) (sich) unterwerfen (dat); unterbreiten (dat); sich fügen (dat, in).

subordinate [sə'bɔ:dnit] Untergebene m, f; untergeordnet; ~ clause gr. Nebensatz m.

subscribe [səb'skraib] spenden; unterschreiben (mit); ~ for Buch vorbestellen; ~ to Zeitung abonnieren; ~r Abonnent(in); teleph. Teilnehmer(in); Spender(in).

subscription [səb'skripʃən] Unterzeichnung f; Abonnement n, Subskription f; (Mitglieds)Beitrag m; Spende f.

subsequent ['sʌbsikwənt] (nach)folgend, später; ~ly hinterher.

subsid|e [səb'said] sich senken; (ein)sinken; sich legen (Wind); ~iary [~'sidjəri] Hilfs...; untergeordnet, Neben...; ~iary (company) Tochtergesellschaft f; ~ize ['sʌbsidaiz] subventionieren; ~y ['sʌbsidi] Subvention f.

subsist [səb'sist] leben (**on** von); **~ence** (Lebens)Unterhalt m, Existenz f.

substance ['sʌbstəns] Substanz f; das Wesentliche.

substandard [sʌb'stændəd] unter der Norm; **~film** Schmalfilm m.

substantial [səb'stænʃəl] wirklich; reichlich (Mahlzeit); namhaft (Summe); wesentlich.

substantive ['sʌbstəntiv] gr. Substantiv n, Hauptwort n.

substitute ['sʌbstitju:t] an die Stelle setzen od. treten (**for** von); (Stell)Vertreter (-in); Ersatz m; **~** Ersatz m [titel m.|
subtitle ['sʌbtaitl] Unter-|
subtle ['sʌtl] fein(sinnig); subtil; scharf(sinnig).

subtract [səb'trækt] abziehen, subtrahieren.

suburb ['sʌbə:b] Vorstadt f, -ort m; **~an** [sə'bə:bən] vorstädtisch, Vorort(s)...

subway ['sʌbwei] (bsd. Fußgänger)Unterführung f; Am. Untergrundbahn f.

succeed [sək'si:d] Erfolg haben; glücken, gelingen; (nach)folgen (**to** dat.).

success [sək'ses] Erfolg m; **~ful** erfolgreich; **~ion** (Nach-, Erb-, Reihen)Folge f; **~ive** aufeinanderfolgend; **~or** Nachfolger(in).

succumb [sə'kʌm] erliegen.

such [sʌtʃ] solche(r, -s); derartig; **~ a man** ein sol-

cher Mann; **~ as** die, welche; wie (zum Beispiel).

suck [sʌk] saugen (an); aussaugen; lutschen (an); **~le** säugen,stillen; **~ling** Säugling m.

sudden ['sʌdn] plötzlich; **all of a ~** ganz plötzlich; **~ly** plötzlich.

suds [sʌdz] pl Seifenschaum m.

sue [sju:] (ver)klagen.

suède [sweid] Wildleder n.

suet [sjuit] Talg m.

suffer ['sʌfə] leiden (**from** an, unter); (er)leiden; büßen; dulden; **~er** Leidende m, f.

suffice [sə'fais] genügen; **~ it to say** es sei nur gesagt.

sufficien|cy [sə'fiʃənsi] genügende Menge; **~t** genügend, genug, ausreichend.

suffix ['sʌfiks] ling. Suffix n, Nachsilbe f.

suffocate ['sʌfəkeit] ersticken.

sugar ['ʃugə] Zucker m; zuckern; **~cane** Zuckerrohr n.

suggest [sə'dʒest] vorschlagen, anregen; hinweisen auf; andeuten; **~ion** Vorschlag m, Anregung f; Hinweis m; Andeutung f; **~ive** anregend; andeutend (**of** acc); vielsagend; zweideutig.

suicide ['sjuisaid] Selbstmord m; Selbstmörder(in).

suit [sju:t] Anzug m; Kostüm n; Karten: Farbe f; jur. Prozeß m; passen; j-m zusagen, bekommen; *j-n* kleiden, *j-m* stehen, passen zu; sich eignen für *od.* zu; **~ yourself** tu, was dir gefällt; **~able** passend, geeignet; **~case** (Hand)Koffer *m.*

suite [swiːt] Gefolge *n*; (Zimmer)Einrichtung *f*; Zimmerflucht *f.*

suitor [ˈsjuːtə] Freier *m*; *jur.* Kläger(in).

sulfur [ˈsʌlfə] *Am. für* sulphur.

sulk [sʌlk] schmollen; **~y** verdrießlich, mürrisch.

sullen [ˈsʌlən] verdrossen, mürrisch; düster.

sulphur [ˈsʌlfə] Schwefel *m.*

sultry [ˈsʌltri] schwül; *fig.* heftig, hitzig.

sum [sʌm] Summe *f*; Betrag *m*; Rechenaufgabe *f*; **do ~** rechnen; *vb:* **~ up** zs.-zählen, addieren; *j-n* abschätzen; zs.-fassen.

summar|ize [ˈsʌməraiz] (kurz) zs.-fassen; **~y** (kurze) Inhaltsangabe, Zs.-fassung *f*, Übersicht *f.*

summer [ˈsʌmə] Sommer *m*; **~ resort** Sommerfrische *f*; **~ school** Ferienkurs *m.*

summit [ˈsʌmit] Gipfel *m.*

summon [ˈsʌmən] auffordern; (zu sich) bestellen; *jur.* vorladen; **~ (up)** Mut *etc.* zs.-nehmen; **~s** [ˈ~z], *pl* **~ses** [ˈ~ziz] Aufforderung *f*; *jur.* Vorladung *f.*

sun [sʌn] Sonne *f*; Sonnen...; (sich) sonnen; **~bath**

Sonnenbad *n*; **~beam** Sonnenstrahl *m*; **~burn** Sonnenbrand *m*, -bräune *f.*

Sunday [ˈsʌndi] Sonntag *m.*

sundial Sonnenuhr *f.*

sundr|ies [ˈsʌndriz] *pl* Verschiedenes; **~y** verschiedene.

sung [sʌŋ] *pp von* sing.

sun-glasses *pl* (a. **a pair of ~**) (e-e) Sonnenbrille.

sunk [sʌŋk] *pp von* sink; **~en** versunken; *fig.* eingefallen.

sun|ny [ˈsʌni] sonnig; **~rise** Sonnenaufgang *m*; **~set** Sonnenuntergang *m*; **~shade** Sonnenschirm *m*; **~shine** Sonnenschein *m*; **~stroke** Sonnenstich *m.*

super| [ˈsuːpə-] übermäßig, über..., über...; übergeordnet, Ober..., ober...; Super... [reichlich.]

superabundant über- [reichlich.]

superb [sju(ː)ˈpəːb] herrlich; ausgezeichnet.

super|ficial [suːpəˈfiʃəl] oberflächlich; **~fluous** [ˈpʌ:fluəs] überflüssig; **~highway** *Am.* Autobahn *f*; **~human** übermenschlich; **~intend** beaufsichtigen, überwachen; **~intendent** Leiter *m*, Direktor *m*; Inspektor *m.*

superior [su(ː)ˈpiəriə] höher; vorgesetzt; besser, hervorragend; überlegen; Vorgesetzte *m*, *f*; **~ity** [ˈ~ˈɔriti] Überlegenheit *f.*

superlative [su(ː)ˈpəːlətiv] höchst; überragend;

(degree) *gr.* Superlativ *m.*

super|man Übermensch *m;* **~market** Supermarkt *m;* **~natural** übernatürlich; **~numerary** [~'nju:-mərəri] überzählig; **~scription** Über-, Aufschrift *f;* **~sonic** Überschall...; **~stition** [~'stiʃən] Aberglaube *m;* **~stitious** abergläubisch; **~vise** ['~vaiz] beaufsichtigen, überwachen; **~visor** Aufseher *m,* Leiter *m.*

supper ['sʌpə] Abendessen *n,* -brot *n;* **the Lord's ~** das Heilige Abendmahl.

supple ['sʌpl] geschmeidig, biegsam.

supplement ['sʌplimənt] Ergänzung *f;* Nachtrag *m;* (Zeitungs- *etc.*)Beilage *f;* ['~ment] ergänzen; **~ary** [~'~] Ergänzungs..., zusätzlich, Nachtrags...

supplication [sʌpli'keiʃən] demütige Bitte, Flehen *n.*

suppl|ier [sə'plaiə] Lieferant(in) *m;* **~y** [~] liefern; versorgen; Lieferung *f;* Versorgung *f; econ.* Angebot *n;* Vorrat *m.*

support [sə'pɔ:t] Stütze *f;* *tech.* Träger *m;* Unterstützung *f;* (Lebens)Unterhalt *m;* (unter)stützen; unterhalten, sorgen für (*Familie etc.*).

suppos|e [sə'pəuz] annehmen, voraussetzen; vermuten; halten für; sollen; **~ed** vermeintlich; angeblich; **~edly** [~idli] vermutlich.

~ition [sʌpə'ziʃən] Voraussetzung *f,* Annahme *f;* Vermutung *f.*

suppress [sə'pres] unterdrücken; **~ion** Unterdrückung *f.*

suppurate ['sʌpjuəreit] eitern.

suprem|acy [su'preməsi] Oberhoheit *f;* Vorherrschaft *f;* Überlegenheit *f;* Vorrang *m;* **~e** [~'pri:m] höchst, oberst, Ober...

surcharge [sə:'tʃɑ:dʒ] überlasten; Zuschlag *od.* Nachgebühr erheben für; ['~] Überlastung *f;* Zuschlag *m;* Nachgebühr *f;* Überdruck *m* (*auf Briefmarken*).

sure [ʃuə] *adj:* **~(of)** sicher, gewiß, überzeugt (von); **feel ~** of sicher *od.* überzeugt sein, daß; **make ~ that** sich (davon) überzeugen, daß; *adv:* **~enough** tatsächlich; **~!** klar!, bestimmt!; **~ly** sicher(lich); **~ty** ['~rəti] Bürge *m;* Bürgschaft *f,* Kaution *f.*

surf [sə:f] Brandung *f.*

surface ['sə:fis] Oberfläche *f;* auftauchen (*U-Boot*).

surf-riding Wellenreiten *n.*

surge [sə:dʒ] Woge *f,* (hohe) Welle; wogen.

surg|eon ['sə:dʒən] Chirurg *m;* **~ery** Chirurgie *f;* Sprechzimmer *n;* **~ery hours** *pl* Sprechstunde(n *pl*) *f;* **~ical** chirurgisch.

surly ['sə:li] mürrisch.

surmise ['sə:maiz] Vermutung *f*; [~'maiz] vermuten.

surmount [sə:'maunt] überwinden; **~ed by** überragt von.

surname ['sə:neim] Familien-, Nach-, Zuname *m*.

surpass [sə:'pɑ:s] *fig.* übersteigen, -treffen; **~ing** unübertrefflich.

surplus [sə:pləs] Überschuß *m*, Mehr *n*; überschüssig, Über(schuß)...

surprise [sə'praiz] Überraschung *f*; überraschen; **~d** überrascht, erstaunt.

surrender [sə'rendə] Übergabe *f*; Kapitulation *f*; Aufgeben *n*; übergeben; aufgeben; sich ergeben (**to** *dat*).

surround [sə'raund] umgeben; **~ings** *pl* Umgebung *f*.

survey [sə:'vei] überblicken; begutachten; *Land* vermessen; ['~vei] Überblick *m*; (Land)Vermessung *f*; (Lage)Karte *f*; **~or** [~'v~] Land-, Feldvermesser *m*, (amtlicher) Inspektor.

surviv|al [sə'vaivəl] Überleben *n*; **~e** überleben; bestehen bleiben; **~or** Überlebende *m, f*.

suscept|ible [sə'septəbl] leicht zu beeindrucken; empfänglich (**to** für); empfindlich (**to** gegen).

suspect [sə'spekt] verdächtigen; vermuten; befürchten; ['sʌspekt] Verdächtige

m, f; verdächtig; **~ed** [~'pektid] verdächtig.

suspend [sə'spend] (auf-) hängen; aufschieben; *Zahlung* einstellen; suspendieren, sperren; **~ed** hängend, Hänge...; schwebend; **~er** Strumpf-, Sockenhalter *m*; *pl Am.* Hosenträger *pl.*

suspens|e [sə'spens] Ungewißheit *f*; Spannung *f*; **~ion** Aufhängung *f*; Aufschub *m*; Einstellung *f*; Suspendierung *f*; *sp.* Sperre *f*; **~ion bridge** Hängebrücke *f*.

suspici|on [sə'spiʃən] Verdacht *m*; **~ous** verdächtig; mißtrauisch.

sustain [səs'tein] stützen, tragen; aushalten; erleiden; unterhalten; versorgen; stärken.

sustenance ['sʌstinəns] (Lebens)Unterhalt *m*; Nahrung *f*; Nährwert *m*.

swab [swɔb] Mop *m*; *med.*: Tupfer *m*; Abstrich *m*; **~ up** aufwischen.

swagger ['swægə] stolzieren; prahlen, renommieren.

swallow ['swɔlou] Schwalbe *f*; (hinunter-, ver-) schlucken; verschlingen.

swam [swæm] *pret von* **swim.**

swamp [swɔmp] Sumpf *m*; überschwemmen (*a. fig.*); **~y** sumpfig.

swan [swɔn] Schwan *m*.

swap [swɔp] *s.* **swop.**

swarm [swɔ:m] Schwarm

m; Schar *f*; schwärmen; wimmeln.

swarthy ['swɔːði] dunkel (-häutig).

swathe [sweið] (ein-, um-) wickeln.

sway [swei] schwanken; (sich) wiegen; schaukeln; beeinflussen.

swear [swɛə] (*irr*) (be-) schwören; fluchen; ~ **s.o.** **in** j-n vereidigen.

sweat [swet] Schweiß *m*; Schwitzen *n*; (*irr*) (aus-) schwitzen; ~**er** Sweater *m*, Pullover *m*; ~**y** verschwitzt.

Swede [swiːd] Schwed|e *m*, -in *f*; 2**ish** schwedisch; Schwedisch *n*.

sweep [swiːp] (*irr*) fegen (*a. fig.*), kehren; gleiten *od.* schweifen über (*Blick*); (majestätisch) einherschreiten *od.* (dahin)rauschen; schwungvolle Bewegung; Schornsteinfeger *m*; ~**er** (Straßen)Kehrer *m*; Kehrmaschine *f*; ~**ing** schwungvoll; umfassend; ~**ings** *pl* Kehricht *m*, Müll *m*.

sweet [swiːt] süß; frisch; lieb, reizend; Bonbon *m*, *n*; *süßer* Nachtisch; *pl* Süßigkeiten *f*; *Anrede*: Liebling *m*; ~**en** (ver)süßen; ~**heart** Schatz *m*, Liebste *m*, *f*; ~**ness** Süße *f*; Sanftheit *f*; Lieblichkeit *f*; ~**pea** Gartenwicke *f*.

swell [swel] (*irr*) (an-) schwellen (lassen); sich (auf)blähen; sich bauschen; aufblähen; *Am.* pri-

ma; ~**ing** Schwellung *f*, Geschwulst *f*.

swept [swept] *pret u. pp von* **sweep**.

swerve [swəːv] (plötzlich) ab- *od.* ausbiegen.

swift [swift] schnell; eilig; flink; ~**ness** Schnelligkeit *f*.

swim [swim] (*irr*) (durch-) schwimmen; **my head** ~**s** mir ist schwind(e)lig; Schwimmen *n*; ~**mer** Schwimmer(in); ~**ming** Schwimmen *n*; Schwimm-...; ~**ming-bath** (*bsd.* Hallen)Schwimmbad *n*; ~**ming-pool** Schwimmbecken *n*; Freibad *n*; ~**suit** Badeanzug *m*.

swindle ['swindl] betrügen; beschwindeln; Schwindel *m*. [*n*.]

swine [swain], *pl* **Schwein** [

swing [swiŋ] (*irr*) schwingen; schwenken; schlenkern; baumeln (lassen); schaukeln; sich drehen (*Tür*); *colloq.* baumeln, hängen; Schwingen *n*; Schwung *m*; Schaukel *f*; ~**boat** Schiffsschaukel *f*; ~ **bridge** Drehbrücke *f*; ~**door** Drehtür *f*.

swirl [swəːl] (herum)wirbeln; Wirbel *m*, Strudel *m*.

Swiss [swis] schweizerisch; Schweizer...; Schweizer (-in) *m*, *f*; **the** ~ *pl* die Schweizer *pl*.

switch [switʃ] *rail.* Weiche *f*; *electr.* Schalter *m*; *rail.* rangieren; *electr.* (um-) schalten; *fig.* wechseln; ~

off ab-, ausschalten; **~ on** an-, einschalten; **~board** Schaltbrett n, -tafel f.

swollen ['swəulən] pp von **swell.**

swoon [swu:n] Ohnmacht f; in Ohnmacht fallen.

swoop [swu:p]: **~ down on** herabstoßen auf, sich stürzen auf.

swop [swɔp] colloq. (ein-, aus)tauschen; Tausch m.

sword [sɔ:d] Schwert n, Degen m.

swor|e [swɔ:] pret, **~n** pp von **swear.** [swim.]

swum [swʌm] pp von

swung [swʌŋ] pret u. pp von **swing.**

syllable ['siləbl] Silbe f.

symbol ['simbəl] Symbol n, Sinnbild n; **~ic(al)** [~'bɔlik(əl)] symbolisch, sinnbildlich; **~ism** Symbolik f.

symmetr|ic(al) [si'me-trik(əl)] symmetrisch, ebenmäßig; **~y** ['simitri] Symmetrie f; fig. a. Ebenmaß n.

sympath|etic [simpə-'θetik] mitfühlend; **~ize** sympathisieren, mitfühlen; **~y** Sympathie f; Mitgefühl n.

symphony ['simfəni] Symphonie f.

symptom ['simptəm] Symptom n.

synchronize ['siŋkrənaiz] synchronisieren.

synonym ['sinənim] Synonym n; **~ous** [si'nɔniməs] synonym, sinnverwandt.

syntax ['sintæks] ling. Syntax f, Satzbau m, -lehre f.

synthe|sis ['sinθisis], pl **~ses** ['~si:z] Synthese f; **~tic** [~'θetik] synthetisch.

syringe ['sirindʒ] Spritze f; (ein)spritzen.

syrup ['sirəp] Sirup m.

system ['sistim] System n; (Eisenbahn-, Straßen- etc.) Netz n; Organismus m, Körper m; **~atic** systematisch.

T

tab [tæb] (Mantel- etc.) Aufhänger m.

table ['teibl] Tisch m; Tafel f; Tabelle f, Verzeichnis n; at **~** bei Tisch; **~cloth** Tischtuch n, -decke f; **~land** Plateau n, Hochebene f; **~spoon** Eßlöffel m; **~spoon(ful)** (ein) Eßlöffel(voll) m.

tablet ['tæblit] Täfelchen n; Stück n (Seife); Tablette f.

tacit ['tæsit] stillschweigend; **~urn** ['~ə:n] schweigsam.

tack [tæk] Stift m, Zwecke f; Heftstich m; heften.

tackle ['tækl] Gerät n, Ausrüstung f; Flaschenzug m; (an)packen.

tact [tækt] Takt m, Feingefühl n; **~ful** taktvoll; **~ics** sg, pl Taktik f; **~less** taktlos.

tadpole ['tædpəul] Kaulquappe f.

tag [tæg] Anhänger m, Schildchen n, Etikett n; etikettieren, auszeichnen; anhängen (**to** an).

tail [teil] Schwanz m, Schweif m; (hinteres) Ende, Schluß m; Rückseite f (e-r Münze); **~-coat** Frack m; **~-light** Rück..., Schlußlicht n.

tailor ['teilə] Schneider m; schneidern; **~-made** Schneider..., Maß...

taint [teint] (verborgene) Anlage (zu e-r Krankheit); **~ed** Fleisch: verdorben.

take [teik] (irr) (an-, ein-, entgegen-, heraus-, hin-, mit-, weg)nehmen; ergreifen; fangen; (hin-, weg)bringen; halten (**for** für); Speisen zu sich nehmen; Platz einnehmen; Fahrt, Zug, Bus etc. nehmen, benutzen; Temperatur messen; phot. Aufnahme machen; Prüfung machen, ablegen; Preis gewinnen; Gelegenheit, Maßnahmen ergreifen; Vorsitz etc. übernehmen; Eid ablegen; Zeit, Geduld erfordern, brauchen; Zeit dauern; **~ along** mitnehmen; **~ from** j-m et. wegnehmen; **~ in** Gast aufnehmen; Zeitung halten; et. kürzer machen, enger machen; fig.: et. in sich aufnehmen; Lage überschauen; colloq. j-n

reinlegen; **be ~n in** reingefallen sein; **~ off** j-n fortbringen; Hut etc. abnehmen; Kleidungsstück ablegen, ausziehen; e-n Tag etc. Urlaub machen; aer. aufsteigen, abfliegen, starten; **~ out** heraus-, entnehmen, entfernen; zum Essen ausführen; **~ over** Amt, Aufgabe etc. übernehmen; **~ to** Gefallen finden an, sich hingezogen fühlen zu; **~ up** auf-, hochheben; aufnehmen; sich befassen mit; Idee aufgreifen; Platz, Zeit etc. in Anspruch nehmen; **~ pp von take**; besetzt; **~-off** aer. Start m.

tale [teil] Erzählung f, Geschichte f; Märchen n.

talent ['tælənt] Talent n, Begabung f; **~ed** begabt.

talk [tɔ:k] Gespräch n; Unterhaltung f; Unterredung f; Vortrag m; sprechen, reden; **~ to** sich unterhalten mit; **~ative** ['~ətiv] geschwätzig.

tall [tɔ:l] groß, hochgewachsen; lang, hoch.

tallow ['tæləu] Talg m.

talon ['tælən] orn. Kralle f, Klaue f.

tame [teim] zahm; folgsam; harmlos; zähmen.

tamper ['tæmpə] **~ with** sich (unbefugt) zu schaffen machen an.

tan [tæn] Lohfarbe f; (Sonnen)Bräune f; lohfarben;

gelbbraun; gerben; bräu-
nen. [gente f.]
tangent ['tændʒənt] Tan-/
tangerine [tændʒə'ri:n]
Mandarine f.
tangle ['tæŋgl] Gewirr n;
Verwicklung f; Durchein-
ander n; verwirren, ver-
wickeln.
tank [tæŋk] Tank m (a.
mil.); Zisterne f, Wasser-
becken n, -behälter m.
tankard ['tæŋkəd] (Bier-)
Krug m.
tanner ['tænə] Gerber m.
tantalizing ['tæntəlaiziŋ]
quälend, verlockend.
tantrum ['tæntrəm] Wut
(-anfall m) f.
tap [tæp] leichtes Klopfen;
Zapfen m; (Wasser-, Gas-,
Zapf)Hahn m; pl mil. Am.
Zapfenstreich m; klopfen,
pochen; an-, abzapfen.
tape [teip] schmales Band,
Streifen m; sp. Zielband n;
(Ton)Band n; **~-measure**
Bandmaß n.
taper ['teipə] v/i ~ off spitz
zulaufen.
tape|**recorder** Tonband-
gerät n; **~ recording**
(Ton)Bandaufnahme f.
tapestry ['tæpistri] Gobe-
lin m.
tapeworm Bandwurm m.
tar [tɑː] Teer m; teeren.
target ['tɑːgit] (Schieß-)
Scheibe f; mil. Ziel n; fig.
Zielscheibe f.
tariff ['tærif] Zolltarif m;
Preisliste f (im Hotel).
tarnish ['tɑːniʃ] matt od.

blind machen; anlaufen
(Metall).
tart [tɑːt] sauer, herb; fig.
scharf; (Obst)Torte f.
tartan ['tɑːtən] Tartan m,
Schottentuch n, -muster n.
task [tɑːsk] Aufgabe f; Arbeit f; **take to ~** j-n ins
Gebet nehmen (for we-
gen). [Quaste f.]
tassel ['tæsəl] Troddel f,]
taste [teist] Geschmack
m; kosten, probieren; (heraus)schmecken; fig. ken-
nenlernen, erleben; **~ful**
geschmackvoll; **~less** ge-
schmacklos; **~y** schmack-
haft; geschmackvoll.
ta-ta ['tæ'tɑː] int. colloq. auf
Wiedersehen!
tattoo [tə'tuː] mil. Zapfenstreich m; Tätowierung f;
tätowieren. [teach.]
taught [tɔːt] pret u. pp von]
taunt [tɔːnt] Spott m; ver-
höhnen, -spotten.
tax [tæks] Steuer f, Abgabe
f; besteuern; **~ation** Be-
steuerung f; Steuern pl; **~
collector** Steuereinneh-
mer m.
taxi|**(-cab)** ['tæksi(-)] Ta-
xe f, Taxi n, (Auto-)
Droschke f; **~-driver** Ta-
xifahrer m; **~ rank** Taxistand m.
tax|**payer** Steuerzahler m;
~-return Steuererklärung f.
tea [tiː] Tee m.
teach [tiːtʃ] (irr) belehren,
unterrichten, j-m et. beibringen; **~er** Lehrer(in).
tea|**cup** Teetasse f; **~-ket-**

tle Tee-, Wasserkessel m.

team [ti:m] Team n, (Arbeits)Gruppe f; Gespann n; sp. Team n, Mannschaft f; **~work** Zs.-arbeit f, Zs.-spiel n, Teamwork n.

teapot Teekanne f.

tear[1] [teə] (irr) zerren; (aus-, zer)reißen; Riß m.

tear[2] [tiə] Träne f.

tearoom Teeraum m, Teestube f.

tease [ti:z] necken, hänseln; ärgern; quälen.

tea|spoon Teelöffel m; **~spoonful** (ein) Teelöffel (-voll) m.

teat [ti:t] Zitze f.

techni|cal ['teknikəl] technisch; Fach...; **~cian** [~'niʃən] Techniker(in); **~que** [~'ni:k] Technik f, Verfahren n.

tedious ['ti:djəs] langweilig; ermüdend.

teens [ti:nz] pl Jugendjahre pl (von 13–19).

teeny ['ti:ni] winzig.

teeth [ti:θ] pl von **tooth**; **~e** [ti:ð] zahnen.

teetotal(l)er [ti:'təutl] Abstinenzler(in).

telegram ['teligræm] Telegramm n.

telegraph ['teligra:f] Telegraf m; telegrafieren; **~ic** [~'græfik] telegrafisch; **~y** [ti'legrəfi] Telegrafie f.

telephone ['telifəun] Telefon n, Fernsprecher m; telefonieren; anrufen; **~ booth** Telefonzelle f; **~ call** Telefongespräch n,

Anruf m; **~ directory** Telefonbuch n; **~ exchange** Fernsprechamt n; **~ kiosk** ['~ 'ki:ɔsk] Telefonzelle f.

tele|printer ['teliprintə] Fernschreiber m; **~scope** ['~skəup] Fernrohr n; **~typewriter** [~'taip-]Fernschreiber m.

televise ['telivaiz] im Fernsehen übertragen.

television ['teliviʒən] Fernsehen n; **on ~** im Fernsehen; **watch ~** fernsehen; **~ set** Fernsehapparat m.

tell [tel] (irr) sagen; erzählen; erkennen; unterscheiden; sagen, befehlen; **~er** (Bank)Kassierer m; **~tale** verräterisch.

temper ['tempə] mäßigen, mildern; Charakter m; Laune f; Wut f; **keep one's ~** sich beherrschen; **lose one's ~** in Wut geraten; **~ament** Temperament n; **~ance** Enthaltsamkeit f; **~ate** [~'rit] gemäßigt; zurückhaltend; **~ature** [~'pritʃə] Temperatur f; Fieber n.

tempest ['tempist] Sturm m; **~uous** [~'pestjuəs] stürmisch.

temple ['templ] Tempel m; anat. Schläfe f.

tempor|al ['tempərəl] zeitlich; weltlich; **~ary** vorläufig, zeitweilig, vorübergehend; Not..., Behelfs...

tempt [tempt] j-n versuchen; verleiten; verlocken; **~ation** Versuchung *f*; **~ing** verführerisch.

ten [ten] zehn; Zehn *f*.

tenacious [ti'neiʃəs] zäh, hartnäckig.

tenant ['tenənt] Pächter *m*; Mieter *m*.

tend [tend] sich bewegen (**to** nach, auf ... zu); *fig*. tendieren, neigen (**to** zu); pflegen; hüten; **~ency** Tendenz *f*, Richtung *f*; Neigung *f*.

tender ['tendə] zart; weich; empfindlich; zärtlich; (formell) anbieten; **~loin** Filet *n*); **~ness** Zartheit *f*; Zärtlichkeit *f*.

tendon ['tendən] Sehne *f*.

tendril ['tendril] Ranke *f*.

tenement-house ['tenimənthaus] *f* Mietshaus *m*.

tennis ['tenis] Tennis (-spiel) *n*; **~-court** Tennisplatz *m*.

tens|e [tens] *gr*. Tempus *n*, Zeitform *f*; (an)gespannt (*a. fig.*); straff; **~ion** Spannung *f*.

tent [tent] Zelt *n*.

tentacle ['tentəkl] *zo*. Fangarm *m*.

tenth [tenθ] zehnte; Zehntel *n*; **~ly** zehntens.

tepid ['tepid] lau(warm).

term [tə:m] (bestimmte) Zeit, Dauer *f*; Amtszeit *f*; Frist *f*; Termin *m*; *jur*. Sitzungsperiode *f*; Semester *n*, Quartal *n*, Trimester *n*; (Fach)Ausdruck *m*, Bezeichnung *f*; *pl*: (Ver-

trags- *etc*.)Bedingungen *pl*; Beziehungen *pl*; **be on good** *od*. **bad ~s with** gut *od*. schlecht stehen mit; (be)nennen, bezeichnen als.

termina|l ['tə:minl] Endstation *f*; **~te** [~eit] begrenzen; (be)enden; **~tion** Beendigung *f*; Ende *n*.

terminus ['tə:minəs] Endstation *f*.

terrace ['terəs] Terrasse *f*; **~d** terrassenförmig (angelegt).

terri|ble ['terəbl] schrecklich; **~fic** [tə'rifik] schrecklich; *colloq*. phantastisch; **~fy** ['terifai] erschrecken.

territor|ial [teri'tɔ:riəl] territorial; Land...; **~y** ['~təri] Territorium *n*, (Hoheits-, Staats)Gebiet *n*.

terror ['terə] Schrecken *m*, Entsetzen *n*; Terror *m*; **~ize** terrorisieren.

test [test] Probe *f*, Untersuchung *f*; Test *m*; (Eignungs)Prüfung *f*; prüfen, testen. [Testament *n*.]

testament ['testəmənt])

testify ['testifai] bezeugen; (als Zeuge) aussagen.

testimon|ial [testi'məunjəl] (Führungs- *etc*.)Zeugnis *n*; **~y** ['~məni] Zeugenaussage *f*.

testy ['testi] gereizt.

text [tekst] Text *m*; Bibelstelle *f*; **~book** Lehrbuch *n*.

textile ['tekstail] Textil..., Gewebe...; *pl* Textilien *pl*.

texture ['tekstʃə] Gewebe *n*; Struktur *f*, Gefüge *n*.

than [ðæn,ðən] als.

thank [θæŋk] danken; (no,) ~ you (nein,) danke; pl Dank m; ~s to dank; ~s! vielen Dank!, danke!; ~ful dankbar; ~less undankbar; 2sgiving (Day) Am. (Ernte)Dankfest n.

that [ðæt, ðət], pl those [ðouz] pron, adj: das; jene(r,-s), der, die, das, der-, die-, dasjenige; solche(r, -s); adv colloq. so; rel pron (that): der, die, das, welche(r, -s); conj daß; damit; weil; da, als.

thatch [θætʃ] Dachstroh n; Strohdach n; mit Stroh decken.

thaw [θɔː] Tauwetter n; (auf)tauen, schmelzen.

the [vor Konsonanten ðə, vor Vokalen ði; betont ðiː] der, die, das; pl die; desto, um so; ... ... je ... desto.

theatre, Am. ~er [θiətə] Theater n; ~rical [θiˈætrikl] Theater... [dir.\
thee [ðiː] Bibel, poet. dich;\
theft [θeft] Diebstahl m.

their [ðeə] pl ihr(e); ~s [~z] der, die, das ihr(ig)e.

them [ðem, ðəm] pl sie (acc); ihnen.

theme [θiːm] Thema n.

themselves [ðəmˈselvz] pl sie selbst; sich (selbst).

then [ðen] dann; damals; denn; damalig; by ~ bis dahin, inzwischen.

theolog|ian [θiəˈləudʒjən] Theologe m; ~y [θiˈɔlədʒi] Theologie f.

theor|etic(al) [θiəˈretik(əl)] theoretisch; ~y [´~ri] Theorie f; Lehre f.   [pie f.\
therapy [θerəpi] Thera-\
there [ðeə] da, dort; darin; (da-, dort)hin; int. da!, na!; ~ is, pl ~ are es gibt, es ist, es sind; ~about(s) da herum; so ungefähr; ~after danach; ~by dadurch; ~fore darum, deshalb; ~upon darauf(hin); ~with damit.

thermo|meter [θəˈmɔmitə] Thermometer n; ~s (bottle, flask) [θɔːmɔs] Thermosflasche f.

these [ðiːz] pl von this.

thes|is [´θiːsis], pl ~es [´~iːz] These f; Dissertation f.

they [ðei] pl sie; man.

thick [θik] dick; dicht; dick(flüssig); legiert (Suppe); ~en (sich) verdicken; (sich) verstärken; legieren; (sich) verdichten; dick(er) werden; ~et [´~it] Dickicht n; ~ness Dicke f, Stärke f; Dichte f.

thief [θiːf], pl thieves [~vz] Dieb(in). [kel m.\
thigh [θai] (Ober)Schen-\
thimble [θimbl] Fingerhut m.

thin [θin] dünn; mager; schwach; fig. spärlich; verdünnen; (sich) lichten; abnehmen.

thine [ðain] Bibel, poet. der, die, das dein(ig)e; dein.

thing [θiŋ] Ding n; Sache f; Gegenstand m.

think
288

think [θiŋk] (*irr*) denken (**of** an); sich vorstellen; halten für; meinen, glauben; überlegen, nachdenken (**about**, **over** über); **~ of** sich erinnern an; sich *et.* (aus)denken; daran denken; halten von; **~ s.th. over** sich *et.* überlegen.

third [θɔːd] dritte; Drittel *n*; **~ly** drittens; **~-party insurance** Haftpflichtversicherung *f*; **~-rate** drittklassig.

thirst [θɔːst] Durst *m*; **~y** durstig; **be ~y** Durst haben.

thirt|een(th) [ˈθɔːˈtiːn(θ)] dreizehn(te); **~ieth** [ˈ~tiiθ] dreißigste; **~y** dreißig; Dreißig *f*.

this [ðis], *pl* **these** [ðiːz] diese(r, -s); dies, das; der, die, das (da).

thistle [ˈθisl] Distel *f*.

thorn [θɔːn] Dorn *m*; **~y** dornig, stach(e)lig.

thorough [ˈθʌrə] gründlich; vollkommen; **~bred** Vollblut(pferd) *n*; Vollblut...; **~fare** Durchfahrt *f*; Durchgangsstraße *f*.

those [ðəuz] *pl von* **that**.

thou [ðau] *Bibel*, *poet.* du.

though [ðəu] obgleich, obwohl, wenn auch; (je-)doch; **as ~** als ob.

thought [θɔːt] *pret u. pp von* **think**; Gedanke *m*; Denken *n*; Überlegung *f*; **~ful** nachdenklich; rücksichtsvoll; **~less** gedan-

kenlos, unüberlegt; rücksichtslos.

thousand [ˈθauzənd] tausend; Tausend *n*; **~th** [ˈ~tθ] tausendste; Tausendstel *n*.

thrash [θræʃ] verdreschen, -prügeln; (um sich) schlagen; sich hin u. her werfen; *s.* **thresh**; **~ing** (Tracht *f*) Prügel *pl*.

thread [θred] Faden *m* (*a. fig.*), Zwirn *m*, Garn *n*; *tech.* Gewinde *n*; einfädeln; durchziehen; sich (hindurch)schlängeln; **~bare** fadenscheinig.

threat [θret] Drohung *f*; **~en** (be-, an)drohen; **~ening** drohend; bedrohlich.

three [θriː] drei; Drei *f*; **~fold** dreifach; **~pence** [ˈθrepəns] *alte Währung:* Dreipencestück *n*; **~score** sechzig; **~stage** dreistufig, Dreistufen...

thresh [θreʃ] dreschen; **~er** Drescher *m*; Dreschmaschine *f*; **~ing** Dreschen *n*; **~ing-machine** Dreschmaschine *f*.

threshold [ˈθreʃhəuld] Schwelle *f*. [**throw**.]

threw [θruː] *pret von*]

thrice [θrais] dreimal.

thrifty [ˈθrifti] sparsam.

thrill [θril] erregen, packen; (er)beben, erschauern; Schauer *m*; (Nerven-) Kitzel *m*, Sensation *f*; **~er** *colloq.* Reißer *m*, Thriller *m*; **~ing** spannend.

thrive [θraiv] (*irr*) gedei-

hen; *fig.* blühen; **~n**
['θrɪvn] *pp von* thrive.

throat [θrəut] Kehle *f*,
Gurgel *f*, Schlund *m*; Hals
m.

throb [θrɔb] pochen, klopfen, hämmern (*Herz etc.*).

throne [θrəun] Thron *m*.

throng [θrɔŋ] Gedränge *n*;
(Menschen)Menge *f*; sich
drängen (in).

throstle ['θrɔsl] Drossel *f*.

throttle ['θrɔtl] (ab-, er-)
drosseln; **~(-valve)** *tech.*
Drosselklappe *f*.

through [θruː] durch;
durchgehend, Durchgangs-
...; **~ carriage** Kurswagen *m*; **~out** überall in;
durch u. durch, ganz u.
gar; **~ train** durchgehen-
der Zug.   [thrive.\

throve [θrəuv] *pret von*\

throw [θrəu] Wurf *m*; (*irr*)
(ab)werfen; schleudern;
würfeln; **~ up** hochwerfen;
(sich) erbrechen; **~n** *pp von*
throw.   [through.\

thru [θruː] *Am.* (für)\

thrum [θrʌm] klimpern
(auf).

thrush [θrʌʃ] Drossel *f*.

thrust [θrʌst] Stoß *m*;
tech.: Druck *m*; Schub *m*;
(*irr*) stoßen.

thud [θʌd] dumpf (auf-)
schlagen; dumpfer (Auf-)
Schlag.

thumb [θʌm] Daumen *m*;
Buch etc. abgreifen *od.*
durchblättern; **~ a lift** per
Anhalter fahren; **~tack**
Am. Reißzwecke *f*.

thump [θʌmp] (dumpfer)
Schlag; schlagen (häm-
mern, pochen) gegen *od.*
auf; (auf)schlagen; pochen
(*Herz*).

thunder ['θʌndə] Donner
m; donnern; **~storm** Gewitter *n*; **~struck** wie vom
Donner gerührt.

Thursday ['θəːzdi] Don-
nerstag *m*.

thus [ðʌs] so; also, somit.

thwart [θwɔːt] durchkreu-
zen.

thy [ðai] *Bibel, poet.* dein(e).

tick [tik] *zo.* Zecke *f*; Inlett *n*; Matratzenbezug *m*;
Ticken *n*; (*Vermerk*)Häk-
chen *n*; ticken; anhaken;
~ off abhaken.

ticket ['tikit] (Eintritts-,
Theater- *etc.*)Karte *f*;
Fahrkarte *f*, -schein *m*;
Flugkarte *f* (Preis- *etc.*)
Schildchen *n*, Etikett *n*;
etikettieren, *Ware* aus-
zeichnen; **~ (automatic)**
machine Fahrkartenau-
tomat *m*; **~ office** *Am.*
Fahrkartenschalter *m*.

tickl|e ['tikl] kitzeln; **~ish**
kitz(e)lig (*a. fig.*).

tid|al wave ['taidl] Flut-
welle *f*; **~e** [taid] Gezeiten *pl*, Ebbe *f* u. Flut *f*;
fig. Strom *m*, Strömung *f*.

tidy ['taidi] ordentlich, sauber; **~ up** aufräumen.

tie [tai] Band *n* (*a. fig.*);
Krawatte *f*, Schlips *m*;
rail. Am. Schwelle *f*; *sp.*
Unentschieden *n*; *fig.* Fessel *f*, Last *f*; (an-, fest)bin-

den; ~ **up** (an-, zs.-, zu-) binden.

tier [tiə] Reihe f, Lage f; *thea.* (Sitz)Reihe f.

tiger ['taigə] Tiger m.

tight [tait] dicht; fest; eng; knapp (sitzend); straff; *fig.* zs.-gepreßt; **~en** eng machen; (sich) straffen; fester werden; **~en (up)** (sich) zs.-ziehen; fest-, anziehen; **~rope** (Draht)Seil n (der Artisten); **~s** pl Trikot n; Strumpfhose f.

tigress ['taigris] Tigerin f.

tile [tail] (Dach)Ziegel m; Kachel f, Fliese f; (mit Ziegeln) decken; kacheln, fliesen.   [erst (als).]

till¹ [til] bis; bis zu; **not ~**}

till² Ladenkasse f.

till³ Boden bestellen, bebauen.   [kippen.]

tilt [tilt] Plane f; (um-)}

timber ['timbə] (Bau-, Nutz)Holz n; Balken m; Baumbestand m, Bäume pl.

time [taim] Zeit f; Uhrzeit f; Frist f; *mus.* Takt m; Mal n; pl mal, ~mal; ~ **is up** die Zeit ist um od. abgelaufen; **for the ~ being** vorläufig; **have a good ~** sich gut unterhalten od. amüsieren; **what's the ~?**, **what ~ is it?** wieviel Uhr ist es?, wie spät ist es?; ~ **and again** immer wieder; **all the ~** ständig, immer; **at a ~** auf einmal, zusammen; **at any ~**, **at all ~s** jederzeit; **at the**

same ~ gleichzeitig, zur selben Zeit; **in ~** rechtzeitig; **in no ~** im Nu, im Handumdrehen; **on ~** pünktlich; *vb:* messen, (ab-)stoppen; zeitlich abstimmen; den richtigen Zeitpunkt wählen od. bestimmen für; **~ly** rechtzeitig; **~table** Fahrplan m; Flugplan m; Stundenplan m.

tim|id ['timid], **~orous** ['~ərəs] furchtsam; schüchtern.

tin [tin] Zinn n; (Blech-, Konserven)Büchse f, Dose f; verzinnen; (in Büchsen) einmachen, eindosen; **~foil** Aluminiumfolie f, Stanniol(papier) n.

tinge [tind3] Färbung f; *fig.* Anflug m, Spur f; (leicht) färben.

tingle ['tiŋgl] prickeln.

tinkle ['tiŋkl] hell (er)klingen; klirren; klingeln mit.

tin|ned Büchsen ..., Dosen ...; **~-opener** Büchsen-, Dosenöffner m.

tint [tint] (Farb)Ton m, Schattierung f; (leicht) färben.

tiny ['taini] winzig.

tip [tip] Spitze f; Mundstück n; Trinkgeld n; Tip m, Wink m; (um)kippen; j-m ein Trinkgeld geben; ~ **(off)** j-m e-n Wink geben; **~ped** mit Mundstück (Zigarette).

tipsy ['tipsi] *colloq.* beschwipst, angeheitert.

tiptoe ['tiptəu] auf Zehenspitzen gehen; **on ~** auf Zehenspitzen.

tire¹ ['taiə] s. **tyre**.

tire² ermüden; müde werden; **~d** müde; erschöpft; *fig.* überdrüssig (**of** *gen*); **~some** ermüdend; lästig.

tissue ['tisju] Gewebe *n*; **~-paper** Seidenpapier *n*.

tit¹ [tit] Meise *f*.

tit²: **~ for tat** wie du mir, so ich dir.

titbit ['titbit] Leckerbissen *m*.

titillate ['titileit] kitzeln.

title ['taitl] (*Buch*)Titel *m*; (*Adels-, Ehren-, Amtsetc.*)Titel *m*; Überschrift *f*; (*Rechts*)Anspruch *m*; **~d** betitelt; ad(e)lig.

titmouse ['titmaus] Meise *f*.

to [tu:, tu, tə] *prp* zu, an, auf, für, gegen, in, mit, nach, vor, (um) zu; bis, (bis) zu, (bis) an; *zeitlich:* bis, bis zu, auf, vor; *adv* zu, geschlossen; **pull ~ Tür** zuziehen; **come ~** (wieder) zu sich kommen; **~ and fro** hin und her, auf und ab.

toad [toud] Kröte *f*.

toast [toust] Toast *m*, gerösteres Brot; Trinkspruch *m*; toasten, rösten; *fig.* trinken auf.

tobacco [tə'bækou] Tabak *m*; **~nist** [-ənist] Tabak(waren)händler *m*.

toboggan [tə'bɔgən] Toboggan *m*; Rodelschlitten *m*; rodeln.

today [tə'dei] heute.

toddle ['tɔdl] unsicher gehen, watscheln.

toe [tou] Zehe *f*; Spitze *f*.

toff|ee, ~y ['tɔfi] Sahnebonbon *m, n*, Toffee *n*.

together [tə'geðə] zusammen; gleichzeitig; *Tage etc.* hintereinander.

toil [tɔil] Mühe *f*, Plackerei *f*; schwer arbeiten.

toilet ['tɔilit] Toilette *f*; **~-paper** Toilettenpapier *n*.

toils [tɔilz] *pl fig.* Schlingen *pl*, Netz *n*.

token ['toukən] Zeichen *n*; Andenken *n*.

told [tould] *pret u. pp* von **tell.**

tolera|ble ['tɔlərəbl] erträglich; leidlich; **~nce** Toleranz *f*; **~nt** tolerant (**of** gegen); **~te** [‿eit] dulden; ertragen; **~tion** Duldung *f*.

toll¹ [toul] schlagen, läuten.

toll² Straßenbenutzungsgebühr *f*, Maut *f*; *fig.* Tribut *m*, Todesopfer *pl*; **~-bar**, **~-gate** Schlagbaum *m*.

tomato [tə'mɑ:tou, *Am.* tə'meitou], *pl* **~es** Tomate *f*.

tomb [tu:m] Grab(mal) *n*; **~stone** Grabstein *m*.

tomcat ['tɔm'kæt] Kater *m*.

tomorrow [tə'mɔrou] morgen; **the day after ~** übermorgen; (*wicht.*).

ton [tʌn] Tonne *f* (*Gewicht*).

tone [toun] Ton *m*, Klang *m*, Laut *m*.

tongs [tɔŋz] *pl* (**a. a pair of ~**)(-e-e) Zange *f*.

tongue [tʌŋ] Zunge *f*; Sprache *f*.

tonic ['tɔnik] Tonikum *n*.

tonight [tə'nait] heute abend; heute nacht.

tonnage ['tʌnidʒ] Tonnengehalt *m*.

tonsil ['tɔnsl] *anat.* Mandel *f*; **~litis** [~si'laitis] Mandelentzündung *f*.

too [tu:] zu, allzu; *nachgestellt:* auch, noch dazu, ebenfalls.

took [tuk] *pret von* take.

tool [tu:l] Werkzeug *n*, Gerät *n*.

tooth [tu:θ], *pl* **teeth** [ti:θ] Zahn *m*; **~ache** Zahnschmerzen *pl*; **~brush** Zahnbürste *f*; **~less** zahnlos; **~paste** Zahnpasta *f*, -creme *f*; **~pick** Zahnstocher *m*.

top [tɔp] Kreisel *m*; oberstes Ende; Oberteil *m*, -seite *f*; Spitze *f* (*a. fig.*); Gipfel *m* (*a. fig.*); Wipfel *m*; Kopf(ende *n*) *m*; *mot.* Verdeck *n*; Stülpe *f* (*am Stiefel etc.*); **at the ~ of** oben an; **on (the) ~ of** oben auf; *adj* oberst; höchst, Höchst..., Spitzen...; **~ secret** streng geheim; *vb* bedecken; überragen; an der Spitze stehen; **~ up** (auf-, nach)füllen.

topic ['tɔpik] Thema *n*.

topple ['tɔpl]: **~** (**down, over** um)kippen.

topsy-turvy ['tɔpsi'tə:vi] auf den Kopf (gestellt); drunter und drüber.

torch [tɔːtʃ] Fackel *f*; Taschenlampe *f*.

tore [tɔː] *pret von* tear¹.

torment ['tɔːment] Qual *f*; [~'ment] quälen.

torn [tɔːn] *pp von* tear¹.

tornado [tɔː'neidəu], *pl* **~es** Wirbelsturm *m*.

torrent ['tɔrənt] Sturzbach *m*; reißender Strom; *fig.* Strom *m*, Schwall *m*.

tortoise ['tɔːtəs] (Land-) Schildkröte *f*.

torture ['tɔːtʃə] Folter(ung) *f*; foltern.

toss [tɔs] (Hoch)Werfen *n*, Wurf *m*; Zurückwerfen *n* (*Kopf*); werfen, schleudern; **~ about** (sich) hin u. herwerfen; **~ up** hochwerfen.

total ['təutl] ganz, gesamt, Gesamt...; total; Gesamtbetrag *m*; sich belaufen auf; **~itarian** [~tæli'tɛəriən] totalitär.

totter ['tɔtə] (sch)wanken, torkeln.

touch [tʌtʃ] Berührung *f*; Verbindung *f*, Kontakt *m*; leichter Anfall, Anflug *m*; (sich) berühren; anrühren, anfassen; *fig.* rühren; **~ down** landen; **~ down** *aer.* Landung *f*; **~ing** rührend; **~y** empfindlich; heikel.

tough [tʌf] zäh (*a. fig.*); grob, brutal.

tour [tuə] (Rund)Reise *f*, Tour(nee) *f* (*a.* (be)reisen.

tourist ['tuərist] Tourist (-in); Touristen..., Fremden(verkehrs)...; ~ **agen-cy, ~ bureau, ~ office** Reisebüro n; Verkehrsverein m.

tournament ['tuǝnǝmǝnt] Turnier n.

tousle ['tauzl] (zer)zausen.

tow [tǝu] Schleppen n; **give s.o. a** ~ j-n abschleppen; **have** od. **take in** ~ ins Schlepptau nehmen; vb: (ab)schleppen.

towards(s) [tǝ'wɔ:d(z)] gegen; auf ... zu, nach ... zu; (als Beitrag) zu.

towel ['tauǝl] Handtuch n.

tower ['tauǝ] Turm m; (hoch)ragen, sich erheben.

town [taun] Stadt f; Stadt-...; ~ **council** Stadtrat m (Versammlung); ~ **coun-cil(l)or** Stadtrat m (Person); ~ **hall** Rathaus n.

tow-rope Schlepptau n; Abschleppseil n.

toy [tɔi] Spielzeug n; pl Spielsachen pl, ~waren pl; Spielzeug..., Kinder...; spielen.

trace [treis] Spur f; nachspüren; verfolgen.

track [træk] Spur f, Fährte f; rail. Gleis n; sp. (Renn-Aschen)Bahn f; Pfad m; nachspüren, verfolgen; ~ **down, ~ out** aufspüren; **~-and-field events** ~ Leichtathletik f; ~ **events** pl Laufdisziplinen pl.

tract|ion-engine ['træk-ʃǝnendʒin] Zugmaschine f; **~or** Traktor m.

trade [treid] Handel m;

Gewerbe n, Handwerk n; Handel treiben, handeln (**in** mit); **~mark** Warenzeichen n; **~r** Händler m, Kaufmann m; **~(s) union** Gewerkschaft f; **~unionist** Gewerkschaftler(in).

tradition [trǝ'diʃǝn] Tradition f; **~al** traditionell.

traffic ['træfik] Verkehr m; Handel m; handeln (**in** mit); **~ island** Verkehrsinsel f; **~ jam** Verkehrsstauung f; **~ light(s** pl) Verkehrsampel f; **~ reg-ulations** pl Verkehrsvorschriften pl; **~ sign** Verkehrszeichen n; **~ warden** mot. appr. Politesse f.

trag|edy ['trædʒidi] Tragödie f; **~ic(al)** tragisch.

trail [treil] Spur f; Pfad m, Weg m; fig. Streifen m; hinter sich herziehen; verfolgen; schleifen; am ~, mot.: Anhänger m; Wohnwagen m.

train [trein] (Eisenbahn-)Zug m; Reihe f, Kette f; Schleppe f (am Kleid); schulen; abrichten; ausbilden; trainieren; **~er** Ausbilder m; Trainer m; **~ing** Ausbildung f; Training n. [Zug m.]

trait [trei] (Charakter-)

traitor ['treitǝ] Verräter m.

tram(-car) [træm(-)] Straßenbahn(wagen m) f.

tramp [træmp] Getrampel n; Wanderung f; Landstreicher m; trampeln; (durch)wandern; **~le** (herum-, zer)trampeln.

tranquil ['træŋkwil] ruhig; ~(l)ity Ruhe f; ~(l)ize beruhigen; ~(l)izer Beruhigungsmittel n.

transact [træn'zækt] erledigen, abwickeln; ~ion Durchführung f; Geschäft n, Transaktion f.

trans|alpine ['trænz'ælpain] transalpin(isch); ~atlantic transatlantisch.

transcend [træn'send] fig.: überschreiten, -steigen; übertreffen.

transcribe [træns'kraib] abschreiben; Kurzschrift übertragen.

transcript ['trænskript] Abschrift f; ~ion Abschrift f; Umschrift f.

transfer [træns'fə:] versetzen; verlegen; übertragen; abtreten; verlegt od. versetzt werden; umsteigen; ['~] Übertragung f; Versetzung f; Verlegung f; Umsteigefahrschein m; ~able [~'fə:rəbl] übertragbar.

transform [træns'fɔ:m] umformen, um-, verwandeln; ~ation Umformung f, Um-, Verwandlung f.

transfus|e [træns'fju:z] Blut übertragen; ~ion [~-ʒən] (Blut)Transfusion f.

transgress [træns'gres] überschreiten; übertreten; verletzen; ~ion Überschreitung f; Übertretung f; Vergehen n; ~or Missetäter(in).

transient ['trænziənt] ver-

gänglich, flüchtig; Am. Durchreisende m, f.

transistor [træn'sistə] Transistor m.

transit ['trænsit] Durchgang(sverkehr) m; econ. Transport m; ~ion [~'siʒən] Übergang m.

transitive ['trænsitiv] gr. transitiv.

translat|e [træns'leit] übersetzen; ~ion Übersetzung f; ~or Übersetzer(in).

translucent [trænz'lu:snt] lichtdurchlässig.

transmi|ssion [trænz'miʃən] Übermittlung f; Übertragung f; Radio etc.: Sendung f; ~t übermitteln; übertragen; senden; ~tter Sendegerät n; Sender m.

transparent [træns'peərənt] durchsichtig.

transpire [træns'paiə] schwitzen; fig. durchsickern.

transplant [træns'pla:nt] um-, verpflanzen; ~(ation) Verpflanzung f.

transport [træns'pɔ:t] befördern, transportieren; ['~] Beförderung f, Transport m; Beförderungsmittel n; ~ation Beförderung f, Transport m.

trap [træp] (in e-r Falle) fangen; Falle f (a. fig.); set a ~ for j—m e-e Falle stellen; ~door Falltür f.

trapeze [trə'pi:z] Trapez n.

trapper ['træpə] Trapper m, Fallensteller m, Pelztierjäger m.

trash [træʃ] *bsd. Am.* Abfall *m*; *fig.* Plunder *m*.

travel ['trævl] (be)reisen; *das* Reisen; *pl* Reisen *pl*; ~ **agency** Reisebüro *n*; ~(**l)er** Reisende *m*, *f*; ~(**l)er's cheque** (*Am.* **check**) Reisescheck *m*; ~(**l)ing bag** Reisetasche *f*.

traverse ['trævə(:)s] durch-, überqueren.

trawl [trɔːl] (Grund-) Schleppnetz *n*; mit dem Schleppnetz fischen; ~**er** Trawler *m*. [lage *f*.]

tray [trei] Tablett *n*; Ab-

treacher|ous ['tretʃərəs] verräterisch, treulos, trügerisch; ~**y** Verrat *m*.

treacle ['triːkl] Sirup *m*.

tread [tred] (*irr*) treten; schreiten; Tritt *m*, Schritt *m*; ~**le** Pedal *n*; ~**mill** Tretmühle *f* (*a. fig.*).

treason ['triːzn] Verrat *m*.

treasure ['treʒə] Schatz *m* (*a. fig.*); Reichtum *m*; (hoch)schätzen; ~ **up** sammeln; ~**r** Schatzmeister *m*.

treasury ['treʒəri] Schatzkammer *f*; Staatsschatz *m*; Staatskasse *f*; ♀ **Department** *Am.* Finanzministerium *n*.

treat [triːt] behandeln; betrachten; bewirten (**to** mit); ~ **s.o. to s.th.** j-m et. spendieren; ~ **of** handeln von; Vergnügen *n*, (Hoch)Genuß *m*; ~**ise** ['-iz] Abhandlung *f*; ~**ment** Behandlung *f*; ~**y** Vertrag *m*.

treble ['trebl] dreifach; (sich) verdreifachen.

tree [triː] Baum *m*.

trefoil ['trefɔil] Klee *m*.

trellis ['trelis] *agr.* Spalier *n*; am Spalier ziehen.

tremble ['trembl] zittern (**with** vor).

tremendous [tri'mendəs] gewaltig; enorm.

trem|or ['tremə] Zittern *n*; Beben *n*; ~**ulous** ['-juləs] zitternd, bebend.

trench [trentʃ] (Schützen-) Graben *m*.

trend [trend] Richtung *f*; *fig.* Tendenz *f*, Trend *m*.

trespass ['trespəs] Übertretung *f*, Vergehen *n*; unbefugt eindringen (**on**, **upon** in); ~**er** Unbefugte *m*, *f*.

tress [tres] Haarlocke *f*, -flechte *f*.

trestle ['tresl] Gestell *n*, Bock *m*.

trial ['traiəl] Versuch *m*, Probe *f*, Prüfung *f* (*a. fig.*); *jur.* Verhandlung *f*, Prozeß *m*; **on** ~ auf Probe.

triang|le ['traiæŋgl] Dreieck *n*; ~**ular** [-'æŋgjulə] dreieckig.

tribe [traib] (Volks)Stamm *m*.

tribun|al [trai'bjuːnl] Gericht(shof *m*) *n*; ~**e** ['trib-juːn] Tribun *m*; Tribüne *f*.

tribut|ary ['tribjutəri] Nebenfluß *m*; ~**e** ['-juːt] Tribut *m* (*a. fig.*).

trick [trik] betrügen; Kniff *m*, List *f*, Trick *m*; Kunststück *n*; Streich *m*; **play a ⟨ on s.o.** j-m e-n Streich spielen.

trickle ['trikl] tröpfeln; rieseln; sickern.

tricycle['traisikl]Dreirad *n*.

trident ['traidənt] Dreizack *m*.

trifl|e ['traifl] Kleinigkeit *f*; spielen; spaßen; **~ing** geringfügig, unbedeutend.

trigger ['trigə] Abzug *m* (*e-r Feuerwaffe*).

trill [tril] Triller *m*; trillern.

trillion ['triljən] Trillion *f*; *Am.* Billion *f*.

trim [trim] schmuck, gepflegt; zurechtmachen; **~ up** heraus)putzen,schmükken; *Hut etc.* besetzen, stutzen, (be)schneiden, trimmen; **~mings** (Besatz *m*; Zutaten *pl*, Beilagen *pl* (*e-r Speise*).

Trinity ['triniti] *eccl.* Dreieinigkeit *f*.

trinket ['triŋkit] (wertloses) Schmuckstück.

trip [trip] (kurze) Reise, Fahrt *f*; Ausflug *m*, (Spritz)Tour *f*; Stolpern *n*; *fig.* Fehler *m*; trippeln; stolpern.

tripe [traip] Kaldaunen *pl*.

triple ['tripl] dreifach; **~ts** ['~its] *pl* Drillinge *pl*.

tripod ['traipɔd] Dreifuß *m*; *phot.* Stativ *n*.

triumph ['traiəmf] Triumph *m*; triumphieren; **~al** ['~mfl] Triumph...; **~ant** triumphierend.

trivial ['triviəl] unbedeu-

tend; trivial, alltäglich.

trod [trɔd] *pret*, **~den** *pp von* **tread**.

troll(e)y ['trɔli] Karren *m*; Tee-, Servierwagen *m*.

trombone[trɔm'bəun]Posaune *f*.

troop [tru:p] Schar *f*, Haufe(n) *m*; *pl mil.* Truppe(n *pl*) *f*; sich scharen *od.* sammeln; (*herein- etc.*)strömen.

trophy ['trəufi] Trophäe *f*.

tropic ['trɔpik] *geogr.* Wendekreis *m*; *pl* Tropen *pl*; **~al** tropisch.

trot [trɔt] Trott *m*, Trab *m*; traben (lassen); trotten.

trouble ['trʌbl] (sich) beunruhigen; j-m Sorgen machen; j-n bitten (**for** um); (sich) bemühen; j-m Mühe machen, plagen; Mühe *f*, Plage *f*; Störung *f* (*a. tech.*); Unannehmlichkeiten *pl*; Schwierigkeit *f*; Not *f*, Sorge(n *pl*) *f*; Leiden *n*, Beschwerden *pl*;*pol.* Unruhe *f*; **ask** *od.* **look for ⟨** das Schicksal herausfordern; **take the ⟨** sich die Mühe machen;**what's the ⟨?** was ist los?; **~some** lästig.

trough [trɔf] Trog *m*.

trousers ['trauzəz] *pl* (*a.* **a pair of ⟨**) (*e-e*) (lange) Hose, Hosen *pl*.

trousseau ['tru:səu] Aussteuer *f*.

trout [traut], *pl* **~(s)** Forelle *f*.

truant ['tru(:)ənt] Schulschwänzer(in); **(play)**

(bsd. die Schule) schwänzen. [stand *m.*]
truce [tru:s] Waffenstill-ſ
truck [trʌk] (offener) Güterwagen; Last(kraft)wagen *m; Am.* Gemüse *n.*
trudge [trʌdʒ] sich (dahin)schleppen, stapfen.
true [tru:] wahr; echt, wirklich; genau; treu; (**it is**) ~ gewiß, freilich, zwar; **come** ~ sich erfüllen.
truly ['tru:li] wirklich; aufrichtig; **yours** ~ Hochachtungsvoll *(Briefschluß).*
trump [trʌmp] Trumpf *m;* übertrumpfen; ~ **up** erdichten.
trumpet ['trʌmpit] Trompete *f;* trompeten; **~er** Trompeter *m.*
truncheon ['trʌntʃən] (Polizei)Knüppel *m.*
trunk [trʌŋk] (Baum-)Stamm *m;* Rumpf *m;* Rüssel *m;* (Schrank)Koffer *m; Am. mot.* Kofferraum *m; pl* Bade-, Turnhose(*n pl*) *f;* **~call** Ferngespräch *n;* **~ exchange** Fernamt *n;* **~line** *rail.* Hauptstrecke *f; teleph.* Fernleitung *f.*
trust [trʌst] Vertrauen *n;* Glaube, *m; jur.* Treuhand (-vermögen *n*) *f; econ.* Trust *m,* Konzern *m;* vertrauen; hoffen; (ver)trauen, sich verlassen auf; **~ee** [~'ti:] Sach-, Verwalter *m,* Treuhänder *m;* **~ful,** **~ing** vertrauensvoll; **~worthy** vertrauenswürdig.
truth [tru:θ], *pl* **~s** [~ðz]

Wahrheit *f;* **~ful** wahr (-heitsliebend).
try [trai] versuchen, probieren; vor Gericht stellen; ~ **on** anprobieren; ~ **out** ausprobieren; *sub:* Versuch *m;* **have a** ~ e-n Versuch machen; **~ing** anstrengend.
tub [tʌb] Faß *n,* Zuber *m,* Kübel *m;* Badewanne *f.*
tube [tju:b] Rohr *n;* (*Am. bsd.* Radio)Röhre *f;* Tube *f;* (Gummi)Schlauch *m;* Tunnel *m;* die (*Londoner*) Untergrundbahn.
tuberculosis [tju(:)bɜ:kju'ləusis] Tuberkulose *f.*
tuck [tʌk] stecken; ~ **in,** ~ **up** (warm) zudecken, *ins* Bett packen; ~ **up** hochschürzen, aufkrempeln.
Tuesday ['tju:zdi] Dienstag *m.*
tuft [tʌft] Büschel *n,* Busch *m;* (*Haar*)Schopf *m.*
tug [tʌg] Zug *m,* Ruck *m; mar.* Schlepper *m;* ziehen, zerren; *mar.* schleppen.
tuition [tju(:)'iʃən] Unterricht *m;* Schulgeld *n.*
tulip ['tju:lip] Tulpe *f.*
tumble ['tʌmbl] fallen, stürzen, purzeln, taumeln; sich wälzen; **~r** Becher *m.*
tummy ['tʌmi] *colloq.:* Bäuchlein *n;* Magen *m.*
tumo(u)r ['tju:mə] Tumor *m.*
tumult ['tju:mʌlt] Tumult *m;* **~uous** [~'mʌltjuəs] stürmisch.
tun [tʌn] Tonne *f,* Faß *n.*

tuna [ˈtuːnə], pl ~(s) Thunfisch m.

tune [tjuːn] Melodie f, Weise f; out of ~ verstimmt; vb: stimmen; ~ in (das Radio) einstellen (to auf); ~ up die Instrumente stimmen.

tunnel [ˈtʌnl] Tunnel m.

turbine [ˈtəːbin] Turbine f.

turbot [ˈtəːbət] Steinbutt m.

turbulent [ˈtəːbjulənt] ungestüm, stürmisch, turbulent.

turf [təːf] Rasen m; Torf m; the ~ (Pferde) Rennbahn f; (Pferde) Rennsport m; mit Rasen bedecken.

Turk [təːk] Türk|e m, -in f.

turkey [ˈtəːki] Truthahn m, -henne f, Pute(r m) f.

Turkish [ˈtəːkiʃ] türkisch; Türkisch n.

turmoil [ˈtəːmɔil] Aufruhr m; Durcheinander n.

turn [təːn] (Um)Drehung f; Reihe(nfolge) f; Biegung f, Kurve f; Wende f; Dienst m, Gefallen m; Zweck m; colloq. Schrecken m; it is my ~ ich bin an der Reihe; by ~s abwechselnd; take ~s sich abwechseln (at in, bei); vb: (sich) (um-, herum)drehen; wenden; zukehren, -wenden; drechseln; lenken, richten; (sich) verwandeln; (sich) verfärben (Laub); sich (ab-, hin-, zu-) wenden; ab-, einbiegen; e-e Biegung machen (Straße); grau etc. werden; ~

away (sich) abwenden; abweisen; ~ back zurückkehren; ~ down Kragen umschlagen; Decke zurückschlagen; Gas kleiner stellen; Radio leiser stellen; ablehnen; ~ off Wasser, Gas abdrehen; Licht, Radio etc. ausschalten, -machen; abbiegen; ~ on Gas, Wasser etc. anstellen; Gerät anstellen; Licht, Radio anmachen, einschalten; ~ out hinauswerfen; abdrehen, ausschalten, -machen; gut etc. ausfallen od. ausgehen; sich herausstellen; ~ over Ware umsetzen; (sich) umdrehen; umwerfen; übergeben (to dat); ~ round (sich) (herum)drehen; ~ to nach rechts etc. abbiegen; sich zuwenden; dat an j-n wenden; ~ up nach oben drehen od. biegen; Kragen hochschlagen; Gas etc. aufdrehen; Radio etc. lauter stellen; fig. auftauchen; ~coat pol. Überläufer(in).

turning Querstraße f, Abzweigung f; ~-point fig. Wendepunkt m.

turnip [ˈtəːnip] (bsd. Weiße) Rübe.

turn-out Gesamtproduktion f; ~over econ. Umsatz m; ~pike Am. gebührenpflichtige Straße; ~stile Drehkreuz n; ~up Brit. Hosenaufschlag m.

turret [ˈtʌrit] Türmchen n.

turtle [ˈtəːtl] (See)Schildkröte f; **~-dove** Turteltaube f. | (Hauer m.)

tusk [tʌsk] Stoßzahn m; |

tutor ['tju:tə] Privat-, Hauslehrer m, Erzieher m; univ. Tutor m; **~ial** [~'tɔːriəl] univ. Tutorenkurs m.

TV ['tiːˈviː] Fernsehen n; Fernsehapparat m.

twang [twæŋ] Schwirren n; näselnde Aussprache; Saiten zupfen, klimpern auf; schwirren; näseln.

tweet [twiːt] zwitschern.

tweezers ['twiːzəz] pl (a. **a pair of ~**) (e-e) Pinzette.

twelfth [twelfθ] zwölfte.

twelve [twelv] zwölf; Zwölf f.

twent|ieth ['twentiiθ] zwanzigste; **~y** zwanzig; Zwanzig f.

twice [twais] zweimal.

twiddle ['twidl] (herum-) drehen; spielen (mit).

twig [twig] (dünner) Zweig.

twilight ['twailait] Zwielicht n; Dämmerung f.

twin [twin] Zwillings...; Doppel...; pl Zwillinge pl.

twine [twain] Schnur f; (sich)schlingen od. winden.

twin-engined zweimotorig.

twinkle ['twiŋkl] funkeln, blitzen; huschen; zwinkern; Blitzen n; (Augen-) Zwinkern n, Blinzeln n.

twirl [twəːl] Wirbel m; wirbeln.

twist [twist] Drehung f; Windung f; Verdrehung f;

(Gesichts)Verzerrung f; Garn n, Twist m; (sich) drehen od. winden; wikkeln; verdrehen; (sich) verzerren od. -ziehen.

twitch [twitʃ] zupfen (an); zucken (mit).

twitter ['twitə] zwitschern.

two [tuː] Zwei f; **put and ~ together** es sich zs.-reimen; jeder; ... **in ~** entzwei...; **~fold** zweifach; **~pence** ['tʌpəns] zwei Pence pl; **~piece** zweiteilig; **~stroke** mot. Zweitakt...; **~way adapter** Doppelstecker m; **~way traffic** Gegenverkehr m.

type [taip] Typ m; Vorbild n, Muster n; Art f; print. Type f, Buchstabe m; **~ (-write)** [irr **write**)] mit der Maschine schreiben; maschineschreiben; **~writer** Schreibmaschine f.

typhoid (fever) ['taifɔid] Typhus m.

typhoon [tai'fuːn] Taifun m. [ber n.]

typhus ['taifəs] Fleckfie-/

typical ['tipikəl] typisch.

typist ['taipist] Stenotypist (-in).

tyrann|ical [ti'rænikəl] tyrannisch; **~ize** [ti'rənaiz] tyrannisieren; **~y** Tyrannei f. [(-in).]

tyrant ['taiərənt] Tyrann/

tyre ['taiə] (Rad-, Auto-) Reifen m.

Tyrole|an [ti'rəuliən], **~se** [tirə'liːz] Tiroler(in); Tiroler...

U

udder ['ʌdə] Euter *n*.

ugly ['ʌglɪ] häßlich; schlimm.

ulcer ['ʌlsə] Geschwür *n*.

ultimate ['ʌltimit] äußerst, letzt; endgültig; End...

ultimat|um [ʌltɪ'meitəm], *pl* **.a** [**.ə**] Ultimatum *n*.

umbrella [ʌm'brelə] Regenschirm *m*.

umpire ['ʌmpaiə] Schiedsrichter *m*.

un- [ʌn-] **un...**, Un...; nicht-..., Nicht...; ent..., auf..., los...

un|abashed unverfroren; unerschrocken; **.abated** unvermindert; **.able** unfähig, außerstande; **.acceptable** unannehmbar; **.accountable** unerklärlich, seltsam; **.accustomed** ungewohnt; nicht gewöhnt (**to** an); **.acquainted: . with** unerfahren in, nicht vertraut mit; **.affected** ungerührt; ungekünstelt, natürlich.

unanimous [ju(:)'næniməs] einmütig, -stimmig.

un|approachable unnahbar; **.ashamed** schamlos; **.asked** ungebeten; **.assisted** ohne Hilfe *od*. Unterstützung; **.assuming** anspruchslos, bescheiden; **.authorized** unberechtigt; unbefugt; **.avoidable** unvermeidlich.

unaware ['ʌnə'wɛə]: **be .**

of *et*. nicht bemerken; **.s** ['.z] unversehens; versehentlich.

un|balanced unausgeglichen; gestört (*Geist*); **.bar** aufriegeln; **.bearable** unerträglich; **.becoming** unkleidsam; unschicklich.

unbeliev|able unglaublich; **.ing** ungläubig.

un|bending unbeugsam; **.bias(s)ed** unbefangen, unparteiisch; **.bidden** unaufgefordert; ungebeten; **.born** (noch) ungeboren; **.bounded** *fig*. grenzenlos; **.broken** ungebrochen; unversehrt, ganz; ununterbrochen; **.button** aufknöpfen; **.called-for** unerwünscht; unpassend; **.canny** ['.kæni] unheimlich; **.cared-for** vernachlässigt; **.ceasing** unaufhörlich; **.certain** unsicher, ungewiß; unzuverlässig; unbeständig; **.challenged** unangefochten.

unchange|able unveränderlich; **.d** unverändert.

unchecked ungehindert.

un|civil unhöflich; **.ized** unzivilisiert.

unclaimed nicht beansprucht; unzustellbar (*bsd*. Brief).

uncle ['ʌŋkl] Onkel *m*.

un|clean unrein; **.comfortable** unbehaglich, ungemütlich; **common** ungewöhnlich; **communicative** wortkarg, verschlossen; **complaining** ohne Murren, geduldig.

unconcern Unbekümmertheit f; Gleichgültigkeit f; **ed** unbeteiligt; unbekümmert; gleichgültig.

un|conditional bedingungslos; **confirmed** unbestätigt.

unconscious unbewußt; bewußtlos; **ness** Bewußtlosigkeit f.

un|constitutional verfassungswidrig; **controllable** unkontrollierbar; unbeherrscht; **conventional** unkonventionell.

unconvinc|ed nicht überzeugt; **ing** nicht überzeugend.

un|couth [ʌnˈkuːθ] ungeschlacht; **cover** aufdecken, freilegen; entblößen; **cultivated**, **cultured** unkultiviert; **damaged** unbeschädigt, unversehrt; **decided** unentschieden; unentschlossen; **deniable** unleugbar.

under [ˈʌndə] prp unter; in (dat); adv unten; darunter; unter; adj in Zssgn: unter, Unter...; **bid** (irr bid) unterbieten; **carriage** aer. Fahrwerk n; mot. Fahrgestell n; **clothes** pl, **clothing** Unterwäsche f; **developed** unterentwickelt; **done** nicht gar;

estimate unterschätzen; **fed** unterernährt; **go** (irr go) durchmachen; sich unterziehen; **graduate** Student(in); **ground** unterirdisch; Untergrund...; Untergrundbahn f; pol. Untergrund (-bewegung f) m; **growth** Unterholz n; **line** unterstreichen; **mine** unterminieren; fig. untergraben; **most** (zu)unterst; **neath** [-ˈniːθ] unter (-halb); unten, darunter; **pass** Unterführung f; **privileged** benachteiligt; **shirt** Unterhemd n; **signed** Unterzeichnete m, f; **sized** zu klein; **staffed** unterbesetzt; **stand** (irr stand) verstehen; (als sicher) annehmen; erfahren, hören; **standable** verständlich; **standing** verständnisvoll; Verstand m; Verständnis n; Einigung f; Bedingung f; **statement** Understatement n, Untertreibung f; **take** (irr take) unternehmen; übernehmen; **taker** Leichenbestatter m, Bestattungsinstitut n; **taking** Unternehmung f; **value** unterschätzen; **wear** Unterwäsche f; **wood** Unterholz n; **world** Unterwelt f.

un|deserved unverdient; **desirable** unerwünscht; **developed** unentwickelt; unerschlossen; **dig-**

nified würdelos; ~diminished unvermindert; ~disciplined undiszipliniert; ~disputed unbestritten; ~disturbed ungestört; ~do (*irr do*) aufmachen; ungeschehen machen; vernichten; ~dreamt-of ungeahnt.

undress (sich) entkleiden *od.* ausziehen; ~ed unbekleidet.

un|due ungehörig; übermäßig; ~dutiful pflichtvergessen; ~easy unbehaglich; unruhig; ~educated ungebildet.

unemploy|ed arbeitslos; *the ~ed pl* Arbeitslose *pl;* ~ment Arbeitslosigkeit *f.* unendurable unerträglich. unequal ungleich; nicht gewachsen (**to** *dat*); ~(l)ed unerreicht.

un|erring unfehlbar; ~even uneben; ungleich (-mäßig); ungerade (*Zahl*); ~eventful ereignislos; ~expected unerwartet; ~failing unfehlbar; unerschöpflich; ~fair ungerecht; unfair; ~faithful un(ge)treu, treulos; ~familiar unbekannt; nicht vertraut; ~fashionable unmodern; ~favo(u)rable ungünstig; ~feeling gefühllos; ~finished unfertig; unvollendet; ~fit ungeeignet, untauglich; ~fold (sich) entfalten *od.* öffnen; enthüllen; ~foreseen unvorhergesehen; ~forget

table unvergeßlich; ~forgiving unversöhnlich; ~forgotten unvergessen.

unfortunate unglücklich; ~ly unglücklicherweise, leider.

un|founded unbegründet; ~friendly unfreundlich; ungünstig; ~furnished unmöbliert; ~generous nicht freigebig; kleinlich; ~gentle unsanft; ~get-at-able ['~get'ætəbl] unzugänglich; ~governable zügellos; wild; ~graceful ungraziös; unbeholfen; ~gracious ungnädig, unfreundlich; ~grateful undankbar; ~guarded unvorsichtig; ~happy unglücklich; ~harmed unversehrt; ~healthy ungesund; ~heard-of unerhört.

unheed|ed unbeachtet; ~ing sorglos.

un|hesitating ohne Zögern; ~hoped-for unverhofft; ~hurt unverletzt.

unicorn ['ju:nikɔːn] Einhorn *n.*

unification [juːnifiˈkeiʃn] Vereinigung *f.*

uniform ['juːnifɔːm] gleich; einheitlich; Uniform *f.* [einseitig.]

unilateral ['juːniˈlætərəl]ʃ unimagina|ble unvorstellbar; ~tive einfallslos.

unimportant unwichtig.

uninhabit|able unbewohnbar; ~ed unbewohnt.

un|injured unbeschädigt;

unverletzt; **~intelligible** unverständlich; **~intentional** unabsichtlich; **~ interesting** uninteressant; **~interrupted** ununterbrochen.

uninvit|ed un(ein)geladen; **~ing** nicht od. wenig einladend.

union ['ju:njən] Vereinigung f; Verbindung f; Einigkeit f; Verband m, Verein m; pol. Union f; Gewerkschaft f; **~ist** Gewerkschaftler(in); **♀ Jack** Union Jack m (britische Nationalflagge).

unique [ju:'ni:k] einzigartig, einmalig.   [m.\

unison ['ju:nizn] Einklang\

unit ['ju:nit] Einheit f; **~e** [~'nait] (sich) vereinigen; verbinden; **~ed** vereint, -einigt; **~y** Einheit f; Einigkeit f.

univers|al [ju:ni'və:səl] allgemein; allumfassend, universal, Universal...; **~e** ['~ə:s] Weltall n, Universum n; **~ity** [~'və:siti] Universität f.

un|just ungerecht; **~kempt** [~'kempt] ungepflegt; ungekämmt; **~kind** unfreundlich; lieblos; **~known** unbekannt; **~lace** aufschnüren; **~lawful** ungesetzlich; **~learn** (irr **learn**) verlernen.

unless [ən'les] wenn ... nicht; außer.

unlike ungleich; anders als; **~ly** unwahrscheinlich.

un|limited unbegrenzt, unbeschränkt; **~load** ab-, aus-, entladen.

unlock aufschließen; **~ed** unverschlossen.

un|looked-for unerwartet; **~loose(n)** lösen, losmachen; **~lucky** unglücklich; **be ~lucky** Pech haben; **~manageable** schwer zu handhaben(d); schwierig; **~manly** unmännlich; **~married** unverheiratet, ledig; **~mistakable** unverkennbar; unmißverständlich; **~moved** unbewegt, ungerührt; **~ natural** unnatürlich; anomal; **~necessary** unnötig; **~noticed**, unbemerkt; **~obtrusive** unaufdringlich, bescheiden; **~occupied** unbesetzt; unbewohnt; **~offending** harmlos, **~official** nichtamtlich, inoffiziell; **~pack** auspacken; **~paid** unbezahlt; **~paralleled** beispiellos, ohnegleichen; **~ pardonable** unverzeihlich; **~perceived** unbemerkt; **~perturbed** ['~pə(:)'tə:bd] ruhig, gelassen; **~pleasant** unangenehm, unerfreulich; **~ polished** unpoliert; fig. ungehobelt; **~polluted** nicht verschmutzt od. verseucht.

unpopular unbeliebt; **~ity** [~'læriti] Unbeliebtheit f.

unpracti|cal unpraktisch;

~sed, *Am.* ~ced ungeübt.
un|precedented beispiellos, noch nie dagewesen;
~**prejudiced** unbefangen, unvoreingenommen; ~**premeditated** unbeabsichtigt; ~**prepared** unvorbereitet; ~**principled** ohne Grundsätze, gewissenlos; ~**productive** unfruchtbar; unergiebig; unproduktiv; ~**profitable** unrentabel; nutzlos; ~**provided**: ~ **for** unversorgt, mittellos; ~**qualified** ungeeignet; unberechtigt; uneingeschränkt.

unquestion|able unzweifelhaft, fraglos; ~**ed** ungefragt; unbestritten.

unreal unwirklich; ~**istic** unrealistisch.

un|reasonable unvernünftig; unmäßig; ~**recognizable** nicht wiederzuerkennen(d); ~**refined** ungeläutert, Roh...; *fig.* ungebildet; ~**reliable** unzuverlässig; ~**reserved** uneingeschränkt; offen(herzig); ~**resisting** widerstandslos; ~**rest** Unruhe *f*; ~**restrained** hemmungslos; ~**restricted** uneingeschränkt, unbeschränkt; ~**ripe** unreif; ~**rival(l)ed** unerreicht; ~**roll** ent-, aufrollen; ~**ruffled** glatt; *fig.* gelassen; ~**ruly** ungebärdig; ~**safe** unsicher; ~**sanitary** unhygienisch.

unsatisf|actory unbefriedigend, unzulänglich; ~**ied** unbefriedigt; unzufrieden.

un|savo(u)ry widerlich, -wärtig; ~**screw** ab-, los-, aufschrauben; ~**scrupulous** bedenken-, gewissen-, skrupellos; ~**seen** ungesehen; ~**selfish** selbstlos; ~**settled** unsicher; unbeständig; unerledigt; unbesiedelt; (geistig) gestört.

unshave|d, ~**n** unrasiert.

unshrink|able nicht einlaufend (*Stoff*); ~**ing** unverzagt.

unskil(l)ful ungeschickt; ~**led** ungelernt.

unsoci|able ungesellig; ~**al** unsozial.

unsolv|able unlösbar; ~**ed** ungelöst.

un|sound ungesund; nicht stichhaltig; verkehrt; ~**speakable** unsagbar.

unspoil|ed, ~**t** unverdorben; nicht verzogen (*Kind*).

unspoken un(aus)gesprochen; ~**of** unerwähnt.

un|stable nicht fest, unsicher; unbeständig; labil; ~**steady** unsicher; schwankend; unbeständig; ~**stressed** unbetont; ~**successful** erfolglos, ohne Erfolg; ~**suitable** unpassend; ungeeignet; ~**sure** unsicher; ~**surpassed** unübertroffen.

unsuspect|ed unverdächtig(t); unvermutet; ~**ing** nichts ahnend, ahnungslos.

unsuspicious nicht argwöhnisch; unverdächtig.
unthink|able undenkbar; **~ing** gedankenlos.
un|tidy unordentlich; **~tie** aufbinden; aufknoten.
until [ən'til] bis; **not ~** erst (als, wenn).
un|timely vorzeitig; ungelegen, unpassend; **~tiring** unermüdlich; **~told** unermeßlich; **~touched** unberührt; *fig.* ungerührt; **~tried** unversucht; **~troubled** ungestört; ruhig; **~true** unwahr; untreu; **~trustworthy** unzuverlässig.
unus|ed ['ʌn'juːzd] unbenutzt, ungebraucht; ['~st] nicht gewöhnt (**to** an); **~ual** ungewöhnlich; ungewohnt.
un|utterable unaussprechlich; **~varying** unveränderlich; **~voiced** *ling.* stimmlos; **~wanted** unerwünscht; **~warranted** [~'wɔrəntid] unberechtigt; ['~'wɔrəntid] unverbürgt; **~wholesome** ungesund, schädlich; **~willing** unwiderwillig, abgeneigt; **~wind** (*irr* **wind**) auf-, widerwillig, abgeneigt; **~wind** (*irr* **wind**) auf-, widerwillig, abgeneigt; wickeln; (sich) abwickeln; **~wise** unklug; **~worthy** unwürdig (**of** *gen*); **~wrap** auswickeln, -packen; **~yielding** unnachgiebig.
up [ʌp] *adv* (her-, hin)auf, aufwärts, nach oben, hoch, in die Höhe, empor; oben; auf ... zu; **~ to** bis (zu);

be **~ to** *et*. vorhaben; j-s Sache sein, abhängen von; *prp* auf ... (hinauf), hinauf, empor; oben an *od.* auf; in das Innere (*e-s Landes*); *adj* oben; hoch; gestiegen; auf(gestanden); aufgegangen (*Sonne*); abgelaufen, um (*Zeit*); **~ and about** wieder auf den Beinen; **what's ~?** *colloq.* was ist los?; **~ train** Zug *m* nach der Stadt; *sub:* **the ~s and downs** die Höhen und Tiefen (*des Lebens*).
up|bringing Erziehung *f;* **~hill** bergan, -auf; *fig.* mühsam; **~holster** [~-'haulstə] *Möbel* polstern; **~holsterer** Polsterer *m;* **~holstery** Polstermaterial *n;* **~keep** Instandhaltung(skosten *pl*) *f.*
upon [ə'pɔn] *s.* **on.**
upper ['ʌpə] ober, Ober..., höher; **2 House** *Brit. parl.* Oberhaus *n;* **~most** oberst, höchst.
up|right auf-, senkrecht, gerade; **~rising** Aufstand *m;* **~roar** Aufruhr *m;* **~set** (*irr* **set**) umwerfen, -stoßen; *Plan etc.* durcheinanderbringen; *Magen* verderben; j-n aus der Fassung bringen, bestürzen; **be ~set** aufgeregt *od.* aus der Fassung *od.* durcheinander sein; **~sidedown** das Oberste zuunterst; verkehrt (herum); **~stairs** die Treppe hin-

auf, (nach) oben; **~start**
Emporkömmling *m*; **~**
stream stromaufwärts; gegen den Strom; **~to-date**
modern; auf dem laufenden; **~ward(s)** ['~wəd(z)]
aufwärts; nach oben.

uranium [ju'reinjəm] Uran
n. [Stadt...]

urban ['ə:bən] städtisch,

urchin ['ə:tʃin] Bengel *m*.

urge [ə:dʒ] drängen; **~ on**
(an)treiben; Drang *m*,
Trieb *m*; **~nt** dringend,
dringlich, eilig.

urine ['juərin] Urin *m*,
Harn *m*.

urn [ə:n] Urne *f*.

us [ʌs, əs] uns.

usage [ju:sidʒ] (Sprach-)
Gebrauch *m*; Behandlung
f; Brauch *m*.

use [ju:s] Gebrauch *m*; Benutzung *f*, Verwendung *f*;
Nutzen *m*; **(of)** no **~** nutz-,
zwecklos; [~z] gebrauchen,
benutzen, an-, verwenden;
~ up auf-, verbrauchen; **~d**
[~zd] gebraucht; [~st] ge-

wöhnt **(to** an); gewohnt
(to zu, *acc*); **~d to** pflegte
zu; **get ~d to** sich gewöhnen an; **~ful** brauchbar, nützlich; **~less** nutz-,
zwecklos, unnütz.

usher ['ʌʃə] Gerichtsdiener
m; Platzanweiser *m*; in
(hinein)führen; **~ette** [~'ret] Platzanweiserin *f*.

usual ['ju:ʒuəl] gewöhnlich, üblich; **as ~** wie gewöhnlich; **~ly** gewöhnlich, meist(ens).

usur|er ['ju:ʒərə] Wucherer
m; **~y** ['~ʒuri] Wucher *m*.

utensil [ju:(')tensl] Gerät *n*.

utili|ty [ju:(')tiliti] Nützlichkeit *f*, Nutzen *m*; **~ze**
(aus)nutzen, sich zunutze
machen.

utmost ['ʌtməust] äußerst.

utter ['ʌtə] äußerst, völlig;
äußern; Seufzer *etc*. ausstoßen; **~ance** Äußerung
f, Ausdruck *m*; Aussprache *f*.

uvula ['ju:vjulə] *anat*.
(Gaumen)Zäpfchen *n*.

V

vacan|cy ['veikənsi] Leere
f; Lücke *f*; freie *od*. offene
Stelle; **~t** leer; frei, unbesetzt (*Zimmer*, *Sitzplatz
etc*.); frei, offen (*Stelle*).

vacate [və'keit, *Am*. 'veikeit] räumen; *Platz* frei
machen; **~ion** (Schul- *etc*.)
Ferien *pl*; *bsd. Am*. Urlaub *m*.

vaccin|ate ['væksineit]

impfen; **~ation** (*bsd*. Pokken)Schutzimpfung *f*; **~e**
['~i:n] Impfstoff *m*.

vacuum ['vækjuəm] Vakuum *n*; **~ bottle** Thermosflasche *f*; **~ cleaner** Staubsauger *m*; **~ flask** Thermosflasche *f*.

vagabond ['vægəbɔnd]
Landstreicher(in).

vagary ['veigəri] Laune *f*.

venal

vague [veig] vag(e), un-
klar.

vain [vein] eitel; vergeblich; in ~ vergebens, vergeblich, umsonst.

vale [veil] Tal n.

valerian [və'liəriən] Bal-
drian m.   [Diener m.\

valet ['vælit] (Kammer-)\

valiant ['væljənt] tapfer.

valid ['vælid] (rechts)gül-
tig; stichhaltig.

valley ['væli] Tal n.

valo(u)r ['vælə] Tapfer-
keit f.

valuable ['væljuəbl] wert-
voll; ~ables pl Wertsa-
chen pl; ~ation Bewertung
f; Schätzungswert m; ~e
['vɔːu] Wert m; (ab)schät-
zen; ~eless wertlos.

valve [vælv] Ventil n;
Klappe f; (Radio)Röhre f.

van [væn] Möbelwagen m;
Lieferwagen m; rail. Gü-
ter-, Gepäckwagen m.

vane [vein] Wetterfahne
f; (Windmühlen-, Pro-
peller)Flügel m.

vanilla [və'nilə] Vanille f.

vanish ['væniʃ] verschwin-
den.

vanity ['væniti] Eitelkeit
f; ~ bag, ~ case Kosme-
tikkoffer m.

vantage ['vɑːntidʒ] Ten-
nis: Vorteil m.

vap|orize ['veipəraiz] ver-
dampfen, -dunsten (las-
sen); ~orous dunstig;
~o(u)r Dampf m; Dunst m.

varia|ble ['vɛəriəbl] ver-
änderlich; ~nce Uneinig-

keit f; be at ~nce uneinig
sein; ~nt abweichend;
Variante f; ~tion Schwan-
kung f, Abweichung f;
Variation f.

varicose vein ['værikəus]
Krampfader f.

varie|d ['vɛərid] bunt,
mannigfaltig; ~ty [və'rai-
əti] Mannigfaltigkeit f,
Vielzahl f; ~ty show
Varietévorstellung f.

various ['vɛəriəs] ver-
schieden(artig); mehrere.

varnish ['vɑːniʃ] Firnis m;
Lack m; firnissen, lackieren.

vary ['vɛəri] (sich) (ver-)
ändern; wechseln (mit et.).

vase [vɑːz, Am. veis, veiz]
Vase f.

vat [væt] Faß n, Bottich m.

vault [vɔːlt] (Keller)Ge-
wölbe n; Gruft f; (Bank-)
Tresor m; sp. Sprung m;
(über)springen; ~ing-
horse Pferd n (Turngerät).

veal [viːl] Kalbfleisch n.

vegeta|ble ['vedʒitəbl] ein
Gemüse n; pl Gemüse n;
~rian [ˌ~'tɛəriən] Vege-
tarier(in); vegetarisch.

vehemen|ce ['viːiməns]
Heftigkeit f; ~t heftig.

vehicle ['viːikl] Fahrzeug n.

veil [veil] Schleier m; (sich)
verschleiern.

vein [vein] Ader f.

velocity [vi'lɔsiti] Ge-
schwindigkeit f.

velvet ['velvit] Samt m;
Samt..., samten, aus Samt.

venal ['viːnl] käuflich.

vend [vend] verkaufen; **~er** (Straßen)Händler *m*, Verkäufer *m*; **~ing machine** (Verkaufs)Automat *m*; **~or** s. **vender, vending machine.**

venera|ble ['venərəbl] ehrwürdig; **~te** ['~eit] verehren; [schlechts...]

venereal [vi'niəriəl] Ge-

Venetian [vi'ni:ʃən] venetianisch; Venetianer(in); **~ blind** (Stab)Jalousie *f*.

vengeance ['vendʒəns] Rache *f*; **with a ~** *colloq.* mächtig, gehörig. [*n.*]

venison ['venzn] Wildbret

venom ['venəm] (Schlangen)Gift *n*; Gehässigkeit *f*; **~ous** giftig.

vent [vent] (Abzugs)Öffnung *f*, (Luft)Loch *n*; Schlitz *m*; **give ~ to** s-*m* Zorn *etc.* Luft machen.

ventilat|e ['ventileit] ventilieren, (be-, ent-, durch-)lüften; **~ion** Ventilation *f*, Lüftung *f*; **~or** Ventilator *m*.

ventriloquist [ven'triləkwist] Bauchredner *m*.

venture ['ventʃə] Wagnis *n*, Risiko *n*; riskieren; (sich) wagen.

veranda(h) [və'rændə] Veranda *f*.

verb [və:b] *gr.* Verb(um) *n*, Zeitwort *n*; **~al** wörtlich; mündlich.

verdict ['və:dikt] *jur.* Urteil *n* (*a. fig.*).

verdure ['və:dʒə] Grün *n*.

verge [və:dʒ] Rand *m*,

Grenze *f*; **on the ~ of** am Rande (*gen*); *vb.*: **~ on** grenzen an.

verify ['verifai] (nach)prüfen; bestätigen.

vermicelli [və:mi'seli] Fadennudeln *pl.*

vermiform appendix ['və:mifo:m] Wurmfortsatz *m*, Blinddarm *m*.

vermin ['və:min] Ungeziefer *n*; *hunt.* Raubzeug *n*.

vernacular [və'nækjulə] Landessprache *f*.

versatile ['və:sətail] vielseitig, wendig.

vers|e [və:s] Vers(e *pl*) *m*; Strophe *f*; **~ed** bewandert; **~ion** Übersetzung *f*; Fassung *f*; Lesart *f*.

vertebra ['və:tibrə], *pl* **~e** ['~i:] *anat.* Wirbel *m*.

vertical ['və:tikəl] vertikal, senkrecht.

very ['veri] sehr; *vor sup*: aller...; genau; bloß; *der, die, das* gleiche; **the ~ best** das allerbeste; **the ~ thing** genau das (richtige); **the ~ thought** der bloße Gedanke.

vessel ['vesl] Gefäß *n* (*a. anat., bot.*); Schiff *n*.

vest [vest] Unterhemd *n*; *bsd. Am.* Weste *f*.

vestry ['vestri] *eccl.*: Sakristei *f*; Gemeindesaal *m*.

vet [vet] *colloq.* Tierarzt *m*.

veteran ['vetərən] alt-, ausgedient; erfahren; Veteran *m*.

veterinary (surgeon) ['vetərinəri] Tierarzt *m*.

veto ['vi:təu], pl ~es Veto n; ablehnen.

vex [veks] ärgern; ~ation Ärger m; ~atious ärgerlich.

via ['vaiə] über, via.

vibrat|e [vai'breit] vibrieren; zittern; ~ion Zittern n, Vibrieren n; Schwingung f.

vicar ['vikə] Vikar m, Pfarrer m; ~age Pfarrhaus n.

vice [vais] Laster n; Schraubstock m; Vize...

vice versa ['vaisi'və:sə] umgekehrt.

vicinity [vi'siniti] Nachbarschaft f, Nähe f.

vicious ['viʃəs] lasterhaft; bösartig, boshaft.

victim ['viktim] Opfer n.

victor ['viktə] Sieger(in); ~ian [~'tɔ:riən] Viktorianisch; ~ious siegreich; Sieges...; ~y Sieg m.

victuals ['vitlz] pl Lebensmittel pl, Proviant m.

Viennese [viə'ni:z] wienerisch, Wiener...; Wiener (-in).

view [vju:] (sich) ansehen; betrachten; Sicht f; Aussicht f, (Aus)Blick m; Ansicht f, Bild n; Meinung f; **in ~ of** angesichts (gen); **on ~** zu besichtigen; ~er Zuschauer(in); ~point Gesichts-, Standpunkt m.

vigil ['vidʒil] Wachen n; Nachtwache f; ~ance Wachsamkeit f; ~ant wachsam.

vigo|rous ['vigərəs] kräf-

tig; energisch; ~(u)r Kraft f, Vitalität f; Energie f.

vile [vail] gemein; abscheulich.

village ['vilidʒ] Dorf n; ~r Dorfbewohner(in).

villain ['vilən] Schurke m, Schuft m; ~ous schurkisch; ~y Niederträchtigkeit f.

vindicat|e ['vindikeit] rechtfertigen; verteidigen; ~ion Rechtfertigung f.

vindictive [vin'diktiv] rachsüchtig.

vine [vain] Wein(stock) m, Rebe f; ~gar ['vinigə] (Wein)Essig m; ~yard ['vinjəd] Weinberg m.

vintage ['vintidʒ] Weinlese f; Jahrgang m (Wein).

violat|e ['vaiəleit] verletzen; Eid etc. brechen; vergewaltigen; ~ion Verletzung f; (Eid- etc.)Bruch m; Vergewaltigung f.

violen|ce ['vaiələns] Gewalt(tätigkeit) f; Heftigkeit f; ~t heftig; gewalttätig, -sam.

violet ['vaiəlit] Veilchen n; violett. [Geige f.]

violin [vaiə'lin] Violine f.)

viper ['vaipə] Viper f, Otter f, Natter f.

virgin ['və:dʒin] Jungfrau f; jungfräulich; Jungfern...; ~ity Jungfräulichkeit f.

viril|e ['virail] männlich; ~ity [~'riliti] Männlichkeit f.

virtu|al ['və:tʃuəl] eigentlich; ~ally praktisch; ~e

virus 310

['ju:, '_ʃu:] Tugend *f*;
Wirksamkeit *f*; **by** *od.* **in
e of** auf Grund (*gen*); **
ous** ['_ʃuəs] tugendhaft.
virus ['vaiərəs] Virus *n, m.*
visa ['vi:zə] Visum *n.*
vise [_] *Am.* Schraubstock *m.*
visib|ility [vizi'biliti] Sicht-
barkeit *f*; *meteor.* Sicht
(-weite) *f*; **_le** sichtbar;
fig. (er)sichtlich.
vision ['viʒən] Sehvermögen *n*, Sehkraft *f*; Vision *f.*
visit ['vizit] besuchen; besichtigen; **~** *n* Besuch *od.*
Besuche machen; Besuch
m; Besichtigung *f*; **pay a
~ to** *j-n* besuchen; **_or** Be-
sucher(in), Gast *m.*
visual ['vizjuəl] Seh...;Ge-
sichts...; visuell; **_ize** sich
vorstellen.
vital ['vaitl] Lebens...; le-
benswichtig; **_ity** [_'tæ-
liti] Lebenskraft *f*, Vitalität *f.*   [amin *n.*\
vitamin ['vitəmin] Vit-\
vivaci|ous [vi'veiʃəs] leb-
haft; **_ty** [_'væsiti] Lebhaftigkeit *f.*   [bendig.\
vivid ['vivid] lebhaft; le-\
vixen ['viksn] Füchsin *f*;
zänkisches Weib.
vocabulary [vəu'kæbju-
ləri] Wörterverzeichnis *n*;
Wortschatz *m.*
vocal ['vəukəl] stimmlich,
Stimm...; *mus.* Vokal...,
Gesang(s)...; **_ist** Sänger
(-in).
vocation [vəu'keiʃən] (innere) Berufung; Beruf *m.*

vogue [vəug] Mode *f*; Be-
liebtheit *f.*
voice [vɔis] Stimme *f*; **_d**
ling. stimmhaft.
void [vɔid] leer; *jur.* ungültig; **~ of** ohne.
volatile ['vɔlətail] *chem.*
flüchtig. [**_es** Vulkan *m.*\
volcano [vɔl'keinəu], *pl*\
volley ['vɔli] Salve *f*,
(Pfeil-, Stein- *etc.*)Hagel
m; *Tennis:* Flugball *m*; *fig.*
Schwall *m.*
volt [vəult] *electr.* Volt *n*;
_age *electr.* Spannung *f.*
voluble ['vɔljubl] rede-
gewandt; fließend (*Rede*).
volume ['vɔljum] Band *m*
(*e-s Buches*); Volumen *n*;
electr. Lautstärke *f.*
volunt|ary ['vɔləntəri]
freiwillig; **_eer** [_'tiə]
Freiwillige *m, f*; sich freiwillig melden; freiwillig
anbieten; sich *e-e Bemerkung* erlauben.
voluptuous [və'lʌptʃuəs]
sinnlich; üppig.
vomit ['vɔmit] (er)bre-
chen; (sich er)brechen.
voracious [və'reiʃəs] gefräßig, gierig.
vote [vəut] (Wahl)Stimme
f; Abstimmung *f*, Wahl *f*;
Wahlrecht *n*; Beschluß *m*;
abstimmen (über); wäh-
len; s-e Stimme abgeben;
~ for stimmen für; **_r**
Wähler(in).
voting ['vəutiŋ] Abstimmung *f*; Stimm(en)...;
Wahl...; **_-paper** Stimm-
zettel *m.*

vouch [vautʃ]: ~ **for** sich verbürgen für; ~**er** Beleg *m*; Unterlage *f*; Gutschein *m*; ~**safe** [~'seif] gewähren; geruhen.

vow [vau] Gelübde *n*; Schwur *m*; geloben; schwören.

vowel ['vauəl] *ling.* Vokal

m, Selbstlaut *m*.

voyage ['vɔiidʒ] *längere* (See-, Flug)Reise.

vulgar ['vʌlgə] gewöhnlich, vulgär.

vulnerable ['vʌlnərəbl] verwundbar.

vulture ['vʌltʃə] Geier *m*.

W

wad [wɔd] (*Watte*)Bausch *m*, Polster *n*; wattieren, auspolstern; zustopfen; ~**ding** Wattierung *f*, Polsterung *f*.

waddle ['wɔdl] watscheln.

wade [weid] (durch)waten.

wafer ['weifə] Waffel *f*; Oblate *f*.

waffle ['wɔfl] Waffel *f*.

waft [wɑːft] wehen; Hauch *m*. {wedeln (mit).}

wag [wæg] wackeln (mit.)}

wage-earner ['weidʒə-ːnə] Lohnempfänger(in); ~**s** ['~iz] *pl* Lohn *m*.

wager ['weidʒə] Wette *f*; wetten.

wag(g)on ['wægən] (*offener* Güter)Wagen.

wail [weil] (Weh)Klagen *n*; (weh)klagen, jammern.

wainscot ['weinskət] (*bsd. untere*) (Wand)Täfelung.

waist [weist] Taille *f*; ~**coat** ['weiskət] Weste *f*; ~**line** Taille *f*.

wait [weit] warten (*for* auf); abwarten; warten auf; ~ **at** (*Am.* **on**) **table** bedienen; ~(**up**)**on**

j–n bedienen; ~**er** Kellner *m*, Ober *m*; ~**ing** Warten *n*; **no** ~**ing** *mot.* Halteverbot *n*; ~**ing-room** Wartezimmer *n*; *rail.* Wartesaal *m*; ~**ress** Kellnerin *f*.

wake [weik] Kielwasser *n* (*a. fig.*); (*irr*): ~ (**up**) aufwachen; (auf)wecken; ~**ful** schlaflos; ~**n** *s.* **wake** (*vb*).

walk [wɔːk] gehen; spazierengehen; (durch)wandern; ~ **about** umhergehen, -wandern; ~ **out** *colloq.* streiken; ~ **out** *on sl.* j–n im Stich lassen; (Spazier)Gang *m*; (Spazier)Weg *m*; ~**er** Spaziergänger(in).

walkie-talkie ['wɔːki-'tɔːki] *colloq.* tragbares Funksprechgerät.

walking papers *pl colloq.* Entlassung(spapiere) *f*; ~**stick** Spazierstock *m*; ~**tour** Wanderung *f*.

walk-out *colloq.* Streik *m*.

wall [wɔːl] Wand *f*; Mauer *f*; ~ **up** zumauern.

wallet ['wɔlit] Brieftasche *f*.

wall|-flower *fig.* Mauer-
blümchen *n*; **~paper** Tapete *f.*

wal|nut ['wɔ:lnʌt] Wal-
nuß(baum *m*) *f.*, **~rus**
['~rəs] Walroß *n.*

waltz [wɔ:ls] Walzer *m*;
Walzer tanzen.

wan [wɔn] blaß, bleich,
fahl. [Stab *m.*]

wand [wɔnd] (Zauber-)∫

wander ['wɔndə] wan-
dern; *fig.:* abschweifen;
phantasieren; **~er** Wanderer *m.*

wane [wein] abnehmen
(*Mond*); *fig.* schwinden.

want [wɔnt] Mangel *m* (of
an); *pl* Bedürfnisse *pl*; be-
dürfen, brauchen; müs-
sen; wünschen; (haben)
wollen, mögen; ermangeln;
it ~s *s.th.* es fehlt an; **~ed**
gesucht; **~ing: be ~** feh-
len; es fehlen lassen (**in**
an).

war [wɔ:] Krieg *m*; Kriegs...

warble ['wɔ:bl] trillern,
singen.

ward [wɔ:d] Mündel *n*;
Abteilung *f*; (Kranken-
haus)Station *f*; (Stadt)Be-
zirk *m*; **~ off** abwehren;
~en Aufseher *m*; Her-
bergsvater *m*; **~er** (Ge-
fangenen)Wärter *m.*

wardrobe ['wɔ:drəub]
Garderobe *f*; Kleider-
schrank *m.*

ware [wɛə] Geschirr *n*; *in
Zssgn:* ...waren *pl*; *pl* Waren; **~house** Lager(haus)
n; Warenlager *n.*

warm [wɔ:m] warm (*a.
fig.*); heiß; *fig.* hitzig; **~
(up)** (auf-, an-, er)wär-
men; sich erwärmen, warm
werden; **~th** [~θ] Wärme *f.*

warn [wɔ:n] warnen (**of,
against** vor); **~ing** Warnung *f*; Kündigung *f.*

warp [wɔ:p] (sich) verziehen (*Holz*).

warrant ['wɔrənt] *et.*
rechtfertigen; garantieren,
verbürgen; Vollmacht *f*;
Rechtfertigung *f*; **~ of
arrest** Haftbefehl *m*; **~y**
Garantie *f*; Berechtigung *f.*

warrior ['wɔriə] Krieger *m.*

wart [wɔ:t] Warze *f.*

wary ['wɛəri] vorsichtig,
wachsam.

was [wɔz, wəz] *1. u. 3. sg
pret von* be; *pass von* be.

wash [wɔʃ] (sich) waschen;
um-, überspülen; **e~n** *Teller
etc.* (ab)waschen; **~ away**
weg-, fortspülen; **~ up**
Geschirr spülen; *sub:* Waschen *n*; Wäsche *f*; Wasch-
...; **~ and wear** pflege-
leicht; **~basin**, *Am.*
~bowl Waschbecken *n*;
~cloth *Am.* Waschlappen
m; **~er** Waschmaschine *f*;
~ing Waschen *n*; Wäsche;
Wasch...; **~ing-machine**
Waschmaschine *f*; **~ing
powder** Waschpulver *n*;
~ing-up Abwasch(en *n*) *m*;

wasp [wɔsp] Wespe *f.*

waste [weist] wüst, öde;
überflüssig; Abfall...; Ver-
schwendung *f*; Wüste *f*,
(Ein)Öde *f*; Abfall *m*; ver-

schwenden; verwüsten; **~away** dahinsiechen, verfallen; **~paper-basket** Papierkorb m; **~pipe** Abflußrohr n.

watch ['wɔtʃ] (Armband-, Taschen-)Uhr f; Wache f; **keep ~** Wache halten, aufpassen; vb: (be)wachen; beobachten; zuschauen; **~ for** warten auf; **~ out** colloq. aufpassen; **~dog** Wachhund m; **~ful** wachsam; **~maker** Uhrmacher m; **~man** (Nacht-)Wächter m.

water ['wɔːtə] Wasser n; pl Gewässer pl; bewässern; sprengen; (be)gießen; tränken; wässern (Mund); tränen (Augen); **~(down)** verwässern (a. fig.); **~bottle** Wasserflasche f; Feldflasche f; **~closet** (Wasser)Klosett n; **~colo(u)r** Aquarell (-malerei f) n; **~course** Wasserlauf m; **~cress** Brunnenkresse f; **~dog** Wasserratte f (Schwimmer); **~fall** Wasserfall m. **watering|-can** Gießkanne f; **~place** Wasserloch n, Tränke f; Bad(eort m) n; Seebad n. **water|-level** Wasserspiegel m; Wasserstand(slinie f) m; **~proof** wasserdicht; Regenmantel m; **~shed** Wasserscheide f; **~side** Küste f, Fluß-, Seeufer n; **~tight** wasserdicht; fig. unangreifbar; **~way**

Wasserstraße f; **~works** sg, pl Wasserwerk(e pl) n; **~y** wässerig.
watt [wɔt] electr. Watt n.
wave [weiv] Welle f; Woge f; Winken n; wellen; schwingen, schwenken; wogen, wehen, flattern; winken (mit); **~ to** j-m zuwinken.
waver ['weivə] (sch)wanken; flackern; [welt].
wavy ['weivi] wellig, gewellt.
wax [wæks] Wachs n; bohnern; zunehmen (Mond).
way [wei] Weg m; Strecke f; Richtung f; Art u. Weise f; (Eigen)Art f; (Aus)Weg m; Hinsicht f; **this ~** hierher, hier entlang; **the other ~ round** umgekehrt; **by the ~** übrigens; **by ~ of** durch; **on the ~, on one's ~** unterwegs; **out of the ~** abgelegen; ungewöhnlich; **give ~** (zurück)weichen; nachgeben; mot. die Vorfahrt lassen (to dat); **have one's own ~** s-n Willen durchsetzen; **lead the ~** vorangehen; **~back** Rückweg m, -fahrt f; **~in** Eingang m; **~ of life** Lebensart f, -weise f; **~ out** Ausgang m; **~side** Wegrand m; **(by the) ~side** am Wege; **~ward** ['~wəd] eigensinnig.
we [wiː, wi] wir.
weak [wiːk] schwach; dünn (Getränk); **~en** schwächen; schwach werden; **~ling**

Schwächling *m*; **~ly**
schwächlich; **~-minded**
schwachsinnig; **~ness**
Schwäche *f*.

wealth [welθ] Reichtum
m; **~y** reich, wohlhabend.

wean [wiːn] entwöhnen.

weapon ['wepən] Waffe *f*.

wear [wεə] (*irr*) *am Körper*
tragen; anhaben; *Hut etc.*
aufhaben; halten, haltbar
sein; *sit gut etc.* tragen;
~ (away, down, off, out)
(sich) abnutzen *od.* abtragen; **~ off** sich verlieren;
~ out erschöpfen; *sub*:
Tragen *n*; (Be)Kleidung *f*;
Abnutzung *f*.

wear|iness ['wiərinis] Müdigkeit *f*; *fig.* Überdruß *m*;
~y müde; ermüden(d).

weasel ['wiːzl] Wiesel *n*.

weather ['weðə] Wetter *n*,
Witterung *f*; **~-beaten**
verwittert; *vom Wetter gegerbt* (*Gesicht*); **~-chart**
Wetterkarte *f*; **~-forecast**
Wetterbericht *m*, -vorhersage *f*.

weave [wiːv] (*irr*) weben,
flechten; **~r** Weber *m*.

web [web] Gewebe *n*; Netz
n; *zo.* Schwimmhaut *f*.

wed [wed] heiraten; **~
ding** Hochzeit *f*; Hochzeits...; **~ding-ring** Ehe-,
Trauring *m*.

wedge [wedʒ] Keil *m*;
(ein)keilen, (-)zwängen.

Wednesday ['wenzdi]
Mittwoch *m*.

weed [wiːd] Unkraut *n*;
jäten; **~-killer** Unkraut-

vertilgungsmittel *n*.

week [wiːk] Woche *f*; **~
in, ~ out** Woche für Woche; **this day ~, today ~**
heute in 8 Tagen; **~day**
Wochentag *m*; **~end** Wochenende *n*; **~ly** wöchentlich.

weep [wiːp] (*irr*) weinen;
tropfen; **~ing willow**
Trauerweide *f*.

weigh [wei] (*a.* **~ out** ab-)
wiegen; *fig.* ab-, erwägen;
~t Gewicht *n*; *fig.*: Last
f; Bedeutung *f*; **~tless**
leicht; schwerelos; **~t-
lifting** *sp.* Gewichtheben
n; **~ty** schwer(wiegend);
wichtig.

weir [wiə] Wehr *n*.

weird [wiəd] unheimlich;
colloq. sonderbar.

welcome ['welkəm] Empfang *m*; willkommen (hei
ßen); *fig.* begrüßen; **you
are ~ to ...** Sie können
gern ...; **(you are) ~!**
gern geschehen!, bitte sehr!

weld [weld] (zs.-)schwei
ßen.

welfare ['welfεə] Wohlfahrt *f*; **~ state** Wohlfahrtsstaat *m*; **~ work**
Fürsorge *f*; **~ worker** Fürsorger(in).

well¹ [wel] Brunnen *m*;
tech. Quelle *f* (*a. fig.*), Bohrloch *n*.

well² gut; wohl; gesund;
~ off wohlhabend; **I am
od. feel ~** ich fühle mich
wohl, es geht mir gut; *int.*
nun!, na!, gut!, schön!;

very ~ (na) gut!; ~**being** Wohl(ergehen) n; ~**born** aus guter Familie; ~**bred** wohlerzogen.

wellingtons ['weliŋtənz] pl Schaft-, Gummistiefel pl.

well-known wohlbekannt; ~**mannered** mit guten Manieren; ~**timed** rechtzeitig, im richtigen Augenblick; ~**to-do** wohlhabend; ~**wisher** Gönner m, Freund m; ~**worn** abgetragen; fig. abgedroschen.

Welsh [welʃ] walisisch; Walisisch n; **the** ~ pl die Waliser pl; ~ **rabbit**, ~ **rarebit** [~ 'reəbit] überbackene Käseschnitte.

wench [wentʃ] veraltet: Mädchen n.

went [went] pret von **go**.

wept [wept] pret u. pp von **weep**.

were [wəː, wə] pret pl u. 2. sg von **be**; pret pass von **be**; subj pret von **be**.

west [west] West(en m); westlich, West...; nach Westen; ~**erly**, ~**ern** westlich; ~**ward(s)** ['~wəd(z)] westwärts.

wet [wet] naß, feucht; ~**through** durchnäßt; Nässe f; Feuchtigkeit f; (irr) naß machen, anfeuchten; ~**nurse** Amme f.

whack [wæk] schlagen; (knallender) Schlag.

whale [weil] Wal m.

wharf [wɔːf] pl a. ~**ves** [~vz] Kai m, Anlegeplatz m.

what [wɔt] was; wie; was für ein(e), welche(r, -s); (das,) was; was!, wie!; was?, wie?; ~ **about** ...? wie steht's mit ...?; ~ **is all this about?** worum handelt es sich eigentlich?; ~ **for?** wofür?, wozu?; ~ **next?** was sonst noch?; ~ **so** ~? na, wenn schon?; ~**(so)ever** was (auch immer), alles was; was auch; welche(r, -s) ... auch (immer).

wheat [wiːt] Weizen m.

wheel [wiːl] Rad n; Steuer (-rad) n; fahren, rollen, schieben; (sich) drehen; ~**barrow** Schubkarren m; ~**chair** Rollstuhl m.

whelp [welp] Welpe m.

when [wen] wann?; wann; wenn; als; ~**(so)ever** immer od. jedesmal wenn.

where [wɛə] wo; wohin; ~ ... **from?** woher?; ~ ... **to?** wohin?; ~**abouts** wo ungefähr; Aufenthalt(s-ort) m; ~**as** während; ~**by** wodurch, womit; ~**fore** weshalb; ~**in** worin; ~**(up)on** worauf; ~**ver** wo (-hin) (auch) immer.

whet [wet] wetzen, schärfen.

whether ['weðə] ob.

which [witʃ] welche(r, -s); der, die, das; was; ~**(so)ever** welche(r, -s) ...(auch) immer.

whiff [wif] Hauch m; Geruch m; Zug m (beim Rauchen).

while [wail] während; Weile *f*, Zeit *f*; **for a ~ e-e** Zeitlang; *vb*: **~ away** sich *die Zeit* vertreiben.

whim [wim] Schrulle *f*, Laune *f*. [mern.]

whimper ['wimpə] wim-\

whims|ical ['wimzikəl] launenhaft, wunderlich; **~y** Laune *f*, Grille *f*.

whine [wain] winseln; wimmern; greinen, jammern.

whinny ['wini] wiehern.

whip [wip] Peitsche *f*; peitschen; verprügeln; schlagen; **~ped cream** Schlagsahne *f*; **~ping** Prügel *pl*; **~ping-top** Kreisel *m*.

whirl [wə:l] wirbeln, sich drehen; Wirbel *m*; Strudel *m*; **~pool** Strudel *m*.

whir(r) [wə:] schwirren.

whisk [wisk] (Staub-, Fliegen)Wedel *m*; *Küche*: Schneebesen *m*; schlagen; **~ away**, **~ off** (ab-, weg-) wischen; *j-n* schnell wegbringen; **~ (away** weg-) huschen, (-)flitzen.

whiskers ['wiskəz] *pl* Backenbart *m*.

whisper ['wispə] flüstern; Geflüster *n*, Flüstern *n*.

whistle ['wisl] pfeifen; Pfeife *f*; Pfiff *m*.

white [wait] weiß; Weiß(e) *n*; Weiße *m*, *f*; **~ coffee** Milchkaffee *m*; **~collar worker** Angestellte *m*, *f*; **~ frost** (Rauh)Reif *m*; **~ heat** Weißglut *f*; **~ lie** fromme Lüge; **~n** weiß

machen *od.* werden; **~ness** Weiße *f*; Blässe *f*; **~wash** Tünche *f*; weißen; *fig.* reinwaschen.

Whit|monday ['wit'mʌndi] Pfingstmontag *m*; **~sun** ['~sn] Pfingst...; **~suntide** Pfingsten *pl*.

whiz(z) [wiz] zischen, sausen, schwirren.

who [hu:, hu] wer?; *colloq.* wem?, wen?; *who*; **relative(r, ~s)** der, die, das.

whodunit [hu:'dʌnit] *sl.* Krimi *m*.

whoever [hu:'evə] wer (auch) immer; jeder, der.

whole [həul] ganz; heil, unversehrt; Ganze *n*; **(up-) on the ~** im ganzen; **~meal bread** Vollkornbrot *n*; **~sale dealer**, **~saler** Großhändler *m*; **~sale trade** Großhandel *m*; **~some** gesund.

wholly ['həuli] ganz.

whom [hu:m] *acc von* **who**.

whoop [hu:p] Schrei *m*, Geschrei *n*; laut schreien; **~ing cough** Keuchhusten *m*.

whore [hɔ:] Hure *f*.

whose [hu:z] *gen sg u. pl von* **who**: wessen?; dessen; deren (*a.* gen *von* **which**).

why [wai] warum, weshalb; **~ so?** wieso?; **that is ~** deshalb; *int.* nun (gut); aber (... doch).

wick [wik] Docht *m*.

wicked ['wikid] böse; schlecht; schlimm; **~ness** Bosheit *f*, Gemeinheit *f*.

wicker| basket ['wikə] Weidenkorb m; **~ chair** Korbstuhl m.

wicket ['wikit] Pförtchen n; *Kricket:* Dreistab m, Tor m.

wide [waid] weit; ausgedehnt; breit; **~ awake** hellwach; *fig.* aufgeweckt; **~n** (sich) verbreitern; (sich) erweitern; **~spread** weitverbreitet.

widow ['widəu] Witwe f; **~er** Witwer m.

width [widθ] Breite f, Weite f.

wife [waif], *pl* **wives** [~vz] (Ehe)Frau f, Gattin f.

wig [wig] Perücke f.

wild [waild] wild; **run ~** wild aufwachsen, verwildern; **~cat** wild *(Streik)*; Schwindel...; **~erness** ['wildənis] Wildnis f, Wüste f; **~fire: like ~** wie ein Lauffeuer.

wil(l)ful ['wilful] eigensinnig; vorsätzlich.

will [wil] Wille m; Wunsch m; Testament n; **~ I, ~ ich, du etc.:** will(st) etc.; **ich, du etc.:** werde, wirst etc.; **~ing** gewillt, willens, bereit. [de f.]

willow ['wiləu] *bot.* Wei-]

wilt [wilt] (ver)welken.

win [win] *(irr)* gewinnen; erlangen; siegen; *sp.* Sieg m.

wince [wins] (zs.-)zucken.

winch [wintʃ] *tech.* Winde f.

wind¹ [wind] Wind m; Blähung f; wittern; **be ~ed** außer Atem sein.

wind² [waind] *(irr)* sich winden *od.* schlängeln; winden, wickeln; **~ up** Uhr aufziehen; **~ing** Windung f; sich windend; **~ing staircase** Wendeltreppe f.

wind-instrument Blasinstrument n. [Winde f.]

windlass ['windləs] *tech.*]

windmill ['winmil] Windmühle f.

window ['windəu] Fenster n; Schaufenster n; **~shade** *Am.* Rouleau n, Jalousie f; **~-shopping: go ~** e-n Schaufensterbummel machen; **~sill** Fensterbrett n.

wind|pipe Luftröhre f; **~-screen**, *Am.* **~-shield** Windschutzscheibe f; **~-screen wiper**, *Am.* **~-shield wiper** Scheibenwischer m; **~y** windig.

wine [wain] Wein m.

wing [wiŋ] Flügel m; Schwinge f; *mot.* Kotflügel m; *aer.* Tragfläche f.

wink [wiŋk] Blinzeln n, Zwinkern n; blinzeln *od.* zwinkern (mit).

winn|er ['winə] Gewinner (-in); Sieger(in); **~ing** siegreich; *fig.* einnehmend; **~ing-post** *sp.* Ziel n; **~ings** *pl* Gewinn m.

wint|er ['wintə] Winter m; überwintern; **~ry** ['~tri] winterlich; *fig.* frostig.

wipe [waip] (ab-, auf-) wischen; (ab)trocknen; **~ off** ab-, wegwischen; **~ out** auswischen; tilgen; (völlig) vernichten.

wire ['waiə] Draht *m*; *colloq.* Telegramm *n*; Draht...; *colloq.* telegraphieren; **~less** drahtlos, Funk...; **~less (set)** Radio(apparat *m*) *n*; **~ netting** Drahtgeflecht *n*.

wiry ['waiəri] drahtig.

wisdom ['wizdəm] Weisheit *f*; **~tooth** Weisheitszahn *m*.   [erfahren.]

wise [waiz] weise, klug,]

wish [wiʃ] Wunsch *m*; wünschen; wollen; **~ s.o. well** *od.* **ill** j-m Gutes od. Böses wünschen; **~ for** (sich) *et.* wünschen.

wistful ['wistful]sehnsüchtig, wehmütig.

wit [wit] Witz *m*; *sg*, *pl* Verstand *m*; **be at one's ~'s end** mit s-r Weisheit am Ende sein.

witch [witʃ] Hexe *f*; **~craft**, **~ery** Hexerei *f*.

with [wið] mit; bei; für; von; durch, vor.

withdraw [wið'drɔ:] (*irr* **draw**) (sich) zurückziehen; Truppen *etc.* abziehen; Geld abheben.

wither ['wiðə] (ver)welken; verdorren (lassen).

with|hold [wið'həuld] (*irr* **hold**) zurückhalten; *et.* vorenthalten; **~in** [~'ðin] in(nerhalb); **~in call** in Rufweite; **~out** [~'ðaut] ohne; **~stand** (*irr* **stand**) widerstehen.

witness ['witnis] Zeug|e *m*, -in *f*; Zeugnis *n*, Beweis *m*; (be)zeugen; Zeuge sein

von; **~box**, *Am.* **~ stand** Zeugenstand *m*, -bank *f*.

witty ['witi] witzig, geistreich.

wives [waivz] *pl von* **wife**.

wizard ['wizəd] Zauberer *m*; Genie *n*.

wobble ['wɔbl] schwanken; wackeln (mit); schlottern (*Knie*).

woe [wəu] Weh *n*, Leid *n*; **~begone** ['_-bigɔn] jammervoll; **~ful** jammervoll, elend.

woke [wəuk] *pret u. pp*, **~n** *pp von* **wake**.

wolf [wulf], *pl* **wolves** [_vz] Wolf *m*; **~ (down)** (gierig) verschlingen.

woman ['wumən], *pl* **women** ['wimin] Frau *f*; weiblich; **~ doctor** Ärztin *f*; **~hood** Frauen *pl*; Weiblichkeit *f*; **~kind** Frauen *pl*; **~ly** fraulich, weiblich.

womb [wu:m] Gebärmutter *f*, Mutterleib *m*; *fig.* Schoß *m*.

women ['wimin] *pl von* **woman**.   [won.]

won [wʌn] *pret u. pp von*]

wonder ['wʌndə] Wunder *n*; Verwunderung *f*; sich wundern; gern wissen mögen, sich fragen; **~ful** wunderbar, -voll.

won't [wəunt] *für* **will not**.

wont [wəunt] Gewohnheit *f*; gewohnt; **be ~ to do** zu tun pflegen; **~ed** gewohnt; üblich.

woo [wu:] werben um.

wood [wud] *oft pl* Wald *m*,

Gehölz n; Holz n; ~cut Holzschnitt m; ~cutter Holzfäller m; ~ed bewaldet, waldig; ~en hölzern (a. fig.); Holz...; ~pecker Specht m; ~wind Holzblasinstrument n; ~work Holzwerk n; Holzarbeit(en pl) f; ~y waldig; holzig.

wool [wul] Wolle f; ~(l)en wollen, Woll...; ~ pl Wollsachen pl; ~(l)y wollig; Woll...

word [wə:d] (in Worten) ausdrücken, formulieren; Wort n; Nachricht f; pl: (Lied)Text m; fig. Wortwechsel m; ~ have a ~ with mit j-m sprechen; ~ing Wortlaut m, Fassung f.

wore [wɔ:] pret von wear.

work [wə:k] Arbeit f; Werk n; pl (Räder-, Trieb-, Uhr)Werk n; pl als sg konstruiert: Werk n, Fabrik f, Betrieb m; at ~ bei der Arbeit; out of ~ arbeitslos; set to ~ an die Arbeit gehen; (a. irr) arbeiten (at, on an); tech. funktionieren, gehen; wirken; fig. gelingen, klappen; verarbeiten; Maschine etc. bedienen; (an-, be)treiben; fig. bewirken; ~ off aufarbeiten; Gefühle abreagieren; ~ out ausrechnen, Aufgabe lösen; Plan ausarbeiten; ~day Werk-, Arbeitstag m; ~er Arbeiter (-in) m; ~house Armenhaus n; Am. Besserungsanstalt f, Arbeitshaus n.

working arbeitend; Arbeits...; Betriebs...; ~ class Arbeiterklasse f; ~ day Werk-, Arbeitstag m; ~ hours pl Arbeitszeit f.

workman (Fach)Arbeiter m; ~ship Kunstfertigkeit f; gute etc. Ausführung.

work|of art Kunstwerk n; ~s council Betriebsrat m; ~shop Werkstatt f.

world [wə:ld] Welt f; ~ly weltlich; irdisch; ~ power pol. Weltmacht f; ~ war Weltkrieg m; ~wide weltweit, auf der ganzen Welt, Welt...

worm [wə:m] Wurm m; ~eaten wurmstichig.

worn [wɔ:n] pp von wear; ~out abgenutzt, abgetragen; verbraucht; erschöpft.

worr|ied ['wʌrid] besorgt, beunruhigt; ~y quälen, plagen; (sich) beunruhigen; (sich) Sorgen machen; Sorge f; Ärger m.

worse [wə:s] comp von bad, evil, ill.

worship ['wə:ʃip] Anbetung f, Verehrung f; Gottesdienst m; verehren, anbeten; ~(p)er Kirchgänger(in).

worst [wə:st] sup von bad, evil, ill.

worsted ['wustid] Kammgarn n; Woll...

worth [wə:θ] Wert m; Verdienst n; wert; ~ reading lesenswert; ~ seeing sehenswert; ~less wertlos

~while der Mühe wert; ~y ['ɔɪ] würdig.

would [wud] *pret u. cond von* will; pflegte(st, -n, -t).

wound¹ [wu:nd] Wunde *f*, Verletzung *f*; verwunden, -letzen (*a. fig.*).

wound² [waund] *pret u. pp von* **wind²**.

wove [wəuv] *pret*, ~n *pp von* **weave**.

wrangle ['ræŋgl] (sich) streiten *od.* zanken; Streit *m*, Zank *m*.

wrap [ræp] wickeln, hüllen; ~ **up** (ein)wickeln, (-)packen, (-)hüllen; **be ~ped up in** *fig.* ganz in Anspruch genommen sein von, ganz aufgehen in; Decke *f*; Schal *m*; Mantel *m*; ~**per** Hülle *f*, Verpackung *f*; (Buch)Umschlag *m*; ~**ping** Verpackung *f*.

wrath [rɔθ] Zorn *m*.

wreath [ri:θ], *pl* ~**s** [~ðz] (*Blumen*)Gewinde *n*, Kranz *m*.

wreck [rek] Wrack *n*; Schiffbruch *m*; vernichten, zerstören; **be ~ed** Schiffbruch erleiden; ~**age** Trümmer *pl*; Wrack(teile *pl*) *n*; ~**ed** gestrandet, gescheitert; schiffbrüchig.

wrecking | **company** *Am.* Abbruchfirma *f*; ~ **service** *Am. mot.* Abschleppdienst *m*.

wren [ren] Zaunkönig *m*.

wrench [rentʃ] reißen, zerren, ziehen; *med.* verren-

ken, -stauchen; ~ **open** aufreißen; *sub:* Ruck *m*; *med.*Verrenkung *f*, -stauchung *f*; Schraubenschlüssel *m*.

wrest [rest] reißen; ~**from** *j-m* entreißen *od. fig.* abringen; ~**le** ringen (mit); ~**ling** Ringkampf *m*, Ringen *n*.

wretch [retʃ] armer Kerl; Schuft *m*; ~**ed** [~id] elend; erbärmlich, schlecht.

wriggle ['rigl] sich winden *od.* schlängeln; zappeln (mit).

wring [riŋ] (*irr*) (~ **out** aus)wringen; *Hände* ringen.

wrinkle ['riŋkl] Runzel *f*; Falte *f*; sich runzeln, runz(e)lig werden; knittern; ~ **up** Stirn runzeln.

wrist [rist] Handgelenk *n*; ~ **watch** Armbanduhr *f*.

writ [rit] Erlaß *m*; *jur.* Verfügung *f*.

write [rait] (*irr*) schreiben; ~ **down** auf-, niederschreiben; ~ **out** (ganz) ausschreiben; *Scheck etc.* ausstellen; ~**r** Schreiber(in); Verfasser(in), Autor(in), Schriftsteller(in).

writhe [raið] sich krümmen.

writing ['raitiŋ] Schreib...; Schreiben *n*; Schrift *f*; Stil *m*; *pl* literarische Werke *pl*; **in** ~ schriftlich; ~**desk** Schreibtisch *m*; ~**paper** Schreib-, Briefpapier *n*.

written ['ritn] *pp von*

write; schriftlich.

wrong [rɒŋ] unrichtig; falsch, verkehrt; **be ~** falsch sein; nicht in Ordnung sein, nicht stimmen; falsch gehen (*Uhr*); unrecht haben; **what is ~ with you?** was ist los mit dir?; *sub*: Unrecht *n*; *vb*:

j-m Unrecht tun.

wrote [rəut] *pret von* **write**.

wrought [rɔːt] *pret u. pp von* **work**; **~-iron** schmiedeeisern; **~-up** erregt.

wrung [rʌŋ] *pret u. pp von* **wring**.

wry [rai] schief, verzerrt.

X, Y

Xmas ['krisməs] *für* **Christmas**.

X-ray ['eks'rei] Röntgenaufnahme *f*; Röntgen...; röntgen.

xylophone ['zailəfəun] Xylophon *n*.

yacht [jɒt] (Segel-, Motor-) Jacht *f*; Segelboot *n*; **~ing** Segeln *n*; Segelsport *m*.

yap [jæp] kläffen.

yard [jɑːd] Yard *n* (= 0,914 *m*); Hof *m*.

yarn [jɑːn] Garn *n*; *colloq*. Seemannsgarn *n*.

yawn [jɔːn] gähnen; Gähnen *n*.

ye[1] [jiː] *alte Form für* **you**.

ye[2] [jiː, ðiː] *alte Form für* **the**.

yea [jei] *veraltet*: ja.

yeah [jei] *sl.* ja.

year [jəː] Jahr *n*; **~ly** jährlich.

yearn [jəːn] sich sehnen.

yeast [jiːst] Hefe *f*.

yell [jel] (gellend) schreien; (gellender) Schrei.

yellow ['jeləu] gelb; Gelb *n*.

yelp [jelp] kläffen, jaulen.

yeoman ['jəumən] freier Bauer.

yes [jes] ja; doch; Ja *n*.

yesterday ['jestədi] gestern; **the day before ~** vorgestern.

yet [jet] noch; bis jetzt; schon; (je)doch, dennoch, trotzdem; **as ~** bis jetzt; **not ~** noch nicht.

yew [juː] Eibe *f*.

yield [jiːld] (ein-, hervor-) bringen; *agr.* tragen; nachgeben, weichen; Ertrag *m*; **~ing** *fig.* nachgiebig.

yoke [jəuk] Joch *n* (*a. fig.*); **~** *pl* (*Ochsen*) Gespann *f*; (an)spannen.

yolk [jəuk] (Ei)Dotter *m, n*, Eigelb *n*.

yonder ['jɒndə] *lit.* dort drüben.

you [juː, ju] du, ihr, Sie; dir, euch, Ihnen; dich, euch, Sie; man.

young [jʌŋ] jung; (Tier-) Junge *pl*; **~ster** ['~stə] Junge *m*.

your [juː] dein(e), euer(e), Ihr(e); **~s** [~z] deine(r, -s), euer, euere(s), Ihre(r, -s),

der, die, das dein(ig)e *od.*
eur(ig)e *od.* Ihr(ig)e; **~self,**
pl **~selves** (du, ihr, Sie)
selbst; dir (selbst), dich,
sich, euch, sich; **by ~self**
allein.

youth [ju:θ], *pl* **~s** [**~**ðz]

Jugend *f*; junger Mann;
Jugend...; **~ful** jung; jugendlich; **~ hostel** Ju-
gendherberge *f*.
Yugoslav ['ju:gəu'slɑ:v]
jugoslawisch; Jugoslaw|e
m, -in *f*; Jugoslawisch *n*.

Z

zeal [zi:l] Eifer *m*; **~ous**
['zeləs] eifrig; eifrig bedacht (**to do** zu tun).
zebra ['zi:brə] Zebra *n*; **~
crossing** Fußgängerüber-
gang *m*, Zebrastreifen *m*.
zenith ['zeniθ] Zenit *m*;
fig. Höhepunkt *m*.
zero ['ziərəu] Null(punkt
m) *f*.
zest [zest] Begeisterung *f*,
Schwung *m*; Reiz *m*.

zigzag ['zigzæg] Zickzack
m.
zip| **code** [zip] *Am.* Post-
leitzahl *f*; **~fastener,~per**
Reißverschluß *m*.
zodiac ['zəudiæk] Tier-
kreis *m*.
zone [zəun] Zone *f*.
zoo [zu:] Zoo *m*.
zoolog|**ical** [zəuə'lɔdʒikəl]
zoologisch; **~y** [**~**'ɔlədʒi]
Zoologie *f*.

A

Aal *m* eel.

Aas *n* carrion, carcass.

ab *prep* from; from ... (on); from ... on(ward[s]); *adv colloq.:* now and then; **von jetzt ~** from now on.

abändern alter, modify.

Abart *f* variety.

Abbau *m* reduction; *Bergbau:* exploitation, working; **2en** reduce; *Maschinen etc.:* dismantle; *Bergbau:* exploit.

ab|beißen bite off; **~bekommen** get off; **s-n Teil** *od.* **et. ~bekommen** get one's share; **~berufen** recall; **~bestellen** countermand; *Zeitung etc.:* cancel one's subscription to; **~biegen** turn off; **nach rechts** *od.* **links ~biegen** turn right *od.* left.

Abbildung *f* picture, illustration.

ab|binden untie, undo; *med.* ligature, tie off; **~blenden** *Scheinwerfer:* dim *od.* dip (*v/i:* the headlights); **2blendlicht** *n* dimmed headlight (*s pl*); **~brechen** break off (*a. fig.*); *Gebäude:* demolish; *Zelt:* strike; *fig.* stop; **~bremsen** slow down *od.* up, brake; **~brennen** burn down; **~**

bringen: j-n ~ von dissuade s.o. from; **~bröckeln** crumble; **~bürsten** brush (off).

Abc *n* ABC, alphabet.

ab|danken resign; *Herrscher:* abdicate; **~decken** uncover; *Tisch:* clear; *zudecken:* cover (up, over); **~dichten** make s.th. watertight, etc., tight.

Abdruck *m* impression, (im)print; **2en** print; *Artikel:* publish.

abdrücken fire.

Abend *m* evening, night; **Guten ~!** Good evening!; **am ~** in the evening; **heute 2** tonight; **morgen** *od.* **gestern 2** tomorrow *od.* last night; **~brot** *n* s. **Abendessen; ~dämmerung** *f* (evening) twilight, dusk; **~essen** *n* evening meal; dinner; *bsd. spätabends:* supper; **~kleid** *n* evening dress *od.* gown; **~kurs** *m* evening classes *pl;* **~land** *n* the Occident; **~mahl** *n eccl.* the (Holy) Communion, *the* Lord's Supper; **2s** in the evening; **~zeitung** *f* evening paper.

Abenteuer *n* adventure; **2lich** *fig.* wild, fantastic.

aber but; **oder ~** otherwise.

Aber|glaube m superstition; **2gläubisch** superstitious.

abermals again, once more.

abfahr|en leave, depart, start; *Schiff:* sail; carry *od.* cart away; **2t** f departure; *mar.* sailing; **2tslauf** m downhill (race).

Abfall m: *oft* **Abfälle** pl waste, refuse, *Am. a.* garbage; **~eimer** m dustbin, *Am.* garbage *od.* trash can; **2en Blätter** etc.: fall (off); *Gelände:* slope (down).

abfällig unfavo(u)rable; disparaging.

Abfallprodukt n by-product; waste product.

ab|fangen catch; *Brief* etc.: intercept; *mot.,* aer. right; **~färben** *Farbe:* run; **~fassen** write, compose, pen; **~fertigen** dispatch; *Zoll:* clear; *Kunden:* serve, attend to; **~feuern** fire (off), discharge.

abfind|en satisfy; *entschädigen:* compensate; **sich ~en mit** resign o.s. to; **2ung** f satisfaction; compensation.

ab|fliegen leave (by plane); *aer.* take off, start; **~fließen** drain *od.* flow off.

Abflug m take-off, start; departure.

Abfluß m flowing off; drain; *See:* outlet; **~rohr** n waste-pipe, drain-pipe.

Abfuhr f fig. rebuff.

abführ|en lead away; *Geld:* pay; **~end** med. laxative, purgative; **2mittel** n laxative. **[schen ~ bottle.)**

abfüllen decant; **in Fla-)**

Abgabe f Ball: pass; *econ.* sale; *Steuer:* tax.

Abgang m departure; *thea.* exit; leaving; **~szeugnis** n (school-)leaving certificate, *Am. a.* diploma.

Abgas n waste gas; *mot.* exhaust (gas).

abgearbeitet worn-out.

abgeben deliver; leave; give; *Arbeit:* hand in; *Ball:* pass; *Erklärung:* make; **sich ~ mit** occupy o.s. with.

abge|bildet in the picture; **~brannt** fig. colloq. hard up, sl. broke; **~griffen** *Buch:* well-thumbed; **~härtet** hardened.

abgehen leave, depart, start; *Brief* etc.: be dispatched; *Weg:* branch off; *Knopf* etc.: come off; fig. go *od.* pass off.

abge|hetzt exhausted; **~legen** remote, distant; **~macht: ~!** it's a deal!; **~magert** emaciated; **~neigt** disinclined, averse; **~nutzt** worn-out.

Abgeordnete m, f deputy, delegate; *Deutschland:* member of the Bundestag *od.* Landtag; *Brit.* Member of Parliament, *Am.* representative.

abge|schlossen fig. complete; complete; **~sehen: ~ von** apart (*Am. a.* aside) from;

~spannt fig. exhausted, tired; **~standen** stale, flat; **~storben** numb; dead; **~stumpft** fig. indifferent; **~tragen** threadbare, shabby.

ab|gewöhnen j–m et.: break od. cure s.o. of s.th.; **sich das Rauchen ~** give up smoking; **~grenzen** mark off; fig. define.

Abgrund m precipice, chasm.

ab|hacken chop od. cut off; **~haken** Liste: tick off; **~halten** hold; **j–n von et. ~halten** keep s.o. from doing s.th.; **~handen: ~ kommen** get lost.

Abhandlung f treatise.

Abhang m slope, incline.

abhängen Bild etc.: take down; rail. uncouple; **~ von** depend (up)on.

abhängig ~ von dependent (up)on; **2keit** f dependence.

ab|härten harden (**gegen** to); **sich ~** harden o.s.; **~hauen** cut od. chop off; colloq. be off; **~heben** teleph. lift (v/i the receiver); cut (the cards); lift od. take off; Geld: (with)draw; **sich ~ von** stand out against; **~heilen** heal (up); **~hetzen: sich ~** rush, hurry.

Abhilfe f remedy.

ab|holen fetch; call od. come for; **~holen lassen** send for; **j–n von der Bahn ~holen** go to meet

s.o. at the station; **~horchen** med. sound; teleph. listen in to; intercept; **e–n Schüler ~hören** hear a pupil's lesson.

Abitur n school-leaving examination.

ab|kaufen buy od. purchase from; **~kehren** sweep off; **sich ~kehren von** turn away from; **~klingen** Schmerz: ease off; **~klopfen** Staub: knock off; Mantel: dust; med. sound; **~knicken** snap od. break off; **~kochen** boil; Milch: scald.

abkommen: ~ von get off; Thema: digress from; **vom Wege ~** lose one's way; **2 n** agreement.

ab|koppeln uncouple; **~kratzen** scrape off; **~kühlen** cool; **sich ~kühlen** cool; fig. cool down.

abkürz|en shorten (Wort etc.: abbreviate; **den Weg ~en** take a short cut; **2ung** f abbreviation; short cut.

abladen unload; Schutt: dump.

Ablage f files pl.

ab|lagern: sich ~ settle; be deposited; **~lassen** drain (off), run (off) Dampf: let off.

Ablauf m Verlauf: course; expiration, end; **nach ~ von** at the end of; **2en** v/t Absätze: wear down; v/i run (off); drain (off), Frist, Paß: expire; Uhr: run down.

Ableben n death, jur. demise.

ab|lecken lick (off); **~le-gen** v/t Kleidung: take off; Akten etc.: file; Geständnis: make; Eid, Prüfung: take; v/i Schiff: sail; take off one's (hat and) coat.

Ableger m layer, shoot.

ablehn|en decline, refuse; Antrag etc.: turn down; **~end** negative; **♀ung** f refusal; rejection.

ableiten divert; fig. derive.

ablenk|en divert (von from); **♀ung** f diversion; distraction. [f delivery.)

abliefer|n deliver; **♀ung** f/

ablös|en detach, remove; take off; mil. relieve; Amtsvorgänger: supersede; **sich ~en** come off; Person: alternate, take turns; **♀ung** f relief.

abmach|en remove, detach; fig. settle, arrange, agree on; **♀ung** f arrangement, settlement, agreement.

abmagern lose weight, grow lean od. thin.

Abmarsch m start; mil. marching off.

abmelden: sich ~ give notice of one's departure.

abmes|sen measure; **♀-sung** f measurement.

ab|montieren take down, dismantle; **~mühen:** sich **~** drudge, toil; **~nagen** gnaw off; Knochen: pick.

Abnahme f decrease, diminution.

abnehme|n v/i Mond: wane; lose weight; decrease; diminish; v/t take off, remove; teleph. Hörer: lift; med. amputate; econ. buy, purchase; **j-m et. ~n** take s.th. from s.o.; **♀r** m econ.: buyer; customer.

Abneigung f aversion, dislike. [(sich) ~ wear out.)

ab|nutzen, ~nützen:/

Abonn|ement n subscription (auf to); **~ent** m subscriber; **♀ieren** subscribe to, take in.

Abordnung f delegation.

ab|pfeifen: das Spiel ~ stop the game; **~pflücken** pick, pluck, gather; **~plagen: sich ~** toil; **~prallen** rebound; **~put-zen** clean; wipe off; **~rasieren** shave off; **~raten: ~ von** dissuade from; advise against; **~räumen** clear (away).

abrechn|en deduct; **mit j-m ~en** get even with s.o.; **♀ung** f settlement (of accounts); deduction.

abreiben rub off; Körper: rub down; polish.

Abreise f departure; **♀n** depart, leave, start.

abreißen v/t tear od. pull off; Gebäude: pull down; v/i break off; Knopf etc.: come off; **♀kalender** m tear-off calendar.

ab|richten Tier: train; Pferd: break (in); **~riegeln** s. **verriegeln.**

Abriß m outline, summary.

ab|rollen unroll; uncoil; unwind; **~rücken** move away; *mil.* march off.

Abruf *m:* **auf ~** on call.

abrunden round (off).

abrupt abrupt.

Abrüstung *f* disarmament.

abrutschen slip off.

Absage *f* cancellation; **~n** cancel, call off.

absägen saw off.

Absatz *m Schuh:* heel; *Treppe:* landing; *print.* paragraph; *econ.* sale.

ab|schaffen abolish; **~schälen** peel (off), pare; **~schalten** switch off, turn off *od.* out, disconnect; **~schätzen** estimate, value.

Abschaum *m* scum; *fig. a.* dregs *pl.*

Abscheu *m* horror, abhorrence; **~lich** abominable, horrid.

abschicken send off, dispatch; post, *bsd. Am.* mail.

Abschied *m* parting, leave-taking; **~ nehmen** take leave (**von** of); **~sfeier** *f* farewell party.

ab|schießen shoot off; *hunt.* shoot, kill; *Waffe:* discharge; *Rakete:* launch; *aer.* (shoot, bring) down; **~schirmen** s: **~ (gegen)** shield (from); screen (from).

Abschlag *m econ.* discount, rebate; **~en** knock (beat, strike) off; *Kopf:* cut off; *Angriff:* beat off, repulse; *Bitte etc.:* refuse;

~(s)zahlung *f* instal(l)-ment.

abschleifen grind off.

Abschlepp|dienst *m* breakdown (*Am.* wrecking) service; **~en** *mot.* tow; **sich ~en mit** trail *od.* toil along with; **~seil** *n* tow(ing)-rope; **~wagen** *m* breakdown lorry, *Am.* wrecking car.

abschließen lock (up); end, finish, complete; *Versicherung:* effect; *Vertrag etc.:* conclude; **e-n Handel ~** strike a bargain; **~d** final; in conclusion.

Abschluß *m* conclusion; **~prüfung** *f* final examination, finals *pl;* **~zeugnis** *n* leaving certificate.

ab|schmieren lubricate, grease; **~schnallen** unbuckle; *Skier:* take off; **~schneiden** cut (off); slice off; **gut** *od.* **schlecht ~schneiden** come off well *od.* badly.

Abschnitt *m math.* segment; *print.* section, paragraph; *Kontroll* **~:** counterfoil, *Am. a.* stub; *Reise:* stage; *Entwicklung:* phase; *Zeit:* period.

ab|schöpfen skim (off); **~schrauben** screw off; **~schrecken** deter; **~schreiben** copy; *Schule:* crib; **~schrift** *f* copy, duplicate; **~schürfen** graze, abrade.

Abschuß *m Rakete:* launching; *aer.* shooting down,

downing; **~rampe** f launching pad od. platform.

ab|schüssig steep; **~schütteln** shake off; **~schwächen** weaken; **~schweifen** digress; **~segeln** set sail, sail off.

abseh|bar: in ~er Zeit in the not-too-distant future; **~en** foresee; **es abgesehen haben auf** aim at; **~en von** refrain from; disregard.

abseits aside, apart; *sp.* off side; **~** (*gen.*) *od.* **von** off.

absende|n send off, dispatch; post, *Am.* mail; **2r** m sender.

absetzen *v/t* set *od.* put down; *j-n:* remove, dismiss; *Passagier:* drop, dismiss; *Waren:* sell; *Theaterstück:* take off; *v/i* stop, pause.

Absicht f intention; **2lich** intentional; on purpose.

absolut absolute.

ab|sondern separate; *med.* secrete; **sich ~sondern** seclude o.s.; **~sorbieren** absorb; **~spenstig: ~machen** entice away (*dat* from); **~sperren** lock (up); *Wasser, Gas:* cut od. shut off; *Straße:* block; **~spielen** play; *Tonband:* a. play back; **sich ~spielen** happen, take place.

Absprung m jump.

abspülen wash off *od.* away; *Geschirr:* wash up.

abstamm|en be descended; **2ung** f descent.

Abstand m distance.

abstauben dust.

absteche|n contrast (**von, gegen** with); **2r** m excursion, trip.

ab|stehen stick out; **~steigen** descend; *Pferd:* dismount, alight; *Fahrrad:* dismount; *Hotel:* put up (in at); **~stellen** put down; *Gas etc.:* turn off; *Auto:* park; **~stempeln** stamp.

Abstieg m descent; *fig.* decline.

abstimm|en vote (**über** on); harmonize (**auf** with); balance; **2ung** f voting; vote.

abstoppen stop.

ab|stoßen push off; *j-n:* repel; **~d** repulsive.

abstreiten deny.

Ab|sturz m fall; *aer.* crash; **2stürzen** fall; *aer.* crash.

absuchen search (**nach** for).   [terous.]

absurd absurd, prepos-∫

Abszeß m abscess.

Abtei f abbey.

Abteil n compartment; **2en** divide; *arch.* partition off; **~ung** f department; *Krankenhaus:* ward; **~ungsleiter** m head of a department.

abtragen *Gebäude:* pull down; *Hügel:* level; *Kleidung:* wear out.

abtreib|en *med.* procure (an) abortion; **2ung** f *med.* abortion.

abtrennen detach, separate; sever.

abtrete|n *Absätze*: wear down; *Gebiet*: cede; *fig.* retire; 2r *m* doormat.

ab|trocknen dry; wipe (dry); **tupfen** mop (up); dab; **wägen** consider carefully, weigh; **wälzen** shift; **wandeln** vary, modify; **warten** wait for.

abwärts down, downward(s).

abwasch|bar washable; 2**becken** *n* sink; **en** *s.* **abspülen.**

Abwässer *pl* sewage *sg*; *Industrie*: waste water *sg.*

abwechs|eln alternate; **einander** *od.* **sich eln** take turns; **elnd** alternate; 2**(e)lung** *f* change; **zur** 2**(e)lung** *f* for a change.

Abwehr *f* defen|ce, *Am.*-se; 2**en** ward off; *Angriff*, *Feind*: repel, repulse.

abweichen deviate.

abweisen refuse, reject; rebuff; **d** unfriendly, cool.

ab|wenden turn away (*a.* **sich**) *Unheil, Blick*: avert; **werfen** throw off; *Bomben*: drop; *Gewinn*: yield.

abwer|ten devaluate; 2**tung** *f* devaluation.

abwesen|d absent; 2**heit** *f* absence.

ab|wickeln unwind, wind off; **wiegen** weigh (out); **wischen** wipe (off); **würgen** *mot.* stall; **zahlen** pay off; 2**zahlung** *f* instal(l)ment.

Abzeichen *n* badge.

ab|zeichnen copy; draw; *Schriftstück*: initial; **ziehen** take off, remove; *math.* subtract, deduct; *Bett*: strip; *Schlüssel*: take out; *mil.* withdraw; go away; *Rauch*: clear away.

Abzug *m* *mil.* withdrawal; *Waffe*: trigger; *math.* deduction; *phot.* print; *print.* proof.

abzüglich less, minus.

abzweig|en: (sich) ** branch off; 2ung** *f* turning, bifurcation.

ach *int.* oh!, ah!; ** so!** oh, I see!

Achse *f* axis (*a. pol.*); *tech.* axle(-tree).

Achsel *f* shoulder; **die** *od.* **mit den n zucken** shrug one's shoulders; **höhle** *f* armpit.

acht eight; **in Tagen** today week, this day week; **vor Tagen** a week ago.

Acht *f* attention; **außer** 2 **lassen** disregard; **sich in** 2 **nehmen** be careful.

achte eighth; 2**l** *n* eighth (part).

achten respect; ** auf** pay attention to; ** darauf, daß** take care (that).

achtens eighth(ly).

Achter *m* (figure) eight; *Rudern*: eight; **bahn** *f* switchback (railway), *Am.* roller coaster.

acht|geben be careful; pay attention (**auf** to); **gib acht!** look out!, watch out!; s. **aufpassen auf**; **⁀los** careless.

Achtung f attention; respect; **⁀!** attention!, caution!; **⁀, Stufe!** mind the step!

acht|zehn(te) eighteen(th); **⁀zig** eighty; **⁀zigste** eightieth.

ächzen groan, moan.

Acker m field; **⁀bau** m agriculture; farming.

addieren add (up).

Adel m nobility, aristocracy; **⁀ig** noble.

Ader f vein; artery.

adieu int. farewell, colloq. cheerio.

Adjektiv n gr. adjective.

Adler m eagle.

adlig noble; **⁀e** m nobleman; peer.

Admiral m admiral.

adoptieren adopt.

Adreßbuch n directory.

Adress|e f address; **⁀ieren** address, direct.

Advent m Advent.

Adverb n gr. adverb.

Affäre f (love) affair; matter, business.

Affe m monkey; **Menschen⁀** ape.

affektiert affected.

Afrika|ner m African; **⁀nisch** African.

After m anus.

Agent m (pol. secret) agent; **⁀ur** f agency.

Aggress|ion f aggression; **⁀iv** aggressive.

Ägyp|ter m Egyptian; **⁀tisch** Egyptian.

ah int. ah!

aha int. aha!, I see!

Ahle f awl.

ähneln be like, resemble.

Ahnen pl ancestors pl, forefathers pl.

ahnen guess; suspect.

ähnlich similar (dat to); like; **⁀keit** f likeness, resemblance, similarity.

Ahnung f presentiment, foreboding; notion, idea; **⁀slos** unsuspecting.

Ahorn m maple(-tree).

Ähre f ear.

Akademi|e f academy; **⁀ker** m university man, bsd. Am. university graduate; **⁀sch** academic.

akklimatisieren: sich ⁀ acclimatize.

Akkord m mus. chord; **im ⁀** econ. by the piece; **⁀arbeit** f piece-work; **⁀lohn** m piece-wages pl.

Akku(mulator) m battery.

Akkusativ m gr. accusative (case).

Akrobat m acrobat.

Akt m act(ion), deed; thea. act; paint. nude.

Akte f document; abgelegte: file; **⁀n** pl a. papers pl; **⁀nmappe** f, **⁀ntasche** f briefcase.

Aktie f share, Am. stock; **⁀ngesellschaft** f joint-stock company, Am. stock corporation.

Aktion f action; mil. operation.

aktiv active; **⁀** n gr. active (voice); **⁀ität** f activity.

aktuell current; up-to-date.

Akusti|k f acoustics pl (Lehre: sg); 2**sch** acoustic.

akut acute.

Akzent m accent; Betonung: a. stress (a. fig.).

akzeptieren accept.

Alarm m alarm; 2**ieren** alarm.

albern silly, foolish.

Album n album.

Alge f alga; seaweed.

Algebra f algebra.

Alibi n alibi.

Alimente pl support sg.

Alkohol m alcohol; 2**frei** non-alcoholic, bsd. Am. soft; 2**isch** alcoholic.

all all; jeder: every; **vor ~em** most of all.

All n the universe.

Allee f avenue.

allein alone; only; ~**stehend** Person: alone in the world; single; Gebäude etc.: isolated; detached.

allemal: ein für ~ once (and) for all.

aller|best very best; ~**dings** indeed; int. certainly!; ~**erst** very first; **zu ~erst** first of all.

Allergie f allergy.

aller|hand, ~lei all kinds od. sorts of; ~**letzt** very last; ~**meist** most; **am ~meisten** most of all; ~**nächst** very next; ~**neu(e)st** very newest; ~**wenigst: am ~en** least of all.

allgemein general; üblich:

common; **im ~en** in general, generally; 2**heit** f general public.

Alliierte m ally.

all|jährlich annual(ly); ~**mählich** gradual(ly); 2**tag** m everyday life, daily routine; ~**täglich** daily; fig. common; ~**zu** (much) too; ~**zuviel** too much.

Alm f alpine pasture, alp.

Almosen pl alms pl.

Alpen pl the Alps pl.

Alphabet n alphabet; 2**isch** alphabetical.

Alptraum m nightmare.

als nach comp.: than; ganz so wie: as; nach Negation: but; zeitlich: when, as; ~ **ob** as if, as though.

also therefore.

alt old; aged; ancient; schal: stale; second-hand.

Altar m altar.

Alte m od. f old man od. woman; **die ~n** pl the old people pl.

Alter n age; **im ~ von** at the age of; **er ist in meinem ~** he is my age.

älter older; senior; **der ~e Bruder** the elder brother; ~**e Dame** elderly lady.

altern grow old, age.

Altersheim n old people's home.

Alter|tum n antiquity; ~**tümer** pl antiquities pl.

ältest oldest; Schwester etc.: eldest.

alt|klug precocious; ~**modisch** old-fashioned; 2**papier** n waste paper; 2-

stadt f old (part of a) town od. city.

Aluminium n aluminium, Am. aluminum; **~folie** f tin foil.

Amateur m amateur.

Amboß m anvil.

ambulan|t: **~er Patient** outpatient; **♀z** f ambulance.

Ameise f ant.

Amerikan|er m American; **♀isch** American.

Amme f (wet-)nurse.

Amnestie f amnesty.

Ampel f hanging lamp; traffic light(s pl).

Ampulle f ampoule.

amputieren amputate.

Amsel f blackbird.

Amt n office; Aufgabe: duty; (telephone) exchange; **♀lich** official.

Amulett n amulet, charm.

amüs|ant amusing, entertaining; **~ieren** amuse; **sich ~ieren** enjoy o.s., have a good time.

an on; at; upon; in; against; to; by; **am 1. März** on March 1st; **von ~** from on.

Analyse f analysis.

Ananas f pineapple.

Anarchie f anarchy.

anatomisch anatomical.

Anbau m agr. cultivation; arch. annex(e), extension; **♀en** grow; arch. add.

anbehalten keep on.

anbei enclosed.

an|beißen bite into; Fisch: bite; **~beten** adore, worship.

Anbetracht m: **in ~** considering.

an|bieten offer; **~binden** bind, tie (up).

Anblick m sight; spectacle; **♀en** look at; glance at.

an|brechen v/t Vorräte: break into; Flasche: open; v/i begin; Tag: break, dawn; **~brennen** burn; **~bringen** bring; fix, attach; **~brüllen** roar at.

An|dacht f devotion; prayers pl; **♀dächtig** devout.

andauern continue, go on; **~d** continual, constant.

Andenken n memory, remembrance; keepsake, souvenir; **zum ~ an** in memory of.

ander other; verschieden: different; folgend: next; **ein ~er** another; **nichts ~es** nothing else; **unter ~em** among other things; **~erseits** on the other hand. [change.]

ändern: (sich) ~ alter,

andernfalls otherwise, (or) else.

anders otherwise; different(ly); else; **~ werden** change; **~wo** elsewhere.

anderthalb one and a half.

Änderung f change; alteration.

andeuten hint; imply.

Andrang m rush, run.

an|drehen Gas etc.: turn on; Licht: a. switch on; **~eignen: sich ~** appropriate, seize; *Kenntnisse*: acquire.

aneinander together; **~geraten** clash.

anekeln disgust, nauseate, sicken.

anerkenn|en acknowledge, recognize; *lobend*: appreciate; **~ung** *f* acknowledg(e)ment, recognition; appreciation.

anfahren start; **j-n ~** run into s.o.; *fig.* snap at s.o.

Anfall *m* fit, attack; **~en** attack.   [to).]

anfällig susceptible **(für** ~

Anfang *m* beginning, start; **~en** begin, start.

Anfänger *m* beginner; learner.

anfangs at the beginning.

Anfangsbuchstabe *m* initial (letter); **großer ~** capital (letter).

an|fassen *packen*: seize; *berühren*: touch; **mit ~fassen** lend a hand; **~fechten** contest, dispute; **~fertigen** make, manufacture; **~feuchten** moisten, wet; **~feuern** *sp.* cheer; **~flehen** implore.

Anflug *m aer.* approach (flight); *fig.* touch.

anforder|n demand; request; **~ung** *f* demand; request; **~ungen** *pl* requirements *pl*.

Anfrage *f* inquiry.

an|freunden: sich ~ make friends; **~fühlen: sich ~** feel.

anführ|en lead; *zitieren*:

quote; *täuschen*: dupe, fool; **~er** *m* (ring)leader; **~ungszeichen** *pl* quotation marks *pl*, inverted commas *pl*.

Angabe *f* declaration, statement; *colloq.* bragging, showing off; **~n** *pl* information *sg*; directions *pl*.

angeb|en declare, state; *einzeln*: specify; *Namen, Grund*: give; *colloq.* brag, show off; **~er** *m colloq.* braggart; **~lich** supposed.

angeboren innate, inborn; *med.* congenital.

Angebot *n* offer; *Auktion*: bid; *econ.* supply.

ange|bracht appropriate, suitable; **~bunden: kurz ~** curt, short; **~heitert** *colloq.* slightly tipsy.

angehen *colloq.*: go on; begin, start; *j-n*: concern; **das geht dich nichts an** that is no business of yours.

angehör|en belong to; **~ige** *pl* relations *pl*, relatives *pl*.

Angeklagte *m, f* the accused, defendant.

Angel *f Tür*: hinge; fishing-rod.

Angelegenheit *f* business, concern, affair, matter.

angelehnt: ~ sein to be ajar.

Angel|gerät *n* fishing-tackle; **~haken** *m* fishhook; **~n** *on fish*; **~rute** *f* fishing-rod; **~schnur** *f* fishing-line.

ange|messen suitable; adequate (*dat* to); **~nehm**

pleasant; ~regt animated, lively; ~sehen respected.

Angesicht n face, countenance; 2s in view of.

angespannt fig. tense.

Angestellte m, f employee; **die ~n** pl the staff sg.

ange|wandt applied; ~wiesen: ~ auf dependent (up)on.

ange|wöhnen: sich ~ take to; 2wohnheit f habit.

Angina f angina, tonsillitis.

Angler m angler.

anglikanisch Anglican.

angreife|n touch; feindlich: attack; Gesundheit: affect; chem. corrode; 2r m aggressor.

angrenzen border (an on).

Angriff m attack, assault.

Angst f fear (vor of); **ich habe ~** I am afraid.

ängst|igen frighten, alarm; ~lich fearful, timid.

anhaben have on.

anhalt|en continue, last; stop; **den Atem ~en** hold one's breath; ~end continuous; 2er m hitchhiker; **per 2er fahren** hitchhike; 2spunkt m clue.

Anhang m appendix, supplement; followers pl.

anhäng|en attach; 2er m adherent, follower; Schmuck: pendant; Schild: label, tag; Wagen: trailer; ~lich devoted, attached.

an|häufen: (sich) accumulate; ~heben lift, raise.

Anhöhe f rise, hill.

anhören listen to; **sich ~** sound.

Ankauf m purchase.

Anker m anchor; 2n anchor.

Anklage f accusation, charge; 2n (gen, wegen) accuse (of), charge (with).

anklammern clip s.th. on; **sich ~** cling (an to).

Anklang m: ~ finden meet with approval.

an|kleben stick on; mit Leim: glue on; mit Kleister: paste on; ~kleiden dress (a. sich); ~klopfen knock (an at); ~knipsen switch on; ~kommen arrive; ~kommen auf depend (up)on; ~kreuzen tick.

ankündig|en announce; 2ung f announcement.

Ankunft f arrival.

an|lächeln, ~lachen smile at.

Anlage f Bau: construction, building; Vorrichtung: installation; Werk: plant; Anordnung: plan, layout; zu e-m Schreiben: enclosure; econ. investment; Fähigkeit: talent; ~n pl grounds pl, park.

anlangen arrive (in, an at); fig. concern.

Anlaß m occasion; cause.

anlasse|n Kleidung: leave od. keep on; Licht etc.: leave on; tech. start; 2r m mot. starter.

anläßlich on the occasion of.

Anlauf m start; sp. run; ℒen start (up); run up; Metall: tarnish; Spiegel etc.: cloud over; mar.call at.

anlege|n put (an to, against); Garten: lay out; Straße: build; Verband: apply; Geld: invest; mar. land; ℒstelle f landing-stage.

anlehnen Tür: leave od. set ajar; (sich) ℒ an lean against od. on.

anleit|en instruct; ℒung f instruction.

anliegen fit close od. tight(ly); ℒ n request.

an|machen colloq. fasten, fix; Feuer: make, light; colloq. Licht: switch on; Salat: dress; ℒmalen paint; ℒmaßend arrogant.

Anmelde|formular n registration form; application form; ℒegebühr f registration fee; ℒn announce; notify; sich ℒn bei make an appointment with; ℒung f registration; appointment.

anmerk|en mark; see, notice; laß dir nichts ℒen! don't give yourself away; ℒung f note; Fußnote: a. footnote.

Anmut f grace, charm; ℒig charming, graceful.

an|nageln nail on; ℒnähen sew on; ℒnähernd approximate.

Annahme f acceptance (a. fig.); fig. assumption.

annehm|bar acceptable;

Preis: reasonable; ℒen accept (a. v/i); take; fig. suppose, assume, Am. guess; sich ℒen e-r Sache od. j-s: take care of s.th. od. s.o.; ℒlichkeit f amenity.

Annonce f advertisement.

anonym anonymous.

Anorak m anorak.

anordn|en arrange; order; ℒung f arrangement; order.

an|packen seize, grasp; ℒpassen adapt, adjust; ℒpflanzen cultivate, plant; ℒprobieren try od. fit on; ℒrechnen charge; credit.

Anrecht n right, title, claim (auf to).

Anrede f address; ℒn address, speak to.

anregen stimulate; suggest; ℒ d stimulating.

Anreiz m incentive.

Anrichte f sideboard; ℒn Speisen: prepare, dress; Schaden: cause.

Anruf m call; ℒen call; teleph. ring up, colloq. phone, Am. call (up).

anrühren touch; mix.

Ansage f announcement; ℒn announce; ℒr(in f) m announcer.

an|schaffen procure; get; purchase; ℒschalten switch od. turn on.

anschau|en look at; view; ℒlich clear, vivid, graphic.

Anschein m appearance; allem ℒ nach = ℒend apparently.

anschicken: sich ℒ, et. zu

tun get ready to do s.th.

Anschlag m touch; *tech.* stop; notice; *Plakat:* placard, poster, bill; (criminal) attempt; **~brett** n notice-board, *Am.* bulletin board; **2en** touch; strike, knock (**an** against); *Plakat:* post *od.* put up.

anschließen connect; **sich ~ j—m:** join; **~d** subsequent (-ly); afterwards.

Anschluß m connection, *a.* connexion; **~ finden an** make friends with; **~ haben an** *rail.*, *Boot:* connect with; **~zug** m connection.

an|schmiegen: sich ~ nestle up to; **~schmieren** (be)smear; *fig. colloq.* cheat; **~schnallen: sich ~** fasten one's seat-belt; **~schnauzen** *colloq.* snap at; **~schneiden** cut; *Thema:* broach; **~schrauben** screw on; **~schreien** shout at.

Anschrift f address.

an|schuldigen accuse; **~schwellen** swell (*a.* fig.); *Fluß:* rise; *fig.* increase; **~schwemmen** wash ashore.

ansehen (take a) look at; see; regard, consider; **2** n prestige; respect.

ansehnlich considerable; good-looking.

an|sengen singe; **~setzen** put (**an** to); **~stücken** add (**an** to); *Termin:* fix, appoint.

Ansicht f sight, view; *fig. s.* **Meinung; ~skarte** f picture postcard; **~ssache** f matter of opinion.

ansied|eln: (sich) ~ settle; **2lung** f settlement.

anspann|en stretch; harness (to the carriage); *fig.* strain; **2ung** f *fig.* strain.

anspielen: ~ auf allude to, hint at.   [spur on.\]

Ansporn m spur; **2en**\}

Ansprache f address, speech.

ansprechen speak to, address; **~d** appealing.

anspringen leap at; *Motor:* start.

Anspruch m claim (**auf** to); **2slos** modest; simple; **2svoll** hard to please, fastidious.   [institution.\]

Anstalt f establishment;\}

An|stand m good manners *pl;* decency, propriety; **2-ständig** decent; respectable; *Preis:* reasonable; **2standslos** readily, without hesitation.

anstarren stare *od.* gaze at.

anstatt instead of.

an|stecken pin on; fasten on; *Ring:* put on; *med.,* fig. infect; **~end** *med.* infectious (*a.* fig.), *Berührung:* contagious; *fig.* catching; **2ung** f infection, contagion.

an|stehen queue (up), line up; **~steigen** rise, ascend; *fig.* increase; **stellen** employ; *colloq. tun:* do; *s.* **an-, einschalten; sich ~ stel-**

len queue (up), line up.

Anstieg m ascent; rise.

an|stiften instigate; ~**stimmen** strike up.

Anstoß m Fußball: kick-off; fig. initiative; ~ **erregen** give offence; ~ **nehmen an** take offence at; 2en push; knock; nudge; **auf j-s Gesundheit** 2en drink (to) s.o.'s health.

anstößig shocking.

anstrahlen illuminate; j-n: beam at.

anstreiche|n paint; Fehler etc.: mark, underline; 2r m house-painter.

anstreng|en exert; strain; Augen: try; j-n: fatigue; **sich** ~**en** exert o.s.; ~**end** strenuous; trying (für to); 2**ung** f exertion, strain, effort.

Anstrich m (coat of) paint.

Anteil m share, portion; ~ **nehmen an** take an interest in; sympathize with; ~**nahme** f interest; sympathy.

Antenne f aerial. [otic.)

Antibiotikum n antibi-)

antik antique.

Antilope f antelope.

Antiquari|at n second-hand bookshop; 2**sch** second-hand.

Antiquität f antiques pl; ~**laden** m antique shop.

antiseptisch antiseptic.

Antlitz n face, countenance.

Antrag m offer, proposal;

parl. motion; ~**steller** m applicant.

an|treffen find; ~**treiben** drift ashore; drive (on); ~**treten** line up; Amt, Erbe: enter upon; Reise: set out on.

Antrieb m drive, propulsion; fig. impulse, drive.

antun: j-m et. ~ do s.th. to s.o.; **sich et.** ~ lay hands on o.s.

Antwort f answer, reply; 2en answer, reply.

an|vertrauen (en)trust; confide; ~**wachsen** take root; fig. increase.

Anwalt m s. **Rechtsanwalt.** (aspirant.)

Anwärter m candidate,)

anweis|en zuweisen: assign; anleiten: instruct; befehlen: direct, order; 2**ung** f assignment; instruction; direction, order.

anwend|en use; apply; 2**ung** f application; use.

anwesen|d present; 2**heit** f presence.

anwidern s. **anekeln.**

Anzahl f number, quantity.

anzahl|en pay on account; 2**ung** f first instal(l)ment, deposit.

anzapfen tap. [sign.)

Anzeichen n symptom,)

Anzeige f notice; Zeitung: advertisement; 2**n** notify; advertise; Instrument: indicate; Thermometer: read; report s.o. to the police.

anziehen Schraube: tighten; *Kleidung*: put on; *j-n*: dress (*a.* **sich**); *fig.* attract; **~d** attractive.

Anzug m suit.

anzüglich personal.

anzünden light, kindle; *Streichholz*: strike; *Gebäude*: set on fire.

apathisch apathetic.

Apfel m apple; **~mus** n apple-sauce; **~saft** m apple juice; **~sine** f orange; **~wein** m cider.

Apostel m apostle.

Apostroph m apostrophe.

Apotheke f chemist's shop, pharmacy, *Am.* drugstore; **~r** m chemist, *Am.* druggist.

Apparat m apparatus; telephone; **am ~!** speaking!; **am ~ bleiben** hold the line.

Appartement n flat, *Am.* apartment.   (to).}

appellieren appeal (**an** f

Appetit m appetite; **~an-regend,** **~lich** appetizing.

applau|dieren applaud; **~s** m applause.

Aprikose f apricot.

April m April.

Aquarell n water-colo(u)r.

Aquarium n aquarium.

Äquator m equator.

Arab|er m Arab; **~isch** Arabian, Arab(ic).

Arbeit f work; labo(u)r; job; **~en** work; labo(u)r; **~er(in** f) m worker; **~ge-ber** m employer; **~neh-mer** m employee.

Arbeits|amt n labo(u)r ex-

change; **~kraft** f worker, hand; **~los** out of work, unemployed; **~lose** m, f unemployed person; **die ~lo-sen** pl the unemployed pl; **~losenunterstützung** f unemployment benefit, *colloq.* dole; **~losigkeit** f unemployment; **~pause** f break; **~platz** m job; **~tag** m workday; **~unfähig** incapable of working; *ständig*: disabled; **~zeit** f working time; working hours pl; **~zimmer** n study.

Archäolog|e m arch(a)eologist; **~ie** f arch(a)eology.

Architekt m architect; **~ur** f architecture.

Archiv n archives pl; record office.

Arena f arena; bullring.

arg bad.

Ärger m *Verdruß*: vexation, annoyance; *Zorn*: anger; **~lich** vexed, angry; annoying, vexatious; **~n** annoy, vex; **sich ~n** be angry.

Arg|wohn m suspicion; **~wöhnisch** suspicious.

Arie f aria.

arm poor.

Arm m arm; *Fluß*: branch.

Armaturenbrett n dashboard.

Armband n bracelet; **~uhr** f wrist watch.

Armee f army.

Ärmel m sleeve; **~kanal** m the (English) Channel.

ärmlich s. armselig.

armselig poor; wretched, miserable; *schäbig*: shabby.

Armut f poverty.

Aroma n flavo(u)r.

Arrest m arrest; **~ bekommen** be kept in.

arrogant arrogant.

Art f kind, sort; *bot.*, *zo.* species; *Weise*: manner, way.

Arterie f artery.

artig good, well-behaved; civil, polite.

Artikel m article (*a. gr.*); *econ. a.* commodity.

Artillerie f artillery.

Artist m performer, artiste.

Arznei f, **~mittel** n medicine.

Arzt m doctor; physician.

Ärzt|in f (woman *od.* lady) doctor; **2lich** medical.

As n ace.

Asche f ash(es pl); **~nbahn** f cinder-track; *mot.* dirttrack; **~nbecher** m ashtray; **~rmittwoch** m Ash Wednesday.

Asiat m Asian, Asiatic; **2isch** Asian, Asiatic.

asozial antisocial; asocial.

Asphalt m asphalt.

Assistent m branch, bough.

Ast m branch, bough.

Aster f aster.

Asthma n asthma.

Astro|naut m astronaut; **~nomie** f astronomy.

Asyl n asylum.

Atelier n studio.

Atem m breath; **außer ~** out of breath; **~ holen**

draw *od.* take breath; **2los** breathless; **~zug** m breath.

Äther m ether.

Athlet m, **~in** f athlete; **2isch** athletic.

atlantisch Atlantic.

atmen breathe.

Atmosphäre f atmosphere.

Atmung f breathing.

Atom n atom; *in Zssgn*: atomic, nuclear; **2ar** atomic; **~bombe** f atomic *od.* atom bomb, A-bomb; **~energie** f atomic *od.* nuclear energy; **~forschung** f atomic *od.* nuclear research; **~kraftwerk** n nuclear power station; **~reaktor** m s. **Reaktor**; **~waffe** f nuclear weapon.

Attent|at n (criminal) attempt; (attempted) assassination; **~äter** m assassin.

Attest n certificate.

Attrappe f dummy.

Attribut n attribute; *gr. a.* attributive.

ätzend corrosive, caustic (*a. fig.*); *fig.* biting.

au *int.* oh!; ouch!

auch also, too; even; **~ nicht** neither, nor.

Audienz f audience.

auf *prp* (*dat*) (up)on; in; at; *prp* (*acc*) on; in; at; to; up; **~ (... zu)** towards; **~ deutsch** in German; *adv* open; **~ und ab gehen** walk up and down, walk to and fro; *int.*: **~!** up!

aufatmen breathe again.

Aufbau m building; construction; ~en erect, build; construct;

auf|bekommen *Tür*: get open; *Aufgabe*: be given; ~**bewahren** keep; preserve; ~**bieten** summon (up); ~**binden** untie; ~**blasen** blow up, inflate; ~**bleiben** sit up; *Tür etc.*: remain open; ~**blenden** *mot.* turn up the headlights; ~**blicken** look up; ~**blühen** blossom (out); ~**brausen** fly into a passion; ~**brechen** break *od.* force open; burst open; *fig.* set out; 2**bruch** *m* departure, start; 2**brühen** *s.* **aufgießen;** ~**bügeln** press, iron; ~**decken** uncover; *Bettdecke*: turn down; *fig.*: expose; disclose; ~**drängen** force *od.* obtrude (up)on; ~**drehen** turn on; ~**dringlich** obtrusive; 2**druck** *m* imprint; *Briefmarken*: surcharge.

aufeinander one upon the other; ~**folgend** successive; consecutive; ~**prallen** collide.

Aufenthalt *m* stay; delay; ~ **haben** *rail.* stop; 2**ge- nehmigung** *f* residence permit; ~**sraum** *m* lounge.

Auferstehung *f* resurrection.

auf|essen eat up; ~**fahren** *Person*: start up; ~**fahren auf** *mot.* run into; 2**fahrt** *f* drive, *Am.* driveway; ~**fallen** be conspicuous; *j-m* ~**fallen** strike *s.o.*;

~**fallend,** ~**fällig** striking; *Kleider*: flashy; ~**fangen** catch.

auffass|en comprehend; *deuten*: interpret; 2**ung** *f* interpretation; view.

auffinden find, discover.

auffordern ask; invite; 2**ung** *f* invitation; request.

auffrischen freshen (up).

aufführ|en *thea.* (re)present, perform; *eintragen*: list, enter; **sich** ~**en** behave; 2**ung** *f thea.* performance.

auffüllen fill up.

Aufgabe *f* task; duty; problem; homework; *Preisgabe*: abandonment; *Geschäfts2*: giving up.

Aufgang *m* ast. rising; staircase.

auf|geben give up; abandon; *Anzeige*: insert; *Brief*: post, *Am.* mail; *Telegramm*: send; *Gepäck*: register, *Am.* check; *Hausaufgabe*: set, *Am.* assign; ~**gehen** open; *Naht*: come open; *hochgehen*: rise.

aufge|legt disposed, in the mood; **gut** *od.* **schlecht** ~**legt** in a good *od.* bad humo(u)r; ~**schlossen** *fig.* open-minded; ~**weckt** *fig.* bright.

auf|gießen *Tee*: infuse, brew, make; ~**greifen** *fig.* take up; ~**haben** *colloq. Hut*: have on; *Aufgabe*: have to do; *Geschäft*: be open; ~**halten** keep open; *anhalten*: stop, detain; *Ver-*

kehr: hold up; **sich ~halten** stay.

aufhänge|n hang (up); *tech.* suspend; **Qr** *m* tab.

auf|heben lift (up); raise; pick up; *aufbewahren:* keep, preserve; *abschaffen:* abolish; *Versammlung:* break up; **~heitern** cheer up; **sich ~heitern** brighten (up); **~hellen: (sich) ~hellen** brighten (up); **~hetzen** incite, instigate; **~holen** make up for; gain (**gegen** on); **~hören** cease, stop, *Am.* quit; **~kaufen** buy up; **~klären** clear up (*a.* **sich**); enlighten (**über** on); **~kleben** paste up; **~knöpfen** unbutton; **~kochen** boil up; **~krempeln** turn *od.* roll up; **~laden** load; *electr.* charge.

Auflage *f Buch:* edition; *Zeitung:* circulation.

auflassen *colloq.:* leave open; *Hut:* keep on.

Auflauf *m* crowd; *Speise:* soufflé; baked sweet *od.* savo(u)ry pudding; *Qn Zinsen:* accrue; *Schiff:* run aground.

auf|legen apply; *Platte:* put on; *Buch:* print, publish; *teleph.* hang up; **~lehnen: sich ~lehnen** rebel, revolt; **~lesen** gather, pick up; **~leuchten** flash (up).

auflös|en undo, loosen; *Versammlung:* break up; *Ehe, Geschäft etc.:* dissolve; *Rätsel:* solve; **(sich) ~en** *chem.* dissolve; **Qung** *f*

(dis)solution; disintegration.

aufmachen open; *Knoten:* undo; *Schirm:* put up.

aufmerksam attentive; **j-n ~ machen auf** call s.o.'s attention to; **Qkeit** *f* attention.

aufmuntern cheer up.

Aufnahme *f Empfang:* reception; *Zulassung:* admission; *phot.* photograph; **e-e ~ machen** take a photograph; **~gebühr** *f* admission fee; **~prüfung** *f* entrance examination.

auf|nehmen take up; *Diktat etc.:* take down; *geistig:* take in; admit; receive; *Verhandlungen etc.:* enter into; *phot.* take; *filmen:* shoot; *mus. etc.:* record; **~passen** *Schule:* be attentive; *vorsichtig sein:* look out; **~passen auf** look after; pay attention to; **~platzen** burst (open).

Aufprall *m* impact; **Qen: ~ auf** crash into.

Aufpreis *m* extra charge.

auf|pumpen pump *od.* blow up; **~räumen** clean up, tidy (*v/i:* up).

aufrecht upright (*a. fig.*), erect; **~erhalten** maintain, uphold.

aufreg|en excite; **sich ~en** get upset (**über** about); **Qung** *f* exoitement.

auf|reiben *Haut:* chafe; *fig.* wear out; **~reißen** *v/t* rip *od.* tear open; *Straße:* tear up; *Tür:* fling open;

Augen: open wide; *v/i* split, burst; **~richten** set up, erect; **sich ~richten** sit up; **~richtig** sincere; candid; **~rollen** roll up; unroll; **~rücken** move up.

Aufruf *m* call, summons; **2en** *j-n*: call *s.o.'s* name.

Aufruhr *m* uproar, tumult; riot, rebellion. [ment.⟩

Aufrüstung *f* (re)arma-⟩

aufsagen recite, repeat.

Aufsatz *m* essay; *Schul2*: composition; *tech.* top.

auf|saugen absorb; **~schieben** slide open; *fig.* put off, postpone, adjourn.

Aufschlag *m* impact; extra charge; *Mantel*: lapel; *Hose*: turn-up; *Ärmel*: cuff; *Tennis*: service; **2en** *v/t* open; *Zelt*: pitch; *v/i* strike, hit; *Tennis*: serve.

auf|schließen unlock, open; **~schneiden** cut open; *Fleisch*: cut up; *colloq.* brag, boast.

Aufschnitt *m* (slices *pl* of) cold meat, *Am.* cold cuts *pl.*

auf|schnüren untie; *Schuh*: unlace; **~schrauben** unscrew; screw (**auf** on); **~schrecken** startle; start (up).

Aufschrei *m* shriek, scream.

aufschrei|ben write down; **~en** cry out, scream.

Aufschrift *f* inscription; *Brief*: address; label.

Aufschub *m* delay.

aufschürfen *Haut*: graze.

Aufschwung *m econ.* boom.

aufsehen look up; **2** *n*

sensation; **2 erregen** cause a sensation; **~erregend** sensational.

Aufseher *m* overseer, supervisor.

aufsetzen put on; *Dokument*: draw up; **sich ~** sit up.

Aufsicht *f* inspection, supervision; **~srat** *m* board of directors.

auf|spannen *Schirm*: put up; **~sparen** save; reserve; **~sperren** unlock; **~spießen** pierce; *mit Hörnern*: gore; **~springen** jump up; *Tür*: fly open; *Haut*: chap; **~stacheln** goad, incite; **~stampfen** stamp (one's foot).

Auf|stand *m* insurrection, uprising, revolt; **~ständische** *m* rebel.

auf|stapeln pile up; **~stecken** pin up; *Haar*: put up; **~stehen** stand up; rise, get up; stand open; **~steigen** rise, ascend; *Reiter*: mount.

aufstellen set *od.* put up; *Kandidaten*: nominate; *Rechnung*: draw up; *Rekord*: set up, establish; **2ung** *f* nomination; list.

Aufstieg *m* ascent; *fig.* rise.

auf|stoßen push open; *Essen*: repeat; *Person*: belch; **2strich** *m* spread; **~stützen** ~ lean (**auf** on); **~suchen** *Ort*: visit; go to see; **~tanken** fill up; (re)fuel; **~tauchen**

emerge; *fig.* turn up; **~tauen** thaw; **~teilen** divide (up).

Auftrag *m* commission; order (*a. econ.*); instruction; **2en Speisen:** serve; *Farbe:* lay on.

auf|treffen strike, hit; **~trennen** undo; **~treten** tread; *thea. etc.:* appear; behave; *Schwierigkeiten:* arise. [impetus, drive.)

Auftrieb *m* buoyancy;)

Auftritt *m thea.* scene (*a. fig.*); *Schauspieler:* appearance.

auf|wachen wake (up); **~wachsen** grow up.

Aufwand *m* expense, expenditure; extravagance.

aufwärmen warm up.

Aufwartefrau *f* charwoman, *Am. a.* cleaning woman.

aufwärts upward(s).

aufwasch|en wash up; 2**~wasser** *n* dishwater.

auf|wecken wake (up); **~weichen** soak; soften; become soft; **~weisen** show.

aufwert|en revalue; 2**ung** *f* revaluation.

auf|wickeln: (**sich**) ~ wind od. roll up; **~wiegeln** stir up, incite; **~wiegen** *fig.* make up for; **~wirbeln** whirl up; *Staub:* raise; **~wischen** wipe up; **~zählen** enumerate.

aufzeichn|en draw; note down; record; 2**ung** *f* note; record.

aufziehen draw *od.* pull

up; *öffnen:* (pull) open; *Uhr etc.:* wind (up); *Kind:* bring up; **j-n** ~ tease s.o.

Aufzug *m* lift, *Am.* elevator; *thea.* act.

aufzwingen: j-m et. ~ force s.th. upon s.o.

Augapfel *m* eyeball.

Auge *n* eye; *Sehkraft:* sight; *bot.* eye, bud; **im** ~ **behalten** keep an eye on; **aus den** ~**n verlieren** lose sight of.

Augen|arzt *m* oculist; **~blick** *m* moment, instant; 2**blicklich** *adj* instantaneous; *vorübergehend:* momentary; *gegenwärtig:* present; *adv* instant(aneous)ly; *at present;* **~braue** *f* eyebrow; **~licht** *n* eyesight; **~lid** *n* eyelid; **~zeuge** *m* eye-witness.

August *m* August.

Auktion *f* auction.

Aula *f* (assembly) hall, *Am.* auditorium.

aus *prp* out of; from; of; for; by; in; ~ **dies em Grunde** for this reason; *adv* out; over; *auf Geräten:* **an** - ~ on - off.

aus|arbeiten work out; *sorgsam:* elaborate; **~atmen** breathe out; **~bauen** extend; develop; **~bessern** repair.

Ausbeute *f* profit; *Ertrag:* yield; *Bergbau:* output; 2**n** exploit (*a. fig.*).

ausbild|en develop; train, instruct; educate; *mil.* drill; 2**ung** *f* development;

training, instruction; education; *mil.* drill.

ausbleiben stay away, fail to appear.

Ausblick *m* outlook, view.

aus|brechen break out; **~breiten** spread (out); stretch; **sich ~breiten** spread.

Ausbruch *m* outbreak (*a. fig.*); *Vulkan:* eruption; *Flucht:* escape; *Gefühl:* outburst.

aus|brüten hatch (*a.fig.*); **~bürsten** brush.

Ausdauer *f* perseverance; **2nd** persevering.

ausdehn|en: (sich) ~ extend; expand; **2ung** *f* extension; expansion.

aus|denken think *s.th.* out; devise, invent; *vorstellen:* imagine; **~drehen** *s.* **ausschalten.**

Ausdruck *m* expression.

ausdrück|en press,squeeze (out); *Zigarette:* stub out; express; **~lich** express.

ausdrucks|los expressionless; *leer:* blank; **~voll** expressive; **2weise** *f* mode of expression; style.

Ausdünstung *f* odo(u)r, smell.

auseinander asunder, apart; broken up; **~brin gen** separate; **~fallen** fall apart; *fig.* break up; **~ge hen** *Versammlung:* break up; *Meinungen:* differ; *Freunde:* part; *Menge:* disperse; **~nehmen** take apart; *tech.* dismantle.

auseinandersetz|en:sich ~ *mit Problem:* grapple with; *j-m:* argue with; **2ung** *f* discussion; argument.   [choice.⟩

auserlesen exquisite.⟩

ausfahr|en go *od.* take for a drive; *Baby:* take out (in the pram); **2t** *f* departure; *Ausflug:* drive, ride; gateway, drive; exit, way out.

ausfall|en fall out; *Maschine etc.:* break down; *nicht stattfinden:* be cancel(l)ed; *Ergebnis:* turn out; **~end** insulting; **2straße** *f* arterial road.

aus|fegen sweep (out); **~findig : ~ machen** find out; **~fließen** flow *od.* run out.

Ausflucht *f:* **Ausflüchte machen** make excuses.

Ausflug *m* excursion, trip.

ausfragen question (**über** about), sound (**über** on).

Ausfuhr *f* export(ation).

ausführen execute, carry out; *econ.* export; *j-n:* take out.

Ausfuhrgenehmigung *f* export permit *od.* licen|ce (*Am.* -se).

ausführlich *adj* detailed; *umfassend:* comprehensive; *adv* in detail, at (some) length.

Ausführung *f* execution; workmanship; model, make.

Ausfuhr|verbot *n* export ban; **~zoll** *m* export duty.

ausfüllen fill in (*bsd. Am.* out).

Ausgabe *f* distribution; *Buch:* edition; *Geld:* expense, expenditure.

Ausgang *m* exit, way out; end; result; **~spunkt** *m* starting-point.

ausgeben give out; *Geld:* spend; **sich ~ für** pass o.s. off for.

ausge|beult baggy; **~bucht** booked up; **~dehnt** extensive, vast.

ausgehen go out; *Haare:* fall out; *Geld, Vorräte:* run out; end.

ausge|lassen frolicsome; **~nommen** except; **~rechnet:** **~ er** he of all people; **~ heute** today of all days; **~schlossen** impossible; **~schnitten** low-necked; **~sucht** exquisite; choice; **~zeichnet** excellent.

ausgiebig abundant, plentiful; *Mahlzeit:* substantial.

aus|gießen pour out; **~gleichen** equalize (*a. sp.*); *Verlust:* compensate; **~gleiten** slip; **~graben** dig out up; excavate.

Ausguß *m* sink.

aus|halten endure, bear, stand; **~händigen** deliver up, hand over.

Aushang *m* notice.

aus|hängen hang *od.* put out; *Tür:* unhinge; **~harren** hold out; **~helfen** help out; **~höhlen** hollow out;

~holen: (mit der Hand) ~ raise one's hand; **~horchen** sound, pump; **~kehren** sweep (out); **~kennen: sich ~ in** (*dat*) know a place; know all about s.th.; **~kleiden** *tech.* line, coat; **~klopfen** beat (out); *Pfeife:* knock out; **~klopfen** *colloq.* *s.* ausschalten; **~kommen: ~ mit** *et.:* manage with; *j-m:* get on with.

Auskunft *f* information; **=~sbüro** *n* inquiry office, *Am.* information desk.

aus|kuppeln declutch; **~lachen** laugh at; **~laden** unload.

Auslage *f* display, show; **~n** *pl* expenses *pl.*

Ausland *n:* **das ~** foreign countries *pl;* **ins** *od.* **im ~** abroad.

Ausländ|er *m,* **~erin** *f* foreigner; **2isch** foreign.

Auslands|aufenthalt *m* stay abroad; **~korrespondent** *m* foreign correspondent; **~reise** *f* journey abroad.

auslass|en *Fett:* render down; *Saum:* let down; *Wort:* leave out, omit; miss out; **2ungszeichen** *n* apostrophe.

aus|laufen leak; end; *mar.* (set) sail; **~leeren** empty.

ausleg|en lay out; *Waren:* a. display; deuten: interpret; *Geld:* advance; **2ung** *f* interpretation. [loan.}

ausleihen lend, *Am.* a.}

Auslese f selection; **2n** pick out, select; *Buch:* finish reading.

ausliefer|n deliver; *Verbrecher:* extradite; **2ung** f delivery; extradition.

aus|löschen *Licht:* put out, switch off; *Feuer etc.:* extinguish (*a. fig.*); wipe out (*a. fig.*); **~lösen** draw lots.

auslöse|n *tech.* release; *Gefangene:* redeem, ransom; *Pfand:* redeem; *fig.* start; **2r** m release.

aus|lüften air; **~machen** *betragen:* amount to; *Feuer:* put out; *Licht etc. s.* **ausschalten;** *vereinbaren:* agree on, arrange; **würde es Ihnen et. ~machen zu ...?** would you mind (*ger*) ...?

Ausmaß n extent.

ausmessen measure.

Ausnahm|e f exception; **2los** without exception; **2weise** (just) for once.

aus|nutzen utilize; *Gelegenheit:* take advantage of; *j-n, et.:* exploit; **~packen** unpack; **~pressen** squeeze (out); **~probieren** try, test.

Auspuff m exhaust; **~gase** pl exhaust fumes pl; **~topf** m silencer; *Am.* muffler.

aus|radieren erase; **~rangieren** discard; **~rasieren: den Nacken ~rasieren** shave the neck clean; **~rauben** rob; **~räumen** empty, clear out; **~rechnen** calculate.

Ausrede f excuse; **2n** finish speaking; **2n lassen** hear *s.o.* out.

ausreichen suffice, be enough; **~d** sufficient.

Ausreise f departure; **2n** leave (a country); **~visum** n exit visa.

aus|reißen pull out; *colloq.* run away; **~renken** dislocate; **~richten** *Botschaft:* give; *erreichen:* accomplish, achieve; **~rotten** exterminate.

Ausruf m cry; exclamation; *ling.* interjection; **2en** cry out, exclaim; **~ezeichen** n, **~ungszeichen** n exclamation mark (*Am. a.* point).

ausruhen (sich) **~** rest.

ausrüst|en fit out, equip; **2ung** f outfit; equipment.

ausrutschen slip.

Aussage f statement; declaration; *jur.* evidence; *gr.* predicate; **2n** state, declare; *jur.* give evidence.

aus|saugen suck (out); **~schalten** *Licht:* switch off; *Gas etc.:* turn off od. out; **~scheiden** eliminate; *med.* secrete; retire (**aus** from); *sp.* drop out; **~scheren** jump the queue; **~schimpfen** scold; **~schlafen** get enough sleep; sleep late.

Ausschlag m *med.* rash; *Zeiger:* deflection; **2en** *v/i Pferd:* kick; *Zeiger:* deflect; *v/t* knock out; *fig.*

reject; ⚲**gebend** decisive.

ausschließ|en shut *od.* lock out; *fig.:* exclude; *ausstoßen:* expel; **⚬lich** exclusive.

Ausschluß *m* exclusion; expulsion.

aus|schmücken decorate; *fig.* embellish; **⚬schneiden** cut out.

Ausschnitt *m Kleid:* (low) neck; *Zeitung:* cutting, clipping; *fig.* section.

ausschreiben write out; *Rechnung* etc.: make out; *Stelle:* advertise.

Ausschreitung *f* excess.

Ausschuß *m* substandard goods *pl*; *Vertretung:* committee.

aus|schütteln shake out; **⚬schütten** pour out; spill; **⚬schweifend** dissolute.

aussehen look; ⚲ *n* look(s *pl*), appearance.

aussein *colloq.:* be out; be over.

außen (on the) outside; **nach ⚬** outward(s).

Außen|bordmotor *m* outboard motor; **⚬handel** *m* foreign trade; **⚬minister** *m* foreign minister, *Brit.* Foreign Secretary, *Am.* Secretary of State; **⚬politik** *f* foreign policy; **⚬seite** *f* outside; **⚬seiter** *m* outsider; **⚬welt** *f* outer *od.* outside world.

außer out of; except; besides; **⚬ wenn** unless; **⚬dem** besides, moreover.

äußere exterior, outer, outward; ⚲ *n* exterior, outside; outward appearance.

außer|gewöhnlich exceptional; **⚬halb** outside, out of; *jenseits:* beyond.

äußerlich external, outward.

äußern utter, express.

außerordentlich extraordinary.

äußerst outermost; *fig.* utmost; extreme(ly).

außerstande unable.

Äußerung *f* utterance, remark.

aussetzen *v/t Belohnung:* offer; *et.*, *j-n*, *sich:* expose (*dat* to); **et. auszusetzen haben** an find fault with; *v/i* stop; *Motor:* a. fail; **mit et. ⚬** interrupt s.th.

Aussicht *f* view (*auf* of); *fig.* chance; **⚲slos** hopeless, desperate.

aus|söhnen: sich ⚬ (mit) become reconciled (with); **⚬sortieren** sort out; **⚬spannen** *fig.* (take a) rest, relax; **⚬sperren** shut out; lock out; **⚬spielen** *v/t Karte:* lead.

Aus|sprache *f* pronunciation, accent; talk, discussion; **⚲sprechen** pronounce; express; finish speaking; **⚬spruch** *m* remark.

aus|spucken spit out; **⚬spülen** rinse.

ausstatt|en furnish, supply; **⚲ung** *f* equipment; furnishings *pl*; *Buch:* get-up.

aus|stehen be outstanding; endure, bear; ~steigen get out od. off, alight.
ausstell|en exhibit, display; Rechnung, Scheck: make out; Paß: issue; 2er m exhibitor; 2ung f exhibition, show.
aussterben die out.
Aussteuer f trousseau.
aus|stopfen stuff, pad; ~stoßen eject; Schrei: utter; Seufzer: heave; fig. expel; ~strahlen radiate; ~strecken stretch (out); ~streichen strike out od. off; ~strömen stream out; Gas, Dampf: escape; Geruch: exhale; ~suchen choose, select.
Austausch m exchange; 2en exchange.
austeilen distribute.
Auster f oyster.
austragen Briefe etc.: deliver; Wettkampf: hold.
Australi|er m Australian; 2sch Australian.
aus|treiben drive out; vertreiben: a. expel; ~treten tread od. stamp out; Schuhe etc.: wear down; ~treten aus leave, resign from; ~trinken drink up; finish; ~trocknen dry (up); Boden, Kehle: parch; ~üben exercise; Beruf: practi|se, Am. ~ce, follow; Einfluß, Druck: exert.
Ausverkauf m sale; 2t sold out; thea. a. full house.
Auswahl f choice, selection; econ. assortment.

auswählen choose, select.
Auswander|er m emigrant; 2n emigrate; ~ung f emigration.
auswärts out of town; von ~ from another place od. town.
aus|waschen wash out; ~wechseln: ~ (gegen) (ex)change (for), replace (by).
Ausweg m way out.
Ausweiche f road widening, Am. turnout; 2n make way (dat for); evade, avoid (a. fig.); 2nd evasive.
Ausweis m identity card; 2en expel; sich 2en prove one's identity; ~papiere pl identification papers pl; ~ung f expulsion.
aus|weiten: (sich) ~ widen, stretch, expand; ~wendig by heart; ~werten evaluate; verwerten: exploit; ~wickeln unwrap; ~wirken: sich ~ auf affect; ~wischen wipe out; ~wringen wring out; ~zahlen pay (out); pay s.o. off; sich ~zahlen pay; ~zählen count (out); 2zahlung f payment.
auszeichn|en mark; fig. distinguish (sich o.s.); 2ung f marking; fig. distinction, hono(u)r; Orden: decoration; award, prize.
ausziehen draw out; Kleid: take off; undress (a. sich); aus e-r Wohnung: move (out).
Auszug m departure; removal; Buch etc.: extract,

excerpt; *Konto*: statement (of account).
Auto *n* (motor-)car; ~**fahren** drive, motor.
Autobahn *f* motorway, *Am.* superhighway, freeway; ~**ausfahrt** *f* (motorway) exit, slip-road; ~**einfahrt** *f* access road, slip-road; ~**gebühr** *f* toll; ~**zubringer** *m* feeder road.
Autobiographie *f* autobiography.
Autobus *m* (motor-)bus; (motor-)coach; ~**bahnhof** *m* bus terminal; ~**haltestelle** *f* bus stop.
Auto|**fähre** *f* car ferry; ~**fahrer** *m* motorist, driver.
Autogramm *n* autograph.
Auto|**händler** *m* car dealer; ~**hilfe** *f* breakdown service; ~**karte** *f* road

map; ~**kino** *n* drive-in cinema.
Automat *m* slot-machine, vending-machine; ~**enrestaurant** *n* automat; ~**ion** *f* automation; 2**isch** automatic.
Auto|**mechaniker** *m* car mechanic; ~**mobil** *n* s.
Auto; ~**mobilklub** *m* automobile association.
Autor *m* author. [rier.⟩
Autoreisezug *m* car-car-⟩
Autorin *f* author(ess).
autori|**sieren** authorize; ~**tär** authoritarian; 2**tät** *f* authority.
Auto|**straße** *f* (motor) road; ~**verkehr** *m* (motor) traffic; ~**verleih** *m* car hire (*Am.* car rental) service; ~**zubehör** *n* (car) accessories *pl.*
Axt *f* ax(e).

B

Baby *n* baby.
Bach *m* brook.
Backbord *n* port.
Backe *f* cheek.
backen bake.
Backen|**bart** *m* (side-)whiskers *pl*, *Am.* sideburns *pl*; ~**zahn** *m* molar (tooth).
Bäcker *m* baker; ~**ei** *f* baker's shop; bakery.
Back|**hähnchen** *n* fried chicken; ~**obst** *n* dried fruit; ~**ofen** *m* oven; ~**stein** *m* brick.
Bad *n* bath; *s.* **Badeort**.

Bade|**anstalt** *f* baths *pl*; ~**anzug** *m* bathing-costume, bathing-suit; ~**hose** *f* (swimming- *od.* bathing-)trunks *pl*; ~**kappe** *f* bathing-cap; ~**mantel** *m* bathrobe; ~**meister** *m* bath attendant; 2**n** *v/t* bathe; *Augen, Wunde*: bathe; *v/i* have *od.* take a bath; *im Freien*: bathe; 2**n gehen** go swimming; ~**ort** *m* spa; seaside resort; ~**strand** *m* (bathing) beach; ~**tuch** *n* bath-towel; ~**wanne** *f* bath(tub);

~zimmer n bathroom.

Bagger m excavator; **2n** excavate.

Bahn f course; railway, Am. railroad; mot. lane; ast. orbit; sp. track; Eis2: rink, Kegel2: alley; **mit der ~** by train; **~damm** m railway (Am. railroad) embankment; **2en: sich e-n Weg ~** force one's way; **~hof** m (railway, Am. railroad) station; **~steig** m platform; **~übergang** m level (Am. grade) crossing.

Bahre f stretcher.

Bai f bay; kleine: creek.

Bakterie f bacterium, germ.

bald soon; fast: almost, nearly; **so ~ wie** as soon as. [rafter.]

Balken m beam; Dach: ∫

Balkon m balcony.

Ball m ball; ball, dance.

ballen Faust: clench.

Ballen m bale; anat. ball.

Ballett n ballet.

Ballon m balloon.

Ball|saal m ballroom; **~spiel** n ball-game.

Bambus m bamboo.

banal commonplace, banal.

Banane f banana.

Band[1] m volume.

Band[2] n band; ribbon; Meß2, Ton2, Ziel2: tape; anat. ligament; fig. bond, tie.

bandagieren bandage.

Bande f gang, band.

bändigen tame; subdue (a. fig.); fig. restrain.

Bandscheibe f interverte-bral disc.

bang(e) anxious, uneasy; **mir ist ~** I am afraid.

Bank f bench; Schul2: desk; econ. bank; **~beamte** m bank clerk od. official; **~ier** m banker; **~konto** n bank(ing) account; **~note** f (bank)note, Am. (bank) bill.

bankrott bankrupt.

Bann m ban; fig. spell.

Banner n banner.

bar: (in) ~ (in) cash.

Bar f bar; nightclub.

Bär m bear.

Baracke f barrack, hut.

barfuß barefoot.

Bargeld n cash, ready money.

barmherzig merciful.

Barometer n barometer.

Barren m metall. bar, ingot; sp. parallel bars pl.

Barriere f barrier.

Barrikade f barricade.

barsch rude, gruff, rough.

Bart m beard; Schlüssel: bit.

bärtig bearded.

Barzahlung f cash payment.

Basar m bazaar.

Basis f base; fig. basis.

Baskenmütze f beret.

Bast m bast; Geweih: velvet.

basteln build.

Batterie f battery.

Bau m building; Tier2: burrow, den, Fuchs: earth.

Bauarbeite|n pl construction work; **~r** m construction worker.

Bauch m abdomen, belly; *Schmer2:* paunch; **~schmerzen** pl, **~weh** n belly-ache sg, gripes pl, stomach-ache sg.

bauen build; construct.

Bauer[1] m farmer.

Bauer[2] n, m (bird-)cage.

Bäuer|in f farmer's wife; **2lich** rustic.

Bauern|haus n farmhouse; **~hof** m farm.

bau|fällig out of repair, dilapidated; **2gerüst** n scaffold(ing); **2herr** m owner; **2holz** n timber, Am. lumber; **2jahr** n: **~1973** 1973 model od. make.

Baum m tree.

baumeln: **~ mit** dangle od. swing s.th.

Baum|stamm m (tree-)trunk; **~wolle** f cotton.

Bauplatz m building plot od. site.

Bausch m wad, pad; **2en:** **sich ~** bulge, swell out.

Bau|stein m brick; Spielzeug: a. (building) block; **~stelle** f building site; **~unternehmer** m building contractor; **~werk** n building.

Bayer m Bavarian; **2isch** Bavarian.

Bazillus m bacillus, germ.

beabsichtigen intend, mean.

beacht|en pay attention to; befolgen: observe; **~lich** considerable.

Beamt|e m, **~in** f official, officer; civil servant.

be|ängstigend alarming; **~anspruchen** claim, demand; Zeit, Raum: take up; tech. stress; **~anstanden** object to; **~antragen** apply for; **~antworten** answer, reply to; **~arbeiten** work (on); **~aufsichtigen** supervise; Kind: look after; **~auftragen** commission; **~bauen** build on; agr. cultivate, till.

beben shake, tremble; Erde: quake.

Becher m cup.

Becken n basin, Am. a. bowl; anat. pelvis.

bedächtig deliberate.

bedanken: sich bei j-m ~ thank s.o.

Bedarf m: **~ (an)** need (of); econ. demand (for); **~haltestelle** f request stop.

bedauerlich deplorable.

bedauern j-n: feel sorry for, pity; et.: regret; **2** n regret; pity; **~swert** pitiable.

bedeck|en cover; **~t** Himmel: overcast.

bedenk|en consider; **~lich** doubtful; dangerous.

bedeuten mean; **~d** important; beträchtlich: considerable.

Bedeutung f meaning; Wichtigkeit: importance; **2slos** insignificant; **2svoll** significant.

bedien|en v/t serve; wait on; tech. operate; Tele-

fon: answer; **sich** ~**en** help o.s.; *v/i* serve; *bei Tisch*: wait at (*Am.* on) table; *Karten*: follow suit; ℓ**ung** *f* service; waiter, waitress; shop assistant (*pl*).

Bedingung *f* condition; ℓ**slos** unconditional.

bedrängen press hard, beset.

bedroh|en threaten; ~**lich** threatening. {*ject.*}

bedrücken depress, de-}

Bedürf|nis *n* need, want; ~**nisanstalt** *f* public convenience, *Am.* comfort station; ℓ**tig** needy, poor.

be|eilen: sich ~ hasten, hurry; ~**eindrucken** impress; ~**einflussen** influence; ~**einträchtigen** impair, injure; ~**end(ig)en** end, finish; ~**erben: j-n** ~ be s.o.'s heir.

beerdig|en bury; ℓ**ung** *f* funeral; ℓ**ungsinstitut** *n* undertakers *pl.*

Beere *f* berry.

Beet *n* bed.

be|fahrbar passable, practicable; ~**fangen** embarrassed; ~**fassen: sich** ~ **mit** engage in, occupy o.s. with; deal with.

Befehl *m* command; order; ℓ**en** command; order.

be|festigen fasten, fix, attach (**an** to); *mil.* fortify; ~**feuchten** moisten.

befinden: sich ~ be; ℓ **2** *n* (state of) health.

befolgen follow; obey.

beförder|n convey, carry; transport; *spedieren*: forward; promote (**zum Major** [to] major); ℓ**ung** *f fig.* promotion.

be|fragen question, interview; ~**freien** free, rescue; ~**freundet:** ~ **sein** be friends.

befriedig|en satisfy; ~**gend** satisfactory; ℓ**gung** *f* satisfaction.

befruchten fertilize.

befugt authorized. [*pl.*]

Befund *m* result; findings}

be|fürchten fear; ~**fürworten** support, advocate.

begab|t gifted, talented; ℓ**ung** *f* gift, talent.

begegn|en: (sich) ~ meet; ℓ**ung** *f* meeting.

be|gehen *Verbrechen*: commit; *Fehler*: make; ~**gehren** desire.

begeister|n: sich ~ **für** become enthusiastic over; ~**t sein** be delighted; ℓ**ung** *f* enthusiasm.

Begier|de *f* desire; ℓ**ig** eager, desirous.

begießen water; *Braten*: baste.

Beginn *m*, ℓ**en** *s.* **Anfang, anfangen.**

be|glaubigen attest, certify; ~**gleichen** pay, settle.

begleit|en accompany; **j-n nach Hause** ~ see s.o. home; ℓ**er** *m* companion; ℓ**ung** *f* company; *mus.* accompaniment.

be|glückwünschen congratulate; ~**gnadigen** pardon; ~gnügen: sich ~ mit be content with; ~graben bury; 2gräbnis n funeral; ~greifen comprehend, understand; ~greiflich: j-m et. ~ machen make s.o. understand s.th.; ~grenzen bound; limit, restrict.

Begriff m idea, notion; im ~ sein zu be about to, be going to.

begründen establish, found; give reasons for.

begrüß|en greet, welcome; 2ung f greeting, welcome.

be|günstigen favo(u)r; ~haart hairy; ~haglich comfortable, cosy, snug; ~halten retain; keep (für sich to o.s.); remember.

Behälter m container; box; Flüssigkeit: tank.

behand|eln treat (a. med.); Thema: deal with; 2lung f treatment.

beharren persist (auf in).

behaupt|en assert (sich o.s.); maintain; 2ung f assertion.

be|heben remove; Schaden: repair; ~helfen: sich ~ mit make shift with; ~ sich ~ ohne do without; ~helfsmäßig temporary, makeshift; ~hend(e) nimble, agile.

beherrsch|en rule (over), govern; Lage etc.: be in control of; Sprache: have command of; sich ~en control o.s.; 2ung f command, control.

be|hilflich: j-m ~ sein help s.o. (bei in); ~hindern hinder; obstruct.

Behörde f mst authorities pl. [tle.]

behutsam cautious; gen-

bei räumlich: by, near; at, with; zeitlich: by, in, during; on; (present) at; ~ Schmidt care of (abbr. c/o) Schmidt; ~ j-m at s.o.'s (house etc.), with s.o.; ~Tag by day; ~ s-r Ankunft on his arrival; ~ Tisch at table; ~ der Arbeit at work; j-n ~m Namen nennen call s.o. by his name; ~ günstigem Wetter weather permitting.

bei|behalten keep up, retain; ~bringen teach; Niederlage, Wunde etc.: inflict (dat on).

Beichte f confession; 2n confess.

beide both; unbetont: two; alle ~ both; e-r von ~n either of them; nur wir ~ just the two of us.

beieinander together.

Beifahrer m (front-seat) passenger; assistant driver; sp. co-driver.

Beifall m approval; applause.

beifügen Brief: enclose.

Beigeschmack m slight flavo(u)r; taste.

Beihilfe f aid; allowance; Stipendium: grant.

Beil n hatchet; chopper; ax(e).

Beilage f Zeitung: supplement; Speisen: vegetables pl, side-dish, colloq. trimmings pl.

beiläufig casual.

beilegen enclose; Streit: settle.

Beileid n condolence.

beimessen attach (dat to).

Bein n leg.

beinah(e) almost, nearly.

beisammen together.

Beisein n presence.

beiseite aside, apart.

beisetz|en bury; 2ung f funeral.

Beispiel n example; zum ~ for example; 2haft exemplary; 2los unexampled.

beißen bite; ~d biting, pungent.

Bei|stand m assistance; 2stehen assist, help.

Beitrag m contribution; share; Mitglieds2: subscription; Zeitung: article; 2en contribute.

beitreten join.

Beiwagen m side-car.

bejahen answer in the affirmative; ~d affirmative.

bejahrt aged.

bekämpfen fight (against); fig. oppose.

bekannt known (dat to); j-n mit j-m ~ machen introduce s.o. to s.o.; 2e m, f acquaintance, mst friend; ~geben announce; ~lich as is generally known; 2machung f publication; public notice; 2schaft f acquaintance.

bekennen admit; confess; sich schuldig ~ jur. plead guilty.

beklag|en lament; sich ~en complain (über of, about); 2te m, f defendant, the accused.

bekleid|en clothe, dress; 2ung f clothing, clothes pl.

be|kommen get; receive; obtain; Zug etc.: catch; Kind: be going to have; Krankheit: get, catch; Hunger etc.: get; j-m: agree with; ~kräftigen confirm; ~laden load; fig. burden.

Belag m covering, coat (-ing); Zunge: fur; Brot: filling, spread. [f siege.]

belagern besiege; 2ung f.

be|langlos unimportant; ~lasten load; Konto: charge, debit; jur. incriminate; fig. burden; ~lästigen molest; trouble, bother; 2lastung f load; jur. burden; ~laufen: sich ~ auf amount to; ~lebt Straße: busy, crowded.

Beleg m document; ~schein: voucher; 2en Platz: reserve; beweisen: prove; Vorlesungen: enrol(l) for; ein Brötchen mit et. 2en put s.th. on a roll, fill a roll with s.th.; ~schaft f personnel, staff; 2t engaged, occupied; Platz: taken; Hotel etc.: full; Stimme: thick, husky; Zunge: coated, furred.

belehren teach; inform.

beleibt corpulent, stout.

beleidig|en offend, *stärker:* insult; **~end** offensive, insulting; **2ung** *f* offen|ce, *Am.* -se, insult.

beleucht|en light (up), illuminate; **2ung** *f* light (-ing); illumination.

Belgi|er *m* Belgian; **2sch** Belgian.

belicht|en *phot.* expose; **2ung** *f phot.* exposure; **2ungsmesser** *m* exposure meter; **2ungszeit** *f* (time of) exposure.

belieb|ig any; *jeder* **~ige** anyone; **~t** popular (*bei* with); **2theit** *f* popularity.

beliefern supply.

bellen bark. [*f* reward.)

belohn|en reward; **2ung** *f*)

be|lügen *j-n* ~ lie to s.o.; **~malen** paint; **~mängeln** find fault with.

bemerk|en notice, perceive; *äußern:* remark; **~kenswert** remarkable (**wegen** for); **2kung** *f* remark.

bemitleiden pity; **~swert** pitiable.

bemüh|en trouble; **sich ~en** trouble (o.s.); endeavo(u)r; **2ung** *f* trouble; endeavo(u)r, effort.

benachrichtig|en inform, notify; *econ.* advise; **2ung** *f* information; notification; *econ.* advice.

benachteilig|en place *s.o.* at a disadvantage; **2ung** *f* disadvantage.

benehmen: sich ~ behave (o.s.); **2** *n* behavio(u)r, conduct.

beneiden envy (*j-n um et.* s.o. s.th.); **~swert** enviable.

benennen name.

Bengel *m* (little) rascal, urchin.

benommen stunned.

benötigen need, want, require.

benutz|en use, make use of; *Bus etc.:* take; **2er** *m* user; **2ung** *f* use.

Benzin *n chem.* benzine; *mot.* petrol, *Am.* gasoline.

beobacht|en observe; *genau:* watch; **2er** *m* observer; **2ung** *f* observation.

bepacken load.

bequem convenient; easy; comfortable; *Person:* easy-going; *faul:* lazy.

berat|en *j-n:* advise; *et.:* discuss (**über et.** s.th.); **sich ~en** confer; **2er** *m* adviser; **2ung** *f* consultation, conference.

berauben deprive (*gen* of).

berechn|en calculate; *econ.* charge; **~end** calculating; **2ung** *f* calculation.

berechtig|en entitle; authorize; **~t** entitled; qualified; *Anspruch:* legitimate.

Bereich *m* area; reach; *fig.* scope, sphere; *Wissenschaft etc.:* field, province; **2ern** enrich (**sich** o.s.).

Bereifung *f* tyres *pl*, (*Am. nur*) tires *pl*.

bereit ready; **~en** prepare; *Freude etc.:* give; **~halten** hold *s.th.* ready; **~s** al ready; 2schaft f readiness; ~stellen place s.th. ready; provide; ~willig ready.

bereuen repent (of).

Berg m mountain; die Haare standen ihm zu ~e his hair stood on end; 2ab downhill (a. fig.); 2~ auf uphill; ~bahn f mountain railway; ~bau m mining. [cue.]

bergen recover; j~n: res-]

berg|ig mountainous; 2~ mann m miner; 2rutsch m landslide; 2steiger m mountaineer, climber.

Bergung f recovery; Menschen: rescue.

Bergwerk n mine.

Bericht m: ~ (über) report (on), account (of); 2en report; Presse: a. cover (über et. s.th.); ~erstatter m reporter; correspondent.

berichtigen correct.

bersten burst (vor with).

berüchtigt notorious (wegen for).

berücksichtigen consider.

Beruf m calling; Gewerbe: trade; vocation, occupation, colloq. job; höherer ~: profession; 2en: sich ~ auf refer to; 2lich professional.

Berufs|ausbildung f vocational od. professional training; ~beratung f vocational guidance; ~kleidung f working clothes pl; ~schule f vocational school; ~sportler m pro-

fessional; 2tätig working; ~tätige m, f employed person; die ~tätigen pl the working people pl.

Berufung f Ernennung: appointment; reference (auf to); ~ einlegen jur. appeal.

beruhen: ~ auf be based on; et. auf sich ~ lassen let a matter rest.

beruhig|en quiet, calm; soothe; sich ~ calm down; 2ungsmittel n sedative. [brated.]

berühmt famous, cele-]

berühr|en touch; 2ung f contact, touch.

Besatzung f crew; mil. occupation troops pl.

beschädig|en damage; 2ung f damage (gen to).

beschaffen procure; provide; Geld: raise; 2heit f state, condition.

beschäftig|en employ, occupy; keep busy; 2ung f employment; occupation.

beschämen make s.o. feel ashamed; ~d shameful; humiliating.

Bescheid m: ~ bekommen be informed; ~ geben let s.o. know; ~ wissen know.

bescheiden modest; 2~ heit f modesty.

bescheinig|en certify, attest; acknowledge; 2ung f certification; Schein: certificate; Quittung: receipt; Bestätigung: acknowledg(e)ment.

be|scheren: j-n ~ give s.o. presents; ~schießen od. shoot at od. on; bombard; ~schimpfen abuse, insult.

Beschlag m metal fitting(s pl); mit ~ belegen seize; monopolize s.o.'s attention; ℒen tech. fit, mount; Pferd: shoe; Fenster, Wand: steam up; Spiegel: cloud over; ℒnahmen seize; confiscate; mil. requisition.

beschleunig|en hasten, speed up; mot. accelerate; ℒung f acceleration.

beschl|ießen end; close; sich entscheiden: resolve, decide; ℒuß m decision.

be|schmieren (be)smear; ~schmutzen soil, dirty; ~schneiden trim, clip; Haare, Hecke etc.: trim; clip; fig. cut down, curtail; ~schönigen gloss over.

beschränk|en confine, limit, restrict; sich ~en auf confine o.s. to; ℒung f limitation, restriction.

beschreib|en Papier: write on; fig. describe; ℒung f description; account.

beschrift|en inscribe; label; ℒung f inscription.

beschuldig|en (gen) accuse (of [doing] s.th., bsd. jur. charge (with); ℒte m, f the accused; ℒung f accusation, charge.

beschützen protect.

Beschwer|de f complaint (a. med.); ℒen burden; sich ℒen complain (über about,

of; bei to); ℒlich tedious.

be|schwichtigen appease, calm (down); ~schwingt elated, elevated; ~schwipst colloq. tipsy; ~schwören et.: take an oath on; j-n: implore, entreat; ~seitigen remove; do away with.

Besen m broom. [by).\
besessen obsessed (von)\
besetz|en occupy (a. mil.); Stelle: fill; thea. cast; Kleid: trim; ℒt engaged, occupied; Platz: taken; Bus etc.: full up; teleph. engaged, Am. busy; ℒung f thea. cast; mil. occupation.

besichtig|en visit, see; inspect (a. mil.); ℒung f visit (gen to); inspection (a. mil.); sightseeing.

besied|eln settle; bevölkern: populate; ℒung f settlement.   [beat.\
besieg|en conquer; defeat,\
Besinnung f reflection; Bewußtsein: consciousness; ℒslos unconscious.

Besitz m possession; ℒen possess; ~er m possessor, owner, proprietor.

besohlen (re)sole.

Besoldung f pay; Beamte: salary.

besonder particular, special; ~s especially; hauptsächlich: chiefly.

besonnen prudent, calm.

besorg|en get, procure; do, manage; ℒnis f apprehension, fear, anxiety; ~niserregend alarming; ~t uneasy, worried (**um** about); 2ung *f*: ~en **machen** go shopping.

besprech|en discuss, talk *s.th.*over; *Buch etc.*: review; 2ung *f* discussion; conference; review.

besspritzen splash, (be-)spatter.

besser better; superior; **um so** ~ all the better; ~n (make) better, improve; **sich** ~ get *od.* become better, improve; 2ung *f* improvement; **gute** 2ung! I wish you a speedy recovery!

best best; ~en **Dank** thank you very much; **am** ~en best.

Bestand *m* (continued) existence; *Vorrat*: stock; ~ **haben** last.

beständig constant, steady; *dauerhaft*: lasting; *Wetter*: settled.

Bestandteil *m* part; component; *Mischung*: ingredient. [strengthen.]

besstärken confirm,

bestätig|en confirm; attest; *Behauptung etc.*: verify; *Empfang*: acknowledge; **sich** ~en prove (to be) true; 2ung *f* confirmation; attestation; verification; acknowledg(e)ment.

Beste *m, f* the best (one); ~ *n* the best (thing).

bestechen bribe.

Besteck *n* knife, fork and spoon; cutlery.

bestehen *Prüfung*: pass;

exist; ~ **auf** insist (up)on; ~ **aus** consist of.

be|stehlen steal from; ~**steigen** *Berg*: climb (up); *Pferd*: mount; *Thron*: ascend.

bestell|en order; *Zimmer etc.*: book, *bsd. Am.* reserve; *j-n*: make an appointment with; *Boden*: cultivate, till; *Grüße*: give; **zu sich** ~en ask to come; 2ung *f* order; booking, *bsd. Am.* reservation.

Bestie *f* beast; *fig. a.* brute.

bestimm|en determine, decide; *Preis*: fix; *Termin, Ort*: *a.* appoint; ~**en für** mean for; ~**t** determined, firm; *Absicht etc.*: definite; certain(ly); 2ungsort *m* destination.

bestraf|en punish (**wegen, für** for); 2ung *f* punishment.

bestrahlen *med.* irradiate.

Bestreb|en *n,* ~**ung** *f* effort.

be|streichen spread; ~**streiten** deny.

bestürz|t dismayed; 2ung *f* consternation, dismay.

Besuch *m* visit; call; *Besucher*: visitor(s *pl*); 2**en** visit; call on; *Schule etc.*: attend; ~**er** *m* visitor, caller; ~**szeit** *f* visiting hours *pl*.

be|tasten touch, feel, finger; ~**tätigen** *tech.* operate; *Bremse*: apply; **sich** ~**tätigen** work, busy o.s.

betäub|en stun (*a. fig.*), daze; *med.*: an(a)esthetize; 2ung *f med.*: an(a)estheti-

zation; *Zustand:* an(a)es-
thesia; *fig.* stupefaction;
ℓungsmittel *n* narcotic,
an(a)esthetic.

Bete *f:* **rote** ~ beetroot, red
beet.

beteilig|en give a share **(an**
in); **sich ~en (an)** take
part (in), participate (in);
ℓte *m, f* person *od.* party
concerned; **ℓung** *f* participation; share.

beten pray.

beteuern protest.

Beton *m* concrete.

beton|en stress; *fig. a.* em-
phasize; **ℓung** *f* stress; *fig.*
emphasis.

be|trachten look at; *fig.*
consider; **~trächtlich** considerable.

Betrag *m* amount, sum;
ℓen amount to; **sich ~en**
behave (o.s.); **~en** *n* be-
havio(u)r, conduct.

betreffen concern; **was ...**
betrifft as for, as to; **~d**
concerning; concerned, in
question.

be|treten step on; *eintreten:*
enter; *verlegen:* embar-
rassed; **~treuen** look after.

Betrieb *m* business, firm;
Fabrik: plant, works *od.*
workshop, *Am. a.* shop; *fig.*
bustle; **außer** ~ out of
order; **in** ~ working.

Betriebs|ferien *pl* works
holidays *pl;* **~leitung** *f*
management; **~rat** *m*
works council; **~unfall** *m*
industrial accident.

be|trinken: sich ~ get

drunk; **~troffen** hit **(von**
by); *fig.* disconcerted.

Be|trug *m* fraud; deceit;
ℓtrügen deceive, cheat;
~trüger *m* cheat, fraud;
impostor.

betrunken drunken; *pred*
drunk; **ℓe** *m, f* drunk.

Bett *n* bed; **~bezug** *m*
plumeau case; **~couch** *f*
studio couch; **~decke** *f*
blanket.

betteln beg **(um** for).

Bett|gestell *n* bedstead; **ℓ-**
lägerig bedridden, con-
fined to bed; **~laken** *n*
sheet.

Bettler *m* beggar.

Bett|uch *n* sheet; **~vorle-**
ger *m* bedside rug; **~wä-**
sche *f* bed-linen; **~zeug** *n*
bedding, bed-clothes *pl.*

betupfen dab.

beugen bend, bow; **sich** ~
bend; *fig.* bow *(dat* to).

Beule *f* bump, swelling; *im*
Blech: dent.

be|unruhigen make *s.o.*
anxious; **sich ~unruhigen**
worry; **~urlauben** give
s.o. time off; *vom Amt:* suspend; **~urteilen** judge.

Beute *f* booty, spoil(s *pl*);
e-s Tieres: prey *(a. fig.).*

Beutel *m* bag; *zo., Tabaks~:*
pouch.

Bevölkerung *f* population.

bevollmächtig|en author-
ize; **ℓte** *m, f* authorized
person *od.* agent, proxy,
deputy.

bevor before.

bevor|stehen be approaching, be near; *Gefahr*: be imminent; **j-m ~stehen** await s.o.; **~zugen** prefer.

bewach|en guard, watch; **♀ung** *f* guard; escort.

bewaffn|en arm; **♀ung** *f* armament; *Waffen*: arms *pl*.

bewahren keep, preserve; **~ vor** save from.

bewähr|en: sich ~ stand the test; **sich ~ als** prove to be; **sich nicht ~** prove a failure; **♀ungsfrist** *f jur.* probation.

be|waldet wooded, woody; **~wältigen** overcome, master; **~wandert** (well) versed.

bewässer|n water; *Land etc.*: irrigate; **♀ung** *f* watering; irrigation.

beweg|en (sich) move, stir; **j-n ~ zu** induce *od.* get s.o. to; **♀grund** *m* motive; **~lich** movable; *Person, Geist etc.*: agile, active; **~t** *Meer*: rough; *Leben*: eventful; *fig.* moved, touched; **♀ung** *f* movement; motion (*a. phys.*); **in ♀ung setzen** set in motion; **~ungslos** motionless.

Beweis *m* proof (**für** *of*); **~e** (*pl*) evidence (*bsd. jur.*); **♀en** prove; **~material** *n* evidence; **~stück** *n* (piece of) evidence; *jur.* exhibit.

bewerb|en: sich ~ um apply for; *kandidieren*: stand for, *Am.* run for; **♀er** *m* applicant; **♀ung** *f* application; candidature;

♀ungsschreiben *n* (letter of) application.

be|werten rate; **~willigen** grant, allow; **~wirken** cause, bring about.

bewirt|en entertain; **~ schaften** *agr.* cultivate, farm; *Gut etc.*: manage, run; *Waren*: manage; *Devisen*: control; **♀ung** *f* entertainment.

bewohn|en inhabit, live in, occupy; **♀er** *m* inhabitant, occupant.

bewölk|en: sich ~ cloud over; **~t** clouded, cloudy, overcast; **♀ung** *f* clouds *pl.*

bewunder|n admire (**wegen** for); **♀ung** *f* admiration.

bewußt deliberate, intentional; **sich ~ sein** be aware of; **~los** unconscious; **♀- sein** *n* consciousness.

bezahl|en pay; *Ware*: pay for; *Schuld*: pay off, settle; **♀ung** *f* payment; settlement. [enchanting.]

bezaubernd charming, }

bezeichn|en mark; describe; call; **~end** characteristic; **♀ung** *f* name.

bezeugen testify (to).

bezieh|en cover; *Wohnung*: move into; *Waren, Zeitung*: get; **ein Kissen ~en** put a clean case on a pillow; **das Bett ~en** put clean sheets on the bed; **sich ~en** cloud over; **sich ~en auf** refer to; **♀ung** *f* relation; **in dieser ♀ung** in this respect; **~ungsweise** respectively; or rather.

Bezirk *n* district, *Am. a.* precinct.

Bezug *m* cover(ing), case; *Kissen: a.* slip; **~ nehmen auf** refer to.

Bezüge *pl* earnings *pl.*

be|zwecken aim at, intend; **~zweifeln** doubt, question.

Bibel *f* Bible.

Biber *m* beaver.

Bibliothek *f* library; **~ar** *m* librarian.

biblisch biblical.

bieg|en: (sich) ~ bend; **um e-e Ecke ~** turn (round) a corner; **~sam** flexible; **2ung** *f* bend.

Biene *f* bee; **~königin** *f* queen bee; **~korb** *m*, **~stock** *m* (bee)hive.

Bier *n* beer; **helles ~** pale beer, ale; **dunkles ~** dark beer; stout, porter; **~deckel** *m* beer-mat; **~krug** *m* beer-mug.

Biest *n* beast, brute.

bieten offer; *Auktion:* bid; **sich ~** offer itself, arise.

Bilanz *f* balance; *Aufstellung:* balance-sheet.

Bild *n* picture, photograph; illustration; *Gemälde:* painting; *fig.* idea.

bilden: (sich) ~ form; *fig.* educate (o.s.).

Bild|erbuch *n* picturebook; **~hauer** *m* sculptor; **2lich** figurative; **~nis** *n* portrait; **~röhre** *f* (television) tube; **~schirm** *m* screen.

Bildung *f* forming, formation; *Aus2:* education.

Billard *n* billiards *sg.*

billig cheap, inexpensive; **~en** approve of; **2ung** *f* approval.

Binde *f* band; *med.* bandage; *s.* **Damenbinde**; **~glied** *n* connecting link; **~haut** *f* *anat.* conjunctiva; **~hautentzündung** *f* conjunctivitis; **2n** bind; tie; *Krawatte:* knot; **2nd** binding; **~r** *m* (neck)tie; **~strich** *m* hyphen.

Bindfaden *m* string; *stärker:* pack-thread.

Bindung *f* binding (*a.* Ski); *fig.* tie, link, bond.

Binnen|land *n* inland, interior; **~schiffahrt** *f* inland navigation.

Biographie *f* biography.

Biologie *f* biology.

Birke *f* birch(-tree).

Birne *f* pear; *electr.* bulb.

bis *räumlich:* to, as far as; *zeitlich:* till, until (*a. cj*), to, by; **zwei ~ drei** two or three; **alle ~ auf** all but, all except.

Bischof *m* bishop.

bisher until now, so far.

Biß *m* bite.

bißchen: ein ~ *adj* a little, a (little) bit of; *adv* a little (bit). **{~morsel.)**

Bissen *m* bite; mouthful,**{**

bissig biting (*a. fig.*); **Achtung, ~er Hund!** beware of the dog.

Bitte *f* request (**um** for); **2n: ~ um** ask for; **bitte**

please; (wie) bitte? (I beg your) pardon?; **bitte (sehr)!** not at all, you're welcome.

bitter bitter.

Bittschrift f petition.

bläh|en med. cause flatulence; Segel: swell; **sich ~en** Segel: swell out; **2un-gen** pl flatulence, wind.

Blam|age f disgrace, shame; **2ieren: sich ~** make a fool of o.s.

blank shining, shiny, bright.

Bläschen n small blister.

Blase f Luft: bubble; Haut: blister (a. tech.); anat. bladder; **2n** blow.

Blas|instrument n wind-instrument; **~kapelle** f brass band.

blaß pale (**vor** with); **~ werden** turn pale.

Blässe f paleness.

Blatt n leaf; Papier2 etc.: sheet; Säge: blade; Karten: hand; (news)paper.

blättern: ~ in leaf through.

Blätterteig m puff pastry.

blau blue; colloq. drunk, tight; **~er Fleck** bruise; **~es Auge** black eye; **2-beere** f bilberry.

bläulich bluish.

Blausäure f prussic acid.

Blech n sheet metal; plate; Back2: baking-sheet; fig. colloq. rubbish; **~büchse** f, **~dose** f tin, Am. can; **~schaden** m mot. body-work damage.

Blei n lead.

bleiben remain, stay; **am Apparat ~** hold the line; **~d** lasting; **~lassen** leave s.th. alone; stop s.th.

bleich pale (**vor** with); **~en** bleach; blanch.

blei|ern (of) lead, leaden (a. fig.); **2stift** m (lead) pencil; **2stiftspitzer** m pencil-sharpener.

Blende f blind; phot. diaphragm, (f-)stop; **~ 8** f-8; **2n** blind, dazzle.

Blick m look, glance; Aussicht: view; **auf den ersten ~** at first sight; **2en** look, glance; **sich 2en lassen** show o.s.

blind blind; Spiegel etc.: dull; **~ werden** go blind; **~er Passagier** stowaway.

Blinddarm m (vermiform) appendix; **~entzündung** f appendicitis.

Blinde m od. f blind man od. woman.

Blinden|anstalt f institute for the blind; **~hund** m guide dog; **~schrift** f braille.

blinke|n shine; Sterne, Licht: twinkle; signal, flash; **2r** m mot. trafficator, indicator.

blinzeln blink, wink.

Blitz m lightning; **~ab-leiter** m lightning-conductor; **2en** flash; sparkle; **es blitzt** it is lightening; **~licht** n flashlight; **~schlag** m (stroke of) lightning; **~schnell** with lightning speed, like lightning;

~würfel m flash cube.

Block m block; *Schreib*2: pad; **~ade** f blockade; **~haus** n log cabin; 2ieren block (up); *Räder*: lock; *Bremsen*: jam; **~schrift** f block letters pl.

blöd(e) imbecile; *dumm*: stupid; 2sinn m rubbish, nonsense; **~sinnig** idiotic, stupid, foolish.

blöken bleat. [(-haired).)

blond blond(e), fair}

bloß bare, naked; mere; only; **~legen** lay bare, expose; **~stellen** expose.

blühen blossom, bloom; *fig.* flourish, thrive.

Blume f flower; *Wein*: bouquet; *Bier*: froth.

Blumen|geschäft n florist's (shop); **~händler** m florist; **~kohl** m cauliflower.

Bluse f blouse.

Blut n blood; 2arm bloodless, *med.* an(a)emic; **~bad** n massacre; **~druck** m blood pressure.

Blüte f blossom, bloom, flower; *fig.* prime, heyday.

Blut|egel m leech; 2en bleed.

Blütenblatt n petal.

Blut|erguß m effusion of blood; **~gruppe** f blood group; 2ig bloody; **~kreislauf** m (blood) circulation; **~probe** f blood test; **~spender** m blood donor; 2stillend styptic, sta(u)nching; **~sverwandte** m, f blood relation; **~transfusion** f blood trans-

fusion; **~ung** f bleeding, h(a)emorrhage; **~vergießen** n bloodshed; **~vergiftung** f blood-poisoning; **~verlust** m loss of blood; **~wurst** f black pudding.

Bö f gust, squall.

Bock m buck; *Ziegen*2: he-goat, billygoat; *Widder*: ram; *Turngerät*: buck; *Gestell*: trestle; 2ig stubborn, obstinate.

Boden m ground; *agr.* soil; *Gefäß, Meer*: bottom; *Fuß*2: floor; *Dach*: loft; **~kammer** f garret, attic; 2los bottomless; *fig.* unbounded; **~schätze** pl mineral resources pl.

Bogen m curve, bend; sweep; *Waffe, Geige*: bow; arch; *Papier*: sheet; 2förmig arched; **~gang** m arcade; **~schießen** n archery; **~schütze** m archer.

Bohle f thick plank, board.

Bohne f bean; **~nkaffee** m coffee.

bohnern polish, wax.

bohre|n bore, drill; 2r m borer, drill.

böig squally, gusty; *aer.* bumpy.

Boiler m boiler, heater.

Boje f buoy.

Bolzen m bolt.

bombardieren bomb, bombard (*a. fig.*).

Bombe f bomb; **~nangriff** m air raid; **~r** m bomber.

Bonbon m, n sweet, *Am.* candy.

Boot _n_ boat; ~**fahrt** _f_
boat trip; ~**sverleih** _m_
boat hire.

Bord¹ _n_ shelf.

Bord² _m_ mar., aer.: **an** ~
on board, aboard; **von** ~
gehen go ashore; ~**stein**
_m_ kerb, Am. curb.

borgen et.: borrow; _j-m_
et.: lend, Am. a. loan.

Borke _f_ bark.

Börse _f_ stock exchange;
Geld²: purse; ~**nkurs** _m_
quotation; ~**nmakler** _m_
stockbroker.

Borste _f_ bristle.

Borte _f_ border; Besatz:
braid.

bösartig malicious, vicious; _med._ malignant.

Böschung _f_ slope, bank.

böse bad, evil, wicked;
zornig: angry; 2 _n_ evil.

boshaft wicked, malicious.

Botani|k _f_ botany; 2**sch**
botanical.

Bote _m_ messenger.

Botschaft _f_ message; Amt:
embassy; ~**er** _m_ ambassador.

Bottich _m_ tub; tun, vat.

Bouillon _f_ beef tea.

box|en box; 2**en** _n_ boxing;
2**er** _m_ boxer; 2**kampf** _m_
boxing-match, fight.

boykottieren boycott.

Branche _f_ line (of business).

Brand _m_ fire, conflagration; _med._ gangrene; Pfl.
blight, mildew; **in** ~ **geraten** catch fire; ~**blase**
_f_ blister; 2**en** surge, break;

~**salbe** _f_ burn ointment;
~**stiftung** _f_ arson; ~**ung**
_f_ surf, breakers _pl._

braten roast; Rost: grill;
Pfanne: fry; Äpfel: bake;
2 _m_ roast (meat); Keule:
joint; 2**fett** _n_ dripping;
2**soße** _f_ gravy.

Brat|... fried _od._ grilled
...; ~**huhn** _n_ roast chicken;
~**kartoffeln** _pl_ fried potatoes _pl_; ~**pfanne** _f_ fry-
ing-pan; ~**röhre** _f_ oven.

Brauch _m_ custom; 2**bar**
useful; 2**en** need, want;
erfordern: require; Zeit:
take.

Braue _f_ eyebrow.

braue|n brew; 2**rei** _f_
brewery. [get a tan.)

braun brown; ~**werden**)

Bräun|e _f_ (sun) tan; 2**en**
brown; Sonne: tan.

Brause _f_ rose; ~(**bad** _n_) _f_
shower(-bath); ~(**limo-
nade**) _f_ fizzy lemonade;
2**n** roar; have a shower.

Braut _f_ fiancée; am Hochzeitstag: bride.

Bräutigam _m_ fiancé; am
Hochzeitstag: bridegroom.

Braut|jungfer _f_ brides-
maid; ~**kleid** _n_ wedding
dress; ~**paar** _n_ engaged
couple; am Hochzeitstag:
bride and bridegroom.

brav honest; _artig:_ good.

brechen break; Strahlen
etc.: refract; _erbrechen:_
vomit.

Brei _m_ pulp; Mus: mash;
Kinder2: pap; 2**ig** pulpy,
pappy.

breit broad, wide; **2e** *f* breadth, width; *geogr.* latitude.

Brems|belag *m* brake lining; **~e** *f* *zo.* gadfly, horsefly; *tech.* brake; **2en** brake; slow down *od.* up; **~spur** *f* skid marks *pl;* **~weg** *m* braking distance.

brenn|bar combustible, inflammable; **~en** burn; be on fire; *Wunde, Augen:* smart; *Nessel:* sting; **2er** *m* burner; **2essel** *f* stinging nettle; **2holz** *n* firewood; **2material** *n* fuel; **2punkt** *m* focus; **2stoff** *m* fuel.

Brett *n* board; shelf.

Brezel *f* pretzel.

Brief *m* letter; **~bogen** *m* (sheet of) notepaper; **~kasten** *m* letter-box, pillarbox, *Am.* mailbox; **2lich** by letter; **~marke** *f* (postage) stamp; **~papier** *n* notepaper; **~tasche** *f* wallet; **~träger** *m* postman, *Am.* mailman; **~um-schlag** *m* envelope; **~wechsel** *m* correspondence.

Brillant *m* brilliant, cut diamond; **2** brilliant.

Brille *f* (**e–e** a pair of) glasses *pl od.* spectacles *pl; Schutz₂:* goggles *pl.*

bringen bring; *fort₂, hin₂:* take; **zu Bett ~** put to bed; **nach Hause ~** see *s.o.* home; **in Ordnung ~** put in order; **zur Welt ~** give birth to.

Brise *f* breeze.

Brit|e *m* Briton; **die ~en** *pl* the British *pl;* **2isch** British.

bröckeln crumble.

Brocken *m* piece; *Erde, Stein:* lump.

Brombeere *f* blackberry.

Bronchitis *f* bronchitis.

Bronze *f* bronze.

Brosche *f* brooch.

Broschüre *f* booklet, brochure.

Brot *n* bread; *Laib:* loaf; **belegtes ~** (open) sandwich; **~aufstrich** *m* spread.

Brötchen *n* roll.

Brotrinde *f* crust.

Bruch *m* *Knochen:* fracture; *med.* hernia; *math.* fraction; *Versprechen:* breach; *Eid, Gesetz:* violation.

brüchig brittle.

Bruch|landung *f* crashlanding; **~rechnung** *f* fractional arithmetic, fractions *pl;* **~stück** *n* fragment; **~teil** *m* fraction.

Brücke *f* bridge; *Teppich:* rug; **~npfeiler** *m* pier.

Bruder *m* brother; *eccl.* (lay) brother, friar.

Brühe *f* broth; *klare:* beef tea; *Suppengrundlage:* stock.

brüllen roar, bellow; *Rinder:* low.

brumm|en *Tier:* growl; *Motor:* purr; *fig.* grumble. **~ig** grumbling.

brünett brunette.

Brunft *f* *s.* **Brunst.**

Brunnen m well; *Quelle*:
spring; *Spring*2: fountain.
Brunst f *männliches Tier*:
rut, *weibliches Tier*: heat;
rutting season. [short.]
brüsk brusque, abrupt; ∫
Brust f breast; chest, *anat.*
thorax; (woman's) breast
(-s *pl*), bosom; **~korb** m
chest, *anat.* thorax; **~**
schwimmen n breast-
stroke; **~warze** f nipple.
Brut f brood, hatch; *Fische*:
fry. [brutality.]
brutal brutal; **2ität** f∫
brüten brood, sit (on eggs);
~ über brood over.
brutto gross.
Bube m *Karten*: knave, jack.
Buch n book; **~druckerei**
f printing office.
Buche f beech(-tree).
buchen book.
Bücher|brett n bookshelf;
~ei f library; **~schrank** m
bookcase.
Buch|fink m chaffinch;
~halter m book-keeper;
~haltung f book-keeping;
~händler m bookseller;
~handlung f bookshop,
Am. bookstore.
Büchse f box, case; *Blech*2:
tin, *Am.* can; *Gewehr*: rifle;
~nfleisch n tinned (*Am.*
canned) meat; **~nöffner** m
tin-opener, *Am.* can opener.
Buchsta|be m letter; **2-**
bieren spell.
Bucht f bay; *kleine*: creek.
Buchung f booking, reservation.

Buck|el m *Höcker*: hump,
hunch; humpback, hunch-
back; **2(e)lig** hump-
backed, hunchbacked.
bücken: **sich ~** bend
(down), stoop.
Bückling m bloater; *fig.*
bow. [place.]
Bude f stall; *colloq.* den,∫
Büfett n sideboard, buffet;
kaltes ~ buffet supper *od.*
lunch.
Büffel m buffalo.
Bug m *mar.* bow; *aer.* nose.
Bügel m *Brille*: bow; *Ta-*
sche: handle; *Kleider*: coat-
hanger, clothes-hanger;
*Steig*2: stirrup; **~brett** n
ironing-board; **~eisen** n
iron; **~falte** f crease;
2frei non-iron; drip-dry;
2n iron, press.
Bühne f platform; *thea.*
stage; **~nbild** n stage
design; setting, décor.
Bullauge n porthole, bull's-
eye.
Bulle m bull.
Bummel m stroll; **2n**
stroll, saunter; *trödeln*:
dawdle, waste time; **~zug**
m *colloq.* slow train.
Bund[1] m (waist-, neck-,
wrist-)band); *pol.* union,
federation, confederacy.
Bund[2] n bundle; *Radies-*
chen: bunch; n, m *Schlüssel*:
bunch.
Bündel n bundle, bunch.
Bundes|... in *Zssgn*: federal
...; **~genosse** m ally;
~kanzler m Federal Chancellor; **~republik** f Fed-

eral Republic; **∼staat** m federal state; **∼wehr** f German Federal Armed Forces pl.

Bündnis n alliance.

Bungalow m bungalow.

Bunker m air-raid shelter.

bunt colo(u)rful; bright, gay; **⊈stift** m colo(u)red pencil, crayon.

Burg f castle.

Bürge m jur.: guarantor; surety; für Einwanderer: sponsor; **⊈n: ∼ für** vouch for; stand surety od. bail for; sponsor s.o.; guarantee s.th.

Bürger m citizen; **∼krieg** m civil war; **∼meister** m mayor; **∼steig** m pavement, Am. sidewalk.

Büro n office; **∼angestellte** m, f clerk; **∼stunden** pl office hours pl.

Bursche m boy, lad, colloq. chap, Am. a. guy.

Bürste f brush; **⊇n** brush.

Bus m s. Autobus.

Busch m bush, shrub.

Büschel n bunch; Haare: tuft; Stroh, Haare etc.: wisp.

buschig bushy.

Busen m bosom, breast(s pl).

Bushaltestelle f bus stop.

Bussard m buzzard.

Buße f Sühne: atonement, penance; **∼geld** n fine.

büßen atone for.

Büste f bust; **∼nhalter** m brassière, colloq. bra.

Butter f butter; **∼blume** f buttercup; **∼brot** n (slice od. piece of) bread and butter; **∼brotpapier** n greaseproof paper; **∼milch** f buttermilk.

C

Café n café, coffee-house.

Camping n camping; **∼platz** m camping-ground, camping-site.

Cello n (violon)cello, 'cello.

Celsius: 5 Grad ∼ (abbr. 5° C) five degrees centigrade. [pagne.]

Champagner m cham-⌡

Champignon m champignon, (common) mushroom.

Chance f chance.

Chaos n chaos.

Charakter m character; **⊈isieren** characterize;

⊈istisch characteristic; **∼zug** m trait.

charm|ant charming; **⊇e** m charm, grace.

Charter|flug m charter flight; **∼maschine** f charter plane.

Chauffeur m chauffeur, driver.

Chef m head, chief, colloq. boss; **∼arzt** m head od. chief physician.

Chemie f chemistry; **∼kalien** pl chemicals pl; **∼ker** m chemist; **⊈sch** chemical.

Chiffre f code, cipher; _Anzeige:_ box number.
Chines|e m Chinese; **◮isch** Chinese.
Chinin n quinine.
Chirurg m surgeon.
Chlor n chlorine; **◮oform** n chloroform.
Cholera f cholera.
Chor m chancel, choir; _Sänger:_ choir; _Gesangsstück:_ chorus.
Christ m Christian; **◮-**

◮baum m Christmas-tree;
◮entum n Christianity;
◮kind n the infant Jesus;
◮lich Christian.
Chrom n chromium.
chronisch chronic.
circa about, approximately.
Conférencier m compère, _Am._ master of ceremonies.
Couch f couch.
Coupé n coupé.
Cousin m, **◮e** f cousin.
Creme f cream.

D

da _adv räumlich:_ there; here; _zeitlich:_ then; _cj begründend:_ as, since, because.
dabei near it _od._ them; with; _im Begriff:_ about, going (**zu** to); _außerdem:_ besides; **◮ bleiben** stick to one's point; **◮sein** be present _od._ there.
dableiben stay, remain.
Dach n roof; **◮decker** m roofer; **◮garten** m roofgarden; **◮kammer** f attic, garret; **◮rinne** f gutter, eaves _pl._
Dachs m badger.
Dachziegel m tile.
Dackel m dachshund.
dadurch for this reason, thus; by it, by that; **◮daß** because.
dafür for it _od._ them; instead, in return, in exchange; **◮ sein** be in favo(u)r of it; **er kann nichts ◮** it is not his fault.

dagegen _adv_ against it _od._ them; _Vergleich:_ by comparison; **ich habe nichts ◮** I have no objection (to it); _cj_ however.
daheim at home.
daher _adv_ from there; _bei Verben der Bewegung:_ ... along; _fig._ hence; _cj_ that is why.
dahin _räumlich:_ there, to that place; _bei Verben der Bewegung:_ ... along; **bis ◮** till then.
dahinter behind it _od._ them; **◮kommen** find out about it; **◮stecken** be behind it.
damal|ig then, of that time; **◮s** then, at that time.
Dame f lady; _beim Tanz:_ partner; _Karten, Schach:_ queen.
Damen|binde f sanitary towel (_Am._ napkin); **◮friseur** m hairdresser; **◮haft** ladylike; **◮toilette** f ladies'

Dativ

room, powder-room.

damit *adv* with *od.* them; *cj* so that; ~ **nicht** lest. [**Deich**: dike, dyke.}

Damm *m* Stau2: dam;}

dämmer|ig dim; ~n dawn (*a. fig. colloq.*: ~m on s.o.); grow dark, 2ung *f* twilight, dusk; *morgens*: dawn.

Dampf *m* steam, vapo(u)r; 2en steam.

dämpfen *Stau, Stoß etc.*: deaden; *Stimme*: lower; *Licht*: soften; *s.* **dünsten**.

Dampf|er *m* steamer; ~ **maschine** *f* steam-engine.

danach after it *od.* them; *später*: afterwards; *entsprechend*: accordingly; **ich fragte ihn** ~ I asked him about it.

Däne *m* Dane.

daneben next to it *od.* them; beside it *od.* them; *außerdem*: besides, moreover.

dänisch Danish.

Dank *m* thanks *pl*; ~*barkeit*: gratitude; **Gott sei** ~! thank God!; 2 owing *od.* thanks to; 2**bar** thankful, grateful; *lohnend*: rewarding; 2en thank; 2e **(schön)** thank you (very much); **nichts zu** 2en don't mention it.

dann then; ~ **und wann** (every) now and then.

daran at (by, in, of, on, to) it *od.* them; **nahe** ~ **sein** be on the point of *ger.*

darauf *räumlich*: on it *od.*

them; *zeitlich*: after (that); ~**hin** thereupon.

daraus out of it *od.* them; from it *od.* them; **was ist** ~ **geworden?** what has become of it?

Darbietung *f* performance. [there.}

darin in it *od.* them; in}

darlegen explain.

Darleh(en) *n* loan.

Darm *m* intestine(s *pl*), bowel(s *pl*), gut(s *pl*).

darstell|en describe;show; 2ung *f* representation.

darüber over it *od.* them; *quer*: across it; *davon*: about it; ~ **hinaus** beyond it; in addition.

darum *adv* (a)round it *od.* them; for it *od.* them; *cj* therefore.

darunter under it *od.* them; beneath it *od.* them; *dazwischen*: among them; *weniger*: less; **was verstehst du** ~? what do you understand by it?

das *s.* **der**; ~ **heißt** that is (to say).

dasein be there *od.* present; exist; 2 *n* existence, being, life.

dasjenige *s.* **derjenige**.

daß that.

dasselbe *s.* **derselbe**.

dastehen stand (there).

Daten *pl* data *pl* (*a. tech.*), facts *pl*; particulars *pl*; ~ **verarbeitung** *f* data processing.

datieren date.

Dativ *m gr.* dative (case).

Dattel f date.

Datum n date.

Dauer f duration; *Fort2*: continuance; period; **von ~ sein** last; 2**haft** lasting; durable; 2**n** continue, last; *Zeitaufwand:* take; 2**nd** lasting; permanent; constant; ~**welle** f permanent wave, *colloq.* perm.

Daumen m thumb.

Daunendecke f eiderdown (quilt).

davon of it od. them; *fort, weg:* off, away; *darüber:* about it.

davor before it od. them, in front of it od. them; **er fürchtet sich ~** he is afraid of it.

dazu to it od. them; *Zweck:* for it od. them; about it; *überdies:* moreover; ~**gehören** belong to it od. them; ~**kommen** arrive; join; be added; ~**tun** add. **dazwischen** between them, (in) between; ~**kommen** happen.

Debatte f debate.

Deck n deck.

Decke f cover(ing); blanket; (travel[l]ing) rug; *Zimmer:* ceiling; ~**l** m lid, cover; (book) cover; 2**n** cover; **den Tisch** 2**n** lay the table.

Deckung f cover.

defekt defective, faulty; 2 m defect, fault.

defini|eren define; 2**tion** f definition.

Defizit n deficit, deficiency.

Degen m sword; *Fechten:* épée.

dehn|bar elastic; ~**en** extend; stretch.

Deich m dam, dyke.

Deichsel f pole, shaft(s pl).

dein your; **der, die, das** ~**e** yours; ~**etwegen** for your sake; because of you.

Dekan m dean.

Deklin|ation f gr. declension; 2**ieren** gr. decline.

Dekor|ateur m decorator; window-dresser; ~**ation** f decoration; (window-) dressing; *thea.* scenery; 2**ieren** decorate; dress.

delikat *köstlich:* delicious; delicate; ~**esse** f delicacy; *Leckerbissen:* a. dainty; 2**essengeschäft** n delicatessen.

Delphin m dolphin.

dementieren deny.

dem|entsprechend accordingly; ~**nach** according to that; therefore; ~**nächst** soon, shortly.

Delle f colloq. dent.

Demokrat m democrat; ~**ie** f democracy; 2**isch** democratic.

demolieren demolish.

Demonstr|ation f demonstration; 2**ieren** demonstrate.

demontieren dismantle.

Demut f humility.

demütig humble; ~**en** humble, humiliate.

denk|bar conceivable, imaginable; ~**en** think; ~**en an** think of; remember;

sich et. ~en imagine s.th.; 2mal *n* monument; Eh-renmal: memorial; ~wür-dig memorable; 2zettel *m fig.* lesson.

denn for, because; **es sei** ~, **daß** unless, except.

deponieren deposit.

dennoch yet, still, never-theless. [against.}

denunzieren inform}

der, die, das the; dem pron that, this; he, she, it; **die** pl these, those, they; rel pron who, which, that.

derartig such.

derb coarse, rough; Schu-he: stout; Person: sturdy; Ausdrucksweise: blunt.

dergleichen: nichts ~ nothing of the kind.

der-, die-, dasjenige he, she, that; **diejenigen** pl those.

der-, die-, dasselbe the same; he, she, it.

desertieren desert.

deshalb therefore; ~, **weil** because.

desinfizieren disinfect.

Dessert *n* dessert, sweet.

destillieren distil.

desto (all, so much) the; ~ **besser** (all) the better; ~ **mehr** (all) the more.

deswegen *s.* **deshalb**.

Detail *n* detail.

Detektiv *m* detective.

deuten interpret; Sterne, Traum: read; ~ **auf** point at.

deutlich clear, distinct.

deutsch German; 2e *m, f* German.

Devisen pl foreign exchange sg od. currency sg.

Dezember *m* December.

dezimal decimal.

Dia *n s.* Diapositiv.

Diagnose *f* diagnosis.

diagonal diagonal.

Dialekt *m* dialect.

Dialog *m* dialog(ue).

Diamant *m* diamond.

Diapositiv *n* slide.

Diät *f* diet. [self.}

dich you; ~ **(selbst)** your-}

dicht thick; Verkehr: heavy; (water)tight; ~ **an** od. **bei** close to.

dichte|n compose od. write poetry, etc.; 2r *m* poet; author.

Dichtung[1] *f* poetry; Prosa: fiction; poem, poetic work.

Dichtung[2] *f tech.* gasket, seal.

dick thick; Person: fat, stout; 2icht *n* thicket; ~köpfig stubborn.

die *s.* **der**; Artikel: pl the.

Dieb *m* thief; ~**stahl** *m* theft, jur. mst larceny.

diejenige *s.* **derjenige**.

Diele *f* board, plank; Vor-raum: hall, Am. a. hallway.

dien|en serve (j-m s.o.); 2er *m* (man-, domestic) servant; 2erin *f* (woman-) servant, maid; 2st *m* ser-vice; 2st **haben** be on duty; **im** od. **außer** 2st on od. off duty.

Dienstag *m* Tuesday.

Dienst|bote *m* (domestic) servant, domestic; 2frei off duty; 2freier Tag day off; **~leistung** f service; 2lich official; **~mädchen** n maid(servant), help; **~stunden** pl office hours pl; 2tuend on duty.

dies, ~er, ~e, ~es this (one); he, she, it; **~e** pl these; they.

dieselbe s. derselbe.

dies|mal this time; for (this) once; **~seits** on this side (gen of).

Differenz f difference.

Diktat n dictation; **~or** m dictator; **~ur** f dictatorship.

diktieren dictate.

Ding n thing; **vor allen ~en** above all.

Diphtherie f diphtheria.

Diplom n diploma, certificate.

Diplomat m diplomat, diplomatist; 2isch diplomatic (a. fig.).

dir (to) you; **~ (selbst)** yourself.

direkt direct; 2ion f management; board of directors; 2or m director, head, manager; Schule: headmaster, Am. principal; 2orin f headmistress, Am. principal; 2rice f manageress; 2übertragung f live broadcast.

Dirig|ent m conductor; 2ieren conduct.

Dirne f prostitute.

Diskont m discount.

Diskothek f discotheque.

diskret discreet; 2ion f discretion.

Diskus m sp. discus.

Disku|ssion f discussion;

2tieren discuss (über et. s.th.). [qualify.]

disqualifizieren dis-}

Distanz f distance (a. fig.); 2ieren: sich ~ von dissociate o.s. from.

Distel f thistle.

Distrikt m district.

Disziplin f discipline.

dividieren divide (durch by).

doch but, though; however, yet; also ~! I knew it!; komm ~ herein! do come in!; nicht ~! don't!; nach negativer Frage: ~! yes, ...

Docht m wick.

Dock n dock.

Dogge f Great Dane.

Dohle f (jack)daw.

Doktor m doctor.

Dokument n document; **~arfilm** m documentary (film).

Dolch m dagger. [preter.}

Dolmetscher m inter-}

Dom m cathedral.

Donner m thunder; 2n thunder; **es donnert** it is thundering; **~stag** m Thursday.

Doppel n duplicate; Tennis: doubles pl; **~bett** n double bed; **~decker** m double-decker; **~gänger** m double; **~punkt** m colon; **~stecker** m two-way adapter; 2t adj double; adv twice; **~zentner** m quintal, 100 kilogram(me)s pl; **~zimmer** n double room.

Dorf n village.

Dorn m thorn (a. fig.).

Schnalle: tongue; *Rennschuhe*: spike; **℈ig** thorny.

Dorsch *m* cod(fish).

dort(over) there; **~her** from there; **~hin** there.

Dose *f* box; *Konserven℈*: tin, *Am.* can; **~nöffner** *m* tin-opener, *Am.* can opener.

Dosis *f* dose (*a. fig.*).

Dotter *m, n* yolk.

Dozent *m* (university) lecturer. [kite.]

Drache *m* dragon; **~n** *m*)

Draht *m* wire; **℈los** wireless; **~seilbahn** *f s.* **Seilbahn.**

drall plump, buxom.

Drama *n* drama; **~tiker** *m* dramatist, playwright; **℈tisch** dramatic.

dran *colloq. s.* **daran; ich bin ~** it's my turn.

Drang *m* pressure; *fig.* urge.

drängen *v/i* be pressing *od.* urgent; *v/t* press (*a. fig.*), push; *fig.* urge; **sich ~** crowd, throng.

drauf *colloq. s.* **darauf; ~ und dran sein** *zu* be on the point of *ger.* [doors.]

draußen outside; out of)

Dreck *m colloq.* dirt; filth; **℈ig** *colloq.*: dirty; filthy.

dreh|bar revolving, rotating; **℈bleistift** *m* propelling pencil; **℈bühne** *f* revolving stage; **~en** turn; *Film*: shoot; **℈stuhl** *m* swivel-chair; **℈tür** *f* revolving door; **℈ung** *f* turn; *um Achse*: rotation.

drei three; **℈eck** *n* triangle; **~eckig** triangular; **~fach**

threefold, treble, triple; **℈rad** *n* tricycle.

dreißig thirty; **~ste** thirtieth.

dreist bold; *frech*: saucy.

dreizehn(te) thirteen(th).

dreschen thresh; *colloq. prügeln*: thrash.

dressieren train.

Drillinge *f* triplets *pl.*

drin *colloq. s.* **darin.**

dringen: **~ auf** insist on; **~ aus** *Geräusch*: come from *od.* through; **~ durch** penetrate, pierce; **~ in** penetrate into; **~d** urgent, pressing; *Verdacht*: strong.

drinnen inside; indoors.

dritte third; **℈l** *n* third; **~ns** thirdly.

Drog|e *f* drug; **~erie** *f* chemist's shop, *Am.* drugstore; **~ist** *m* chemist, *Am.* druggist.

drohen threaten, menace.

dröhnen roar; boom.

Drohung *f* threat, menace.

drollig amusing, comical.

Dromedar *n* dromedary.

Droschke *f s.* **Taxi.**

Drossel *f* thrush; **℈n** *tech.* throttle.

drüben over there, yonder.

drüber *colloq. s.* **darüber.**

Druck *m* pressure; *Hände℈*: squeeze; *print.* print(ing); **~buchstabe** *m* block letter; **℈en** print.

drücken *v/t* press, push; *Hand etc.*: squeeze; **sich ~ vor** *colloq. Arbeit etc.*: shirk; *v/i Schuh*: pinch; *Wetter*: oppressive, close.

Druck|er *m* printer; **~erei**

f printing office; **knopf** *m* snap-fastener; **sache** *f* printed matter; **schrift** *f* block letters *pl.*

drum *colloq. s.* **darum.**

drunter *colloq. s.* **darunter; es geht ~ und drüber** everything is topsy-turvy.

Drüse *f* gland.

Dschungel *m* jungle.

du you.

ducken: sich ~ crouch.

Dudelsack *m* bagpipes *pl.*

Duft *m* scent, fragrance, perfume; **en** smell (**nach** of); **end** sweet-smelling, fragrant.

dulden endure; suffer; tolerate, put up with.

dumm stupid; **heit** *f* stupidity; stupid *od.* foolish action; **kopf** *m* fool.

dumpf musty, stuffy; *Ton, Schmerz:* dull.

Düne *f* dune, sand-hill.

Dung *m* dung, manure.

dünge|n dung, manure; *bsd. künstlich:* fertilize; **r** *m s.* **Dung**; *Kunstdünger:* fertilizer.

dunkel dark; *trüb:* dim; *fig.* obscure; *Vorstellung etc.:* faint, vague; **es wird ~** it is growing *od.* getting dark; **2 n ~heit** *f* dark(ness).

dünn thin; *Luft:* rare.

Dunst *m* haze, mist.

dünsten steam; *Fleisch, Obst etc.:* stew.

dunstig hazy, misty.

Dur *n* major (key).

durch through; by; **aus**

absolutely, quite; **aus nicht** not at all; **blättern** leaf through.

Durchblick *m:* **~ auf** view of; **en** look through.

durch|bohren pierce; *durchlöchern:* perforate; **brechen** break through; break apart *od.* in two; **brennen** *Sicherung:* blow; **dringen** penetrate; pierce.

durcheinander in confusion *od.* disorder; **2** *n* mess, confusion; **bringen** confuse; *Begriffe:* mix up.

durchfahr|en go (pass, drive) through; **2t** *f* passage (through); *Tor:* gate(way); **2t verboten!** no thoroughfare.

Durchfall *m* diarrh(o)ea; **en** fall through; *Examen:* fail; *thea.* be a failure.

durchführen lead *od.* take through; *vollenden:* carry out *od.* through; *verwirklichen:* realize.

Durchgang *m* passage; **kein ~!** no thoroughfare; private; **sverkehr** *m* through traffic.

durchgebraten well done.

durchgehen go through; *Pferd:* bolt; *prüfen:* go *od.* look through; **d** continuous; **der Zug** through train.

durchgreifen *fig.* take drastic measures *od.* steps; **d** drastic; radical.

durch|halten keep up; hold out; **hauen** chop

through; *fig.* give *s.o.* a good hiding; **~kommen** come *od.* pass through; *Kranker:* pull through; *Examen:* pass; **~kreuzen** *Plan etc.:* cross, thwart; **~lassen** let pass *od.* through; **~lässig** pervious (to *light, etc.*), permeable (to *water, etc.*); **~laufen** run *od.* pass through; *Schuhe etc.:* wear out; *Stufen, Abteilungen etc.:* pass through; **~lesen** read through; **~leuchten** shine through; *med.* X-ray; **~löchern** perforate; **~machen** go through; 2messer *m* diameter; **~näßt** soaked, drenched; **~queren** cross, traverse.

Durchreise *f* journey *od.* way through; 2n travel *od.* pass through; 2nde *m*, *f* person travel(l)ing through, *Am. a.* transient.

durch|reißen tear (asunder *od.* in two); 2sage *f* announcement; **~schauen** look through; *fig.* see through.

durchscheinen shine through; **~d** translucent.

Durchschlag *m* carbon (copy); 2en *f* pierce; *Kugel:* penetrate; **~papier** *n* carbon(-paper). [through.]

durchschneiden cut∫

Durchschnitt *m* average; **im ~** on an average; 2lich *adj* average; *ordinary;* *adv* on an average; *normally.*

durch|sehen see *od.* look through; look *s.th.* over, go over *s.th.*; **~setzen** put through; *mit Gewalt:* force through; **sich ~setzen** get one's way; be successful; **~sichtig** transparent; clear; **~sickern** seep through; **~sieben** sieve, sift; **~sprechen** discuss, talk over; **~stöbern** ransack, rummage; **~streichen** strike *od.* cross out; **~suchen** search; **~wachsen** *Speck:* streaky; **~weg** throughout, without exception; **~wühlen** ransack, rummage; 2zug *m* draught, *Am.* draft; **~zwängen:** **sich ~** squeeze *o.s.* through.

dürfen: ich darf I am allowed to; I may; **du darfst nicht** you must not.

dürftig poor; scanty.

dürr dry; *Boden etc.:* barren, arid; *mager:* lean, skinny; 2e *f* dryness; barrenness.

Durst *m* thirst (*nach* for); **~ haben** be thirsty; 2ig thirsty.

Dusche *f* shower(-bath); 2n have a shower(-bath).

Düse *f* nozzle; *aer.* jet; **~nflugzeug** *n* jet aircraft *od.* plane, *colloq.* jet; **~njäger** *m aer.* jet fighter.

düster dark, gloomy (*a. fig.*); *Licht:* dim.

Dutzend *n* dozen.

dynamisch dynamic(al).

Dynamit *n* dynamite.

Dynamo *m* dynamo, generator.

D-Zug *m* express (train).

E

Ebbe f ebb(-tide), low tide.

eben adj even; flach: plain, level; math. plane; adv exactly; just.

Ebene f plain; math. plane; fig. level.

eben|falls also, likewise; ~so just as; ~soviel just as much od. many; ~sowenig just as little od. few.

Eber m boar.

ebnen v level; fig. smooth.

Echo n echo.

echt genuine; Farbe: fast; Dokument: authentic.

Eck|ball m sp. corner-kick; ~e f corner; Kante: edge; s.

Eckball ; **2ig** angular; ~platz m corner-seat; ~zahn m canine tooth.

edel noble; **2stein** m precious stone; jewel, gem.

Efeu m ivy.

egal colloq. s. gleich.

Egge f harrow; **2n** harrow.

egoistisch selfish.

ehe before.

Ehe f marriage; Ehestand: a. matrimony; ~bruch m adultery; ~frau f wife; 2lich conjugal; Kind: legitimate. [old.]

ehemalig former, ex-...;

Ehe|mann m husband; ~paar n married couple.

eher sooner; lieber: rather; je ~, desto besser the sooner the better.

Ehe|ring m wedding ring; ~scheidung f divorce; ~

schließung f marriage.

Ehre f hono(u)r; **2n** hono(u)r.

Ehren|bürger m honorary citizen; ~gast m guest of hono(u)r; ~mitglied n honorary member; ~wort n word of hono(u)r;

ehr|erbietig respectful; 2furcht f: ~ (vor) respect (for); awe (of); 2gefühl n sense of hono(u)r; 2geiz m ambition; ~geizig ambitious. [honesty.]

ehrlich honest; **2keit** f.]

Ehrung f hono(u)r.

Ei n egg; physiol. ovum.

Eiche f oak(-tree); ~l f acorn.

Eichhörnchen n squirrel.

Eid m oath.

Eidechse f lizard.

eidesstattlich: ~e Erklärung statutory declaration.

Eidotter m, n (egg) yolk.

Eier|becher m egg-cup; ~kuchen m omelet(te), pancake; ~schale f egg-shell.

Eifer m zeal, eagerness; ~sucht f jealousy; 2süchtig jealous (auf of).

eifrig eager; keen.

Eigelb n (egg) yolk.

eigen own; besonder: particular; peculiar; ~artig peculiar; ~händig with one's own hands; ~mächtig arbitrary; without authority; **2name** m proper name; ~s expressly; specially.

Eigenschaft f quality; Sa-chen: property; **in s-r** **als** in his capacity as.
eigensinnig obstinate.
eigentlich actual; proper.
Eigen|tum n property; **tümer** m owner, proprietor. [self-willed.)
eigenwillig individual; {
eignen: sich für od. **zu** be suited for.
Eil|bote m express (messenger); **brief** m express letter.
Eile f haste, hurry; **2n** hasten, hurry; Brief, Angelegenheit: be urgent.
eilig hasty, speedy; dringend: urgent; **es haben** be in a hurry.
Eilzug m fast train.
Eimer m bucket, pail.
ein one; a, an; **ander** one another, each other.
ein|äschern burn to ashes; Leiche: cremate; **atmen** breathe, inhale.
Ein|bahnstraße f one-way street; **band** m binding, cover.
ein|bauen build in; **berufen** call; mil. call up, Am. draft.
Einbettzimmer n single room.
einbiegen: in turn into; **nach** turn to.
einbild|en: sich et.. **imag-ine, think; 2ung** f imagination; Dünkel: conceit.
einbreche|n break through; break in; **n in** Haus: break into; **2r** m

nachts: burglar; tagsüber: housebreaker.
Einbruch m housebreaking; burglary.
ein|bürgern naturalize; **büßen** lose; **deutig** clear.
eindringen: en enter; penetrate (into); **lich** urgent.
Ein|druck m impression; **2drücken** push in; **2drucksvoll** impressive.
ein|er, e, (e)s one.
einerlei s. gleich; 2 n monotony, humdrum.
einerseits on the one hand.
einfach simple, plain; Mahlzeit: frugal; Fahr-karte: single, Am. one-way; **2heit** f simplicity.
Einfahrt f entry; entrance; s. **Autobahneinfahrt.**
Einfall m mil. invasion; fig. idea, inspiration; **2en** fall in, collapse; **2en in** mil. invade; **j-m 2en** occur to s.o.
ein|fangen catch, capture, seize; **farbig** Stoff: self-colo(u)red, plain; **fassen** edge, border; **fetten** grease.
Einfluß m influence; **2-reich** influential.
einfrieren freeze (in).
Ein|fuhr f import(ation); **2führen** econ. import; introduce; in ein Amt: instal(l).
Eingang m entrance; von Waren: arrival.
einge|bildet imaginary; dünkelhaft: conceited; **2-**

borene m, f native; **fallen** sunken, hollow.

eingehen come in, arrive; *bot.*, *zo.* die; *Material*: shrink; **auf** agree to; *Einzelheiten*: enter into.

Eingemachte n preserved fruit; preserves pl.

eingeschrieben registered.

Eingeweide pl intestines pl, bowels pl; *Tiere*: entrails pl.

eingewöhnen: sich acclimatize, settle down.

ein|gießen pour (out); **gießen in** pour into; **greifen** intervene; interfere.

Eingriff m med. operation.

einhängen hang up.

einheimisch native; **2e** m, f native; resident.

Einheit f unity; *phys.*, *math.*, *mil.* unit; **2lich** uniform.

einholen catch up with; *Zeitverlust*: make up for; buy.

einig united; **sein** agree; **sich nicht sein** differ; **e** some, several; **en** unite; **sich en** come to an agreement; **ermaßen** to some extent; somewhat; **es** something; **2ung** f union; agreement. [one year's...]

einjährig one-year-old;

Einkauf m purchase; **2en** buy, purchase; **2en gehen** go shopping; **stasche** f shopping bag; **szentrum** n shopping cent|re (*Am.* -er).

ein|kehren put up *od.* stop (in at); **kleiden** clothe.

Einkommen n income; **steuer** f income-tax.

Einkünfte pl income sg.

einlad|en load (in); invite; **2ung** f invitation.

Einlaß m admission; *Zutritt*: admittance.

einlassen let in, admit.

Einlauf m med. enema; **2en** *Zug*: pull in; *Schiff*: enter the harbo(u)r; *Material*: shrink.

einlege|n pickle; *Film* **n** load a camera; **2sohle** f insole, sock.

Einleitung f introduction.

ein|liefern: in ein Krankenhaus take to hospital; **lösen** *Wechsel*: hon-o(u)r; *Scheck*: cash; **machen** preserve; *in Dosen*: tin, *Am.* can.

einmal once; one day; **auf** all at once; **nicht** not even; **ig** fig. unique.

einmischen: sich meddle, interfere.

Einmündung f junction.

Ein|nahme f taking; **nahmen** pl takings pl, receipts pl; **2nehmen** take; *Geld*: earn, make, *bei Geschäften etc.*: take; *Platz*: take up, occupy.

ein|ordnen put in its place; *Briefe etc.*: file; **packen** pack (up); *einwickeln*: wrap up; **pflanzen** plant; **reiben** rub (*s.th.* in); **reichen** send *od.* hand in.

Einreise f entry; **geneh-**

migung f entry permit; ~visum n entrance visa.

ein|reißen tear; Haus: pull down; ~renken med. set; fig. put od. set right.

einricht|en fit up, equip; Wohnung: furnish; fig. arrange; 2ung f establishment; equipment; furniture; institution.

eins one.

einsam lonely, solitary; 2keit f loneliness, solitude.

einsammeln collect.

Einsatz m inset, insertion; Spiel2: stake.

ein|schalten switch od. turn on; sich ~ schalten intervene; ~schenken pour (out); ~schicken send in; ~schlafen fall asleep; ~schläfern lull to sleep; Tier: put to sleep; ~schlagen Nagel: drive in; zerbrechen: break, smash; einwickeln: wrap up; Weg: take; Blitz, Geschoß: strike; ~schließen lock in od. up; umgeben: enclose; mil. surround; fig. include; ~schließlich including; ~schmieren grease; ~schneiden: ~ in cut into; ~schneidend fig. drastic.

Einschnitt m cut; Kerbe: notch).

einschränken restrict, confine; Ausgaben: reduce, cut down; sich ~ economize.

Einschreibe|brief m registered letter; 2n register; Mitglied: enrol(l); Post:

register; sich 2n enter one's name.

ein|schreiten intervene; ~schüchtern intimidate; ~sehen fig. see, understand; ~seitig one-sided; pol. unilateral; ~senden send in; ~setzen begin; Kälte etc.: set in; put in, insert; Geld: stake; use; Leben: risk; sich ~setzen für stand up for; support.

Einsicht f fig. insight, judiciousness; 2ig judicious, sensible. [fig. taciturn.)

einsilbig monosyllabic;)

ein|sinken sink (in); ~sparen save; ~sperren shut od. lock up; imprison.

Einspruch m objection, protest; jur. appeal; ~ erheben (gegen) object (to), protest (against).

einspurig single-lane.

einst once.

ein|stecken pocket (a. fig.); Brief: post, Am. mail; ~steigen: in get into; Bus: get on; alles ~! all aboard!

einstell|en Arbeitskräfte: engage, employ, hire; aufgeben: give up; Zahlungen etc.: stop, cease; ~en (auf) Mechanismus: adjust (to); Radio: tune in (to); die Arbeit ~en strike, colloq. down tools; sich ~en appear; sich ~en auf be prepared for; adapt o.s. to; 2ung f engagement; Zahlungen: stoppage; adjustment; innere: attitude.

ein|stimmig unanimous;

stöckig one-stor|eyed, -ied.

ein|studieren study; *thea.* rehearse; **2sturz** *m* collapse; **2stürzen** fall in, collapse. [being.⟩

einstweilen for the time⟩

ein|tauchen: ~ **in** dip *od.* plunge into; **tauschen** exchange (**gegen** for).

einteil|en divide (**in** into); classify; **ig** one-piece; **2ung** *f* division; classification.

eintönig monotonous.

Eintracht *f* harmony.

eintragen enter; *amtlich:* register; **sich:** sign.

einträglich profitable.

ein|treffen arrive; *sich erfüllen:* come true; **treten** enter; *fig.* happen; **treten in** join.

Eintritt *m* entry, entrance; *Einlaß:* admittance; **frei!** admission free; ~ **verboten!** no admittance; **geld** *n* entrance fee, admission (fee); **skarte** *f* admission ticket.

ein|trocknen dry up; ~ **verstanden:** ~ **sein** agree.

Einwand *m* objection.

Einwander|er *m* immigrant; **2n** immigrate; **ung** *f* immigration.

einwandfrei perfect.

ein|weichen soak, **weihen** inaugurate; **j-n** ~ **weihen in** initiate s.o. in; **wenden** object (**gegen** to); **werfen** throw in (*a. fig.*); *Fenster:* smash, break;

Brief: post, *Am.* mail; *Münze:* insert.

einwickel|n wrap (up); **2papier** *n* wrapping-paper.

einwilligen consent; **2-gung** *f* consent.

einwirken: ~ **auf** act (up-on; *beeinflussen:* influence.

Einwohner *m*, **in** *f* inhabitant; resident.

Einwurf *m* sp. throw-in; *Briefkasten:* slit; *Automat:* slot; *Einwand:* objection.

Einzahl *f* gr. singular.

einzahl|en pay in; **2ung** *f* payment; *Bank:* deposit.

einzäunen fence (in).

Einzel *n* Tennis: mst singles *pl*; **handel** *m* retail trade; **heiten** *pl* particulars *pl*, details *pl*; **2n** single; *für sich allein:* individual; *abgetrennt:* separate; *Schuh etc.:* odd; **im 2nen** in detail; **zimmer** *n* single room.

einziehen draw in; *Erkundigungen:* make (**über** on, about); *Mieter:* move in; ~ **in** *Mieter:* move into.

einzig only; single; *alleing:* sole, **artig** unique.

Eis *n* ice; *Speise2:* ice-cream; **bahn** *f* skating-rink; **bär** *m* polar bear; **diele** *f* ice-cream parlo(u)r.

Eisen *n* iron.

Eisenbahn *f* railway, *Am.* railroad; **er** *m* railway-man.

Eisenwaren *pl* ironmon-

gery *sg*, *bsd. Am.* hardware *sg.*

eisern iron, of iron.
eis|gekühlt iced; chilled;
2**hockey** *n* ice hockey;
∼**ig** icy (*a. fig.*); ∼**kalt** ice-
cold, icy; 2**kunstlauf** *m*
figure-skating; 2**lauf(en)** *m*
skating; 2**läufer** *m* skater; 2**würfel** *m* ice cube;
2**zapfen** *m* icicle.
eitel vain; 2**keit** *f* vanity.
Eit|er *m* matter, pus; 2**e-**
rig purulent; 2**ern** fester,
suppurate.
Eiweiß *n* white of egg; *biol.,*
chem.: protein; albumen.
Ekel *m* disgust, loathing,
2**erregend** nauseating,
sickening; 2**haft** disgusting, repulsive; 2**n: sich** ∼
(vor) be nauseated (at);
fig. be disgusted (with),
feel disgust (at).
Ekzem *n* eczema.
elastisch elastic.
Elch *m* elk, moose.
Elefant *m* elephant.
elegant elegant, smart.
Elektri|ker *m* electrician;
2**sch** electric(al).
Elektrizität *f* electricity;
∼**werk** *n* power-station,
power-house.
Elektro|gerät *n* electric
appliance; 2**nisch** elec-
tronic.
Element *n* element.
Elend *n* misery; *Not:* a.
need, distress; 2 miserable,
wretched; needy, dis-
tressed; ∼**sviertel** *n*
slums *pl.*

elf eleven.
Elfenbein *n* ivory.
elfte eleventh.
Ellbogen *m* elbow.
Elster *f* magpie.
Eltern *pl* parents *pl*; ∼**teil**
m parent.
Email *n*, ∼**le** *f* enamel.
Emigrant *m*, ∼**in** *f* emigrant.
Empfang *m* reception (*a.*
Radio); *Erhalt:* receipt;
2**en** receive.
Empfänger *m* receiver (*a.*
Radio); *Geld*2: payee;
*Brief*2: addressee.
empfänglich susceptible
(**für** to).
Empfangs|bestätigung *f*
(acknowledg[e]ment of) receipt; ∼**chef** *m* 2**dame** *f*
receptionist; ∼**schalter** *m*
reception desk.
empfehl|en recommend
(j-m et. s.th. to s.o.);
2**ung** *f* recommendation;
Gruß: compliments *pl.*
empfind|en feel; ∼**lich**
sensitive (**gegen** to); *Per-*
son: touchy; 2**ung** *f* sensation, feeling.
empor|ragen tower, rise;
∼**steigen** rise, ascend.
empör|t indignant,
shocked; 2**ung** *f* indigna-
tion.
emsig busy, industrious.
Ende *n* end; **am** ∼ at *od.* in
the end; eventually; **zu**
sein be at an end; be over;
zu ∼ **gehen** end; *knapp*
werden: run short; be low.
End|ergebnis *n* final re-

sult; ₂**gültig** final; ₂**lich** finally, at last; ₂**los** endless; ∼**runde** f, ∼**spiel** n sp. final; ∼**station** f terminus, terminal; ∼**summe** f (sum) total; ∼**ung** f gr. ending.

Energ|ie f energy; ₂**isch** vigorous, energetic.

eng narrow; *Kleidung*: tight; *dicht*: close; *innig*: intimate.

Engel m angel.

Engländer m Englishman; **die** ∼ pl the English pl.

englisch English.

Engpaß m defile, narrow pass; *fig.* bottle-neck.

engstirnig narrow-minded.

Enkel m grandchild; grandson; ∼**in** f granddaughter.

enorm enormous.

Ensemble n mus. ensemble; *thea.* company.

entbehr|en do without, spare; *vermissen*: miss; ∼**lich** dispensable; *überflüssig*: superfluous; ₂**ung** f want, privation.

Entbindung f med. delivery, confinement; ∼**heim** n maternity hospital.

entdeck|en discover; ₂**er** m discoverer; ₂**ung** f discovery.

Ente f duck.

ent|eignen expropriate, dispossess; ∼**erben** disinherit; ∼**fallen**: **j—m** ∼ fig. escape s.o.; ∼**falten** unfold (*a.* **sich**); *Fähigkeiten*: develop.

entfern|en remove; **sich** ∼**en** withdraw; ∼**t** distant, remote; ₂**ung** f removal; distance; ₂**ungsmesser** m phot. range-finder.

entfliehen flee, escape.

entführ|en kidnap; *Flugzeug*: hijack; ₂**er** m kidnap(p)er; *Flugzeug*: hijacker; ₂**ung** f kidnap(p)ing.

entgegen prp contrary to; against; adv towards; ∼**gehen** go to meet; ∼**gesetzt** opposite; fig. contrary; ∼**kommen** come to meet; fig. meet s.o. ('s wishes); ∼**kommend** obliging; ∼**nehmen** accept, receive; ∼**sehen** look forward to; ∼**strecken** hold od. stretch out (*dat* to).

ent|gegnen reply; ∼**gehen** escape; ∼**gleisen** be derailed; ∼**gleiten**: **j—m** ∼ slip from s.o.'s hands.

enthalt|en contain, hold; **sich** ∼**en** (gen) abstain od. refrain from; ∼**sam** abstinent; ₂**ung** f abstention.

enthüllen uncover; *Denkmal*: unveil; fig. reveal, disclose.

enthusiastisch enthusi-∼**ent|kleiden** (**sich**) ∼ undress; ∼**kommen** escape; get away; ∼**laden** unload; (**sich**) ∼**laden** discharge.

entlang along.

entlass|en dismiss, discharge; ₂**ung** f dismissal, discharge.

ent|lasten relieve; exonerate; ~laufen run away (*dat* from); ~legen remote, distant; ~lüften ventilate; ~mutigen discourage; ~nehmen take (*dat* from); ~nehmen aus *fig.* gather from; ~reißen snatch away (*dat* from); ~rinnen escape (*dat* from).

entrüst|en fill with indignation; **sich ~en** be indignant (**über** at *s.th.*, with *s.o.*); **~et** indignant; **2ung** *f* indignation.

entschädig|en compensate; **2ung** *f* compensation.

entscheid|en: (sich) ~ decide; **~end** decisive; *kritisch:* crucial; **2ung** *f* decision.

entschließ|en: (sich) ~ decide, make up one's mind; **~schlossen** resolute, determined; **2schluß** *m* resolution, decision, determination.

entschuldig|en excuse; **sich ~en** apologize (**bei** to); **2ung** *f* excuse; apology; *int.* sorry!, (I beg your) pardon!

Entsetz|en *n* horror; **2lich** horrible, terrible.

entsinnen: sich ~ remember.

entspann|en: sich ~ relax; *pol.* ease (off); **2ung** *f* relaxation; *pol.* easing.

entsprechen (*dat*) correspond (to, with); *Beschreibung:* answer (to); *Anforderungen etc.:* meet; **~d** cor-

responding; *angemessen:* appropriate (*dat* to).

entspringen *Fluß:* rise.

entsteh|en arise, originate; **2ung** *f* origin. [distinct.⟩

entstellen disfigure; *fig.⟩*

enttäusch|en disappoint; **2ung** *f* disappointment.

entweder: ~ ... oder either ... or.

ent|weichen escape; **~wenden** steal, pilfer; **~werfen** *Vertrag:* draft; *Muster:* design; *flüchtig:* sketch, outline; *Garten:* plan.

entwerten devaluate; *Briefmarke, Fahrkarte:* cancel; **2er** *m* cancel(l)ing machine; **2ung** *f* devaluation; cancel(l)ation.

entwick|eln: (sich) ~ develop; **2lung** *f* development.

ent|wirren disentangle; **~wischen** *colloq.:* **j–m ~** give s.o. the slip.

Entwurf *m* draft; design; sketch; plan.

ent|ziehen deprive (**j–m et.** s.o. of *s.th.*); **~ziffern** make out.

entzück|end delightful, charming; **~t** delighted.

entzünd|en light, kindle; **sich ~en** *med.* become inflamed; **~et** inflamed; **2ung** *f* inflammation.

entzwei asunder, in two.

Epidemie *f* epidemic.

Epilog *m* epilog(ue).

Episode *f* episode.

Epoche *f* epoch.

er he; *Sache:* it.

Erbarmen n pity, mercy.

erbärmlich pitiful; *elend:* miserable.

erbarmungslos merciless, relentless.

erbaue|n build, construct; **2r** m builder, constructor.

Erbe¹ m heir.

Erbe² n inheritance, heritage; **2n** inherit.

erbeuten capture.

Erb|in f heiress; **2lich** hereditary.

er|blicken see; **2blinden** go blind; **~brechen: sich ~** vomit.

Erbschaft f inheritance.

Erbse f pea.

Erd|beben n earthquake; **~beere** f strawberry; **~boden** m earth, ground; **~e** f earth; *Bodenart:* ground, soil; **2en** electr. earth; **~geschoß** n ground (*Am.* first) floor; **~kugel** f globe; **~kunde** f geography; **~nuß** f peanut; **~öl** n (mineral) oil; **~reich** n ground, earth.

erdrosseln strangle.

erdrücken crush to death; **~d** fig. overwhelming.

Erd|rutsch m landslide (a. pol.), landslip; **~teil** m continent.

er|dulden suffer, endure; **~eignen: sich ~** happen.

Ereignis n event; **2reich** eventful.

erfahr|en learn, hear; *erleben:* experience; *adj* experienced, expert; **2ung** f experience.

erfassen seize, grasp.

erfind|en invent; **2er** m inventor; **2ung** f invention.

Erfolg m success; *Ergebnis:* result; **2los** unsuccessful; **2reich** successful.

erforder|lich necessary; **~n** require, demand.

Erforschung f exploration.

erfreu|en please; *entzücken:* delight; **~lich** pleasant; delightful.

erfrier|en freeze to death; **2ung** f frost-bite.

erfrisch|en refresh; **2ung** f refreshment.

er|froren frost-bitten; **~füllen** fulfil(l); *Pflicht:* perform; *Bitte:* comply with; *Forderungen:* meet; **~gänzen** complete; *nachträglich hinzufügen:* supplement; *Warenlager:* replenish; **~geben** show, prove, yield; **sich ~geben** surrender; **sich ~geben in** resign o.s. to.

Ergebnis n result, outcome; *sp.* result, score; **2los** unsuccessful.

ergehen: über sich ~ lassen suffer; **wie ist es ihm ergangen?** how did he fare?

ergiebig productive, rich.

ergreif|en seize, grasp; *Verbrecher:* capture; *Gelegenheit, Maßnahme:* take; *Flucht:* take to; *Beruf:* take up; *fig.* move, touch;

2ung f capture, seizure.

erhalt|en obtain; *Nachricht etc.*: receive; *bewahren*: preserve, keep; *unterstützen*: support; **gut** ~ in good condition *od.* condition.

erheb|en lift, raise; **sich** ~**en** rise; **~lich** considerable.

er|hellen light (up); **~hitzen** heat; **~hoffen** hope for.

erhöh|en raise; *fig.* increase; **2ung** f elevation; *fig.* increase; *Preise, Lohn*: rise.

erhol|en: sich ~ recover; (take a) rest, relax; **2ung** f recovery; *Entspannung*: relaxation, rest.

erinner|n: j-n ~ **an** remind s.o. of; **sich** ~ remember; **2ung** f remembrance (**an** of), recollection.

erkält|en: sich (stark) ~ catch (a bad) cold; **2ung** f cold.

erkenn|en recognize; *wahrnehmen*: perceive (*a. fig.*), see; *fig.* realize; **2tnis** f perception, realization.

Erker m bay.

erklär|en explain; *aussprechen*: declare, state; **2ung** f explanation; statement; declaration.

erkrank|en fall ill, be taken ill (**an** with); **2ung** f falling ill; illness, sickness.

erkundig|en: sich ~ make inquiries; inquire (**nach**

j-m: after, for, *et.*: about); **2ung** f inquiry.

Er|laß m decree; **2lassen** remit; dispense (**j-m et.** s.o. from s.th.); *Verordnung*: issue; *Gesetz*: enact.

erlaub|en allow, permit; **2nis** f permission.

erläutern explain.

erleb|en experience, have; see; *Schlimmes*: go through; **2nis** n experience; adventure.

erledigen settle; manage; finish.

erleichter|n ease, lighten; *fig.* make easy; *Not, Schmerz*: relieve; **2ung** f relief.

er|leiden suffer; endure; **~lernen** learn; **~lesen** choice; excellent.

Erlös m proceeds *pl.*

erloschen extinct.

erlös|en release, deliver (**von** from); **2ung** f release, deliverance; *eccl.* redemption.

er|mächtigen authorize; **~mahnen** admonish.

ermäßig|en reduce; **2ung** f reduction.

ermessen estimate; judge; **2** n judg(e)ment; discretion.

ermitt|eln ascertain, find out; *jur.* investigate; **2lungen** *pl jur.* investigations *pl*, inquiries *pl*.

ermöglichen make possible.

ermord|en murder; *meuchlerisch*: assassinate; **2ung**

f murder; assassination.

er|müden tire; get tired *od.* fatigued; **~muntern** encourage.

ermuti|gen encourage; **2-gung** *f* encouragement.

ernähr|en feed; *unterhalten:* support; **sich ~en von** live on; **2ung** *f* food, nourishment, nutrition.

erennen|en appoint; **2ung** *f* appointment.

erneu|ern renew; **~t** *adj* renewed; *adv* once more.

ernst serious, grave; **2** *m* seriousness; **im 2** in earnest; **~haft**, **~lich** serious.

Ernte *f* harvest; *Ertrag:* crop; **~dankfest** *n* harvest festival; **2n** harvest, gather, reap (*a. fig.*).

erober|n conquer; **2ung** *f* conquest.

eröffn|en open; **2ung** *f* opening.

erpress|en blackmail; **2er** *m* blackmailer; **2ung** *f* blackmail.

erraten guess.

erreg|en excite; *verursachen:* cause; **2ung** *f* excitement.

erreich|bar within reach; *fig.* attainable, available; **~en** reach; *Zug etc.:* catch; *fig.* achieve, attain.

Ersatz *m* replacement; substitute; *Schaden2:* compensation, damages *pl*; **~teil** *n* spare (part).

erschaffen create.

erschein|en appear; **2en** *n* appearance; **2ung** *f* appearance; phenomenon.

er|schießen shoot (dead); **~schlagen** kill; **~schließen** *Bauland:* develop.

erschöp|fen exhaust; **2-fung** *f* exhaustion.

erschrecken frighten, scare; be frightened.

erschütter|n shake; *fig. a.* move; **2ung** *f* *fig.* shock.

erschweren make (more) difficult.

erschwinglich reasonable.

ersetzen replace; substitute; *Auslagen:* refund; *Schaden:* compensate.

erspar|en save; **j—m et. ~en** spare s.o. s.th.; **2nisse** *pl* savings *pl*.

erst first; *nicht früher als:* not till *od.* until; *nicht mehr als:* only.

erstarr|en grow stiff, stiffen; **~t** *Finger:* stiff, numb.

erstatten *Auslagen:* refund; *Bericht ~* report.

Erstaufführung *f* first night *od.* performance, première.

Erstaun|en *n* astonishment; **2lich** astonishing, amazing; **2t** astonished.

erst|e, **~er**, **~es** first; **2e Hilfe** first aid; *s.* **Mal**.

erstechen stab.

erstens first(ly).

ersticken suffocate, choke.

erstklassig first-class.

er|strecken: sich ~ extend, stretch; **sich ~ über**

a. cover; ~**suchen** request; ~**teilen** give.

Ertrag *m* yield; *Einnahmen:* proceeds *pl*, returns *pl*; 2**en** bear, endure, stand.

erträglich tolerable.

er|tränken drown; ~**trinken** be drowned, drown; ~**wachen** wake (up).

erwachsen grown-up, adult; 2**e** *m, f* grown-up, adult.

er|wägen consider; ~**wähnen** mention; ~**wärmen** warm, heat.

erwart|en await, wait for; expect; 2**ung** *f* expectation.

er|weisen prove; *Achtung:* show, pay; *Dienst:* render; *Gefallen:* do; **sich** ~**weisen als** prove (to be); ~**weitern (sich)** expand, enlarge, extend, widen.

erwerb|en acquire; ~**slos** unemployed.

erwidern *Besuch etc.:* return; answer, reply.

erwünscht desired; *wünschenswert:* desirable.

erwürgen strangle.

Erz *n* ore.

erzähl|en tell; narrate; 2**ung** /narration; *Literatur:* (short) story, narrative.

Erz|bischof *m* archbishop; ~**engel** *m* archangel.

erzeug|en produce; make, manufacture; 2**nis** *n* product; *agr. a.* produce.

erzie|hen bring up; educate; *Tier:* train; 2**her** *m*

educator; teacher; 2**hung** *f* upbringing; education; *Lebensart:* breeding; 2**hungsanstalt** *f* approved school, reformatory.

erzielen obtain; *Preis:* realize; *sp.* score; *Einigung:* reach, arrive at.

es it; he; she.

Esche *f* ash(-tree).

Esel *m* donkey; *fig.* ass; ~**sohr** *n fig.* dog-ear.

eßbar eatable, edible.

Esse *f* chimney.

essen eat; **zu Mittag** ~ (have) lunch; *Hauptmahlzeit:* dine, have dinner; **zu Abend** ~ dine, have dinner; *bsd. spätabends:* sup, have supper; **auswärts** ~ eat *od.* dine out; **et. zu Mittag** *etc.* ~ have s.th. for lunch, *etc.*; 2 *n* eating; *Kost:* food; *Mahlzeit:* meal; lunch, dinner, supper.

Essig *m* vinegar.

Eß|löffel *m* soup-spoon; ~**tisch** *m* dining-table; ~**waren** *pl* victuals *pl*, food; ~**zimmer** *n* dining-room.

Etage *f* floor, stor(e)y; ~**bett** *n* bunk bed.

Etat *m* budget.

Etikett *n* label, ticket.

etliche some, several.

Etui *n* case.

etwa *vielleicht:* perhaps, by any chance; *ungefähr:* about, *Am. a.* around.

etwas *indef pron* something; *verneinend, fragend:* anything; *adj* some; *adv* a little; somewhat.

euch you.

eu|er your; **~(e)re** your.

Eule f owl.

Europä|er m European; **♀isch** European.

Euter n udder.

evangeli|sch evangeli(cal); Protestant, *Deutschland:* a. Lutheran; **♀um** n gospel.

eventuell possible; possibly, perhaps.

ewig eternal; everlasting, perpetual; **auf ~** for ever; **♀keit** f eternity.

exakt exact.

Examen n exam(ination).

Exemplar n specimen; *Buch:* copy.

exerzieren drill.

Exil n exile.

Exist|enz f existence; **♀ie-ren** exist; subsist.

Expedition f expedition.

Experiment n experiment; **♀ieren** experiment.

explo|dieren explode, burst; **♀sion** f explosion; **~siv** explosive.

Export m export(ation); **♀ieren** export.

extra extra.

extrem extreme.

F

Fabel f fable; **♀haft** marvel(l)ous.

Fabrik f factory, works *sg, pl;* **~at** n make; *Erzeugnis:* product.

...fach *in Zssgn:* ...fold.

Fach n compartment, partition, shelf; *Schub♀:* drawer; *ped.* subject; **~arbeiter** m skilled worker; **~arzt** m specialist (**für** in).

Fächer m fan.

Fach|gebiet n branch, field, province; **~kennt-nisse** pl specialized knowledge *sg;* **~mann** m expert.

Fackel f torch.

fad(e) *ohne Geschmack:* insipid, tasteless; *schal:* stale; *fig.* dull, boring.

Faden m thread (*a. fig.*).

fähig capable, able; **♀keit** f (cap)ability; talent, faculty.

fahl pale, pallid.

fahnd|en: ~ nach search for; **♀ung** f search.

Fahne f flag; banner; *mil.* a. colo(u)rs *pl.*

Fahrbahn f roadway.

Fähre f ferry(-boat).

fahren v/i *Person, Fahrzeug:* drive, go; *Radfahrer:* ride, cycle; *mar.* sail; **mit der Bahn ~** go by train; *v/t Wagen:* drive; *Fahrrad:* ride.

Fahrer m driver; **~flucht** f hit-and-run driving.

Fahr|gast m passenger; *Taxi:* fare; **~geld** n fare; **~gestell** n *mot.* chassis; *aer. s.* **Fahrwerk; ~karte** f ticket; **~kartenautomat** m (automatic) ticket(-vending) machine; **~karten-schalter** m booking-office, *Am.* ticket office; **♀lässig** careless; **~lehrer** m driving

fassen

instructor; **~plan** m timetable, *Am. a.* schedule; 2**planmäßig** on time *od.* schedule; **~preis** m fare; **~rad** n bicycle, *colloq.* bike; **~schein** m ticket; **~schule** f driving school, school of motoring; **~stuhl** m lift, *Am.* elevator; **~stunde** f driving lesson.

Fahrt f ride, drive; *Reise:* journey; *Vergnügungs*2: trip.

Fährte f track (*a. fig.*).

Fahr|werk n *aer.* undercarriage, landing-gear; **~zeug** n vehicle.

Fakultät f *univ.* faculty.

Falke m hawk, falcon.

Fall m fall; *gr., jur., med.* case; **auf alle Fälle** in all events; **auf jeden ~** in any case; **auf keinen ~** on no account.

Falle f trap.

fallen fall, drop; *mil.* be killed; *Flut:* subside; **~ lassen** drop.

fällen *Baum:* fell, cut down; *Urteil:* pass.

fallenlassen drop.

fällig due.

falls if, in case.

Fallschirm m parachute.

falsch false; *verkehrt:* wrong; *Geld:* counterfeit; *Person:* deceitful; **~ gehen** *Uhr:* be wrong; **~ verbunden!** *teleph.* sorry, wrong number.

fälschen forge, fake; *Geld:* counterfeit. [money.]

Falschgeld n counterfeit∫

Fälschung f forgery; counterfeit; fake.

Falt|e f fold; *Rock etc.:* pleat; *Hose:* crease; *Gesicht:* wrinkle; 2**en** fold; **die Hände** 2**en** clasp one's hands; **~er** m butterfly; moth; 2**ig** wrinkled.

familiär familiar; informal.

Familie f family.

Familien|angehörige m, f member of a family; **~name** m surname, family name, *Am. a.* last name; **~stand** m marital status.

fanatisch fanatic(al).

Fang m catch; 2**en** catch.

Farb|... colo(u)r ...; **~e** f colo(u)r; *Malerfarbe:* paint; *Farbstoff:* dye; *Gesicht:* complexion; *Karten:* suit; 2**echt** colo(u)r-fast.

färben colo(u)r; *Stoff, Haare etc.:* dye.

farb|ig colo(u)red; *Glas:* tinted, stained; **~los** colo(u)rful; **~los** colo(u)rless; 2**stift** m s. **Buntstift;** 2**ton** m shade.

Färbung f colo(u)ring; *leichte Tönung:* shade.

Farn m, **~kraut** n fern.

Fasan m pheasant.

Fasching m carnival.

Fas|er f fib|re, *Am.* -er; 2**(e)rig** fibrous; 2**ern** fray (out).

Faß n cask, barrel; *Bottich:* tub, vat; **~bier** n draught beer.

Fassade f façade, front.

fassen seize, take hold of; catch; *enthalten:* hold;

Schmuck: set; *fig.* grasp, understand; **sich ~** compose o.s.; **sich kurz ~ be** brief.

Fassung *f Edelsteine:* setting; *Brille:* frame; *electr.* socket; *schriftlich:* draft (-ing); *Wortlaut:* wording, version; **die ~ verlieren** lose one's self-control; **aus der ~ bringen** disconcert; **2slos** disconcerted.

fast almost, nearly.

fasten fast.

Fastnacht *f* Shrove Tuesday, Mardi gras.

fauchen spit.

faul rotten; bad; *Person:* lazy; **~en** rot, go bad, decay.

faulenze|n idle, laze, loaf; **2r** *m* sluggard, lazy-bones.

Faulheit *f* laziness.

Fäulnis *f* rottenness, decay.

Faul|pelz *m s.* **Faulenzer; ~tier** *n* sloth.

Faust *f* fist; **~handschuh** *m* mitt(en); **~schlag** *m* blow with the fist, punch.

Favorit *m* favo(u)rite.

Februar *m* February.

fechten fence.

Feder *f* feather; *Schreib2:* pen; *tech.* spring; **~ball-spiel** *n* badminton; **~bett** *n* eiderdown; **~gewicht** *n* featherweight; **~halter** *m* penholder; **2nd** springy, elastic; **~ung** *f mot.* springs *pl;* **~vieh** *n* poultry.

Fee *f* fairy.

fegen sweep.

fehlen be absent; be miss-

ing; lack, be lacking; **sie fehlt uns** we miss her; **was fehlt Ihnen?** what is the matter with you?

Fehler *m* mistake, error; *tech.* defect, flaw; **2frei** faultless, perfect; *tech.* flawless; **2haft** faulty, defective; incorrect.

Fehl|geburt *f* miscarriage, abortion; **~schlag** *m fig.* failure; **2schlagen** *fig.* fail, miscarry; **~zündung** *f mot.* misfire, backfire.

Feier *f* ceremony; celebration; **~abend** *m:* **~ machen** finish; **2lich** solemn; **2n** celebrate; **~tag** *m* holiday.

feig(e) cowardly.

Feige *f* fig.

Feig|heit *f* cowardice; **~ling** *m* coward.

Feile *f* file; **2n** file.

feilschen haggle.

fein fine; delicate; *Qualität:* high-grade; choice; *Unterschied:* subtle.

Feind *m* enemy; **2lich** hostile; **~schaft** *f* enmity, *stärker:* animosity; **2selig** hostile.

fein|fühlig sensitive; **2-heit** *f* fineness; delicacy; **2-kost** *f* delicatessen *sg, pl;* **2-schmecker** *m* gourmet.

Feld *n* field; *Schach:* square; **~flasche** *f* water-bottle, *Am.* canteen; **~stecher** *m s.* **Fernglas; ~webel** *m* sergeant; **~weg** *m* (field) path.

Felge *f* felloe; *mot.* rim.

Fell n skin, fur; *lebender Tiere*: coat; *Schaf*: fleece.

Fels m rock; **∼block** m rock, boulder; **∼en** m rock; **∼ig** rocky.

Fenster n window; **∼brett** n window-sill; **∼laden** m shutter; **∼rahmen** m window-frame; **∼scheibe** f (window-)pane.

Ferien pl holiday(s pl), Am. vacation sg; *parl.* recess; *jur.* vacation, recess; **∼dorf** n holiday village; **∼wohnung** f holiday flat.

Ferkel n young pig; *fig.* pig.

fern far, distant, remote; **2amt** n trunk (Am. long-distance) exchange; **∼bleiben** remain od. stay away (dat from); **2e** f distance; remoteness; **∼er** further (-more), in addition; **2gespräch** n trunk (Am. long-distance) call; **∼gesteuert** Rakete: guided; Flugzeug etc.: remote-controlled; **2glas** n (ein a pair of) field-glasses pl; binoculars pl; **2heizung** f district heating; **2licht** n mot. full (headlight) beam; **2rohr** n telescope; **2schreiber** m teleprinter, Am. teletypewriter; **2sehapparat** m s.

Fernseher / **2sehen** n television; **∼sehen** watch television; **2seher** m television set; **2sehzuschauer** n television viewer; **2sicht** f view; **2sprechamt** n telephone exchange, Am. a. central; **2sprechzelle** f

telephone kiosk (Am. booth); **2verkehr** m long-distance traffic.

Ferse f heel.

fertig ready; finished; *Kleidung*: ready-made; **∼bringen** manage; **∼machen** finish, complete; **(sich) ∼machen** get ready; **2stellung** f completion.

Fessel f chain, fetter; *anat.* ankle; *Pferd*: pastern; *fig.* bond, fetter, tie; **2n** chain; *fig.* fascinate; **2nd** fascinating.

fest firm (a. fig.); solid; *Schlaf*: sound. [feast.]

Fest n celebration; *eccl.*

fest|binden fasten, tie (**an** to); **∼halten** hold on (**an** to); **∼halten an** fig. cling to; **sich ∼halten an** hold on to; **2land** n mainland, continent; **∼legen: sich ∼ auf** commit o.s. to; **∼lich** festive; **∼machen** fix, fasten; *mar.* moor (**alle: an** to); **2nahme** f arrest; **∼nehmen** arrest; **∼schnallen** strap down; **∼setzen** fix, set; **2spiele** pl festival sg; **∼stehen** stand firm; *fig.* be certain; **∼stellen** find out; see, perceive; **2tag** m festive day; holiday; **2ung** f fortress; **2zug** m procession.

fett fat; *Boden*: rich; **2** n fat; grease (a. tech.); **2fleck** m grease-spot; **∼ig** fat; *Haut*: oily; *Haare, Finger*: greasy.

Fetzen m shred; *Lumpen*: rag.

feucht damp, moist; _Luft:_ humid; 2igkeit _f_ moisture; dampness; _Luft:_ humidity.

Feuer _n_ fire; _fig._ ardo(u)r; ~**alarm** fire-alarm; ~**bestattung** _f_ cremation; 2~**fest** fire-proof, fire-resistant; 2**gefährlich** inflammable; ~**leiter** _f_ fire-escape; ~**löscher** _m_ fire-extinguisher; ~**melder** _m_ fire-alarm; 2n shoot, fire; ~**wehr** _f_ fire-brigade, _Am. a._ fire department; _Fahrzeug:_ fire-engine; ~**wehrmann** _m_ fireman; ~**werk** _n_ (display of) fireworks _pl;_ ~**zeug** _n_ (cigarette-)lighter.

feurig fiery; _fig. a._ ardent.

Fibel _f_ primer.

Fichte _f_ spruce; ~**nnadel** _f_ pine needle.

Fieber _n_ temperature, fever; ~ **haben** _s._ **fiebern;** 2**haft** feverish; 2n have _od._ run a temperature; ~**thermometer** _n_ clinical thermometer.

fiebrig feverish.

Figur _f_ figure; _Schach:_ chessman, piece.

Filet _n_ fillet.

Filiale _f_ branch.

Film _m_ _Überzug:_ film, thin coating; _phot._ film; _Spiel2:_ film, (moving) picture, _Am. a._ motion picture, _colloq._ movie; ~**aufnahme** _f_ _Vorgang:_ filming, shooting; _Einzelszene:_ shot; 2**en** film, shoot; ~**kamera** _f_ cine-camera, film (_Am._ motion-picture _od._ movie) camera;

~**schauspieler(in** _f_) _m_ film _od._ screen actor (_od._ actress), _Am. colloq._ movie actor (_od._ actress); ~**theater** _n_ cinema, _Am._ motion-picture theater.

Filter _m, tech. n_ filter; 2n filter; ~**zigarette** _f_ filter-tipped cigarette.

Filz _m_ felt.

Finale _n sp._ final(s _pl_); _mus., thea._ finale.

Finanz|**amt** _n_ tax _od._ revenue office; _England:_ a. office of the Inspector of Taxes; ~**en** _pl_ finances _pl;_ 2**iell** financial; 2**ieren** finance; ~**minister** _m_ Minister of Finance, _Brit._ Chancellor of the Exchequer, _Am._ Secretary of the Treasury.

finden find; discover; _der Ansicht sein:_ think.

Finger _m_ finger; ~**abdruck** _m_ fingerprint; ~**hut** _m_ thimble; _bot._ foxglove.

Fink _m_ finch.

Finn|**e** _m_ Finn; 2**isch** Finnish. 2**nis** _f_} darkness).

finster dark; gloomy; 2**nis** _f_}

Firma _f_ firm, business, company.

firmen _eccl._ confirm.

First _m_ _arch._ ridge.

Fisch _m_ fish; ~**dampfer** _m_ trawler; 2**en** fish; ~**er** _m_ fisherman; ~**erdorf** _n_ fishing-village; ~**fang** _m_ fishing; ~**gräte** _f_ fishbone; ~**händler** _m_ fishmonger, _Am._ fish dealer.

fix quick; clever, smart.

flach flat; *seicht*: shallow.

Fläche f surface; *geom.* area; *ebene* ~ plane.

Flachland n plain.

Flachs m flax.

flackern flicker.

Flagge f flag.

Flamme f flame; *lodernde*: blaze.

Flanell m flannel; ~**hose** f flannels pl.

Flanke f flank.

Flasche f bottle; *Taschen*~: flask.

Flaschen|bier n bottled beer; ~**öffner** m bottle-opener; ~**zug** m pulley.

flattern flutter; *Haare etc.*: stream, fly.

flau weak, feeble, faint; *econ.* dull, slack.

Flaum m down, fluff, fuzz.

Flaute f dead calm; *econ.* dullness, slack period.

Flechte f *Haar*: braid, plait; *bot., med.* lichen; 2**n** braid, plait; *Korb, Kranz*: weave.

Fleck m *Schmutz, zo.*: mark, spot; *Öl*: smear; *Blut, Wein, Kaffee*: stain; *Tinte*: stain, blot; *Stelle, Ort*: place, spot; *Flicken*: patch; *fig.* blemish, spot, stain; ~**enwasser** n spot *od.* stain remover; 2**ig** spotted; stained.

Fledermaus f bat.

Flegel m flail; *Person*: lout, boor.

flehen: ~ um plead for.

Fleisch n flesh; *Schlacht*2: meat; *Frucht*2: pulp; ~

brühe f meat-broth; *klare*: beef tea; ~**er** m butcher; ~**erei** f butcher's shop; 2**ig** fleshy; *bot.* pulpy; ~**konserven** pl tinned (*Am.* canned) meat *sg.*

Fleiß m diligence, industry; 2**ig** diligent, industrious, hard-working.

fletschen: die Zähne ~ *Tier*: bare its teeth.

Flick|en m patch; 2**en** patch; *Schuhe, Dach etc.*: mend, repair; ~**werk** n patchwork.

Flieder m lilac. [bowtie.}

Fliege f fly; *Krawatte*:}

fliegen fly.

Fliegen|gewicht n flyweight; ~**pilz** m fly agaric.

Flieger m airman, pilot.

fliehen flee, run away (**vor** from).

Fliese f tile.

Fließ|band n assembly line; *Förderband*: conveyor-belt; 2**en** flow; *Leitungswasser etc.*: run; 2**end** *Verkehr*: moving; *Rede*: fluent.

flimmern glimmer, glitter; *Film*: flicker.

flink quick, nimble, brisk.

Flinte f shot-gun.

Flirt m flirtation; 2**en** flirt.

Flitter m spangles pl, sequins pl; ~**wochen** pl honeymoon *sg.*

Flock|e f flake; *Wolle*: flock; 2**ig** fluffy, flaky.

Floh m flea.

Floß n raft.

Flosse f fin; *Robbe*: flipper.

Flöte f flute.

flott quick, brisk; gay, lively; *Kleidung*: smart, stylish.

Flotte f fleet; *Kriegs♭*: navy; **~nstützpunkt** m naval base.

Fluch m curse; *Schimpfwort*: curse, swear-word; **♭en** swear, curse.

Flucht f flight (**vor** from); escape (**aus** from).

flücht|en flee (**nach, zu** to); run away; *Gefangener*: escape; **~ig** fugitive (a. fig.); *kurz*: fleeting; *oberflächlich*: careless, superficial; *chem.* volatile; **♭ling** m fugitive; *pol.* refugee; **♭lingslager** n refugee camp.

Flug m flight; **im ~(e)** rapidly, quickly.

Flügel m wing; *Propeller etc.*: blade, vane; *mus.* grand piano.

Fluggast m (air) passenger.

flügge fully-fledged.

Flug|gesellschaft f airline (company); **~hafen** m airport; **~kapitän** m captain; **~karte** f ticket; **~linie** f airline; **~lotse** m air traffic controller; **~platz** m airfield; **~sicherung** f air traffic control; **~steig** m gate, channel; **~verkehr** m air traffic; **~zeit** f flying time.

Flugzeug n aircraft, aeroplane, *colloq.* plane, *Am. a.* airplane; **~kanzel** f cockpit; **~rumpf** m fuselage, body; **~träger** m aircraft

carrier; **~unglück** n air crash *od.* disaster.

Flunder f flounder.

flunkern fib, tell a fib.

Flur m hall.

Fluß m river, stream; flow (-ing); *fig.* fluency, flux; **♭ab(wärts)** downstream; **♭auf(wärts)** upstream; **~bett** n river bed.

flüssig fluid, liquid; *Metall*: molten, melted; *Stil*: fluent; **♭keit** f fluid, liquid.

flüstern whisper.

Flut f flood; high tide, (flood-)tide; *fig.* flood, torrent; **~licht** n floodlight; **~welle** f tidal wave.

Fohlen n foal; *männliches*: colt; *weibliches*: filly.

Föhre f pine.

Folge f sequence, succession; *Hörfunkserie*: instal(l)-ment, part; *Reihe*: series; *Ergebnis*: consequence, result; **♭en** follow; *als Nachfolger*: succeed (**j-m** s.o.; **auf** to); *sich ergeben*: follow, ensue (**aus** from); *gehorchen*: obey (**j-m** s.o.); **♭lich** therefore; **♭sam** obedient.

Folie f foil.

Folter f torture; **♭n** torture.

Fön m electric hair-dryer.

Fonds m fund(s pl).

Fontäne f fountain.

Förderband n conveyor-belt.

fordern demand; *Entschädigung*: claim; *Preis*: ask.

fördern further, advance; *Bergbau*: haul, raise.

Forderung f demand; *An-spruch*: claim.

Forelle f trout.

Form f form; *Gestalt*: figure, shape; *tech.* mo(u)ld; *sp.* form, condition; **2al** formal; **~alität** f formality; **~at** n size; **~el** f formula; **2en** form; *Material*: shape, fashion.

förmlich formal.

formlos formless, shapeless; *fig.* informal.

Formular n form, *Am. a.* blank.

formulieren formulate; *Frage etc.*: word, phrase.

forsch vigorous, energetic; *draufgängerisch*: smart, dashing.

forsch|en: **~ nach** search for; **2er** m researcher, research worker; *Entdecker*: explorer; **2ung** f research (work).

Forst m forest.

Förster m forester.

fort *weg*: away, gone; *weiter*: on; *verloren*: gone, lost; **~bestehen** continue; **~fahren** depart, leave; *mit dem Auto etc.*: a. drive off; *fig.* continue, keep on; **~führen** continue, carry on; **~gehen** go (away), leave; **~geschritten** advanced; **~laufend** consecutive, continuous); **~pflanzen** sich **~** propagate, reproduce; **~schaffen** take away, remove; **~schreiten** advance, proceed, progress; **2schritt** m progress; **~**

schrittlich progressive; **~setzen** continue, pursue; **2setzung** f: **~ folgt** to be continued; **~während** adj continuous; adv constantly, always.

Foto n colloq. photo; **~apparat** m camera; **~graf** m photographer; **~grafie** f photography; photo (-graph); **2grafieren** photograph; take a photo (-graph) of.

Fotokopie f photostat.

Foyer n bsd. thea. foyer.

Fracht f goods pl; freight; *mar. a.* cargo; *Gebühr*: carriage, *aer.*, *mar.*, *Am.* freight; **~er** m freighter.

Frack m dress coat, tailcoat.

Frage f question; *gr.*, *rhet.* interrogation; *Problem*: problem, point; **~bogen** m questionnaire; *für Antragsteller*: form; **2n** ask; *ausfragen*: question; **~zeichen** n question-mark.

fraglich doubtful, uncertain; *betreffend*: in question.

Fragment n fragment.

fragwürdig doubtful, dubious.

frankieren stamp.

Franse f fringe.

Franz|ose m Frenchman; **die ~osen** pl the French pl; **2ösisch** French.

Frau f woman; *Dame*: lady; *Ehe2*: wife; **~ X** Mrs X; **~enarzt** m gyn(a)ecologist.

Fräulein n young lady; teacher; shop-assistant; waitress; ~ **X** Miss X.
frech impudent, colloq. saucy; **2heit** f impudence, colloq. sauciness.
frei free (**von** from, of); nicht besetzt: vacant; Feld: open; ~**er Tag** day off.
Frei|bad n outdoor swimming pool; ~**e** n: **im** ~**n** in the open (air), outdoors; **ins**~ into the open(air), outdoors; **2geben** release; **j-m 2geben** give s.o. time off; **2gepäck** n free luggage (allowance); **2haben** have a holiday; im Büro etc. have a day off; ~**hafen** m free port; **2handel** m free trade; ~**heit** f liberty, freedom; ~**karte** f free ticket; **2lassen** release, set free od. at liberty; **gegen Kaution 2lassen** release on bail; ~**lassung** f release; ~**lauf** m freewheel.
freilich admittedly; bejahend: certainly, of course.
Frei|lichtbühne f open-air theat|re (Am. -er); ~**lichtkino** n open-air cinema, bsd. Am. outdoor od. drive-in theater; **2machen** Post: prepay, stamp; ~**maurer** m freemason; **2mütig** frank; **2sprechen** acquit; ~**stoß** m Fußball: free kick; ~**tag** m Friday; **2willig** voluntary; ~**willige** m volunteer; ~**zeit** f free (spare, leisure) time.

fremd strange; ausländisch: foreign, alien (a. fig.).
Fremde[1] f distant od. foreign parts; **in der** ~ abroad.
Fremde[2] m, f stranger; Ausländer: foreigner.
Fremden|führer m guide; ~**heim** n boarding house; ~**verkehr** m tourism; ~**verkehrsbüro** n tourist office (bureau, agency); ~**zimmer** n room.
fremd|ländisch foreign, exotic; **2sprache** f foreign language; **2wort** n foreign word.
Frequenz f frequency.
fressen eat; colloq. devour.
Freud|e f joy; Vergnügen: pleasure; **2estrahlend** radiant with joy; **2ig** joyful; happy; **2los** cheerless.
freuen: es freut mich I am glad od. pleased; **sich** ~ **über** be pleased about od. with, be glad about; **sich** ~ **auf** look forward to.
Freund m (boy)friend; ~**in** f (girl)friend; **2lich** friendly, kind, nice; Zimmer: cheerful; ~**schaft** f friendship.
Friede(n) m peace.
Fried|hof m cemetery, graveyard, churchyard; **2lich** peaceful.
frieren freeze; Fenster etc.: freeze over; **mich friert I** am cold, I feel cold.
frisch fresh; Eier: newlaid; Wäsche: clean; Brot:

new; **~ gestrichen!** wet (*Am.* fresh) paint!

Friseu|r *m* hairdresser; *Herren*:barber;**~se** *f*(woman) hairdresser.

frisier|en: j-n ~ do *od.* dress s.o.'s hair; **sich ~** do one's hair; **2salon** *m* hairdressing saloon.

Frist *f* (fixed, limited) period of time; term; *jur.* respite.

Frisur *f* hair-style, hair-do.

froh glad; cheerful, gay.

fröhlich cheerful, happy.

fromm pious; *Gebet:* devout.

Frömmigkeit *f* piety.

Front *f arch.* front, façade; *mil.* front,line; *fig.* frontal; *Zusammenstoß:* head-on; **~antrieb** *m mot.* frontwheel drive.

Frosch *m* frog.

Frost *m* frost; **~beule** *f* chilblain.

frösteln feel chilly.

frostig frosty; *fig.* cold.

frottier|en rub down; **2tuch** *n* Turkish towel.

Frucht *f* fruit; **2bar** fertile; fruitful.

früh early; **am ~en Morgen** in the early morning; **~ aufstehen** rise early; **heute ~** this morning; **2aufsteher** *m* early riser, *colloq.* early bird; **~er** earlier; former; formerly, in former times; **~estens** at the earliest; **2geburt** *f* premature birth; premature baby *od.* animal;**2jahr**

n, **~ling** *m* spring; **~morgens** early in the morning; **~reif** precocious.

Frühstück *n* breakfast; **Zimmer mit ~** bed and breakfast; **2en** (have) breakfast.

Fuchs *m* fox; *Pferd:* sorrel.

Füchsin *f* she-fox, vixen.

Fuge *f tech.* joint.

fügen: sich ~ in submit to.

fühl|bar *fig.* sensible, noticeable; **~en: (sich) ~** feel; **2er** *m* feeler.

führen *v/t* lead, guide, conduct, show; *Geschäft etc.:* run; *Waren:* deal in; *Leben:* lead; *Tagebuch etc.:* keep; *Krieg:* make, wage; *v/i Pfad etc.:* lead, go (**nach, zu** to); *sp.* (hold the) lead; **~ zu** lead to, result in; **~d** leading, prominent.

Führer *m* leader (*a. pol.*); *Fremden*2: guide; *Reise*2: guide(-book); **~schein** *m mot.* driving licence, *Am.* driver's license.

Führung *f* leadership; management; *Besichtigung:* conducted tour; *Benehmen:* conduct, behavio(u)r; *sp.* lead; **in ~ liegen** lead; **~szeugnis** *n* certificate of good conduct.

Fuhrunternehmer *m* carrier.

füllen fill; *Zahn:* stop, fill; *Kissen, Geflügel etc.:* stuff.

Füllen *n s.* Fohlen.

Füll|er *m colloq.,* **~feder (-halter** *m*) *f* fountain-pen;

~ung f filling; *Zahn*: stopping, filling; stuffing; *Tür*: panel.

Fundament n foundation; *fig.* basis.

Fund|büro n lost-property office; **~sachen** pl lost property sg.

fünf five; **2eck** n pentagon; **2kampf** m sp. pentathlon; **2linge** pl quintuplets pl; **~te** fifth; **2tel** n fifth (part); **~tens** fifthly, in the fifth place; **~zehn(te)** fifteen(th); **~zig** fifty; **~zigste** fiftieth.

Funk m radio, wireless.

Funke m spark; *fig. a.* glimmer; **2ln** sparkle, glitter; *Stern*: twinkle, sparkle; **~n** m bsd. fig. s. **Funke**.

funk|en radio, transmit; **2er** m radio od. wireless operator; **2gerät** n radioset; **2signal** n radio signal; **2spruch** m radio od. wireless message; **2station** f radio od. wireless station; **2streifenwagen** m radio patrol car.

Funktion f function; **~är** m functionary, official; **2ieren** work; **nicht2ieren** *Lift*: be out of order.

für for; in exchange od. return for; **Schritt ~ Schritt** step by step; **Tag ~ Tag** day after day.

Furche f furrow; *Wagenspur*: rut.

Furcht f fear, dread; **aus ~ vor** for fear of; **2bar** terrible, dreadful.

fürcht|en fear, dread; **sich ~en vor** be afraid od. scared of; **~erlich** terrible.

furcht|los fearless; **~sam** timid, timorous.

Fürsorge f care; **öffentliche ~** public welfare (work); **soziale ~** social welfare (work); **~erziehung** f corrective training; **~r(in** f) m (social) welfare worker.

Fürsprache f intercession; **~sprecher** m intercessor.

Fürst m prince; **~entum** n principality.

Furt f ford.

Furunkel m boil, furuncle.

Fuß m foot; **zu ~** on foot; **zu ~ gehen** walk; **~abstreifer** m door-scraper, door-mat.

Fußball m football; (association) football, *colloq. u. Am.* soccer; **~platz** m football ground; **~spiel** n football match; **~spieler** m football player, footballer.

Fuß|boden m floor(ing); **~bremse** f mot. footbrake.

Fußgänger m pedestrian; **~übergang** m pedestrian crossing; **~unterführung** f subway; **~zone** f pedestrian precinct od. zone.

Fuß|gelenk n ankle joint; **~note** f footnote; **~pfad** m footpath; **~sohle** f sole of the foot; **~spur** f foot-

print; *mehrere*: track; **~tritt** *m* kick; **~weg** *m* footpath.
Futter¹ *n* food; *Vieh*♀: feed; *Trocken*♀: fodder.
Futter² *n* lining.
Futteral *n Brille etc.*: case; *Schirmhülle*: cover; *Messer*: sheath.
fütter|n feed; *Kleid*: line; **♀ung** *f* feeding.
Futur *n gr.* future (tense).

G

Gabe *f* gift, present; *Almosen*: alms.
Gabel *f* fork; **♀n: sich ~** fork, bifurcate.
gackern cackle.
gaffen gape; stare.
Gage *f* salary.
gähnen yawn.
Galerie *f* gallery.
Galgen *m* gallows *sg*.
Galle *f* bile; gall; **~nstein** *m* gall-stone, bile-stone.
Gallert *n*, **~e** *f* jelly.
Galopp *m* gallop; *kurzer*: canter; **♀ieren** gallop; canter.
Gang *m* walk; *tech.* running, working; *Boten*♀: errand; *Verlauf*, *Mahlzeit*: course; *Flur*: corridor; *zwischen Sitzreihen*: gangway, *bsd. Am.* aisle; *mot.* gear; **erster (zweiter, dritter, vierter) ~** low *od.* bottom (second, third, top) gear; **in ~ bringen** *od.* **setzen** set going *od.* in motion; **~art** *f* gait, walk; *Pferd*: pace; **~schaltung** *f* gear-change.
Gans *f* goose.
Gänse|blümchen *n* daisy; **~braten** *m* roast goose; **~haut** *f fig.* goose-flesh, *Am. a.* goose pimples *pl*; **~rich** *m* gander.
ganz *adj* all; *ungeteilt*: entire, whole; *vollständig*: complete, total, full; **den ~en Tag** all day (long); *adv* quite; entirely.
gänzlich complete, total, entire.
Ganztagsbeschäftigung *f* full-time job *od.* employment.
gar *Speisen*: done; **~ nicht** not at all; **~ nichts** nothing at all.
Garage *f* garage.
Garantie *f* guarantee, *jur.* guaranty; **♀ren** guarantee.
Garbe *f* sheaf.
Garde *f* guard.
Garderobe *f* wardrobe; cloakroom, *Am.* checkroom; *thea.* dressing-room; **~nmarke** *f* check.
Gardine *f* curtain.
gären ferment.
Garn *n* yarn; thread; cotton.
Garnele *f* shrimp, prawn.
garnieren garnish.
Garnison *f* garrison.
Garnitur *f* set.
garstig nasty.
Garten *m* garden.

Gärtner m gardener; ~ei f market-garden; nursery.

Gas n gas; ~ geben mot. accelerate; ~ wegnehmen mot. decelerate; 2förmig gaseous; ~hahn m gastap; ~heizung f gas-heating; ~herd m gas-stove, Am. gas range; ~leitung f gas-mains pl; ~ofen m gas-oven; ~pedal n accelerator (pedal), Am. gas pedal.

Gasse f lane, alley.

Gast m guest; visitor; Wirtshaus: customer; ~arbeiter m foreign worker.

Gästezimmer n guest-room; spare (bed)room.

gast|freundlich hospitable; 2freundschaft f hospitality; 2geber m host; 2geberin f hostess; 2haus n, 2hof m restaurant; inn, (small) hotel; ~lich hospitable; 2spiel n thea. guest performance; 2stätte f, 2stube f restaurant; 2wirt m innkeeper, landlord; 2wirtschaft f restaurant; public house, colloq. pub.

Gas|werk n gas-works sg; ~zähler m gas-meter.

Gatt|e m husband; ~in f wife.

Gattung f bot., zo. genus; fig. kind, sort, type.

Gaul m (old) nag.

Gaumen m anat. palate.

Gauner m scoundrel, sl. crook.

Gaze f gauze.

Gazelle f gazelle.

Geächtete m, f outlaw.

Gebäck n feines: pastry, fancy cakes pl; s. **Plätzchen.**

gebären give birth to.

Gebäude n building, edifice.

geben give; Karten: deal; **es gibt** there is, there are; **was gibt es?** what is the matter?; **gegeben werden** thea. be on.

Gebet n prayer.

Gebiet n territory; Bezirk: district; Fläche: area; Fach-2: field; Wissens2: province; Interessen2: sphere.

Gebilde n shape; structure.

gebildet educated; cultured, cultivated.

Gebirg|e n mountains pl; 2ig mountainous; ~skette f, ~szug m mountain chain od. range.

Gebiß n (set of) teeth; künstliches: (set of) artificial od. false teeth, denture; Zaum: bit.

geboren born; ~er Deutscher German by birth; ~e Smith née Smith.

geborgen safe.

Gebot n order, command; **die Zehn** ~e pl eccl. the Ten Commandments pl; ~sschild n mandatory sign.

Gebrauch m use; 2en use; 2t second-hand; ~sanweisung f directions pl od. instructions pl for use; ~twagen m used od. second-hand car.

Gebrech|en n defect; **2-lich** fragile; *schwach:* infirm. [lowing.]

Gebrüll n roaring; *Rind:*]

Gebühr f *Kosten:* charge; *Post:* rate; *amtliche:* fee; **2en** be due (*dat* to); **2en-frei** free of charge; **2en-pflichtig** liable to charges.

Geburt f birth; **.enkontrolle** f birth-control.

gebürtig: ~ aus a native of.

Geburts|datum n date of birth; **.jahr** n year of birth; **.ort** m place of birth, birth-place; **.tag** m birthday; **.urkunde** f birth certificate.

Gebüsch n bushes *pl*, undergrowth.

Gedächtnis n memory.

Gedanke m thought; idea; **2nlos** thoughtless; **.nstrich** m dash; **2nvoll** thoughtful.

Ge|därme *pl* entrails *pl*, bowels *pl*; intestines *pl*; **.deck** n cover; menu; **2-deihen** thrive, prosper.

gedenk|en think of; intend; *ehrend:* commemorate; **2tafel** f (commemorative) plaque.

Gedicht n poem.

Gedräng|e n crowd, throng; **2t** crowded, packed.

gedrückt *fig.* depressed.

Geduld f patience; **2en: sich ~** have patience; **2ig** patient.

ge|ehrt hono(u)red; *Brief:* **Sehr .ehrter Herr N.!**

Dear Sir, Dear Mr N.; **.eignet** fit; suitable.

Gefahr f danger, peril; risk; **auf eigene ~** at one's own risk.

gefähr|den endanger; risk; **.lich** dangerous.

Gefährt|e m, **.in** f companion.　　　　　[gradient.]

Gefälle n fall, descent,]

Gefallen[1] m favo(u)r.

Gefallen[2] n: **~ finden an** take (a) pleasure in, take a fancy to *od.* for; **2 please; es gefällt mir** I like it; **sich et. 2 lassen** put up with s.th.

gefällig pleasing, agreeable; obliging; kind; **2keit** f kindness; favo(u)r.

gefangen captive; imprisoned; **2e** m, f prisoner, captive; **.nehmen** take prisoner; *fig.* captivate; **2schaft** f captivity, imprisonment.

Gefängnis n prison, jail, gaol; **.strafe** f sentence *od.* term of imprisonment.

Gefäß n vessel (*a. anat.*).

gefaßt composed; **~ auf** prepared for.

Ge|fecht n *mil.* engagement, action; **.fieder** n plumage, feathers *pl.*

gefleckt spotted.

Geflügel n fowl, poultry.

gefräßig greedy, voracious.

gefrier|en freeze; **2fach** n deep-freeze; **2fleisch** n frozen meat; **2punkt** m freezing-point; ⎰**truhe** *f* deep-freeze.

gefügig pliable.

Gefühl *n* feel; *Empfindung*: feeling (*a. fig.*), sensation; *Gemütsregung*: emotion; ⎰**los** unfeeling; insensible; ⎰**voll** sentimental.

gegen towards; against; *jur., sp.* versus; *vergleichend*: compared with; *als Entgelt*: (in exchange) for; *Medikament*: for; *ungefähr*: about, *Am.* around.

Gegenangriff *m* counter-attack.

Gegend *f* region, area.

gegeneinander against one another *od.* each other.

Gegen|gewicht *n* counter-balance, counterpoise; **⤷gift** *n* antidote, antitoxin; **⤷leistung** *f* return (service), equivalent; **⤷licht** *n phot.* against the light; **⤷lichtblende** *f phot.* lense hood; **⤷maßnahme** *f* counter-measure; **⤷mittel** *n* remedy, antidote; **⤷satz** *m* contrast; opposition; **im ⤷satz zu** in contrast to *od.* with, in opposition to; **⤷seite** *f* opposite side; **⤷seitig** mutual, reciprocal; **⤷spieler** *m* opponent, antagonist; **⤷stand** *m* object; *fig.* subject, topic; **⤷stück** *n* counterpart; **⤷teil** *n* contrary, reverse; **im ⤷teil** on the contrary.

gegenüber opposite; **⤷stehen** be faced with, face.

Gegen|wart *f* presence; *jetzige Zeit*: present time; *gr.* present (tense); **⤷wärtig** (at) present; **⤷wert** *m* equivalent; **⤷wind** *m* head wind; **⤷zug** *m* corresponding train. [ponent.]

Gegner *m* adversary, op-⎰

Gehackte *n* minced meat.

Gehalt[1] *m* content.

Gehalt[2] *n* salary, **⤷serhöhung** *f* rise (in salary), *Am.* raise. [ful.⎰]

gehässig malicious, spite-⎰

Gehäuse *n* box; case.

geheim secret; ⎰**dienst** *m* secret service; ⎰**nis** *n* secret; mystery; **⤷nisvoll** mysterious.

gehen go; *zu Fuß*: walk; *weg.*: leave; *Maschine*: go, work; *Uhr*: go; *Ware*: sell; *Wind*: blow; **wie geht es Ihnen?** how are you?

Geheul *n* howling.

Gehilf|e *m*, **⤷in** *f* assistant.

Gehirn *n* brain(s *pl*); **⤷erschütterung** *f* concussion (of the brain).

Gehöft *n* farm.

Gehölz *n* wood, coppice.

Gehör *n* hearing; ear.

gehorchen obey.

gehör|en belong (*dat*, **zu** to); **⤷ig** *adj* proper, right; *colloq.* good; *adv colloq.* thoroughly. [obedience.⎰]

gehorsam obedient; ⎰ *m*

Geh|steig *m*, **⤷weg** *m* pavement, *Am.* sidewalk.

Geier *m* vulture.

Geige *f* violin, *colloq.* fiddle; **⤷r(in** *f*) *m* violinist.

Geisel f hostage.

Geiß f (she-, nanny-)goat; **~bock** m he-goat, billy-goat.

Geist m spirit; mind, intellect; wit; *Gespenst*: ghost.

geistes|abwesend absent-minded; **~gegenwärtig**; **~ sein** have the presence of mind; *schlagfertig*: be quick-witted; **~gestört** mentally disturbed; **~krank** insane, mentally ill; **2zustand** m state of mind.

geistig intellectual, mental; **~e Getränke** pl spirits pl.

geistlich spiritual; **2e** m clergyman; minister.

geistreich witty; ingenious; spirited.

Geiz m avarice; **~hals** m miser; **~ig** niggardly, stingy.

Ge|jammer n lamentation(s pl); **~kreisch** n screaming, shrieking; **~lächter** n laughter.

gelähmt paralysed, crippled.

Gelände n area; *Boden*: ground; *Landschaft*: country; *mil.* terrain; **~lauf** m cross-country run.

Geländer n railing(s pl), banisters pl; *Balkon*: balustrade.

gelassen calm, composed.

Gelatine f gelatin(e).

ge|läufig common; familiar; **~launt**: **gut** od. **schlecht ~ sein** be in a

good od. bad humo(u)r od. mood.

Geläut(e) n ringing; *Kirchenglocken*: chimes pl.

gelb yellow; **2sucht** f jaundice.

Geld n money; **~anlage** f investment; **~ausgabe** f expense; **~buße** f fine; **~schein** m banknote, *Am.* bill; **~schrank** m strong-box, safe; **~sendung** f remittance; **~strafe** f fine; **~stück** n coin; **~wechsel** m exchange of money.

Gelee n, m jelly.

gelegen situated; *passend*: convenient.

Gelegenheit f occasion; *günstige*: opportunity; **~skauf** m bargain.

gelegentlich occasional.

gelehr|ig docile; **~t** learned; **2te** m learned man, scholar.

Geleise n s. Gleis.

Geleit n escort; **2en** v/t accompany; conduct; *bsd. schützend*: escort; **~zug** m *mar.* convoy.

Gelenk n joint; **2ig** supple.

gelernt skilled, trained.

Geliebte m lover; f mistress. {it mildly.}

gelinde: **~ gesagt** to put}

gelingen succeed; **es gelingt mir zu** I succeed in ger.

gellend shrill, piercing.

geloben vow, promise.

gelten be valid; *Geld*: be current; **~ als** pass for; **~ für** apply to; **~ lassen** let

pass; ~d: ~ machen An-
spruch, Recht: assert.

Gelübde n vow.

gelungen successful.

gemächlich leisurely, comfortable, easy.

Gemahl m husband; ~in f
wife.

Gemälde n painting, picture; ~galerie f picture-
gallery.

gemäß according to; ~igt
moderate; temperate (a.
geogr.).

gemein common; mean.

Gemeinde f community;
eccl. parish; in der Kirche:
congregation; ~rat m mu-
nicipal council; Person:
municipal council(l)or.

Gemein|heit f meanness;
mean trick; 2sam com-
mon; ~schaft f com-
munity.   [mal; grave.\

gemessen measured; for-\

Gemisch n mixture; ~t-
warenhandlung f gro-
cery.

Gemse f chamois.

Gemurmel n murmur(ing).

Gemüse n vegetable(s pl);
grünes: greens pl; ~händ-
ler m greengrocer.

gemütlich good-natured;
comfortable, snug, cosy;
2keit f snugness; cosi-
ness.

Gemüts|bewegung f
emotion; ~verfassung f,
~zustand m state of
mind.

genau exact, accurate; pre-
cise; just; 2igkeit f ac-

curacy, exactness; preci-
sion.

genehmig|en approve;
grant; 2ung f grant; ap-
proval; licen|ce, Am. -se;
permit; Erlaubnis: per-
mission.

geneigt inclined (zu to).

General m general; ~be-
vollmächtigte m econ.:
universal agent; general
manager; ~direktor m
managing director; ~kon-
sulm consul-general; ~kon-
sulat n consulate-general;
~probe f dress rehearsal;
~streik m general strike;
~vollmacht f full power
of attorney.

Generation f generation.

Generator m generator.

genes|en recover (von
from); 2ung f recovery.

genial brilliant.

Genick n nape of the neck,
(back of the) neck.

genieren: sich ~ feel od.
be embarrassed.

genieß|bar eatable; drink-
able; ~en enjoy.

Genitiv m gr. genitive
(case).

genormt standardized.

Genosse m pol. comrade;
~nschaft f association;
co(-)operative (society).

genug enough, sufficient.

genüg|en be enough; ~end
sufficient; ~sam Essen:
frugal; bescheiden: modest.

Genugtuung f satisfaction.

Genus n gr. gender.

Genuß m von Nahrung:

consumption; *Essen:* eating, *Trinken:* drinking; *Vergnügen:* enjoyment, pleasure; *Hoch*2: treat; **~mittel** *n* semi-luxury.

Geo|graphie *f* geography; **~logie** *f* geology; **~metrie** *f* geometry.

Gepäck *n* luggage, *Am.* baggage; **~annahme** *f* luggage (registration) office *od.* counter; **~aufbewahrung** *f* left-luggage office *od.* counter, *Am.* checkroom; **~ausgabe** *f* luggage office *od.* counter; **~kontrolle** *f* luggage inspection, *Am.* baggage check; **~netz** *n* luggage-rack, *Am.* baggage rack; **~schein** *m* luggage receipt (slip, ticket), *Am.* baggage check; **~schließfach** *n* luggage locker; **~stück** *n* piece of luggage; **~träger** *m* porter; *Fahrrad:* carrier; **~wagen** *m* luggage-van, *Am.* baggage car.

gepflegt neat; *Garten:* well-kept.

Ge|plapper *n* babble, chatter(ing); **~plauder** *n* chat(ting), small talk; **~polter** *n* rumble.

gerade *adj* straight (*a. fig.*); *Zahl etc.:* even; *direkt:* direct; *Haltung:* upright, erect; *adv* straight; just; **~ dabei sein, et. zu tun** be just doing s.th.; **~ an dem Tage** on that very day; 2 *f* straight line; **~aus** straight on *od.* ahead; **~**

heraus frankly; **~(n)wegs** straight, directly; **~zu** almost, really.

Gerät *n* tool, implement, utensil; *Radio:* set; *Apparat:* apparatus.

geraten come, fall, get; **(gut) ~** turn out well.

Geratewohl *n:* **aufs ~** at random.

geräumig spacious.

Geräusch *n* noise; 2**los** noiseless; 2**voll** noisy.

gerben tan.

gerecht just; *rechtschaffen:* righteous; 2**igkeit** *f* justice; righteousness.

Gerede *n* talk; gossip; *Gerücht:* rumo(u)r.

gereizt irritable.

Gericht *n Küche:* dish, course; *jur. s.* Gerichtshof; 2**lich** legal.

Gerichts|barkeit *f* jurisdiction; **~hof** *m* law-court, court of justice; **~saal** *m* court-room; **~verhandlung** *f* trial; **~vollzieher** *m* bailiff.

gering little, small; *s.* geringfügig; **~er** inferior, less, minor; **~fügig** insignificant, trifling, slight; **~schätzig** contemptuous; 2**schätzung** *f* contempt; **~st** least.

gerinnen clot; *Milch:* curdle; *Blut:* coagulate, congeal.

Gerippe *n* skeleton.

gern(e) willingly, gladly; **~ haben** *od.* **mögen** be fond of, like.

Geröll n scree, detritus.

Gerste f barley; **~nkorn** n med. sty(e).

Geruch m smell, odo(u)r; angenehmer: scent; **2los** odo(u)rless; scentless.

Gerücht n rumo(u)r.

geruhsam peaceful, quiet.

Gerümpel n lumber, junk.

Gerund(ium) n gr. gerund.

Gerüst n scaffold(ing).

gesamt whole, entire, total, all; **2ausgabe** f complete edition; **2betrag** m sum total; **2schule** f comprehensive school.

Gesandt|e m envoy; **~schaft** f legation.

Gesang m singing; Lied: song.

Gesäß n seat, buttocks pl.

Geschäft n business; Laden: shop, Am. store; **2ig** busy, active; **2lich** adj business...; adv on business.

Geschäfts|... business...; **~führer** m manager; **~mann** m businessman; **~partner** m (business) partner; **~räume** pl business premises pl; **~reise** f business trip; **~schluß** m closing-time; **nach ~schluß** a. after business hours; **~zeit** f office od. business hours pl.

geschehen happen, occur, take place; in events pl.

gescheit clever, intelligent, bright.

Geschenk n present, gift;

~packung f gift-box.

Geschicht|e f story; tale; Wissenschaft: history; **2lich** historical.

Geschick n fate, destiny; skill; **~lichkeit** f skill; **2t** skil(l)ful.

Geschirr n dishes pl; Porzellan: china; Steingut: earthenware, crockery; Pferde: harness.

Geschlecht n sex; kind, species; Familie: family; gr. gender; **2lich** sexual.

Geschlechts|krankheit f venereal disease; **~teile** pl genitals pl; **~verkehr** m sexual intercourse.

geschliffen cut; fig. polished.

Geschmack m taste (a. fig.); Aroma: flavo(u)r; **2los** tasteless; pred fig. in bad taste; **2voll** tasteful; pred fig. in good taste.

geschmeidig supple, lithe.

Geschnatter n cackle, cackling.

Geschöpf n creature.

Geschoß n projectile, missile; Stockwerk: stor(e)y, floor.

Geschrei n cries pl; shouting; fig. noise, fuss.

Geschütz n gun, cannon.

Geschwader n mil.: mar. squadron; aer. wing, Am. group.

Geschwätz n idle talk; Klatsch: gossip; **2ig** talkative.

geschweige: ~ (denn) let alone.

geschwind fast, quick, swift.

Geschwindigkeit f quickness; _Tempo:_ speed; **~beschränkung** f speed limit; **~überschreitung** f speeding.

Geschwister pl brother's (pl) and sister's (pl).

Geschworene m, f juror; **die ~n** pl the jury sg.

Geschwulst f swelling; tumo(u)r.

Geschwür n abscess, ulcer.

Gesell|e m journeyman; **~en: sich zu j-m ~** join s.o.; **2ig** social, sociable.

Gesellschaft f society; company (a. econ.); party; **j-m ~ leisten** keep s.o. company; **~er(in** f) m econ. partner; **2lich** social.

Gesellschafts|reise f conducted tour; package(d) tour; **~spiel** n party od. round game.

Gesetz n law; **~buch** n code; statute-book; **~entwurf** m bill; **~geber** m legislator; **~gebung** f legislation; **2lich** lawful, legal; **2lich geschützt** patent, registered.

gesetzt ernst: sedate; **~ den Fall ...** supposing :..

gesetzwidrig unlawful, illegal.

Gesicht n face; _Miene:_ countenance.

Gesichts|ausdruck m expression, countenance; **~farbe** f complexion; **~punkt** m point of view;

~züge pl features pl, lineaments pl.

Gesindel n rabble, mob.

Gesinnung f mind; sentiment(s pl).

gespannt tense (a. fig.); _Seil:_ tight, taut; fig. intent, eager; _Aufmerksamkeit:_ close; _Verhältnis:_ strained.

Gespenst n ghost; **2isch** ghostly.

Gespräch n talk, conversation; teleph. call; **2ig** talkative.

Gestalt f form, shape; _Körperbau:_ figure; **2en** form, shape (a. fig.); arrange, organize.

geständ|ig: ~ sein confess; **2nis** n confession.

Gestank m stench.

gestatten allow, permit; **~ Sie!** allow me!, excuse me!

gestehen confess.

Ge|stein n rock, stone; **~stell** n stand, rack, shelf; _Rahmen:_ frame.

gest|ern yesterday; **~rig** of yesterday, yesterday's.

Gestrüpp n brush(wood), undergrowth.

Gestüt n stud (farm).

Gesuch n application; _Bittschrift:_ petition.

gesund sound; healthy; **~ werden** get well; **~er Menschenverstand** common sense.

Gesundheit f health.

Gesundheits|amt n public lic health department; **2schädlich** unhealthy, unwholesome; **~zustand** m state of health.

Getränk n drink, beverage.

Getreide n corn, grain.

Getriebe n mot. gear; **automatisches ~** automatic transmission; **~schaden** m gear defect.

Ge|tue n fuss; **~tümmel** m turmoil.

getupft dotted, spotted.

Gewächs n growth (a. med.); Pflanze: plant; **~haus** n greenhouse, hothouse.

ge|wachsen: j-m ~ sein be a match for s.o.; **e-r Sache ~ sein** be equal to s.th.; **~wagt** risky; bold.

Gewähr f guarantee, security; **Qen** grant, allow; **Qleisten** guarantee.

Gewahrsam m custody, safe-keeping.

Gewalt f power; authority; Zwang: force; violence; **mit ~** by force; **Qig** powerful, mighty; **Qsam** adj violent; adv a. forcibly; **Qsam öffnen** force open, open by force; **Qtätig** violent.

Gewand n garment; wallendes: robe; bsd. eccl. vestment. [clever.]

gewandt agile, nimble;}

Gewässer n water(s pl).

Gewebe n fabric; feines: tissue (a. anat., fig.); Webart: texture.

Gewehr n gun; rifle.

Geweih n horns pl, antlers pl.

Gewerb|e n trade, business; **Qlich** commercial, industrial; **Qsmäßig** professional.

Gewerkschaft f trade(s) union, Am. labor union; **~ler** m trade-unionist; **Qlich** trade-union.

Gewicht n weight; fig. importance; **~heben** n weight-lifting; **Qig** weighty.

gewillt willing.

Ge|wimmel n throng; **~winde** n thread.

Gewinn m gain; econ. gains pl, profit; Lotterie: prize; SpielQ: winnings pl; **Qbringend** profitable; **Qen** win; fig. gain; **~er** m winner.

gewiß certain; **~!** certainly! Am. sure!

Gewissen n conscience; **Qhaft** conscientious; **Qlos** unscrupulous; **~sbisse** pl remorse sg.

Gewißheit f certainty.

Gewitter n (thunder-) storm; **Qn: es gewittert** there is a thunderstorm.

gewöhnen accustom (an to); **sich ~ an** get used to.

Gewohnheit f habit.

gewöhnlich ordinary, usual; unfein: common, vulgar.

gewohnt customary, habitual.

Gewölbe n vault.

gewunden winding.

Gewürz n spice; **~gurke** f pickled gherkin.

Gezeiten pl tide(s pl).

geziert affected.

Gezwitscher n chirping, twittering. [strained.]

gezwungen forced, con-

Gicht f gout.

Giebel m gable.

Gier f greed; **2ig** greedy.

gieß|en pour; *tech.* cast, found; *Blumen*: water; **es ~t** it is pouring (with rain); **2erei** f foundry; **2-kanne** f watering-can.

Gift n poison; *Schlangen*2: venom (a. fig.); poisonous; venomous (a. fig.); **~pilz** m poisonous mushroom, toadstool; **~schlange** f venomous snake; **~zahn** m poison-fang.

Gipfel m summit, top; *Spitze*: peak; **~konferenz** f summit meeting.

Gips m plaster (of Paris); **~abdruck** m, **~verband** m med. plaster cast.

Giraffe f giraffe.

Girlande f garland.

Girokonto n current account. [drift.]

Gischt m, f spray; spin-

Gitarre f guitar.

Gitter n lattice; *Fenster*: grating.

Glanz m brightness; lust|re, *Am.* -er; *fig.* splendo(u)r.

Gläser pl s. **Brille; 2n** vitreous; glassy.

glasieren glaze; *Kuchen*: ice, frost.

glasig glassy. [glass.]

Glasscheibe f pane of

glatt smooth (a. fig.); *glitschig*: slippery.

Glätte f smoothness (a. fig.); slipperiness. [*Am.* glaze.]

Glatteis n glazed frost,

glätten smooth.

glattrasiert clean-shaven.

Glatze f bald head.

Glaube m faith, belief (**an** in); **2n** believe; *meinen*: think, suppose, *Am.* a. guess; **~nsbekenntnis** n creed.

glaubhaft plausible.

Gläubiger m creditor.

glaubwürdig credible.

gleich adj equal; same; *eben*: level; **zur ~en Zeit** at the same time; adv alike, equally; so.: immediately, directly, at once; **~ groß** the same height; **~gegenüber** just opposite; **es ist ~ acht (Uhr)** it is close on od. nearly eight (o'clock); **~altrig** (of) the same age; **~berechtigt** having equal rights; **~bleibend** constant, steady; **~en** equal; *ähneln*: resemble; **~falls** also, likewise; **2gewicht** n balance (a. fig.); **~gültig** indifferent (**gegen** to); **es ist mir ~gültig** I don't care; **2gültigkeit** f indifference; **~lautend** identical; **~mäßig** regular; *Verteilung etc.*: equal; **~namig** of the same name; **2strom** m direct current; **2ung** f math. equation; **~wertig** of the same value, of equal value; **~zeitig** simultaneous.

Gleis n rails pl, line(s pl), track(s pl).

gleit|en glide, slide; **⚲flug** m glide.

Gletscher m glacier; **~spalte** f crevasse.

Glied n anat. limb; Kette: link (a. fig.); **⚲ern** arrange; divide; **~maßen** pl limbs pl, extremities pl.

glimmen smo(u)lder.

glimpflich: ~ davonkommen get off lightly.

glitschig slippery.

glitzern glitter, glisten.

Globus m globe.

Glocke f bell.

Glocken|spiel n carillon, chime(s pl); **~turm** m belfry, bell tower.

glotzen colloq. stare.

Glück n fortune; good luck; happiness; **auf gut ~** on the off chance; **~ haben** be lucky; **viel ~!** good luck!; **zum ~** fortunately.

Glucke f sitting hen.

glücken s. gelingen.

gluckern gurgle.

glücklich fortunate; happy; **~erweise** fortunately.

glucksen gurgle.

Glück|sspiel n game of chance; **⚲strahlend** radiant(ly happy); **~wunsch** m congratulation(s pl); good wishes pl; **herzlichen ~wunsch zum Geburtstag!** many happy returns (of the day)!

Glüh|birne f bulb; **⚲en** glow; **⚲end** glowing; Eisen: red-hot; Kohle: live;

fig. ardent; **⚲(end)heiß** burning hot; **~lampe** f bulb; **~wein** m mulled wine od. claret; **~würmchen** n glow-worm.

Glut f heat; glow (a. fig.); embers pl; fig. ardo(u)r.

Gnade f grace; favo(u)r; mercy; **~ngesuch** n petition for mercy.

gnädig gracious; merciful; Anrede: **~e Frau** Madam.

Gold n gold (a. fig.); **~barren** m gold bar od. ingot; **⚲en** gold; fig. golden; **⚲ig** fig. sweet, lovely, Am. a. cute; **~schmied** m goldsmith; **~währung** f gold standard.

Golf[1] m geogr. gulf.

Golf[2] n golf; **~platz** m golf-course, (golf-)links pl; **~schläger** m (golf-)club; **~spiel** n golf; **~spieler** m golfer.

Gondel f gondola; car.

gönne|n: j-m et. allow s.o. s.th.; neidlos: not to (be)grudge s.o. s.th.; **~rhaft** patronizing.

Gorilla m gorilla.

Gosse f gutter (a. fig.).

Gott m God; **⚲heit:** god, deity; **~ sei Dank!** thank God!; **um ~ willen!** for God's sake!

Gottes|dienst m (divine) service; **~lästerung** f blasphemy.

Gottheit f deity, divinity.

Gött|in f goddess; **⚲lich** divine.

Götze m idol.

Gouvern|ante f governess; ~**eur** m governor.

Grab n grave; tomb.

Graben m ditch; mil. trench; 2dig; Tier: burrow.

Grab|gewölbe n vault, tomb; ~**inschrift** f epitaph; ~**mal** n monument; tomb, sepulch|re, Am. -er: ~**stein** m tombstone; gravestone.

Grad m degree; mil. etc.: grade, rank; **15 ~ Kälte** od. **minus** 15 degrees below zero; ~**einteilung** f graduation. [earl.]

Graf m count; in England:]

Gräfin f countess.

Grafschaft f county.

Gram m grief, sorrow.

Gramm n gram(me).

Grammati|k f grammar; 2**sch** grammatical.

Granate f mil. shell; Gewehr2, Hand2: grenade.

Granit m granite.

graphisch graphic.

Gras n grass; 2**en** graze.

gräßlich hideous, atrocious.

Grat m ridge, edge.

Gräte f (fish)bone.

Gratifikation f gratuity, bonus. [charge.]

gratis gratis, free of]

gratulieren congratulate; **j-m zum Geburtstag ~** wish s.o. many happy returns (of the day).

grau grey, bsd. Am. gray.

grauen: **mir graut vor** I shudder at, I dread; 2 n

horror; ~**haft** horrible.

Graupe|n pl pot-barley; ~**ln** pl soft hail sg.

grausam cruel; 2**keit** f cruelty.

graus|en s. **grauen;** ~**ig**]

graziös graceful.

greifen seize, grasp, catch hold of; **um sich ~** spread.

Greis m old man; ~**in** f old woman.

grell Licht: glaring; Farbe, Muster: loud.

Grenze f boundary; Staats2: frontier, border; 2**n: ~ an** border on; fig. a. verge on; 2**nlos** boundless.

Grenzübergang m frontier od. border crossing (-point).

Griech|e m Greek; 2**isch** Greek; arch. Grecian.

griesgrämig morose, sullen.

Grieß m semolina.

Griff m grip, grasp; Tür, Messer etc.: handle; Schwert: hilt.

Grille f cricket; fig. whim.

Grimasse f grimace; ~**n schneiden** pull faces.

grimmig grim; fierce.

grinsen: ~ **(über)** grin (at); höhnisch: sneer (at); 2 n grin; sneer.

Grippe f influenza, colloq. flu. [rough; rude.]

grob coarse (a. fig.);]

grölen colloq. bawl.

Groll m grudge, ill will; 2**en: j-m ~** bear s.o. a grudge od. ill will.

Groschen m penny.

groß large; *dick, weit, erwachsen:* big; *hochgewachsen:* tall; *fig.* great, grand; *Hitze:* intense; *Kälte:* severe; *Verlust:* heavy; **im ∼en (und) ganzen** on the whole; **∼er Buchstabe** capital (letter); **∼artig** great, grand; **Ωaufnahme** *f Film:* close-up.

Größe *f* size; *Körper*Ω: height; *bsd. math.* quantity; *Bedeutung:* greatness; *Person:* celebrity; *thea.* star.

Groß|eltern *pl* grandparents *pl*; **∼handel** *m* wholesale trade; **∼händler** *m* wholesale dealer, wholesaler; **Ωjährig** of age; **Ωjährig werden** come of age; **∼jährigkeit** *f* majority; **∼macht** *f* great power; **∼mutter** *f* grandmother; **Ωspurig** arrogant; **∼stadt** *f* large town *od.* city; **Ωstädtisch** *of od.* in a large town *od.* city.

Groß|vater *m* grandfather; **∼wild** *n* big game; **Ωziehen** *Kind:* bring up; *Kind, Tier:* rear, raise; **Ωzügig** liberal, generous.

grotesk grotesque.

Grotte *f* grotto.

Grübchen *n* dimple.

Grube *f* pit; *Bergbau: a.* mine. [(over).]

grübeln brood (**über** on,)

Gruft *f* tomb, vault.

grün green; **∼anlage** *f* (public) park (*s pl*).

Grund *m* soil; *Gewässer:* bottom (*a. fig.*); *Beweg*Ω:

motive; reason (*gen,* **für** of, for); **∼ausbildung** *f* basic training; **∼bedingung** *f* basic *od.* fundamental condition; **∼begriffe** *pl* rudiments *pl*; **∼besitz** *m* (landed) property; **∼besitzer** *m* landowner.

gründen found, establish; **Ωr** *m* founder.

Grund|fläche *f math.* base; *Zimmer etc.:* area; **∼gebühr** *f* basic fee; *teleph.* rental; **∼gedanke** *m* basic *od.* fundamental idea; **∼lage** *f* foundation; **Ωlegend** fundamental, basic.

gründlich thorough; *Kenntnisse:* profound.

grund|los *fig.* unfounded; **Ωmauer** *f* foundation.

Gründonnerstag *m* Maundy Thursday.

Grund|regel *f* fundamental rule; **∼riß** *m* ground-plan; **∼satz** *m* principle; **Ωsätzlich** on principle; **∼schule** *f* primary school; **∼stein** *m* foundation-stone; **∼stück** *n* plot (of land); (building) site; premises *pl*; **∼stücksmakler** *m* estate agent, *Am.* realtor.

Gründung *f* foundation, establishment.

grundverschieden entirely different.

grunzen grunt.

Grupp|e *f* group; **Ωieren** group.

grus(e)lig creepy, weird.

Gruß *m* greeting; *bsd. mil., mar.* salute.

Grüße pl regards pl; respects pl; compliments pl; ⌐n greet; bsd. mil. salute; ⌐n Sie ihn von mir remember me to him.

Grütze f grits pl, groats pl.

gucken look; peep, peer.

Gulasch n goulash.

gültig valid; legal; Münze: current; Fahrkarte: valid, available; ⌐keit f validity; currency; availability.

Gummi m gum; m Radier⌐: (India-)rubber; ⌐band n elastic (band); ⌐eren gum; ⌐knüppel m truncheon, Am. club; ⌐sohle f rubber sole; ⌐stiefel pl wellingtons pl, Am. rubbers pl.

günstig favo(u)rable; im ⌐sten Fall at best.

Gurgel f throat; ⌐n gargle, gurgle.

Gurke f cucumber; Gewürz⌐: gherkin. [strap.⌐

Gurt m girdle, belt; Trage⌐:]

Gürtel m belt, girdle.

Guß m tech. founding, casting; Regen: downpour, shower; ⌐eisern cast-iron.

gut adj good; ⌐es Wetter fine weather; ⌐ werden get well; fig. turn out well; ganz ⌐ not bad; schon ⌐! never mind!, all right!; adv well; ⌐ aussehen be good-looking.

Gut n possession, property; Land⌐: estate.

Gut|achten n (expert) opinion; ⌐achter m expert; ⌐artig good-natured; med. benign.

Gute n: ⌐s tun do good; alles ⌐! all the best!

Güte f goodness, kindness; econ. quality; in ⌐ amicably; meine ⌐! good gracious!

Güter pl goods pl; ⌐bahnhof m goods station, Am. freight depot od. yard; ⌐wagen m (goods) waggon, Am. freight car; ⌐zug m goods (Am. freight) train.

gut|gelaunt good-humo(u)red; ⌐haben n credit (balance); ⌐heißen approve (of); ⌐herzig kind (-hearted).

Gutsbesitzer m owner of an estate.

Gutschein m credit note; coupon, Beleg: voucher.

Guts|haus n farm-house; ⌐hof m estate, farm.

gutwillig willing.

Gymnasi|ast m appr. grammar-school boy; ⌐um n appr. grammar-school.

Gymnasti|k f gymnastics pl; ⌐sch gymnastic.

Gynäkologe m gyn(a)ecologist.

H

Haar n, ⌐e pl hair sg; sich die ⌐e schneiden lassen have one's hair cut; ⌐bürste f hairbrush; ⌐

festiger m setting-lotion; **2ig** hairy; in Zssgn: ...-haired; **~klemme** f hair grip, Am. bobby pin; **~nadel** f hairpin; **~nadelkurve** f hairpin bend; **~schnitt** m haircut; **~spray** m, n hair spray od. lacquer; **~wäsche** f shampoo; **~waschmittel** n shampoo; **~wasser** n hair-lotion. [ings pl.]

Habe f property; belong- **haben** have.

habgierig avaricious.

Habicht m (gos)hawk.

Hack|e f hoe; Ferse: heel; **2en** hack; Fleisch: mince; Holz: chop; **~fleisch** n mince(d meat).

Hafen m harbo(u)r, port; **~arbeiter** m docker, long-shoreman; **~stadt** f (sea-)port.

Hafer m oats pl; **~brei** m (oatmeal) porridge; **~flocken** pl oat flakes pl, rolled oats pl; **~schleim** m gruel.

Haft f Gewahrsam: custody; Gefängnis: imprisonment, confinement; **2bar** responsible, jur. liable; **2en** stick, adhere (an to); **2en für** answer for, be liable for.

Häftling m prisoner.

Haft|pflichtversicherung f third-party insurance; **~ung** f jur. liability.

Hagel m hail; fig. a. volley; **~korn** n hailstone; **2n** hail; **~schauer** m (brief) hailstorm.

hager lean, gaunt.

Hahn m orn., tech. cock; Haus: rooster; Wasser2: tap, Am. a. faucet.

Hai(fisch) m shark.

häkeln crochet.

Haken m hook; Kleider2: a. peg; fig. snag, catch.

halb half; e-e **~e Stunde** half an hour; **ein ~es Jahr** six months pl; um **~ vier** at half past three; **2finale** n sp. semifinal; **~gar** underdone, rare; **~ieren** halve; **2insel** f peninsula; **2kreis** m semicircle; **2kugel** f hemisphere; **~laut** adj low, subdued; adv in an undertone; **2mond** m half-moon, crescent; **2pension** f dinner, bed and breakfast; **2schuh** m shoe; **2tagsarbeit** f part-time job od. employment; **~wüchsig** adolescent; **2zeit** f sp. half (-time).

Hälfte f half.

Halfter m, n halter.

Halle f hall; Hotel: lobby, lounge.

hallen resound, ring.

Hallenbad n indoor swimming-pool.

Halm m blade; Getreide: stem, stalk; Stroh: straw.

hallo int. hallo!

Hals m neck; Kehle: throat; **~ über Kopf** head over heels; **~band** n necklace; Tier: collar; **~entzündung** f sore throat; **~kette** f necklace; **~schlag-**

ader f carotid; **~schmerzen** pl: **~ haben** have a sore throat; **2starrig** stubborn, obstinate; **~tuch** n neckerchief; Schal: scarf.

Halt m hold; Stütze: support; **2bar** durable, lasting.

halten v/t hold; keep; Rede: make, deliver; **~ für** take for; **viel** od. **wenig ~ von** think highly od. little of; sich **~** last; v/i stop.

Halt|er m keeper, owner; für Geräte etc.: holder; **~estelle** f stop; **2machen** stop; **~ung** f deportment, carriage; fig. attitude (**gegenüber** towards).

Halteverbot n no stopping; **eingeschränktes ~** no waiting.

Hammel m wether; **~fleisch** n mutton.

Hammer m hammer; **~werfen** n hammer throw.

hämmern hammer.

Hampelmann m jumping jack.

Hamster m hamster.

Hand f hand; **i-m die ~ geben** od. **schütteln** shake hands with s.o.; **~arbeit** f manual labo(u)r od. work; needlework; **~ball** m handball; **~brause** f handshower; **~bremse** f handbrake.

Händedruck m handshake.

Handel m commerce; Geschäftsverkehr: trade; traffic; abgeschlossener: bargain; **2n** act; feilschen:

bargain (**um** for); **2n mit** deal od. trade in; **2n von** deal with, be about.

Handels|beziehungen pl trade relations pl; **~gesellschaft** f (trading) commercial school, business college od. school.

Hand|feger m hand-brush; **~fläche** f palm; **2gearbeitet** hand-made; **~gelenk** n wrist; **~gemenge** n scuffle; **~gepäck** n hand-luggage, Am. baggage; **2haben** handle, manage; **~koffer** m suitcase.

Händler m dealer.

handlich handy.

Handlung f act(ion), deed; thea. action, plot; econ. shop, Am. store; **~sweise** f conduct.

Hand|schellen pl handcuffs pl; **~schrift** f handwriting; manuscript; **2schriftlich** handwritten; **~schuh** m glove; **~tasche** f handbag, Am. purse; **~tuch** n towel; **~voll** f handful; **~werk** n (handi)craft; **~werker** m workman; **~werkzeug** n tools pl.

Hanf m hemp.

Hang m slope, incline; fig. inclination, tendency.

Hänge|brücke f suspension bridge; **~matte** f hammock.

hängen hang (**an** on); an **j-m ~** be attached od. devoted to s.o.; **~bleiben**

get caught (**an** on, in).

Happen *m* morsel, bite; snack.

Harfe *f* harp. [offensive.]

harmlos harmless, in-

Harmonie *f* harmony; **2eren** harmonize; **2sch** harmonious.

Harn *m* urine; **blase** *f* (urinary) bladder.

Harpune *f* harpoon.

hart hard; *fig.: a.* harsh; severe.

Härte *f* hardness; *fig.: Unbill: a.* hardship; *Strenge:* severity.

Hart|geld *n* coin(s *pl*); **2näckig** obstinate, stubborn.

Harz *n* resin.

Hase *m* hare.

Haselnuß *f* hazelnut.

Hasenscharte *f* harelip.

Haß *m* hatred.

hassen hate.

häßlich ugly; *fig. a.* nasty.

hastig hasty, hurried.

Haube *f* bonnet; cap; hood; *mot.* bonnet, *Am.* hood.

Hauch *m* breath; *fig.* touch; **2en** breathe.

Haue *f* *colloq.* hiding, spanking; **2n** hew; chop; *verhauen:* beat.

Haufen *m* heap, pile; *fig. colloq.* crowd.

häuf|en heap, pile (up), accumulate; **sich en** pile up, accumulate; *fig.* increase; **ig** frequent.

Haupt *n* head; *fig. a.* leader; **bahnhof** *m* main *od.* central station; **darstel-**

ler(in *f*) *m* lead(ing man *od.* lady); **eingang** *m* main entrance; **fach** *n* main subject, *Am.* major; **film** *m* feature (film); **gewinn** *m* first prize.

Häuptling *m* chief(tain).

Haupt|mann *m* captain; **merkmal** *n* characteristic feature; **quartier** *n* headquarters *pl*; **rolle** *f* lead (-ing part); **sache** *f* main thing; **2sächlich** main; **satz** *m* gr. main clause; **stadt** *f* capital; **straße** *f* high street, *Am.* main street; **Hauptverkehrs.straße:** main road *od.* street; **verkehrszeit** *f* rush *od.* peak hours *pl.*

Haus *n* house; home; **nach e** home; **zu e** at home; **angestellte** *f* domestic (servant); **apotheke** *f* medicine-chest, medicine-cabinet; **arbeit** *f* housework; **arzt** *m* family doctor; **aufgaben** *pl* homework *sg*; **besitzer** *m* houseowner, landlord; **bewohner** *m* occupant of a house; **flur** *m s.* Flur; **frau** *f* housewife; **halt** *m* household; **hälterin** *f* housekeeper; **haupt** *n* head of a family; *Besitzer:* landlord. [lar.]

Hausierer *m* hawker, ped-

häuslich domestic.

Haus|meister *m* caretaker, janitor; **ordnung** *f* rules *pl* of the house; **schlüssel** *m* latchkey, front-door key;

~schuh *m* slipper; **~tier** *n* domestic animal; **~tür** *f* front door; **~wirt** *m* landlord; **~wirtin** *f* landlady.

Haut *f* skin; *Tier*♀: hide; **~ausschlag** *m* rash; **~farbe** *f* colo(u)r of the skin; **~schere** *f* (e~e a pair of) cuticle scissors *pl.*

Hebamme *f* midwife.

Hebebühne *f* lifting platform.

Hebel *m* lever.

heben lift, raise; heave; **sich ~** rise, go up.

hebräisch Hebrew.

Hecht *m* pike.

Heck *n mar.* stern; *aer.* tail; *mot.* rear.

Hecke *f* hedge.

Heer *n* army; *fig. a.* host.

Hefe *f* yeast.

Heft *n* exercise book; *Zeitschrift*: issue, number.

heften fasten, fix (**an** to); *Saum*: baste.

heftig violent, fierce; passionate; *Regen etc.*: heavy; *Schmerzen*: severe.

Heft|klammer *f* staple; **~pflaster** *n* adhesive od. sticking plaster; **~zwecke** *f* s. Reißzwecke.

hegen *fig.* have, entertain.

Heide¹ *m* heathen.

Heide² *f* heath; **~kraut** *n* heather, heath.

Heidelbeere *f* bilberry, blueberry.

heidnisch heathen(ish).

heikel *Person*: particular; *Problem etc.*: delicate, awkward.

heil safe, unhurt; whole.

Heiland *m* Savio(u)r, Redeemer.

Heil|anstalt *f* sanatorium, *Am.* ~ sanitarium; **2bar** curable; **2en** cure; heal (up).

heilig holy; *Gott geweiht*: sacred (*a. fig.*); **Heiliger Abend** = **2abend** *m* Christmas Eve; **2e** *m, f* saint.   [medicine.)

Heilmittel *n* remedy;)

heim home; **2** *n* home; **2arbeit** *f* outwork.

Heimat *f, ~land* *n* mother country, native land; **2los** homeless; **~ort** *m* home town *od.* village.

Heim|fahrt *f* journey home, homeward journey; **2isch** home, local, domestic; *bot., zo. etc.*: native; **sich 2isch fühlen** feel at home; **2kehren, 2kommen** return home; **2lich** secret; **~reise** *f* s. Heimfahrt; **2tückisch** malicious; treacherous; **2wärts** homeward(s); **~weg** *m* way home; **2weh** *n:* ~ **haben** be homesick.

Heirat *f* marriage; **2en** marry; get married; **~santrag** *m* offer *od.* proposal of marriage.

heiser hoarse, husky.

heiß hot; **mir ist ~** I am *od.* feel hot.

heißen be called; *bedeuten*: mean; **wie ~ Sie?** what is your name?; **willkommen ~** welcome.

heiter *Wetter*: bright; *Himmel*: a. clear; *Person*: cheerful, gay.

heiz|en *Zimmer etc.*: heat; *Ofen*: light; 2er m fireman; 2körper m radiator; 2material n fuel; 2öl n fuel oil; 2ung f heating.

Held m hero.

helfen help, assist, aid; ~ gegen be good for.

Helfer m helper, assistant; ~shelfer m accomplice.

hell *Klang, Stimme*: clear; *Licht*: bright; *Haare*: light, fair; *Farben*: light; *Bier*: pale; 2seher(in f) m clairvoyant.

Helm m helmet.

Hemd n shirt.

hemm|en *Bewegung etc.*: check, stop; *behindern*: hamper; 2ung f stoppage, check; *psych.* inhibition; ~ungslos uncontrolled, unrestrained.

Hengst m stallion.

Henkel m handle, ear.

Henne f hen.

Henker m executioner.

her here; ago; **von ... ~** from.

herab down; ~lassen let down, lower; ~lassend condescending; ~setzen reduce; ~steigen climb down, descend.

heran close, near; ~kommen come *od.* draw near; approach (a. *fig.*); ~wachsen grow (up) (**zu** into).

herauf up (here); upstairs; ~ziehen pull up.

heraus out (here); **zum Fenster ~** out of the window; ~bekommen get out; *Geld*: get back; *fig.* find out; ~bringen bring *od.* get out; *fig.* ~finden find out, discover; ~fordern challenge; ~geben give back, restore; *Zeitung etc.*: edit; *Buch*: publish; *Vorschriften*: issue; *Geld*: give change (**auf** for); 2geber m editor; publisher; ~kommen come out; be published; ~ragen project, jut out; ~stellen put out; ~sich ~stellen als turn out *od.* prove to be; ~strecken put out; ~treten come *od.* step out; *Augen*: protrude; ~ziehen pull out; *Zahn*: a. extract.

herb *Geschmack*: tart; *Wein*: dry; *Gesichtszüge*: austere.

herbeieilen come hurrying; ~holen fetch.

Herberge f shelter, lodging; inn.   [fall.}

Herbst m autumn, *Am. a.*}

Herd m stove.

Herde f herd; *Schaf 2, Gänse 2 etc.*: flock.

herein in (here); ~! come in!; ~fallen *fig.* be taken in; ~legen *fig.* take in.

Her|fahrt f journey here; 2fallen: ~ über attack; ~gang m course of events; 2geben give up; return.

Hering m herring.

her|kommen come here; 2kunft f origin; *Person*: a. birth.

Heroin n heroin.

Herr m lord, master; gentleman; eccl. the Lord; **~ Maier** Mr Maier; **mein ~ Sir**; **m-e ~en** gentlemen.

Herren|friseur m men's hairdresser, barber; **~haus** n manor-house; **~schneider** m men's tailor; **~toilette** f (gentle)men's cloakroom. [pare.]

herrichten arrange; pre-}

Herrin f mistress; lady.

herrisch imperious.

herrlich glorious, splendid.

Herrschaft f rule, dominion; Macht: control; von Dienstboten: master and mistress.

herrsche|n rule; Monarch: reign; fig. be, prevail; **2r** m ruler; sovereign, monarch.

her|rühren, ~stammen: **~von** come from; **~stellen** make, manufacture, produce; **2stellung** f manufacture, production.

herüber over (here), across.

herum (a)round; about; **~führen** show (a)round; **~lungern** loaf od. hang about; **~reichen** pass od. hand round.

herunter down (here); downstairs; **von oben ~** down from above; **~kommen** come down(stairs) fig.: come down in the world; deteriorate.

hervor out, forth; **~bringen** bring out, produce(a. fig.); Früchte: yield; Wort:

utter; **~gehen** be clear od. apparent (aus from); **~heben** fig. stress, emphasize; **~holen** produce; **~ragen** project; **~ragend** fig. outstanding; **~rufen** fig. arouse, evoke; **~stechend** fig. striking.

Herz n anat. heart (a. fig.); Karten: heart(s pl); **~anfall** m heart attack; **~enslust** f: **nach ~** to one's heart's content; **~fehler** m cardiac defect; **2haft** hearty; **2ig** lovely, Am. a. cute; **~infarkt** m cardiac infarction; **2krank** having heart trouble; **2lich** cordial, hearty; **2los** heartless.

Herzog m duke; **~in** f duchess; **~tum** n duchy.

Herz|schlag m heartbeat; Herzversagen: heart failure; **~verpflanzung** f heart transplant.

Hetze f hurry, rush; **2n** hurry, rush; agitate.

Heu n hay.

Heuch|elei f hypocrisy; **2eln** feign; **~ler** m hypocrite.

heulen howl; cry.

Heu|schnupfen m hayfever; **~schrecke** f grasshopper, locust.

heut|e today; **~e abend** this evening, tonight; **~e früh**, **~e morgen** this morning; **~e in acht Tagen, ~e in e-r Woche** today od. this day week; **~e vor acht Tagen, ~e vor e-r Woche** a week ago to-

day; **~ig** this day's, today's;
~gegenwärtig: present; **~zu-
tage** nowadays, these days.

Hexe f witch; **~nschuß** m
lumbago.

Hieb m blow; **~e** pl hiding
sg, thrashing sg. [way!}
hier here; **~entlang!** this}
hier|auf on it od. this; after
this od. that, then; **~aus**
from it od. this; **~bei** here,
in this case; **~durch**
through this; hereby;
~für for it od. this; **~her**
here, hither; **bis ~her** as
far as here; **~in** in this;
~mit with it od. this, here-
with; **~nach** after it od.
this; dementsprechend: according to this; **~über** over
it od. this; over here; Thema: about it od. this; **~von**
of od. from it od. this.

Hilfe f help; Beistand: aid,
assistance; relief **(für** to);
Erste ~ first aid; **~ruf** m
shout (call, cry) for help.

hilflos helpless.

Hilfs|arbeiter m unskilled
worker od. labo(u)rer; **2be-
dürftig** needy; **2bereit**
helpful, ready to help; **~
mittel** n aid; tech. device.

Himbeere f raspberry.

Himmel m sky; eccl., fig.
heaven; **2blau** sky-blue;
~fahrt f eccl. ascension (of
Christ); Ascension-day;
~srichtung f direction.

himmlisch heavenly.

hin: ~ und her to and fro,
Am. back and forth; **~
und wieder** now and

again od. then; **~ und zurück** there and back.

hinab down; **~steigen**
climb down, descend.

hinauf up (there); upstairs; **~gehen** go up
(-stairs); Preise, Lohne etc.:
go up, rise; **~steigen**
climb up, ascend.

hinaus out; **~begleiten**
show out; **~gehen** go od.
walk out; **~schieben** fig.
put off, postpone; **~wer-
fen** throw out; j-n: turn
od. throw out; **~zögern**
put off.

Hin|blick m: **im ~ auf** in
view of, with regard to; **2-
bringen** take there.

hindern hinder; **~ an** prevent from ger; **2is** n sp.
etc.: obstacle.

hindurch through; zeitlich: all through, through-
out.

hinein in(to); **~gehen** go
in; **~gehen** in go into;
hold.

hinfahr|en j-n: drive od.
take there; et.: take there;
2t f journey od. way there.

hin|fallen fall (down); **2-
flug** m outward flight; **~
führen** lead od. take there;
2gabe f devotion; **~ge-
ben:** give o.s. to; widmen: devote o.s. to; **~
gehen: ~ (zu)** go (to); Pfad
etc.: lead (to); **~halten**
hold out; j-n: put s.o. off.

hinken limp.

hin|legen lay od. put
down; **sich ~ legen** lie

down; **nehmen** ertragen: put up with; **Qreise** f journey there, outward journey; **richten** execute; **setzen** set od. put down; **sich setzen** sit down; **sichtlich** with regard to; **stellen** place; abstellen: put down.

hinten behind; at the back; am Ende: in the rear.

hinter behind; **Qbein** n hind leg; **Qbliebene** pl the bereaved pl; Angehörige: surviving dependants pl; **einander** one after the other; **gehen** deceive; **Qgrund** m background; **Qhalt** m ambush; **her** zeitlich: afterwards; **Qkopf** m back of the head; **legen** leave (behind); **legen** n m colloq. behind, bottom; **Qrad** n rear od. back wheel; **Qtreppe** f backstairs pl; **Qtür** f back door.

hinüber over (there); quer: across.

Hin- und Rückfahrkarte f return ticket.

hinunter down (there); downstairs; **schlucken** swallow. {out.}

Hinweg m way there od.}

hinweg away, off; **kommen: über** get over; **setzen: sich über** ignore.

Hin|weis m hint; Anhaltspunkt: indication; **Qweisen: j-n auf** draw od. call s.o.'s attention to;

auf point at od. to; **Qwerfen** throw down; **Qziehen: sich** stretch (bis zu to); zeitlich: drag on.

hinzu in addition; **fügen** add; **kommen** be added; **ziehen** Arzt: call in.

Hippie m hippie, hippy.

Hirn n brain(s pl fig.).

Hirsch m stag, hart; Gattung: deer; **kuh** f hind.

Hirt m herdsman; Schaf2, fig.: shepherd.

hissen hoist.

historisch historic(al).

Hitze f heat; **welle** f heatwave, hot spell.

hitz|ig Person: hot-tempered, hot-headed; Debatte: heated; **Qkopf** m hothead; **Qschlag** m heatstroke.

Hobel m plane; **Qn** plane.

hoch high; Turm, Baum: tall; Strafe: heavy, severe; Alter: great, old; **oben** high up; **Q** n highpressure area, anticyclone.

Hoch|achtung f high esteem od. respect; **Qachtungsvoll** respectful; Brief: yours faithfully od. sincerely, bsd. Am. yours truly; **betrieb** m intense activity, rush; **druck** m high pressure; **druckgebiet** n s. Hoch; **Qebene** f plateau, tableland; **form** f: in in top form; **gebirge** n high mountains pl; **haus** n multistor(e)y building; skyscraper; **konjunktur** f boom; **⊾mut** *m* arrogance; ⚬mütig arrogant, haughty; **⊾ofen** *m* blast-furnace; **⊾saison** *f* peak season, height of the season; **⊾schule** *f* university; academy; **⊾sommer** *m* midsummer; **⊾spannung** *f* high tension *od.* voltage; **⊾sprung** *m* high jump.

höchst *adj* highest; *äußerst*: extreme; *adv* highly, most, extremely.

Hochstapler *m* impostor.

höchst|ens *n* at (the) most, at best; ⚬**form** *f* top form; ⚬**geschwindigkeit** *f* maximum speed; *mot.* speed limit; ⚬**leistung** *f* *sp.* record (performance)/*Maschine*: maximum output.

Hoch|verrat *m* high treason; **⊾wasser** *n* flood; ⚬**wertig** high-grade.

Hochzeit *f* wedding; *Trauung*: a. marriage; **⊾sgeschenk** *n* wedding present; **⊾sreise** *f* honeymoon.

hocke|n squat; **⊾r** *m* stool.

Höcker *m* *Kamel*: hump; *Buckel*: hump, hunch.

Hoden *pl* testicles *pl.*

Hof *m* court(yard); farm; *Fürsten2*: court; *ast.* halo.

hoffen hope **(auf** *für*)); **⊾t-lich** I hope, let's hope.

Hoffnung *f* hope; ⚬**slos** hopeless.

höflich polite, civil, courteous; ⚬**keit** *f* courtesy.

Höhe *f* height; *aer.*, *ast.*, *geogr.* altitude; *An2*: hill; *Rechnung*: amount; *Sum-*

me: size; *Strafe*: severity; *mus.* pitch; **in die ⊾** up (-wards).

Hoheitsgebiet *n* (sovereign) territory.

Höhen|kurort *m* high-altitude health resort; **⊾lage** *f* altitude; **⊾luft** *f* mountain air; **⊾zug** *m* mountain range.

Höhepunkt *m* *fig.* climax.

hohl hollow.

Höhle *f* cave, cavern; *Tier2*: den, lair.

Hohl|maß *n* measure of capacity; **⊾raum** *m* hollow, cavity. [rision.⎱

Hohn *m* scorn; *Spott*: de-⎰

höhn|en sneer, jeer (**über** at); **⊾isch** scornful; *spottend*: sneering, derisive.

holen fetch; go for; *besorgen*: get; **⊾ lassen** send for; **sich e-e Krankheit ⊾** catch a disease.

Holländ|er *m* Dutchman; ⚬**isch** Dutch.

Hölle *f* hell.

holper|ig bumpy, rough, uneven; **⊾n** jolt, bump.

Holunder *m* elder.

Holz *n* wood; *Nutz2*: timber, *bsd. Am.* lumber.

hölzern wooden.

Holz|hauer *m* woodcutter, *Am. a.* lumberjack; ⚬**ig** woody; **⊾kohle** *f* charcoal; **⊾schnitt** *m* woodcut; **⊾schuh** *m* clog; **⊾wolle** *f* wood-wool, *Am.* excelsior.

Honig *m* honey.

Honorar *n* fee.

Hopfen *m* hop.

hopsen hop, jump.

Hör|apparat *m* hearing aid; **2bar** audible.

horchen listen; eavesdrop.

Horde *f* gang.

höre|n *v/t* hear; *Radio:* listen (in) to; *Vorlesung:* attend; *erfahren:* hear, learn; *v/i* hear (**von** from); *zuhören:* listen; **~n auf** listen to; **schwer ~n** be hard of hearing; **2r** *m* hearer; *Rundfunk:* listener(-in); *univ.* student; *teleph.* receiver.

Horizont *m* horizon, skyline; **2al** horizontal.

Horn *n* horn.

Hörnchen *n* croissant.

Hornhaut *f* horny skin; *anat. Auge:* cornea.

Hornisse *f* hornet.

Horoskop *n* horoscope.

Hör|saal *m* lecture-room (-hall, -theat|re, *Am.* -er); **~spiel** *n* radio play; **~weite** *f*: **in ~** within earshot.

Hose *f* (e-e a pair of) trousers *pl od. Am.* pants *pl.*

Hosen|anzug *m* trouser *od.* pant suit; **~schlitz** *m* fly; **~tasche** *f* trouser-pocket; **~träger** *pl* (**ein Paar a** pair of) braces *pl od. Am.* suspenders *pl.*

Hospital *n* hospital.

Hostess *f* hostess.

Hostie *f eccl. the* Host.

Hotel *n* hotel; **~führer** *m* hotel guide; **~halle** *f* hall, lobby, lounge, foyer; **~pension** *f* private hotel.

Hubraum *m* cubic capacity.

hübsch pretty, nice; *Männer:* good-looking, handsome. [copter.)

Hubschrauber *m* heli-)

Huf *m* hoof; **~eisen** *n* horseshoe.

Hüft|e *f* hip; **~gelenk** *n* hip-joint; **~gürtel** *m* girdle.

Hügel *m* hill; **2ig** hilly.

Huhn *n* fowl, hen; *junges:* chicken.

Hühnchen *n* chicken.

Hühner|auge *n* corn; **~stall** *m* hen-house, hencoop.

Hülle *f* cover(ing), wrapper; *Buch:* jacket; *Schirm:* sheath; **2n** wrap, cover.

Hülse *f Schote:* pod; *Getreide:* husk; *Geschoß:* case; **~nfrüchte** *pl* pulse *sg.*

human humane.

Hummel *f* bumble-bee.

Hummer *m* lobster.

Humor *m* humo(u)r; **~ist** *m* humorist; **2istisch** humorous.

humpeln limp.

Hund *m* dog.

Hunde|hütte *f* dog-kennel; **~kuchen** *m* dog-biscuit; **~leine** *f* lead, leash.

hundert hundred; **2jahrfeier** *f* centenary, *Am. a.* centennial; **~ste** hundredth.

Hündin *f* bitch.

Hundstage *pl* dog-days *pl.*

Hüne *m* giant.

Hunger *m* hunger; **~ be-**

kommen get hungry; ~ **haben** be *od.* feel hungry; ₂**n** hunger; ~**snot** *f* famine.

hungrig hungry.
Hupe *f* horn; ₂**n** hoot.
hüpfen hop, skip.
Hürde *f* hurdle.
Hure *f* whore, prostitute.
huschen slip, dart; *kleines Tier:* scurry, scamper.
hüsteln cough slightly.
husten cough; ₂ *m* cough.
Hut *m* hat.
hüten guard, protect; *Scha-*

fe etc.: tend; **sich** ~ **vor** beware of.
Hütte *f* hut; cabin; *tech.* smelting works *sg.*
Hydrant *m* hydrant.
hydraulisch hydraulic.
Hygien|e *f* hygiene; ₂**isch** hygienic.
Hymne *f* hymn.
Hypno|se *f* hypnosis; ₂-**tisieren** hypnotize.
Hypothek *f* mortgage.
Hypothese *f* hypothesis.
Hysteri|e *f* hysteria; ₂**sch** hysterical.

I

ich I.
Ideal *n* ideal; ₂ ideal.
Idee *f* idea, notion.
identi|fizieren identify; ~**sch** identical; ₂**tät** *f* identity.
Ideologie *f* ideology.
Idiot *m* idiot; ₂**isch** idiotic.
Idol *n* idol.
Igel *m* hedgehog.
ignorieren ignore.
ihm (to) him; (to) it.
ihn him; it.
ihnen *pl* (to) them; **Ihnen** *sg, pl* (to) you.
ihr *pers pron* you; (to) her; *poss pron* her; *pl* their; ₂ *sg, pl* your.
illegal illegal.
Illustrierte *f* (illustrated) magazine. [snack-bar.}
Imbiß *m* snack; ~**stube** *f*{
Imker *m* bee-keeper.
immer always; ~ **mehr** more and more; ~ **noch**

still; ~ **wieder** again and again; **für** ~ for ever, for good; ~**zu** all the time.
Immobilien *pl* immovables *pl*, real estate *sg*; ~**makler** *m* estate agent, *Am.* realtor.
immun immune.
Imperativ *m gr.* imperative (mood).
Imperfekt *n gr.* imperfect (tense). [perialism.}
Imperialismus *m* im-{
impf|en inoculate; *bsd. gegen Pocken:* vaccinate; ~-**schein** *m* certificate of vaccination *od.* inoculation; ₂**stoff** *m* serum; vaccine; ₂**ung** *f* inoculation; vaccination. [press s.o.}
imponieren j-m ~ im-{
Import *m* import(ation); ₂**ieren** import.
imprägnieren waterproof.
impulsiv impulsive.

imstande: ~ **sein** be able.

in *räumlich: wo?* in, at; *innerhalb:* within; *wohin?* into, in; ~ **der Schule** at school; ~ **die Schule** to school; *zeitlich:* in, at, during; with.

inbegriffen included, inclusive (of).

indem whilst, while; *Mittel:* by ger.

Inder *m* Indian.

Indianer *m* (Red) Indian.

Indikativ *m gr.* indicative (mood).

indirekt indirect.

indisch Indian.

individu|ell individual; 2-**um** *n* individual.

Indizien *pl,* **~beweis** *m* circumstantial evidence *sg.*

Industri|alisierung *f* industrialization; **~e** *f* industry; *attr* industrial.

ineinander into one another.

Infektion *f* infection; **~skrankheit** *f* infectious disease. (mood).)

Infinitiv *m gr.* infinitive

infizieren infect.

Inflation *f* inflation.

infolge owing *od.* due to; **~dessen** consequently.

Informa|tion *f* information; 2**ieren** inform.

Ingenieur *m* engineer.

Ingwer *m* ginger.

Inhaber *m* owner, proprietor; *Wohnung:* occupant; *Laden:* keeper; *Paß, Amt etc.:* holder.

Inhalt *m* contents *pl;* **~s-**

verzeichnis *n* list (*Buch:* table) of contents.

Initiative *f* initiative; **die** ~ **ergreifen** take the initiative.

Injektion *f* injection.

inklusive *s.* inbegriffen.

Inland *n* home (country); *Landesinnere:* inland.

inländisch inland, home, domestic.

Inlett *n* tick.

inmitten in the midst of.

innen inside, within; **nach** ~ inwards.

Innen|minister *m* Minister of the Interior, *Brit.* Home Secretary, *Am.* Secretary of the Interior; **~politik** *f* domestic policy; **~seite** *f* inner side, inside; **~stadt** *f* city (cent|re, *Am.* -er).

inner interior; inner; *med., pol.* internal; 2**e** *n* interior; **~halb** within; **~lich** inwardly; *bsd. med.* internally.

innig intimate, close.

inoffiziell unofficial.

Insasse *m* inmate; *Fahrgast:* occupant, passenger.

Inschrift *f* inscription.

Insekt *n* insect.

Insel *f* island.

Inser|at *n* advertisement, *colloq.* ad; 2**ieren** advertise.

insgesamt altogether.

insofern: ~ **als** in so far as.

Inspektion *f* inspection.

Install|ateur *m* plumber; fitter; 2**ieren** instal(l).

instand: ~ **halten** keep in good order; *tech.* maintain; ~ **setzen** repair.

Instinkt *m* instinct.

Institut *n* institute.

Instruktion *f* instruction.

Instrument *n* instrument.

Inszenierung *f thea.* staging, production.

Intellektuelle *m, f* intellectual, highbrow.

intelligen|t intelligent; 2z *f* intelligence.

Intendant *m* director.

intensiv intensive, intense.

interess|ant interesting; 2e *n* interest (**an, für** in); 2ent *m* interested person *od.* party; *econ.* prospective buyer; ~**ieren** interest (**für** in); **sich ~ie-ren für** be interested in.

Internat *n* boarding-school. [tional.]

international interna-

inter|pretieren interpret; 2punktion *f* punctuation; 2view *n* interview.

intim intimate.

intolerant intolerant.

intransitiv *gr.* intransitive.

Invalide *m* invalid.

Invasion *f* invasion.

invest|ieren invest; 2i-tion *f* investment.

inwie|fern in what way *od.* respect; ~**weit** how far, to what extent.

inzwischen in the mean-time, meanwhile.

irdisch earthly; worldly; *sterblich:* mortal.

Ire *m* Irishman; **die ~n** *pl* the Irish *pl.*

irgend *in Zssgn:* some...; any...; ~**ein(e)** some(one); any(one); ~**einer** *s.* ~**je-mand;** ~ **etwas** something; anything; ~ **je-mand** someone; anyone; ~**wann** some time (or other); ~**wie** somehow; anyhow; ~**wo** somewhere; anywhere.

irisch Irish. [ironic(al).]

Iron|ie *f* irony; 2isch

irre confused; mad, insane; 2 *m, f* lunatic; mental patient; ~**führen** *fig.* mislead; ~**n** *err; räumlich:* wander; **sich ~n** be mistaken (**in** *j-m:* in, *et.:* about); be wrong.

irritieren irritate; confuse.

Irrsinn *m* insanity, madness; 2ig insane, mad.

Irr|tum *m* error, mistake; **im ~tum sein** be mistaken; 2tümlich(erwei-se) by mistake.

Ischias *m, n* sciatica.

Islam *m* Islam.

Isolier|band *n* insulating tape; 2en isolate; insulate; ~**ung** *f* isolation; insulation. [Israeli.]

Israeli *m* Israeli; 2sch

Italie|ner *m* Italian; 2-nisch Italian.

J

ja yes; **wenn ~** if so.
Jacht f yacht.
Jacke f jacket.
Jackett n jacket.
Jagd f hunt(ing); shoot(-ing); **Verfolgung**: chase; s. **Jagdrevier**; **~aufseher** m gamekeeper, Am. game warden; **~hund** m hound; **~revier** n huntingground, shoot; **~schein** m shooting licen|ce, Am. -se.
jagen hunt; shoot; **rasen**: rush, dash; **verfolgen**: chase.
Jäger m hunter.
Jaguar m jaguar.
jäh precipitous, steep; **plötzlich**: sudden, abrupt.
Jahr n year; **seit ~en** for years; **mit 18 ~en, im Alter von 18 ~en** at (the age of) eighteen; **~elang** for years; **~elange Erfahrung** (many) years of experience.
Jahres|bericht m annual report; **~tag** m anniversary; **~zahl** f date, year; **~zeit** f season, time of the year.
Jahr|gang m age-group; **Wein**: vintage; **~hundert** n century.
...jährig in Zssgn: ...-year-old, of ... (years).
jährlich adj annual, yearly; adv every year.
Jahr|markt m fair; **~zehnt** n decade.
jähzornig hot-tempered.

Jalousie f (Venetian) blind, Am. a. window shade.
Jammer m: **es ist ein ~** it is a pity.
jämmerlich miserable, wretched.
jammern lament (um for, over); moan; **greinen**: whine.
Januar m January.
Japan er m Japanese; **die ~er** pl the Japanese pl; **2isch** Japanese.
jäten weed.
Jauche f liquid manure.
jawohl yes; certainly.
je ever; at any time; **~ zwei** two each; **sie bekamen zwei Äpfel** each they received two apples each; **~ nachdem** it depends; **~ mehr, desto besser** the more the better; **~ länger, ~ lieber** the longer the better; **~ Pfund** a pound.
jed|er m, **~e, ~es** every; **~er beliebige**: any; **~er einzelne**: each; **von zwei ~en**: either; **~en zweiten Tag** every other day; **~enfalls** at all events, in any case; **~ermann** everyone, everybody; **~erzeit** always; **~esmal** each od. every time.
jedoch however, yet.
jemals ever; at any time.
jemand someone, somebody; **fragend, verneint**: anyone, anybody.

jen|er, **~e**, **~es** that (one); **~e** pl those pl.

jenseits on the other side (of); beyond, across.

jetzt now, at present; **bis ~** until now, so far; **erst ~** only now; **von ~ an** from now on.

jeweils at a time.

Jockei m jockey.

Jod n iodine.

Joghurt m, n yog(ho)urt.

Johannisbeere f currant.

Journalist m journalist.

jubeln rejoice, exult.

Jubiläum n anniversary.

juck|en itch; **2reiz** m itch.

Jude m Jew.

jüdisch Jewish.

Jugend f youth; young people pl; **~amt** n youth welfare department; **~fürsorge** f youth welfare; **~heim** n youth club; **~herberge** f youth hostel; **~kriminalität** f juvenile delinquency; **2lich** youthful, young; **~liche(m)** youth, teenager; f teenager.

Jugoslaw|e m Yugoslav; **2isch** Yugoslav.

Juli m July.

jung young.

Junge¹ m boy, youngster, lad; Karten: knave, jack.

Junge² n Hund: puppy; Katze: kitten; Fuchs, Bär etc.: cub.

jungenhaft boyish.

jünger younger, junior; 2 m disciple.

Jung|fer f: **alte ~** old maid, spinster; **~frau** f virgin; **~geselle** m bachelor; **~gesellin** f bachelor girl.

Jüngling m youth, young man.

jüngst adj youngest; Zeit: (most) recent, latest; **das 2e Gericht, der 2e Tag** the Last Judg(e)ment, the Day of Judg(e)ment; adv recently, lately.

Juni m June.

junior junior.

Jurist m lawyer, jurist; law-student.

Jury f jury.

Justiz f (administration of) justice; **~minister** m Minister of Justice; Brit. Lord Chancellor, Am. Attorney General; **~ministerium** n Ministry of Justice; Am. Department of Justice.

Juwel|en pl jewel(le)ry; **~ier** m jewel(l)er.

Jux m colloq. joke.

K

Kabel n cable.

Kabeljau m cod(fish).

Kabine f cabin; Friseur etc.: cubicle; Fahrstuhl: car.

Kabinett n pol. cabinet,

government.

Kabriolett n cabriolet, convertible.

Kachel f tile.

Kadaver m carcass.

Käfer m beetle.

Kaffee m coffee; ~satz m coffee-grounds pl.

Käfig m cage. [naked.]

kahl Mensch: bald; bare,

Kahn m boat; Last2: barge.

Kai m quay, wharf.

Kaiser m emperor.

Kajüte f cabin.

Kakao m cocoa; bot. cacao.

Kakt|ee f, ~us m cactus.

Kalb n calf; ~fleisch n veal; ~sbraten m roast veal.

Kalender m calendar.

Kalk m lime.

Kalorie f calorie.

kalt cold; **mir ist** ~ I am cold; ~blütig cold-blooded.

Kälte f cold(ness); s. **Grad**; ~welle f cold spell od. wave.

Kamel n camel.

Kamera f camera.

Kamerad m comrade, companion, colloq. pal; ~schaft f comradeship.

Kamille f camomile.

Kamin m chimney; fireplace; ~sims m, n mantelpiece.

Kamm m comb; Hahn: comb, crest; Welle: crest; Gebirge: ridge.

kämmen comb.

Kammer f (small) room; ~musik f chamber music.

Kampagne f campaign.

Kampf m combat, fight (a. fig.); struggle (a. fig.).

kämpfe|n fight, struggle; 2r m fighter.

Kampfrichter m judge.

Kanal m künstlicher: canal; natürlicher: channel (a. tech., fig.); Abzug: sewer, drain; ~isation f Flüsse: canalization; Städte etc.: sewerage; 2isieren canalize; sewer.

Kanarienvogel m canary (-bird).

Kandid|at m candidate; 2ieren be a candidate.

kandiert candied, crystallized.

Känguruh n kangaroo.

Kaninchen n rabbit.

Kanister m can.

Kanne f Kaffee2, Tee2: pot; Milch2 etc.: can.

Kanon m mus. round, catch.

Kanone f cannon, gun.

Kante f edge.

Kantine f canteen.

Kanu n canoe.

Kanzel f eccl. pulpit; aer. cockpit.

Kanzler m chancellor.

Kap n cape, headland.

Kapazität f capacity; fig. authority.

Kapelle f eccl. chapel; mus. band.

Kapital n capital; ~anlage f investment; ~ismus m capitalism; ~ist m capitalist; ~verbrechen n capital crime.

Kapitän m captain.

Kapitel n chapter.

kapitulieren surrender.

Kaplan m chaplain.

Kappe f cap.

Kapsel f capsule; case.

kaputt colloq.: broken; *Lift etc.*: out of order; *erschöpft*: tired od. fagged (out); **~gehen** colloq.: break; **~machen** colloq.: break; ruin.

Kapuze f hood; *eccl.* cowl.

Karaffe f carafe; *Wein*, *Likör*: decanter.

Karawane f caravan.

Kardinal m cardinal; **~zahl** f cardinal number.

Karfreitag m Good Friday.

kariert check(ed), chequered, *Am.* checkered.

Karies f caries.

Karikatur f caricature, cartoon.

Karneval m carnival.

Karo n square, check; *Karten*: diamond(s pl).

Karosserie f mot. body.

Karotte f carrot.

Karpfen m carp.

Karre f, **~n** m cart.

Karriere f career.

Karte f card.

Kartei f card-index; file; **~karte** f index-card, filing-card.

Kartoffel f potato; **~brei** m mashed potatoes pl.

Karton m Pappe: cardboard, pasteboard; *Schachtel*: cardboard box, carton.

Karussell n roundabout, merry-go-round, *Am. a.* car(r)ousel.

Karwoche f Holy od. Passion Week.

Käse m cheese.

Kaserne f barracks sg.

Kasperle n, m Punch; **~theater** n Punch and Judy show.

Kasse f cash-box; *Laden*2: cash register, till; *Bank*: cash-desk, pay-desk; *thea. etc.*: box-office.

Kassen|arzt m appr. panel doctor; **~patient** m appr. panel patient; **~zettel** m sales slip (*Am.* check).

Kassette f phot., tech. cassette; *Geld*2: box; *Schmuck*2: case; **~nfilm** m cartridge film.

kassiere|n take (the money); *Beitrag*: collect; **2r(in** f) m cashier; *Bank*: a. teller; collector.

Kastanie f chestnut.

Kästchen n small box od. case; casket.

Kasten m box; case.

Kasus m gr. case.

Katalog m catalog(ue).

Katarrh m cold, catarrh.

Katastrophe f disaster.

Kategorie f category.

Kater m male cat, tomcat; colloq. s. **Katzenjammer**.

Kathedrale f cathedral.

Katholi|k m Catholic; **2sch** Catholic.

Katze f cat; **~njammer** m colloq. hangover.

kauen chew.

kauern crouch, squat.

Kauf m purchase; **günstiger ~** bargain; **2en** buy, purchase.

Käufer m buyer; customer.

Kaufhaus n department store.

käuflich fig. venal.

Kaufmann m businessman; merchant; shopkeeper, bsd. grocer, Am. a. storekeeper. [gum.}

Kaugummi m chewing-}

kaum hardly, scarcely.

Kaution f security; jur. bail.

Kaviar m caviar(e).

keck bold; saucy, cheeky.

Kegel m Spiel: skittle, pin; math., tech. cone; ~bahn f skittle (Am. bowling) alley; 2förmig conic(al), cone-shaped; 2n play (at) skittles od. ninepins, Am. bowl. [larynx.}

Kehle f throat; ~kopf m}

Kehre f (sharp) bend od. turn; 2n sweep, brush; ~icht m, n sweepings pl.

keifen nag, scold.

Keil m wedge; ~er m wild boar.

Keim m germ; 2en Samen: germinate; sprießen: sprout; 2frei sterilized, sterile.

kein: ~(e) no; ~e(r, ~s) none, no one, nobody; ~er von beiden neither (of the two); ~er von uns none of us; ~esfalls, ~eswegs not at all; ~mal not once.

Keks m, n biscuit, Am. cooky; ungesüßt: cracker.

Kelch m cup; bot. calyx.

Kelle f Suppen2: ladle; Maurer2: trowel.

Keller m cellar; ~geschoß n basement.

Kellner m waiter; ~in f waitress.

kennen know, be acquainted with; ~enlernen get od. come to know; j~n: meet s.o.; 2er m expert; Kunst2, Wein2: connoisseur; 2tnis f knowledge; 2zeichen n mark, sign; mot. registration (number), Am. license number; ~zeichnen mark; fig. characterize.

kentern capsize.

Keramik f ceramics sg.

Kerbe f notch. [guy.}

Kerl m colloq. chap, Am.}

Kern m Nuß: kernel; Kirsche etc.: stone, Am. pit; Orange, Apfel etc.: pip; Erd2: core; phys. nucleus; in Zssgn: nuclear, atomic; fig. core, heart; **Kern...** s.a. **Atom...**; ~energie f nuclear energy; ~gehäuse n core; 2gesund thoroughly healthy; ~spaltung f nuclear fission.

Kerze f candle.

Kessel m kettle; boiler.

Kette f chain; Berg2: a. range; Hals2: necklace.

Ketten|raucher m chainsmoker; ~reaktion f chain reaction.

keuchen pant, gasp; 2-**husten** m (w)hooping cough.

Keule f club; Fleisch: leg.

kichern giggle, titter.

Kiefer[1] m jaw(-bone).

Kiefer[2] f bot. pine.

Kiel m mar. keel.

Kieme f gill. [ble.}

Kies m gravel; ~el m peb-}

Kilo|(gramm) n kilo-gram(me); ~meter m kilomet|re, Am. -er; ~watt n kilowatt.

Kind n child; Klein²: baby.

Kinder|arzt m p(a)e-diatrician; ~bett n Gitter²: cot, Am. crib; ~garten m kindergarten, day nursery; ~lähmung f polio(myelitis); ²los child-less; ~mädchen n nurse; ~wagen m perambulator, colloq. pram, Am. baby carriage; ~zimmer n nurs-ery.

Kind|heit f childhood; ²isch childish; ²lich child-like.

Kinn n chin.

Kino n cinema, colloq. the pictures pl, Am. motion-picture theater, colloq. the movies pl.

Kippe f colloq. stub, Am. a. butt; ²n tip (over); tilt.

Kirche f church.

Kirchen|gemeinde f par-ish; ~schiff n nave; ~stuhl m pew.

Kirch|gänger m church-goer; ²lich church; ~turm m steeple, ohne Spitze: church-tower.

Kirsche f cherry.

Kissen n cushion, Kopf²: pillow; ~tenz² crate.}

Kiste f box, chest; Lat-}

Kitsch m (sentimental) rub-bish, trash. [putty.}

Kitt m cement; Glaser²: }

Kittel m smock; overall; Arzt²: (white) coat.

kitten cement; putty.

kitz|eln tickle; ~(e)lig ticklish (a. fig.).

klaffen gape, yawn.

kläffen yap, yelp.

Klage f complaint; Weh²: lament; jur. action, suit; ²n complain; jur. take le-gal action.

Kläger m jur. plaintiff.

kläglich pitiful, piteous; miserable.

klamm Hände etc.: numb.

Klamm f ravine, gorge.

Klammer f clamp, cramp; Büro²: (paper-)clip; Wä-sche²: (clothes-)peg; typ. bracket, runde: a. paren-thesis; ²n: sich ~ an cling to (a. fig.).

Klang m sound; ringing.

Klappe f flap; ²n v,t: nach oben ~ tip up; nach unten ~ lower, put down; v i click, bang; colloq. come off well.

Klapper f rattle; ²n clat-ter, rattle (mit et. s.th.); ~schlange f rattlesnake.

Klapp|messer n clasp-knife, jack-knife; ~sitz m tip-up seat; ~stuhl m fold-ing chair.

Klaps m slap.

klar clear; bright; plain; offenkundig: evident.

klären clarify; fig. clear up.

Klasse f class; Schul²: class, form, Am. a. grade; ~nzimmer n classroom, schoolroom.

klassisch classic(al).

Klatsch m fig. colloq. gossip; **2en** v/t: **Beifall** ~ applaud (j-m s.o.); v/i splash; applaud, clap; colloq. gossip.

Klaue f claw; fig. clutch.

Klavier n piano.

kleb|**en** v/t glue, paste, stick; v/i stick, adhere (**an** to); **~end** adhesive; **~rig** sticky; **2stoff** m adhesive.

Klee m clover, trefoil.

Kleid n dress, frock; gown; **2en** v: **j~n** ~ suit od. become s.o.; **sich** ~ dress (o.s.).

Kleider pl clothes pl; **~bügel** m coat-hanger; **~bürste** f clothes-brush; **~haken** m clothes-peg; **~schrank** m wardrobe.

Kleidung f clothes pl.

klein little (nur attr), small; **2bildkamera** f miniature camera; **2bus** m minibus; **2geld** n (small) change; **2igkeit** f trifle; **2kind** n infant, baby; **~laut** subdued; **~lich** narrow-minded; geizig: mean; **2stadt** f small od. country town; **~städtisch** small-town, provincial; **2wagen** m small car, minicar.

Klemme f tech. clamp; Haar: (hair) grip, Am. bobby pin; **in der ~ sitzen** colloq. be in a jam; **2n** Tür etc.: stick; **sich die Finger 2n** pinch od. nip one's fingers.

Klempner m plumber.

Klette f bur(r).

klettern climb.

Klient m client.

Klima n climate; **~anlage** f: **mit** ~ air-conditioned.

klimpern jingle; mus. strum.

Klinge f blade.

Klingel f bell; **~knopf** m bell-push; **2n** ring (the bell).

klingen sound; ring.

Klinik f hospital, clinic.

Klinke f (door)handle.

Klippe f cliff, crag.

klirren Kette: clank, jangle; Schlüssel: jingle; Gläser, Münzen: clink, chink.

klobig clumsy.

klopfen beat; knock; **auf die Schulter** ~ tap; **es klopft** there's a knock at the door.

Klops m meatball.

Klosett n lavatory, (water-)closet, W.C., toilet; **~papier** n toilet-paper.

Kloß m dumpling; fig. lump.

Kloster n cloister; Mönchs-2: monastery; Nonnen-2: convent, nunnery.

Klotz m block, log.

Klub m club.

Kluft f cleft; chasm (a. fig.).

klug clever; intelligent.

Klumpen m lump; Erd2 etc.: clod.

knabbern nibble, gnaw.

Knabe m boy, lad.

knacken crack.

Knall m crack; bang; Waffe: report; **2en** crack; bang; Korken: pop.

knapp tight; spärlich:

scanty; *Stil*: concise; *Vorsprung, Sieg*: narrow; *Zeit*: short; **werden** run short.

knarren creak.

knattern roar.

Knäuel *m, n* ball.

Knauf *m* knob.

Knebel *m* gag; **2en** gag.

kneif|en pinch; **2zange** *f* (e–e a pair of) pincers *pl.*

Kneipe *f colloq.* pub, local.

kneten knead.

Knick *m* fold, crease; *Kurve*: bend; **2en** fold, crease; bend; *brechen*: break.

Knicks *m* curts(e)y; **e–n machen = 2en** (drop a) curts(e)y (**vor** to).

Knie *n* knee; **2en** kneel; **scheibe** *f* knee-cap; **strumpf** *m* knee-length sock. [trick, knack.]

Kniff *m* crease, fold; *fig.*}

knipsen *colloq.* clip, punch; *phot.* take a snapshot of.

Knirps *m* little chap.

knirschen crunch; **mit den Zähnen ~** grind one's teeth.

knistern crackle; *Seide etc.*: rustle.

knittern crease, wrinkle.

Knoblauch *m* garlic.

Knöchel *m Fuß*: ankle; *Finger*: knuckle.

Knoch|en *m* bone; **enbruch** *m* fracture; **2ig** bony.

Knödel *m* dumpling.

Knolle *f* tuber; *Zwiebel*: bulb.

Knopf *m* button.

knöpfen button.

Knopfloch *n* buttonhole.

Knorpel *m* cartilage, gristle.

Knospe *f* bud; **2n** bud.

Knoten *m* knot; **2** knot; **punkt** *m* rail. junction.

knüpfen tie, knot; *Bedingungen*: attach (**an** to).

Knüppel *m* cudgel.

knurren growl, snarl; *Magen*: rumble.

knusprig crisp, crunchy.

Koch *m* cook; **buch** *n* cookery-book, *Am.* cookbook; **2en** *v/t Wasser, Eier, Fisch*: boil; *Fleisch, Gemüse*: cook, boil; *Kaffee, Tee etc.*: make; *v/i Wasser etc.*: boil; *Tätigkeit*: cook, do the cooking; **er** *m* cooker.

Köch|in *f* cook.

Koch|nische *f* kitchenette; **topf** *m* pot, saucepan.

Köder *m* bait; **2n** bait.

Koffer *m* (suit)case; trunk; **radio** *n* portable radio (set); **raum** *m mot.* boot, *Am.* trunk. [dy, cognac.}

Kognak *m* French bran-}

Kohl *m* cabbage.

Kohle *f* coal; *electr.* carbon; **nsäure** *f* carbonic acid; **nstoff** *m* carbon; **papier** *n* carbon-paper.

Koje *f* berth, bunk.

Kokosnuß *f* coconut.

Koks *m* coke.

Kolben *m Gewehr*: butt; *tech.* piston.

Kolik *f* colic.

Kolleg|e *m*, **in** *f* colleague.

435

Konjugation

Kolonie f colony.

Kolonne f column; *Wagen*2: convoy.

Kombi|nation f combination; *Fußball etc.*: move; **~wagen** m estate car, *Am.* station wagon.

Komfort m comfort; **2abel** comfortable.

Komi|k f humo(u)r, fun; **~ker** m comedian; **2sch** comic(al), funny; *fig.* odd.

Komitee n committee.

Komma n comma; **sechs ~ vier** six point four.

Kommando n *mil.* command; *Befehl(e)*: a. order (-s *pl*); *Abteilung*: detachment.

kommen come; *an...*: arrive; **~ lassen** *j-n*: send for; *et.*: order; **~ auf** remember; **um et. ~** lose s.th.

Komment|ar m commentary, comment; **2ieren** comment on.

Kommiss|ar m *Polizei*: superintendent; **~ion** f commission; *Ausschuß*: a. committee.

Kommode f chest of drawers, *Am.* bureau.

Kommunis|mus m communism; **~t** m communist; **2tisch** communist.

Komöd|iant m comedian; **~ie** f comedy.

Kompanie f company.

Komparativ m *gr.* comparative (degree).

Kompaß m compass.

komplett complete.

Komplex m complex; *Gebäude*: block.

Komplikation f complication.

Kompliment n compliment.

Komplize m accomplice.

komplizier|en complicate; **~t** complicated; *Problem etc.*: complex.

kompo|nieren compose; **2nist** m composer; **2sition** f composition.

Kompott n stewed fruit.

Kompromiß m compromise.

kondens|ieren condense; **2milch** f evaporated milk.

Kondition f sp. condition.

Konditional m *gr.* conditional (mood).

Konditor|ei f confectionery, café; **~waren** *pl* confectionery sg.

Konfekt n sweets *pl*, *Am.* candy; chocolates *pl*.

Konfektion f ready-made clothes *pl*.

Konferenz f conference.

Konfession f denomination.

Konfirmation f confirmation.

Konfitüre f preserves *pl*, (whole-fruit) jam.

Konflikt m conflict.

konfrontieren confront.

konfus confused.

Kongreß m congress.

König m king; **~in** f queen; **2lich** royal; **~reich** n kingdom.

Konjug|ation f *gr.* conjugation; **2ieren** *gr.* conjugate.

15*

Konjunkt|ion f gr. conjunction; ~iv m gr. subjunctive od. conjunctive (mood); ~ur f economic od. business situation.

Konkurr|ent m competitor, rival; ~enz f competition (a. sp.); competitor(s pl), rival(s pl); 2enzfähig able to compete; Preise: competitive; 2ieren compete.

Konkurs m bankruptcy.

können know; be allowed od. permitted to; ~ Sie Deutsch? do you speak German?; ich kann I can, I am able to; es kann sein it may be.

konsequen|t consistent; 2z f consistency; Folge: consequence.

konservativ conservative.

Konserven f tinned (Am. canned) food sg; ~büchse f, ~dose f tin, Am. can.

konservieren preserve.

Konsonant m consonant.

konstru|ieren gr. construe; tech.: construct; entwerfen: design; 2ktion f tech.: construction; design. [consulate.]

Konsul m consul; ~at n∫

Konsum m consumption; Laden: co-operative, colloq. co-op; ~ent m consumer; ~güter pl consumer('s) goods pl.

Kontakt m contact; ~ aufnehmen get in touch.

Kontinent m continent.

Konto n account.

Kontrast m contrast.

Kontroll|e f control; Aufsicht: supervision; Prüfung: check; ~eur m inspector; rail. conductor; 2ieren control; supervise; check. [sation.]

Konversation f conver-∫

konzentrieren: (sich) ~ concentrate.

Konzert n concert; Musikstück: concerto; ~saal m concert-hall.

Konzession f concession; licen|ce, Am. -se.

Kopf m head; fig. brains pl; ~bedeckung f headgear; ~ende n head, top; ~hörer m headphone; ~kissen n pillow; ~nicken n nod; ~salat m lettuce; ~schmerzen pl headache sg; ~sprung m header; ~tuch n head-scarf; 2über head first; ~weh n headache. [2ren copy.)

Kopie f copy, duplicate;∫

Kopilot m aer. co-pilot; mot. co-driver.

Koralle f coral.

Korb m basket; ~möbel f wicker furniture sg.

Korken m cork; ~zieher m corkscrew. [men: seed.)

Korn n grain, corn; Sa-∫

körnig granular; in Zssgn: ...-grained.

Körper m body; ~bau m physique; 2behindert (physically) disabled, handicapped; 2lich bodily, physical; ~pflege f hygiene.

korrekt correct; **2ur** f correction.

Korrespond|ent m correspondent; **2ieren** correspond.

korrigieren correct.

Korsett n corset.

Kosename m pet name.

Kosmetik f beauty culture; **∼erin** f beautician, cosmetician; **∼salon** m beauty parlo(u)r.

Kost f food, fare; *Beköstigung:* board; diet; **2bar** costly, expensive; *fig.* valuable, precious.

kosten¹ taste, try, sample.

kosten² cost; *Zeit:* take; **2** pl cost(s pl); *Ausgaben:* expenses pl; **∼los** free (of charge).

köstlich delicious.

Kost|probe f sample; **2spielig** expensive.

Kostüm n costume; suit.

Kot m excrement.

Kotelett n chop.

Kotflügel m mudguard, *Am. a.* fender.

Krabbe f crab; shrimp.

krabbeln crawl.

Krach m crash; *Lärm:* noise; *Streit:* quarrel, *colloq.* row; **2en** crash.

krächzen croak.

Kraft f strength; *Natur2:* force; *electr.,* *tech.* power; *Tat2:* energy; **in ∼ treten** come into operation *od.* force; **∼brühe** f beef tea; **∼fahrer** m driver, motorist; **∼fahrzeug** n motor vehicle.

kräftig strong (*a. fig.*); powerful; *Essen:* substantial.

kraft|los feeble, weak; **2stoff** m fuel; petrol, *Am.* gas(oline); **2wagen** m motor vehicle; **2werk** n power-station.

Kragen m collar.

Krähe f crow; **2n** crow.

Kralle f claw; *Raubvogel:* talon.

Krampf m cramp; *stärker:* spasm, convulsion; **∼ader** f varicose vein; **2haft** convulsive; *fig.* forced.

Kran m crane.

krank ill, *bsd. Am.* sick; **∼ werden** fall ill; **2e** m, f sick person, patient.

kränken offend, hurt.

Kranken|bett n sickbed; **∼haus** n hospital; **∼kasse** f health insurance scheme; **∼pfleger** m male nurse; **∼schwester** f nurse; **∼versicherung** f health *od.* sickness insurance; **∼wagen** m ambulance; **∼zimmer** n sick-room.

krank|haft morbid; **2heit** f illness, sickness; *bestimmte:* disease.

kränklich sickly, ailing.

Kranz m wreath; garland.

kratzen (sich) ∼ scratch (o.s.). [*sp.* crawl.)

kraulen scratch (gently); f

kraus curly, crisp.

Kraut n herb; *Kohl:* cabbage.

Krawall m riot.

Krawatte f (neck)tie.

Krebs *m zo.* crayfish; *med.* cancer.

Kredit *m* credit.

Kreide *f* chalk.

Kreis *m* circle (*a. fig.*); district; **~bahn** *f* orbit.

kreischen screech, scream.

Kreisel *m* (whipping-)top.

kreis|en (move in a) circle, revolve, rotate; *aer.*, *Vogel:* circle; *Blut:* circulate; **~förmig** circular; **2lauf** *m* circulation; **2laufstörung** *f* circulatory disturbance; **~rund** circular; **2verkehr** *m* roundabout traffic.

Krem *f* cream.

Krempe *f* brim.

Kreuz *n* cross; crucifix; *anat.* small of the back; *Karten:* club(s *pl*); **2.** **~und quer** in all directions.

kreuz|en cross; **sich ~en** cross, intersect; **2fahrt** *f* cruise; **~igen** crucify; **2otter** *f* common viper, adder; **2schmerzen** *pl* backache *sg*; **2ung** *f* cross-roads *sg*; *bot.*, *zo.* cross(breed); **2verhör** *n*: **ins ~ nehmen** cross-examine; **~worträtsel** *n* crossword (puzzle).

kriech|en creep, crawl; **2spur** *f mot.* creeper lane.

Krieg *m* war.

kriegen *colloq.*: get; *fangen:* catch.

Kriegs|beschädigte *m* disabled veteran; **~gefangene** *m* prisoner of war; **~gefangenschaft** *f* cap-

tivity; **~verbrechen** *n* war crime.

Kriminal|beamte *m* criminal investigator, plainclothes man; **~film** *m* crime film, thriller; **~polizei** *f* criminal investigation department; **~roman** *m* detective story, crime novel.

kriminell criminal; **2e** *m* criminal.

Krippe *f* crib, manger; *Kinderhort:* crèche.

Krise *f* crisis.

Kriti|k *f* criticism; *thea. etc.:* review; **~ker** *m* critic; **2sch** critical; **2sieren** criticize.

kritzeln scrawl, scribble.

Krokodil *n* crocodile.

Krone *f* crown; *Adels2:* coronet.

krönen crown. [lier.)

Kronleuchter *m* chande-)

Krönung *f* coronation.

Kropf *m* goit|re, *Am.* -er.

Kröte *f* toad.

Krücke *f* crutch.

Krug *m* jug, pitcher; mug.

Krume *f* crumb.

Krümel *m* small crumb.

krumm crooked; bent.

krümm|en bend; *Finger*, *Arm:* crook; **2ung** *f* bend; curve; *Fluß*, *Weg:* turn, wind; *Erde*, *anat.*: curvature.

Krüppel *m* cripple.

Kruste *f* crust.

Kruzifix *n* crucifix.

Kubikmeter *m, n* cubic met|re, *Am.* -er.

Küche *f* kitchen; cuisine.

Kuchen *m* cake.

Küchen|herd *m* (kitchen) range, stove; **~schrank** *m* dresser.

Kuckuck *m* cuckoo.

Kufe *f* aer. skid; *Schlitten etc.*: runner.

Kugel *f* ball; *Gewehr etc.*: bullet; *math., geogr.* sphere; *sp.* shot; **2förmig** spherical; **~gelenk** *n* tech., anat. ball-and-socket joint; **~lager** *n* ballbearing(s *pl*); **~schreiber** *m* ball(-point) pen; **~stoßen** *n* shot-put.

Kuh *f* cow.

kühl cool; chilly; **~en** cool; chill; **~er** *m* mot. radiator; **2schrank** *m* refrigerator, *colloq.* fridge.

kühn bold, daring.

Kuhstall *m* cow-house.

Küken *n* chick(en).

kultivieren cultivate.

Kultur *f* agr. cultivation; culture, civilization; **2ell** cultural; **~film** *m* documentary film.

Kümmel *m* caraway.

Kummer *m* grief, sorrow; *Verdruß:* trouble.

kümmer|lich miserable, wretched; **~n** sorrow, worry; **sich ~n um** look after, take care of; see (to it).

Kunde *m* customer, client; **~ndienst** *m* service.

Kundgebung *f* pol. rally.

kündig|en cancel; *Vertrag:* denounce; **j-m ~en** give s.o. notice; **2ung** *f* notice.

Kund|in *f* customer, client; **~schaft** *f* customers *pl*, clients *pl*.

Kunst *f* art; *Fertigkeit:* skill; **~ausstellung** *f* art exhibition; **~dünger** *m* fertilizer; **~händler** *m* art dealer; **~leder** *n* imitation leather.

Künstler *m*, **~in** *f* artist; *mus., thea.:* performer; **2isch** artistic.

künstlich artificial; false (*a. Zähne etc.*); synthetic.

Kunst|seide *f* rayon, artificial silk; **~stoff** *m* synthetic material, plastics *sg*; **~stück** *n* feat; trick; **2voll** artistic, elaborate; **~werk** *n* work of art.

Kupfer *n* copper; **~stich** *m* copperplate (engraving).

Kuppe *f* rounded hilltop; *Nagel etc.:* head.

Kuppel *f* dome, cupola.

kupp|eln couple; *mot.* declutch; **2lung** *f* tech. coupling; *mot.* clutch; **2lungspedal** *n* clutch pedal.

Kur *f* cure.

Kurbel *f* crank.

Kürbis *m* pumpkin.

Kur|gast *m* visitor; **2ieren** cure; **~ort** *m* health resort, spa; **~park** *m* park, gardens *pl*.

Kurs *m* course (*a. fig.*); *Börse:* price; *Wechsel* 2: rate of exchange; *Lehrgang:* course, class; *pol.* policy, line; **~buch** *n* railway (*Am.* railroad) guide.

kursieren circulate.
Kurswagen m through carriage.
Kurtaxe f visitor's tax.
Kurve f curve; bend.
kurz short; *zeitlich*: brief; **~e Hose** shorts pl; **sich ~ fassen** be brief *od.* concise; **vor ~em** a short time ago.
kürzen shorten (**um** by); *Buch etc.*: abridge; *Ausgaben*: cut, reduce.
Kurz|film m short film; **2fristig** *Kredit*: short-term; *Absage*: at short notice; **~geschichte** f short story; **~nachrichten** pl news summary sg.

kürzlich recently.
Kurz|parkzone f limited parking zone; **~schluß** m short circuit; **~schrift** f shorthand; **2sichtig** short-sighted, near-sighted; **~waren** pl haberdashery sg, *Am. a.* notions pl; **~welle** f short wave.
Kusine f cousin.
Kuß m kiss.
küssen kiss.
Küste f shore, coast.
Küster m verger, sexton.
Kutsche f carriage, coach; **~r** m coachman.
Kutte f cowl.
Kutter m cutter.
Kuvert n envelope.

L

Labor n laboratory; **~ant** (-in f) m laboratory assistant; **~atorium** n laboratory.
Lache f pool, puddle.
lächeln smile; **2** n smile.
lachen laugh; **2** n laugh (-ter).
lächerlich ridiculous.
Lachs m salmon.
Lack m varnish; *Vor:* varnish; **~leder** n patent leather.
laden load; *electr.* charge.
Laden m shop, *Am.* store; *Fenster:* shutter; **~dieb** m shop-lifter; **~kasse** f till; **~schluß** m closing time; **~tisch** m counter.
Ladung f load, freight; *mar.* cargo; *electr.* charge.

Lage f situation (*a. fig.*); position (*a. fig.*); **in der ~ sein zu** be able to.
Lager n couch, bed; *Vorrat:* store, stock; *mil. etc.:* camp, encampment; *s.* **Lagerhaus; auf ~** on hand, in stock; **~feuer** n campfire; **~haus** n warehouse, store-house; **2n** v/i *mil.* (en)camp; *econ.* be stored; v/t *econ.* store, warehouse; **~raum** m store-room; **~ung** f storage.
Lagune f lagoon.
lahm lame; **~en** be lame (**auf** in).
lähm|en paraly|se, *Am.* -ze; **2ung** f paralysis.
Laib m loaf.
Laie m layman; amateur.

Laken n sheet.

lallen babble.

Lamm n lamb.

Lampe f lamp; ～schirm m lamp-shade.

Land n *Festl.*: land; country; an～ gehen go ashore; auf dem ～(e) in the country; ～ebahn f runway; 2～einwärts upcountry, inland; 2en land.

Länder|kampf m, ～spiel n international match.

Landes|grenze f national border, frontier; ～innere n interior, upcountry; ～regierung f (*Deutschland*: Land) government.

Land|karte f map; ～kreis m rural district.

ländlich rural, rustic.

Land|schaft f countryside; *bsd. paint.* landscape; ～smann m (fellow-)countryman, compatriot; ～straße f highway; road; ～streicher m vagabond, tramp; ～tag m Landtag, Land parliament.

Landung f landing; ～steg m gangway.

Land|weg m: auf dem ～(e) by land; ～wirt m farmer; ～wirtschaft f agriculture, farming; 2wirtschaftlich agricultural.

lang long; *Person*: tall.

Länge f length; tallness; *geogr.* longitude.

langen *colloq.*: be enough; ～ nach reach for.

Langeweile f boredom.

lang|fristig long-term; ～

jährig: ～e Erfahrung many years of experience.

länglich longish, oblong.

längs along(side).

lang|sam slow; 2schläfer m late riser; 2spielplatte f long-play record.

längst long ago *od.* since.

Langstreckenlauf m long-distance run *od.* race.

langweil|en bore; sich ～en be bored; ～ig boring, dull; ～ige **Person** bore.

Lang|welle f long wave; 2wierig protracted, lengthy.

Lappen m rag; *Staub*2: duster; *Wisch*2 *etc.*: cloth; *anat., bot.* lobe.

Lärche f larch.

Lärm m noise; 2en make a noise; 2end noisy.

Larve f mask; *zo.* larva.

Lasche f tongue.

lassen let; *be～*: leave; allow, permit; let; *veran～*: make; laß das! don't!; drucken ～ have printed.

lässig easy; careless.

Last f load; burden; *Gewicht*: weight; ～auto n s.

Last(kraft)wagen m; 2en: ～ auf weigh *od.* press on.

Laster n vice.

lästern: ～ über speak ill of. [noying.}

lästig troublesome; an-}

Last|kahn m barge; ～(kraft)wagen m lorry, *Am.* truck.

Latein n Latin; 2isch Latin.

Laterne f lantern; streetlamp; **~npfahl** m lamp-post.

Latte f lath; Zaun: pale.

Lätzchen n bib, feeder.

Laub n foliage, leaves pl; **~baum** m deciduous tree.

Laube f arbo(u)r, bower.

Lauch m leek.

lauern lurk, watch.

Lauf m Gewehr: barrel; Fluß: course (a. fig.); run; sp. a. heat; **~bahn** f career; **2en** run; gehen: walk; **2enlassen:** j-n ~ let s.o. go.

Läufer m runner (a. Teppich); Fußball: half-back.

Laufmasche f ladder, Am. a. run.

Lauge f lye.

Laun|e f humo(u)r, mood, temper; whim; **2enhaft, 2isch** moody.

Laus f louse.

lauschen listen (dat to); heimlich: eavesdrop.

laut adj loud; noisy; adv aloud, loud(ly); prp according to; **2** m sound; **~en** Text: run.

läuten ring; **es läutet** the bell is ringing.

laut|los noiseless, soundless; Stille: hushed; **2schrift** f phonetic transcription; **2sprecher** m loud-speaker; **2stärke** f volume. [warm.}

lauwarm tepid, luke-}

Lava f lava.

Lavendel m lavender.

Lawine f avalanche.

leben live; be alive; **leb wohl!** good-bye!, fare-

well!; **von et.** ~ live on s.th.; **2** n life; stir, bustle; **am 2 alive; am 2 bleiben** survive; **ums 2 kommen** lose one's life; **~dig** fig. lively.

Lebens|alter n age; **~bedingungen** pl living conditions pl; **~gefahr** f danger to life; **~gefahr!** danger!; **2gefährlich** dangerous (to life); **~haltungskosten** pl cost sg of living; **2länglich** for life; **~lauf** m personal record, curriculum vitae; **2lustig** gay, merry; **~mittel** pl food sg, groceries pl; **~mittelgeschäft** n grocer's (shop), Am. grocery; **~standard** m standard of living; **~unterhalt** m: s-n ~ **verdienen** earn one's living; **~versicherung** f life assurance, Am. life insurance; **2wichtig** vital, essential; **~zeichen** n sign of life. [cod-liver oil.}

Leber f liver; **~tran** m}

Lebewesen n living being od. creature.

Lebewohl n farewell.

leb|haft lively; vivid; Interesse: keen; **~los** lifeless.

leck leaky; **~sein** leak.

lecken lick; leak.

lecker dainty, delicious; **2bissen** m dainty, delicacy.

Leder n leather.

ledig single, unmarried; Kind: illegitimate.

leer empty; vacant; Seite etc.: blank; **2e** f emptiness;

~en empty; clear out; pour out; 2lauf m neutral gear.

legal legal, lawful.

legen v/t lay; place, put; **sich** ~ *Wind etc.*: abate, calm down; v/i *Henne*: lay.

Legende f legend.

Lehm m loam.

Lehn|e f *Arm*2: arm; *Rükken*2: back; 2en lean, rest (**an, gegen** against); (**sich**) 2**en an** lean against; ~**sessel** m, ~**stuhl** m armchair, easy chair.

Lehrbuch n textbook.

Lehre f doctrine; science; *Warnung*: lesson; apprenticeship; **in der** ~ **sein bei** be apprenticed to; 2n teach, instruct.

Lehrer m teacher, instructor; ~**in** f teacher.

Lehr|fach n subject; ~**herr** m master, sl. boss; ~**ling** m apprentice.

Leib m body; *Bauch*: belly, *anat.* abdomen; *Mutter*2: womb; ~**chen** m bodice, ~**esübungen** pl physical exercises pl; ~**gericht** n favo(u)rite dish; ~**schmerzen** pl s. Bauchschmerzen; ~**wache** f, ~**wächter** m bodyguard.

Leiche f (dead) body, corpse; ~**nschauhaus** n morgue.

leicht light (a. fig.); *einfach*: easy; 2**athlet** m athlete; 2**athletik** f athletics pl, Am. track and field events pl; ~**gläubig** credulous; 2**igkeit** f lightness; fig. a.

ease; 2**sinn** m carelessness; ~**sinnig** careless.

leid: es tut mir ~ I am sorry; **er tut mir** ~ I am sorry for him; 2 n grief, sorrow; ~**en** suffer (**an** from); (**nicht**) ~**en können** (dis)like; 2**en** n suffering; *med.* complaint; ~**end** ailing. [2**lich** passionate.]

Leidenschaft f passion;∫

leid|er unfortunately; 2**tragende** m, f mourner.

Leih|bücherei f lending-library, circulating library; 2**en** lend; (**sich**) 2**en** borrow; ~**haus** n pawnshop; ~**wagen** m hire(d) car.

Leim m glue; 2**en** glue.

Leine f line; *Hunde*2: leash.

leinen (of) linen; 2 n linen; 2**schuh** m canvas shoe.

Leinwand f paint. canvas; *Kino*: screen.

leise low, soft; ~**r stellen** turn down.

Leiste f ledge; *anat.* groin.

leisten do; *Dienst, Hilfe*: render; **ich kann mir das** ~ I can afford it; **Widerstand** ~ offer resistance.

Leistung f performance; achievement; *Arbeits*2: output; *Versicherung*2: benefit.

Leit|artikel m leading article, leader, editorial; 2**en** lead, guide; conduct (a. phys., mus.); run, manage.

Leiter[1] m conductor; manager.

Leiter² f ladder.

Leitung f *Stromkreis:* circuit; *teleph.* line; *Rohr*♀: pipe; *Führen:* guidance; *fig.* management, administration; **~srohr** n conduitpipe; **~swasser** n tap water.

Lekt|ion f lesson; **~üre** f reading; books pl.

Lende f loin(s pl.).

lenk|en direct; *mar.* steer; *Fahrzeug:* a. drive; **2rad** n steering-wheel; **2stange** f handlebar; **2ung** f steering-gear.

Leopard m leopard.

Lerche f lark.

lernen learn.

Lese|buch n reader; **~lampe** f reading-lamp; **2n** read; *agr.* gather; **~r(in** f) m reader; **2rlich** legible; **~zeichen** n book-mark.

letzt last; final.

leucht|en shine; *schimmern:* gleam; **~end** shining, bright; luminous; **2er** m candlestick; *s.* Kronleuchter; **2reklame** f neon sign; **2turm** m lighthouse; **2ziffer** f luminous figure.

leugnen deny.

Leute pl people pl; *einzelne:* persons pl.

Lexikon n dictionary; encyclop(a)edia.

Libelle f dragon-fly.

liberal liberal.

Licht n light; **~ machen** switch *od.* turn on the light(s); **~bild** n photo

(-graph); **2empfindlich** sensitive to light; *phot.* sensitive.

lichten *Wald:* clear; **den Anker ~** weigh anchor; **sich ~** thin.

Licht|hupe f headlight flash(er); **~maschine** f dynamo; **~reklame** f neon sign; **~schalter** m (light) switch; **~strahl** m ray *od.* beam of light.

Lichtung f clearing.

Lid n (eye)lid.

lieb dear (a. *Anrede*); *nett:* nice, kind; *Kind:* good.

Liebe f love; **2n** love.

liebenswürdig kind.

lieber rather, sooner; **~ haben** prefer, like better.

Liebes|brief m love-letter; **~paar** n lovers pl.

liebevoll loving, affectionate.

Lieb|haber m lover (a. *fig.*); **2kosen** caress; **2lich** lovely, charming; **~ling** m darling; favo(u)rite; *Kind, Tier:* pet; *Anrede:* darling; **2los** unkind; *nachlässig:* careless; **~ste** m, f darling; sweetheart.

Lied n song.

liederlich slovenly.

Liefer|ant m supplier, purveyor; **~auto** n s. **Lieferwagen; 2bar** available; **2n** deliver; supply; **~ung** f delivery; supply; *Ware:* consignment; **~wagen** m delivery van.

Liege f couch; *Garten*♀: bedchair.

liegen lie; *Haus etc.*: be (situated); **~ nach** face; **es liegt an ihm** it is up to him; **~bleiben** stay in bed; *Arbeit etc.*: stand over; **~lassen** leave (behind).

Liege|stuhl *m* deck chair; **~wagen** *m* couchette coach.

Lift *m* lift, *Am.* elevator.

Liga *f* league.

Likör *m* liqueur, cordial.

lila lilac.

Lilie *f* lily.

Limonade *f* orangeade; lemonade. [sedan.)

Limousine *f* saloon car,)

Linde *f* lime(-tree), linden.

lindern alleviate, soothe; *Not:* relieve.

Lineal *n* ruler. [ber.)

Linie *f* line; *Bus etc.*: num-)

link left; **2e** *f* left; **~isch** awkward, clumsy.

links (on *od.* to the) left; **nach ~** to the left; **2händer** *m* left-hander.

Linse *f bot.* lentil; *opt.* lens.

Lippe *f* lip; **~nstift** *m* lipstick.

lispeln lisp.

List *f* ruse, trick.

Liste *f* list; roll.

listig cunning, crafty.

Liter *m, n* lit|re, *Am.* -er.

litera|risch literary; **2tur** *f* literature.

Lizenz *f* licen|ce, *Am.* -se.

Lob *n* praise; **2en** praise; **2enswert** praiseworthy.

Loch *n* hole; **2en** perforate, pierce; *Karten:* punch;

~er *m* punch, perforator; **~karte** *f* punch(ed) card.

Locke *f* curl, ringlet.

locken decoy (*a. fig.*); *fig.* allure, entice.

Lockenwickler *m* curler.

locker loose; slack; **~n** loosen (*a.* sich), slacken; relax.

lockig curly.

Löffel *m* spoon.

Loge *f thea.* box.

Loggia *f* loggia.

logisch logical.

Lohn *m* wages *pl*; *fig.* reward; **~empfänger** *m* wage-earner; **2en: sich ~** pay; **2end** profitable; *fig.* rewarding; **~erhöhung** *f* rise (in wages), *Am.* raise; **~steuer** *f* wage(s) tax; **~stopp** *m* wage-freeze.

lokal local; **2** *n* restaurant; public house, *Am.* saloon.

Lokomotiv|e *f* (railway) engine; **~führer** *m* engine-driver, *Am.* engineer.

Lorbeer *m* laurel, bay.

Los *n* lot; lottery ticket; *fig.* fate, destiny, lot.

los loose, free; **was ist ~?** what is the matter?; **~ sein** be rid of; **~! los** (on, ahead)!; **~binden** untie.

Lösch|blatt *n* blotting-paper; **2en** extinguish, put out; wipe off; *Tonband:* erase; *Feuer, Durst:* quench; *mar.* unload.

lose loose.

Lösegeld *n* ransom.

losen cast *od.* draw lots (**um** for).

lösen loosen, untie; *Karte*: buy; *fig.* solve; *Verlobung*: break off; *Vertrag*: annul, cancel; **(sich) ~** *chem.* dissolve; **sich ~** loosen.

los|fahren depart, drive off; **~gehen** go od. be off; **~lassen** let go.

löslich soluble.

los|lösen detach; **~machen** unfasten, loosen; **~reißen** tear off; **sich ~reißen** *fig.* tear o.s. away.

Lösung *f* solution (*a. fig.*).

loswerden *prit* get rid of.

Lot *n* plumb(-line), plummet.

löten solder.

Lotse *m mar.* pilot.

Lotterie *f* lottery.

Lotto *n* numbers pool, lotto.

Löw|e *m* lion; **~in** *f* lioness.

loyal loyal.

Luchs *m* lynx.

Lücke *f* gap; **Qnhaft** incomplete; **Qnlos** complete.

Luft *f* air; **frische ~ schöpfen** take the air; **in die ~ sprengen** blow up; **~angriff** *m* air raid; **~blase** *f* air-bubble; **~brücke** *f* air lift; **Qdicht** airtight; **~druck** *m* atmospheric od. air pressure.

lüften air; *Hut*: raise.

Luft|fahrt *f* aviation, aeronautics *sg*; **~kissen** *n* air cushion; **Qkrank** airsick; **~kurort** *m* climatic health resort; **Qleer: ~er Raum**

vacuum; **~linie** *f* bee-line, *Am. a.* air line; **~loch** *n* air pocket; **~matratze** *f* airbed; **~post** *f* air mail; **~pumpe** *f* bicycle pump; **~röhre** *f* windpipe; **~stützpunkt** *m* air base.

Lüftung *f* ventilation.

Luft|veränderung *f* change of air; **~verkehr** *m* air traffic; **~verkehrsgesellschaft** *f* airway, *Am.* airline; **~waffe** *f* air force; **~weg** *m*: **auf dem ~** by air, **~zug** *m* draught, *Am.* draft.

Lüg|e *f* lie, falsehood; **Qen** lie; **~ner(in** *f*) *m* liar.

Luke *f* hatch.

Lump *m* cad, rogue.

Lumpen *m* rag.

Lunge *f* lungs *pl*; **~nentzündung** *f* pneumonia; **~nflügel** *m* lung.

Lupe *f* magnifying glass.

Lust *f* pleasure, delight; lust; **~ haben zu** feel like *ger*.

lüstern lewd.

lust|ig merry, gay; *belustigend*: amusing, funny; **sich ~ig machen über** make fun of; **Qspiel** *n* comedy.

lutschen suck.

luxuriös luxurious.

Luxus *m* luxury; **~artikel** *m* luxury; **~hotel** *n* luxury hotel. [gland.〕

Lymphdrüse *f* lymph〕

Lyrik *f* (lyric) poetry.

M

machen make; do; *herstellen*: make, produce, manufacture; *Prüfung*: sit for; *Rechnung*: come *od.* amount to; **wieviel macht das?** how much is it?; **das macht nichts!** never mind!, that's (quite) all right!; **da(gegen) kann man nichts machen** it cannot be helped; **ich mache mir nichts daraus** I don't care about it; **sich et. ~ lassen** have s.th. made; **na, mach schon!** *colloq.* hurry up!

Macht *f* power (*a.* Staat), *stärker*: might; authority.

mächtig powerful (*a. fig.*); mighty; *riesig*: huge.

machtlos powerless.

Mädchen *n* girl; maid (-servant); **~name** *m* girl's name; *Frau*: maiden name.

Made *f* maggot, mite; **2ig** maggoty, full of mites.

Magazin *n* magazine.

Magen *m* stomach; **~beschwerden** *pl* stomach trouble *sg*; **~bitter** *m* bitters *pl*; **~geschwür** *n* gastric ulcer; **~schmerzen** *pl* stomach-ache *sg*.

mager meag|re, *Am. ~*er (*a. fig.*); *Mensch, Tier, Fleisch*: lean; **2milch** *f* skim(med) milk.

magnetisch magnetic.

mähen cut, mow, reap.

Mahl *n* meal.

mahlen grind, mill.

Mahlzeit *f* meal.

Mähne *f* mane.   [ish.]

mahnen remind, admon-]

Mai *m* May; **~baum** *m* maypole; **~glöckchen** *n* lily of the valley; **~käfer** *m* cockchafer.

Mais *m* maize, Indian corn, *Am.* corn.

Majestät *f* majesty.

Major *m* major.

makellos immaculate.

Makler *m* broker.

Mal *n* mark, sign; time; **zum ersten ~** for the first time.

mal times; multiplied by.

male|n paint; **2r** (*in f*) *m* painter; **2rei** *f* painting.

Malz *n* malt.

Mama *f* mam(m)a, mammy, ma.

man one, you, we; they, people.

manch, ~er, ~e, ~es many a; **~e** *pl* some, several; **~mal** sometimes, at times.

Mandant *m* client.

Mandarine *f* tangerine.

Mandel *f bot.* almond; *anat.* tonsil; **~entzündung** *f* tonsillitis.

Manege *f* (circus-)ring.

Mangel *m* want, lack, deficiency; *Knappheit*: shortage; *Fehler*: defect; **~haft** defective; unsatisfactory; **~ware** *f*: **~ sein** to be scarce.

Manieren *pl* manners *pl.*

Mann m man; *Ehe*2: husband.

Männ|chen n zo. male; orn. cock; 2lich male; gr. masculine; [team.}

Mannschaft f crew; sp.}

Manöver n manoeuvre, Am. maneuver.

Mansarde f attic, garret.

Manschette f cuff; ~knopf m cuff-link.

Mantel m (over)coat.

Manuskript n manuscript.

Mappe f portfolio, briefcase; *Aktendeckel*: folder.

Märchen n fairy-tale.

Marder m marten.

Margarine f margarine, colloq. marge.

Marinade f marinade.

Marine f marine; *Kriegs*2: navy.

Marionette f puppet.

Mark[1] f *Geld*: mark.

Mark[2] n anat. marrow; bot. pith.

Marke f *Brief*2 etc.: stamp; *Fabrikat*: brand.

markieren mark.

Markise f awning.

Markt m market.

Marmelade f jam; *Orangen*2: marmalade.

Marmor m marble.

Marsch m march (a. mus.); 2ieren march.

Märtyrer m martyr.

März m March.

Marzipan n marzipan, marchpane.

Masche f mesh; *Strick*2: stitch; ~ndraht m wire netting.

Maschine f machine; *Motor*: engine; aer. plane; 2ll mechanical.

Maschinen|gewehr n machine-gun; ~schaden m engine trouble.

Masern pl measles pl.

Mask|e f mask; ~enball m fancy-dress od. masked ball; 2ieren: sich ~ put on a mask.

Maß[1] n measure; *Verhältnis*: proportion; *Mäßigung*: moderation; ~e pl measurements pl.

Maß[2] f *Bier*: appr. quart.

Massaker n massacre.

Maßanzug m tailor-made suit.

Masse f mass; *Haupt*2: bulk; *Substanz*: substance; *Volk*: crowd; e-e ~ a lot of.

massieren massage, knead.

massig massy, bulky.

mäßig moderate; *Ergebnis* etc.: poor. [massif.}

massiv massive, solid; 2 n}

maß|los immoderate; 2~nahme f measure, step; 2stab m measure, rule(r); *Karte*: scale; fig. standard; ~voll moderate.

Mast m mast.

mästen fatten, feed; *Geflügel*: stuff, cram.

Material n material.

Mathematik f mathematics sg, pl; ~er m mathematician. [formance.}

Matinee f morning per-}

Matratze f mattress.

Matrose m sailor, seaman.

Matsch m mud, slush.

matt *schwach*: faint, feeble; *trübe*: mat(t); *Auge, Licht*: dim; *Schach*: (check)mate.

Matte *f* mat.

Mattscheibe *f* screen.

Mauer *f* wall.

Maul *n* mouth; **~esel** *m* hinny; **~korb** *m* muzzle; **~tier** *n* mule; **~wurf** *m* mole. [son.}

Maurer *m* bricklayer, ma-}

Maus *f* mouse.

Maximum *n* maximum.

Mechani|k *f* mechanics *mst sg*; **~ker** *m* mechanic; **2sch** mechanical; **~smus** *m* mechanism.

meckern bleat; *fig. colloq.* grumble.

Medaill|e *f* medal; **~on** *n* locket.

Medikament *n* medicine.

Medizin *f* medicine, **2isch** medical; *heilkräftig*: medicinal; *Seife etc.*: medicated.

Meer *n* sea, ocean; **~enge** *f* strait(s *pl*); **~esspiegel** *m* sea level; **~rettich** *m* horseradish; **~schwein-chen** *n* guinea-pig.

Mehl *n* flour.

mehr more; **ich habe nichts ~** I have nothing left; **~deutig** ambiguous; **~ere** several, some; **~fach** repeated; **2heit** *f* majority; **~malig** repeated; **~mals** several times, repeatedly; **2wertsteuer** *f* value-added tax; **2zahl** *f* majority; *gr.* plural.

meiden avoid.

Meile *f* mile.

mein my.

Meineid *m* perjury.

meinen think, believe, *Am. a.* reckon, guess; *äußern*: say; *sagen wollen*: mean.

meinetwegen for my sake; *int.* I don't mind *od.* care!

Meinung *f* opinion; **meiner ~ nach** in my opinion; **j-m (gehörig) die ~ sagen** give s.o. a piece of one's mind; **~sverschiedenheit** *f* difference of opinion; disagreement.

Meise *f* titmouse.

Meißel *m* chisel.

meist most; **am ~en** most (of all); **~ens** mostly.

Meister *m* master; *sp.* champion; **~schaft** *f* sp. championship; **~werk** *n* masterpiece.

melancholisch melancholy.

meld|en announce; inform; *amtlich*: notify; report; **sich ~en** report (bei to); *Schule*: put up one's hand; answer the telephone; *sp.* enter; **2ung** *f* announcement; report; *Behörde*: registration; *sp.* entry.

melken milk. [air.}

Melodie *f* melody, tune,}

Melone *f* melon.

Menge *f* quantity, amount; *Menschen2*: crowd; **e-e ~** plenty of, lots of.

Mensch *m* human being; man; *einzelner*: person, individual; **die ~en** *pl* people *pl*, mankind *sg*; **kein ~** nobody.

Menschen|affe *m* ape; **~kenntnis** *f* knowledge of human nature; **~leben** *n* human life; **2leer** deserted; **~menge** *f* crowd; **~rechte** *pl* human rights *pl*; **2scheu** shy.

Menschheit *f* mankind.

menschlich human; *fig.* humane; **2keit** *f* humanity.

Menstruation *f* menstruation. [*od.* dinner.]

Menü *n* menu, set lunch

merk|en notice, perceive; **sich et. ~en** remember s.th.; **2mal** *n* characteristic, feature; **~würdig** strange, odd.

Meß|band *n* tape-measure; **2bar** measurable.

Messe *f* fair; *eccl.* mass; **~gelände** *n* fairground.

messen measure.

Messer *n* knife.

Messing *n* brass.

Metall *n* metal; **~waren** *pl* hardware *sg.* [-er.]

Meter *m*, *n* met|re, *Am.*

Methode *f* method; technique. [scher(ei).]

Metzger *m*, **~ei** *f* s. Flei-

Meuterei *f* mutiny.

mich me; **~ (selbst)** myself.

Mieder *n* bodice; *Korsett:* corset; **~waren** *pl* foundation garments *pl*.

Miene *f* countenance, air.

Miet|e *f* rent; *für bewegliche Sachen:* hire; **2en** rent; *Wagen, Boot:* hire;

~er *m* tenant; *einzelner Zimmer:* lodger; **2frei** rentfree; **~shaus** *n* block of flats, *Am.* apartment house; **~vertrag** *m* lease; **~wagen** *m* hire(d) car; **~wohnung** *f* flat, *Am.* apartment.

Mikro|phon *n* microphone, *colloq.* mike; **~skop** *n* microscope.

Milch *f* milk; *Fisch*2: milt, soft roe; **~glas** *n* frosted glass; **2ig** milky; **~kaffee** *m* white coffee; **~kännchen** *n* (milk-)jug; **~reis** *m* rice pudding; **~zahn** *m* milk-tooth.

mild mild; soft, gentle; **~ern** soften; *Schmerz:* soothe, alleviate.

Milieu *n* surroundings *pl*, environment. [army.]

Militär *n* the military,

Milli|arde *f* billion; *früher Brit.* milliard; **~meter** *m*, *n* millimet|re, *Am.* -er; **~on** *f* million; **~onär** *m* millionaire.

Milz *f* spleen.

minder less; **2heit** *f* minority; **~jährig** under age.

minderwertig inferior; **2keitskomplex** *m* inferiority complex.

mindest least; *geringst:* slightest; *kleinst:* minimum; **~ens** at least.

Mine *f* mine; *Bleistift:* lead; *Ersatz~:* refill.

Mineral *n* mineral; **~öl** *n* mineral oil, petroleum; **~wasser** *n* mineral water.

Minirock m miniskirt.

Minister m minister, Brit. a. secretary (of state), Am. secretary; **~ium** n ministry, Brit. a. office, Am. department.

minus minus, less; s. **Grad.**

Minute f minute.

mir (to) me.

misch|en mix, mingle; blend; Karten: shuffle; **2~ling** m half-breed; **2ung** f mixture.

miß|achten disregard, ignore; **2bildung** f deformity; **~billigen** disapprove (of); **2brauch** m abuse; falsche Anwendung: misuse; **2erfolg** m failure; **2geschick** n bad luck, misfortune; Panne etc.: mishap; **2handlung** f illtreatment.

Mission f mission; **~ar** m missionary.

Miß|kredit m: in **~ bringen** bring discredit upon; **2lingen** fail; **2mutig** illhumo(u)red; discontented; **~stand** m nuisance, grievance; **2trauen** distrust; **2trauisch** distrustful, suspicious; **~verständnis** n misunderstanding; **2verstehen** misunderstand; Absichten etc.: mistake.

Mist m dung, manure; fig. colloq. rubbish.

Mistel f mistletoe.

Misthaufen m dunghill.

mit with; **2arbeit** f co(-)operation; **2arbeiter** m colleague; **~bringen** bring

(with one); **2bürger** m fellow-citizen; **~einander** with each other; together; **2esser** m med. blackhead; **~fahren:** mit j-m **~** go with s.o.; j-n **~ lassen** give s.o. a lift; **~fühlend** sympathetic; **~geben** give s.o. s.th. (to take along); **2gefühl** n sympathy; **~gehen:** mit j-m **~** go with s.o.

Mitglied n member; **~schaft** f membership.

Mit|inhaber m partner; **~kommen** come along.

Mitleid n compassion, pity; sympathy; **2ig** compassionate.

mit|machen take part in; erleben: go through; **~machen bei** join in; **2mensch** m fellow creature; **~nehmen** take along (with one); fig. exhaust; **j-n** (im Auto) **~nehmen** give s.o. a lift; **2reisende** m, f fellow-travel(l)er; **2schüler(in** f) m schoolfellow, schoolmate; **~spielen** join in a game; sp. be on the team; thea. be in the cast.

Mittag m midday, noon; **heute 2** at noon today; **zu ~ essen** lunch, dine; **2essen** n lunch(eon); Hauptmahlzeit: dinner; **2s** at noon.

Mittags|pause f lunch hour; **~tisch** m dinnertable; s. **Mittagessen.** **~zeit** f noon. [Am. -er.]

Mitte f middle; cent|re,f)

mitteil|en oommunicate; **j-m et. ~en** inform s.o. of s.th.; **2ung** f communication; information.

Mittel n means sg, pl, way; **Heil2:** remedy **(gegen** for**);** Durchschnitt: average; **~ pl** means pl, money sg; **~alter** n Middle Ages pl; **2alterlich** medi(a)eval; **~finger** m middle finger; **2groß** of medium height; medium-sized; **2los** destitute; **2mäßig** mediocre; **~punkt** m cent|re, Am. -er; **~stürmer** m sp. cent|re (Am. -er) forward.

mitten: ~ in (auf, unter) in the midst od. middle of.

Mitternacht f midnight.

mittler middle; average.

Mittwoch m Wednesday.

Mitwisser m confidant; jur. accessary.

mixen mix.

Möbel pl furniture sg; **~stück** n piece of furniture; **~wagen** m furniture (Am. moving) van.

möblieren furnish.

Mode f fashion, vogue; **~artikel** pl fancy goods pl, novelties pl. [pattern.}

Modell n model; Muster:}

Mode(n)schau f fashion parade od. show.

mod(e)rig musty, mo(u)ldy.

modern modern; fashionable; **~isieren** modernize.

Mode|salon m fashion house; **~schmuck** m costume jewel(le)ry.

modisch fashionable.

mogeln colloq.: cheat.

mögen wollen: want; gern **~:** like, be fond of; **nicht ~** dislike; **ich möchte wissen** I should like to know; **ich möchte lieber I** would rather.

möglich possible; **so bald wie ~, ~st bald** as soon as possible; **2keit** f possibility.

Mohammedaner m Muslim, Moslem.

Mohn m poppy.

Möhre f carrot.

Mohrrübe f carrot.

Mokka m mocha.

Mole f mole, jetty.

Molkerei f dairy.

Moll n minor (key).

mollig colloq.: snug, cosy; dicklich: plump. [stant.}

Moment m moment, in-}

Monarchie f monarchy.

Monat m month; **2lich** monthly. [friar.}

Mönch m monk; Bettel2:}

Mond m moon; **~fähre** f lunar module; **~finsternis** f lunar eclipse; **~schein** m moonlight.

Mono|log m monolog(ue), soliloquy; **2ton** monotonous.

Montag m Monday.

Mont|age f mounting, fitting; Zusammenbau: assemblage; **~eur** m fitter; **2ieren** mount, fit; assemble.

Moor n bog, swamp; **2ig** boggy, marshy.

Moos n moss.
Moped n moped.
Moral f morals pl; Lehre: moral; mil. etc.: morale.
Morast m mud; 2ig muddy.
Mord m murder (an of).
Mörder m murderer.
Morgen m morning; am ~ s. **morgens; guten ~!** good morning!; 2 tomorrow; 2 früh tomorrow morning; .dämmerung f dawn, daybreak; .rock m dressing-gown; 2s in the morning.
morgig tomorrow's.
Morphium n morphia, morphine.
morsch rotten, decayed.
Mörtel m mortar.
Mosaik n mosaic.
Moschee f mosque.
Moskito m mosquito.
Moslem m Muslim, Moslem. [Apfel2: cider.]
Most m must, grape-juice;
Mostrich n mustard.
Motiv n motive, reason; paint., mus. motif.
Motor m motor, engine; .boot n motor-boat; .haube f bonnet, Am. hood; .rad n motorcycle; .radfahrer m motor-cyclist; .roller m (motor-)scooter; .schaden m engine trouble.
Motte f moth.
Möwe f gull.
Mücke f gnat, midge.
müde tired, weary.
muffig musty.

Mühe f trouble, pains pl; j-m ~ machen give s.o. trouble; sich ~ geben take pains; 2los effortless, easy; 2voll hard, laborious.
Mühle f mill.
mühsam laborious.
Mulde f depression, hollow.
Mull m gauze, mull.
Müll m dust, refuse, rubbish, Am. a. garbage; ~abfuhr f refuse (Am. garbage) disposal od. collection; .eimer m dustbin, Am. garbage od. ash can.
Müller m miller.
Mülltonne f s. **Mülleimer.** [(mit by).]
multiplizieren multiply)
Mund m mouth; .art f dialect.
münden: ~ in Fluß: flow into; Straße: lead into.
mündig: ~ (werden come) of age.
mündlich adj oral, verbal; adv orally, by word of mouth.
Mundstück n mouthpiece; Zigarette: tip.
Mündung f mouth, ins Meer: estuary; Feuerwaffe: muzzle. [wash.]
Mundwasser n mouth-)
Munition f ammunition.
munter wach: awake; leb-haft, fröhlich: lively, merry.
Münz|e f coin; Hartgeld: (small) change; Gedenkmünze: medal; .fernsprecher m coin-box od. pub-

lic telephone; **~wechsler** *m* change giver.

mürbe tender; *Gebäck:* crisp, short.

murmel|n mumble, murmur; **2tier** *n* marmot.

murren grumble.

mürrisch surly, sullen.

Mus *n* pap; stewed fruit.

Muschel *f* mussel; *Schale:* shell; *teleph.* earpiece.

Museum *n* museum.

Musik *f* music; **2alisch** musical; **~automat** *m* juke-box; **~er** *m* musician; **~instrument** *n* musical instrument; **~kapelle** *f* band.

Muskat *m*, **~nuß** *f* nutmeg.

Muskel *m* muscle; **~kater** *m colloq.:* **~ haben** be muscle-bound; **~zerrung** *f* pulled muscle.

Muskul|atur *f* muscles *pl;* **2ös** muscular.

Muße *f* leisure; spare time.

müssen: ich muß I must, I have to.

Muster *n* model; design, pattern; *Probestück:* specimen, sample; *fig.* model, example; **2n** pattern; *prüfen:* examine.

Mut *m* courage; **2ig** courageous; **2maßlich** supposed.

Mutter *f* mother; *Schraube:* nut; **~leib** *m* womb.

mütterlich motherly, maternal.

mutter|los motherless; **2-mal** *n* birthmark, mole; **2sprache** *f* mother tongue.

mutwillig wanton, mischievous.

Mütze *f* cap.

mysteriös mysterious.

Mythologie *f* mythology.

N

Nabe *f* hub.

Nabel *m* navel.

nach *prp* after; to(wards), for; *Reihenfolge:* after; *Zeit:* after, past; according to; *adv* after; **~ und ~** little by little, gradually.

nachahmen imitate, copy; *fälschen:* counterfeit.

Nachbar *m,* **~in** *f* neighbo(u)r; **~schaft** *f* neighbo(u)rhood, vicinity.

nachdem after, when; **je ~ (, wie)** according as.

nach|denken think *(über*

over, about); **~denklich** pensive; **2druck** *m fig.* stress, emphasis; **~drücklich: ~ betonen** emphasize; **~eifern** emulate.

nacheinander one after the other.

nacherzäh|len retell; **2-lung** *f* story retold.

Nachfolger *m* successor.

nachforsch|en investigate; **2ung** *f* investigation.

Nachfrage *f* inquiry; *econ.* demand; **2n** inquire.

nach|fühlen: es j-m *(turn to)*

feel od. sympathize with s.o.; **⸥füllen** refill; **⸥geben** give way; fig. give in, yield; **⸥gebühr** f surcharge; **⸥gehen** follow; Uhr: be slow; **⸥giebig** fig. yielding, compliant; **⸥haltig** lasting.

nachher afterwards.

Nachhilfeunterricht m private lesson(s pl), coaching.

nachholen make up for.

Nachkomme m descendant; **⸥n** pl bsd. jur. issue sg; **⸥n** follow.

Nachkriegs... post-war ...

Nachlaß m econ. reduction, discount; jur. assets pl, estate.

nach|lassen Wind, Schmerz etc.: abate; Interesse, Kräfte: flag; **⸥lässig** careless, negligent; **⸥laufen** run after; **⸥lesen** look up; **⸥lösen** take a supplementary ticket; **⸥machen** s. **nachahmen**.

Nachmittag m afternoon; **am ⸥** = **⸥s** in the afternoon.

Nach|nahme f cash on delivery; **⸥name** m surname, last name; **⸥porto** n surcharge; **⸥prüfen** verify; check; **⸥rechnen** check.

Nachricht f news sg; Botschaft: message; Bericht: report.   [tice).⸥

Nachruf m obituary (no-⸥

nach|sagen repeat; **⸥saison** f dead od. off season;

⸥schicken s. **nachsenden**; **⸥schlagen** look up; **⸥schlüssel** m skeleton key; **⸥schub** m supplies pl; **⸥sehen** v/i look after; **⸥sehen ob** (go and) see whether; v/t examine, inspect; check; look up; **⸥senden** send on, forward (dat to); **⸥sichtig** indulgent, forbearing; **⸥silbe** f gr. suffix; **⸥sitzen: ⸥müssen** be kept in; **⸥speise** f dessert.

nächst next; Entfernung, Beziehung: nearest.

nachstellen Uhr: put back; tech. readjust.

Nächstenliebe f charity.

Nacht f night; in der **⸥** s. **nachts**; gute **⸥!** good night!; **⸥dienst** m nightduty.

Nachteil m disadvantage; **⸥ig** disadvantageous.

Nachthemd n nightdress, nightgown; Männer: nightshirt.

Nachtigall f nightingale.

Nachtisch m sweet, dessert.

Nacht|lokal n nightclub; **⸥portier** m night-porter.

nachträglich later.

nacht|s at od. by night; **⸥schicht** f night-shift; **⸥tisch** m bedside table; **⸥wächter** m (night-)watchman.

nach|wachsen grow again; **⸥weis** m proof; **⸥weisen** prove; **⸥welt** f posterity; **⸥wirkung** f after-effect; **⸥wort** n epilog(ue); **⸥zäh-**

len count over (again); check; **Zzahlung** *f* additional payment.

Nacken *m* nape (of the neck), neck.

nackt naked, nude, bare.

Nadel *f* needle; **Steck2,** **Haar2** etc.: pin; **~baum** *m* conifer(ous tree).

Nagel *m* nail; **Beschlag:** stud; **~lack** *m* nail-varnish; **~lackentferner** *m* nail-varnish remover; **~schere** *f* (e-e a pair of) nail-scissors *pl.*

nage|n gnaw; **~n an** gnaw at; **Knochen:** pick; **2tier** *n* rodent.

nah(e) near, close (**bei** to).

Nähe *f* nearness; vicinity; **in der ~** close by *od.* to.

nähen sew, stitch.

näher nearer, closer; **Weg:** shorter; **~n: sich ~** approach.

Näh|garn *n* cotton; **~maschine** *f* sewing-machine; **~nadel** *f* needle.

nahr|haft nutritious, nourishing; **2ung** *f* food, nourishment; **2ungsmittel** *pl* food *sg,* victuals *pl.*

Naht *f* seam; *med.* suture.

Nähzeug *n* sewing-kit.

naiv naive, native, simple.

Nam|e *m* name; **~enstag** *m* name-day; **2entlich** by name; especially.

nämlich that is (to say).

Napf *m* bowl, basin.

Narbe *f* scar.

Narko|se *f* narcosis; **~tikum** *n* narcotic.

Narr *m* fool; jester.

Närr|in *f* fool(ish woman); **2isch** foolish, silly.

Narzisse *f* narcissus; **gelbe ~** daffodil.

nasal nasal.

naschen: gern ~ have a sweet tooth.

Nase *f* nose.

Nasen|bluten *n* nosebleeding; **~loch** *n* nostril; **~spitze** *f* tip of the nose.

Nashorn *n* rhinoceros.

naß wet.

Nässe *f* wet(ness).

naßkalt damp and cold, raw.

Nation *f* nation.

national national; **2hymne** *f* national anthem; **2ität** *f* nationality; **2itäts(kenn)zeichen** *n* mot. nationality plate; **2mannschaft** *f* national team.

Natter *f* adder, viper.

Natur *f* nature; **~forscher** *m* naturalist; **~gesetz** *n* law of nature, natural law; **2getreu** true to nature; lifelike; **~kunde** *f* biology.

natürlich *adj* natural; unaffected; *adv* naturally, of course.

Natur|schutzgebiet *n,* **~schutzpark** *m* national park, wild-life (p)reserve; **~wissenschaft** *f* (natural) science; **~wissenschaftler** *m* (natural) scientist.

Nebel *m* mist; *stärker:* fog.

neben beside; compared with; **~an** next door; **2ausgang** *m* side-exit;

bei by the way; besides; **2beruf** m, **2beschäftigung** f side-line; **~einander** side by side; **2eingang** m side-entrance; **2fach** n subsidiary subject, Am. minor (subject); **2fluß** m tributary; **2gebäude** n adjoining building; Anbau: annex(e); **2kosten** pl extra charges pl, extras pl; **2produkt** n by-product; **2sächlich** unimportant; **2satz** m gr. subordinate clause; **2straße** f by-road, side-road; **2tisch** m next table; **2wirkung** f side-effect; **2zimmer** n adjoining room.

neblig foggy; misty.

Necessaire n case.

necken tease, banter.

Neffe m nephew.

negativ negative.

Neger m Negro; **~in** f Negress.

nehmen take. [ous.)

Neid m envy; **2isch** envi-)

neig|en: (sich) ~ bend, incline; **~ zu** be inclined od. given to; **2ung** f inclination (a. fig.), slope.

nein no. [wirz: clove.)

Nelke f carnation; Ge-)

nennen name, call; mention; **sich ... ~** be called ...; **~swert** worth mentioning.

Neon n neon.

Nerv m nerve; **j-m auf die ~en fallen** od. **gehen get** on s.o.'s nerves.

Nerven|arzt m neurologist; **~heilanstalt** f, **~kli-**

nik f mental hospital; **~system** n nervous system; **~zusammenbruch** m nervous breakdown.

nerv|ös nervous; **2osität** f nervousness.

Nerz m mink.

Nessel f nettle.

Nest n nest.

nett nice; pretty; kind.

netto net.

Netz n net; fig. network; **~anschluß** m mains supply; **~haut** f retina; **~karte** f area season ticket.

neu new; kürzlich: recent; modern; **~este Nachrichten** latest news; **von ~em** anew, afresh; **was gibt es 2es?** what is the news?, Am. what is new?; **~artig** novel; **2bau** m new building; **~geboren** new-born; **2gier(de)** f curiosity; **~gierig** curious; **2heit** f novelty; **2igkeit** f (e-e a piece of) news sg; **2jahr** n New Year('s Day); **~lich** the other day, recently; **2mond** m new moon.

neun nine; **~te** ninth; **2tel** n ninth part; **~tens** ninthly; **~zehn(te)** nineteen (-th); **~zig** ninety; **~zigste** ninetieth.

neutr|al neutral; **2alität** f neutrality; **2um** n gr. neuter.

Neuzeit f modern times pl.

nicht not; **~ mehr** no more, no longer.

Nichte f niece. [smoker.)

Nichtraucher m non-)

nichts nothing.

Nichtschwimmer m non-swimmer.

nicken nod.

nie never.

nieder adj low; fig. inferior; adv down; **~geschlagen** dejected; downcast; **2-kunft** f confinement; **~lage** f defeat; **~lassen**: **sich ~** sit down; Vogel: alight; settle; **2lassung** f settlement; Zweiggeschäft: branch, agency; **~legen** lay off. put down; Amt: resign; **sich ~legen** lie down, go to bed; **2schlä-ge** pl meteor. precipitation sg; rain sg; **~schlagen** knock down, floor; Augen: cast down; Aufstand: put down; **2ung** f lowlands pl.

niedlich sweet, nice, pretty.

niedrig low (a. fig.).

niemals never, at no time.

niemand nobody, no one; **2sland** n no-man's-land.

Niere f kidney.

niesel|**n: es ~t** it is drizzling; **2regen** m drizzle.

niesen sneeze.

nippen sip (**an** at).

nirgends nowhere.

Nische f niche, recess.

nisten nest.

Niveau n level; fig. a. standard. **[dard.]**

noch still; yet; **~ ein** another, one more; **~ ein-mal** once more od. again; **~ etwas?** anything else?; **~ immer** still; **~ nicht** not yet; **~ nie** never before; **~ mals** once more od. again.

Nominativ m gr. nominative (case).

nominieren nominate.

Nonne f nun. **[flight.]**

Nonstopflug m non-stop

Nord(en m) north.

nördlich northern, northerly.

Nord|**ost(en** m) northeast; **~pol** m North Pole; **~see** f North Sea; **~west(en** m) northwest.

nörgeln nag.

Norm f standard; Regel: rule; **2al** normal; gewohnt: regular; Maß, Gewicht, Zeit: standard.

Not f need, distress; want; trouble; Elend: misery.

Notar m mst notary public.

Not|**ausgang** m emergency exit; **2behelf** m makeshift; **~bremse** f emergency brake; rail. communication cord; **~durft** f: **s-e ~ verrichten** relieve o.s.; **2dürftig** scanty, poor; temporary.

Note f note; Zensur: mark.

Not|**fall** m emergency; **2-falls** if necessary.

notieren make a note of, note down. **[need.]**

nötig necessary; **~ haben**

Notiz f notice; Vermerk: note; **~buch** n notebook.

not|**landen** make an emergency landing; **2landung** f emergency landing; **~lei-dend** needy, distressed; **~ruf** m teleph. emergency call; **2rutsche** f aer. emergency chute; **2signal** n

emergency *od.* distress signal; **2wehr** *f* self-defence; *Am.* -se; **wendig** necessary; **2zucht** *f* rape.
Novelle *f* novelette.
November *m* November.
Nu *m*: **im ~** in no time.
nüchtern sober; *sachlich*: matter-of-fact.
Nudel *f* noodle.
null zero; **zwei zu ~** two-nil; **2** *f* zero, nought, cipher; *teleph.* O [əu], zero; **2punkt** *m* zero.
numerieren number.
Nummer *f* number; *Zeitung etc.*: a. copy; *Größe*: size; **~nschild** *n mot.* num-

ber plate.
nun now, at present; **~?** well?
nur only; but; *bloß*: merely; **~ noch** only.
Nuß *f* nut; **~kern** *m* kernel; **~knacker** *m* nutcracker.
Nüstern *pl* nostrils *pl.*
Nutzen *m* use; *Gewinn*: profit, gain; *Vorteil*: advantage; **2 s. nützen.**
nütz|en *v/i* be of use; **es ~t nichts zu** it is no use *ger*; *v/t* make use of; *Gelegenheit*: seize; **~lich** useful; advantageous.
nutzlos useless.
Nylon *n* nylon.

O

o *int.* oh!, ah!
Oase *f* oasis.
ob whether, if.
Obdach *n* shelter, lodging; **2los** homeless.
oben above; up; at the top; upstairs; **von ~** from above; **~an** at the top; **~auf** on the top; on the surface; **~erwähnt**, **~genannt** above-mentioned.
ober upper, higher.
Ober *m* (head) waiter.
Ober|arm *m* upper arm; **~arzt** *m* senior physician; **~befehlshaber** *m* commander-in-chief; **~fläche** *f* surface; **2flächlich** superficial; **2halb** above; **~hemd** *n* shirt; **~kellner** *m* head waiter; **~kiefer** *m* upper jaw; **~körper** *m* up-

per part of the body; **~lippe** *f* upper lip; **~schenkel** *m* thigh; **~schule** *f* secondary school, *Am. appr.* (senior) high school.
oberst uppermost, top (-most); highest; **2** *m* colonel.
obgleich (al)though.
Obhut *f* care, custody.
Objekt *n* object (*a.gr.*).
objektiv objective; **2** *n phot.* lens.
Obst *n* fruit; **~garten** *m* orchard; **~händler** *m* fruiterer.
obszön obscene, filthy.
obwohl (al)though.
Ochse *m* ox; **~nfleisch** *n* beef.
öd(e) deserted, desolate.
oder or.

Ofen

Ofen *m* stove; *Back2*; oven; **~rohr** *n* stove-pipe.

offen open (*a. fig.*); *Stelle*: vacant; *fig.* frank, outspoken; **~bar** obvious; **~lassen** leave open; **~sichtlich** evident, obvious.

offensiv offensive.

offenstehen stand open.

öffentlich *adj* public; **~er Dienst** civil service; *adv* publicly, in public; **2keit** *f* publicity; the public.

offiziell official.

Offizier *m* officer.

öffn|en (sich) ~ open; **2er** *m* opener; **2ung** *f* opening.

oft often, frequently.

öfter (more) often.

oh *int.* o(h)!

ohne without; **~dies** anyhow, anyway.

Ohn|macht *f med.* unconsciousness; **in ~macht fallen** faint; **2mächtig** powerless; *med.* unconscious; **2mächtig werden** faint.

Ohr *n* ear.

Öhr *n* eye.

Ohren|arzt *m* ear specialist; **2betäubend** deafening; **~schmerzen** *pl* earache *sg.*

Ohr|feige *f* box on the ear(s); **~läppchen** *n* lobe of the ear; **~ring** *m* earring.

Oktober *m* October.

Öl *n* oil; **2en** oil; *tech. a.* lubricate; **~gemälde** *n* oil-painting; **2heizung** *f* oil-heating; **2ig** oily.

Olive *f* olive.

olympisch Olympic; **2e Spiele** *pl* Olympic Games *pl.*

Omelett *n* omelet(te).

Omnibus *m* s. **Autobus.**

Onkel *m* uncle.

Oper *f* opera; opera-house.

Operation *f* operation.

Operette *f* operetta.

operieren: j~n ~ operate (up)on s.o.; **sich ~ lassen** undergo an operation.

Opernglas *n* opera-glasses *pl.* [2n sacrifice.]

Opfer *n* sacrifice; victim; **2n** sacrifice.

Opposition *f* opposition.

Optiker *m* optician.

Optimist *m* optimist; **2isch** optimistic.

Orange *f* orange; **~ade** *f* orangeade; **~nmarmelade** *f* marmalade.

Orchester *n* orchestra.

Orchidee *f* orchid.

Orden *m* order (*a. eccl.*); medal, decoration.

ordentlich tidy; *richtig*: proper; *tüchtig*: good, sound.

ordinär common, vulgar.

ordn|en put in order; arrange; **2er** *m* file; **2ung** *f* order; class; **in 2ung bringen** put in order; **2ungszahl** *f* ordinal number.

Organ *n* organ. [tion.]

Organisation *f* organiza-

organisch organic.

organisieren organize.

Organismus *m* organism; *biol. a.* system.

Orgel f organ.

orientalisch oriental.

orientier|en: sich ∼ orientate o.s.; **Qung** f orientation; **die Qung verlieren** lose one's bearings.

Origin|al n original; **Qal** original; **Qell** original; **kunstvoll:** ingenious.

Orkan m hurricane.

Ort m place; village; town.

Orthopäde m orthop(a)edist.

örtlich local.

Ortschaft f place, village.

Orts|gespräch n teleph. local call; **∼kenntnis** f knowledge of a place; **Q-**

kundig familiar with the locality; **∼zeit** f local time.

Öse f eye; Schuh: eyelet.

Ost(en m) east.

Oster|ei n Easter egg; **∼hase** m Easter bunny od. rabbit; **∼n** n Easter.

Österreich|er m Austrian; **Qisch** Austrian.

östlich eastern, easterly; **∼ von** east of.

Otter[1] m otter.

Otter[2] f adder, viper.

Ouvertüre f overture.

oval oval.

Oxyd n oxide; **Qieren** oxidize.

Ozean m ocean.

P

Paar n pair; Ehe**Q** etc.: couple; **Q:** **ein ∼ a** few, some; **Qen: (sich) ∼** mate; **Qweise** in pairs.

Pacht f lease; **Qen** (take on) lease, rent.

Pächter m, **∼in** f lessee, leaseholder, tenant.

Päckchen n small parcel, Am. a. package; **ein ∼ Zigaretten** a pack(et) of cigarettes.

pack|en pack (up); derb fassen: grip, grasp, clutch; **Qpapier** n brown paper; **Qung** f pack(age), packet; med.: pack; Breipackung: poultice; **e-e Qung Zigaretten** s. Päckchen.

pädagogisch pedagogic(al).

Paddel n paddle; **∼boot** n

canoe; **Qn** paddle, canoe.

Paket n parcel, package.

Palast m palace.

Palm|e f palm(-tree); **∼sonntag** m Palm Sunday.

panieren bread, crumb.

Panik f panic.

Panne f breakdown, mot. a. engine trouble; Reifen**Q:** puncture; fig. mishap; **∼dienst** m mot. breakdown service.

Panorama n panorama.

Panther m panther.

Pantoffel m slipper.

Panzer m armo(u)r; mil. tank; zo. shell; **∼schrank** m safe.

Papa m papa, colloq. dad (-dy).

Papagei m parrot.

Papier n paper; **∼e** pl pa-

pers *pl*, documents *pl*;
Ausweis: papers *pl*, identity card *sg*; **~geld** *n* paper-money; banknotes *pl*, *Am.* bills *pl*; **~korb** *m* waste-paper-basket; **~waren** *pl* stationery *sg*.

Pappe *f* pasteboard, cardboard.

Pappel *f* poplar.

Papp|karton *m*, **~schachtel** *f* cardboard box, carton.

Paprika *m* paprika; **~schoten** *pl* peppers *pl*.

Papst *m* pope.

Parade *f* parade.

Paradies *n* paradise.

Paragraph *m jur.* article, section; *print.* paragraph.

parallel parallel.

Parfüm *n* perfume, scent.

Park *m* park; **2en** park; **2en verboten!** no parking!

Parkett *n* parquet; *thea.* stalls *pl*, *Am.* orchestra.

Park|gebühr *f* parking fee; **~haus** *n* parking garage; **~lücke** *f* parking space; **~platz** *m* (car-)park, parking lot; **~uhr** *f mot.* parking meter; **~verbot(sschild)** *n* no parking (sign).

Parlament *n* parliament.

Parodie *f* parody.

Partei *f* party; **2isch** partial; **2los** independent.

Parterre *n s.* Erdgeschoß.

Partie *f Spiel:* game; *mus.* part. [gue(r)rilla.]

Partisan *m* partisan,

Partizip *n gr.* participle.

Partner *m*, **~in** *f* partner; **~schaft** *f* partnership.

Parzelle *f* plot, lot.

Paß *m* pass (*a. Fußball etc.*); *Reise*2: passport.

Passage *f* passage.

Passagier *m* passenger.

Passant *m*, **~in** *f* passer-by. [(-graph).]

Paßbild *n* passport photo

passen fit; *zusagen:* suit (j-m s.o.); *bequem sein:* be convenient; **~ zu** go with, match; **~d** fit, suitable; convenient.

passier|bar passable; **~en** *v/i* happen; *v/t* pass; **2schein** *m* pass, permit.

passiv passive; **2** *n gr.* passive (voice).

Paste *f* paste.

Pastete *f* pie. [ize.]

pasteurisieren pasteur-]

Pate *m* godfather; godchild; **2** *f* godmother; **~kind** *n* godchild.

Patent *n* patent.

Patient *m*, **~in** *f* patient.

Patin *f* godmother.

Patriot *m* patriot.

Patrone *f* cartridge.

Patsche *f fig. colloq.:* **in der ~ sitzen** be in a scrape.

patzig rude, saucy.

Pauke *f* kettle-drum.

Pauschal|e *f* lump sum; **~reise** *f* package(d) tour; **~summe** *f* lump sum.

Pause *f* break, interval, intermission; *kurze:* pause; *thea.* interval, *Am.* intermission; *Schul*2: break, *Am. a.* recess; **2los** uninterrupted, incessant.

Pavian m baboon.

Pavillon m pavilion.

Pech n pitch; fig. colloq. bad luck; ~vogel m colloq. unlucky fellow.

Pedal n pedal.

pedantisch pedantic.

peinlich embarrassing; gewissenhaft: particular.

Peitsche f whip.

Pell|e f skin, peel; ~kartoffeln pl potatoes pl (boiled) in their jackets.

Pelz m fur; Kleidung: mst furs pl; ~mantel m fur coat; ~mütze f fur cap; ~stiefel pl fur-lined boots pl.

pendeln rail. commute.

Pension f (old-age) pension; boarding-house; ~at n boarding-school; ~ieren pension (off); sich 2ieren lassen retire; ~sgast m boarder.

perfekt perfect; 2 n gr. perfect (tense).

Pergament n parchment.

Periode f period (a. med.).

Perle f pearl; Glas2: bead; 2n sparkle.

Perlmutt n, ~er f mother-of-pearl.

Person f person; für zwei ~en for two.

Personal n staff, personnel; ~abteilung f personnel department; ~ausweis m identity card; ~chef m personnel officer od. manager; ~ien pl particulars pl, personal data pl;

~pronomen n gr. personal pronoun.

Personen|wagen m (motor-)car; ~zug m passenger train.

persönlich personal; Brief: private; 2keit f personality.

Perücke f wig.

Pest f plague.

Petersilie f parsley.

Petroleum n petroleum; Lampen2: paraffin (oil), kerosene.

Pfad m path; ~finder m Boy Scout; ~finderin f Girl Guide (Am. Scout).

Pfahl m stake, post, pile.

Pfand n pledge; Flaschen2: deposit.

pfänden distrain upon.

Pfann|e f pan; ~kuchen m pancake.

Pfarr|er m priest; clergyman, parson; vicar; Dissenterkirche: minister; ~gemeinde f parish; ~haus n parsonage; rectory, vicarage.

Pfau m peacock.

Pfeffer m pepper; ~kuchen m gingerbread; ~minze f peppermint; 2n pepper; ~streuer m pepper-castor.

Pfeife f whistle; Orgel etc.: pipe; (tobacco) pipe; 2n whistle; Wind, Radio: howl.

Pfeil m arrow.

Pfeiler m pillar.

Pferd n horse; zu ~e on horseback.

Pferde|rennen n horse-race; **~stall** m stable; **~stärke** f horsepower.

Pfiff m whistle.

Pfifferling m chanterelle.

pfiffig clever, artful.

Pfingst|en n Whitsun(tide); **~montag** m Whit Monday; **~sonntag** m Whit Sunday.

Pfirsich m peach.

Pflanze f plant; **2n** plant.

Pflaster n plaster; *Straße*: pavement; **2n** pave; **~stein** m paving-stone; *Kopfstein*: cobble(-stone).

Pflaume f plum; *Back2*: prune.

Pflege f care; *med.* nursing; *fig.* cultivation; **~eltern** pl foster-parents pl; **~heim** n nursing home; **~kind** n foster-child; **2n** nurse; *fig.* cultivate; **sie pflegte zu sagen** she used to say; **2leicht** wash and wear; **~r** m male nurse; **~rin** f nurse.

Pflicht f duty; **~fach** n compulsory subject.

Pflock m peg. [pluck.}

pflücken pick, gather,}

Pflug m plough, *Am.* plow.

pflügen plough, *Am.* plow.

Pforte f gate, door.

Pförtner m gate-keeper; door-keeper, porter.

Pfosten m post.

Pfote f paw.

Pfropfen m stopper; plug; *med.* clot (of blood).

pfui int. fie!, for shame!

Pfund n pound. [botch.}

pfuschen colloq. bungle,}

Pfütze f puddle, pool.

Phantas|ie f imagination, fancy; **2ieren** med. be delirious, rave; **2tisch** fantastic.

Phase f phase, stage.

Philolog|e m, **~in** f philologist.

Philosoph m philosopher; **~ie** f philosophy.

phlegmatisch phlegmatic.

phonetisch phonetic.

Phosphor m phosphorus.

Photo... s. **Foto...**

Photokopie f s. **Fotokopie.**

Physik f physics sg; **2alisch** physical; **~er** m physicist.

physisch physical.

Pian|ist m pianist; **~o** n piano.

Pick|el m med. pimple; **2(e)lig** pimpled, pimply.

picken pick, peck.

Picknick n picnic.

Pik n spade(s pl).

pikant spicy, piquant.

Pilger m pilgrim.

Pille f pill.

Pilot m pilot.

Pilz m fungus; mushroom.

Pinguin m penguin.

Pinsel m brush.

Pinzette f (e-e a pair of) tweezers pl.

Pionier m pioneer; mil. engineer.

Piste f course; aer. runway.

Pistole f pistol, Am. a. gun.

placieren place; **sich ~** sp. be placed.

Plage f trouble, nuisance; ℓn trouble, bother; **sich** ℓn toil, drudge.

Plakat n poster, placard, bill.

Plakette f plaque.

Plan m plan; *Absicht:* a. design, intention.

Plane f awning.

planen plan.

Planet m planet.

Planke f plank, board.

plan|los adj aimless; adv at random; ℓmäßig adj systematic; adv as planned.

planschen splash, paddle.

Plantage f plantation.

plappern colloq. prattle.

plärren colloq.: blubber; *schreien:* bawl.

Plastik[1] f sculpture.

Plasti|k[2] n plastic(s sg); ℓsch plastic.

plätschern splash; *Wasser:* ripple, murmur.

platt flat, level, even; colloq. flabbergasted.

Platte f plate; dish; *Stein:* flag; *Metall, Stein, Holz:* slab; *Tisch:* top; *Schall₂:* disc, record; **kalte ~** cold meat.

plätten iron.

Platten|spieler m record-player; **~teller** m turntable.

Plattform f platform.

Platz m place; spot; *Raum:* room, space; *Lage, Bau₂:* site; *Sitz:* seat; square, runder: circus; **ist hier noch ~?** is this seat taken?; **den dritten ~ belegen**

sp. come in third; **~anweiserin** f usherette.

Plätzchen n biscuit, *Am.* cookie.

platz|en burst (a. fig.), split; ℓkarte f ticket for a reserved seat; ℓregen m downpour.

Plauder|ei f chat, talk; oberflächliche: small talk; ℓn (have a) chat.

pleite colloq. broke.

Plisseerock m pleated skirt.

Plomb|e[1] f (lead) seal; *Zahn:* stopping, filling; ℓieren seal; stop, fill.

plötzlich sudden.

plump clumsy.

plündern plunder, loot.

Plural m gr. plural.

plus plus.

Plusquamperfekt n gr. pluperfect (tense).

Pöbel m mob, rabble.

pochen knock, rap; *Herz:* throb, thump.

Pocken pl smallpox sg; **~schutzimpfung** f vaccination.

Podium n podium, platform.

Poesie f poetry.

Pokal m sp. cup; **~endspiel** n cup-final; **~spiel** n cup-tie.

pökeln corn, salt.

Pol m pole; ℓar polar.

Pole m Pole.

Police f policy.

polieren polish.

Politi|k[2] f policy; *Staat:* politics sg, pl; **~ker** m pol-

itician; *führender*: statesman; 2sch political
Politesse f *mot. appr.*
traffic warden.
Politur f polish.
Polizei f police *pl;* ~be-
amte m police-officer;
~revier n police-station;
~streife f police patrol;
~stunde f closing time.
Polizist m policeman, *sl.*
bobby, cop; ~in f police-
woman.
polnisch Polish.
Polster n pad; cushion;
~möbel *pl* upholstered
furniture *sg;* 2n upholster,
stuff; *wattieren*: pad, wad;
~sessel m easy chair.
poltern rumble.
Pommes frites *pl* chips *pl,*
Am. French fried potatoes
pl.
Pony n pony; m fringe.
populär popular.
Por|e f pore; 2ös porous;
permeable.
Porree m leek.
Portemonnaie n purse.
Portier m porter.
Portion f portion, share;
bei Tisch: helping, serving;
zwei ~en ... : ... for two.
Porto n postage; 2frei
post-free.
Porträt n portrait.
Portugies|e m Portuguese;
die ~en *pl* the Portuguese
pl; 2isch Portuguese.
Porzellan n china.
Posaune f trombone.
Position f position.
positiv positive.

possessiv *gr.* possessive.
Post f post, *Am.* mail; mail,
letters *pl;* = ~amt n post
office; ~anweisung f
postal order; ~beamte m
post office official; ~bote m
postman, *Am.* mailman.
Posten m post, place; *An-
stellung:* job; *mil.* sentry,
sentinel.
Post|fach n post office
box; ~karte f postcard,
Am. a. postal card; ~
kutsche f stage-coach; 2-
lagernd poste restante;
~leitzahl f postcode, *Am.*
zip code; ~scheck m postal
cheque (*Am.* check);
~schließfach n post office
box; ~sparbuch n post
office savings-book;
~stempel m postmark;
2wendend by return of
post; ~wertzeichen n
stamp.
Pracht f splendo(u)r.
prächtig splendid.
Prädikat n *gr.* predicate.
prahlen brag, boast.
praktisch practical; useful,
handy; ~er Arzt general
practitioner.
Praline f chocolate.
prall tight; *drall:* plump;
Sonne: blazing.
Prämie f premium; bonus.
präparieren prepare.
Präposition f *gr.* preposition.
Präsens n *gr.* present
(tense).
Präsident m president;
Vorsitzender: a. chairman.

prasseln *Feuer:* crackle; *Regen etc.:* patter.

Präteritum *n* gr. preterit(e) (tense).

Praxis *f* practice.

predig|en preach; **2er** *m* preacher; **2t** *f* sermon.

Preis *m* price; cost; *Auszeichnung:* award; prize; **~ausschreiben** *n* competition.

Preiselbeere *f* cranberry.

Preis|erhöhung *f* rise *od.* increase in price(s); **2gekrönt** prize; **~nachlaß** *m* discount; **~stopp** *m* price-freeze; **2wert:** ~ **sein** be a bargain. [bruise.)

Prellung *f* contusion,)

Premiere *f* première, first night.

Press|e *f* press; *Saft2:* squeezer; *Zeitungen:* the press; **2en** press; squeeze.

prickeln prickle, tingle.

Priester *m* priest.

prima *colloq.* swell.

primitiv primitive, crude.

Prinz *m* prince; **~essin** *f* princess.

Prinzip *n* principle.

Prise *f:* e-e ~ a pinch of.

Pritsche *f* plank bed.

privat private; **2adresse** *f* home address; **2klinik** *f* private hospital, nursing home; **2schule** *f* private school.

Privileg *n* privilege.

pro per; ~ **Jahr** per annum; ~ **Person** each; ~ **Stück** a piece.

Probe *f* trial, test; *Waren:*

sample, specimen; *thea.* rehearsal; **~exemplar** *n* specimen copy; **~fahrt** *f* test drive; **~flug** *m* test flight; **2n** *thea.* rehearse.

probieren try, test; *Speisen:* taste.

Problem *n* problem.

Produ|kt *n* product; *agr. a.* produce; **~ktion** *f* production; *Menge:* output; **2ktiv** productive; **2zieren** produce.

Prof|essor *m* professor; **~i** *m sp.* pro(fessional).

Profil *n* profile; *Reifen:* tread.

profitieren profit (**von** by).

Programm *n* program (-me).

Projekt *n* project; **~ion** *f* projection; **~ionsapparat** *m,* **~or** *m* projector.

Prolog *m* prolog(ue).

Promille *n* per thousand; *colloq.* pro mille content.

prominent prominent.

Pronomen *n* gr. pronoun.

Propeller *m* aer. (air-) screw, propeller.

prophezeien prophesy, predict.

Prosa *f* prose.

Prospekt *m* prospectus, leaflet, brochure.

prost *int.* cheers!

Prostituierte *f* prostitute.

Protest *m* protest; **~ant** *m* Protestant; **2antisch** Protestant; **2ieren** protest.

Prothese *f* artificial limb; *Zahn2:* denture.

Protokoll n record; Versammlungs♀: minutes pl.
protzig showy.
Proviant m provisions pl.
Provinz f province.
Provis|ion f commission; ♀orisch provisional.
provozieren provoke.
Prozent n per cent; ~satz m percentage.
Prozeß m process; jur. lawsuit, action.
Prozession f procession.
prüde prudish.
prüf|en Schüler etc.: examine; try, test; kontrollieren: check; ~end Blick: searching; ♀er m examiner; ♀ung f examination, colloq. exam; test.
Prügel m cudgel, club; ~pl colloq. beating sg, thrashing sg; ♀n beat, thrash; **sich** ♀n (have a) fight.
pst int. hush!
Psychi|ater m psychiatrist; ♀sch psychic(al).
Psycholog|e m psychologist; ~ie f psychology; ♀isch psychological.
Publikum n the public; Zuhörer: audience; Zuschauer: spectators pl, crowd; Leser: readers pl.
Pudding m pudding.
Pudel m poodle.
Puder m powder; ~dose f compact; ♀n powder; **sich** ♀n powder o.s.; ~quaste

f powder-puff; ~zucker m powdered sugar.
Pullover m pullover, sweater.
Puls m pulse; ~ader f artery; ~schlag m beat, pulsation.
Pult n desk.
Pulver n powder.
Pumpe f pump; ♀n pump.
Punkt m point (a. fig.); Tüpfelchen: dot; print., ling. full stop, period; Stelle: spot, place; ~ zehn Uhr 10 (o'clock) sharp.
pünktlich punctual.
Punsch m punch.
Pupille f pupil.
Puppe f doll; zo. chrysalis, pupa.
pur pure; Getränk: neat.
Püree n purée, mash.
purpur|n, ~rot purple.
Purzel|baum m somersault; ♀n tumble.
Pustel f pustule, pimple.
pusten puff, pant; blasen: blow.   [turkey(-cock).}
Pute f turkey(-hen); ~r m}
putz|en clean, cleanse; wipe; Schuhe: polish, Am. shine; **sich die Nase** ~en blow od. wipe one's nose; **sich die Zähne** ~en brush one's teeth; ♀frau f charwoman.
Pyjama m pyjamas pl, Am. a. pajamas pl.
Pyramide f pyramid.

Q

Quacksalber m quack (doctor).

Quadrat n square; 2isch square; ~meter m, n square me|tre, Am. -er.

quaken quack; Frosch: croak.   [agony.]

Qual f pain, torment;]

quälen torment (a. fig.); torture; fig. bother.

Qualifi|kation f qualification; 2zieren: (sich) ~ qualify.

Qualität f quality.

Qualle f jelly-fish.

Qualm m (dense) smoke; 2en smoke.

qualvoll very painful; agonizing.

Quantität f quantity.

Quarantäne f quarantine.

Quark m curd(s pl).

Quartal n quarter.

Quartett n quartet(te).

Quartier n accommodation.

Quaste f tassel; Puder2: (powder-)puff.

Quatsch m colloq. nonsense, sl. rot.

Quecksilber n mercury, quicksilver.

Quelle f spring; source (a. fig.); Öl2: well; 2n gush, well.

quer crosswise; ~ über across; 2straße f crossroad; zweite 2straße rechts second turning to the right.

quetsch|en squeeze; med. contuse, bruise; 2ung f contusion, bruise.

quieken squeak, squeal.

quietschen squeak,squeal; Tür: creak; Bremsen: screech.

quitt quits, even.

Quitte f quince.

quitt|ieren Rechnung: receipt; aufgeben: quit, abandon; 2ung f receipt.

Quote f quota; share.

R

Rabatt m discount, rebate.

Rabbiner m rabbi.

Rabe m raven.

rabiat violent.

Rache f revenge, vengeance.

Rachen m throat.

rächen revenge (sich o.s.).

Rad n wheel; s. Fahrrad.

Radar m, n radar.

radfahre|n cycle, (ride a) bicycle; 2r m cyclist.

radier|en rub out, erase; Kunst: etch; 2gummi m (India-)rubber.

Radieschen n (red) radish.

radikal radical.

Radio n radio, wireless; im ~ on the radio; 2aktiv

radio(-)active; **apparat**
m radio(-set), wireless (set).
Radius m radius.
Rad|kappe f hub cap; **~
rennen** n cycle race; **~
spur** f rut.
raffiniert refined; fig. clever, cunning.
Ragout n ragout, stew.
Rahm m cream.
Rahmen m frame; 2 frame.
Rakete f rocket.
rammen ram.
Rampe f ramp.
Ramsch m junk, trash.
Rand m edge, border,
margin; bsd. Gefäß: brim;
Gefäß, Brille: rim; Stadt:
outskirts pl; fig. verge,
brink.
Rang m rank (a. mil.);
thea. circle, Am. balcony.
rangieren rail. shunt,
switch.
Ranke f tendril; 2n: **sich ~**
creep, climb.
Ranzen m satchel.
ranzig rancid, rank.
Rappe m black horse.
rar rare, scarce.
rasch quick, swift; prompt.
rascheln rustle.
rasen rage, storm, rave;
race, speed, colloq. scorch;
~d raving; Tempo: scorch-
ing; Schmerzen: agonizing;
Kopfschmerzen: splitting.
Rasen m lawn.
Raserei f colloq.: rage,
fury; madness; mot. speeding.
Rasier|apparat m (safe-
ty) razor; **~creme** f shav-

ing-cream; 2en shave;
sich 2en (**lassen** get a)
shave; **~klinge** f razor-
blade; **~messer** n razor;
~pinsel m shaving-brush;
~seife f shaving-soap; **~
wasser** n after-shave lotion.
Rasse f race; zo. breed.
rasseln rattle.
Rassen|trennung f racial
segregation; **~unruhen** pl
race riots pl.
rasserein s. reinrassig.
Rast f rest; break, pause;
2en rest; 2los restless;
~platz m mot. picnic area,
lay-by; **~stätte** f rest-
house.
Rat m advice, counsel; Ausweg: way out; Körper-
schaft: council, board; Person: council(l)or.
Rate f instal(l)ment; **in ~n**
by instal(l)ments.
raten advise, counsel;
guess.
Ratenzahlung f payment
by instal(l)ments.
Rat|geber m adviser; **~
haus** n town (Am. a. city)
hall.
Ration f ration, allowance;
2alisieren rationalize;
2ieren ration.
rat|los at a loss; **~sam**
advisable.
Rätsel n riddle, puzzle;
mystery; 2haft puzzling;
mysterious.
Ratte f rat.
rattern rattle.
Raub m robbery; 2en rob.

Räuber m robber.
Raub|mord m murder with robbery; **~tier** n beast of prey; **~überfall** m hold-up; armed robbery; **~vogel** m bird of prey.
Rauch m smoke; **2en** smoke; **2en verboten!** no smoking!; **~er** m, **~erabteil** n smoker.
räuchern smoke, cure.
rauchig smoky.
raufe|n fight; **2rei** f fight.
rauh rough; *Klima*: inclement, raw; *Stimme*: hoarse; **2reif** m white frost, hoarfrost.
Raum m room; space; area; **~anzug** m space suit.
räumen clear; *Gebiet*: leave; *Wohnung*: vacate.
Raum|fahrt f astronautics sg., pl; **~flug** m space flight; **~inhalt** m volume; **~kapsel** f capsule.
räumlich of space, spatial.
Raumschiff n spaceship, spacecraft.
Raupe f caterpillar.
Rausch m intoxication; **e-n ~ haben** be drunk; **2en** rustle; *Wind*: sough; sweep (**aus** from); **2end** n narcotic, drug, *colloq.* dope. [one's throat.]
räuspern: sich ~ clear
Razzia f raid.
reagieren react (**auf** to); *fig. a.* respond (**auf** to).
Reaktor m (nuclear) reactor.
real real; **~istisch** realistic; **2ität** f reality.

Rebe f vine.
Rebell m rebel; **2ieren** rebel, revolt, rise.
Rebhuhn n partridge.
Rechen m rake.
Rechen|aufgabe f sum, (arithmetical) problem; **~fehler** m arithmetical error, miscalculation; **~schaft** f: **~ablegen über** account for; **zur ~ ziehen** call to account.
rechn|en do sums, reckon; **~en auf** count *od.* rely (up)on; **2ung** f calculation; reckoning; *Waren*: invoice; *Gasthaus*: bill, *Am.* check.
recht right; **~ haben** be right.
Recht n right (**auf** to); *jur.* law; *fig.* justice.
Rechte f right hand.
Rechteck n rectangle; **2ig** rectangular.
recht|fertigen justify; **2fertigung** f justification; **~lich** legal; **~mäßig** legal, lawful, legitimate.
rechts (on *od.* to the) right; **nach ~** to the right.
Rechtsanwalt m lawyer, *Am. a.* attorney; solicitor.
Rechtschreibung f orthography, spelling.
rechtskräftig valid, legal; *Urteil*: final.
recht|wink(e)lig right-angled; **~zeitig** punctual; on time.
Reck n horizontal bar.
recken stretch (**sich** o.s.).
Redakt|eur m editor;

~ion f editorial staff, editors pl.

Rede f speech; zur ~ stellen take to task (wegen for); give away; talk.

redlich honest, upright.

Red|ner m speaker; 2~selig talkative.

reduzieren reduce.

Reederei f shipping company od. firm.

reell respectable, honest; Ware: good; Angebot: fair.

reflektieren reflect.

reflexiv gr. reflexive.

Reform f reform; 2~ieren reform.

Regal n shelf.

rege active, lively; busy.

Regel f rule; med. menstruation; 2~mäßig regular; 2~n regulate; arrange; settle; ~ung f regulation; arrangement; settlement.

regen: (sich) ~ move, stir.

Regen m rain; ~bogen m rainbow; ~bogenhaut f iris; ~mantel m raincoat; ~schauer m shower; ~schirm m umbrella; ~tag m rainy day; ~tropfen m raindrop; ~wasser n rainwater; ~wetter n rainy weather; ~wurm m earthworm; ~zeit f rainy season.

Regie f direction.

regier|en reign; govern; 2~ung f government; Amtsperiode: Am. administration; Monarchie: reign.

Regiment n regiment.

Regisseur m director.

registrieren register, record.

regne|n rain; es ~t it is raining; ~risch rainy.

regulieren regulate, adjust.

regungslos motionless.

Reh n roe deer; roe; weiblich: doe; ~bock m roebuck; ~geiß f doe; ~kitz n fawn.

Reib|e f, ~eisen n grater; 2~en rub; ~ung f friction.

reich rich (an in); wealthy.

Reich n empire; Natur2: kingdom; poet. realm.

reichen v/t Speise: serve; j-m et. ~ hand od. pass s.th. to s.o.; v/i reach; genügen: suffice; das reicht! that will do!

reich|haltig rich; ~lich ample, abundant; ~lich Zeit plenty of time; 2~tum m riches pl; wealth; 2~weite f reach; mil. range.

Reif m white frost, hoarfrost.

reif ripe, mature; ~en} [ripen, mature.}

Reifen m hoop; Auto2: tyre, (Am. nur) tire; ~druck m tyre pressure; ~panne f puncture, Am. a. flat.

Reife|prüfung f s. Abitur; ~zeugnis n s. Abschlußzeugnis.

Reihe f row; line; Serie: series; Anzahl: number; thea. row; der ~ nach in turn; ~nfolge f order.

Reiher m heron.

Reim m rhyme; 2en: (sich) ~ rhyme.

rein pure; clean; clear; ~igen clean; 2igung f cleaning; (dry) cleaners pl; **chemische** 2igung drycleaning; ~lich clean(ly); 2machefrau f charwoman; ~rassig purebred, thoroughbred.

Reis m rice.

Reise f journey; mar. voyage; Rund2: tour; kurze: trip; ~andenken n souvenir; ~büro n travel agency od. bureau; ~führer m guide(-book); ~gesellschaft f (tourist) party; ~leiter m courier; 2n travel, journey; ~nde m, f passenger; tourist; econ. commercial travel(l)er; ~necessaire n dressingcase; ~paß m passport; ~scheck m travel(l)er's cheque (Am. check); ~tasche f travel(l)ing bag; ~ziel n destination.

reiß|en tear; ~end rapid; 2nagel m s. Reißzwecke; 2verschluß m zipfastener, zipper, Am. a. slide fastener; 2wecke f drawing-pin, Am. thumbtack.

reit|en ride; 2er m rider; geübter: horseman; 2hose f riding-breeches pl; 2pferd n riding-horse; 2stiefel pl riding-boots pl.

Reiz m charme, attraction; med. irritation; 2bar irritable; 2en irritate (a.

med.); provoke; anziehen: attract; Karten: bid; 2end charming, Am. cute; lovely; 2voll attractive.

Reklam|ation f complaint; ~e f advertising; Anzeige: advertisement, colloq. ad.

Rekord m record.

Rekrut m recruit.

relativ relative; 2pronomen n gr. relative pronoun.

Religi|on f religion; 2ös religious; pious.

Reling f rail.

Reliquie f relic.

Renn|bahn f racecourse, Am. race track; 2en run, race; ~en n run(ning); race; ~fahrer m racing driver; racing cyclist; ~läufer m ski racer; ~pferd n racehorse; ~rad n racing bicycle; ~sport m racing; ~stall m racing stable; ~wagen m racing car.

renovieren Haus: renovate; Zimmer: redecorate.

Rente f Jahres2: annuity; (old-age) pension.

Rentier n reindeer.

Rentner m (old-age) pensioner.

Reparatur f repair; ~werkstatt f repair shop; mot. a. garage, service station.

reparieren repair.

Report|age f coverage; ~er m reporter.

Reptil n reptile.

Republik f republic; ~aner m republican; 2anisch republican.

Reserve f reserve; ~rad n spare wheel; ~tank m reserve tank.

reservier|en Platz: keep; ~en lassen book, reserve; ~t reserved (a. fig.).

Residenz f residence.

resignieren resign.

Respekt m respect.

Rest m rest, remainder; Speise: leftover.

Restaurant n restaurant.

rest|lich remaining; ~los entirely, completely.

rette|n save (vor from); deliver, rescue (aus from); 2r m rescuer, deliverer.

Rettich m radish.

Rettung f rescue.

Rettungs|boot n lifeboat; ~gürtel m lifebelt; ~mannschaft f rescue party; ~ring m life-buoy.

Reue f repentance, remorse.

Revier n district, quarter.

Revision f jur. appeal.

Revolution f revolution; ~är m revolutionary; 2är revolutionary.

Revolver m revolver, Am. colloq. a. gun.

Rezept n prescription; Koch2: recipe (a. fig.).

Rezeption f reception desk.

Rhabarber m rhubarb.

Rheuma n, ~tismus m rheumatism.

Rhythmus m rhythm.

richten tech. adjust; Waffe: point (auf at); direct (auf,

an to); **sich ~ nach** conform to, act according to; depend on.

Richter m judge.

richtig right, correct; gehörig: proper; ~ gehen Uhr: be right; ~ stellen put od. set right.

Richtlinien f directions pl.

Richtung f direction; ~anzeiger m mot. indicator, trafficator.

riechen smell (nach of; an at).

Riegel m bar, bolt; Seife: bar, cake; Schokolade: bar.

Riemen m strap; Gürtel, tech.: belt; Ruder: oar.

Riese m giant.

Riff n reef.

Rille f groove.

Rind n Ochse: ox; Kuh: cow; ~er pl cattle pl.

Rinde f bark; Käse: rind; Brot: crust.

Rind|erbraten m roast beef; ~fleisch n beef.

Ring m ring.

Ringelnatter f ring-snake.

ring|en Hände: wring; wrestle; fig. a. struggle; **nach Atem ~en** gasp (for breath); 2er m wrestler; 2kampf m wrestling (-match); 2richter m referee.

Rinne f groove, channel; 2en run, flow; tröpfeln: drip; ~stein m gutter.

Rippe f rib.

Risiko n risk.

risk|ant risky; ~ieren risk.

Riß m rent, tear; *Sprung:* crack; *Haut:* chap.

Ritt m ride.

Ritter m knight.

Ritze f chink; ♀n scratch.

Rival|e m, ⊾in f rival.

Robbe f seal.

Robe f robe; gown.

Roboter m robot.

robust robust, sturdy.

röcheln rattle.

Rock m skirt.

rodel|n sled(ge), *Am. a.* coast; ♀**schlitten** m sled, sledge; *sp.* toboggan.

roden clear.

Rogen m (hard) roe, spawn.

Roggen m rye.

roh raw; rough, rude; cruel; brutal; ♀**kost** f uncooked vegetarian food. [reed.⎱

Rohr n tube, pipe; *Schilf:*⎰

Röhre f tube, pipe; *Radio:* valve, *Am.* tube.

Rohstoff m raw material.

Roll|aden m rolling shutter; ⊾**bahn** f runway.

Rolle f roll; *tech. a.* roller; *thea.* part, role; ⊾ **Garn** reel of cotton, *Am.* spool of thread; ♀n roll; *aer.* taxi; ⊾**r** m (motor-)scooter.

Roll|film m roll film; ⊾**kragen** m turtle neck; ⊾**schuh** m roller-skate; ⊾**stuhl** m wheelchair; ⊾**treppe** f escalator.

Roman m novel.

romantisch romantic.

römisch Roman.

röntgen X-ray; ♀**aufnahme** f, ♀**bild** n X-ray; ♀**strahlen** pl X-rays pl.

rosa pink.

Rose f rose.

Rosen|kohl m Brussels sprouts pl; ⊾**kranz** m rosary.

rosig rosy.

Rosine f raisin.

Roß n horse.

Rost m rust.

Rost m grate; *Brat*♀: gridiron, grill; ⊾**braten** m sirloin steak.

rosten rust.

rösten roast, grill; *Brot:* toast; *Kartoffeln:* fry.

rost|frei rustless; stainless; ⊾**ig** rusty.

rot red; ⊾ **werden** blush; ⊾**blond** sandy.

Rote Kreuz n Red Cross.

röten: (sich) ⊾ redden.

rotieren rotate, revolve.

Rot|kohl m red cabbage; ⊾**stift** m red pencil; ⊾**wein** m red wine; claret; ⊾**wild** n red deer.

Roulade f roulade (of beef).

Rouleau n s. **Rolladen;** blind, *Am.* (window) shade.

Route f route.

Routine f routine.

Rübe f beet; **rote** ⊾ red beet, beetroot; **gelbe** ⊾ carrot.

Rubin m ruby.

Ruck m jerk, jolt.

Rückblick m retrospect.

rücken move; shift; **näher** ⊾ approach.

Rücken m back; ⊾**lehne** f back; ⊾**mark** n spinal cord; ⊾**schwimmen** n backstroke; ⊾**wind** m following wind, tail wind; **~wirbel** m dorsal vertebra.

Rück|erstattung f restitution, refund; **~fahrkarte** f return (ticket), Am. round-trip ticket; **~fahrt** f return journey od. trip; **auf der ~fahrt** on the way back; **2fällig: ~ werden** relapse; **~flug** m return flight; **2gängig: ~ machen** cancel; **~grat** m spine, backbone; **~halt** m support; **~kehr** f return; **~licht** n tail-light, rear light od. lamp; **~porto** n return postage; **~reise** f return journey, journey back od. home.

Rucksack m knapsack, rucksack.

Rück|schlag m set-back; **~schritt** m retrogression; pol. reaction; **~seite** f back, reverse; **2sichtslos** inconsiderate; skrupellos: ruthless; unbekümmert: reckless; **2sichtsvoll** considerate; **~sitz** m backseat; **~spiegel** m rearview mirror; **~spiel** n return match; **~stand** m arrears pl; chem. residue; **2ständig** old-fashioned; **~tritt** m resignation; **~trittbremse** f backpedal-(l)ing brake, Am. coaster brake; **2wärts** back, backward(s); **~wärtsgang** m reverse (gear); **~weg** m way back; **2wirkend** retrospective; **~**

~zahlung f repayment; **~zug** m retreat.

Rudel n troop; Wölfe: pack; Rehe: herd.

Ruder n oar; mar.: rudder; helm; aer. rudder; **~boot** n row(ing)-boat; **2n** row.

Ruf m call (a. fig.); cry, shout; Leumund: reputation; **2en** call; cry, shout; **2en lassen** send for; **~nummer** f telephone number.

Rüge f rebuke, reprimand.

Ruhe f rest; sleep; Stille: quiet(ness), calm; Gelassenheit: composure; **in ~ lassen** leave od. let alone; **2los** restless; **2n** rest; sleep; **~pause** f pause; **~stand** m: **im ~** retired; **~störung** f disturbance (of the peace); **~tag** m restday.

ruhig quiet, calm.

Ruhm m glory; fame.

Rühr|ei n pl scrambled eggs pl; **2en** stir, move; fig. touch, move, affect; **sich ~en** stir, move; **2end** touching, moving; **~ung** f emotion, feeling.

Ruin m ruin; decay; **~e** f ruin(s pl); **2ieren** ruin.

rülpsen belch.

Rum m rum.

Rummel m colloq. bustle; **~platz** m amusement park.

rumpeln colloq. rumble.

Rumpf m anat. trunk, body; mar. hull, body; aer. fuselage, body.

rund adj round; circular;

adv about; ~ **um** (a)round;
2blick *m* panorama; **2e** *f*
round; *sp.* lap; *Boxen:*
round; *Polizist:* beat; **2-**
fahrt *f* s. **Rundreise;** **2-**
flug *m* sightseeing *od.*
local flight.

Rundfunk *m* broadcast
(-ing); *Anstalt:* broad-
casting company; *s.* **Ra-**
dio; ~**gerät** *n* s. **Radio-**
apparat; ~**hörer** *m* lis-
tener(-in); *pl a.* (radio)
audience *sg*; ~**sender** *m*
broadcasting *od.* radio station; ~**sendung** *f* broadcast; ~**sprecher** *m* broad-
caster, (radio) announcer.

Rund|gang *m* tour, round;
2herum round about, all
(a)round; **2lich** roundish;
plump; ~**reise** *f* circular
tour, round trip, sightseeing trip; ~**schreiben** *n*

circular (letter).

Runz|el *f* wrinkle; **2(e)lig**
wrinkled; **2eln: die Stirn**
~ frown.

rupfen pick; *Geflügel:*
pluck.

Rüsche *f* ruffle, frill.

Ruß *m* soot.

Russe *m* Russian.

Rüssel *m* *Elefant:* trunk;
Schwein: snout.

rußig sooty.

russisch Russian.

rüsten: sich ~ (zu) prepare *od.* get ready (for).

rüstig vigorous, strong.

Rüstung *f* armo(u)r; *mil.*
armament.

Rute *f* rod; *Gerte:* switch.

Rutsch|bahn *f,* ~**e** *f* slide,
chute; **2en** glide, slide; **2ig**
slippery.

rütteln jog, jolt; **an der**
Tür ~ rattle at the door.

S

Saal *m* hall.

Saat *f* seed (*a. fig.*); *junge*
Pflanzen: growing crops *pl.*

Säbel *m* sab|re, *Am.* -er.

Sabotage *f* sabotage.

Sach|bearbeiter *m* offi-
cial in charge; **2dienlich**
relevant; ~**e** *f* thing; affair,
matter; ~**en** *pl* *Besitz:*
things *pl*, belongings *pl*;
2gemäß proper; ~**kennt-**
nis *f* expert knowledge;
2kundig expert; **2lich**
matter-of-fact, business-
like; objective.

sächlich *gr.* neuter.

Sach|register *n* (subject)
index; ~**schaden** *m* damage to property.

sacht soft, gentle.

Sach|verhalt *m* facts *pl*
(of the case); ~**verstän-**
dige *m, f* expert, authority.

Sack *m* sack, bag; ~**gasse** *f*
blind alley, cul-de-sac; *fig.*
deadlock.

säen sow.

Saft *m* juice; *Bäume etc.:*
sap; **2ig** juicy.

Sage *f* legend, myth.

Säge *f* saw; ~**mehl** *n* saw-
dust.

sagen say; *mitteilen*: tell.

sägen saw.

Sahne f cream.

Saison f season; **~zu-schlag** m seasonal surcharge.

Saite f string, chord; **~instrument** n string(ed) instrument.

Sakko m, n (lounge) jacket.

Salat m salad; *Kopf2*: lettuce.

Salbe f ointment.

Salz n salt; 2en salt; 2ig salt(y); **~kartoffeln** pl boiled potatoes pl; **~säure** f hydrochloric acid; **~streuer** m salt-castor; **~wasser** n salt water.

Same(n) m seed; *biol.* sperm.

samm|eln gather; collect; 2ler m collector; 2lung f collection; *fig.* composure.

Samstag m Saturday.

Samt m velvet.

sämtlich all; complete.

Sanatorium n sanatorium, *Am. a.* sanitarium.

Sand m sand.

Sandale f sandal.

Sand|bank f sandbank; 2ig sandy.

sanft soft; gentle, mild.

Sänger m, **~in** f singer.

sanitär sanitary.

Sanitäter m ambulance man, first-aider.

Sankt Saint, *abbr.* St.

Sard|elle f anchovy; **~ine** f sardine. [casket.]

Sarg m coffin, *Am. a.*

Satellit m satellite.

Satire f satire.

satt: sich ~ essen eat one's fill; **ich bin ~** I have had enough; **et. ~ haben** *colloq.* be fed up with s.th.

Sattel m saddle; 2n saddle.

sättigend substantial.

Satz m *Sprung*: leap, bound; *ling.* sentence, clause; *Tennis*: set; *Boden2*: dregs pl, grounds pl; *Garnitur*: set; **~ung** f statute; **~zeichen** n punctuation mark.

Sau f sow.

sauber clean; *ordentlich*: neat, tidy; 2keit f cleanness; tidiness, neatness; **~machen** clean.

säubern clean(se); *Zimmer*: tidy, clean.

sauer sour; acid; *Gurke*: pickled; *fig. colloq.* peeved; 2milch f curdled milk; 2stoff m oxygen; 2teig m leaven.

saufen drink; *colloq.* booze.

Säufer m *colloq.* drunkard, boozer.

saugen suck.

säug|en suckle; nurse; 2e-tier n mammal; 2ling m baby.

Säule f column, pillar.

Saum m seam, hem; *Rand*: border, edge.

Sauna f sauna.

Säure f acidity (*a. Magen-*2); *chem.* acid.

sausen rush, dash.

Saxophon n saxophone.

Schabe f cockroach; 2n scrape.

schäbig shabby; *fig. a.* mean.

Schach *n* chess; **~brett** *n* chessboard; **~figur** *f* chessman; **2matt** checkmate; **~spiel** *n* (game of) chess.

Schacht *m* shaft; *Bergbau:* a. pit.

Schachtel *f* box.

schade: es ist ~ it is a pity; **wie ~!** what a pity!

Schädel *m* skull; **~bruch** *m* fractured skull.

schaden injure, harm, hurt; **2** *m* damage (**an** to); *körperlicher:* injury; **2ersatz** *m* compensation; *Geldsumme:* damages *pl;* **2freude** *f* malignant delight; **~froh** gloating.

schadhaft damaged; *Rohr:* leaking; *Zähne:* decayed.

schäd|igen damage; *j-n:* injure; **~lich** harmful, injurious; **2linge** *pl* vermin *pl.*   [ram.]

Schaf *n* sheep; **~bock** *m*]

Schäfer *m* shepherd; **~hund** *m* sheepdog; *deutscher:* Alsatian.

schaffen create; *befördern:* convey, carry; take; *bewältigen:* manage.

Schaffner *m rail.* guard, *Am.* conductor; *Bus:* conductor; *Straßenbahn, Bus:* conductor.

Schaft *m* shaft; *Gewehr:* stock; *Stiefel:* leg; **~stiefel** *pl* high boots *pl,* wellingtons *pl.*

schal stale; *fade:* insipid.

Schal *m* scarf; *Woll2:* comforter.

Schale *f* bowl, dish; *Waage:* scale; shell; *Früchte:* skin, peel; **~n** *pl* parings *pl; Kartoffeln:* peelings *pl.*

schälen pare, peel; **sich ~** *Haut:* peel *od.* come off.

Schall *m* sound; **2dicht** soundproof; **2en** sound; *klingen, dröhnen:* ring, peal; **~mauer** *f* sound barrier; **~platte** *f* record.

schalt|en switch; *mot.* change gear; **2er** *m* switch; *rail.* booking-office, ticket-office; *Post, Bank:* counter; *Auskunftsschalter:* desk; **2hebel** *m* gear lever; *tech., aer.* control lever; **2jahr** *n* leap-year; **2tafel** *f* switchboard, control panel.

Scham *f* shame.

schämen: sich ~ be *od.* feel ashamed (*gen,* **wegen** of).

Scham|gefühl *n* sense of shame; **2haft** bashful; **~los** shameless.

Schande *f* shame, disgrace.   [graceful.]

schändlich shameful, dis-]

Schanze *f* ski-jump.

Schar *f* troop, band; *Gänse etc.:* flock; **2en: sich ~ um** gather *od.* flock round.

scharf sharp; pungent; *Pfeffer:* hot; *Augen, Gehör, Verstand:* sharp, keen; **~ sein auf** be keen on.

schärfen sharpen.

Scharf|schütze *m* sharpshooter, sniper; **~sinn** *m* acumen.

Scharlach m scarlet fever; 2rot scarlet.

Scharnier n hinge, joint.

Schärpe f sash.

scharren scrape; *Huhn:* scratch; *Pferd:* paw.

Schatt|en m shadow; **~ierung** f shade; 2ig shady.

Schatz m treasure; *fig.* sweetheart, darling.

schätzen estimate, value (**auf** at); *würdigen:* appreciate; *hoch.:* esteem.

Schau f show; exhibition.

Schauder m shudder, shiver.

schauen look (**auf** at).

Schauer m *Regen etc.:* shower; *s.* **Schauder;** 2lich dreadful, horrible.

Schaufel f shovel; *Kehr* 2: dustpan; 2n shovel.

Schaufenster n shop-window; **~bummel** m ~-n ~ **machen** go window-shopping.

Schaukel f swing; *Boot:* rock; **~pferd** n rocking-horse; **~stuhl** m rocking-chair, *Am. a.* rocker.

Schaum m foam; *Bier:* froth, head; *Seife:* lather.

schäumen foam; *Seife:* lather; *Wein:* sparkle.

Schaum|gummi n, m foam (rubber); 2ig frothy; **~stoff** m expanded plastics *pl.*

Schauplatz m scene.

Schauspiel n spectacle; *thea.* play; **~er** m actor;

~erin f actress.   [check.)

Scheck m cheque, *Am.*

Scheibe f disc, disk; *Brot etc.:* slice; *Fenster:* pane; *Schieß* 2: target; **~nbremse** f disc brake; **~nwischer** m windscreen (*Am.* windshield) wiper.

Scheid|e f sheath, scabbard; *anat.* vagina; 2en separate; **sich** 2en **lassen von** j-m divorce *s.o.;* **~ung** f divorce.

Schein m certificate; *Quittung:* receipt; banknote, *Am. a.* bill; *fig.* appearance; 2bar seeming, apparent; 2en shine; *fig.* seem, appear, look; 2heilig hypocritical; **~werfer** m headlight; *thea.* spotlight.

Scheiße f *vulg.* shit.

Scheit n log.

Scheitel m *Frisur:* parting; 2n part.

scheitern fail, miscarry.

Schellfisch m haddock.

Schelm m rogue; 2isch arch, roguish, mischievous.

schelten scold.

Schema n scheme; pattern.

Schemel m stool.

Schenke f pub(lic house).

Schenkel m *Ober* 2: thigh; *Unter* 2: shank.

schenken give.

Scherbe f, **~n** m (broken) piece, fragment.

Schere f (e-e a pair of) scissors *pl;* *Krebs etc.:* claw; 2n clip, shear; *Haare:* cut; *Bart:* shave.

Schereien pl trouble sg.

Scherz m joke; **2en** joke; **2haft** joking.

scheu shy, timid; 2 f shyness; Furchtsamkeit: timidity; **~en** v/i shy (**vor** at); v/t shun, avoid.

Scheuer|lappen m floorcloth; **~leiste** f skirting-board; 2n scour, scrub; wund reiben: chafe.

Scheune f barn.

Scheusal n monster.

scheußlich abominable.

Schi m etc. s. **Ski** etc.

Schicht f layer (a. geol.); Arbeits2: shift; (social) class, rank; **2en** pile.

schick chic, stylish.

schicken send.

Schicksal n fate, destiny.

Schiebe|dach n sliding roof; **~fenster** n sash-window; 2n push, shove; **~tür** f sliding door.

Schiedsrichter m Tennis: umpire; Fußball etc.: referee.

schief sloping, slanting; awry; Gesicht, Mund: wry.

Schiefer m slate; Splitter: splinter; **~tafel** f slate.

schiefgehen go wrong.

schielen squint.

Schienbein n shin(-bone).

Schiene f rail; med. splint; 2n splint.

schieß|en fire; shoot; **ein Tor** 2 score a goal; **2erei** f shooting; **2scheibe** f target; **2stand** m shooting-gallery, shooting-range.

Schiff n ship, vessel; **~ahrt** f navigation; **2bar** navigable; **~bruch** m: **~ erleiden** be shipwrecked; 2**brüchig** shipwrecked.

schikanieren tyrannize.

Schild n sign(-board); Namens2: nameplate; Etikett: label; Mützen2: peak; **~drüse** f thyroid gland.

schildern describe; 2**ung** f description.

Schildkröte f Land2: tortoise; See2: turtle.

Schilf(rohr) n reed.

Schimm|el m Pferd: white horse; Pilz: mo(u)ld; 2**eln** mo(u)ld; 2(e)lig mo(u)ldy.

schimmern glimmer, gleam.   [zee.)

Schimpanse m chimpan-)

schimpf|en scold; 2**wort** n swearword, abusive word.

Schindel f shingle.

schinden sweat; **sich ~** drudge, slave, sweat.

Schinken m ham.

Schirm m umbrella; Lampe: shade; Mütze: peak; **~mütze** f peaked cap.

Schlacht f battle (**bei** of); 2**en** slaughter, butcher; **~feld** n battlefield; **~schiff** n battleship.

Schlacke f cinder.

Schlaf m sleep; **~anzug** m (ein a pair of) pyjamas pl od. Am. pajamas pl.

Schläfe f temple.

schlafen sleep; **~ gehen, sich ~ legen** go to bed.

schlaff slack; limp; Muskeln: flabby; bot. limp.

schlaf|los sleepless; **⌀losigkeit** f sleeplessness, *med.* insomnia; **⌀mittel** n soporific.

schläfrig sleepy, drowsy.

Schlaf|sack m sleeping-bag; **⌀tablette** f sleeping-pill; **⌀wagen** m sleeping-car; **⌀zimmer** n bedroom.

Schlag m blow (a. fig.); *flache Hand:* slap; *tech.* stroke; *electr.* shock; *med.* apoplexy, stroke; **⌀ader** f artery; **⌀anfall** m apoplexy, stroke; **⌀baum** m barrier(s pl); **⌀en** strike, beat, hit; *Faust:* punch; *flache Hand:* slap; *Bäume:* fell; *besiegen:* beat, defeat; *Uhr:* strike; **⌀er** m pop (-ular) song; hit.

Schläger m rowdy; *Kriket:* bat; s. *Golf-, Tennisschläger;* **⌀ei** f fight.

schlag|fertig good at repartee; **⌀sahne** f whipped cream; **⌀wort** n slogan; **⌀zeile** f headline; **⌀zeug** n percussion (instruments pl).

Schlamm m mud; **⌀ig** muddy.

Schlamp|e f slut, slattern; **⌀ig** slovenly, slipshod.

Schlange f zo.: snake; serpent (a. fig.); *Menschen⌀:* queue, *Am. a.* line; **⌀ stehen** queue up, *Am. a.* line up.

schlängeln: sich ⌀ worm one's way *od.* o.s.; *Weg:* wind; *Fluß:* meander.

schlank slender, slim; **⌀-**

heitskur f: **e–e ⌀ machen** slim.

schlau clever, cunning.

Schlauch m tube; *Spritz⌀:* hose; *Auto⌀ etc.:* inner tube; **⌀boot** n rubber boat; **⌀los** tubeless.

Schlaufe f loop.

schlecht adj bad (a. verdorben); wicked; **mir ist ⌀** I feel sick; adv badly, ill.

schleichen creep; *heimlich:* sneak, steal.

Schleier m veil (a. fig.); *Dunst:* a. haze.

Schleife f loop; *Band⌀:* bow; *Kranz⌀:* streamer.

schleifen drag, trail; *Messer etc.:* whet; *Steine:* cut.

Schleim m slime; *med.* mucus, phlegm; **⌀haut** f mucous membrane; **⌀ig** slimy (a. fig.); mucous.

schlemmen feast.

schlendern stroll, saunter.

schlenkern dangle, swing.

Schleppe f train; **⌀en** drag (**sich** o.s.); carry; *mar.* tug; **⌀lift** m T-bar-lift.

Schleuder f sling, catapult, *Am. a.* slingshot; *Trocken⌀:* spin-drier; **⌀n** v/t fling, hurl; *Wäsche:* spin-dry; v/i *mot.* skid.

Schleuse f sluice; *Kanal:* lock.

schlicht plain, simple; modest; a. settle.

schließ|en shut, close; *Fabrik:* shut down; *Geschäft:* shut up; *Vertrag, Rede:* conclude; **⌀fach** n post office box; *rail.* locker; ~**lich** finally, at last.

schlimm bad; serious; *wund:* bad, sore; ~**er** worse; **am** ~**sten** (the) worst.

Schling|e *f* loop; sling (*a. med.*); *zusammenziehbare:* noose; *hunt.* snare (*a. fig.*); ~**el** *m* rascal; **2en** wind, twist; ~**pflanze** *f* creeper, climber.

Schlips *m* (neck)tie.

Schlitten *m* sled(ge); *sp.* toboggan; *Pferde2:* sleigh; ~**fahrt** *f* sleigh-ride.

Schlittschuh *m* skate; ~ **laufen** skate; ~**läufer** *m* skater.

Schlitz *m* slit; *Einwurf2:* slot; **2en** slit, slash.

Schloß *n* Tür, Gewehr: lock; *arch.* castle, palace.

Schlosser *m* locksmith.

schlottern shake (**vor** with).

Schlucht *f* gorge, ravine.

schluchzen sob.

Schluck *m* draught; ~**auf** *m* hiccup, hiccough; **2en** swallow; ~**en** *m s.* **Schluckauf.**

Schlummer *m* slumber; **2n** slumber.

Schlund *m* pharynx, throat.

schlüpf|en slip, slide; **2er** *m* knickers *pl*, drawers *pl*; panties *pl*, briefs *pl*; ~**rig** slippery.

schlurfen shuffle.

schlürfen sip; drink *od.* eat noisily.

Schluß *m* close, end; *Ab2,*

~**folgerung:** conclusion.

Schlüssel *m* key; ~**bein** *n* collarbone; ~**bund** *m, n* bunch of keys; ~**loch** *n* keyhole.

Schluß|folgerung *f* conclusion; ~**licht** *n s.* **Rücklicht;** ~**runde** *f sp.* final.

schmächtig slender, slim.

schmackhaft palatable, savo(u)ry.

schmal narrow; *Gestalt:* slender, slim; *Gesicht:* thin; **2spur** *f* narrow ga(u)ge. [*ne2:* lard.]

Schmalz *n* grease; *Schwei-*∫

Schmarotzer *m* parasite.

schmatzen eat noisily, smack one's lips.

schmecken taste; ~ **nach** taste of; **schmeckt es?** do you like it?; **das schmeckt mir** I enjoy this.

schmeichel|haft flattering; ~**n** flatter (**j-m** s.o.).

schmeißen *colloq.* throw, fling, hurl; *Tür:* slam.

schmelzen melt; *Metall:* smelt, fuse.

Schmerbauch *m* paunch.

Schmerz *m* pain (*a. pl*), *anhaltender:* ache; *fig.* grief, sorrow; **2en** pain (*a. fig.*), hurt; ache; *fig.* grieve, afflict; **2haft**, **2lich** painful; **2los** painless; **2stillendes Mittel** anodyne.

Schmetter|ling *m* butterfly; **2n** dash; *singen:* warble.

Schmied *m* (black)smith; ~**e** *f* forge, smithy; **2en**

forge; *Pläne:* make, devise.

schmiegen: sich ~ an nestle up to.

schmier|en smear; *tech.* grease, oil, lubricate; *aufstreichen:* spread (**auf** on); *kritzeln:* scrawl, scribble; **~ig** greasy; dirty; filthy.

Schminke *f* make-up; 2n make up; **sich** 2n make (o.s.) up.

schmollen sulk, pout.

Schmor|braten *m* pot roast; 2en stew (*a. fig.*).

Schmuck *m* ornament; decoration; jewel(le)ry, jewels *pl*; 2 neat, smart.

schmücken adorn, decorate.

schmuggeln smuggle.

schmunzeln smile amusedly.

Schmutz *m* dirt, filth; 2en soil, get dirty; **~fleck** *m* smudge, stain; 2ig dirty, filthy; [beak.]

Schnabel *m* bill, *gebogen:*}

Schnalle *f* buckle; 2n buckle; *festschnallen:* strap.

schnapp|en snap, snatch; **nach Luft ~en** gasp for breath; 2**schuß** *m* snapshot.

Schnaps *m* strong liquor, *Am. a.* schnap(p)s.

schnarchen snore.

schnattern cackle.

schnauben snort; **(sich) die Nase ~** blow one's nose.

schnaufen pant, puff, blow.

Schnauze *f* muzzle, snout; *Kanne:* spout.

Schnecke *f* snail; *Nackt*2: slug.

Schnee *m* snow; **~ball-schlacht** *f* snowball fight; 2**bedeckt** *Berg:* snowcapped; **~flocke** *f* snowflake; **~gestöber** *n* snowflurry; **~glöckchen** *n* snowdrop; **~kette** *f* snow *od.* tyre chain; **~mann** *m* snowman; **~matsch** *m* slush; **~pflug** *m* snowplough, *Am.* snowplow; **~sturm** *m* snowstorm, blizzard; **~wehe** *f* snowdrift; 2**weiß** snow-white.

Schneide *f* edge; 2n cut; carve; **~r** *m* tailor; 2**rin** *f* dressmaker; **~zahn** *m* incisor. [it is snowing.]

schnei|en snow; **es ~t**}

Schneise *f* lane.

schnell quick, fast, swift; rapid; *baldig:* speedy; **(mach)** ~! be quick!, hurry up!; **~en** jerk; 2**hefter** *m* folder; 2**igkeit** *f* speed; 2**imbiß** *m* snack(-bar); 2**straße** *f* *Am.* expressway; 2**zug** *m* express (train).

schnippisch pert.

Schnitt *m* cut; *Kleid etc.:* cut, make, style; *fig.* average; **~blumen** *pl* cut flowers *pl*; **~e** *f* slice; **~lauch** *m* chives *pl*; **~muster** *n* pattern; **~punkt** *m* (point of) intersection; **~wunde** *f* cut, gash.

Schnitzel[1] *n* cutlet; **Wiener ~** cutlet Viennese style.

Schnitzel[2] *n, m colloq.* scrap.

485

Schrift

schnitzen carve, cut.

Schnorchel m s(ch)norkel.

schnüffeln sniff, nose.

Schnuller m dummy, comforter. [jerker.)

Schnulze f colloq. tear-}

Schnupfen m cold, catarrh.

schnuppern sniff.

Schnur f string, line.

Schnurr|bart m m(o)ustache; 2en purr.

Schnürsenkel m shoelace, shoestring.

Schock m shock; 2ieren shock.

Schokolade f chocolate.

Scholle f Erd2: clod; Eis2: floe; ichth. plaice.

schon already; **~ lange** for a long time; **~ gut!** all right!

schön beautiful; Mann: handsome; Wetter: fair, fine.

schonen spare; take care of; Kräfte: husband.

Schönheit f beauty.

Schonzeit f close season.

Schopf m tuft; orn. a. crest.

schöpf|en scoop, ladle; Mut: take; Hoffnung: find; **Verdacht ~en** become suspicious; 2er m creator; 2erisch creative; 2ung f creation.

Schorf m scab.

Schornstein m chimney; mar., tech. funnel; 2feger m chimney-sweep(er).

Schoß m lap; Mutterleib: womb; Rock2: tail.

Schote f pod.

Schotte m Scot, Scotch-

man, Scotsman; die ~n pl the Scotch pl.

Schotter m (road-)metal.

schottisch Scotch, Scottish.

schräg slanting, sloping.

Schramme f scratch.

Schrank m cupboard; wardrobe.

Schranke f barrier (a. fig.); rail. a. gate.

Schraube f screw; mar. screw(-propeller); 2nschrauben|mutter** f nut; **~schlüssel** m spanner, wrench; **~zieher** m screwdriver.

schrecklich terrible.

Schrei m cry; lauter: shout; Angst2: scream.

schreiben write; spell; **mit der Maschine ~** type (-write); 2n letter.

Schreib|feder f pen; **~heft** n exercise-book; **~maschine** f typewriter; **~material** n s. Schreibwaren; **~papier** n writing-paper; **~tisch** m (writing-)desk; **~ung** f spelling; **~waren** pl writing-materials pl, stationery sg; **~warengeschäft** n stationer's (shop).

schreien cry; lauter: shout; angstvoll: scream.

Schreiner m s. Tischler.

Schrift f (hand)writing; print. type; 2lich written, in writing; **~steller** m author, writer; **~stück** n piece of writing, paper, document; **~wechsel** m correspondence.

schrill shrill, piercing.

Schritt *m* step; **~ fahren!** slow down!, dead slow!

schroff rugged, jagged; *steil*: steep; *fig.* harsh.

Schrot *m, n* crushed grain; *Munition*: (small) shot; **~flinte** *f* shotgun.

Schrott *m* scrap(-iron).

schrubben scrub, scour.

schrumpfen shrink.

Schub|fach *n* drawer; **~karre**(*n m*) *f* wheelbarrow; **~kraft** *f* thrust; **~lade** *f* drawer.

schüchtern shy, timid.

Schuft *m* scoundrel, rascal; **2en** *colloq.* drudge, slave.

Schuh *m* shoe; **~anzieher** *m* shoehorn; **~bürste** *f* shoe-brush; **~creme** *f* shoe-cream, shoe-polish; **~geschäft** *n* shoe-shop; **~größe** *f* size (of shoe); **~sohle** *f* sole; **~spanner** *m* shoe-tree.

Schul|arbeit *f* homework; **~bank** *f* (school-)desk; **~bildung** *f* education; **~buch** *n* school-book.

Schuld *f Geld*2: debt; *Vergehen*: guilt; *Fehler*: fault; **ich bin** 2 it is my fault; **2bewußt** guilty; **2en:** **j-m et. ~** owe so. s.th.; **j-m Dank ~** be indebted to s.o. **(für** for).

schuldig guilty; **~ sprechen** find guilty; **2e** *m, f* guilty person; culprit.

schuldlos innocent.

Schule *f* school; **höhere ~** secondary school, *Am.*

appr. (senior) high school; **2n** train, school.

Schüler *m* schoolboy, pupil; **~in** *f* schoolgirl, pupil.

Schul|ferien *pl* holidays *pl*, *Am.* vacation *sg*; **~fernsehen** *n* educational TV; **2frei: heute haben wir ~** there's no school today; **~freund(in** *f)* *m* schoolfriend, schoolfellow; **~funk** *m* school broadcasts *pl*; **~mappe** *f* satchel; **2-pflichtig** of school age; **~schwänzer** *m* truant; **~stunde** *f* lesson.

Schulter *f* shoulder; **~blatt** *n* shoulder-blade.

Schulzeugnis *n* report.

Schund *m* trash, rubbish.

Schuppe *f zo.* scale; **~n** *pl* dandruff *sg*.

Schuppen *m* shed.

Schurke *m* scoundrel, villain. [pinafore.]

Schürze *f* apron; *Kinder:*

Schuß *m* shot; *Munition*: round; *kleine Portion*: dash; **~waffe** *f* firearm; **~wunde** *f* gunshot wound.

Schuster *m* shoemaker.

Schutt *m* rubbish, refuse; *Trümmer*: debris; **~abladeplatz** *m* dump.

Schüttel|frost *m* shivering-fit; **2n** shake.

schütten pour; **es schüttet** it is pouring with rain.

Schutz *m* protection; *Zuflucht*: shelter; **~blech** *n* mudguard, *Am.* fender.

schützen protect; shelter.
Schutz|engel m guardian angel; **~heilige** m, f patron saint; **~impfung** f protective inoculation; *Pocken*: vaccination; **2los** unprotected; *wehrlos*: defen|celess, *Am.* -seless; **~umschlag** m (dust-)jacket.
schwach weak; faint; feeble.
Schwäch|e f weakness; **2en** weaken; **2lich** weakly; *zart*: delicate, frail.
schwach|sinnig weakminded, feeble-minded; **2strom** m weak current.
Schwager m brotherin-law. [law.}
Schwägerin f sister-in-}
Schwalbe f swallow.
Schwall m flood; *Worte*: torrent.
Schwamm m sponge.
Schwan m swan.
schwanger pregnant; **2schaft** f pregnancy.
schwanken stagger, totter; *Zweige etc.*: sway; *Preise*: fluctuate; *zögern*: waver.
Schwanz m tail.
schwänzen: die Schule ~ play truant.
Schwarm m *Bienen etc.*: swarm; *Vögel*: a. flight, flock; *Fische*: school, shoal; *Person*: idol, hero.
schwärmen *Bienen etc.*: swarm; **~für** adore.
Schwarte f rind.
schwarz black; **~es Brett** notice-board, *Am.* bulletin board; **2brot** n brown

bread; **2weißfilm** m black-and-white film.
schwatzen chat(ter).
schwätze|n chat(ter); **2r(in** f) m chatterbox; gossip.
Schwebe|bahn f aerial railway *od.* ropeway; **2n** be suspended; *Vogel, aer.*: hover (a. *fig.*); *gleiten*: glide; **in Gefahr 2n** be in danger.
Schwed|e m Swede; **2isch** Swedish. [sulfur.}
Schwefel m sulphur, *Am.*}
Schweif m tail.
schweig|en be silent; **2en** n silence; **~end** silent; **~sam** taciturn.
Schwein n pig, hog.
Schweine|braten m roast pork; **~fleisch** n pork; **~stall** m pigsty (a. *fig.*).
Schweiß m sweat, perspiration; **2en** *tech.* weld.
Schweizer m Swiss; **2isch** Swiss.
schwelen smo(u)lder.
schwelgen| in revel in.
Schwell|e f threshold; **2en** swell; **~ung** f swelling.
schwenken swing; *Hut*: wave; *spülen*: rinse.
schwer heavy; *Wein etc.*: strong; *schwierig*: hard, difficult; *ernst*: serious; **2 Pfund ~ sein** weigh two pounds); **~arbeiten** work hard; **~fällig** slow; *unbeholfen*: clumsy; **2gewicht** n heavy-weight; **~hörig** hard of hearing; **2kraft** f gravity; **2kranke** m, f seriously ill person; **2-**

punkt m cent|re (Am. -er) of gravity; fig. emphasis.
Schwert m sword.
schwer|verdaulich indigestible, heavy; **~verständlich** difficult to understand; **~verwundet** seriously wounded; **~wiegend** fig. weighty, serious.
Schwester f sister; Kranken2: nurse.
Schwieger|eltern pl parents-in-law pl; **~mutter** f etc. mother-in-law, etc.
schwielig callous.
schwierig difficult, hard; 2keit f difficulty, trouble.
Schwimm|bad n swimming bath, swimming pool; 2en swim; Gegensatz: float; **~er(in)** f m swimmer; **~flosse** f flipper; **~gürtel** m lifebelt; **~haut** f web; **~weste** f life-jacket.
Schwindel m med. giddiness, dizziness; colloq. swindle; **~anfall** m fit of dizziness; 2n cheat, swindle. [2ig giddy, dizzy.)
Schwindl|er m swindler.}
Schwinge f wing; 2n swing.
Schwips m: e-n ~ haben colloq. be tipsy.
schwitzen sweat, perspire.
schwören swear.
schwül sultry, close.
Schwung m swing; fig. energy, drive; 2voll full of drive; lively.
Schwur m oath; **~gericht** n appr. Crown Court.
sechs six; 2eck n hexagon;

~eckig hexagonal; **~te** sixth; 2tel n sixth (part); **~tens** sixthly, in the sixth place.
sech|zehn(te) sixteen(th); **~zig** sixty; **~zigste** sixtieth.
See¹ m lake.
See² f sea, ocean; **an der ~** at the seaside; **~bad** n seaside resort; **~gang** m: hoher ~ rough sea; **~hund** m seal; 2krank seasick.
Seel|e f soul; 2isch psychic(al).
See|macht f naval power; **~mann** m seaman, sailor; **~meile** f nautical mile; **~not** f distress (at sea); **~reise** f voyage; **~streitkräfte** pl naval forces pl.
Segel n sail; **~boot** n sailing-boat; sp. yacht; **~fliegen** n gliding; **~flugzeug** n glider; 2n sail; sp. yacht; **~schiff** n sailing-ship, sailing-vessel; **~tuch** n canvas.
Segen m blessing (a. fig.), bsd. eccl. benediction.
Segler m yachtsman.
segnen bless.
sehen v/i see; **~ auf** look at; **~ nach** look after; v/t see; notice; watch; observe; 2swert worth seeing; 2swürdigkeiten pl sights pl.
Sehne f sinew, tendon; Bogen: string. [for.)
sehnen: sich **~ nach** long}
Sehn|enzerrung f strained tendon; 2ig sinewy.
sehn|lich ardent; anxious; 2sucht f longing, yearning.

sehr very; *mit vb*: (very) much, greatly.

seicht shallow.

Seid|**e** *f* silk; **~enpapier** *n* tissue (paper); **~ig** silky.

Seife *f* soap.

Seifen|**pulver** *n* soap-powder; **~schaum** *m* lather; **suds** *pl*.

seifig soapy.

Seil *n* rope; **~bahn** *f* funicular (railway); cableway.

sein¹ his; her; its.

sein² *be*: **bestehen**: exist; **2** *n* being; existence.

seiner|**seits** for his part; **~zeit** then; in those days.

seit since; **~ drei Wochen** for three weeks; **~dem** *adv* since then; ever since; **~ig** since.

Seite *f* side; *Buch*: page.

Seiten|**straße** *f* side-road; **~wind** *m* side-wind.

seit|**lich** lateral; **~wärts** sideways.   [tary.}

Sekretär *m*, **~in** *f* secre-}

Sekt *m* champagne.

Sektor *m* sector; *fig*. field.

Sekunde *f* second.

selbst *pron*: **ich ~** (I) myself; **von ~** *Person*: of one's own accord; *Sache*: by itself, automatically; *adv* even.

selbständig independent; **2keit** *f* inde pendence.

Selbst|**bedienung** *f* self-service; **~beherrschung** *f* self-command, self-control; **~bestimmung** *f* self-determination; **2bewußt** self-confident; **2gemacht** home-made; **~gespräch** *n*

soliloquy, monolog(ue); **2los** unselfish, disinterested; **~mord** *m* suicide; **2sicher** self-confident; **2süchtig** selfish; **2tätig** self-acting, automatic; **~unterricht** *m* private study; **2verständlich** of course, naturally; **~verteidigung** *f* self-defen|ce, *Am*. -se; **2vertrauen** *n* self-confidence; **~verwaltung** *f* self-government, autonomy.

selig *eccl*. blessed; *verstorben*: late; *fig*. overjoyed.

Sellerie *m*, *f* celery.

selten *adj* rare, scarce; *adv* rarely, seldom.

seltsam strange, odd.

Semester *n* term.

Semikolon *n* semicolon.

Seminar *n univ.* seminar; *Priester*: seminary.

Semmel *f* roll.

Senat *m* senate.

send|**en** send, forward; *Funk etc.*: transmit; *Rundfunk*: broadcast; *Fernsehen*: *a*. telecast; **2er** *m* transmitter; broadcasting station; **2ung** *f econ.* consignment, shipment; broadcast; telecast.

Senf *m* mustard.   [ing.}

sengen singe; *a* parch-}

Senk|**e** *f* depression, hollow; **2en** lower; *Kopf*: bow; **sich 2en** sink; *Decke etc.*: sag; **2recht** vertical, perpendicular.

Sensation *f* sensation.

Sense *f* scythe.

sensibel sensitive.

sentimental sentimental.

September *m* September.

Serie *f* series; *Satz*: set.

Serpentine *f* serpentine.

Serum *n* serum.

Service[1] *n* service, set.

Service[2] *m*, *n* service.

servieren serve.

Serviette *f* (table-)napkin.

Sessel *m* armchair, easy chair; *lift* *m* chair-lift.

setzen set, place, put; *pflanzen*: plant; *sich* ~ sit down, take a seat; *Vögel*: perch; *Bodensatz etc.*: settle; ~ *auf Rennpferd*: back.

Seuche *f* epidemic (disease).

seufze|**n** sigh; 2r *m* sigh.

sexuell sexual.

sich oneself; *sg* himself, herself, itself; *pl* themselves; *sg* yourself, *pl* yourselves; *einander*: each other, one another.

Sichel *f* sickle.

sicher safe, secure (**vor** from); *gewiß*: certain, sure; 2heit *f* safety; security; certainty.

Sicherheits|**gurt** *m* seatbelt; ~nadel *f* safety-pin; ~schloß *n* safety-lock.

sicher|**n** secure; guarantee; ~stellen secure; 2ung *f* safeguard; *tech.* safety device; *electr.* fuse.

Sicht *f* visibility; *Aus*2: view; **in** ~ **kommen** come into view, come in sight; 2bar visible; 2lich visibly; ~vermerk *m* visa,

visé; ~weite *f* visibility.

sickern trickle, ooze, seep.

sie she; *pl* they; 2 *sg*, *pl* you.

Sieb *n* sieve; *Sand*: riddle.

sieben[1] sieve, sift; *Sand etc.*: riddle.

sieben[2] seven.

siebte seventh; 2l *n* seventh (part); ~ns seventhly, in the seventh place.

sieb|**zehn(te)** seventeen(th); 2zig seventy; ~zigste seventieth.

siedeln settle.

siede|**n** boil; 2punkt *m* boiling-point.

Sied|**ler** *m* settler; ~lung *f* settlement; *Stadtrand*: housing estate.

Sieg *m* victory; *sp. a.* win.

Siegel *n* seal; *privat*: signet.

sieg|**en** be victorious; *sp.* win; 2er *m* conqueror; *sp.* winner. [signal.⟩

Signal *n* signal; 2isieren⟩

Silbe *f* syllable. [silver.⟩

Silber *n* silver; 2n (of)⟩

Silhouette *f* silhouette; *Stadt*: *a.* skyline. [Eve.⟩

Silvester *n* New Year's⟩

Sinfonie *f* symphony.

singen sing.

Singular *m gr.* singular.

Singvogel *m* songbird, songster. [down.⟩

sinken sink; *Preise*: go⟩

Sinn *m* sense; *Verstand*: mind; *Bedeutung*: sense, meaning.

Sinnes|**änderung** *f* change of mind; ~organ *n* sense-organ.

sinn|**lich** sensual; ~los

senseless; futile, useless.

Sippe f *Stamm*: tribe; (blood-)relations pl;family.

Sirup m syrup, Am. sirup.

Sitte f custom, habit; **⁓n** pl morals pl.

sittlich moral.

Situation f situation.

Sitz m seat; **⁓en** sit, be seated; *passen*: fit; **⁓en bleiben** remain seated; **⁓platz** m seat; **⁓ung** f meeting, conference.

Skala f scale; *Radio*: dial.

Skandal m scandal.

Skelett n skeleton.

skeptisch sceptical, Am. skeptical.

Ski m ski; **⁓ laufen** od. **fahren** ski; **⁓fahrer** m, **⁓läufer** m skier; **⁓lift** m ski-lift; **⁓springen** n ski-jumping.

Skizz|e f sketch; **2ieren** sketch, outline.

Sklave m slave.

Skrupel m scruple; **2los** unscrupulous.

Skulptur f sculpture.

Slalom m slalom.

Smaragd m emerald.

Smoking m dinner-jacket, Am. a. tux(edo).

so so, thus; like this od. that; *vergleichend*: as; **⁓ein** such a; **⁓bald**: **⁓ (wie od. als)** as soon as.

Socke f sock; **⁓l** m pedestal; **⁓nhalter** m suspender, Am. garter.   [water.]

Soda(wasser) n soda-⫂

Sodbrennen n heartburn.

soeben just (now).

sofort at once; immediately.

Sog m suction; *aer.* wake; *mar.* undertow.

so|gar even; **⁓genannt** so-called.

Sohle f sole; *Tal*: bottom.

Sohn m son.

solange as long as.

solch such.

Sold m pay.

Soldat m soldier.

Söldner m mercenary.

solid(e) solid; *fig. a.* sound.

Solist m, **⁓in** f soloist.

Soll n debit; *Produktions2*: target.

sollen: ich sollte I should, I ought to; **er soll** he shall; he is said to.

Sommer m summer; **2lich** summer(y); **⁓schlußverkauf** m summer sale(s pl); **⁓sprossen** f freckles pl; **⁓(s)zeit** f summertime.

Sonde f probe (a. med.).

Sonder|angebot n special offer; **⁓ausgabe** f special (edition); **2bar** strange, odd; **⁓fahrt** f special; **⁓ling** m crank, odd person; **2n** but; **⁓zug** m special (train).

Sonnabend m Saturday.

Sonne f sun; **2n: sich ⁓** sun o.s., bask in the sun.

Sonnen|aufgang m sunrise; **⁓bad** n sun-bath; **⁓brand** m sunburn; **⁓brille** f (e-e a pair of) sunglasses pl; **⁓finsternis** f solar eclipse; **⁓licht** n sunlight; **⁓öl** n suntan lotion; **⁓schein** m sunshine; ~**schirm** m sunshade; ~**stich** m sunstroke; ~**strahl** m sunbeam; ~**uhr** f sundial; ~**untergang** m sunset.

sonnig sunny.

Sonntag m Sunday.

sonst otherwise, *mit pron* else; **wer** ~? who else?; **wie** ~ as usual; ~ **nichts** nothing else.

Sorge f care; sorrow; uneasiness, anxiety; **sich** ~**n machen um** be anxious *od.* worried about; **mach dir keine** ~**n** don't worry.

sorgen: ~ **für** care for, provide for; **dafür** ~, **daß** see (to it) that; **sich** ~ **um** worry about.

sorg|fältig careful; ~**los** carefree; careless.

Sort|e f sort, kind, species; **2ieren** (as)sort; arrange; ~**iment** n assortment.

Soße f sauce; *Braten*2: gravy.

Souvenir n souvenir.

Souveränität f sovereignty.

so|viel as much; ~**weit** as far as; ~**wieso** in any case, anyway.

sowjetisch Soviet.

sowohl: ~ ... **als (auch)** both ... and, ... as well as.

sozial social; ~**demokratisch** Social Democratic; **2ist** m socialist; ~**istisch** socialist.

Soziussitz m pillion.

sozusagen so to speak.

Spalt m crack, crevice; ~**e**

f s. **Spalt**; *print.* column; **2en: (sich)** ~ split.

Span m chip, shaving.

Spange f clasp; (hair-)slide; *Armreif:* bangle.

Spani|er m Spaniard; **2sch** Spanish.

Spann m instep; ~**e** f span; *econ.* margin; **2en** stretch; tighten; be (too) tight; **2end** exciting, thrilling; ~**ung** f tension (*a. fig.*); *electr.* voltage; *tech.* strain, stress; ~**weite** f spread.

Spar|buch n savings-bank book; **2en** save; economize; ~**er** m saver.

Spargel m asparagus.

Spar|kasse f savings-bank; ~**konto** n savings account.

spärlich scanty.

sparsam economical.

Spaß m fun; joke; **2en** joke, make fun; ~**vogel** m wag.

spät late; **zu** ~ (too) late; **wie** ~ **ist es?** what time is it?

Spaten m spade.

spätestens at the latest.

Spatz m sparrow.

spazieren walk, stroll; ~**fahren** v/i go for a drive; v/t take for a drive; *Baby:* take out for a walk; ~**gehen** go for a walk.

Spazier|fahrt f drive, ride; ~**gang** m walk, stroll; **e-n** ~**gang machen** go for a walk; ~**gänger** m walker.

Specht m woodpecker.

Speck m bacon.
Spediteur m forwarding agent; **Möbel:** (furniture) remover.
Speer m spear; sp. javelin.
Speiche f spoke.
Speichel m spit(tle), saliva.
Speicher m garret, attic.
speien spit; vomit, be sick.
Speise f food, nourishment; **Gericht:** dish; **~eis** n ice-cream; **~kammer** f larder, pantry; **~karte** f bill of fare, menu; **2n** v/i s. essen; v/t feed; **~röhre** f gullet; **~saal** m od. shut off; **~wagen** m dining-car, diner; **~zimmer** n dining-room.
spekulieren speculate.
Spende f gift; contribution; **2n** give; donate.
Sperling m sparrow.
Sperr|e f barrier; rail. barrier, Am. gate; sp. suspension; **2en** close; **Licht etc.:** cut od. shut off; **Scheck:** stop; sp. suspend; **~holz** n plywood; **2ig** bulky; **~stunde** f closing time.
Spesen pl expenses pl.
speziali|sieren: sich ~ specialize (auf in); **2st** m specialist; **2tät** f speciali(t)y.
speziell special, particular.
Spiegel m mirror, looking-glass; **~bild** n reflection; **~ei** n fried egg; **2n** shine; **sich 2n** be reflected.
Spieg(e)lung f reflection.
Spiel n play; sp. game;

Wettkampf: match; **auf dem ~ stehen** be at stake; **aufs ~ setzen** jeopardize; **~automat** m slot-machine; **~bank** f casino; **2en** play; gamble; **2end** fig. easily; **~er** m player; gambler; **~feld** n (playing-)field; **~film** m feature film od. picture; **~gefährte** m playfellow, playmate; **~karte** f playing-card; **~marke** f counter, chip; **~plan** m program(me); **~platz** m playground; **~regel** f rule of the game); **~sachen** f toys pl; **~verderber** m spoil-sport; **~waren** pl toys pl; **~zeug** n toy(s pl).
Spieß m spear, pike; **Brat2:** spit.
Spinat m spinach.
Spind m, n cupboard; locker.
Spinn|e f spider; **2en** spin; fig. colloq. be crazy, sl. be nuts; **~webe** f cobweb.
Spion m spy; **~age** f espionage.
Spirale f spiral.
Spirituosen pl spirits pl.
spitz pointed; sharp; **Winkel:** acute; **2e** f point; **Nase, Finger:** tip; **Turm:** spire; **Berg etc.:** peak, top; **Gewebe:** lace; **fig.:** head; top; **~en** point, sharpen; **~findig** subtle; **2name** m nickname.
Splitter m splinter, shiver; **2n** splinter, shiver.
Sporn m spur.

Sport m sport; fig. hobby; ~treiben go in for sport; ~kleidung f sportswear; ~lehrer m games-master; ~ler m sportsman; ~lerin f sportswoman; 2lich sporting; Figur: athletic; ~nachrichten pl sports news pl; ~platz m sports field; stadium; ~tauchen n skin-diving; ~verein m sports-club; ~wagen m sports-car; folding pram, Am. stroller.

Spott m mockery; derision; scorn; 2billig colloq. dirt-cheap; 2en: ~ über mock od. sneer at.

spöttisch mocking, sneering; ironical.

Sprach|e f Fähigkeit: speech; language; ~führer m phrase-book; ~kenntnisse pl knowledge sg of foreign languages; 2los speechless.

Spray m, n spray; Gerät: a. atomizer.

sprech|en speak; talk; 2er m speaker; Ansager: announcer; Wortführer: spokesman; 2stunde f consulting-hours pl, surgery hours pl; 2stundenhilfe f receptionist; 2zimmer n consulting-room, surgery.

spreizen spread (out).

spreng|en sprinkle; water; blow up; burst open; 2stoff m explosive; 2ung f blowing-up; explosion.

sprenkeln speckle, spot.

Sprichwort n proverb.
sprießen sprout.

Spring|brunnen m fountain; 2en jump, leap; Ball: bounce; Schwimmen: dive; burst, crack, break.

Spritze f syringe; Injektion: injection; 2n sprinkle; water; splash; med. inject; 2n aus spurt from; ~r m splash.

spröde brittle; fig. coy.

Sproß m shoot, sprout.

Sprosse f rung, step.

Sprößling m offspring.

Sprotte f sprat.

Spruch m saying.

Sprudel m mineral water; 2n bubble; effervesce.

sprüh|en v/t spray, sprinkle; v/i Funken: fly; es ~t it is drizzling; 2regen m drizzle.

Sprung m jump, leap, bound; Schwimmen: dive; Riß: crack; ~brett n spring-board; ~schanze f ski-jump.

Spucke f colloq. spit(tle); 2n spit. [coil.]

Spule f spool, reel; electr.]

spül|en v/t rinse; wash (up); v/i flush the lavatory; 2mittel n detergent.

Spur f trace (a. fig.); mehrere: track; Wagen: rut; fig. sign.

spüren feel; sense.

Staat m state; government.

Staats|angehörige m, f national, citizen, bsd. Brit. subject; ~angehörigkeit f nationality; citizenship;

~anwalt m public prosecutor, Am. prosecuting attorney; ~bürger m citizen; ~dienst m civil service; ~mann m statesman; ~oberhaupt n head of (the) state.

Stab m staff (a. fig.); Metall, Holz: bar; pole.

stabil stable.

Stachel m prickle; Biene: sting; ~beere f gooseberry; ~draht m barbed wire.

stach(e)lig prickly, thorny.

Stadi|on n stadium; ~um n stage, phase.

Stadt f town; city.

Städter m townsman; ~ pl townspeople pl.

Stadt|gebiet n urban area; ~gespräch n local call.

städtisch municipal.

Stadt|mitte f town od. city cent|re, Am. -er; ~plan m town plan, map of the town; ~rand m outskirts pl; ~rat m town council; Person: town council(l)or; ~rundfahrt f sightseeing tour; ~teil m, ~viertel n quarter.

Staffel|ei f easel; ~lauf m relay race.

Stahl m steel.

Stall m stable.

Stamm m stem; Baum: trunk; Volks♀: race; Eingeborenen♀: tribe; ~baum m family tree, pedigree (a. zo.); ♀eln stammer; ♀en: ~ aus come from; zeitlich: date from; ~gast m regular customer od. guest, colloq. regular.

stämmig stocky, squat.

Stammkunde m regular customer.

stampfen v/t mash; v/i stamp; Pferd: paw.

Stand m stand; position; Verkaufs♀: stall; Höhe: level; Wettkampf: score; ~bild n statue.

Ständer m stand.

Standes|amt n registry office; ♀amtlich: ~e Trauung civil marriage.

stand|haft firm; ~halten resist. [stant.]

ständig permanent; con-]

Stand|licht n parking light(s pl); ~ort m position; ~punkt m point of view.

Stange f pole; Metall: rod, bar; Fahne: staff.

Stanniol n tin foil.

stanzen punch, stamp.

Stapel m pile, stack; ♀n pile (up), stack.

stapfen plod.

Star m orn. starling; med. cataract; thea. etc.: star.

stark strong; dick: stout; ~e Erkältung bad cold; ~er Raucher heavy smoker.

Stärke f strength; chem. starch; ♀n strengthen (a. fig.); Wäsche: starch; **sich** ♀n take some refreshment(s). [rent.]

Starkstrom m heavy cur-]

starr rigid (a. fig.); stiff; Blick: fixed; ~en stare

(auf at); ~köpfig obstinate; 2krampf *m* tetanus.

Start *m* start (a. fig.); aer. take-off; Rakete: lift-off; ~bahn f runway; 2bereit ready to start; aer. ready for take-off; 2en v/i start; aer. take off; Rakete: lift off; v/t start; Rakete: launch.

Station f station; Kranken2: ward.

Statistik f statistics pl.

Stativ n tripod.

statt instead of; ~ dessen instead; ~ zu instead of ger.

Stätte f place, spot.

stattfinden take place.

stattlich stately, impressive; Summe: considerable.

Statue f statue.

Statut n statute.

Staub *m* dust.

Staubecken n reservoir.

staub|en make dust; ~ig dusty; 2sauger *m* vacuum cleaner; 2tuch n duster.

Stau|damm *m* dam; 2en dam (up); **sich** 2en accumulate; gather; Fahrzeuge: become jammed.

staunen be astonished (**über** at).

Staupe f distemper.

Stausee *m* reservoir.

stechen prick; Insekten: sting; Floh, Mücke: bite; Sonne: burn; ~d Blick: piercing; Schmerz: stabbing.

Steckdose f (wall) socket.

stecken v/t stick, put; v/i

sich befinden: be; stick, be stuck; 2 *m* stick; ~bleiben get stuck; ~lassen leave; 2pferd n hobbyhorse; fig. hobby. [pin.]

Steck|er *m* plug; ~nadel f)

Steg *m* footbridge.

stehen stand; sich befinden: be; geschrieben ~: be written; kleiden: suit, become; **wie steht's mit ...?** what about ...?; ~ **bleiben** remain standing; ~bleiben stop; ~lassen leave s.o. standing; Essen: leave untouched.

Stehlampe f floor-lamp.

stehlen steal. [room.]

Stehplatz *m* standing-)

steif stiff (a. fig.); numb (**vor Kälte** with cold).

Steig|bügel *m* stirrup; 2en rise; increase; Nebel: ascend; 2ern raise; increase; heighten; ~ung f rise; gradient, Am. grade.

steil steep.

Stein *m* stone; ~bruch *m* quarry; ~gut n crockery, earthenware; 2ig stony; ~pilz *m* yellow boletus; ~schlag *m* falling rocks pl.

Stelle f place; Fleck: spot; Punkt: point; Behörde: authority; Buch: passage; Arbeit: colloq. job; **freie** ~ vacancy; **ich an deiner** ~ if I were you.

stellen put, place; set (a. Uhr, fig.); Bedingungen: make; Frage: ask, put.

Stellung f position, posture; Beruf: position; Rang:

position, rank; **~nahme** f opinion, comment; **2slos** unemployed.

Stellvertreter m substitute; deputy.

stemmen Gewicht: lift; **sich ~gegen** press against; fig. resist od. oppose s.th.

Stempel m stamp; bot. pistil; **2n** stamp.

Stengel m stalk, stem.

Steno f colloq., **~graphie** f shorthand; **2graphieren** write (in) shorthand; **~typistin** f shorthand-typist.

Steppdecke f quilt.

sterb|en die (**an** of); **~lich** mortal.

steril sterile.

Stern[1] m star (a. fig.); **~enbanner** n Star-Spangled Banner, Stars and Stripes pl; **~schnuppe** f shooting star; **~warte** f observatory.

stet|ig constant; steady; **~s** always.

Steuer[1] n mar. helm, rudder; mot. (steering-)wheel.

Steuer[2] f tax; duty.

Steuer|beamte m revenue officer; **~bord** n starboard; **~erklärung** f taxreturn; **2frei** tax-free; Waren: duty-free; **~knüppel** m aer. control lever od. stick; **~mann** m mar. helmsman; Boot: coxswain; für see, navigate; mot. drive; fig. direct, control; **~rad** n steeringwheel; **~ruder** n helm; rudder; **~ung** f steering; **~zahler** m taxpayer.

Stich m prick; Insekten: sting, bite; Messer: stab; Nähen: stitch; Karten: trick; Kupfer2: engraving; **im ~ lassen** desert, forsake; **2haltig: ~ sein** hold water; **~probe** f random test od. sample; **~tag** m fixed day; **~wort** n headword; note; thea. cue.

stick|en embroider; **~ig** stuffy, close; **2stoff** m nitrogen.

Stiefel m boot.

Stief|mutter f etc. stepmother, etc.; **~mütterchen** n pansy.

Stiel m handle; Axt: haft; Besen: stick; bot. stalk.

Stier m bull; **~kampf** m bullfight.

Stift n pin; peg; pencil; **2en** endow; give, donate.

Stil m style.

still still, quiet, silent; **~!** silence!; **2e** f stillness, quiet(ness), silence; **~gen** Fabrik etc.: shut down; Verkehr: stop; **~en** Schmerz: soothe; Hunger, Neugier: appease; Durst: quench; Blut: sta(u)nch; Säugling: nurse; **~halten** keep still; **~schweigend** fig. tacit; **~stehen** standstill, stop.

Stimm|band n vocal c(h)ord; **2berechtigt** entitled to vote; **~e** f voice; Wähler: vote; **2en** v/t tune; v/i be true od. right; Summe: be correct; **2en für** vote for; **2recht** n right to vote; **~ung** f mood, humo(u)r; **~zettel** m ballot, voting-paper.

stinken stink (**nach** of).

Stipendium n scholarship.

Stirn f forehead, brow; fig. cheek; **~runzeln** n frown.

stöbern colloq. rummage (about).

stochern stoke; pick.

Stock m stick; Rohr♀: cane; Takt♀: baton; Bienen♀: beehive; **~werk** n stor(e)y, floor; **erster ~** first (Am. second) floor.

stock|en stop; Milch etc.: curdle (a. fig.); Stimme, falter; Verkehr: be blocked; **♀werk** n stor(e)y, floor.

Stoff m substance; material, fabric, textile; Material, Zeug: material, stuff; cloth.

stöhnen groan, moan.

stolpern stumble, trip.

stolz proud; haughty; **♀** m pride.

stopf|en v/t stuff; Pfeife: fill; Geflügel: cram, stuff; Strümpfe: darn; v/i med. constipate, be constipating; **♀garn** n darning-cotton; **♀nadel** f darning-needle.

Stoppel f stubble.

stopp|en stop; Zeit: time, clock; **♀uhr** f stop-watch.

Stöpsel m stopper, plug.

Storch m stork.

stören v/i be intruding; v/t disturb; belästigen: trouble.

störrisch stubborn.

Störung f disturbance; trouble (a. tech.); break-down.

Stoß m push, shove; Schlag:

blow, knock; Schwimm♀: stroke; Erschütterung: shock; Wagen: jolt; Haufen: pile, heap; **~dämpfer** m shock-absorber; **♀en** push, shove; knock, strike; **(sich) ♀en an** strike od. knock against; **♀en an** adjoin, border on; **♀en auf** come across; Widerstand: meet with; **~stange** f bumper; **~verkehr** m rush-hour traffic.

stottern stammer; Motor: sputter.

Straf|anstalt f prison; **♀-bar** punishable, criminal; **~e** f punishment; jur., sp., fig. penalty; jur. sentence; **♀en** punish.

straff tight; fig. strict.

Strafraum m sp. penalty area.

Strahl m ray (a. fig.); Licht: a. beam; Blitz: flash; Wasser etc.: jet; **♀en** radiate; shine; fig. beam; **~ung** f radiation, rays pl.

Strähne f Haar: lock, strand.

stramm tight.

strampeln kick.

Strand m beach; **am ~** on the beach; **♀en** strand; **~hotel** n beach hotel; **~kleidung** f beachwear; **~korb** m beach-basket, beach-chair; **~promenade** f promenade, Am. boardwalk.

Strang m cord (a. anat.); rope.

Strapaz|e f exertion, fatigue; **2ierfähig** durable, for hard wear.

Straße f road, highway; street; _Meerenge_: strait; **auf der ~** in the street.

Straßen|arbeiten pl road works pl; **~bahn** f tram (-car), _Am._ streetcar; **~beleuchtung** f street lighting; **~café** n pavement (_Am._ sidewalk) café; **~karte** f road map; **~kreuzung** f cross-roads sg; **~schild** n street od. road sign; **~wacht** f A.A. (= Automobile Association) patrol (-man).

sträuben _Federn_: ruffle up; **sich ~** _Haare_: stand on end; **sich ~ gegen** struggle od. kick against.

Strauch m shrub, bush.

straucheln s. **stolpern.**

Strauß m orn. ostrich; _Blumen_: bunch, bouquet.

streben v. **nach** strive for.

Strecke f stretch; route; distance; _rail. etc._: line; **2n** stretch, extend; _verdünnen_: dilute; **sich ~** **2n** stretch (o.s.).

Streich m trick, prank; **2eln** stroke, caress; **2en** rub; paint; s. **aus-**, **bestreichen**; **mit der Hand über et.** **2en** pass one's hand over s.th.; **~holz** n match; **~orchester** n string band od. orchestra.

Streife f patrol(man); **2n** stripe, streak; _berühren_: brush; _Thema_: touch (up)on; roam; **~n m** stripe,

unregelmäßiger: streak; _Land etc._: strip; **~nwagen** m police od. patrol car.

Streik m strike, _Am._ a. walkout; **2en** strike, _Am._a. walk out.

Streit m quarrel; dispute; conflict; **2en: (sich) ~** quarrel; **~kräfte** pl(armed) forces pl.

streng severe, stern (a. _Blick etc._); _genau_: strict.

streuen strew, scatter.

Strich m stroke; _Linie_: line.

Strick m cord; rope; **2en** knit; **~jacke** f cardigan; **~nadel** f knitting-needle; **~waren** pl knitwear sg; **~zeug** n knitting.

Striemen m weal, wale.

Stroh n straw; _Dach_: thatch; **~halm** m straw.

Strom m stream (a. fig.), (large) river; _electr._ current.

strömen stream; flow, run; _Regen, Menschenmenge_: pour.

Strom|kreis m circuit; **~schnelle** f rapid.

Strömung f current.

Strophe f verse.

Strudel m swirl, whirlpool.

Struktur f structure.

Strumpf m stocking; **~halter** m suspender, _Am._ garter; **~haltergürtel** m girdle; **~hose** f tights pl.

struppig shaggy.

Stube f room; **~nmädchen** n chambermaid.

Stück n piece (a. _mus._); fragment; _Vieh_: head;

Zucker: lump; *thea.* play.

Stud|ent m, **~in** f student, undergraduate.

Stud|ie f study; **~ieren** study, read; **~ium** n study, *allgemeiner*: studies pl.

Stufe f step; *Grad*: degree; *Entwicklung*: stage; **~nweise** gradual.

Stuhl m chair, seat; **~bein** n leg of a chair; **~gang** m *med.* stool, movement; **~lehne** f back of a chair.

stumm dumb, mute.

Stummel m stump; *Zigarette etc.*: stub, butt.

Stummfilm m silent film.

stümperhaft bungling, clumsy.

stumpf blunt; *Sinne*: dull; apathetic; **2** m stump, stub; **~sinnig** stupid, dull.

Stunde f hour; *Unterrichts*-**2**: lesson, *Am. a.* period.

Stunden|kilometer m kilomet|re (*Am.* -er) per hour; **2lang** *adv* for hours (and hours); *adj*: **nach 2langem Warten** after hours of waiting; **~lohn** m wages pl per hour; **~plan** m timetable, *Am.* schedule; **2weise** by the hour.

stündlich hourly.

Sturm m storm.

stürm|en storm; *Wind*: rage; rush; **2er** m sp. forward; **~isch** stormy.

Sturz m fall; *Regierung etc.*: overthrow; *Preis*-**2**: slump.

stürzen fall; *eilen*: rush; *Regierung*: overthrow.

Sturzhelm m crash-helmet.

Stute f mare.

Stütze f support.

stutzen v/t *Haare*: crop; *Bart*: trim; *Flügel, Hecke*: clip; *Baum*: lop; v/i start (**bei** at).

stützen support (a. *fig.*); **sich ~ auf** lean on.

stutzig: **~ machen** make suspicious.

Stützpunkt m base.

Subjekt n gr. subject; **2iv** subjective.

Substantiv n gr. noun, substantive.

Substanz f substance.

subtrahieren subtract.

Suche f search (**nach** for); **auf der ~ nach** in search of; **2n** *Rat etc.*: seek; **2n (nach)** search for, look for.

Sucht f mania; addiction.

süchtig: **~ sein** be addicted to *drugs, etc.*; **2e** m, f addict.

Süd|**(en** m) south; **~früchte** pl citrus and other tropical fruits pl; **2lich** south (-ern), southerly; **~ost(en** m) southeast; **~pol** m South Pole; **~west(en** m) southwest.

Sühne f atonement.

Sülze f brawn, jellied meat.

Summe f sum (a. *fig.*), (sum) total; *Betrag*: amount.

summen buzz, hum.

Sumpf m swamp, bog, marsh; **2ig** swampy, boggy, marshy.

Sünde f sin; **∼bock** m colloq. scapegoat; **∼r** m sinner.

Super|(benzin) n super; **∼lativ** m gr. superlative (degree); **∼markt** m supermarket.

Suppe f soup; **∼nschüssel** f tureen; **∼nteller** m soupplate.

süß sweet (a. fig.); **∼en** sweeten; **ℒigkeiten** pl sweets pl; **ℒspeise** f sweet; **ℒwasser** n fresh water.

Symbol n symbol; **ℒisch** symbolic(al). [ric(al).\
symmetrisch symmet-\
sympathisch lik(e)able; **er ist mir ∼** I like him.

Symphonie f symphony.

Symptom n symptom.

Synagoge f synagogue.

synchronisieren synchronize; **Tonfilm:** a. dub.

synthetisch synthetic.

System n system; **ℒatisch** systematic(al); methodical.

Szene f scene.

T

Tabak m tobacco.

Tabelle f table.

Tablett n tray; **∼e** f tablet. [ometer.\
Tachometer m, n speed-\

Tadel m reproof, rebuke; **ℒlos** faultless; excellent; **ℒn** reprove, rebuke.

Tafel f slab; **Gedenk∼:** plaque, tablet; **Schiefer∼:** slate; **Schul∼:** blackboard; **Anschlag∼:** notice-board; **Am.** billboard; **Schokolade:** bar; dinner-table; **∼geschirr** n dinner-service, dinner-set.

Täf(e)lung f wainscot, panel(l)ing.

Tag m day; **am** od. **bei ∼e** by day; **guten ∼!** how do you do?; good morning!; good afternoon!

Tage|buch n diary; **ℒlang** for days (together); **ℒn** hold a meeting.

Tages|anbruch m: **bei ∼**

at daybreak od. dawn; **∼ausflug** m day excursion od. trip; **∼kurs** m current rate; **∼licht** n daylight.

täglich daily.

tagsüber during the day.

Tagung f meeting.

Taille f waist.

Takt m mus. time, measure; mot. stroke; fig. tact; **∼ik** f tactics sg, pl; **ℒlos** tactless; **∼stock** m baton; **ℒvoll** tactful.

Tal n valley.

Talent n talent, gift.

Talg m suet; ausgelassener: tallow.

Talisman m talisman, charm.

Tang m seaweed.

Tank m tank; **ℒen** get some petrol (Am. gasoline); **∼er** m tanker; **∼stelle** f petrol station, Am. gas od. filling station; **∼wart** m pump attendant.

Tanne f fir(-tree); ~n-zapfen m fir-cone.

Tante f aunt.

Tanz m dance; 2en dance.

Tänzer m, ~in f dancer; partner.

Tapete f wallpaper.

tapezieren paper.

tapfer brave; courageous.

Tarif m tariff.

tarn|en camouflage; bsd. fig. disguise; 2ung f camouflage.

Tasche f bag; pocket.

Taschen|buch n pocket-book; ~dieb m pickpocket; ~geld n pocket-money; ~lampe f (pocket) torch, flashlight; ~messer n pocket-knife; ~tuch n (pocket-)handkerchief; ~uhr f pocket-watch.

Tasse f cup.

Taste f key; 2n grope (nach for, after); sich 2n feel od. grope one's way.

Tat f action, act, deed; Straf2: offen|ce, Am. ~se; crime; 2enlos inactive.

Täter m perpetrator.

tätig active; busy; 2keit f activity; occupation, job.

tat|kräftig active; 2ort m scene of a crime.

Tätowierung f tattoo.

Tat|sache f fact; 2sächlich actual, real.

tätscheln pet, pat.

Tatze f paw.

Tau[1] n rope, cable.

Tau[2] m dew.

taub deaf; Finger: numb.

Taube f pigeon.

taubstumm deaf and dumb; 2e m, f deaf mute.

tauch|en dip; dive; U-Boot: submerge; 2er m diver; 2sieder m immersion heater; 2sport m skin-diving.

tauen melt; es taut it is thawing; dew is falling.

Tauf|e f baptism, christening; 2en baptize, christen; ~pate m godfather; f = ~patin f godmother.

taug|en be good (zu for); (zu) nichts ~en be good for nothing; ~lich good, fit, useful.

taumeln reel, stagger.

Tausch m exchange, barter; 2en exchange, barter.

täusch|en deceive; sich ~en be mistaken; ~end striking; 2ung f deception.

tausend thousand; ~ste thousandth.

Tauwetter n thaw.

Taxe f Gebühr: fee; s. Taxi.

Taxi n taxi(-cab); cab; ~fahrer m taxi-driver, cab-driver; ~stand m cabstand, taxi rank.

Technik f technology, engineering; Fertigkeit: skill, workmanship; Verfahren: technique; ~er m technician.

technisch technical; ~e Hochschule college of technology. [cakes pl.]

Tee m tea; ~gebäck n tea-

Teer m tar; 2en tar.

Teesieb n tea-strainer.

Teich m pond, pool.

Teig m dough, paste; ~**waren** pl farinaceous foods pl.

Teil m, n part; An2: portion, share; **zum** ~ partly, in part; 2**bar** divisible; ~**chen** n particle; 2**en** divide; fig. share; 2**haben** participate, (have a) share (**an** in); ~**haber** m partner; ~**nahme** f participation; sympathy; 2**nahmslos** indifferent; apathetic; 2**nehmen**: ~ **an** take part in, participate in; ~**nehmer** m participant; teleph. subscriber; 2s partly; ~**ung** f division; 2**weise** partly, in part.

Teint m complexion.

Telefon n telephone, colloq. phone; ~**buch** n telephone directory; ~**gespräch** n (tele)phone call; 2**ieren** (tele)phone; 2**isch** over the od. by (tele)phone; ~**istin** f (telephone) operator; ~**zelle** f telephone kiosk, call-box, Am. telephone booth; ~**zentrale** f (telephone) exchange.

telegrafieren wire; Übersee: cable; 2**isch** by telegram od. wire; by cable.

Telegramm n telegram, wire; Übersee: cable(gram).

Teller m plate.

Tempel m temple.

Temperament n temperament; 2**voll** spirited.

Temperatur f temperature; j-s ~ **messen** take s.o.'s temperature.

Tempo n time; Gangart: pace; Geschwindigkeit: speed.

Tendenz f tendency, trend.

Te nis n tennis; ~**platz** m tennis-court; ~**schläger** m (tennis-)racket.

Teppich m carpet.

Termin m appointed time od. day; jur., econ. date.

Terrasse f terrace.

Territorium n territory.

Terror m terror; 2**isieren** terrorize.

Testament n (last) will; eccl. Testament.

testen test.

Tetanus m tetanus.

teuer dear (a. fig.), expensive; **wie** ~ **ist es?** how much is it?

Teufel m devil.

Text m text; Lied: words pl; Oper: book, libretto.

Textilien pl textiles pl.

Theater n theat|re, Am.-er; ~**besucher** m playgoer; ~**kasse** f box-office; ~**stück** n play.

Theke f bar, counter.

Thema n theme, subject; Gesprächs2: topic.

Theologie f theology.

theoretisch theoretic(al); 2**ie** f theory.

Therapie f therapy.

Thermometer n thermometer. [mos (flask).]

Thermosflasche f ther-∫

Thrombose f thrombosis.
Thron m throne.
Thunfisch m tunny, tuna.
ticken tick.
tief deep (a. fig.); Seufzer, Schlaf etc.: profound; niedrig: low; 2 n meteor. depression; 2druckgebiet n low-pressure area; 2e f depth (a. fig.); ~gekühlt deep-frozen; 2kühlfach n, 2kühltruhe f deep-freeze.
Tier n animal; beast; ~arzt m veterinary (surgeon), colloq. vet, Am. a. veterinarian; ~garten m zoological gardens pl, zoo; 2isch animal; ~kreis m ast. zodiac; ~park m s. Tiergarten.
Tiger m tiger; ~in f tigress.
tilgen wipe out; Schuld: extinguish. [flesh.]
Tinte f ink; ~nfisch m cut-
Tip m hint, tip.
tippen knock: type; ~ an tip; ~ auf tap on.
Tisch m table; bei ~ at table; nach ~ after dinner; ~decke f table-cloth; ~ler m joiner; Möbel: cabinetmaker; ~tennis n table-tennis; ~tuch n tablecloth; ~zeit f dinnertime; lunch-hour.
Titel m title; ~bild n cover (picture); ~blatt n titlepage. [spruch.)
Toast m toast (a. Trink-
tob|en rage, storm; Kinder: romp; ~süchtig raving mad.

Tochter f daughter.
Tod m death.
Todes|anzeige f obituary (notice), ~opfer n death, casualty; ~strafe f capital punishment, death penalty.
tödlich deadly; fatal.
todmüde dead tired.
Toilette f toilet; lavatory; ~nartikel pl toilet articles pl; ~npapier n toilet-paper.
tolerant tolerant.
toll mad, crazy; ~en romp; 2wut f rabies.
tolpatschig colloq. awkward, clumsy.
Tomate f tomato.
Ton[1] m clay.
Ton[2] m sound; mus. tone, einzelner: note; Betonung: accent, stress; ~abnehmer m pick-up; 2angebend leading; ~art f mus. key; ~band n tape; ~bandgerät n tape recorder.
tönen v/i sound, ring; v/t tint (a. Haar), tone.
Ton|fall m intonation, accent; ~film m sound film.
Tonne f tun; barrel; Regen2: butt; Gewicht, mar. ton.
Topf m pot.
Tor n gate; Fußball etc.: goal; Skisport: gate.
Torf m peat.
töricht foolish, silly.
torkeln reel, stagger.
Tor|latte f crossbar; ~lauf m Skisport: slalom;

⁓linie f goal-line; **⁓pfosten** m gate-post; sp. goal-post; **⁓schütze** m scorer.

Torte f fancy cake, layer-cake.

Torwart m goalkeeper.

tosen roar.

tot dead (a. fig.); **⁓er Punkt** fig. deadlock.

total total, complete.

Tote m od. f dead man od. woman; (dead) body, corpse; **die ⁓n** pl the dead pl.

töten kill; murder.

Totenschein m death certificate.   [pools pl.]

Toto m, colloq. n football]

Totschlag m manslaughter, homicide; **2en** kill.

toupieren back-comb.

Tour f tour (durch of).

Tourist m tourist; **⁓enklasse** f tourist class; **⁓in** f tourist.

Tournee f tour.

traben trot.   [form.]

Tracht f costume; uni-f

trächtig with young, pregnant.

Tradition f tradition.

Trag|bahre f stretcher; **2bar** portable; Kleidung: wearable; fig. bearable.

träge lazy, indolent.

tragen carry; Kleidung: wear; stützen: support; Früchte: bear (a. fig.).

Träger m carrier; Gepäck2: porter; (shoulder-)strap; tech. support, girder.

Tragfläche f aer. wing.

trag|isch tragic; **2ödie** f tragedy.

Tragtüte f carrier bag.

Train|er m trainer; coach; **⁓ing** n training; **⁓ingsanzug** m track suit.

Traktor m tractor.

trampeln trample, stamp.

Träne f tear; **2n** water.

tränken water; et.: soak.

Transfusion f transfusion.

Transistorgerät n transistor set.

transitiv gr. transitive.

Transport m transport(ation), conveyance, carriage; **2ieren** transport, convey, carry.

Traube f bunch of grapes; Beere: grape; **⁓nsaft** m grape-juice; **⁓nzucker** m grape-sugar, glucose, dextrose.

trauen marry; trust (j-m s.o.); **sich** ⁓ dare.

Trauer f sorrow; mourning; **⁓feier** f obsequies pl; **⁓kleidung** f mourning; **2n** mourn (um for); **⁓spiel** n tragedy.

Traum m dream.

traurig sad.

Trau|ring m wedding-ring; **⁓schein** m marriage certificate od. lines pl; **⁓ung** f marriage, wedding; **⁓zeuge** m witness to a marriage.

treff|en hit; strike; begegnen: meet; Vorkehrungen: take; **nicht ⁓en** miss; **e-e Entscheidung ⁓en** come to a decision; **2en** n meeting; ♤**punkt** m meeting-place.

treib|en v/t drive; drift; *Knospen:* put forth; *fig.* impel, urge; v/i drive; drift; *im Wasser:* float; *bot.* shoot; ♤**haus** n hothouse; ♤**riemen** m driving-belt; ♤**stoff** m s. **Kraftstoff.**

trenn|en separate; *abtrennen:* sever; *teleph.* cut off, disconnect; **sich ♤en** separate, part; ♤**ung** f separation; disconnection; ♤**wand** f partition.

Treppe f staircase, (e–e **e**) flight of) stairs pl.

Treppen|absatz m landing; **♤geländer** n banisters pl; **♤haus** n staircase; **♤stufe** f stair, step.

Tresor m safe; strong-room. [on); kick.)

treten tread, step (**auf ♤**)

treu faithful; loyal; ♤**e** f faithfulness; loyalty, **♤los** faithless; disloyal.

Tribüne f platform; *sp.* grandstand.

Trichter m funnel; crater.

Trick m trick.

Trieb m *bot.* sprout, (new) shoot; *Natur♤:* instinct; (sexual) urge; **♤kraft** f motive power; *fig.* driving force; **♤wagen** m railcar. [shirt.)

Trikot n tights pl; (e-s **)**

trink|bar drinkable; ♤**becher** m drinking-cup; **♤en** drink; **♤en auf** drink (to); toast; ♤**er** m drinker; ♤**geld** n tip; ♤**spruch** m

toast; ♤**wasser** n drinking-water.

trippeln trip.

Tritt m tread, step; *Fuß♤:* kick; **♤brett** n running-board.

Triumph m triumph; ♤**ieren** triumph.

trocken dry (*a. Wein*); *Boden:* arid; ♤**haube** f (hair-)dryer; ♤**heit** f dryness; aridity; **♤legen** drain; *Baby:* change (the napkins od. Am. diapers); ♤**obst** n dried fruit.

trocknen dry.

Troddel f tassel.

trödeln colloq. dawdle.

Trog m trough.

Trommel f drum; *tech. a.* cylinder; ♤**fell** n *anat.* eardrum; ♤**n** drum.

Trompete f trumpet.

tropfen drop, drip; ♤ m drop.

tropisch tropical.

Trost m comfort, consolation.

trösten console, comfort.

trostlos disconsolate; *Gegend etc.:* desolate; *fig.* wretched.

Trottel m colloq. idiot.

trotten colloq. trot.

trotz in spite of, despite; ♤ m defiance; **♤dem** nevertheless; **♤ig** defiant; sulky.

trüb(e) muddy; *Licht, Augen:* dim; *Farbe, Wetter:* dull.

Trubel m bustle.

trübsinnig gloomy.

trügerisch treacherous.

Truhe f chest.

Trümmer pl ruins pl; *Schutt*: debris sg; *Unfall*: wreckage sg. ((card).)

Trumpf m *Karten*: trump.

Trunkenheit f drunkenness, intoxication; **~ am Steuer** drunken driving.

Trupp m troop, gang; **~e** f troop; *thea.* company.

Truthahn m turkey(-cock).

Tschechoslowak|e m Czechoslovak; **~isch** Czechoslovak. (losis.)

Tuberkulose f tubercu-(losis.)

Tuch n cloth; s. **Hals-, Kopf-, Staubtuch.**

tüchtig clever, good; *fähig*: efficient; capable.

tückisch treacherous; malicious, spiteful.

Tugend f virtue.

Tulpe f tulip.

Tumor m tumo(u)r.

Tümpel m pool.

Tumult m tumult, uproar.

tun do; make; *wohin* ~: put; **zu ~ haben** be busy; **so ~, als ob** pretend to.

Tunke f sauce; **2n** dip, steep.

Tunnel m tunnel.

tupfen dab; spot, dot; **2** m dot, spot.

Tür f door.

Turbine f turbine.

Türk|e m Turk; **2isch** Turkish.

Türklinke f doorhandle.

Turm m tower; *Kirch*2: a. steeple; **~spitze** f spire; **~springen** n high-diving.

Turn|anzug m gym-dress; **2en** do gymnastics; **~er** m gymnast; **~halle** f gym (-nasium).

Turnier n tournament.

Turn|schuh m gym-shoe; **~verein** m gymnastic od. athletic club.

Tür|rahmen m door-case, door-frame; **~schild** n door-plate.

Tusche f India(n) ink; **2ln** whisper.

Tüte f (paper-)bag.

Typ m type; *tech.* a. model.

Typhus m typhoid (fever).

typisch typical (für of).

Tyrann m tyrant; **2isieren** tyrannize (over), bully.

U

U-Bahn f s. **Untergrundbahn.**

übel adj evil, bad; **mir ist ~** I am od. feel sick; adv ill, badly; **2** n evil; **2keit** f sickness, nausea; **~nehmen** take s.th. ill od. amiss. [ti|se, Amer. -ce.]

üben exercise; (ein) ~: prac-

über over, above; *e-n Fluß etc.*: across; *reisen* ~: via, by way of; more than; **sprechen ~** talk about od. of; **nachdenken ~** think about; **schreiben ~** write on; **~all** everywhere.

über|anstrengen overstrain (sich o.s.); **~bie-**

ten fig. beat, surpass.
Überblick m survey (über of); ˷en overlook, survey.
über|bringen deliver; ˷dauern outlast, outlive; ˷drüssig weary od. sick (gen of); ˷eilt precipitate, rash.
übereinander one upon the other; ˷schlagen: **die Beine** ˷ cross one's legs.
überein|kommen agree; ˷stimmen: ˷ (mit) Person: agree (with); 2˷correspond (with, to); 2˷stimmung f agreement; correspondence.
überfahr|en v/i cross; v/t run over; Signal: run; 2t f passage; Fluß: crossing.
Überfall m hold-up; assault; 2en hold up; assault.
überfällig overdue.
Überfallkommando n flying (Am. riot) squad.
über|fliegen fly over od. across; fig. glance over; ˷fließen overflow; 2fluß m abundance, superfluity; ˷flüssig superfluous; ˷fluten overflow, flood.
überführ|en transport, convey; Verbrecher: convict (gen of); 2ung f overpass.
überfüllt crammed; mit Menschen: overcrowded.
Übergang m crossing; fig. transition; ˷zeit f period of transition.
über|geben deliver, hand

over; mil. surrender; **sich** ˷geben vomit, be sick; ˷gehen in pass into; 2gewicht n overweight; ˷greifen: ˷ auf spread to; ˷handnehmen increase, be rampant; ˷hängen v/i overhang; v/t s. **umhängen**; ˷haupt: wenn ˷ if at all; ˷ nicht not at all; ˷ kein no ... whatever; ˷heblich presumptuous, arrogant.
überhol|en overtake, pass; ausbessern: overhaul; ˷t outmoded, out of date; ˷verbot n no overtaking.
über|kleben paste over; ˷kochen boil over; ˷lassen: j-m et. ˷ let s.o. have s.th.; fig. leave s.th. to s.o.; ˷lasten overload; fig. overburden; ˷laufen run over, Kochendes: boil over; mil. desert (zu to); adj overcrowded.
überleben survive; 2de m, f survivor.
überleg|en (sich) ˷ consider, think about; ˷ es sich anders ˷ change one's mind; ˷en adj superior (dat to; an in); 2ung f consideration, reflection.
Über|lieferung f tradition; 2listen outwit; 2mäßig immoderate; 2morgen the day after tomorrow; 2müde overtired; 2mütig wanton, frolicsome; 2nächst the next but one; 2nächste Woche the week after next.

übernacht|en stay overnight; **2ung** /night's lodging; **2ung und Frühstück** bed and breakfast.
über|natürlich supernatural; **~nehmen** take over; *Verantwortung:* assume; *Führung:* take; **~prüfen** check; *j-n:* screen; **~queren** cross; **~ragen** tower over; *fig.* tower above.
überrasch|en surprise; *ertappen:* catch (**bei** at, in); **~end** surprising, unexpected; **2ung** /surprise.
über|reden persuade; **~reichen** present; **2reste** *pl* remains *pl;* **~rumpeln** (take by) surprise.
Überschallgeschwindigkeit /supersonic speed.
über|schätzen overrate; **~schlagen** *Seiten:* skip; *Kosten:* make a rough estimate of); *sich* **~schlagen** tumble over; *Wagen:* turn over; *Stimme:* become high-pitched; **~schlagen** *adj* lukewarm, tepid; **~schneiden:** *sich* **~**overlap (*a. fig.*); **~schreiten** cross; *fig.* transgress; *Geschwindigkeit, Anweisungen:* exceed; **2schrift** /heading, title; headline; **2schuß** *m* surplus; **2schwemmung** /flood(ing).
Übersee... oversea(s).
übersehen overlook(*a. fig.*).
übersetz|en translate (**in** into); **2er** *m* translator; **2ung** /translation.

Übersicht /survey (**über** of); summary; **2lich** clear.
über|siedeln remove (**nach** to); **~springen** jump, clear; *Seite etc.:* skip; **~stehen** *v/i* jut out, project; *v/t Unglück:* survive; *Krankheit:* get over; **~steigen** climb over; *fig.* exceed; **~stimmen** outvote.
Überstunden *pl* overtime *sg;* **~ machen** work overtime.
überstürz|en rush, hurry; **~t** precipitate, rash.
übertrag|bar transferable; *econ.* negotiable; *med.* communicable; **~en** *Blut:* transfuse; *tech., med., Rundfunk:* transmit; *Rundfunk:* broadcast; **im Fernsehen ~en** televise; *adj* figurative.
übertreffen *j-n:* excel; *j-n, et.:* surpass, exceed.
übertreib|en exaggerate; **2ung** /exaggeration.
über|treten transgress, violate; **~trieben** exaggerated; **2tritt** *m* going over (**zu** to); *eccl.* conversion; **~völkert** overpopulated; **~vorteilen** overreach, do; **~wachen** supervise, control; *polizeilich:* shadow.
überwältigen overcome, overwhelm; **~d** overwhelming.
überweis|en *Geld:* remit (**an** to); **2ung** /remittance.

über|winden overcome; **sich ~winden zu** bring o.s. to; **2zahl** f: **in der ~** superior in numbers.

überzeug|en convince (**von** of); **2ung** f conviction.

überziehen put *s.th.* on; cover; *Bett:* put clean sheets on; *Konto:* overdraw.

üblich usual, customary.

U-Boot n submarine, *Deutschland:* a. U-boat.

übrig left, remaining; **die ~en** pl the others pl, the rest sg; **~bleiben** be left, remain; **~ens** by the way; **~lassen** leave.

Übung f exercise, practice; **~shang** m nursery slope.

Ufer n shore; *Fluß:* bank; **am** od. **ans ~** ashore.

Uhr m clock; *Armband2:* watch; **um vier ~** at four o'clock; **~armband** n watch-strap; **~macher** m watch-maker; **~zeiger** m hand.

Uhu m eagle-owl.

ulkig funny.

Ulme f elm.

um round, about; **~ seinetwillen** for his sake; **~ zu** (in order) to; *s.* **besser.**

um|ändern change, alter; **~armen (sich)** embrace; **~bauen** rebuild, reconstruct; **~blättern** turn over; **~bringen** kill (**sich** o.s.); **~buchen** rebook (**auf den ... for the...**).

umdreh|en turn over; **~ sich** turn round; **2ung** f tech. revolution.

umfallen fall down.

Umfang m circumference; *Leib, Stamm:* girth; *fig.* extent; **2reich** extensive.

um|formen remodel, transform (*a. electr.*); **2frage** f inquiry; poll.

Umgang m company; **~ haben mit** associate with; **~sformen** pl manners pl; **~ssprache** f colloquial speech.

umgeb|en surround; *adj* surrounded (**von** with, by); **2ung** f *Stadt:* environs pl; *Milieu:* surroundings pl, environment.

umgeh|en: ~ mit use; *j-m:* deal with; **2ungsstraße** f bypass, ringroad.

um|gekehrt *adj* reverse, inverted; *adv* vice versa; **~graben** dig up; **2hang** m wrap, cape; **~hängen: sich den Mantel ~** put one's coat round one's shoulders.

umher about, (a)round; **~blicken** look about (one).

um|kehren return, turn back; **~kippen** upset, tilt (*v/i a.* over); **~klammern** clasp; *Boxen:* clinch; **~klappen** turn down, fold (back).

Umkleide|kabine f dressing-cubicle; **2n: sich ~** change. **[(bei** in).**]**

umkommen be killed

Umkreis m: im ~ von within a radius of.

Umlauf m circulation; ~bahn f orbit.

umleit|en divert; 2ung f diversion, detour.

um|liegend surrounding; ~pflügen plough, Am. plow.

umrech|nen convert; 2nungskurs m rate of exchange.

um|ringen surround; ~riß m outline; ~rühren stir; 2satz m econ.: turnover; Absatz: sales pl; Einnahme(n): return(s pl); ~schalten switch (over); ~schauen: sich ~ s. umsehen.

Umschlag m Brief: envelope; cover, wrapper; Buch: jacket; Hose: turn-up, Am. a. cuff; med. feuchter ~: compress; Brei 2: poultice; 2en v/t econ.: turn up; Kragen: turn down; v/i turn over, upset; Boot: capsize; upset; Wetter, fig.: change.

um|schnallen buckle on; 2schrift f Phonetik: transcription; ~schütten pour into another vessel; decant; verschütten: spill; 2schwung m Gesinnung: revulsion; Wetter etc.: change; ~sehen: sich ~ look back; look round; look about (nach for); ~sein colloq. Zeit: be up; Ferien etc.: be over.

umsonst gratis, free of charge; vergebens: in vain.

Umstand m circumstance; unter diesen Umständen under the circumstances; in anderen Umständen sein be expecting.

umständlich long-winded, tedious; Methode a.: roundabout; Person: fussy.

um|steigen change; ~stellen shift about od. round; Währung, Produktion: convert; umzingeln: surround; sich ~ stellen adapt od. accommodate o.s. (auf to); ~stimmen: j-n ~ change s.o.'s mind; ~stoßen knock over; upset (a. Plan); 2sturz m subversion, overthrow; ~stürzen upset, overturn.

Umtausch m exchange; in andere Währung: conversion; 2en exchange; convert.

um|wandeln transform, change; ~wechseln change; ~weg m detour.

Umwelt f environment; ~verschmutzung f environmental pollution.

um|werfen upset, overturn; ~wickeln wind round; ~ziehen (re)move (nach to); sich ~ziehen change; ~zingeln surround; 2zug m procession; removal, move.

unabhängig independent; 2keit f independence.

un|absichtlich unintentional; ~achtsam careless.

unan|gebracht inappropriate; *pred a.* out of place; **~genehm** unpleasant; *peinlich:* awkward; **un-nehmlichkeiten** *pl* trouble *sg*, inconvenience *sg;* **~sehnlich** unsightly; *unscheinbar:* plain; **~ständig** indecent, *stärker:* obscene. **un|appetitlich** unappetizing; distasteful; **~artig** naughty.

unauf|fällig inconspicuous; **~hörlich** incessant, continuous; **~merksam** inattentive.

unausstehlich unbearable, insufferable.

unbarmherzig merciless, unmerciful.

unbe|absichtigt unintentional; **~achtet** unnoticed; **~baut** *agr.* untilled; *Gelände:* undeveloped; **~deutend** insignificant; **~dingt** by all means; **~fahrbar** impracticable, impassable; **~friedigend** unsatisfactory; **~friedigt** dissatisfied; disappointed; **~fugt** unauthorized; incompetent; **~greiflich** incomprehensible; **~grenzt** unlimited, boundless; **~gründet** unfounded; **~haglich** uneasy, uncomfortable; **~herrscht** unrestrained, lacking in self-control; **~holfen** clumsy, awkward; **~kannt** unknown; **~kümmert** unconcerned; **~liebt** unpop-

ular; **~merkt** unnoticed; **~quem** uncomfortable; *lästig:* inconvenient; **~rührt** untouched; **~schränkt** unrestricted; absolute; **~schreiblich** indescribable; **~ständig** unsettled; **~stechlich** incorruptible; **~stimmt** indeterminate, indefinite; *unsicher:* uncertain; *Gefühl:* vague; **~teiligt** unconcerned; indifferent; not involved; **~wacht** unguarded; **~waffnet** unarmed; **~weglich** motionless; **~wohnt** uninhabited; *Gebäude:* unoccupied, vacant; **~wußt** unconscious; **~zahlbar** priceless, invaluable; **~zahlt** unpaid.

unbrauchbar useless.

und so; **na ~?** so what?

un|dankbar ungrateful; *Aufgabe:* thankless; **~deutlich** indistinct; **~dicht** leaky.

undurch|dringlich impenetrable; *Gesicht:* impassive; **~lässig** impervious, impermeable; **~sichtig** opaque; *fig.* mysterious.

un|eben uneven; *Weg:* bumpy; **~echt** false; *Schmuck:* imitation, counterfeit; *Bild etc.:* fake; **~ehelich** illegitimate; **~empfindlich** insensitive **(gegen** to); **~endlich** endless, infinite.

unent|behrlich indispensable; ~geltlich gratuitous, gratis; free (of charge); ~schieden undecided; ~schieden unenden sp. end in a draw od. tie; ~schlossen irresolute.

uner|bittlich inexorable; ~fahren inexperienced; ~freulich unpleasant; ~hört unheard-of, outrageous; ~kannt unrecognized; ~klärlich inexplicable; ~laubt unauthorized; verboten: illegal; ~meßlich immense; ~müdlich indefatigable; Anstrengungen: untiring; ~reicht unrival(l)ed, unequal(l)ed; ~schöpflich inexhaustible; ~schrokken intrepid, fearless; ~setzlich irreplaceable; ~träglich intolerable; ~wartet unexpected; ~wünscht unwanted.

unfähig incapable (zu of ger); unable; inefficient. Unfall m accident.

un|faßbar inconceivable; ~förmig shapeless, misshapen; ~frankiert unstamped; ~freiwillig involuntary; Humor: unconscious; ~freundlich unfriendly, unkind; Klima, Wetter: disagreeable; Zimmer, Tag: cheerless; ~fruchtbar unfruitful, sterile; ~fug m mischief.

Ungar m Hungarian; 2isch Hungarian.

unge|bildet uneducated;

~bräuchlich unusual; ~bührlich improper; ~bunden fig. free.

Ungeduld f impatience; 2ig impatient.

unge|eignet unfit; Person: a. unqualified; Augenblick: inopportune; ~fähr adj approximate, rough; adv approximately, roughly, about; ~fährlich harmless; ~fällig disobliging; ~heizt cold.

ungeheuer vast, huge, enormous; 2 n monster.

unge|hindert unhindered, free; ~hörig improper; ~horsam disobedient; ~kürzt unabridged; ~legen inconvenient; ~lenk awkward, clumsy; ~lernt unskilled; ~mütlich uncomfortable; ~nau inaccurate, inexact; ~nießbar uneatable; undrinkable; colloq. Person: unbearable; ~nügend insufficient; ~pflegt unkempt; ~rade odd.

ungerecht unjust (gegen to); 2igkeit f injustice.

ungern unwillingly, grudgingly.

unge|schickt awkward, clumsy; ~schützt unprotected; ~setzlich illegal, unlawful; ~stört undisturbed, uninterrupted; ~sund unhealthy, unwholesome.

ungewiß uncertain; j-n im ungewissen lassen keep s.o. in suspense; 2-

heit f uncertainty; *Spannung:* suspense.

unge|wöhnlich unusual, uncommon; **2ziefer** n vermin; **~zogen** rude, uncivil; *Kind:* naughty; **~zwungen** free (and easy).

ungläubig incredulous.

unglaub|lich incredible; **~würdig** untrustworthy; incredible.

ungleich unequal, different; **~mäßig** uneven; irregular.

Unglück n misfortune; *schweres:* calamity, disaster; *bad od.* ill luck; **2lich** unfortunate, unlucky; unhappy; **2licherweise** unfortunately; **~sfall** m misadventure; accident.

un|gültig invalid; *Geld:* not current; **~günstig** unfavo(u)rable; disadvantageous; **~handlich** unwieldy, bulky; **~heilbar** incurable; **~heimlich** uncanny; *fig.* tremendous; **~höflich** impolite, uncivil; **~hörbar** inaudible; **~hygienisch** insanitary.

Uniform f uniform.

uninteressant uninteresting, boring.

Union f union.

Universität f university.

Universum n universe.

unkennt|lich unrecognizable; **2nis** f ignorance.

un|klar not clear; obscure; *Antwort:* vague; **2kosten** pl costs pl, expenses pl; **2-**

kraut n weed; **~leserlich** illegible; **~logisch** illogical; **~lösbar** insoluble; **~manierlich** unmannerly; **~mäßig** immoderate; *Trinken:* intemperate; **2menge** f enormous *od.* vast quantity.

Unmensch m monster, brute; **2lich** inhuman, brutal.

un|mißverständlich unmistakable; **~mittelbar** immediate, direct; **~möbliert** unfurnished; **~modern** unfashionable; **~möglich** impossible; **~moralisch** immoral; **~mündig** under age; **~natürlich** unnatural; *geziert:* affected; **~nötig** unnecessary.

unordentlich untidy; **2nung** f disorder, mess.

un|parteiisch impartial, unbias(s)ed; **~passend** unsuitable; improper; *unangebracht:* inappropriate; **~passierbar** impassable; **~päßlich** indisposed, unwell; **~persönlich** impersonal; **~praktisch** unpractical; **~pünktlich** unpunctual; **~rasiert** unshaved, unshaven.

unrecht wrong; **~haben** be wrong; **2** n: **zu ~** wrongly; *j-m* **~tun** wrong s.o.; **~mäßig** unlawful.

un|regelmäßig irregular; **~reif** unripe, immature.

Unruh|e f restlessness; *pol.* unrest; *fig.:* uneasiness;

alarm; **~en** pl disturbances pl, riots pl; **2ig** restless; *Meer:* rough; *fig.* uneasy.

uns (to) us; **~ (selbst)** ourselves.

un|sachlich not objective; irrelevant; **~sauber** dirty; *fig. a.* unfair; **~schädlich** harmless; **~scharf** blurred; **~schätzbar** invaluable; **~scheinbar** plain; **~schicklich** improper, indecent; **~schlüssig** irresolute. [**2ig** innocent.⟩

Unschuld f innocence;⟩ **unselbständig** dependent (on others).

unser our; ours.

un|sicher unsteady; *gefährlich:* insecure; uncertain; **~sichtbar** invisible; **2inn** m nonsense; **~sittlich** indecent; **~sozial** unsocial; **~sterblich** immortal; **2timmigkeit** f discrepancy; *Meinungsverschiedenheit:* dissension; **~sympathisch** disagreeable; **er ist mir ~sympathisch** I don't like him; **~tätig** inactive; idle.

unten below; downstairs; **von oben bis ~** from top to bottom.

unter prp below, under; *zwischen:* among; *weniger als:* less than; *adj* lower.

Unter|arm m forearm; **~bewußtsein** n: **im ~** subconsciously; **2bieten** Rekord: lower, beat; **2binden** stop.

unterbrech|en interrupt;

Reise: break, *Am. a.* stop over; **2ung** f interruption; break, *Am. a.* stopover.

unter|bringen place; accommodate, lodge; **~dessen** (in the) meantime, meanwhile; **~drücken** suppress; *unterjochen:* oppress; **~einander** one beneath the other; among one another; **~entwickelt** underdeveloped.

unterernähr|t underfed, undernourished; **2ung** f malnutrition.

Unter|führung f subway, *Am.* underpass; **~gang** m *ast.* setting; *Schiff:* sinking; *fig.* ruin; **~gebene** m, f inferior, subordinate; **2gehen** *ast.* set; sink.

Untergrund m subsoil; *pol.* underground; **~bahn** f underground (railway), *London:* tube, *Am.* subway.

unterhalb below, underneath.

Unterhalt m maintenance; *Lebens2:* subsistence, livelihood; **2en** maintain; support; *zerstreuen etc.:* entertain, amuse; **sich 2en** converse, talk; **sich gut 2en** enjoy o.s.; **~ung** f conversation, talk; entertainment.

Unter|hemd n vest, undershirt; **~holz** n undergrowth; **~hose** f (e-e a pair of) drawers pl od. pants pl; **2irdisch** underground; **~kiefer** m lower jaw; **~kunft** f accommodation, lodging; **~lage** f base; _Schreibunterlage:_ pad; **~lagen** pl documents pl; **2lassen** omit, neglect; **2leib** m abdomen, belly; **2liegen** (_dat_) be defeated (by), _sp. a._ lose (to); **~lippe** f lower lip; **~mieter** m lodger.

unternehm|en undertake; **2en** n enterprise; _econ._ business; **2er** m entrepreneur; _Werkvertrag:_ contractor; _Arbeitgeber:_ employer; industrialist; **~ungslustig** enterprising.

Unter|offizier m noncommissioned officer; **~redung** f conversation, interview.

Unterricht m instruction, lessons pl; **2en** instruct, teach; **2en von** inform _s.o._ of; **~sstunde** f lesson, period.

Unter|rock m slip; **2schätzen** underestimate; **2scheiden** distinguish; **sich 2scheiden** differ; **~schenkel** m shank.

Unterschied m difference; **2lich** different; varying.

unterschlag|en embezzle; **2ung** f embezzlement.

unter|schreiben sign; **2schrift** f signature; **2seeboot** n s. **U-Boot;** **2setzt** squat, stocky; **~st** lowest, undermost; **2stehen: sich ~** dare; **~stellen** _Auto:_ garage, park; **2stellen** take shelter

(**vor** from); **~streichen** underline.

unterstüt|zen support; **2zung** f support; assistance, aid; _Beihilfe:_ relief.

untersuch|en inquire into, investigate (_a. jur._); **prüfen:** examine (_a. med._); explore; **2ung** f inquiry (_gen_ into), investigation (_a. jur._); examination (_a. med._); exploration; **2ungshaft** f detention (on remand).

Unter|tasse f saucer; **2tauchen** dive; duck (_a. v/t_); _fig._ disappear; **~teil** n, m lower part; **~titel** m subtitle; _Film: a._ caption; **~wäsche** f underclothes pl, underclothing, underwear; **2wegs** on the _od._ one's way; **2werfen** subject (_dat_ to); **sich 2werfen** submit (_dat_ to); **2würfig** subservient; **2zeichnen** sign; **2ziehen** put on underneath; **sich e-r Operation 2ziehen** undergo an operation.

un|tragbar unbearable; **~trennbar** inseparable; **~treu** unfaithful; **~tröstlich** inconsolable; **2tugend** f vice.

unüber|legt inconsiderate, thoughtless; **~sichtlich** unclear, obscure; _Kurve:_ blind; **~windlich** insurmountable.

ununterbrochen uninterrupted; _unaufhörlich:_ incessant.

unver|ändert unchanged; ~antwortlich irresponsible; ~besserlich incorrigible; ~bindlich not binding; Frage: non-committal; ~daulich indigestible; ~dient undeserved; ~einbar incompatible; ~geßlich unforgettable; ~gleichlich incomparable; ~heiratet unmarried, single; ~käuflich not for sale; ~letzt uninjured, unhurt; ~meidlich inevitable; ~mutet unexpected; ~nünftig unreasonable.

unverschämt impudent; 2heit f impudence, cheek. unver|ständlich unintelligible; unbegreiflich: incomprehensible; ~zeihlich unpardonable; ~züglich immediate, instant.

unvoll|endet unfinished; ~kommen imperfect; ~ständig incomplete.

unvor|bereitet unprepared; ~eingenommen unprejudiced; ~hergesehen unforeseen; ~sichtig incautious; unklug: imprudent; ~stellbar unimaginable; ~teilhaft unprofitable; unbecoming.

unwahr untrue; 2heit f untruth; ~scheinlich improbable, unlikely. un|weit: ~ gen od. von not far from; ~wesentlich immaterial (für to); 2wetter n tempest; violent thunderstorm; ~wichtig unimportant.

unwider|ruflich irrevocable; ~stehlich irresistible. unwiederbringlich irretrievable. Unwill|e(n) m indignation; 2ig indignant; unwilling; 2kürlich involuntary. un|wirksam ineffective; ~wirtlich inhospitable; ~wissend ignorant; ~wohl unwell, indisposed; ~würdig unworthy (gen of); ~zählig innumerable. unzer|brechlich unbreakable; ~trennlich inseparable.

Un|zucht f sexual offen|ce, Am. ~se; 2züchtig obscene.

unzufrieden discontented, dissatisfied; 2heit f discontent, dissatisfaction.

unzu|gänglich inaccessible; ~länglich insufficient; ~rechnungsfähig irresponsible; ~sammenhängend incoherent; ~verlässig unreliable.

üppig bot. luxuriant, exuberant; Essen: sumptuous; Figur: voluptuous.

ur|alt very old; 2aufführung f première.

Uran n uranium.

Urenkel m etc. greatgrandson, etc.

Urheber m author.

Urin m urine.

Urkunde f document, deed; certificate.

Urlaub m leave (of absence) (a. mil.); Ferien:

holiday(s *pl*), *bsd. Am.* vacation; **~er** *m* holiday-maker, *Am.* vacationist.

Urne *f* urn.

Ur|sache *f* cause; *Grund:* reason; **keine ~sache!** don't mention it, you are welcome; **~sprung** *m* ori-gin, source; **2sprünglich** original.

Urteil *n* judg(e)ment; *Strafmaß:* sentence; **2en** judge (**über** *j*-n |of| s.o.); **~sspruch** *m* verdict.

Urwald *m* prim(a)eval *od.* virgin forest.

V

Vakuum *n* vacuum.

Vanille *f* vanilla.

Varieté *n* variety theatre, music-hall, *Am.* vaude-ville theater.

Vase *f* vase.

Vater *m* father; **~land** *n* mother country.

väterlich fatherly, pater-nal. [Prayer.]

Vaterunser *n* the Lord's

Vegeta|rier *m* vegetarian; **2risch** vegetarian; **~tion** *f* vegetation.

Veilchen *n* violet.

Vene *f* vein.

Ventil *n* valve; *fig.* vent, outlet; **~ation** *f* ventila-tion; **~ator** *m* ventilator, fan.

verabred|en agree upon, arrange; *Ort, Zeit:* appoint, fix; **sich ~en** make an ap-pointment; **2ung** *f* ap-pointment; *colloq.* date.

verab|scheuen abhor, de-test; **~schieden: sich ~ (von)** take leave (of), say good-bye (to).

ver|achten despise; **2acht-lich** contemptible; **2ach-tung** *f* contempt; **~allge-**

meinern generalize; **~al-tet** out of date.

veränder|lich changeable, variable; **~n: (sich)** **~** alter, change; **2ung** *f* change, alteration.

veranlassen cause.

veranstalt|en organize; **2ung** *f* event; *sp.* event, meeting, *Am.* meet.

verantwort|en take the re-sponsibility for; **sich ~en** **für** answer for; **~lich** re-sponsible; **j-n ~lich ma-chen für** hold s.o. respon-sible for; **2ung** *f* responsi-bility; **~ungslos** irrespon-sible.

ver|arbeiten make; pro-cess; *fig.* digest; **~ärgern** vex, annoy.

Verb *n gr.* verb.

Verband *m med.* dressing, bandage; association, union; **~(s)kasten** *m* first-aid box; **~(s)zeug** *n* dress-ing (material), first-aid kit.

ver|bannen banish (*a. fig.*), exile; **~bergen** conceal, hide (**sich** o.s.).

verbesser|n improve; be-richtigen: correct; **2ung** *f* improvement; correction.

verbeug|en *v.refl.* ~ bow (**vor** to); **Qung** *f* bow.

ver|biegen twist; **~bieten** forbid, prohibit; **~billigen** reduce in price, cheapen.

verbind|en *med.* dress, bind up; link (**mit** to), join; connect (*a. teleph.*); *teleph.* put *s.o.* through (**mit** to); **Qung** *f* union; combination; connection, *a.* connexion (*a. teleph., rail., tech.*); *Verkehrsweg:* communication; *chem.* compound; **sich in Qung setzen mit** get in touch with.

ver|blassen fade; **~blüffen** amaze, perplex; **~blühen** fade, wither; **~bluten** bleed to death; **~borgen** hidden.

Verbot *n* prohibition; **~schild** *n* prohibition sign.

Verbrauch *m* consumption (**an** of); **Qen** consume, use up; **~er** *m* consumer; **Qt** *Luft:* stale.

Verbreche|n *n* crime, offen|ce, *Am.* -se; **~r** *m* criminal; **Qrisch** criminal.

verbreite|n: **sich ~** spread; **~rn: sich ~widen**, broaden.

verbrenn|en burn; *Leiche:* cremate; **Qung** *f* burning; cremation; *med.* burn.

ver|bringen spend, pass; **~brühen** scald (**sich** o.s.).

verbünde|n: sich ~ ally o.s. (**mit** to, with); **Qte** *m, f* ally, confederate.

ver|bürgen: sich ~ für

vouch for; **~büßen: e-e Strafe ~** serve a sentence.

Verdacht *m* suspicion.

verdächtig suspicious; **~en** suspect; **Qung** *f* suspicion.

verdamm|en condemn; **~t** damned; *int. colloq.* damn (it)!; **~t kalt** beastly cold.

ver|dampfen evaporate; **~danken: j-m et.** ~ owe s.th. to s.o.

verdau|en digest; **~lich: leicht ~** easy to digest, light; **Qung** *f* digestion; **Qungsstörung** *f* indigestion.

Verdeck *n mot.* hood, top; **Qen** cover; hide.

ver|derben spoil; *Fleisch etc.:* go bad; **sich den Magen ~derben** upset one's stomach; **~deutlichen** make plain *od.* clear; **~dienen** earn; *fig.* merit, deserve.

Verdienst¹ *m* earnings *pl; Gewinn:* gain, profit.

Verdienst² *n* merit.

ver|doppeln: (sich) double; **~dorben** *Fleisch:* tainted; *Magen:* upset; *fig.* corrupt; **~drängen** displace; *psych.* repress; **~drehen** distort, twist (*a. fig.*); *Augen:* roll; **~dreifachen: (sich)** triple; **~dunkeln** darken (*a.* sich); **~dünnen** dilute; **~dunsten** evaporate; **~dursten** die of thirst.

verehr|en adore; revere;

eccl. worship; 2er *m* admirer; worship(p)er; 2ung *f* adoration; reverence; worship. [*gen:* swear.]
vereidigen swear in; *Zeu-*
Verein *m* society, association; club.
vereinbar|en agree upon, arrange; 2ung *f* agreement, arrangement.
vereinfachen simplify.
vereinig|en: (sich) ~ unite; 2ung *f* union; society, association.
ver|engen: (sich) ~ narrow; **~erben** leave; *biol.* transmit.
verfahren proceed; **sich ~** lose one's way; 2 *n* procedure; *jur.* proceedings *pl;* *tech.* process.
Verfall *m* decay (*a. fig.*); 2en decay (*a. fig.*); *Haus etc.: ~* dilapidate; *ablaufen:* expire. [colo(u).r.]
verfärben: sich ~ change
verfass|en write; 2er *m* author; 2ung *f* condition; *pol.* constitution.
verfaulen rot, decay.
verfilm|en film; 2ung *f* film *od.* screen adaptation.
verfluch|en curse; **~t** damned; *int. colloq.* damn (it)!
verfolge|n pursue (*a. fig.*); *bsd. pol.* persecute; *Spuren:* follow; 2er *m* pursuer.
verfrüht premature.
verfüg|bar available; **~en** decree, order; **~en über** have at one's disposal; 2ung *f* decree, order; dis-

posal; **j-m zur 2ung stehen** *od.* **stellen** be *od.* place at s.o.'s disposal.
verführ|en seduce; **~risch** seductive; tempting.
vergangen gone, past; 2heit *f* past; *gr.* past (tense).
Vergaser *m* carburet(t)or.
vergeb|en *Preis:* award; *Auftrag:* place; forgive; **~lich** *adj* vain; *adv* in vain.
vergehen pass; 2 *n* offen|ce, *Am.* -se.
ver|gessen forget; leave; **~geßlich** forgetful; **~geuden** dissipate, squander.
vergewalti|gen rape; 2gung *f* rape.
ver|gewissern: sich ~ make sure (*gen* of); **~gießen** shed; *verschütten:* spill.
vergift|en poison (*a. fig.*); 2ung *f* poisoning.
Vergleich *m* comparison; *jur.* compromise; 2bar comparable; 2en compare.
vergnüg|en amuse; **sich ~en** amuse *od.* enjoy o.s.; 2en *n* pleasure, enjoyment; **~t** merry, gay.
ver|golden gild; **~graben** bury; **~griffen** *Ware:* sold out; *Buch:* out of print.
vergrößer|n enlarge (*a. phot.*); *opt.* magnify; **sich ~n** increase; 2ung *f phot.* enlargement; 2ungsglas *n* magnifying glass.
verhaft|en arrest; 2ung *f* arrest.
verhalten: sich ~ *Sache:*

be; *Person:* behave; ⚥ *n* behavio(u)r, conduct.

Verhältnis *n* proportion, rate, relation; *colloq.* love-affair; **~se** *pl* conditions *pl*, circumstances *pl*; *Mittel:* means *pl*; **~mäßig** comparatively, relatively; proportionally.

verhand|eln negotiate; ⚥**~lung** *f* negotiation; *jur.* trial.

ver|hängnisvoll fatal, disastrous; **~härmt** care-worn; **~haßt** hated; *Sache:* hateful, odious; **~hauen** *colloq.* thrash; **~heerend** disastrous; **~heilen** heal (up); **~heimlichen** hide, conceal; **~heiraten: sich ~** marry; **~hindern** prevent; **~höhnen** ridicule, mock.

Verhör *n* interrogation, examination; **~en** examine, interrogate; **sich ⚥en** hear wrong.

ver|hungern starve; *Um-gang, Geschlechts⚥:* inter-course; ⚥**en** *Bus etc.:* run; ⚥**en** *mit* associate *od.* mix with.

ver|hungern starve; **~hüten** prevent; **~irren: sich ~** lose one's way; **~jagen** drive away.

Verkauf *m* sale; ⚥**en** sell; **zu ⚥en** for sale.

Verkäuf|er *m* shop-assistant, *Am.* (sales)clerk, salesman; **~erin** *f* shop-assistant, *Am.* (sales)clerk, saleswoman; ⚥**lich** for sale.

Verkehr *m* traffic; *Um-gang, Geschlechts⚥:* inter-course; ⚥**en** *Bus etc.:* run; ⚥**en** *in* frequent; ⚥**en** *mit* associate *od.* mix with.

Verkehrs|ader *f* arterial road; **~ampel** *f* traffic light(s *pl*); **~büro** *n* tourist office; **~hindernis** *n* obstruction; **~insel** *f* traffic island; **~minister** *m* Minister of Transport; **~mittel** *n* (means *pl* of) conveyance *od.* transport, *Am.* transportation; **~polizist** *m* traffic policeman *od.* constable, *Am. a.* traffic cop; **~schild** *n* traffic *od.* road sign; **~stauung** *f,* **~stokkung** *f* traffic block (congestion, jam); **~teilnehmer** *m* road user; **~unfall** *m* traffic accident; **~verein** *m* tourist office; **~vorschrift** *f* traffic regulation; **~zeichen** *n* traffic *od.* road sign.

ver|kehrt inverted, upside down; *fig.* wrong; **~kennen** mistake, misjudge; **~klagen** sue (**auf, wegen** for); **~kleiden** disguise (**sich** o.s.); *tech.* face; **~kommen** decayed; *sittlich:* depraved, corrupt; **~krachen** *colloq.:* **sich ~ mit** fall out with; **~krüppelt** crippled; **~künden** announce; *Urteil:* pronounce; **~kürzen** shorten.

Verlag *m* publishing house, the publishers *pl*.

verlangen demand, require; **~ nach** ask for; ⚥ *n* desire.   [tend.⟩

verlängern lengthen; ex-

Verlängerung *f* lengthening; extension; **~sschnur**

f extension cord; **～swoche**
f extra week.

ver|langsamen slacken,
slow down; **～lassen** leave;
forsake, abandon; **sich ～
lassen auf** rely on; **～läß-
lich** reliable.

Verlauf *m* course; **2en**
Vorgang: go; *Straße etc.:*
run; **sich 2en** lose one's
way; *Menge:* disperse.

verlege|n mislay; transfer,
remove; *Kabel etc.:* lay;
Termin: put off, postpone;
Buch: publish; *adj* embarrassed; **at a loss (um** for);
2nheit *f* embarrassment;
Klemme: difficulty; **2r** *m*
publisher.

ver|leihen lend, *Am. a.*
loan; *gegen Miete:* hire *od.*
let out; *Preis:* award; **～
lernen** unlearn, forget; **～
lesen** read out; *Namen:*
call over; **sich ～lesen** read
wrong.

verletz|en hurt **(sich** o.s.),
injure; *fig. a.* offend; **2te**
m, *f* injured person; **die
2ten** *pl* the injured *pl;*
2ung *f* injury.

verleugnen deny, disown.

verleumd|en slander;
2ung *f* slander, defama-
tion, *jur. a.* libel.

verlieb|en: sich ～ in fall
in love with; **～t** in love **(in**
with); *Blick:* amorous.

verlieren lose; *Blätter etc.:*
shed.

verlob|en: sich ～ become
engaged **(mit** to); **2te** *m*
fiancé; *f* fiancée; **die 2ten**

pl the engaged couple *sg;*
2ung *f* engagement.

ver|lockend tempting; **～
loren** lost; *fig.* forlorn; **～
lorengehen** be lost; **～lo-
sen** raffle; **2lust** *m* loss; **～
machen** bequeath, leave;
2mählung *f* wedding,
marriage; **～mehren** in-
crease; **sich ～mehren** increase; *zo.* multiply; **～
meiden** avoid; **2merk** *m*
note, entry; **～messen**
measure; *Land:* survey;
adj presumptuous; **～mie-
ten** let, rent; *jur.* lease;
Boote etc.: hire (out); **zu
～mieten** on *od.* for hire;
Haus: to (be) let; **～mi-
schen** mix, mingle, blend;
～missen miss; **～mißt**
missing.

vermitt|eln *v/t* procure;
Eindruck etc.: give; *v/i*
mediate **(zwischen** be-
tween); intercede **(bei**
with; **für** for); **2ler** *m*
mediator, go-between; **2-
lung** *f* mediation; intercession; *teleph.* (telephone)
exchange.

Vermögen *n* ability, power; *Besitz:* property; *Geld:*
fortune.

vermut|en suppose, *Am.
a.* guess; **～lich** presumable; **2ung** *f* supposition.

ver|nachlässigen neglect;
～nehmen hear, learn;
jur. examine, interrogate;
～neigen: sich ～ bow
(vor to); **～neinen** deny;
answer in the negative.

vernicht|en destroy; 2ung f destruction.

Ver|nunft f reason; 2nünftig sensible; reasonable (a. Preis).

veröffentlich|en publish; 2ung f publication.

ver|ordnen med. order, prescribe; ~pachten rent, jur. lease.

verpack|en pack (up); wrap up; 2ung f packing; Material: a. wrapping.

ver|passen miss; ~pfänden pawn, pledge; ~pflanzen transplant (a. med.).

verpfleg|en board; feed; 2ung f food; board.

ver|pflichten oblige; engage; sich ~pflichten bind o.s.; ~pfuschen colloq. bungle, botch); ~prügeln colloq. thrash; 2putz m plaster.

Ver|rat m betrayal; pol. treason; 2raten (sich) ~ betray (o.s.), give (o.s.) away; ~räter m traitor.

ver|rechnen: sich ~ miscalculate; fig. make a mistake; ~regnet rainy, wet.

verreis|en go on a journey; ~t away, out of town.

verrenk|en dislocate (sich et. s.th.), luxate; sich den Hals ~en fig. crane one's neck, rubberneck; 2ung f dislocation, luxation.

ver|riegeln bolt, bar; ~ringern diminish, lessen (a. sich); Geschwindigkeit: slow up od. down; ~rosten rust.

verrück|en move, shift; ~t mad, crazy (a. fig.: nach about); 2te m lunatic, madman; f lunatic, madwoman.

verrutschen slip.

Vers m verse.

versage|n v/t deny (j-m et. s.o. s.th.); v/i fail; break down; 2n n, 2r m failure.

versalzen oversalt.

versamm|eln assemble; sich ~eln assemble, meet; 2ung f assembly, meeting.

Versand m dispatch, Am. a. shipment; Post: posting; ~geschäft n, ~haus n mail-order business od. house.

ver|säumen Pflicht: neglect; verpassen: miss; Zeit: lose; ~schaffen procure, get; sich ~schaffen obtain, get; Geld: raise; ~schärfen ~ get worse; ~schenken give away; ~schicken send (away), dispatch, forward; ~schieben zeitlich: put off, postpone.

verschieden different; ~artig various.

ver|schiffen ship; ~schimmeln get mo(u)ldy, Am. a. mo(u)ld; ~schlafen oversleep (v/i); adj sleepy, drowsy; 2schlag m shed; ~schlagen adj cunning; ~schlechtern deteriorate, make worse; sich ~schlechtern deteriorate, get worse; ~schließen lock;

Haus: lock up; **~schlimmern** make worse; **sich ~schlimmern** get worse; **~schlingen** devour(*a.fig.*); **~schlossen** closed, shut; *fig.* reserved; **~schlucken** swallow; **sich ~schlucken** choke; **℈schluß** *m* fastener; *Pfropfen:* plug; *Stöpsel:* stopper; *phot.* shutter; **~schmelzen** *v/i* melt, blend; *v/t tech.* fuse (*a. fig.*); *fig.* merge (**mit** in); **~schmerzen** get over (the loss of); **~schmieren** smear; blur; **~schmutzen** soil, dirty; *Luft, Wasser:* pollute; **~schneit** snow-covered; *Berggipfel:* *a.* snow-capped; **~schnüren** tie up; **~schollen** missing; **~schonen** spare; **~schreiben** *med.* prescribe (**gegen** for); **sich ~schreiben** make a slip of the pen; **~schrotten** scrap; **~schuldet** indebted, in debt; **~schütten** spill; *j-n:* bury alive; **~schweigen** conceal; **~schwenden** waste, squander; **~schwiegen** discreet; **~schwimmen** become blurred; **~schwinden** disappear, vanish; **~schwommen** vague (*a. fig.*); *phot.* blurred.

Verschwör|er *m* conspirator; **~ung** *f* conspiracy, plot.

versehen *Haushalt:* look after; **mit** *et.* **~** provide with; **sich ~** make a mistake; **℈** *n* oversight, mistake, slip; **aus ℈ =** **~tlich** by mistake.

Versehrte *m, f* disabled person.

ver|senden send, dispatch, forward; **~sengen** singe; scorch; **~setzen** shift, move; *Beamte:* transfer; *Schule:* move up, *Am.* promote; *verpfänden:* pawn; *antworten:* reply; **~setzen in Lage etc.:** put *od.* place into; **~seuchen** contaminate.

versicher|n assure (*a. Leben*); *beteuern:* protest; *Leben, Eigentum:* insure; **sich ~n** insure *od.* assure o.s.; **℈te** *m, f* the insured; **℈ung** *f* assurance; insurance (company).

Versicherungs | gesellschaft *f* insurance company; **~police** *f* insurance policy.

ver|sickern trickle away; **~sinken** sink.

Version *f* version.

versöhn|en reconcile; **sich (wieder) ~en** become reconciled; **℈ung** *f* reconciliation.

versorg|en provide, supply; **℈ung** *f* supply.

verspät|en: sich ~ be late; **~et** belated; **℈ung** *f:* **~ haben** be late.

ver|speisen eat (up); **~sperren** lock (up); bar, block (up), obstruct (*a. Sicht*); **~spotten** scoff at, ridicule; **~sprechen** prom-

ise; sich **~sprechen**
make a slip of the tongue;
2sprechen f promise; **~**
staatlichen nationalize.

Verstand m understanding; intelligence, intellect;
Geist: mind, wits pl; *Ver-*
nunft: reason.

verständ|igen inform, no-
tify; **sich ~igen** fig. come
to an understanding;
2igung f understanding,
agreement; *teleph.* com-
munication; **~lich** intelli-
gible; understandable; **2-**
nis n comprehension, understanding.

verstärk|en reinforce;
strengthen; *Ton:* amplify;
steigern: intensify; **2er** m
amplifier; **2ung** f rein-
forcement.

verstaub|en get dusty; **~t**
dusty.

verstauch|en: sich den
Fuß ~ sprain one's foot;
2ung f sprain.

verstauen stow away.

Versteck n hiding-place;
2en hide (a. sich), conceal.

verstehen understand, *col-*
loq. get; *einsehen:* see; *be-*
greifen: comprehend; *Spra-*
che: know; **ich verstehe!**
I see!; **sich mit j-m gut**
~ get on well with s.o.

Versteigerung f auction
(-sale).

verstell|bar adjustable;
~en adjust; *versperren:* bar,
block (up), obstruct.

ver|steuern pay duty od.
tax on; **~stimmt** out of

tune; *colloq.* cross; **~stoh-**
len furtive.

verstopf|en plug (up); **~t**
Straße: blocked, congest-
ed; *med.* constipated;
2ung f med. constipation.

verstorben late, deceased;
2e m, f the deceased.

Verstoß m offen|ce, Am.
-se; 2en offend.

ver|streichen *Zeit:* pass,
elapse; *Frist:* expire; **~**
streuen scatter; **~stüm-**
meln mutilate; **~stum-**
men grow silent od. dumb.

Versuch m attempt; trial;
experiment; **2en** try, attempt; *kosten:* taste; **~ung**
f temptation.

ver|tagen (sich) **~** ad-
journ; **~tauschen** ex-
change.

verteidig|en defend (sich
o.s.); **2er** m defender;
jur. counsel for the de-
fen|ce, Am. **-se;** *Fußball:*
full-back; **2ung** f de-
fen|ce, Am. **-se; 2ungs-**
minister m Minister of
Defence, Am. Secretary of
Defense.

verteilen distribute.

vertief|en (sich) **~** deep-
en; **sich ~ in** fig. become
absorbed in; **2ung** f hollow.

vertikal vertical.

Vertrag m contract; *pol.*
treaty; **2en** endure, bear,
stand; **diese Speise 2e**
ich nicht this food does
not agree with me; **sich**
gut 2en get on well.

vertrau|en trust (**j—m** s.o.); **2en** n confidence, trust; **~lich** confidential; **~t** intimate, familiar.

vertreiben drive away; expel (**aus** from); **sich die Zeit ~** pass one's time.

vertret|en represent; substitute for; **Ansicht:** hold; **2er** m representative; *econ.* commercial travel(l)er, *bsd. Am.* travel(l)ing salesman.

ver|trocknen dry up; **~trösten** put off.

verunglück|en have an accident; **tödlich ~en** be killed in an accident; **2te** m, f casualty.

ver|unreinigen s. **verschmutzen**; **~untreuen** embezzle; **~ursachen** cause.

verurteil|en condemn (*a. fig.*); sentence; **2ung** f *jur.* conviction.

ver|vielfältigen duplicate; **~vollkommnen** perfect; **~vollständigen** complete.

verwahr|lost neglected; **2ung** f charge, custody.

verwalt|en administer, manage; **2er** m administrator; manager; *Gutsverwalter:* steward; **2ung** f administration, management.

verwand|eln change (*a. sich*), turn, transform; **2lung** f change, transformation.

verwandt related (**mit** to); **2e** m, f relative, relation; **2schaft** f relationship;

Verwandte: relations *pl.*

verwarnen caution.

verwechs|eln mistake (**mit** for); confound, mix up, confuse; **2(e)lung** f mistake.

ver|wegen bold; **~weigern** deny, refuse.

Verweis m reprimand; rebuke, reproof; reference (**auf** to); **2en:** **j—n ~ auf** *od.* **an** refer s.o. to.

verwelken fade, wilt, wither.

verwend|en use, employ; *Zeit etc.:* spend (**auf** on); **2ung** f use, employment.

ver|werfen reject; **~werten** turn to account, utilize; **~wirklichen** realize.

verwirr|en confuse; **2ung** f confusion.

ver|wischen blur; *Spuren:* cover up; **~witwet** widowed; **~wöhnen** spoil; **~worren** confused.

verwund|bar vulnerable (*a. fig.*); **~en** wound.

Verwund|ete m wounded (soldier), casualty; **~ung** f wound, injury.

ver|wünschen curse; **~wüsten** devastate; **~zählen: sich ~** miscount; **~zaubern** bewitch, enchant; **~zehren** consume.

Verzeichnis n list, catalog(ue); register.

verzeih|en pardon, forgive; **~en Sie!** excuse me!; **2ung** f: **~!** I beg your pardon!, sorry!

verzerren distort; **sich ~** become distorted.

Verzicht m renunciation (**auf** of); **~en** renounce (**auf** et. s.th.); do without.

Verzierung f decoration, ornament.

verzinsen pay interest on.

verzöger|n delay; **sich ~** be delayed; **~ung** f delay.

verzollen pay duty on; **haben Sie et. zu ~?** have you anything to declare?

verzweifeln despair; **~elt** hopeless; *aussichtslos:* desperate; **~lung** f despair.

verzweigen: sich ~ ramify; *Straße:* branch.

Veto n veto.

Vetter m cousin.

Vieh n livestock; cattle; **~zucht** f stock-farming, cattle-breeding.

viel much; **~e** pl many.

viel|beschäftigt verybusy; **~fach** multiple; **~leicht** perhaps, maybe; **~mehr** rather; **~sagend** significant; **~seitig** many-sided, versatile; **~versprechend** promising.

vier four; **~eck** n square, quadrangle; **~eckig** square; **~linge** pl quadruplets pl; **~taktmotor** m fourstroke engine; **~te** fourth.

Viertel n fourth (part); quarter; **~ fünf, (ein) ~ nach vier** a quarter past four; **drei ~ vier** a quarter to four; **~finale** n sp. quarter-finals pl; **~jahr** n

three months pl, quarter (of a year); quarter; **~jährlich** adj quarterly; **2**adv every three months, quarterly; **~pfund** n quarter of a pound; **~stunde** f quarter of an hour.

viertens fourthly.

vierzehn fourteen; **~Tage** pl a fortnight sg, two weeks pl; **~te** fourteenth.

vierzig forty; **~ste** fortieth.

Villa f villa.

violett violet.

Violine f violin.

Visum n visa, visé.

Vitamin n vitamin.

Vizepräsident m vice-president.

Vogel m bird; **~perspektive** f bird's-eye view; **~scheuche** f scarecrow.

Vokab|el f word; **~ular** n vocabulary.

Vokal m vowel.

Volk n people; nation.

Volks|hochschule f adult evening classes pl; **~lied** n folk song; **~musik** f folk music; **~republik** f people's republic; **~schule** f appr. elementary od. primary school; **~stamm** m tribe; **~tanz** m folk-dance; **~wirtschaft** f economics sg; political economy.

voll adj full; gefüllt: filled; ganz: whole, complete, entire; Figur, Gesicht: full, round; adv fully, in full.

voll|automatisch fully automatic; **2bad** n bath;

2bart *m* full beard; **2beschäftigung** *f* full employment; **~enden** finish, complete; **~endet** perfect; **~füllen** fill (up); **~gepfropft** crammed, packed; **~gießen** fill (up).

völlig entire, complete.

voll|jährig of age; **2jährigkeit** *f* majority; **~klimatisiert** (fully) air-conditioned; **~kommen** perfect; **2macht** *f*: **~ haben** be authorized; **2milch** *f* whole milk; **2mond** *m* full moon; **2pension** *f* full board; **~schlank** plump, stout; **~ständig** complete; **~stopfen** stuff, cram; **~tanken** *mot.* fill up; **~zählig** complete.

Volt *n* volt.

Volumen *n* volume.

vor|*räumlich, zeitlich*: from; *Genitiv*: of; *Passiv*: by.

vor *räumlich*: in front of, before; *zeitlich*: before; **~ acht Tagen** a week ago; **5 Minuten ~ 12** five minutes to (*Am.* of) twelve.

Vor|abend *m* eve; **~ahnung** *f* presentiment, foreboding.

voran (*dat*) at the head (of), in front (of), before; **Kopf ~** head first; **~gehen** lead the way, precede.

Voranmeldung *f* advance reservation.

Vorarbeiter *m* foreman.

voraus (*dat*) in front (of), ahead (of); **im ~** in advance, beforehand; **~ge-**

hen *s.* **vorangehen**; **~gesetzt**: **~, daß** provided that; **~sagen** foretell, predict; forecast; **~schicken** send on in advance; **~sehen** foresee; **2setzung** *f* presupposition; **~sichtlich** presumable, probable; **2zahlung** *f* advance payment. [reserve.]

Vorbehalt *m* reservation, }

vorbei *räumlich*: by, past (**an** *s.o., s.th.*); *zeitlich*: over, past, gone; **~fahren** drive past; **~gehen** pass, go by; **~gehen an** pass; **~lassen** let pass.

vorbereit|en prepare; **2ung** *f* preparation.

vorbestellen order in advance; *Zimmer etc.*: book.

vorbeugen *v/i* prevent (**e-r Sache** *s.th.*); *v/t u.* **sich ~** bend forward; **~d** preventive.

Vorbild *n* model; *fig. a.* pattern; **2lich** exemplary.

vorbringen bring forward; *Meinung etc.*: advance; *äußern*: say.

vorder front, fore; **2achse** *f* front axle; **2bein** *n* foreleg; **2grund** *m* foreground; **2rad** *n* front wheel; **2seite** *f* front; *Münze*: obverse; **2sitz** *m* front seat; **~st** foremost; **2teil** *n, m* front.

vor|dringen advance; **2druck** *m* form, *Am. a.* blank; **~ehelich** pre-marital; **~eilig** hasty, rash, precipitate; **~eingenom-**

men prejudiced; **~enthalten** keep back, withhold (j—m et. s.th. from s.o.); **~erst** for the time being; **2fahr** *m* ancestor.

vorfahr|en drive up; **2t** *f* right of way; **2t(s)straße** *f* major road.

Vorfall *m* incident, event.

vorfinden find.

vorführ|en *jur.* bring (*dat* before); demonstrate; show, present; **2ung** *f* demonstration; presentation; showing; *thea.*, *Film:* performance.

Vor|gang *m* incident, event; process; **~gänger** *m* predecessor; **~garten** *m* front garden; **2geben** pretend; **~gebirge** *n* promontory; **2gehen** lead the way; *Uhr:* be fast, gain; *verfahren:* proceed; *sich ereignen:* go on, happen; **~gesetzte** *m* superior; **2gestern** the day before yesterday.

vorhaben intend, be going to *do* s.th.; **2** *n* intention; plan; project.

vorhanden available; **~ sein** exist; **2sein** *n* presence, existence.

Vor|hang *m* curtain; **~hängeschloß** *n* padlock.

vorher before, previously; in advance; **~gehend** preceding. [inant.) **vorherrschend** predominant.

vor|hin a short while ago; **~ig** last; **~jährig** of last year, last year's; **2kennt-**

nisse *pl:* mit guten **~n** in well-grounded in.

vorkomm|en be found; *passieren:* occur, happen; **2en** *n* occurrence.

Vorkriegs- pre-war ...

vorlad|en summon; **2ung** *f* summons.

Vor|lage *f* copy; *Muster:* pattern; *parl.* bill; *Unterbreitung:* presentation; *Fußball:* pass; **2lassen** let pass; *empfangen:* admit; **2läufig** *adj* provisional, temporary; *adv* for the time being; **2laut** forward, pert; **~leben** *n* past (life).

vorlege|n produce; present; j—m et. **~** lay (place, put) s.th. before s.o.; **2r** *m* rug.

vorles|en j—m et. **~** read (out) s.th. to s.o.; **2ung** *f* lecture (über *on*).

vorletzt last but one; **~e Nacht** the night before last.

Vor|liebe *f* preference; **~marsch** *m* *mil.* advance; **2merken** make a note of; reserve.

Vormittag *m* morning; **am ~ = 2s** in the morning.

Vormund *m* guardian.

vorn in front; **nach ~** forward; **von ~** from the front; from the beginning.

Vorname *m* Christian name, first name, *Am.* a. given name.

vornehm distinguished; *edel:* noble; elegant; **~tun** give o.s. airs; **~en:** sich et. ~ resolve to do s.th.

vornherein: von ~ from the first of. start.

Vorort *m* suburb; **~(s)zug** *m* suburban train.

Vor|rang *m:* **~ haben vor** take precedence over, have priority over; **~rat** *m* store, stock (**an** of); **Vorräte** *pl a.* provisions *pl*, supplies *pl*; **2rätig** *econ.* on hand, in stock; **~recht** *n* privilege; **~richtung** *f* device; **2rücken** *v/t* move forward; *v/i* advance; **~runde** *f sp.* preliminary round; **~saison** *f* dead *od.* off season; **~satz** *m* intention; **2sätzlich** intentional, deliberate; *bsd. jur.* wil(l)ful; **~schein** *m:* **zum ~ kommen** appear, turn up.

Vorschlag *m* proposal, suggestion; **2en** propose, suggest.

Vor|schlußrunde *f sp.* semi-final; **~schrift** *f* regulation(s *pl*); **2schriftsmäßig** according to regulations; **~schule** *f* preschool; **~schuß** *m* advance; **2sehen** design; plan; **sich 2sehen** take care, be careful; **sich 2sehen vor** (be on one's) guard against.

Vorsicht *f* caution; *Behutsamkeit:* care; **~!** look out!, be careful!; **~, Stufe!** mind the step!; **2ig** cautious; careful; **~smaßnahme** *f:* **~n treffen** take precautions.

Vorsilbe *f gr.* prefix.

Vorsitz *m* chair, presidency; **~ende** *m* chairman, president.

vorsorgen provide.

Vorspeise *f* hors d'œuvre.

Vorspiel *n* prelude (*a. fig.*); **2en** j-m et. ~ play s.th. to s.o.

Vor|sprung *m arch.* projection; *sp.* lead; *fig.* start, advantage (**vor** of); **2stadt** *f* suburb; **~stand** *m* managing committee *od.* board; **2stehen** project, protrude.

vorstell|en *v Uhr:* put on; introduce (j-n j-m s.o. to s.o.); **sich ~en bei** have an interview with; **sich et. ~en** imagine s.th.; **2ung** *f* introduction, presentation; *thea.* performance; *fig.* idea.

Vor|strafe *f* previous conviction; **2täuschen** feign, pretend.

Vorteil *m* advantage; **2haft** advantageous (**für** to).

Vortrag *m* lecture; **e-n ~ halten** (give a) lecture; **2en** *Gedicht:* recite; *Meinung:* express.

vortreten step forward; protrude.

vorüber *räumlich:* by, past; *zeitlich:* over; **~gehen** pass, go by; **~gehend** passing; *zeitweilig:* temporary; **2gehende** *m* passer-by.

Vor|urteil *n* prejudice; **~verkauf** *m thea.* advance booking; **wand** m pretext, preten|ce, Am. -se.

vorwärts forward, onward, on; **~!** go ahead!; **~kommen** (make) progress.

vor|weisen produce, show; **~werfen:** j-m et. **~** reproach s.o. with s.th.; **~wiegend** chiefly, mainly, mostly.

Vorwort n foreword; des Autors: preface.

Vorwurf m reproach; j-m e-n **~** od. **Vorwürfe machen** reproach s.o. (**wegen** with); **2svoll** reproachful.

Vor|zeichen n omen; **2zeigen** produce, show; **2zeitig** premature; **2ziehen** Vorhänge: draw; fig. prefer; **~zug** m preference; **Vorteil:** advantage; Wert: merit; **2züglich** excellent, exquisite.

vulgär vulgar.

Vulkan m volcano.

W

Waag|e f balance, (e-e a pair of) scales pl; **2(e)-recht** horizontal, level.

Wabe f honeycomb.

wach awake; **~ werden** wake up; **2e** f watch, guard (a. Person); Polizei~wache: police-station; **~en** (keep) watch; sit up (**bei** with).

Wacholder m juniper; **~branntwein** m gin.

Wachs n wax.

wachsam watchful.

wachsen[1] wax.

wachsen[2] grow; fig. increase.

Wächter m guard; bsd. Nacht2: watchman.

Wacht|posten m sentry; **~turm** m watch-tower.

wack(e)lig shaky; Möbel: rickety; **~eln** shake; Tisch etc.: wobble; Zahn: be loose.

Wade f calf.

Waffe f weapon (a. fig.); **~n** pl a. arms pl.

Waffel f bsd. Eis2: wafer.

Waffenstillstand m armistice, truce.

wagen venture (a. sich); risk; sich getrauen: dare.

Wagen m carriage; Kraft2: car; rail. s. **Waggon**; **~heber** m jack; **~papiere** pl car documents pl; **~spur** f rut.

Waggon m (railway) carriage, Am. (railroad) car.

Wahl f choice; alternative; Auslese: selection; pol. election.

wähle|n choose; pol. elect (v/i vote); teleph. dial; **2r** m voter; **2risch** particular.

Wahl|fach n optional subject, Am. elective; **~kampf** m election campaign; **~kreis** m constituency; **2los** indiscriminate;

~recht n franchise; **~urne** f ballot-box.

Wahnsinn m insanity, madness (a. fig.); 2**ig** insane, mad.

wahr true; *wirklich:* real.

während prp during; *cj* while; *Gegensatz:* whereas.

Wahr|heit f truth; 2**nehmbar** perceptible; 2**nehmen** perceive, notice; *Gelegenheit:* avail o.s. of; *Interessen:* look after; **~sagerin** f fortune-teller; 2**scheinlich** probably, most od. very likely; **~scheinlichkeit** f probability, likelihood.

Währung f currency.

Wahrzeichen n landmark.

Waise f orphan; **~nhaus** n orphanage.

Wal m whale.

Wald m wood, forest; 2**ig** wooded, woody.

Wall m mil. rampart; *Erd2:* mound.

Wallach m gelding.

Wallfahrt f pilgrimage.

Walnuß f walnut.

Walze f roller; cylinder.

wälzen (sich) ~ roll.

Walzer m waltz.

Wand f wall.

Wandel m change; 2**n:** sich ~ change.

Wander|er m wanderer; hiker; 2**n** wander; hike; **~ung** f walking-tour, hike; **~weg** m footpath.

Wand|gemälde n mural (painting); **~lung** f change; **~schrank** m wall-cup-

board; **~tafel** f blackboard.

Wange f cheek.

wanke|lmütig fickle, inconstant; **~n** totter, stagger.

wann when; s. **dann**; **seit ~?** how long ?, since when ? [*colloq.* tub.)

Wanne f tub; bath(tub),)

Wanze f bug, *Am. a.* bedbug. [arms *pl.*)

Wappen n coat of arms,)

Ware f commodity; **~n** pl a. goods pl, merchandise sg, wares pl.

Waren|haus n department store; **~lager** n stock; *Raum:* warehouse; **~probe** f sample; **~zeichen** n trademark.

warm warm, *Essen:* hot.

Wärm|e f warmth; *phys.* heat; 2**en** warm; **~flasche** f hot-water bottle.

Warn|dreieck n mot. warning triangle; 2**en:** ~ **(vor)** warn (of, against), caution (against); **~signal** n danger signal; **~ung** f warning, caution.

warten wait (auf for).

Wärter m attendant; *Wächter:* guard; *Tier2:* keeper; *Pfleger:* (male) nurse.

Warte|saal m, **~zimmer** n waiting-room.

Wartung f maintenance.

warum why. [nipple.)

Warze f wart; *Brust2:* f

was what; **~ kostet das?** how much is this ?

wasch|bar washable; 2**becken** n wash-basin, *Am.* washbowl.

Wäsche f wash(ing); *the* laundry; Tisch2, Bett2: linen; Unter2: underwear; **~klammer** f clothes-peg, clothes-pin; **~leine** f clothes-line.

waschen wash; **sich ~** (have a) wash; **(sich) die Haare ~** wash *od.* shampoo one's hair; **~ und legen** a shampoo and set.

Wäscherei f laundry.

Wasch|lappen m face-cloth, Am. washcloth; **~maschine** f washing-machine, washer; **~pulver** n washing powder; **~raum** m wash-room.

Wasser n water; **~ball-spiel** n water-polo; **~dampf** m steam; 2dicht waterproof; *bsd. mar.* watertight; **~fall** m waterfall; **~flugzeug** n seaplane; **~graben** m ditch; **~hahn** m tap, Am. a. faucet.

wässerig watery.

Wasser|kraftwerk n hydroelectric power station *od.* plant; **~leitung** f water-pipe(s pl).

wässern Heringe etc.: soak.

Wasser|pflanze f aquatic plant; **~rohr** n water-pipe; 2scheu afraid of water; **~ski** m: **~ fahren** water-ski; **~sport** m aquatic sports pl; **~stiefel** m pl waders pl; **~stoff** m hydrogen; **~stoffbombe** f hydrogen bomb, H-bomb; **~weg** m waterway; **auf dem ~** by water;

~welle f water-wave; **~werk** n waterworks sg, pl.

wäßrig watery.

waten wade.

watscheln waddle.

Watt n electr. watt.

Watte f cotton-wool; surgical cotton. [loom.]

web|en weave; 2stuhl m

Wechsel m change; Geld-zuwendung: allowance; econ. bill (of exchange); **~geld** n change; **~kurs** m rate of exchange; 2n change; variieren: vary; Worte: exchange; **~strom** m alternating current; **~stube** f exchange office.

wecke|n wake (up), rouse (a. fig.); 2r m alarm-clock.

wedeln Skisport: wedel; **~ mit wag.** [... nor.]

weder ~ ... noch neither

Weg m way (a. fig.); Straße: road; Pfad: path; Spazier2: walk.

weg away, off; **~gegangen, verloren:** gone; **ich muß ~** colloq. I must be off; **~blei-ben** stay away, drop off; **~bringen** take away; Sachen: a. remove. [to.]

wegen because of, on

weg|fahren v/t cart away; v/i leave; im Wagen: drive away; **~fallen** be omitted; **~gehen** go away; Ware: sell; **~jagen** drive away; **~lassen** let s.o. go; Sache: leave out, omit; **~laufen** run away; **~nehmen** take s.th. away; Zeit, Raum: take up; **~räumen** clear

away; **~schaffen** remove.
Wegweiser m signpost;
fig. guide.
weg|werfen throw away;
~wischen wipe off.
weh sore; **~ tun** ache; hurt
(sich o.s.); **j-m ~ tun**
hurt s.o.
Wehen *pl* labo(u)r *sg.*
wehen blow.
wehmütig wistful.
Wehr n weir.
Wehr|dienst m military
service; **~dienstverwei-**
gerer m conscientious ob-
jector; **2en: sich ~** defend
o.s.; **2los** defenceless, *Am.*
defenseless.
Weib n woman; *Ehefrau:*
wife; **~chen** n *zo.* female;
2lich female; *gr.*, *Wesens-*
art: feminine.
weich soft (*a. fig.*); *Fleisch:*
tender; *Ei:* soft-boiled.
Weiche *pl* rail.: switch; **~n**
pl a. points *pl.*
weichen¹ give way, yield
(*dat* to).
weichen² soak.
Weide f *bot.* willow; *agr.*
pasture; **~land** n pasture;
2n pasture, graze.
weiger|n: sich ~ refuse;
2ung f refusal.
weihen *eccl.* consecrate.
Weiher m pond.
Weihnachten n Christmas.
Weihnachts|abend m
Christmas Eve; **~baum**
m Christmas-tree; **~ge-**
schenk n Christmas present; **~lied** n (Christmas)
carol; **~mann** m Father

Christmas, Santa Claus.
Weih|rauch m incense; **~**
wasser n holy water.
weil because; since, as.
Weile f: **e-e ~** a while.
Wein m wine; **~stock** f: vine;
~beere f grape; **~berg** m
vineyard; **~brand** m bran-
dy.
weinen weep (**um, vor**
for), cry (**vor** *Freude:* for,
Schmerz: with).
Wein|faß n butt, winecask;
~karte f wine-list; **~lese** f
vintage; **~rebe** f vine;
~stock m vine; **~traube** f
s. Traube.
weise wise.
Weise f *mus.* melody, tune;
fig. manner, way.
weisen: ~ auf point at *od.*
to; **von sich ~** reject; *Be-*
schuldigung: deny.
Weis|heit f wisdom; **~**
heitszahn m wisdom-
tooth.
weiß white; **2brot** n white
bread; **2e** m white (man);
2wein m white wine.
Weisung f direction, direc-
tive.
weit *adj* wide; vast;
Reise, Weg: long; *adv* far,
wide(ly); **~ entfernt** far
away; **bei ~em** by far;
von ~em from a distance;
~ab far away.
weiter *adj* further; *Kosten*
etc.: additional, extra; **~e**
fünf Wochen another five
weeks; *adv* furthermore,
moreover; **~!** go on!;
nichts ~ nothing more;

und so ~ and so on; ~**fahren** drive on; go on; ~**geben** pass (an to); ~**gehen** go on (a. fig.); move on; ~**kommen** get on; ~**können** be able to go on; ~**machen** carry on.

weit|sichtig far-sighted; 2**sprung** m long (Am. broad) jump; ~**verbreitet** widespread.

Weizen m wheat; ~**mehl** n wheaten flour.

welch interr pron what, which; ~**er?** which one?; rel pron who, which, that. **Wellblech** n corrugated iron.

Welle f wave; tech. shaft. **wellen: (sich)** ~ wave; 2**länge** f wave length; 2**linie** f wavy line; 2**reiten** n surf-riding, surfing.

wellig wavy.

Welt f world; ~**all** n universe; 2**berühmt** world-famous; ~**krieg** m world war; 2**lich** worldly; dies-seitig: secular, temporal; ~**meister** m world champion; ~**raum** m space; ~**reise** f journey round the world; ~**rekord** m world record; 2**stadt** f metropolis; 2**weit** world-wide.

wem to whom, whom (colloq. who) ... to; **von** ~ who(m) from.

wen whom, colloq. who.

Wende f turn; 2n v/t turn (about, round); **bitte** 2**n!** please turn over!; **sich** 2**n an** turn to; Aus-

kunft etc.: apply to (**wegen** for); v/i mot. turn; ~**punkt** m turning-point.

wenig little; ~**e** pl few pl; ~**er** less; pl fewer; math. minus; **am** ~**sten** least (of all); ~**stens** at least.

wenn when; bedingend: if.

wer who; auswählend: which; **von euch?** which of you?; ~ **auch immer** who(so)ever.

Werbe|fernsehen n commercial television; ~**funk** m commercial broadcasting; 2**n für** advertise; ~**um** court; ~**sendung** f commercial.

Werbung f publicity, advertising.

werden become, get; all-mählich: grow; plötzlich blaß etc.: turn; **was will er (einmal)** ~? what is he going to be?; **ich werde fahren** I shall drive; s. gesund od. krank.

werfen throw (mit s.th.; **nach** at); zo. Junge: throw; Schatten, Blick: cast.   [yard.]

Werft f dockyard, ship-]

Werk n work; tech. works pl; Fabrik: works sg, pl, factory; ~**meister** m foreman; ~**statt** f workshop; ~**tag** m workday; 2**tags** on weekdays; ~**zeug** n tool, implement; feines: instrument.

wert worth; würdig: worthy (gen of); **nichts** ~

worthless; 2 m value, worth; 2gegenstand m article of value; ~los worthless, valueless; 2papiere pl securities pl; 2sachen pl valuables pl; ~voll valuable, precious.

Wesen n Lebe2: being, creature; Natur: nature, character; 2tlich essential.

weshalb why.

Wespe f wasp.

wessen whose; what ... of.

Weste f waistcoat; econ. u. Am. vest.

West|(en m) m west; 2lich west(erly); Einfluß etc.: western.

Wett|bewerb m competition; ~e f bet; 2en bet; mit j-m um et. 2en bet s.o. s.th.

Wetter n weather; ~bericht m weather forecast; ~lage f weather conditions pl; ~leuchten n sheet-lightning; ~vorhersage f weather forecast.

Wett|kampf m contest, competition; ~kämpfer m contestant; ~lauf m, ~rennen n race; ~rüsten n armament race; ~streit m contest.

wichtig important; 2keit f importance. [change.]

wickeln wind; Baby:]

Widder m ram.

wider against, contrary to; 2haken m barb; ~legen refute, disprove; ~lich repugnant, repulsive; ekelhaft: disgusting; ~setzen:

sich ~ oppose; ~spenstig refractory; ~sprechen contradict; 2spruch m contradiction; opposition; 2stand m resistance (a. electr.), opposition; ~standsfähig resistant; ~strebend reluctant; ~wärtig disgusting; 2wille m aversion, dislike; Ekel: disgust; ~willig reluctant.

widmen dedicate; devote (sich o.s.). [like.]

wie how; Vergleich: as;]

wieder again; immer ~ again and again; s. hin; 2aufbau m reconstruction, rebuilding; ~aufnehmen resume; ~bekommen get back; ~bringen bring back; give back; ~erkennen recognize (an by); ~finden find again; recover; ~geben give back, return; darbieten etc.: render; ~gutmachen make up for; ~herstellen restore; ~holen repeat; 2holung f repetition; ~kommen come back, return; ~sehen (sich) ~ see od. meet again; 2sehen n reunion; auf 2sehen! good-bye!

Wiege f cradle.

wiegen¹ weigh.

wiegen² rock; 2lied n lullaby.

wiehern neigh, whinny.

Wiese f meadow.

wieso why. [how many.]

wieviel how much; vor pl]

wild wild; savage; 2 *n* game; 2**dieb** *m* poacher; 2**hüter** *m* game-keeper; 2**leder** *n* suède; 2**nis** *f* wilderness, wild; 2**schwein** *n* wild boar.

Wille *m* will; **s-n ~n durchsetzen** have one's way; **~nskraft** *f* will-power.

willkommen welcome.

wimmeln swarm (**von** with).

wimmern whimper, whine.

Wimpel *m* pennant, pennon.

Wimper *f* (eye)lash.

Wind *m* wind.

Windel *f* napkin, *Am.* diaper.

winden wind, twist; **sich ~ vor** writhe with.

wind|ig windy; 2**mühle** *f* windmill; 2**pocken** *pl* chicken-pox *sg*; 2**schutzscheibe** *f* windscreen, *Am.* windshield; 2**stille** *f* calm; 2**stoß** *m* blast of wind, gust.

Windung *f* winding, turn; *Weg:* bend.

Wink *m* sign; *fig.* hint.

Winkel *m math.* angle; *Ecke:* corner, nook.

winken signal (*dat* to); *her~:* beckon; wave.

winseln whimper, whine.

Winter *m* winter; **im ~ in** winter; 2**lich** wintry; **~schlußverkauf** *m* winter sale(s *pl*); **~sport** *m* winter sports *pl*.

winzig tiny, diminutive.

Wipfel *m* (tree-)top.

wir we.

Wirbel *m* whirl, swirl; *Luft, Wasser:* eddy; *anat.* vertebra; 2**n** whirl; **~säule** *f* spinal column; **~sturm** *m* cyclone, tornado.

wirk|en beruhigend **~** have a soothing effect; **~lich** real; 2**lichkeit** *f* reality; **~sam** effective; 2**ung** *f* effect; **~ungsvoll** effective.

wirr confused; *Rede:* incoherent; *Haare:* dishevel(l)ed.

Wirt *m* host; landlord, innkeeper; **~in** *f* hostess; landlady.

Wirtschaft *f* housekeeping; *Gemeinwesen:* economy; *s.* **Wirtshaus**; **~erin** *f* housekeeper; 2**lich** economic; *haushälterisch:* economical; **~sminister** *m* Minister for Economic Affairs.

Wirtshaus *n* pub(lic house), inn.

wisch|en wipe; *Staub* **~** dust; 2**lappen** *m* dish-cloth; floorcloth.

wissen know; 2 *n* knowledge.

Wissenschaft *f* science; **~ler** *m* scientist; 2**lich** scientific.

wissen|swert worth knowing; **~tlich** knowingly.

witter|n scent, smell; 2**ung** *f* weather; *hunt.* scent. [widower.}

Witwe *f* widow; **~r** *m* }

Witz m wit; *Spaß*: joke; 2ig witty; funny.
wo where.
Woche f week.
Wochen|ende n weekend; 2lang for weeks; ~lohn m weekly pay od. wages pl; ~markt m weekly market; ~schau f newsreel; ~tag m weekday.
wöchentlich weekly; **einmal ~** once a week.
wo|durch by what?, how?; by which, whereby; ~für for what?, what ... for?; (in return) for which.
Woge f wave (a. fig.).
wogegen against what?; against which.
wo|her from where?, where ... from?; ~hin where (... to)?
wohl well; *vermutend*: I suppose; **leben Sie ~!** farewell!; 2 n: **auf Ihr ~!** your health!; **zum ~!** *colloq.* cheers!; 2**befinden** n well-being, (good) health; 2**fahrt** f welfare; 2**habend** well-to-do; ~**schmeckend** savo(u)ry, tasty; 2**stand** m prosperity; 2**tätigkeit** f charity; ~**tuend** pleasant; ~**verdient** well-deserved; 2**wollen** n goodwill, benevolence; *Gunst*: favo(u)r.
Wohn|block m s. **Wohnhaus;** 2**en** live (**in** in, at; **bei** j-m with s.o.); ~**haus** n block of flats, *Am.* apartment house; 2**haft** resident, living; ~**ort** m domicile; ~**sitz** m residence; ~**ung** f flat, *Am.* apartment; ~**wagen** m caravan, *Am.* trailer; ~**zimmer** n sitting-room, living-room.
wölben: (sich) ~ arch.
Wolf m wolf.
Wolke f cloud.
Wolken|bruch m cloudburst; ~**kratzer** m skyscraper; 2**los** cloudless.
wolkig cloudy, clouded.
Woll|decke f blanket; ~**e** f wool.
wollen wish, desire; want; be willing; intend, be going to; *im Begriff sein*: be about to; **lieber ~** prefer.
Wollstoff m wool(l)en fabric; ~**e** f/ wool(l)ens pl.
wo|mit with what?, what ... with?; with *od.* by which; ~**nach** what ... for?; ~**ran** by what?; by which?; ~**ran denkst du?** what are you thinking of?; ~**rauf** on what?, what ... on?; *danach:* whereupon, after which; ~**rauf wartest du?** what are you waiting for?; ~**raus** what ... from?; from which; ~**rin** in what?; in which, wherein.
Wort n word; *Ausdruck:* }
Wörterbuch n dictionary. } [expression.]
wörtlich literal.
wort|los without a word; 2**schatz** m vocabulary; 2**stellung** f *gr.* word order; 2**wechsel** m dispute.
wo|rüber what ... about?; ~**rum** about what?, what ... about?; about *od.* for

which; ⁓rum handelt es sich? what is it about? ⁓von what ... from od. of?; what ... about?; of od. from which; ⁓vor what ... of?; of which; ⁓zu what ... for?

Wrack n wreck.

wringen wring.

Wucher m usury; 2n grow exuberantly, ⁓ung f med. growth.

Wuchs m growth; figure.

Wucht f force; 2ig heavy.

wühlen dig; Schwein: 2voll wulstig thick.

wund sore; ⁓e Stelle sore; 2e f wound.

Wunder n miracle; fig. a. wonder, marvel; 2bar wonderful, marvel(l)ous; 2n surprise, astonish; sich 2n be surprised od. astonished (über at); 2schön very beautiful, 2voll wonderful. [tetanus.]

Wundstarrkrampf m]

Wunsch m wish, desire; Bitte: request.

wünschen wish, desire; ⁓swert desirable.

Würde f dignity.

würdig worthy (gen of); ⁓en appreciate. [ter.]

Wurf m throw, cast; zo. lit-]

Würfel m cube; Spiel2: die (pl dice); 2n (play) dice; ⁓zucker m lump sugar.

Wurfgeschoß n missile.

würgen v/t choke, strangle; v/i choke; Erbrechen: retch.

Wurm m worm; 2stichig worm-eaten, wormy.

Wurst f sausage.

Würstchen n (small) sausage.

Würze f Gewürz: spice; Aroma: seasoning, flavo(u)r.

Wurzel f root.

würz|en spice, season, flavo(u)r; ⁓ig spicy, well-seasoned.

wüst desert, waste; wirr: confused; roh: rude; 2e f desert, wilderness.

Wut f rage, fury.

wüten rage; ⁓d furious, bsd. Am. a. mad.

X, Y

x-beliebig: jede(r, -s) ⁓ ... any ...

x-mal many times, sl. umpteen times.

x-te: zum ⁓n Male for the umpteenth time.

Yacht f yacht.

Z

Zack|e f, ⁓en m (sharp) point; Zinke: prong; Fels: jag; 2ig jagged.

zaghaft timid.

zäh tough; = ⁓flüssig viscid, viscous, sticky.

Zahl

Zahl f number; *Ziffer:* figure; cipher; **2bar** payable.
zählbar countable.
zahlen pay; *Restaurant:* ~ (, bitte)! the bill (*Am.* the check), please!
zähle|n count; **~n zu** count among; **2r** m meter.
Zahl|karte f *appr.* moneyorder form; **2los** innumerable, countless; **2reich** *adj* numerous; *adv* in great number; **~tag** m pay-day; **~ung** f payment; **~ungsbedingungen** pl terms pl of payment; **~ungsmittel** n currency.
zahm tame, domesticated.
zähmen tame, domesticate.
Zahn m tooth; *tech.* tooth, cog; **e-n ~ bekommen** cut a tooth; **~arzt** m dentist; **~bürste** f toothbrush; **~creme** f toothpaste; **~fleisch** n gums pl; **2los** toothless; **~lücke** f gap between the teeth; **~pasta** f toothpaste; **~rad** n cogwheel; **~radbahn** f rack-railway; **~schmerzen** pl toothache sg; **~stocher** m toothpick.
Zange f (**e-e a pair of**) tongs pl; *med., zo.* forceps sg, pl.
zanken scold (**mit j-m s.o.**); **sich ~** quarrel.
zänkisch bickering, nagging.
Zäpfchen n *anat.* uvula; *med.* suppository.
Zapf|en m plug; *Pflock:* peg, pin; *Spund:* bung;

Drehzapfen: pivot; *bot.* cone; *Sern* cap; **~hahn** m tap, *Am.* faucet; **~säule** f petrol pump.
zappeln struggle; *vor Unruhe:* fidget.
zart tender, soft, delicate; *sanft:* gentle.
zärtlich tender, loving; **2keit** f tenderness; *Liebkosung:* caress.
Zauber m spell, charm, magic (*alle a. fig.*); *fig.* enchantment; **~er** m sorcerer, magician; **2haft** *fig.* enchanting; **~künstler** m conjurer; **2n** v/t conjure.
Zaum m bridle.
zäumen bridle.
Zaumzeug n bridle.
Zaun m fence; **~pfahl** m pale. [crossing.}
Zebrastreifen m zebra
Zeche f score, bill; *Bergbau:* mine; coal-pit, colliery.
Zeh m, **~e** f toe; **~enspitze** f: **auf ~n** on tiptoe.
zehn ten; **2kampf** m decathlon; **2te** m tenth; **2tel** n tenth (part); **~tens** tenthly.
Zeichen n sign, token; *Merk2:* mark; *Signal:* signal; **~block** m drawingblock; **~papier** n drawing-paper; **~stift** m pencil, crayon; **~trickfilm** m animation, animated cartoon.
zeichn|en draw; **2er** m draftsman, draughtsman; designer; **2ung** f drawing; design; *zo.* marking.

Zeige|finger *m* forefinger, index (finger); **2n** show, point out; demonstrate; point (**auf** *a*: **nach** to); **~r** *m* Uhr: hand.

Zeile *f* line.

Zeit *f* time; *s.* **Zeitraum**: **freie ~** spare time; **laß dir ~!** take your time; **~abschnitt** *m* period; **~alter** *n* age; **2gemäß** modern, up-to-date; **~genosse** *m* contemporary; **2genössisch** contemporary; **2ig** *adj* early; *adv* on time; **~karte** *f* season-ticket, *Am.* commutation ticket; **2lich** *adj* temporal; *adv* as to time; **2lich zusammenfallen** coincide; **~lupenaufnahme** *f* Film: slow-motion picture; **~punkt** *m* moment; **~raum** *m* period, space (of time); **~schrift** *f* journal, periodical, magazine; **~ung** *f* (news)paper, journal.

Zeitungs|kiosk *m* newsstand; **~notiz** *f* press item; **~verkäufer** *m* newsvendor.

Zeit|verlust *m* loss of time; **~verschwendung** *f* waste of time; **~vertreib** *m* pastime; **2weise** at times; **~zeichen** *n* time-signal.

Zelle *f* cell; **~stoff** *m*, **~ulose** *f* cellulose.

Zelt *n* tent; **2en** camp; go camping; **~lager** *n* camp; **~platz** *m* camping-ground.

Zement *m* cement.

Zensur *f* censorship; *Schu-*

le: mark, *Am. a.* grade.

Zentimeter *m, n* centimet|re, *Am.* -er.

Zentner *m* centner, metric hundredweight (*50 kilograms*).

zentral central; **2e** *f* central (office); *teleph.* (telephone) exchange; **2heizung** *f* central heating.

Zentrum *n* cent|re, *Am.* -er.

zerbrech|en break (to pieces); **sich den Kopf ~en** rack one's brains; **~lich** breakable, fragile.

zer|bröckeln crumble; **~drücken** crush; *Kleid:* crease.

Zeremonie *f* ceremony.

Zerfall *m* decay; **2en** fall to pieces, decay (*a. fig.*).

zer|fetzen tear to pieces; **~fließen** melt; **~fressen** eat; *chem.* corrode; **~gehen** melt; **~kauen** chew; **~kleinern** cut up; mince; **~knirscht** contrite; **~knittern** (c)rumple, wrinkle, crease; **~knüllen** crumple up; **~kratzen** scratch; **~legen** take apart *od.* to pieces; *Fleisch:* carve; **~lumpt** ragged; **~mahlen** grind; **~platzen** burst; explode; **~quetschen** crush, squash; *bsd. Kartoffeln:* mash; **~reiben** grind, pulverize; **~reißen** *v/t* tear, rip up; *v/i* tear; *Seil etc.:* break.

zerr|en drag; tug; *med.* strain; **2ung** *f med.* strain.

zer|sägen saw up; **~schel-**

len be smashed; *Schiff:* be
wrecked; **~schlagen** break
od. smash (to pieces); **~**
schmettern smash; **~**
schneiden cut in two; cut
up; **~setzen: (sich)** ~ de-
compose; **~splittern** split,
splinter; **~springen** burst;
Glas: crack.

zerstäube|n spray; ₂r *m*
sprayer, atomizer.

zerstör|en destroy; ₂er *m*
destroyer (*a. mar.*); ₂ung
f destruction.

zerstreu|en disperse, scatter
(*a. sich*); *Zweifel etc.*:
dissipate; **sich** ~ *en* fig.
amuse o.s.; **~t** *fig.* absent
(-minded); ₂ung *f* diver-
sion, amusement.

zer|stückeln cut up; **~tei-**
len divide; **~treten** tread
down; crush; **~trümmern**
smash; **~zaust** tousled.

Zettel *m* slip (of paper);
*Preis*₂ *etc.*: ticket; *Klebe*₂
label.

Zeug *n* stuff (*a. fig. contp.*);
material; things *pl*; **dum-**
mes ~! nonsense!; rubbish!

Zeuge *m* witness; ₂en
biol. beget; **~enaussage** *f*
testimony, evidence; **~in** *f*
(female) witness; **~nis** *n*
jur. testimony, evidence;
Bescheinigung: certificate;
(school) report, *Am.* report
card.

Zickzack *m* zigzag; **im** ~
fahren *etc.* zigzag.

Ziege *f* (she-)goat, nanny
(-goat).

Ziegel *m* brick; *Dach*₂:

tile; **~stein** *m* brick.

Ziegen|bock *m* he-goat;
~leder *n* kid; **~peter** *m*
mumps.

ziehen *v/t* pull; draw (*a.*
Strich); *Hut:* take off; *Gra-*
ben: dig; *Zahn:* extract;
Aufmerksamkeit
auf sich ~ attract attention; **sich** ~ extend, stretch;
sich in die Länge ~ drag
on; *v/i* pull (**an** at); puff
(**an** *Zigarre etc.*: at); *um-*
ziehen: (re)move (**nach**
to); *Vögel:* migrate; *Tee:*
infuse, draw; **es zieht**
there is a draught (*Am.*
draft).

Ziehharmonika *f* accor-
dion.

Ziel *n* aim (*a. fig.*); **~schei-**
be: mark, target (*a. fig.*);
sp. winning-post; *mil.* objective; *Reise*₂: destination; *fig.* end, purpose; **~**
band *n* tape; ₂**bewußt**
purposeful; ₂**en** (take)aim
(**auf** at); ₂**los** aimless;
~scheibe *f* target.

ziemlich *adj* considerable;
adv pretty, fairly, rather.

Zier *f*, **~de** *f* ornament; *fig.*
a. hono(u)r (**für** to); ₂**en:**
sich ~ be affected; be
prudish; ₂**lich** dainty.

Ziffer *f* figure, digit; **~**
blatt *n* dial(-plate), face.

Zigarette *f* cigaret(te).

Zigarre *f* cigar.

Zigeuner *m*, **~in** *f* gipsy.

Zimmer *n* room; apartment; **~mädchen** *n* chambermaid; **~mann** *m* car-

penter; **~vermieterin** f landlady.

zimperlich prudish; squeamish.

Zimt m cinnamon.

Zink n zinc.

Zinke f tooth; *Gabel:* prong.

Zinn n tin.

Zins|en pl interest sg; **~fuß** m rate of interest.

Zipfel m corner.

Zirkel m circle (a. *fig.*); *math.* (**ein** (a pair of) compasses pl.

zirkulieren circulate.

Zirkus m circus.

zischen hiss; *schwirren:* whiz(z).   [quote.]

Zit|at n quotation; **2ieren**]

Zitrone f lemon; **~nlimonade** f lemonade.

zittern tremble, shake (**vor** with).

zivil civil(ian); *Preis:* reasonable; **2** n s. **Zivilkleidung; 2bevölkerung** f civilians pl; **2isation** f civilization; **2ist** m civilian; **2kleidung** f civilian, plain clothes pl; **2personen** pl civilians pl.

zögern hesitate.

Zoll[1] m inch.

Zoll[2] m (customs) duty; *Behörde:* the Customs pl; **~abfertigung** f customs clearance; **~amt** n customs-house; **~beamte** m customs official; **~erklärung** f customs declaration; **2frei** duty-free; **~kontrolle** f customs examination;

2pflichtig liable to duty, dutiable.

Zone f zone.

Zoo m zoo.

Zoologie f zoology.

Zopf m plait, pigtail, braid.

Zorn m anger; **2ig** angry.

zottig shaggy.

zu prp *Richtung:* to, toward(s), up to; *Ort:* at, in; *Zweck:* for; **~ Weihnachten** at Christmas; *adv* too; *colloq.* closed, shut; **Tür!** close *od.* shut the door!; *mit inf:* **ich habe ~ arbeiten** I have to work.

Zubehör n, m fittings pl; *tech.* accessories pl.

zubereit|en prepare; **2ung** f preparation.

zu|binden tie up; **~blinzeln** wink at.

Zucht f discipline; *bot.* growing; *zo.:* breeding; breed.

züchte|n breed; *bot.* grow; **2r** m breeder; grower.

Zuchthaus n convict prison, *Am.* penitentiary; **~strafe** f imprisonment, penal servitude.

zucken jerk; twitch (**mit** et. s.th.); *vor Schmerz:* wince; *Blitz:* flash; *s.* **Achsel.**

Zucker m sugar; **~dose** f sugar-basin, *Am.* sugar bowl; **2krank** diabetic; **2n** sugar; **~rohr** n sugarcane; **~rübe** f sugar-beet.

Zuckungen pl convulsions pl.

zudecken cover (**sich** o.s.).

zudem besides, moreover.
zu|drehen turn off; ~**dringlich** importunate.
zuerst (at) first.
Zufahrt f approach; ~**straße** f approach (road).
Zu|fall m chance; 2**fällig** adj accidental; attr a. chance; adv by accident, by chance; ~**flucht** f refuge, shelter.
zufrieden content(ed), satisfied; 2**heit** f contentment, satisfaction; ~**stellen** satisfy.
zu|frieren freeze up od. over; ~**fügen** add; inflict (j-m [up]on s.o.); 2**fuhr** f supply.
Zug m draw, pull; procession; orn. migration; rail. train; Gesichts2: feature; Charakter2: trait; Luft2, Trinken: draught, Am. draft; Schach: move; Rauchen: puff.
Zu|gabe f extra; thea. encore; ~**gang** m entrance; access (a. fig.); 2**gänglich** accessible (**für** to) (a. fig.); 2**geben** add; admit; 2**gehen** colloq. Tür etc.: close, shut; geschehen: happen; 2**gehen auf** walk up to.
Zügel m rein (a. fig.); 2**los** fig. unbridled; 2**n** rein; fig. bridle, check.
Zu|geständnis n concession; 2**getan** attached (dat to).
zug|ig draughty, Am. drafty; 2**kraft** f tech.

traction; fig. draw, appeal.
zugleich at the same time.
Zugluft f draught, Am. draft.
zugreifen help o.s.
zu|grunde~**gehen** perish; ~ **richten** ruin.
Zugschaffner m s. Schaffner.
zugunsten in favo(u)r of.
Zug|verbindung f train connection; ~**vogel** m bird of passage.
Zuhause n home.
zuheilen heal up.
zu|hören listen (dat to); 2**r** m hearer, listener; 2**r** pl audience sg.
zu|jubeln cheer; ~**kleben** paste up; ~**knallen** v/i Tür: bang shut, slam (to); v/t slam (to); ~**knöpfen** button (up); ~**kommen**: ~ **auf** come up to.
Zu|kunft f future; gr. future (tense); 2**künftig** adj future; adv in future.
zu|lächeln smile at; 2**lage** f extra pay; Gehalt: rise, Am. raise; ~**lassen** colloq. leave shut; j-n: admit (a. fig.); 2**lassung** f admission; licen|ce, Am. ~se; ~**letzt** finally; last; ~**liebe**: j-m ~ for s.o.'s sake; ~**machen** colloq.: close, shut; button (up).
zumindest at least.
zumut|en: j-m et. ~ demand s.th. from s.o.; 2**ung** f unreasonable demand; impertinence.

zunächst first of all; *vorerst:* for the present.
Zu|nahme *f* increase; **~name** *m* surname.
zünd|en kindle; *bsd. mot.* ignite; **2holz** *n* match; **2kerze** *f* spark(ing)-plug; **2schlüssel** *m* ignition key; **2ung** *f* ignition.
zunehmen increase (**an** in); *Person:* put on weight.
Zuneigung *f* affection.
Zunge *f* tongue.
zunichte: **~ machen** destroy.
zu|nicken nod to; **~pak-ken** grip, clutch.
zupfen pluck (**an** at).
zurechnungsfähig *jur.* responsible.
zurecht|finden: sich ~ find one's way; **~kommen: ~ mit** *et.:* manage; **~machen** *colloq.* get ready, prepare; **(sich) ~machen** make up.
zureden: j-m **~** coax s.o., encourage s.o.
zurück back; *rückwärts:* backward(s); *hinten:* behind; **~bekommen** get back; **~bleiben** remain od. stay behind; fall od. lag behind; **~blicken** look back; **~bringen** bring back; **~drängen** push back; *fig.* repress; **~erstatten** *Auslagen:* refund; **~fahren** drive back; *fig.* start back; **~fliegen** fly back; **~führen** lead back; **~führen auf** attribute to; **~geben** give back, return,

restore; **~gehen** go back; return; *fig.* diminish, decrease; **~gezogen** retired; **~halten** hold back; **~haltend** reserved; **~holen** fetch back; **~kommen** come back, return; **~lassen** leave (behind); **~legen** put back; lay aside; *Entfernung:* cover; **~nehmen** take back; *Worte etc.:* withdraw, retract; **~prallen** rebound; **~schicken** send back; **~schlagen** *v/t* repel; *Bettdecke:* turn down; *v/i* hit back; **~schrecken** shrink (back) (**vor** from); **~setzen** put back; *fig.* slight, neglect; **~stellen** put back (a. *Uhr*); *fig.* defer, postpone; **~stoßen** push back; *fig.* repel, repulse; **~treten** step od. stand back; resign (**von** *Amt:* from); recede (**von** *Vertrag:* from); **~weisen** decline, reject; **~werfen** throw back; *fig.* set back; **~zahlen** pay back (a. *fig.*); **~ziehen** draw back; *fig.* withdraw; **sich ~ziehen** retire, withdraw; *mil.* retreat.
Zuruf *m* shout; **2en** shout (j-m et. s.th. at to s.o.).
Zusage *f* promise; *Einwilligung:* assent; **2n** *v/t* promise; *v/i* accept an invitation; j-m **2n** suit s.o.
zusammen together; at the same time; **2arbeit** *f* co-operation; *Gemeinschaft:* team-work; **~ar-**

beiten work together; co-operate; **~binden** bind together; **~brechen** break down; *völlig:* collapse; **2bruch** *m* breakdown; collapse; **~drücken** compress, press together; **~fallen** fall in, collapse; *zeitlich:* coincide; **~fassen** summarize, sum up; **2fassung** *f* summary; **~gehören** belong together; **~hang** *m* connection, *a.* connexion; *textlich:* context; **~hängen** *v/i* be connected; *v/t* hang together; **~klappen** fold up; **~kommen** meet; **2kunft** *f* meeting; **~legen** fold up; *Geld:* club together, pool; **~nehmen:** sich **~** pull o.s. together; **~packen** pack up; **~passen** match, harmonize; **2prall** *m* collision; **~prallen** collide; **~rechnen** add up; **~rücken** *v/t* move together; *v/i* close up; **~schlagen** *Hände:* clap; beat *s.o.* up; **~setzen** put together; *tech.* assemble; sich **~setzen aus** consist of; **~stellen** put together; *Liste etc.:* compile; **2stoß** *m* collision; *fig. a.* clash; **~stoßen** collide; *fig. a.* clash; **~treffen** meet; *zeitlich:* coincide; **~zählen** add *od.* count up; **~ziehen** contract (*a.* sich).

Zu|satz *m* addition; *Beimischung:* admixture; *Ergänzung:* supplement; **2sätzlich** additional.

zuschau|en look on, watch; **2er** *m* spectator, looker-on, onlooker; **2erraum** *m thea.* auditorium.

zuschicken send (*dat* to).

Zuschlag *m* extra charge; surcharge (*a. Post*); *rail.* excess fare; **2en** hit, strike; *s.* **zuknallen.**

zu|schließen lock (up); **~schnappen** *Hund:* snap; *Tür:* snap to; **~schneiden** cut out; cut (to size); **~schrauben** screw on; **2schrift** *f* letter; **2schuß** *m* allowance; subsidy; **~sehen** *s.* **zuschauen; ~sehends** visibly; **~senden** *s.* **zuschicken; ~setzen:** j-m **~** press *s.o.* (hard).

zusicher|n: j-m et. **~** assure *s.o.* of *s.th.*; **2ung** *f* assurance.

zu|spitzen: sich **~** *fig.* come to a crisis; **2stand** *m* condition, state.

zustande: ~ bringen achieve; **~ kommen** come off.

zuständig competent.

zustehen be due (*dat* to).

zustell|en deliver; **2ung** *f* delivery.

zustimm|en (*dat*) agree (to *s.th.*) with *s.o.*); consent (to *s.th.*); **2ung** *f* consent.

zu|stöpfen stop up, plug (up); **~stoßen** j-m **~** happen to *s.o.*; **~stürzen: ~ auf** rush at.

Zutaten *pl* ingredients *pl.*

zuteil|en allot, apportion;

ℒung f allotment; ration.

zu|tragen: sich ~ happen; **~traven:** j-m et. ~ credit s.o. with s.th.; **~traulich** confiding, trustful, trusting; *Tier:* friendly, tame.

zutreffen be true; **~ auf** be true of; **~d** right, correct.

zutrinken: j-m ~ raise one's glass to s.o., drink (to) s.o.'s health.

Zutritt m access; *Einlaß:* admission; **~ verboten!** no admittance!

zuverlässig reliable; **ℒ-keit** f reliability.

Zuversicht f confidence; **ℒlich** confident.

zuviel too much.

zuvor before, previously; **~kommen:** j-m od. e-r Sache ~ anticipate s.o. od. s.th.; **~kommend** obliging.

Zuwachs m increase.

zu|weilen sometimes; **~weisen** assign; **~wenden: (sich)** ~ turn (dat. to [-wards]); **~wenig** too little; **~werfen** *Tür:* slam (to); j-m et. **~werfen** throw to s.o.; *Blick:* cast at s.o.; **~winken** wave to; beckon to s.o.; **~ziehen** v/t draw together; *Vorhänge:* draw; *Arzt etc.:* consult; **sich ~ziehen** incur; *med.* catch; v/i move in; **~züglich** plus.

Zwang m compulsion; *Gewalt:* force; **ℒlos** informal.

zwanzig twenty; **~ste** twentieth.

zwar indeed, it is true; **und ~** that is.

Zweck m aim, end, purpose; **keinen ~ haben** be of no use.

Zwecke f tack; *Reiß~:* drawing-pin, *Am.* thumbtack.

zweck|los useless; **~mäßig** expedient, suitable.

zwei two; **ℒbettzimmer** n double room; **~deutig** ambiguous; **~erlei** of two kinds, two kinds of; **~fach** double, twofold.

Zweifel m doubt; **ℒhaft** doubtful, dubious; **ℒlos** doubtless; **ℒn** doubt (an e-r Sache s.th.; an j-m s.o.).

Zweig m branch (a. fig.); **kleiner ~** twig; **~geschäft** n, **~niederlassung** f, **~stelle** f branch.

Zwei|kampf m duel, single combat; **ℒmal** twice; **ℒmotorig** twin-engined; **ℒseitig** two-sided; *Vertrag etc.:* bilateral; **~sitzer** m two-seater; **ℒsprachig** bilingual; **ℒstöckig** two-stor|eyed, -ied.

zweit second; **aus ~er Hand** second-hand; **wir sind zu ~** there are two of us.

zwei|teilig *Anzug:* two-piece; **~tens** secondly.

Zwerchfell n diaphragm.

Zwerg m dwarf.

Zwetsch(g)e f plum.

zwicken pinch, nip.

Zwieback m rusk, zwieback. [bulb.)

Zwiebel f onion; Blumen∫

Zwie|licht n twilight; ~spalt m conflict; ~tracht f discord.

Zwilling|e pl twins pl; ~s... twin ...

zwingen force; compel.

Zwinger m kennel; Zucht: kennel(s pl).

zwinkern wink, blink.

Zwirn m thread, cotton; ~s-faden m thread.

zwischen zweien: between; mehreren: among; ~durch colloq. in between; for a change; 2ergebnis n intermediate result; 2fall m incident; 2landung f aer. intermediate landing, stop, Am. a. stopover; **(Flug) ohne** 2landung non-stop (flight); 2raum m space, interval; 2stecker m adapter; 2stück n intermediate piece; adapter; 2wand f partition; 2zeit f interval; in der 2zeit meantime.

zwitschern twitter, chirp.

zwölf twelve; um ~ (Uhr) at twelve (o'clock); (um) ~ Uhr mittags (at) noon; (um) ~ Uhr nachts (at) midnight; ~te twelfth.

Zylind|er m top hat; math., tech. cylinder.

zynisch cynical.

Zypresse f cypress.

Alphabetical List of the German Irregular Verbs

Infinitive — Preterite — Past Participle

backen – backte (buk) – ge-backen

bedingen – bedang (bedingte) – bedungen (*conditional*: bedingt)

befehlen – befahl – befohlen

beginnen – begann – begonnen

beißen – biß – gebissen

bergen – barg – geborgen

bersten – barst – geborsten

bewegen – bewog – bewogen

biegen – bog – gebogen

bieten – bot – geboten

binden – band – gebunden

bitten – bat – gebeten

blasen – blies – geblasen

bleiben – blieb – geblieben

bleichen – blich – geblichen

braten – briet – gebraten

brauchen – brauchte – gebraucht (*v/aux* brauchen)

brechen – brach – gebrochen

brennen – brannte – gebrannt

bringen – brachte – gebracht

denken – dachte – gedacht

dreschen – drosch – gedroschen

dringen – drang – gedrungen

dürfen – durfte – gedurft (*v/aux* dürfen)

empfehlen – empfahl – empfohlen

erlöschen – erlosch – erloschen

erschrecken – erschrak – erschrocken

essen – aß – gegessen

fahren – fuhr – gefahren

fallen – fiel – gefallen

fangen – fing – gefangen

fechten – focht – gefochten

finden – fand – gefunden

flechten – flocht – geflochten

fliegen – flog – geflogen

fliehen – floh – geflohen

fließen – floß – geflossen

fressen – fraß – gefressen

frieren – fror – gefroren

gären – gor (*fig.* gärte) – gegoren (*fig.* gegärt)

gebären – gebar – geboren

geben – gab – gegeben

gedeihen – gedieh – gediehen

gehen – ging – gegangen

gelingen – gelang – gelungen

gelten – galt – gegolten

genesen – genas – genesen

genießen – genoß – genossen

geschehen – geschah – geschehen

gewinnen – gewann – gewonnen

gießen – goß – gegossen

gleichen – glich – geglichen

gleiten – glitt – geglitten

glimmen – glomm – geglommen

graben – grub – gegraben

greifen – griff – gegriffen

haben – hatte – gehabt

halten – hielt – gehalten

hängen – hing – gehangen

hauen – haute (hieb) – gehauen

heben – hob – gehoben

heißen – hieß – geheißen

helfen – half – geholfen

kennen – kannte – gekannt

klingen – klang – geklungen

kneifen – kniff – gekniffen

kommen – kam – gekommen

können – konnte – gekonnt (*v/aux* können)

kriechen – kroch – gekrochen

laden – lud – geladen

lassen – ließ – gelassen (*v/aux* lassen)

laufen – lief – gelaufen

leiden – litt – gelitten

leihen – lieh – geliehen

lesen – las – gelesen

liegen – lag – gelegen

lügen – log – gelogen

mahlen – mahlte – gemahlen

meiden – mied – gemieden

melken – melkte (molk) – gemolken (gemelkt)

messen – maß – gemessen

mißlingen – mißlang – mißlungen

mögen – mochte – gemocht (*v/aux* mögen)

müssen – mußte – gemußt (*v/aux* müssen)

nehmen – nahm – genommen

nennen – nannte – genannt

pfeifen – pfiff – gepfiffen

preisen – pries – gepriesen

quellen – quoll – gequollen

raten – riet – geraten

reiben – rieb – gerieben

reißen – riß – gerissen

reiten – ritt – geritten

rennen – rannte – gerannt

riechen – roch – gerochen

ringen – rang – gerungen

rinnen – rann – geronnen

rufen – rief – gerufen

salzen – salzte – gesalzen (gesalzt)

saufen – soff – gesoffen

saugen – sog – gesogen

schaffen – schuf – geschaffen

schallen – schallte (scholl) – geschallt (*for erschallen a.* erschollen)

scheiden – schied – geschieden

scheinen – schien – geschienen

schelten – schalt – gescholten

scheren – schor – geschoren
schieben – schob – geschoben
schießen – schoß – geschossen
schinden – schund – geschunden
schlafen – schlief – geschlafen
schlagen – schlug – geschlagen
schleichen – schlich – geschlichen
schleifen – schliff – geschliffen
schließen – schloß – geschlossen
schlingen – schlang – geschlungen
schmeißen – schmiß – geschmissen
schmelzen – schmolz – geschmolzen
schneiden – schnitt – geschnitten
schrecken – schrak – *rare:* geschrocken
schreiben – schrieb – geschrieben
schreien – schrie – geschrie(e)n
schreiten – schritt – geschritten
schweigen – schwieg – geschwiegen
schwellen – schwoll – geschwollen
schwimmen – schwamm – geschwommen
schwinden – schwand – geschwunden
schwingen – schwang – geschwungen

schwören – schwor – geschworen
sehen – sah – gesehen
sein – war – gewesen
senden – sandte – gesandt
sieden – sott – gesotten
singen – sang – gesungen
sinken – sank – gesunken
sinnen – sann – gesonnen
sitzen – saß – gesessen
sollen – sollte – gesollt (*v/aux* sollen)
spalten – spaltete – gespalten (gespaltet)
speien – spie – gespie(e)n
spinnen – spann – gesponnen
sprechen – sprach – gesprochen
sprießen – sproß – gesprossen
springen – sprang – gesprungen
stechen – stach – gestochen
stecken – steckte (stak) – gesteckt
stehen – stand – gestanden
stehlen – stahl – gestohlen
steigen – stieg – gestiegen
sterben – starb – gestorben
stieben – stob – gestoben
stinken – stank – gestunken
stoßen – stieß – gestoßen
streichen – strich – gestrichen
streiten – stritt – gestritten
tragen – trug – getragen
treffen – traf – getroffen
treiben – trieb – getrieben
treten – trat – getreten
triefen – triefte (troff) – getrieft

552

trinken – trank – getrunken

trügen – trog – getrogen

tun – tat – getan

verderben – verdarb – verdorben

verdrießen – verdroß – verdrossen

vergessen – vergaß – vergessen

verlieren – verlor – verloren

verschleißen – verschliß – verschlissen

verzeihen – verzieh – verziehen

wachsen – wuchs – gewachsen

wägen – wog (*rare*: wägte) – gewogen(*rare*: gewägt)

waschen – wusch – gewaschen

weben – wob – gewoben

weichen – wich – gewichen

weisen – wies – gewiesen

wenden – wandte – gewandt

werben – warb – geworben

werden – wurde – geworden (worden*)

werfen – warf – geworfen

wiegen – wog – gewogen

winden – wand – gewunden

wissen – wußte – gewußt

wollen – wollte – gewollt (*v*/*aux* wollen)

wringen – wrang – gewrungen

ziehen – zog – gezogen

zwingen – zwang – gezwungen

* only in connection with the past participles of other verbs, e.g. *er ist gesehen worden* he has been seen.

Some Important German Phonetic Symbols

[a] as in French *cart*
[e:] as in *day*
[ɛ] as in *fair*
[ɛ:] same sound but long
[o] as in *molest*
[o:] same sound but long and closer
[ø:] as in French *feu*
[ø] same sound but short
[œ] as in French *neuf*
[y] as in French *sur*
[y:] same sound but long

[aɪ] as in *while*
[ɔY] as in *boy*
[ç] an approximation of this sound may be found by saying [ij] and emitting a strong current of breath
[x] as in Scotch *loch*
[:] indicates full length of vowel
[ʔ] glottal stop
['] main stress

German Proper Names

Aachen ['ɑ:xən] *n* Aachen, Aix-la-Chapelle.

Adler ['ɑ:dlər] *Austrian psychologist.*

Adria ['ɑ:dria] *f* Adriatic Sea.

Afrika ['ɑ:frika] *n* Africa.

Allgäu ['algɔY] *n* Al(l)gäu (*region of Bavaria*).

Alpen ['alpən] *pl* Alps *pl.*

Amerika [a'me:rika] *n* America.

Ärmelkanal ['ɛrməlkanɑ:l] *m* English Channel.

Asien ['ɑ:zjən] *n* Asia.

Atlantik [at'lantik] *m* Atlantic.

Australien [aʊ'strɑ:ljən] *n* Australia.

Bach [bax] *German composer.*

Baden-Württemberg ['bɑ:dən'vyrtəmbɛrk] *n Land of the German Federal Republic.*

Barlach ['barlax] *German sculptor.*

Basel ['bɑ:zəl] *n* Bâle, Basle.

Bayern ['baɪərn] *n* Bavaria (*Land of the German Federal Republic*).

Becher ['bɛçər] *German poet.*

Beckmann ['bɛkman] *German painter.*

Beethoven ['be:tho:fən] *German composer.*

Berlin [bɛr'li:n] *n* Berlin.

554

Bern [bɛrn] *n* Bern(e).

Bloch [blɔx] *German philosopher.*

Böcklin ['bœkliːn] *German painter.*

Bodensee ['boːdənzeː] *m* Lake of Constance.

Böhm [bøːm] *Austrian conductor.*

Böhmen ['bøːmən] *n* Bohemia.

Böll [bœl] *German author.*

Bonn [bɔn] *n capital of the German Federal Republic.*

Brahms [braːms] *German composer.*

Braunschweig ['braunʃvaik] *n* Brunswick.

Brecht [brɛçt] *German dramatist.*

Bremen ['breːmən] *n* Land of the German Federal Republic.

Bruckner ['bruknər] *Austrian composer.*

Daimler ['daimlər] *German inventor.*

Deutschland ['dɔytʃlant] *n* Germany.

Diesel ['diːzəl] *German inventor.*

Döblin [døˈbliːn] *German author.*

Dolomiten [doloˈmiːtən] *pl the* Dolomites *pl.*

Donau ['doːnau] *f* Danube.

Dortmund ['dɔrtmunt] *n* industrial city in West Germany.

Dresden ['dreːsdən] *n capital of Saxony.*

Dünkirchen ['dyːnkirçən] *n* Dunkirk.

Dürer ['dyːrər] *German painter.*

Dürrenmatt ['dyrənmat] *Swiss dramatist.*

Düsseldorf ['dysəldɔrf] *n* capital of North Rhine-Westphalia.

Egk [ɛk] *German composer.*

Eichendorff ['aiçəndɔrf] *German poet.*

Eiger ['aigər] *Swiss mountain.*

Einstein ['ainʃtain] *German physicist.*

Elbe ['ɛlbə] *f German river.*

Elsaß ['ɛlzas] *n* Alsace.

Engels ['ɛŋəls] *German philosopher.*

Essen ['ɛsən] *n* industrial city in West Germany.

Europa [ɔyˈroːpa] *n* Europe.

Feldberg ['fɛltbɛrk] *German mountain.*

Fontane [fɔnˈtaːnə] *German author.*

Franken ['fraŋkən] *n* Franconia.

Frankfurt ['fraŋkfurt] *n* Frankfort.

Freud [frɔyt] *Austrian psychologist.*

Frisch [friʃ] *Swiss author.*

Garmisch ['garmiʃ] *n* health resort in Bavaria.

Genf [gɛnf] *n* Geneva; *...er See im* Lake of Geneva.

Goethe ['gø:tə] *German poet.*

Grass [gras] *German author.*

Graubünden [grau'byndən] *n the Grisons.*

Grillparzer ['grilpartsər] *Austrian dramatist.*

Gropius ['gro:pjus] *German architect.*

Großglockner [gros-'glɔknər] *Austrian mountain.*

Grünewald ['gry:nəvalt] *German painter.*

Haag [ha:k]: *Den ~ The Hague.*

Habsburg *hist.* ['ha:psburk] *n Hapsburg (German dynasty).*

Hahn [ha:n] *German chemist.*

Hamburg ['hamburk] *n Land of the German Federal Republic.*

Händel ['hɛndəl] *Handel (German composer).*

Hannover [ha'no:fər] *n Hanover (capital of Lower Saxony).*

Harz [ha:rts] *m Harz Mountains pl.*

Hauptmann ['hauptman] *German dramatist.*

Haydn ['haidən] *Austrian composer.*

Hegel ['he:gəl] *German philosopher.*

Heidegger ['haidegər] *German philosopher.*

Heidelberg ['haidəlbɛrk] *n university town in West Germany.*

Heine ['hainə] *German poet.*

Heisenberg ['haizənbɛrk] *German physicist.*

Heißenbüttel ['haisənbytəl] *German poet.*

Helgoland ['hɛlgolant] *n Heligoland.*

Hesse ['hɛsə] *German poet.*

Hessen ['hɛsən] *n Hesse (Land of the German Federal Republic).*

Hindemith ['hindəmit] *German composer.*

Hohenzollern *hist.* [ho:ən-'tsɔlərn] *n German dynasty.*

Hölderlin ['hœldərli:n] *German poet.*

Inn [in] *m affluent of the Danube.*

Innsbruck ['insbruk] *n capital of the Tyrol.*

Jaspers ['jaspərs] *German philosopher.*

Jung [juŋ] *Swiss psychologist.*

Jungfrau ['juŋfrau] *f Swiss mountain.*

Kafka ['kafka] *Czech poet.*

Kant [kant] *German philosopher.*

Karajan ['ka:rajan] *Austrian conductor.*

Karlsruhe [karls'ru:ə] *n city in South-Western Germany.*

Kärnten ['kɛrntən] *n Carinthia.*

Kassel ['kasəl] *n Cassel.*

Kästner ['kɛstnər] *German author.*

Kiel [ki:l] *n capital of Schleswig-Holstein.*

Klee [kle:] *German painter.*

Kleist [klaɪst] *German poet.*

Koblenz ['ko:blɛnts] *n Coblenz, Koblenz.*

Kokoschka [ko'kɔʃka] *German painter.*

Köln [kœln] *n Cologne.*

Konstanz ['kɔnstants] *n Constance.*

Leibniz ['laɪbnits] *German philosopher.*

Leipzig ['laɪptsiç] *n Leipsic.*

Lessing ['lɛsiŋ] *German poet.*

Liebig ['li:biç] *German chemist.*

Lothringen ['lo:triŋən] *n Lorraine.*

Lübeck ['ly:bɛk] *n city in West Germany.*

Luther ['lutər] *German religious reformer.*

Maas [ma:s] *f Meuse.*

Mahler ['ma:lər] *Austrian composer.*

Main [maɪn] *m German river.*

Mainz [maɪnts] *n Mayence (capital of Rhineland-Palatinate).*

Mann [man] *name of three German authors.*

Marx [marks] *German philosopher.*

Matterhorn ['matərhɔrn] *Swiss mountain.*

Meißen ['maɪsən] *n Meissen.*

Meitner ['maɪtnər] *German female physicist.*

Memel ['me:məl] *f frontier river in East Prussia.*

Menzel ['mɛntsəl] *German painter.*

Mies van der Rohe ['mi:sfandər'ro:ə] *German architect.*

Mittelmeer ['mitəlme:r] *n Mediterranean (Sea).*

Moldau ['mɔldaʊ] *f Bohemian river.*

Mörike ['mø:rikə] *German poet.*

Mosel ['mo:zəl] *f Moselle.*

Mössbauer ['mœsbaʊər] *German physicist.*

Mozart ['mo:tsart] *Austrian composer.*

München ['mynçən] *n Munich (capital of Bavaria).*

Naab [na:p] *f German river.*

Neisse ['naɪsə] *f German river.*

Niedersachsen ['ni:dərzaksən] *n Lower Saxony (Land of the German Federal Republic).*

Nietzsche ['ni:tʃə] *German philosopher.*

Nordrhein-Westfalen ['nɔrtraɪnvest'fa:lən] *n North Rhine-Westphalia (Land of the German Federal Republic).*

Nordsee ['nɔrtze:] *f German Ocean, North Sea.*

Nürnberg ['nyrnbɛrk] *n Nuremberg.*

Oder ['o:dər] *f German
river.*

Orff [ɔrf] *German composer.*

Ostende [ɔst'ɛndə] *n* Ost-
end.

Österreich ['ø:stəraiç] *n*
Austria.

Ostsee ['ɔstze:] *f* Baltic.

Pfalz [pfalts] *f* Palatinate.

Planck [plaŋk] *German
physicist.*

Pommern ['pɔmərn] *n*
Pomerania.

Prag [prɑ:g] *n* Prague.

Preußen *hist.* ['prɔysən] *n*
Prussia.

Regensburg ['re:gəns-
burk] *n* Ratisbon.

Rhein [rain] *m* Rhine.

Rheinland-Pfalz ['rain-
lant'pfalts] *n* Rhineland-
Palatinate (*Land of the
German Federal Republic*).

Rilke ['rilkə] *Austrian poet.*

Röntgen ['rœntgən] *German physicist.*

Ruhr [ru:r] *f German river;*
Ruhrgebiet ['ru:rgəbi:t]
*n industrial centre of West
Germany.*

Saale ['za:lə] *f German
river.*

Saar [za:r] *f affluent of the
Moselle;* **Saarbrücken**
[za:r'brykən] *n capital of
the Saar;* **Saarland** ['za:r-
lant] *n* Saar (*Land of the
German Federal Republic*).

Sachsen ['zaksən] *n* Saxony.

Schiller ['ʃilər] *German
poet.*

Schlesien ['ʃle:zjən] *n* Sile-
sia.

Schleswig-Holstein
['ʃle:sviç'hɔlʃtain] *n Land
of the German Federal Re-
public.*

Schopenhauer ['ʃo:pən-
hauər] *German philosopher.*

Schubert ['ʃu:bərt] *Austrian composer.*

Schumann ['ʃu:man] *German composer.*

Schwaben ['ʃva:bən] *n*
Swabia.

Schwarzwald ['ʃvarts-
valt] *m* Black Forest.

Schweiz [ʃvaits] *f: die ~*
Switzerland.

Siemens ['zi:məns] *German inventor.*

Spranger ['ʃpraŋər] *German philosopher.*

Steiermark ['ʃtaiərmark]
f Styria.

Stifter ['ʃtiftər] *Austrian
author.*

Storm [ʃtɔrm] *German
poet.*

Strauß [ʃtraus] *Austrian
composer.*

Strauss [ʃtraus] *German
composer.*

Stuttgart ['ʃtutgart] *n
capital of Baden-Württem-
berg.*

Thoma ['to:ma] *German
author.*

Thüringen ['ty:riŋən] *n*
Thuringia.

Tirol [ti'ro:l] *n* the Tyrol.

Trakl ['trɑːkəl] *Austrian poet.*

Vierwaldstätter See [fiːr-'valtʃtɛtərʔzeː] *m* Lake of Lucerne.

Wagner ['vɑːgnər] *German composer.*
Wankel ['vaŋkəl] *German inventor.*
Weichsel ['vaɪksəl] *f* Vistula.
Weiß [vaɪs] *German dramatist.*
Weizsäcker ['vaɪtszɛkər] *German physicist.*

Werfel ['vɛrfəl] *Austrian author.*
Weser ['veːzər] *f German river.*
Westdeutschland *pol.* ['vɛstdɔʏtʃlant] *n* West Germany.
Wien [viːn] *n* Vienna.
Wiesbaden ['viːsbɑːdən] *n* capital of Hesse.

Zeppelin ['tsɛpəliːn] *German inventor.*
Zuckmayer ['tsukmaɪər] *German dramatist.*
Zweig [tsvaɪg] *Austrian author.*
Zürich ['tsyːrɪç] *n* Zurich.

German Abbreviations

Abb. *Abbildung* illustration.

Abf. *Abfahrt* departure, *abbr.* dep.

Abk. *Abkürzung* abbreviation.

Abt. *Abteilung* department, *abbr.* dept.

a. D. *außer Dienst* retired.

AG *Aktiengesellschaft* joint-stock company, *Am.* (stock) corporation.

allg. *allgemein* general.

a. M. *am Main* on the Main.

Ank. *Ankunft* arrival.

Art. *Artikel* article.

atü *Atmosphärenüberdruck* atmospheric excess pressure.

bes. *besonders* especially.

Betr. *Betreff, betrifft* subject, re.

Bhf. *Bahnhof* station.

BRD *Bundesrepublik Deutschland* Federal Republic of Germany.

bzw. *beziehungsweise* respectively.

C *Celsius* Celsius, *abbr.* C.

ca. *circa, ungefähr, etwa* about, approximately, *abbr.* c.

CDU *Christlich-Demokratische Union* Christian Democratic Union.

CSU *Christlich-Soziale Union* Christian Social Union.

DB *Deutsche Bundesbahn* German Federal Railway.

DDR *Deutsche Demokratische Republik* German Democratic Republic.

DGB *Deutscher Gewerkschaftsbund* Federation of German Trade Unions.

d. h. *das heißt* that is, *i. e.*

DIN, Din *Deutsche Industrie-Norm(en)* German Industrial Standards.

Dipl. *Diplom* diploma.

DM *Deutsche Mark* German Mark.

DRK *Deutsches Rotes Kreuz* German Red Cross.

ev. *evangelisch* Protestant.

e. V. *eingetragener Verein* registered association, incorporated, *abbr.* inc.

E(W)G *Europäische (Wirtschafts)Gemeinschaft* European (Economic) Community, *abbr.* E(E)C.

Fa. *Firma* firm; *letter:* Messrs.

FDP *Freie Demokratische Partei* Liberal Democratic Party.

Forts. *Fortsetzung* continuation.

Frl. *Fräulein* Miss.

geb. *geboren* born; *geborene ... née;* *gebunden* bound.

Gebr. *Gebrüder* Brothers.

gest. *gestorben* deceased.

gez. *gezeichnet* signed, *abbr.* sgd.

GmbH *Gesellschaft mit beschränkter Haftung* limited liability company, *abbr.* Ltd., *Am.* closed corporation under German law.

Hbf. *Hauptbahnhof* central or main station.

i, A. *im Auftrage* for, by order, under instruction.

inkl. *inklusive, einschließlich* inclusive.

Ing. *Ingenieur* engineer.

Inh. *Inhaber* proprietor.

jr., jun. *junior, der Jüngere* junior, *abbr.* jr, jun.

kath. *katholisch* Catholic.

Kfm. *Kaufmann* merchant.

kfm. *kaufmännisch* commercial.

Kfz. *Kraftfahrzeug* motorvehicle.

kW *Kilowatt* kilowatt, *abbr.* kw.

Lkw. *Lastkraftwagen* lorry, truck.

lt. *laut* according to.

MEZ *mitteleuropäische Zeit* Central European Time.

n. Chr. *nach Christus* After Christ, *abbr.* A. D.

No., Nr. *Numero, Nummer* number, *abbr.* No.

PKW, Pkw. *Personenkraftwagen* (motor-)car.

Prof. *Professor* professor.

PS *Pferdestärke(n)* horsepower, *abbr.* H.P., h.p.; *postscriptum, Nachschrift* postscript, *abbr.* P. S.

Rel. *Religion* religion.

S. *Seite* page.

s. *siehe* see, *abbr.* v., vid. (· vide).

sen. *senior, der Ältere* senior.

sog. *sogenannt* so-called.

SPD *Sozialdemokratische Partei Deutschlands* Social Democratic Party of Germany.

St. *Stück* piece; *Sankt* Saint.

St(d)., Stde. *Stunde* hour, *abbr.* h.

Str. *Straße* street, *abbr.* St.

Tel. *Telefon* telephone; *Telegramm* wire, cable.

TH *Technische Hochschule* technical university or college.

u. *und* and.

UKW *Ultrakurzwelle* ultrashort wave, very high frequency, *abbr.* VHF.

U/min. *Umdrehungen in der Minute* revolutions per minute, *abbr.* r.p.m.

usw. *und so weiter* and so on, *abbr.* etc.

v. *von, vom* of; from; by.

V *Volt* volt; *Volumen* volume.

v. Chr. *vor Christus* Before Christ, *abbr.* B. C.

vgl. *vergleiche* confer, *abbr.* cf.

z. B. *zum Beispiel* for instance, *abbr.* e. g.

z. T. *zum Teil* partly.

zus. *zusammen* together.